Social Work
with the Aging

Social Work with the Aging

The Challenge and Promise of the Later Years

SECOND EDITION

Louis Lowy

Boston University

Longman
New York & London

Social Work with the Aging
The Challenge and Promise of the Later Years
Second Edition

Longman Inc., 1560 Broadway, New York, N.Y. 10036
Associated companies, branches, and representatives
throughout the world.

Developmental Editor: Irving E. Rockwood
Editorial and Design Supervisor: Jennifer C. Barber
Production Supervisor: Ferne Y. Kawahara
Composition: C. L. Hutson Co., Inc.
Printing and Binding: The Alpine Press, Inc.

Library of Congress Cataloging in Publication Data

Lowy, Louis.
   Social work with the aging.

   Bibliography: p.
   Includes index.
   1. Social work with the aged—United States.
2. Aged—United States.   I. Motenko, Aluma K.
II. Title
HV1461.L69 1985   362.6   84-15479
ISBN 0-582-28461-9

Manufactured in the United States of America
Printing: 9 8 7 6 5 4 3 2 1   Year: 93 92 91 90 89 88 87 86 85

To the memory of my parents,
who were not allowed to become old

Contents

Preface

From July 26 to August 6, 1982, over 1,100 delegates of member states of the United Nations, international bodies, and nongovernmental organizations met in Vienna to consider the progressive aging of the world's population—a fundamental demographic shift produced by declines in fertility, reduced infant mortality, and, to some degree, increased longevity. The tasks before the delegates were to assess the significance of aging trends for national development and to launch an action program to ensure the growing number of older persons security and opportunities for participation in society.

The World Assembly on Aging was convened to promote awareness of massive demographic shifts, in particular to identify their significance for developing countries. But equally important, the Assembly aimed to clarify the practical implications of these trends for policymakers. One implication made explicit is that increases in the absolute and relative numbers of older persons will have a wide-reaching impact on socioeconomic development, including such factors as productivity, consumption, savings, and patterns of government expenditure. A second implication of vital significance lies in the humanitarian sphere: A concerted effort will be needed to plan health, family support, housing, employment, income security, and educational services for greatly increased numbers of older persons. It is clear that higher proportions and growing numbers of the aging will necessitate fundamental adjustments in economic and social infrastructure. These adjustments, requiring decades to implement, must be initiated now.

As one mechanism for stimulating such forward planning, national representatives were asked to deliver statements in the course of the general debate, which took stock of demographic trends and described policies for the aging in the context of their own sociocultural traditions. These statements afforded countries an opportunity to assess their policies in the light of experiences of other nations and thus to identify new solutions and common issues.

The growing number of older people in all countries of the world has tremendous implications for the demographic distribution and is of major significance for the economic, political, social, and cultural changes in all classes, groups, and societies. The meaning of the slogan "demography is destiny" can be better understood when we consider these circumstances. Although gerontology is still in a relative state of infancy, we notice many efforts of research—nationally and internationally— as well as many systematic attempts to analyze social practice experiences that contradict stereotypic notions and myths about growing older and about being older. More empirically verified knowledge about the processes of aging has become the order of the day. We recognize more and more that aging is a process in the total life cycle, and older people are increasingly viewed as a part of a total society, yet to be integrated.

As a social worker I have been involved in working with older people for over thirty years. I have seen their concerns, worries, failures, successes, joys, and tragedies; their problems, successes, weaknesses, and strengths. I have been engaged in direct practice in nursing homes, long-term care facilities, multiservice centers, and educational and leisure-time programs, and have been able to witness the manifold creative talents of older people. I have worked with families who were able to negotiate intrafamily and intergenerational conflicts. I have worked with volunteers, young and old, and have found that successful dialogues and activities among and between generations are not only desirable but are eminently possible. Besides providing direct care and professional assistance, collaboration with formal/ informal networks is indispensable, and continuing emphasis must be placed on the activation and involvement of older people themselves in shaping their present and future.

My experiences in large-scale social work practice have demonstrated that mobilization of the potentials of people of all ages can lead to new goals and activities. My involvement as advisor to many public services, especially to the Department of Elder Affairs of the Commonwealth of Massachusetts, has been invaluable in learning about the complexities of social policy shaping and implementation. Such participation has offered me many opportunities to link micro- (small-), mezzo-(medium-), and macro-(large-scale) levels of social work.

The White House Conferences on Aging in 1961, 1971, and 1981 have brought to public awareness the fact that aging is an important part of the human condition. Physicians, social workers, nurses, members of the allied health professions, theologians, pastoral counselors, educators, teachers, and citizens from all strata of society, religious, ethnic, and racial groups have learned that understanding the aging process is vital to obtaining answers to the ever-baffling question "What is life all about?"

I have also been engaged in gerontological research, teaching, and practice abroad, as visiting professor to various universities in Europe, conducting annual seminars at the "Staffelnhof" in Lucerne, Switzerland, and working with the Caritas organization and Meinwerk Institute in West Germany in their department of gerontology. These activities have been broadening and have deepened my appreciation for the impact of gerontological social work.

In the United States, social work with the aging is coming of age. The National Association of Social Workers has established a Task Force on Aging, and the Council on Social Work Education has developed a National Committee on Gerontology and Social Work Education. Leadership in schools of social work on the undergraduate and graduate levels has blossomed. An appreciable array of conferences and institutes have been held in the last few years and there is hardly a group or organization of social workers that does not concern itself with the needs, tasks, and problems of the elderly.

The advent of the "sandwich generation" has alerted social workers that it is not just the elderly population that requires attention, but that the total family, the kin network, must be addressed. The advent of the *Journal of Gerontological Social Work* is a significant milestone in recognizing the field of aging as a legitimate arena of social work practice. The increasing emphasis on permeating the curricula of schools of social work and the design of concentrations in social work with the aging augur well for the future. More important, infusion of the topic of aging in all areas of the social work curriculum in human behavior and the social environment, policy, practice, field education, and research has begun. Many continuing education programs have sprung up throughout the country. Despite cutbacks in funding, gerontology centers continue to maintain themselves and have become more sophisticated. Social work research in the field of aging is making significant contributions, particularly in the psychosocial arena of gerontology. We can point to changes of widespread significance that have occurred since the first edition of this book was written.

Despite these changes, myths and stereotypes about age and aging still abound. The fact that the aging are not *them* but *us* has by no means penetrated all strata of our society. The emergence of the elderly woman as a major focus of attention is beginning to dawn on policymakers, researchers, and practitioners. The heterogeneity of the elderly rather than their homogeneity has become acknowledged.

Since the first edition of this book was published, a series of new textbooks has appeared. It is difficult to quantify the enormous amount of gerontological material that has emerged since the 1970s and continues to emerge almost daily. Given these developments it has become imperative to revise the first edition of this book. Although the basic organization has been maintained, information and data have been updated and new developments in social work and gerontology have been incorporated.

Because it is impossible to list all people who have assisted in this task, let me point out those who have been particularly involved in helping me with the revision of the text. Ellen Janice Kane, a graduate student of social work and a staff member of the Boston University Gerontology Center, has done a great deal of work to update information and to bring new data to bear, as well as to revise topics that needed changing.

Special thanks and acknowledgment are due to Aluma Motenko, former director of the Area Agency in Brockton, Massachusetts, and currently a doctoral student in Boston University's newly developed interdisciplinary social work/sociology Ph.D. program, as well as adjunct assistant professor at Boston University School of Social Work. She has written the new chapter, "Working with Families," which includes issues pertaining to the family "in the middle" and to family members as providers of support services, as well as how these issues relate to working with the family in the home and in community and institutional care programs.

I want to express acknowledgment and thanks to my secretary, Marie Gerace, who has made it possible for a manuscript that is devoid of mysteries and in excellent shape to be delivered to the publisher.

I would like to thank Irving Rockwood, executive editor of Longman, Inc., who has given encouragement and shown patience, and who was particularly helpful in the preparation of this second edition as were David Estrin and Jennifer Barber, the editorial assistant and production editor, respectively.

Plato has already stated that the most appropriate response to the experiences of growing old is neither resignation or continuation of middle-aged commitments, but the adoption of values and activities different from those appropriate to the first periods in life. This view affirms that the "third age" makes possible the discovery of values and meanings different in character from those accessible during earlier periods. It affirms that the insights and values achievable in the later years are related to worldly needs and interests. Plato asserts that full participation of the old in the political arena and other areas of social responsibility is essential for the public good.

The "third age" is an integral stage of the whole life span. Our needs for survival, growth, and development and for achieving a sense of autonomy and meaning have to be met continuously. It is our task as social workers to infuse our values and beliefs about human dignity and social justice in working with the aging and their families and to utilize their resources and talents in making life better and more beautiful for everybody.

Louis Lowy

Preface to the First Edition

This book is intended primarily for those practitioners engaged in social work with older persons and for those undergraduate and graduate students who are preparing for such work. Today, with more people than ever before living beyond 65 years of age, the question arises "For what purpose?" In an increasingly secularly oriented society, people find it harder and harder to find meaning and purpose in living.

Robert Butler, who won a Pulitzer Prize for his *Why Survive? Being Old in America*, challenges our society to face up to its responsibilities toward its older citizens. George L. Maddox has stated: "In a society which values youthfulness and productivity, older people have the capacity simultaneously to fascinate, to trouble, and to embarrass. Older people are a commentary on what it means to be finite. Older people live on a frontier which every man sooner or later must explore." It may well be that the presence of older people reminds the rest of the population that life exacts it due from everyone and that meaning and purpose are necessary if every person is to face up to life's trials and tribulations and its seemingly unfathomable path. Those who are younger are reminded that they too will face the tasks and challenges of the later years—for which few precedents exist.

The presence of older people poses new demands on all of us. We must reconceptualize the life cycle and our accustomed modes of thinking about the distribution of work and play, the uses of time throughout life, the relationships among three and four generations of family members, and their new statuses and roles. We must reconsider economic productivity, the consumption and distribution of goods and services, and the engagement, reengagement, and disengagement of people in various societal enterprises in the light of lifetimes that now last between

70 and 80 years for many, if not yet all, Americans. The harvest of our discriminatory practices is evidenced by the fact that many nonwhites do not yet share this life expectancy. We need new individual and societal perspectives so that we may harness the opportunities of longer life. Instead of viewing aging as a problem, we should view it as an opportunity for human fulfillment and a force for greater contribution toward a more humane society.

Because social work is always interposed in mediating the natural tensions between individual strivings for need fulfillment and societal demands and expectations, there is a magnificent opportunity to search for new ground and new modes of utilizing the enormous resource potential of older persons. Here is a challenge for social work, not merely to pick up the pieces of mistaken or mismanaged social policies but to assume leadership in extending the frontier of human endeavors in the service of a more equitable, just, and humane social order. The problems of old age arise out of the interplay among biological, physiological, and psychological changes, and out of societal inequities, ageism, social demands or neglect, family growth, role changes, and developmental tasks required of all people as they grow older. Eventually, all of us have to face death; we must reflect on death if we are to achieve the sense of ultimate identity and integrity that comes with having left a mark on our life's journey.

Work with the aging can be exciting, whether it is in direct practice or through policy shaping and administration; whether with one person, with ten, or with hundreds; whether in a large bureaucracy or in a small informal agency; whether in an institution or in a community setting. In addition to the frustration and elation, the defeats and victories, the disappointing periods and the gratifying moments of all social work, one extra ingredient makes work with the aging uniquely exciting and rewarding: It brings together the past, the present, and the future in uniting us with people through time and space. We become aware of the march of generations, the continuity of history, and the unity of people, in spite of their uniqueness and variability. In their common heritage and destiny, we see a cosmic unity and a strength by which the human spirit continuously struggles to find an answer to the question "Why survive?"

The conceptual development of practical social work has proceeded at an uneven pace. This is reflected in work with the aging and, consequently, in this book, which attempts to pull together much of the writing and practical wisdom about work with the aging at a particular time in history. Its aim is to encourage many more such attempts, thus contributing to the further development of social work practice in general. I am indebted to many people who helped me shape my ideas, attitudes, and feelings in my learning experiences, in teaching, and in my practice, and to those who helped me organize and set down my thoughts in this book. Here ranks first and foremost Werner W. Boehm, director of the International Center at Rutgers University and editor of the Harper Series in Social Work, who was instrumental in getting me to write this book and who encouraged me greatly in developing this text. He has been a guiding spirit throughout the editorial process and was most helpful in negotiating aspects of this enterprise.

I am grateful to all the persons who have had a share in my development as a social worker, gerontologist, and educator. I am sure they are aware of their influence and their contributions as fellow practitioners, teachers, and learners. They include students in my classes and courses, administrators and officials, members of groups and organizations, clients, colleagues, and friends. I would like to acknowledge the special contribution of Ellen Orlen, assistant professor at Boston University, who skillfully applied the process–action model to working with individual older persons and is primarily responsible for the material and the writing of Chapter 10, although I assume full responsibility for its content. She proved to be an exemplary social worker–gerontologist in work and deed. Special thanks are due also to Diane Perlmutter, who assisted greatly in the preparation of the literature and the case materials, as did Elizabeth Zoob and Jane Matlow. The interest, enthusiasm, and competence they manifested are great rewards to their former teacher and present colleague. Alexandra Thacher demonstrated her know-how and flair as manuscript editor and proofreader; Marcessia Gelawtski, Janet Keylor, and Donna Gold were indefatigable typists, patiently deciphering my graphological mysteries and producing the final manuscript copy. Acknowledgment is made to Anne Freed, Fannie Allen, and Leonard Serkess for their accommodating assistance, and to all those students who gave helpful critical reactions to this text.

Special thanks are also due to Arthur Farber of the University of Washington, Sheldon Gelman of Pennsylvania State University, Mary O'Day of the University of California at Berkeley, and Robert Morris of Brandeis University for their thoughtful readings and valuable suggestions for revisions, many of which were incorporated in the final draft. Last but not least, I want to express deep appreciation to my wife, Ditta, not only for her painstaking efforts in the revision phase of the manuscript but also for her support and encouragement throughout the writing of this book.

May the present and future aging population be the ultimate beneficiaries of this volume, as we teach and learn together and make life an exciting and rewarding adventure for all of us, since we become *they*, and *they* are *we*, thus forging a unity of experience that creates a common spiritual bond.

Louis Lowy

*Social Work
with the Aging*

Tho' much is taken, much abides; and tho'
We are not now that strength which in old days
Moved earth and heaven, that which we are, we are—
One equal temper of heroic hearts,
Made weak by time and fate, but strong in will
To strive, to seek, to find, and not to yield.

Tennyson, "Ulysses"

Are the old really human beings? Judging by the way our society treats them, the question is open to doubt. Since it refuses them what they consider the necessary minimum, and since it deliberately condemns them to extreme poverty, to slums, to ill health, loneliness and despair, it asserts that they have neither the same needs nor the same rights as other members of the community. In order to soothe its conscience, our society's ideologists have invented a certain number of myths—myths that contradict one another, by the way—which induce those in the prime of life to see the aged not as fellow beings but as another kind of being altogether.

Simone de Beauvoir, The Coming of Age

Introduction

The Western conception of aging is dominated by a view of aging as a process of the inevitable decline of a person, a process that is "biological rather than spiritual, social, or cultural; unfavorable rather than favorable; universal and eternal rather than differential and variable; and unmanageable rather than manageable."[1] In our daily encounters with people, in the mass media, and in almost all aspects of daily living, we are still confronted with such a view of aging, overtly, or covertly and subtly. It is small wonder, therefore, that our own attitudes toward this process and toward the aged population have been shaped by such views. We may not always be aware of such attitudes in ourselves, but they do exist and are held quite tenaciously by large segments of the population in the United States. Because social workers are part of this society, we must assume that they are also influenced by the prevailing societal views concerning aging and the aged.

It has been an axiom of social work that its practitioners must be aware of their own attitudes toward people of all walks of life, and that they must come to terms with their prejudices and blind spots as they carry out their work with people of diverse racial, ethnic, religious, socioeconomic, and age groups. A premium is placed on the development of self-awareness, including knowledge of one's own attitudes and feelings toward older people and, even more significantly, toward one's own aging process and ultimate death. Obviously, social workers who work with the elderly, either in direct services or in planning, organizing, and administrative functions, must come to terms with their future roles in society as they grow old themselves. While they are likely to reflect Western attitudes in their practice as well as in their personal lives, they are expected to examine this orientation and to conduct an authentic search for a different view as they meet the challenges of working with an aging population.

A Point of View

The major point of view of this volume is that aging is a continuous process whose cumulative effects are manifested at a later stage in the life cycle. Life is marked by a series of developmental stages that can be distinguished and differentiated—infancy, childhood, youth, the middle years, old age.[2,3] Being old, therefore, is a normal phenomenon for those who reach this stage in life—at this time, more people than ever before in history in many societies. Probably one of the great evolutionary achievements of the twentieth century is that large segments of the population live to a ripe old age, and the potential exists for all of mankind to fulfill this aspiration. At that stage in the life cycle, the tasks incumbent upon old age have to be struggled with and, as far as possible, mastered. This is not different from the way children, young adults, and middle-age adults have to grapple with their tasks, attempting to master them as they mature and partake of the adventure of life.

The biology of aging is but one aspect of the process; others are the psychological, social, cultural, and spiritual factors. Older people—various, differentiated, and heterogeneous—can be grouped together only as a generation that shares a common history and has experienced the same events. People born in 1900, 1905, or 1910 have lived through the same historical events (i.e., constitute a cohort), reacting in their own particular way based on their personality; genetic makeup; position in family constellations; group affiliations; membership in religious, racial, ethnic, or socioeconomic group; and many other psychological, social, cultural, and spiritual factors. To paraphrase Henry A. Murray's saying, an older person is like all older persons, like some older person, like no older person.[4] The later years of life make demands that have to be met but also offer rewards—notwithstanding the fact that in our society the negatives still outweigh the positives; this is not inherent in aging, but in the way our society treats the elderly.

Every society needs a population mix; a share of the young, middle-aged, and old blend past, present, and future and assure a continuing culture. Every society experiences social problems from demographic shifts in the population; from unequal distribution of scarce resources and conflicting demands placed upon these resources; from technological changes and various societal responses to them; and from increasing aspirations and new value orientations accompanied by new adaptive responses by different age groups who have different stakes, investments, interests, and time perspectives.

This text provides an overview for the social worker who works with older people individually or with members of families, groups, organizations, or communities. Research efforts are presented that illuminate our present knowledge about various aspects of aging and about the heterogeneous elderly population in the United States. Practice experiences gathered by social workers in their work with the aging are discussed, and from these a number of generalizable practice principles are deduced that can be applied in different ways. Since the state of the art of social work in general, and social work with the aging in particular, does not yet allow for systematic, coherent prescriptions for practice, this book hopes to assist everyday practitioners in performing their tasks by consolidating the relevant literature and by stimulating them to use additional sources that became available, to increase their knowledge base and engage in research efforts that can yield more validated and reliable practice theory.

Organization of the Book

This volume is essentially organized around the *Working Definition of Social Work Practice*, originally developed by the Commission of Social Work Practice of the National Association of Social Workers in 1958 and further refined by William Gordon in 1962[5] and by this author in 1966.[6] The five major components which comprise the *Working Definition* are values, purposes, sanctions, knowledge, and intervention. These themes have proven valuable in analyzing and understanding social work practice.

In Chapter 2, a brief historical review depicts both the reluctance to work with the elderly and the impetus of such work, from the milestone 1958 Conference in Aspen cosponsored by the Council on Social Work Education—which for the first time identified social work with the aging as a distinct field of practice—to subsequent developments by the Council and the National Association of Social Workers (NASW) with regard to enhancing this field of practice. The roles of the American Public Welfare Association, the Family Service Association, the Gerontological Society, and other national organizations and individuals in promoting social work practice with the aged are briefly described.

Chapter 3 provides data on the older and younger elderly population as regards life expectancy; geographic, ethnic, and racial distribution; social characteristics; marital status; and health, income, housing, and education. Changes in demographic factors since the turn of the century relative to the population growth, sex ratio, and mobility of our elderly population are compared to data compiled by the United Nations regarding other countries.

Chapter 4 outlines a social work continuum. The framework is based on the *Working Definition of Social Work Practice* referred to above. Against a societal rationale for the existence and practice of social work, its five components (values, purposes, sanctions, knowledge, and intervention) are delineated and are shown to be interrelated as they affect the way social workers approach and carry out their activities with the elderly. Chapters 5 to 12 discuss these components in greater detail. Chapter 5 posits that all social work practice is guided by preferred stances of thinking, feeling, and doing. Those values pertaining to human nature, to the relationship of people, and to society's relation to its members and the processes of helping are major categories. Under these are central values such as human worth and dignity, the uniqueness of the individual, and self-determination.

Varying values held toward the elderly in our change-oriented society are related within the context of a work ethic and materialistic individualism. Major emphasis is placed, for instance, on unproductivity stereotypes, sexual and senility myths, and family prejudices. Implications for the value stance of social work practice with the elderly are drawn. The process of helping older people is contrasted to the process of helping younger people. The conclusion illustrates a dominant belief in the youth-oriented American society that older people "have had it" and are mostly in need of custodial services. Social workers have begun to examine these assumptions, and there is evidence that many of their attitudes have reflected the societal bias.

Chapter 6 deals with the three major goals that span the practice continuum: curing, preventing, and enhancing. On one end of the continuum is the amelioration of debilitating, disabling, or crisis conditions that demand intervention. On the other end is the enhancement and development of strengths and capacities for self-actualization. The continuum avoids rigidity, since treating problems and modifying social conditions can also lead to preventive actions against the spread of these same problems and conditions; and prevention, in turn, may lead to growth and development for the elderly person as well as for the person's family, friends, and colleagues.

Chapter 7 discusses the fact that since work with the aged, like all social work practice, is sanctioned by society, most social work activities are carried out in public and private social welfare agencies, community services, home care, congregate residences for the elderly, nursing homes, institutional facilities, etc. It refers to the "aging network" and its components.

Because there are many books on the market covering the growing body of knowledge in gerontology, justice no longer can be done in a text of this type. Therefore, Chapter 8 has been considerably abbreviated and consists primarily of relevant aspects of biological, physiological, and medical knowledge, as well as psychological and sociological topics of which social workers have to be aware. References that are readily available for immersion in the body of gerontological knowledge are highlighted.

Chapter 9 introduces an analytic mode of thinking about intervention. The five dimensions outlined are (1) definition of targets of the elderly in their social environment; (2) specification of goals on a continuum of treatment, action, and development; (3) steps in the process, including exploration and reconnaissance of the situation or problem, or need identification and assessment, focused goal formulation, development of a plan of action, use of feedback, and evaluation; (4) activities involved in formal, informal, and life-space interviews, group meetings, and conferences, and techniques and skills for psychological support, anticipatory guidance, information-giving, use of program media, marshaling of community and technical resources, etc.; and (5) performance of major roles—enabler, broker, advocate, and expert.

This analytic mode of thinking about social work intervention is elaborated in a process-action model based on the time flow of problem-solving engagements between social workers and elderly clients, whether they are individuals or members of groups or organizations. The four major sequences are entry, defining the task, working on the task, and termination. Entry includes the following spiral-like processes: (1) contacting and providing access to available services, (2) maximizing motivation and minimizing resistance to the use of services, and (3) establishing an initial helping relationship that results in (4) formulating a service contract between parties. Defining the task involves (5) building on the helping relationship and maintaining it and (6) defining the situation by postulating a need, a problem to be solved, or a condition to be improved. This process of assessment brings into sharper focus more specific goals for the subsequent encounters and moves towards (7) task formulation. This phase ends with a plan of how to work on the task, who will be involved, and what resources will be used.

Working on the task demands (8) the use of the strengths of the elderly client, resources of family members and peers in the immediate surroundings, community resources, and (9) the skills of the social worker in enabling, brokering, and advocating. Termination of the task includes (10) terminating the relationships, possible further referrals to other helping sources, a review of the contract and its termination, and (11) an evaluation of outcome. Evaluation, it will be noted, is a continuing process that permeates all phases and yields feedback for inputs throughout this process.

Chapter 10 describes and analyzes various approaches to working with individual older persons using the analytic framework introduced in Chapter 9, adding new materials on case-management and working in the hospice.

Chapter 11 is an additional chapter, "Working with Families" written by Aluma Motenko. After defining "family" in a new demographic context, it addresses the question "who is the client?" and focuses on the manifold tasks of the family in providing services to its elderly members and the stress accompanying caregiving functions. Social work intervention in the "entry phase" is followed by "defining and working on seven major tasks," leading to the "termination phase." The chapter concludes with several case illustrations that elucidate the seven major tasks of social work practice with family members.

Chapter 12 updates and elaborates the process of group work with the elderly, and Chapter 13 addresses community organizing and grass-roots development. Chapter 14 speaks to the role of social work in developing social policy and concludes with a discussion of present-day issues in the social work profession related to the field of aging.

Let me conclude here with a formulation by Leopold Rosenmayr: "Because the end of life comes closer as we grow older, we come to feel that the realization of our goals and dreams is only partially possible. At the same time we must be ready to engage in taking risks, because without risk taking there can be no freedom."[7] Rosenmayr formulates the hypothesis that "the greater the courage the more highly developed the sense of conscientiousness and the capacity for late freedom, the greater the opportunity for creativity."[8] As I stated in my review of his book *Die Späte Freiheit* for *The Gerontologist*, "Living is a unitary process, to love and to be loved, and to be accepted by others enables older people to adapt, to change and to fully mature during this stage of the life process."[9] Studying gerontology as a separate multidiscipline has produced appreciable knowledge of aging, but it also has fostered a trend toward segregating the aged and separating the later years from the total life span. This view has also been expressed by Binstock and other American gerontologists. We must continue to build theories and develop empirical research about aging, but we must also incorporate a total life-span perspective in our study of aging. For the first time, our humanists have achieved some ascendancy in gerontology to effect a balance between the empirically/scientifically oriented and the humanist-oriented gerontologists, a position that social workers have always advocated, since social workers have the unique advantage of combining the humanistic with the scientific. It is its caring philosophy and its caring practice that makes social work unique, to be a pioneer and a contributor with other disciplines and professions to advance the "state of the art" for the benefit of people of all ages.

References

1. Michel Philbert, in James D. Manney, Jr., *Aging in American Society* (Institute of Gerontology, University of Michigan, Wayne State University Press, 1974), p. 9.
2. Charlotte Bühler, "Old Age and Fulfillment of Life with Considerations of the Use of Time in Old Age," *Acta Psychologia* (1961), pp. 12, 126–148.
3. Erik Erikson, *Childhood and Society* (New York: Norton, 1963).
4. Henry A. Murray and Clyde Kluckhohn, *Personality in Nature, Society and Culture* (New York: Knopf, 1949), chap. 2.
5. William Gordon, "A Critique of the Working Definition," *Social Work*, vol. 1, no. 4 (1962).
6. Louis Lowy, "A Study of Incorporation of a Professional Role" (Unpublished doctoral dissertation, Harvard University, 1966).
7. Leopold Rosenmayr, *Die Späte Freiheit* (Berlin: Severin and Siedler Verlag, 1983), p. 264. Quote translated by Louis Lowy.
8. Ibid.
9. Louis Lowy, Book Review of "The Late Freedom," *The Gerontologist*, vol. 24, no. 4 (Fall 1984).

2

Historical Notes
on Social Work
with the Aging

At the end of World War II, Ollie Randall, a pioneer in work with the elderly and a recipient of many awards for her leadership, wrote: "There is a definite lag between the acceptance of the facts [concerning the aged] and any understanding of their implications."[1] The facts are the increasing longevity and individuality of aging people, and the implications are the effects of these phenomena on planning, programs, implementation, and outcome.

Prior to 1945, not much had been happening in social work with the aging. In 1926, a paper entitled "Provisions for Care of the Aged" with a relevant bibliography was published by the Russell Sage Foundation.[2] In the 1929 *Social Work Yearbook*, Rose Head Richards described the aged as a "dependent group"; and although social work had been sporadically caring and planning for the aged over the years, the overriding approach, which viewed such endeavor as "a form of work that has not lost its appeal to the generous," was clearly a charitable one.[3] In 1930, the Deutsch Foundation sponsored a conference on care of the aged[4] and in 1937, the New York Committee on Mental Hygiene of the Family Welfare Association of America provided a series of weekly lectures for professionals working with the aged that culminated in their publication of *Mental Hygiene in Old Age*. In the next few years, books and papers on housing, institutional care, and the implications of the Social Security Act of 1935 appeared.

Increased attention to the elderly was fostered by the founding of the Gerontological Society in 1945—a forum for professionals working with the aged and for promoting research. It began publication of *The Gerontologist* and *The Journal of Gerontology*, major periodicals in the field.

At the National Conference of Social Work in 1947, Rose McHugh spoke of the essentials of "A Constructive Program for the Aged," emphasizing the dignity and integrity of the individual and the community's responsibility to provide planned coordinated services;[5] and Raymond Hilliard[6] stressed the causes of dependency and chronic illness in old age rather than the treatment of symptoms—although, in the same year the New York School of Social Work (now the Columbia University School of Social Work) sponsored a conference on the "Social Treatment of the Older Person." In 1949, Ruth Hill described in the *Social Work Yearbook* a "beginning interest" in the welfare of older people by voluntary social welfare agencies, and at the same time admitted to the lack of a body of experience in casework with the aged.[7] Schools of social work did not offer any special courses, although there were a number of field work placements in social agencies serving older clients.

Wilma Donahue in 1950 spoke about "Age with a Future" at the National Conference on Social Welfare.[8] She stated that the increasing number of older people represented a national asset that our society could not afford to ignore, and recommended research, program evaluations, education for professional personnel in aging, retraining, adult education programs, special conferences, and campaigns to arouse public interest in the field. Later in 1950, the Federal Security Agency mounted a campaign to launch a national conference on aging.

Articles in the 1952 *Social Work Yearbook* openly referred to the reluctance of family service agencies to work with the elderly, despite their assumed responsibility to do so. Group work with the aged was first mentioned by Herbert Shore in 1952 in "Group Work Program Development in Homes for the Aged."[9] An important contribution to group work practice with the aged was made in a book by Susan H. Kubie and Gertrude Landau.[10] Also during that year the Welfare Council of Metropolitan Chicago sponsored a community project for the aged. Since older persons had disposable time on their hands, often referred to as "leisure," they were attracted to group programs offered by group service and recreational agencies, such as settlement houses, YMCAs, Jewish community centers, and neighborhood houses. Group work with older persons became a more pronounced activity than casework or community organization in the 1950s.

Elizabeth Wickenden in 1953 wrote the seminal volume *The Needs of Older People and Public Welfare Services To Meet Them.*[11] She discussed the effects of changing family patterns, industrialization, the lengthening life span, and population distribution, and bemoaned the lack of commitment to the care of the aged by social welfare agencies, community groups, and social workers.

In 1954, Helen Francis Turner et al. discussed in the paper "Serving the Older Person: A Multiple Approach by the Family Agency" the utility of casework, education for family life, homemaker services, and private residence programs;[12] and in 1955, the Review Committee of the Family Service Association of America listed "casework with the aged" as one of their top three priorities.

In 1957 William Posner asked, in the provocative paper, "Adapting and Sharpening Social Work Knowledge and Skills in Serving the Aging," why there was a lag in developing social services for the aged.[13] He concluded that the attitudes of social workers toward the aged and the development of programs for and with the elderly go hand in hand: social workers must lead the way and change their own and society's attitudes toward the aging if progress in helping them is to be made.

The Aspen Conference

In September 1958, the Council on Social Work Education, with support from the Ford Foundation, sponsored the landmark "Seminar on Aging" in Aspen, Colorado. Billed as an experiment in communication and cooperation on questions of training and preparation, its goals were fourfold: (1) to assess the social service needs of older people and to identify the responsibility of schools of social work to prepare personnel for this field of practice; (2) to provide, as a resource for curriculum building, a general overview of the growing body of knowledge now available from different disciplines; (3) to stimulate review of present educational programs in schools of social work in order to strengthen curriculum content relevant to work with the aging; (4) to initiate collaborative efforts by educators and practitioners, to develop field instruction opportunities, to produce teaching materials, and to promote more effective preparation and use of volunteers for service to the aging.

A series of papers by well-known experts presented at the Aspen Conference dealt with numerous aspects of work with the aging. The pros and cons of this specialization were discussed, and finally the participants identified social work with the aging as a distinct field of practice. The proceedings of the Conference were subsequently published and have served as valuable references for the further development of educational materials on aging and for stimulating curricular and training activities on the part of schools of social work and social welfare agencies.[14]

The National Institute of Mental Health (a participating agency at the conference) made a limited number of scholarships available to master's degree students of social work in order to encourage recruitment of students and promote content regarding aging in the curriculum. The Aspen seminar was indeed a milestone in social work with the aging.

The National Council on Aging

Leadership by the National Council on Aging, established in 1960, grew out of a committee on aging initiated by the National Social Welfare Assembly. The Council became "a central national resource that works with and through other organizations to develop interest in work with older people and to design methods that can be used in programs that are designed to meet their varied needs."[15] The Council and other national organizations sponsored a seminar that published *Casework with the Aging*, a useful reference volume of papers by well-known social work practitioners and educators.[16] This seminar was the first organized effort to relate social work methods to work with the elderly. It attempted to overcome the disabling attitudes toward the aging that continue to persist among social caseworkers.

The goals were a fourfold thrust: (1) to identify the scope and special elements of casework with the aging; (2) to delineate the body of knowledge and skills that are relevant and needed; (3) to identify content and methods of staff development that will render more effective casework services to older people; and (4) to determine areas of agency planning and administration that require adaptation in order to increase the delivery of casework services to elderly clients.

During the following year, the Council took the initiative again and succeeded in enlisting the cooperation of the National Association of Social Workers, the National Institute of Mental Health, and the American Public Welfare Association to cosponsor a seminar whose goals for group work practice were the same as those defined at the casework seminars a year earlier. Prominent group work practitioners, coordinators, and social scientists presented papers and held workshops. The compilations of these deliberations resulted in the publication of *Social Group Work with Older People*, a major bibliographical reference for group work with older people.[17]

The subject of a third seminar, also held in 1961, was *Community Organization and Planning for Older Adults*. It was conducted at Brandeis University in Waltham, Massachusetts, and was cosponsored by seven organizations—National Council on Aging, American Public Welfare Association, the Bureau of Old Age and Services Insurance, the Bureau of Public Assistance, Family Service Association, National Institute of Mental Health, and the United Community Chests and Councils of America. The issues discussed included content and scope of approaches, required modifications of planning and action to assure opportunities and services to meet the needs of the aging, and relationships between agencies and community-wide planning bodies.

The aforementioned publication compiled the deliberations of community organization experts, social planners, and agency administrators and was used during the early and middle 1960s. It became obvious that much work needed to be done in collaboration with social scientists to define, conceptualize, and distill a practice theory of community organizations and an application for work with the elderly in particular. The conceptualization efforts in the field of community organization during the 1960s obviously could not have been incorporated in the work of this seminar as yet.

In addition to these landmark seminars, the National Council on Aging also had assumed a major role in the creation, program design, and development of multipurpose senior centers. The Hodson Center, operated by the New York Department of Public Welfare and directed by Gertrude Landau, is credited with being the first institution in the field; it has served as a model in the rapid spread of social programs. The Sirovitch Center, also in New York City; the Leisure Lounge in Bridgeport, Connecticut; a center in Cleveland, Ohio; the San Francisco Center; and Little House in Menlo Park, California, were also pioneering efforts. The National Council on Senior Centers was founded and became an affiliate of the National Council on Aging.

The Stormy 1960s

The first White House Conference on Aging in 1961 set the tone for increasing federal involvement with the conditions of the elderly population as a part of our national policy. As a result of the recommendations of this Conference, the nation could no longer ignore one tenth of its people. In 1963, John F. Kennedy addressed the House of Representatives on "The Elderly Citizens of Our Nation," the first time a president had ever delivered such an address to Congress. A historic moment in the field of aging had arrived. Drawing on the outcome of the Conference, the President discussed the social, physical, psychological, and economic status of the aged in America. He made recommendations on social welfare measures, housing plans, employment opportunities, health care legislation, tax benefits, and community action, and he ended with a plea to improve an already "proud and hopeful national record in many other social arenas by providing for our aged as well."[18]

The Central Bureau for the Jewish Aged sponsored an institute on "Dynamic Factors in the Role of the Caseworker in Work with the Aged" in October 1961 in New York City. Dedicated to the memory of William Posner, the institute dealt with basic issues in casework with the aging, the role of the caseworker, professional attitudes and behavior in practice with the aging, community organizations for services to the aged, social work education, and group work.

Shortly thereafter, the Project on Aging was initiated by Family Service Association of America and headed by Theodore Eisenstadt. Edna Wasser, the associate director, pioneered in conceptualizing casework with the aging. In a paper she discussed the need for social workers to take on a commitment to serve the aged and to acquire the necessary knowledge and skill to do so effectively.[19] The Project developed five training institutes geared to developing casework services in family service agencies, and proposed to increase community planning for the aged through voluntary and public programs. The publication of Edna Wasser's *Creative Approaches to Casework with the Aging* resulted from this project.[20]

In May 1964, the National Institute of Mental Health, the Michigan Department of Mental Health, and the University of Michigan School of Social Work cosponsored a workshop on "Social Work Practice with the Aging and Its Implications for Mental Health," whose primary objectives were to identify common problems and improve the quality of social work practice with the aging and the aged. The goals included individual and agency programs aimed at the prevention of social and emotional breakdowns and the development of practice principles and mental health concepts applicable to the aged and their families, as well as program principles regarding the development, integration, and continuum of services.

Meanwhile the national growth of the senior centers continued to a significant degree. In the early 1960s over 500 were listed by the National Council on Aging, and social workers assumed major directional and staffing responsibilities in them. The senior center movement is closely linked with the expansion of social work activities in gerontology and the engagement of the elderly through group work. Social workers also became involved with senior power groups and served as catalysts, advisors, consultants, and advocates.[21]

The American Public Welfare Association in 1966 sponsored the California Project on Aging. The outcomes of this project included programs to upgrade the skills and knowledge base of workers in public welfare agencies in order to change their attitutdes, make more effective use of staff through improved supervision, and achieve higher worker expectations for elderly clients. Margaret Blenkner in a paper at the fifteenth annual meeting of the Gerontological Society in Miami Beach in 1962 offered a new theoretical perspective when she suggested that social workers should view aging as a developmental process against which they can diagnose, set goals for, and treat their clients.[22] This view was further developed in a later paper by Allen Pincus.[23]

From 1968 to 1969, the Family Service Association of America sponsored another project entitled "Social Work Team with Aging—Family Service Centers," whose aim it was to test the effectiveness of a team approach, an innovative method for improving services to clients and their families. Meanwhile, many social workers were providing short-term and long-term care for the elderly in institutional settings. The expansion of nursing homes with the passage of Medicare and Medicaid and a mandate for the inclusion of social work consultation (rescinded later by Congress) called for an increase in workers. Social workers in the field were still small in number, but their ranks increased during the 1960s when schools of social work began to offer special courses on work with the aging.

The Florence Heller School of Brandeis University developed a doctoral program in social welfare and aging; Boston University School of Social Work and a few other schools, notably the State University School of Social Work in San Diego and Wayne State at Michigan, started concentrations in aging. Social workers in collaboration with other fields became actively engaged in setting up multidiscipline gerontology centers in universities. Elaine Brody devoted a great deal of effort to conceptualizing practice and testing principles in the Philadelphia Geriatric Center, reporting findings, and stimulating further research. In 1970, she urged social work education to exercise leadership and challenge rather than reflect the prevalent attitudes and approaches toward the aged; she stressed the need for education, training, and workers.[24]

At the National Conference on Social Welfare in 1970, Virginia Southwood presented a paper called "Closing a Policy-Services Gap in Service for the Aging," based on a project begun in 1967 in rural Missouri. The project had focused on direct service claims from the offices of private physicians, had depended on community organization to establish an improved social climate for the aging, and had used a team approach by social workers and a physician, supplemented by a medical-social aide whose area was new careers. The project was found by those involved to be "a workable way [both] to close the policy-services gap in service to the aging and also to teach a generalist approach to the practice of social work."

The 1970s: Dawn of a New Phase

Some of the policy resolutions of the second White House Conference in 1971 found their way into national legislation. The aged had become visible and had gained somewhat reluctant recognition as a segment of the population that was likely to increase in numbers if not yet in power. The senior power movement had made Congress aware of the political potential of older voters. Pioneering days were over, an era had ended, and with the dawn of the 1970s a new phase began in the field of aging. The elderly would now be included as part of the nation, due to the slow recognition that the young of today will be the elderly of tomorrow—that the old are not them, but us!

Elaine Brody wrote in 1971: "The aged should be a prime social work target group for preventative, supportive, and restorative services, but that unfortunately the emphasis has been on the necessity of aging people to fit into the system rather than the system's bending to the needs of the aging. There was a lag in coordination among practice, research, education, policy, and planning."[25] This theme was echoed in an article by Elaine Brody and Stanley Brody in 1974.[26]

In 1971, the Gerontological Society sponsored a workshop on "Bridging the Gap Between Social Work Education and Practice with the Aging," in Houston, Texas. Some salient themes emerged: research findings needed implementation to make the lives of the aging more meaningful; policy issues in physical and mental health could not be separated from the daily living conditions of the individual; there was a need for a team approach and for the education and training of competent practitioners by schools of social work so that services to older people would enable them to function at their highest capacities.

A second workshop, on curriculum building, was cochaired by Elaine Brody and Walter Beattie, Jr., two of the earlier pioneers in gerontology who now assumed major leadership responsibility in the field.[27] This workshop continued where the first left off and laid out specific guidelines for setting up concentrations in aging in schools of social work and for prodding the Council on Social Work Education, graduate and undergraduate schools, and social agencies to take a leap forward in gerontological training efforts.

On the theme of education for social work with the aging, Sheldon Tobin (1973) published a paper outlining a dual role in which the educator-advocate must simultaneously develop a core training program on aging, induce other faculty members to add gerontological content to their teaching material, build interdisciplinary bridges with other academic units, and influence other educational institutions in the formulation of educational policy on aging.[28]

This author and Leo Miller wrote of the farsightedness of the 1958 conference in Aspen but deplored the slow pace of curriculum development, urging that all social work students be exposed to increased knowledge of the aging process, including physical, social, and psychological components, as well as to the interface between those processes and the political and economic systems. They stated that aging should be dealt with philosophically, in terms of values relevant to life and death issues, and concluded that schools of social work should secure leadership within themselves for developing programs in gerontology and should set examples for other professional schools to follow.[29]

In 1974, the Council on Social Work Education sponsored another seminar entitled "Alternative Educational Models for Social Work Practice with the Aging." Administrators and practitioners participated in Portland, Oregon, and took stock of increased course offerings and curriculum content in aging. They also recognized the necessity to move now with vigor and determination to make sure content on aging and skill acquisition were given a firm place in direct services, in policy decisions, and in the administration of social work education.

Into the 1980s: Consolidation and Further Movement

It would seem that social work educators have indeed taken an active role in providing gerontological knowledge to their students. By 1981, in a survey to which 71 percent of U.S. graduate social work schools responded, 36 percent of these programs reported offering gerontological specializations and 30 percent reported offering certificates in aging. However, the mission of imparting knowledge of and sensitivity to the issues of aging is far from complete. The same survey revealed that nearly half of American schools of social work still offer only one or no course in aging. Realizing the importance of this mission, leaders of the 1981 annual meeting of the Council on Social Work Education formed the National Committee for Gerontology in Social Work Education. By January 1983, the Committee had more than 150 members representing thirty-eight states and more than seventy universities.[30] Among issues cited by spokespersons for the committee that must be confronted in gerontological social work education for the 1980s are the need to include concepts of preventive health care in social work curriculum, the need to expose all students to older adults in their field work experience, and the need to eliminate ageist content from all social work curricula.[31]

Already in 1972, the National Council on Aging prepared a paper, "The Multi-Purpose Senior Center, a Model Community Action Program," describing the rationale for the various components that make up a senior center:

[The senior center] can serve as an agent for change, for understanding, for service and for action. . . .

. . .

. . . [It can be] a place where all the elderly, but especially the elderly poor, can socialize, learn skills, receive needed personal services, find opportunities for work, and receive encouragement in their quest for self-expression, self-direction, and social action.[32]

For agencies trying to create a multipurpose senior center, this paper offered information on organizing, programs, staffing, outreach, and financing. In 1975 this author referred to the senior center as a major community facility to bring together the old and young in a setting that older people can call their own—where they are hosts and not just guests.[33]

Jordon I. Kosberg urged social workers to view the problems of aging in the light of the ageism in our society and to concentrate on the development of trained, knowledgeable, farsighted, enlightened professionals and on advocacy on behalf of the aged.[34] It was not until 1974 that the National Association of Social Workers (NASW) established the Council on Social Work Services to the Aging to concentrate on gerontological practice and broad social policy concerns. In 1976, its chairman,

William Bell, recommended that the council be continued beyond the cut-off date of June 1976 as a task force on aging to make its work an integral part of the Association. For the first time in its history, the NASW in March 1977 issued a proposed policy statement on aging that was adopted by its delegate assembly in the fall of 1977. This statement was prepared by its National Task Force on Aging in consultation with the Midwest Coalition of NASW.

The statement says that social work has shared in the ageism practices against the elderly as have other professional disciplines, and that it has "failed to recognize its unique contributions among the professions to the improvement of the quality of life for older Americans." After spelling out the utility of casework, group work, and community organization skills of the profession to advance the well-being of the elderly, the policy proposal addresses a series of areas of public concern such as economic security, employment and retirement, health care, long-term care, living arrangements, transportation, social and other supportive services, rural and minority elderly, involvement of the elderly in planning and administration of programs, and research and training endeavors.[35] Various organizations are now committed to developing gerontological social policy, social work education, casework, group work, community planning and organization, and research activities.

For example, the *Journal of Gerontological Social Work* appeared on the scene in 1980, and a regular section entitled "Practice Concepts" was introduced in *The Gerontologist*, the journal of the Gerontological Society of America (GSA) in December 1982. As well, the Council on Social Work Education (CSWE) cosponsored the 1982 annual meeting of the National Council on the Aging (NCoA), and the 1982 annual meeting of the GSA featured a session entitled "Social Work Practice: Unique Contributions to Programs and Services to the Aged."

Aging has become a "hot topic," as evidenced by the proliferation of media attention to the elderly as well as a plethora of new publications (including both popular and scholarly periodicals and books) and organizations devoted to the interests of the elderly. Aging organizations have had a powerful impact in promulgating progressive policy. The Leadership Council of Aging Organizations (LCAO), was formed in 1978 when six national organizations formed a "coalition committed to representing the elderly's interests in the federal policy arena."[36] The LCAO, which has grown to include twenty-two member organizations, provided strong leadership at the 1981 White House Conference on Aging. As well, the grass-roots efforts of the Older Women's League (OWL) resulted in adding a committee to that conference specifically to address the concerns of older women.

The United Nations declared the 1980s the "Age of Aging," and for the first time in history, an international meeting on aging was held, when representatives of over 120 nations gathered in Vienna in 1982 under the auspices of the United Nations at a "World Assembly on Aging." UN Secretary-General Javier Perez de Cuellar called the event "one of the few occasions when an issue of global impact of such importance is being faced by the international community at a relatively early stage—before it is too late."[37] The Assembly set up a trust fund to provide technical assistance to developing nations and called for world-wide emphasis on

Table 2.1. Time Line

	→1850	→1900	→1930	→1940
Social History	—Wave of immigration —Economic depression (1890) —Industrial revolution —Labor union movement	—World War I (psychoanalytic theory emerges) —Depression	—Old age viewed as social problem —Depression continues	—World War II
Development of Social Work as a Profession	—Charity organization societies —Almshouses —Voluntary social agencies —Settlement houses —Development of case records and concept of investigation	—Development of social agencies with specific functions —Voluntary agencies focus on psychology of individual —Fee for service instituted in private realm	—Development of rehabilitative techniques —Professionalism of the field —Establishment of public welfare departments	—Social group work methods

	—Case conference procedure	—Private institutional nursing homes —Schools of social work emerge (areas of study identified)		—National Mental Health Act
Development of Social Policy for Elderly or Directly Affecting Elderly	—First private retirement pensions	—Retirement plans in public sector —Old age disability insurance for civil service employees —Old age pension laws —Provision of care by family legally enforced —State old age assistance programs	—Social Security Act (old age assistance, old age insurance) —Establish public welfare departments —Housing and Community Development Act —Railroad Retirement Act	
Development of Social Work Services to Elderly Clients	—Almshouses —Charity organization societies		—Eligibility workers to screen recipients of Social Security benefits	—Founding of Gerontological Society

(Continued)

Table 2.1 (Continued)

	→ 1950	→ 1960	→ 1970	→ 1980
Social History	—Korean War	—Vietnam War —Civil rights movement		—Reagan presidency —Redefinition by federal government regarding social policy and programs —Reaganomics
Development of Social Work as a Profession	—Council of Social Work Education —1955 National Association of Social Workers founded —Community Organization and Planning Committee	—New welfare rights group —1962 fields of service; social problems emerge as focus	—Community organization and social action become significant —Emergence of research and systematic knowledge building	—Redefinition of "cause and function" —Emergence of licensing and vendorship —Diversity of profession and search for unity —Accountability —Increasing systematization efforts of knowledge base

Development of Social Policy for Elderly or Directly Affecting Elderly	—Settlements —Golden Age Center	—Old Age Assistance (Title I of Social Security Act expanded social services to elderly) —First White House Conference on Aging —Medicare —Medicaid —Older Americans Act —Food Stamp Act	—Comprehensive Service Amendments to Older Americans Act —Social Service Title XX —Social Security Insurance —Second White House Conference on Aging —Amended Food Stamp Act —Medicare extended to include disabled and chronic kidney diseases	—Second and Third White House Conferences on Aging —Block grants for Title XX —Social Security Amendments of 1983 ("Rescue") —Reauthorization of Older Americans Act —Medicare changes —Long-term care issues —Hospices emerge, inclusion in medical insurance; life enrichment programs grow —Mandatory retirements give way slowly
Development of Social Work Services to Elderly Clients		—Old Age Assistance provides social services; Older Americans Act provides social services	—Establishment of Council on Social Work Services to the Aging by NASW	—Establishment of National Committee for Gerontology in Social Work Education —Council on Social Work Education Grant on Social Work Curricula and Gerontology Project

SOURCE: R. E. Dunkle, "The Historical Perspective on Social Service Delivery," *Journal of Gerontological Social Work*, Vol. 7, No. 3, May 1984, p. 7. Adapted (extended to 1980) by Louis Lowy.

preventive health care, reduction of health costs, maintaining elders' independence as long as possible, providing support for the "sandwich generation," providing a guaranteed minimum standard of income for all elderly, and for international exchange of information in gerontology. Tarek Shuman was appointed permanent UN Executive Secretary of the World Assembly on Aging to carry out the UN mandate of the Vienna International Plan of Action on Aging.

As with the country as a whole, and indeed the entire world, social work has begun to perceive the aged as a significant population group with particular needs, tasks, and problems. Although the involvement of social work in this field is sporadic and still shows signs of reluctance, there are also signs that its commitment to the well-being of the elderly has become more than rhetorical affirmation. In the social work history of the stormy 1960s, the reordering of priorities became as much an issue as the reconceptualization of methods. The conceptual unity of clinical practice and program policy has been fostered by leaders in the profession today without underplaying or denying the existence of tensions between clinicians and activists.

The NASW proposes the following guidelines to improve elderly services in the 1980s:[38]

1. Promote self-determination
2. Strengthen family and community supports
3. Meet social service needs of all age groups
4. Provide continuum of social care for chronically impaired persons
5. Meet unique concerns and interest in older persons

Expanded roles for gerontological social workers have emerged in many innovative practice settings, including

- the hospice
- respite care
- adult day care
- long-term care
- home health care
- advocacy, including working for recognition of the serious need for support services for the "sandwich generation"

Table 2.1 illustrates the historical developments of social history, the development of social work as a profession, and the development of social policy and social-work services for the elderly.

More students than ever are choosing work with the aging as a first priority and seeking careers as social workers in gerontology. Multidisciplinary efforts are more of a reality in gerontology than in many other social fields. Many social workers find this approach congenial and feel very much at home with it. While working with the elderly is still not considered the top of the status ladder and probably never will be, it is now recognized that this significant client and target population has a right to quality services and that practice with the aging will affect the whole of social work practice in the immediate and long-range future.

References

1. Ollie Randall, "The Aged," *Social Work Yearbook*, vol. 8 (1945), p. 36.
2. Bulletin 75.
3. Rose Head Richards, "The Aged," *Social Work Yearbook*, vol. 1 (1929), p. 31.
4. I. M. Rubinow, "The Care of the Aged," *Proceedings of the Deutsch Foundation Conference* (1930).
5. *National Conference of Social Work Proceedings* (1947), pp. 391–401.
6. "Planning Services for the Aged: Part 1, by the State Welfare Department," NCSW *Proceedings* (1947), pp. 402–410.
7. *NCSW Proceedings*, vol. 10 (1949), pp. 44–45.
8. "Social Work in the Current Scene," *National Conference of Social Work Proceedings*, vol. 77 (1950), pp. 70–86.
9. *Social Service Review*, vol. 26, no. 2 (1952), pp. 181–194.
10. *Group Work with the Aged* (New York: International Universities Press, 1953).
11. Chicago: American Public Welfare Association, 1953.
12. *Social Casework*, vol. 35, no. 7 (1954), pp. 299–308.
13. *Social Work*, vol. 2, no. 4 (October 1957), pp. 37–42.
14. Council on Social Work Education (CSWE), *Toward Better Understanding of the Aging and Social Work Education for Better Services to the Aging* (Aspen, 1958).
15. *Encyclopedia of Social Work*, 16th issue, vol. 1 (New York: NASW, 1971) p. 54.
16. Proceedings of the seminar held at Arden House, Harriman Campus, Columbia University, October 30–November 4, 1960, *Social Casework*, vol. 42 (May and June 1961), pp. 215–290.
17. Proceedings of the seminar in New Paltz, New York, June 1961 (New York: NASW, 1963).
18. *Congressional Record* (September 1963).
19. "The Sense of Commitment in Serving Older Persons," *Social Casework*, vol. 45, no. 8 (October 1964), pp. 443–449.
20. *Project on Aging* (New York: Family Service Association of America, 1966).
21. Jean Maxwell, Leo Laks, Sebastian Tine, Louis Lowy, Beverly Diamond, Florence Vickery, Morris Levin, Peter Tarrell, Fannie Allen, Betty Rank, Rebecca Eckstein, Herbert Shore, Jerome Kaplan, James H. Woods, Gertrude Landau, Susan Kubie, Godfrey Frankel, Morris Cohen constitute a partial list of early pioneers in the senior center movement and in social group work with older adults.
22. "Developmental Considerations and the Older Client."
23. "Toward a Developmental View of Aging for Social Work," *Social Work*, vol. 12, no. 3 (July 1967), pp. 33–41.
24. Elaine Brody, "Serving the Aged: Educational Needs as Viewed by Practice," *Social Work*, vol. 15, no. 4 (October 1970), pp. 42–51.
25. Elaine Brody, "Aging," *Encyclopedia of Social Work*, vol. 16 (1971).
26. "Decade for Decision for the Elderly," *Social Work*, vol. 19, no. 5 (1974), pp. 544–554.

27. "Curriculum Building in Aging," a Social Work Education Workshop sponsored by the Gerontological Society, San Juan, Puerto Rico, 1972.
28. "The Educator as Advocate: The Gerontologist in an Academic Setting," *Journal of Education for Social Work*, vol. 9, no. 3 (Fall 1973), pp. 94–98.
29. Louis Lowy and Leo Miller, "Toward a Greater Movement for Gerontology in Social Work Education," *The Gerontologist*, vol. 14, no. 6 (December 1974), pp. 466–467.
30. *Social Work Agenda*, vol. 2, no. 1 (January 1983).
31. Ibid.
32. Lowy and Miller, op. cit., pp. 1 and 41.
33. Louis Lowy, "The Senior Center—A Major Community Facility Today and Tomorrow," *Perspectives on Aging*, NCOA (May 1975).
34. "A Social Problems Approach to Gerontology," *Social Work Education* (Winter 1976), pp. 78–84.
35. *NASW News* (National Association of Social Workers), Washington, D.C., vol. 22, no. 3 (March 1977), pp. 17–18.
36. *Association for Gerontology in Higher Education (A.G.H.E.) Newsletter*, vol. 4, no. 3 (Fall 1981), p. 4.
37. Irma Schechter (ed.), *Aging Services News* (August 1982), p. 1.
38. *Social Work Agenda*, vol. 1, no. 1 (January 1982), p. 2.

3

Every Ninth American . . .

Fact Sheet on Aging in the United States

Two hundred years ago, when we declared our independence, the colonies had a total population estimated at about 2.5 million. Virginia was the most populous with about 0.5 million. Pennsylvania was next with about 0.3 million. Then came North Carolina, Massachusetts, Maryland, New York, and Connecticut, ranging down in that order to about 0.2 million, with the remaining colonies following. Life expectancy at birth was probably about 38 or 39 years so that the older population numbered about 50,000 or 2 percent of the total.

By 1900, there were 3 million older Americans—those aged 65 and over (65+)—comprising 4 percent of the total population, or every twenty-fifth American. As of mid-1975, 22.4 million older persons made up better than 10 percent of the over 213 million total civilian resident population—or every tenth American. Projections prepared by Herman Brotman based on Census Bureau data indicate that in 1982 there were 26.8 million older Americans (11.6% of the population or every ninth American); by the year 2000, 35 million Americans will exceed age 65, comprising 13.1% of the population or every eighth American; and by the year 2050, 67 million Americans or 21.7% of the population will account for every fifth American!

Table 3.1. Population Percentages for the United States: 1910–2050

	1910	1930	1940	1950
Young (under 18)	38.0	38.8	34.4	31.1
Work force (18–64)	57.7	55.8	58.7	60.8
Old (65+)	4.3	5.4	6.9	8.1

SOURCE: *Chartbook on Aging in America*, 1981 White House Conference on Aging.

In 1980, the largest concentrations of older persons—13 percent or more of a state's total population—occur in eight states: Florida (17.3), Arkansas (13.7), Iowa (13.3), Kansas (13.0), Missouri (13.2), and Nebraska (13.1), South Dakota (13.2), and Rhode Island (13.4). California and New York each had more than 2 million older people and Pennsylvania, Florida, Texas, Illinois and Ohio each had more than a million.

Almost a quarter of the nation's older population live in just three States (California, New York, and Florida). Adding five more States (Pennsylvania, Texas, Illinois, Ohio, and Michigan) brings the eight-State total equal to almost half the older people in the United States. It takes 12 more States (New Jersey, Massachusetts, Missouri, Indiana, Wisconsin, North Carolina, Tennessee, Minnesota, Georgia, Virginia, Alabama, and Washington—a total of 20) to account for just under three quarters of the older population and an additional 10 (a total of 30) to include 90 percent. The remaining 10 percent of the 65+ population lives in the remaining 21 States (including the District of Columbia).

What is this population like, and how does it change?[1]

This chapter answers the above question by providing statistical information on the aging population that includes the following: (1) population characteristics in the United States, such as life expectancy, growth projections, geographic distributions, and race and ethnicity data; (2) social characteristics, such as marital status and sex ratios; (3) economic status; (4) education levels, (5) housing and living arrangements and conditions; (6) health status and death rates; and (7) some international statistics for comparison and some projections for the year 2000.

Population Characteristics in the United States

There are approximately 26.8 million Americans who are 65 years of age and older: 10.8 million men and 16.0 million women. The ratio of women to men is as follows:

W/M for ages 65 to 74: 131/100
W/M at age 85+: 229/110

Table 3.1. (*continued*)

1960	1970	2000	2020	2050
35.8	34.3	26.5	24.6	24.8
55.0	55.9	61.7	59.8	58.1
9.2	9.9	12.2	15.6	17.6

Each day 5,200 individuals enter the ranks of the elderly; this amounts to 1.9 million each year. Each day 3,600 die; this amounts to 1.1 million each year. Thus, the aged population grows by 1,600 per day or almost 600,000 per year. This rate is equivalent to adding a city the size of Little Rock, Arkansas, to the United States each year. If all the aged lived in one state, it would be the largest state in the Union. Since 1900, the elderly population has grown from 3 million to 26.8 million. The total population of the United States has increased three times since 1900. The elderly have multiplied eight times. This is due to persons living longer and curtailment of younger people entering the country. (See Table 3.1.)

The following material was prepared by Herman B. Brotman, consultant to the Special Committee on Aging, United States Senate, and former Assistant to the Commissioner on Aging, Department of Health, Education, and Welfare:

GROWTH IN NUMBERS

During the 70 years between 1900 and 1970, the total population of the United States grew to almost three times its size in 1900 while the older part grew to almost seven times its 1900 size—and is still growing faster than the under-65 portion. Between 1960 and 1970, older Americans increased in number by 21 percent as compared with 13 percent for the under-65 population (a further 15 percent versus 6 percent in 1970–1976).

The fastest growth rates, more than 50%, in 1970–1980 occurred in Arizona, Florida, Nevada, Hawaii, South Carolina, Arkansas and New Mexico. Florida, with considerable in-migration of older persons, had and still has the highest proportion of older people, 14.5 percent in 1970 and 17.3 percent in 1980. California is now the State with the largest number of older people, 2,415,000, outnumbering New York, 2,161,000, which was first in 1970.

TURNOVER

The older population is not a homogeneous group nor is it static. Every day approximately 5,200 Americans celebrate their 65th birthday; every day approximately 3,600 persons aged 65 + die. The net increase is about 1,600 a day or 600,000 a year but the 5,200 "newcomers" each day are quite different from those already

65 + and worlds apart from those already centenarians who were born during or shortly after the Civil War.

AGE

In 1980, most older Americans were under 75 (61 percent); half were under 73; and more than a third (34.4 percent) were under 70. Over 2.2 million Americans are 85 years of age or over. Accurate data on the number of centenarians is not available but in June 1980, 15,258 persons who produced some proof of age are 100 + and receiving social security benefit payments.[2]

The older population itself is aging, according to the White House Conference on Aging *Chartbook of Aging in America*. Currently, the 75 + age group is the fastest growing age group in the U.S. It is expected to continue to grow rapidly for another 30 years, lag behind the growth of the 65–74 age group as "baby boomers" reach age 65, then grow most rapidly again as the baby boomers themselves reach and pass age 75.[3]

Increasingly, older people are subdivided into the younger-older (chronologically between 60 and 74), and the older-older groups (75 +). It is this latter group of the aging population that more and more commands special attention by gerontologists, notably Bernice Neugarten, and by the federal government through the Federal Council on the Aging. This council believes that special programs and services ought to be available as an entitlement for the oldest of the old.

Some salient statistics can be summarized as follows:

- In 1980, one in every nine persons in the U.S. was 65 + (25.5 million men and women).
- Between 1900 and 1982, the percentage of the U.S. population aged 65 + almost tripled (4.1 percent in 1900 and 11.6 percent in 1982) while the number increased almost ninefold (from 3 million to 26.8 million).
- The older population is expected to increase 30 percent to 35 million by the year 2000. If the present low birth rate continues, these 35 million will be 13.4 percent of the total population of about 260 million. If the birth rate should continue to decline, they would represent 14.2 percent of a total population of about 246 million.[4]

Life Expectancy and Growth of Older Population

Median ages: men, 69.5;   women, 77.2

Life Expectancy. As shown in Table 3.2, average life expectancy in 1978 at birth was 73.3 years, 69.5 for males but close to 8 years longer or 77.2 for females. At age 65, average remaining years of life were 16.3, 14.0 for men, but 4.4 years longer or 18.4 for women. The 26-year increase in life expectancy at birth since 1900 results from the wiping out of most of the killers of infants and of the young— little improvement has occurred in the upper ages when chronic conditions and

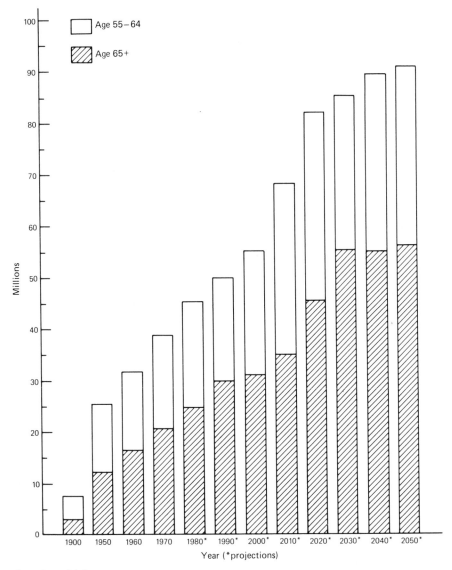

Figure 3.1. Number of persons aged 55 and over, by age group—1900, and 1950 to 2050. Source: *Chartbook on Aging in America*, 1981 White House Conference on Aging, p. 3.

Table 3.2. Average Life Expectancy in the United States

Age	1900	1939	1949
At birth	47.3	63.7	68.0
At age 65	11.9	12.8	12.8

SOURCE: Public Health Service, National Center for Health Statistics. *Vital Statistics of the United States: 1970, Volume II—Mortality*, pt. A. (Washington, D.C.: Government Printing Office, 1974), Tables 5-1 and 5-5.
* *Chartbook on Aging in America*, 1981 White House Conference on Aging.

diseases become the major killers. More people now reach 65 but, once there, they live only 4.4 years longer than did their ancestors who reached that age in the past.[5]

Figure 3.1 shows graphically the numerical growth of the U.S. aging population until 1980 and further projections of its growth until the year 2050. These projections, however, assume a continuation of the current death rates.

Table 3.3 indicates the changes in the 65+ population according to sex ratio since the turn of the century until 1975 and projects this ratio until the year 2000.

Geographic Distribution

In 1980, about half (45.4 percent) of persons aged 65+ lived in the six most populous states—California, Illinois, New York, Ohio, Pennsylvania, Texas—and Florida (the eighth most populous). Each of these states had more than 1 million older persons. The 65+ population in two states (California and New York) is over 2 million. It is expected that in 1986 California and New York will have over 2 million elderly citizens and that there will be 1 million in Florida, Illinois, Ohio, Pennsylvania, and Texas. California had the most elderly in 1980, but not the highest percentage relative to the rest of its population. All age groups are growing in number in those states.

The percentages of over-65 population in 1980 for the various states and the District of Columbia are as shown in Table 3.4.

Race and Ethnicity

In 1980, the nonwhite population was 16.8 percent of the total population, but only 10.2 percent of those 65 years of age and older. There is a difference in life expectancy between the white and nonwhite populations. The nonwhite population 65 years of age and older was 2.6 million in 1980.

Table 3.2. (*continued*)

1955	1959	1970	1974	1978*
69.6	69.9	70.9	71.9	73.3
14.2	14.4	15.2	15.6	16.3

1978 Life Expectancy for nonwhite: men, 65.0;   women, 73.6

Blacks. The number of blacks 65 years of age and older will increase because their standard of living, medical care, and nutrition is improving. The number reported in 1980 was 2,086,000. As expected, most were females (57.6 percent), most resided in the South (60.8 percent), and 66 percent lived in metropolitan areas. New York, the second most populous state in 1970, had the largest population of older blacks (7.6 percent), followed by Texas, the third most populous state, with 7 percent. California, the most populous state in terms of population, had the smallest proportion of older blacks (4.7 percent). Although comprising more than 16.8 percent of the total population, black people make up only 10.2 percent of the older age group. The effects of institutionalized racism fall most heavily on black men—their life expectancy of 65.0 years is 4.5 years less than that of white men, and in addition it has been declining.[6]

East Asian-Americans. The majority of East Asian-Americans (primarily Japanese, Chinese, Filipino, Korean, and Samoan) live in California and Hawaii as a result of immigration directly to those areas. Immigration policies have profoundly affected the lives of elderly Asian-Americans, particularly with regard to family life and male-female sex ratios. In 1960 there were 12,415 elderly Chinese over 65 years of age, about 7 percent of the total Chinese-American population. The figure increased to 26,889 in 1970. Males outnumbered females by 30 percent, reflecting pre-World War II immigration laws that prohibited women and children from accompanying men to the United States.

Japanese-Americans appear to have provided their elderly with greater family support and economic security, since they were not so severely restricted from bringing their families with them upon immigrating. In 1970, 46,888 Japanese-Americans, or 8 percent of the total Japanese-American population, were over 65 years of age. With four men for every three women, the proportion of elderly living with a spouse was 68 percent.[7]

American Indians. The 1970 census counted 827,000 American Indians and the 1980 Census estimated that 418,000 persons 65+ accounted for 5.3 percent of

Table 3.3. Changes in the 65+ Population by Sex Ratio

Year	Total	Men	Women	Ratio Women/Men
1900	3,080,000	1,555,000	1,525,000	98/100
1930	6,634,000	3,325,000	3,309,000	100/100
1970	19,972,000	8,367,000	11,605,000	139/100
1975	22,400,000	9,172,000	13,228,000	144/100
2000*	35,036,000	13,734,000	21,302,000	155/100

SOURCE: *Facts About Older Americans, 1976*, U.S. Dept. of Health, Education, and Welfare, DHEW Publ. No. (OHD) 77-20006. (Washington, D.C.: U.S. Government Printing Office, 1976.)
* From Herman B. Brotman, "Summary Table 'A': Middle Series Projections, All Ages and 65+, By Race and Sex, 1982-2050." November 1982.

Table 3.4. Summary: States by Percent of Total State Population Aged 65+, 1980

Percent	State	Number
17.3	Florida	1
13.4–14.3	Arkansas, Rhode Island	2
12.4–13.3	Iowa, Missouri, South Dakota, Nebraska, Kansas, Pennsylvania, Massachusetts, Maine, Oklahoma	9
11.4–12.3	New York, North Dakota, West Virginia, Wisconsin, Minnesota, Connecticut, New Jersey, District of Columbia, Mississippi, Oregon, Vermont	11
11.3*	Alabama, Arizona, Tennessee	3
10.3–11.2	Kentucky, New Hampshire, Illinois, Ohio, Indiana, Montana, Washington	7
9.3–10.2	California, North Carolina, Delaware, Idaho, Michigan, Louisiana, Texas, Georgia, Maryland, Virginia	10
8.3–9.2	South Carolina, New Mexico, Colorado	3
7.3–8.2	Nevada, Wyoming, Hawaii, Utah	4
2.9	Alaska	1
	Total	51

SOURCE: *Every Ninth American (1982)*. An Analysis for the Chairman of the Select Committee on Aging, House of Representatives, 97th Congress, 2nd Session, July 1982, p. 42.
* National average.

Native Americans. But with an average life expectancy of 44 years, one-third shorter than the national average, it seems a wonder that any Indians survive to be 65.

Indians are the poorest people in the land. In 1964, one-half of the families had incomes of less than $2,000 per year. Three-fourths had less than $3,000. Unemployment in 1967 on reservations reached 37.3 percent, compared with 2.3 percent for non-Indians. Hunger, malnutrition, substandard housing, poor health, lack of urgently needed services, and the emotional problems inherent in a changing culture are constant problems. If such poverty is the rule, we can be certain the elderly are even poorer. The traditional kinship support of the family is unfeasible when the family itself has no resources. The elderly are left impoverished—particularly if their children leave the reservation,[8,9] which is often necessary for them to realize any sort of job opportunity. Wages are often minimal, barely covering basic needs; thus, children who leave are unable to support additional family members and equally unable to send money back to the reservation. The young Indian thus leaves his aging parents with no economic base. The tribe is also unable to assume the responsibility and care of the elderly because economically it is no better off.[10] Some aged Native Americans get small amounts of "land claim money" for land leased to cattle ranchers or oil companies, but these checks are often insufficient to live on and may render the recipients ineligible for public welfare.

The U.S. government has to some degree, however, recognized the severe plight and unique needs of Native Americans. A separate title was established under the Older Americans Act Amendments of 1978 (and reauthorized in 1984) to provide Indian tribes and tribal organizations with direct funding for social and nutritional services. These monies are not always available to urban Indians, however, due to requirements that populations be "clustered" rather than dispersed throughout the metropolitan area, which is often the case.

Mexican-Americans (Chicanos). Statistical estimates of 1970 suggest that the total Mexican-American population numbers approximately 4,500,000, and 1978 data indicate the elderly constitute 3.7 percent of the Mexican-American population. About 86 percent live in urban areas, primarily in five southwestern states — Arizona, California, Colorado, New Mexico, and Texas. The elderly make up an estimated 4 percent of the Mexican-American population. Life expectancy is low.[11]

Mexican-Americans, due to patterns of segregation and other factors, have been the most successful in retaining their culture and language.[12] An estimated 58 percent of the Mexican-American population was born in Mexico and 42 percent are second- and third-generation Americans, most of whom were born and still live in one of the southwestern states. Although Mexican-Americans cling to the ideal of extended family living, young urban Mexican-Americans are often unable to care for their elders in the traditional way. Human Service personnel tend to overlook these problems, believing that the extended family cares for its own. The problem is exacerbated by the fact that the guilt-ridden younger generation Mexican-Americans tend to conceal their problems.[13]

Social Characteristics

Implications for the Family

"America's trend toward an older population has dramatically changed the nature of family structure. Three and four generation families have become increasingly common, with an estimated one third of all persons 65 + having at least one grandchild and one fourth of persons 58–59 having one or more surviving parents."[14] Neither is it uncommon for elderly to outlive their adult offspring.

Traditionally, middle-aged offspring, in most cases women, have taken care of their aging parents. Today, many more of these daughters are in the work force and/or struggling with supporting and educating their own offspring at the same time. More of their parents live into old age today, many of them suffering chronic illnesses that necessitate ongoing care. Also, due to high unemployment and an uncertain economy, middle-aged adults are increasingly placed in the position of supporting their adult offspring for longer than ever before. The question arises, therefore, of just how long the "sandwich generation" can stand the squeeze. It becomes obvious just how critical this question is when one realizes that 80 percent of the care that is given to our elders is given by their families.[15]

Marital Status, Sex Ratios, and Ethnicity

In the elderly population, most men are married and most women are widows. There are 40,600 marriages each year in which one or both of the parties are 65 years of age or older. In 1980, most older men were married (78 percent) and most older women were widows (51 percent). There were more than five times as many widows as widowers. About one-third of the older married men had wives under 65 years of age (34 percent).

> Among women aged 75 +, almost 70% are widows. In 1979, the marriage rate for older women was almost six times that of the older brides, partly because there are progressively fewer males than females in progressively older age groups and partly because men tend to marry younger than themselves. About 75% of the brides and grooms were previously widowed. More elderly whites than blacks are married (39 vs. 33% of women and 79 vs. 65% of males). An increasingly widening difference in life expectancy of men and women has resulted in a growing disparity in rates of elderly widows and widowers; from 1950 to 1979 the ratio has grown from two to one to four to one.[16]

Table 3.5 shows marital status by sex and age group, for 1980.

In addition to delineating sex ratios family status of the older population can also be classified by ethnicity, as shown in Table 3.6. These figures affirm the heterogeneity among the aging population and refute the still prevailing assumptions of a "homogeneous older population."

Table 3.5. Marital Status, by Sex and Age Group, 1980*

Sex and marital status	Number (thousands)				Percent distribution			
	45–54	55–64	65–74	75+	45–54	55–64	65–74	75+
Male:								
Total	10,962	9,870	6,549	3,234	100.0	100.0	100.0	100.0
Married	9,347	8,414	5,346	2,244	85.3	85.2	81.6	69.4
Not married	1,615	1,457	1,204	989	14.8	14.8	18.4	30.6
Single†	699	565	357	142	6.4	5.7	5.5	4.4
Widowed	176	397	557	776	1.6	4.0	8.5	24.0
Divorced	740	495	290	71	6.8	5.0	4.4	2.2
Female:								
Total	11,670	11,034	8,549	5,411	100.0	100.0	100.0	100.0
Married	9,222	7,713	4,282	1,264	79.0	69.9	50.1	23.4
Not married	2,447	3,321	4,266	4,147	21.0	30.1	49.9	76.6
Single†	552	504	480	344	4.7	4.6	5.6	6.4
Widowed	821	2,082	3,444	3,677	7.0	18.0	40.3	67.9
Divorced	1,074	735	342	126	9.2	6.7	4.0	2.3
Ratio:‡								
Total	106	112	131	167				
Married	99	92	80	56				
Not married	152	228	354	419				
Single†	79	89	134	242				
Widowed	466	524	618	474				
Divorced	145	148	118	177				

SOURCE: *Every Ninth American*, p. 25.

* The impact of differential life expectancies by sex may be illustrated by a theoretic application of life expectancies in 1978 to an assumed 100 marriages in 1980 where all grooms are aged 25 and all brides are aged 20.

† Never married.

‡ Women per 100 men.

Table 3.6. Familial Status of Persons Aged 65 and Older by Ethnicity, Age, and Sex: 1979*

| Ethnicity, Sex, and Age | Familial Status† as % of Total Population | | | | Total Population (in thousands) |
| | In Primary Family | | Primary Individual | Secondary Individual | |
	Total	Primary Family Head			
White					
Male					
65–74	86.1	81.7	12.5	1.4	5,726
75 and Over	77.8	71.7	21.0	1.1	2,872
Female					
65–74	62.2	7.4	36.7	1.1	7,557
75 and Over	46.8	8.5	52.3	0.9	4,795
Black					
Male					
65–74	71.3	65.3	21.6	7.1	558
75 and Over	71.2	48.1	23.5	5.3	254
Female					
65–74	59.9	19.0	37.8	2.0	757
75 and Over	54.6	17.9	42.2	2.8	385
Hispanic‡					
Male					
65–74	82.8	77.8	16.7	0.6	157
75 and Over	76.7	60.6	17.7	3.5	93
Female					
65–74	73.3	14.5	25.2	0.5	192
75 and Over	76.1	6.4	22.0	1.9	97

SOURCE: *Minority Aging: Sociological and Social Psychological Issues*, Ron C. Manuel (ed.), (Westport, Conn.: Greenwood Press, 1982), pp. 42–43.

* Data source: United States Bureau of the Census, 1980a.

† A primary family includes the person who maintains the household. A subfamily is a unit of a primary family, excluding but related to the household head, consisting of a married couple (with or without children) or one parent with single children (under 18 years). While a primary individual maintains a household and lives either alone or with nonrelatives, a secondary individual lives in a household or group quarters with nonrelatives.

‡ Hispanics may be either black or white.

Economic Status

Income and Poverty

Older persons have half the income of their younger counterparts. In 1980, half of the 9.2 million families headed by an older person had incomes of less than $12,881 ($22,548 for families with under-65 heads); the median income of 8.0

million older persons living alone or with nonrelatives was $5,095 ($10,526 for younger unrelated individuals). Some 3.9 million, or approximately 15 percent of the elderly, lived in households with incomes below the official poverty threshold for that kind of household. This is a considerable improvement over the 4.7 million, or a quarter of the elderly, in 1970 and results primarily from the increases in social security benefits. Women and minority aged are heavily overrepresented among the aged poor. Many of the aged poor became poor after reaching old age because of the half to two-thirds cut in income from earnings that results from retirement from the labor force. About 32 percent of the aged couples could not afford the costs of the theoretic retired couple budget prepared by the Bureau of Labor Statistics for a modest but adequate intermediate standard of living ($9,434 in 1980).[17]

Figure 3.2 shows the 1978 figures for median money income by age and family status.

The aged still constitute the fastest growing poverty group. Regardless of previous means and previous socioeconomic status, one may be thrown into poverty for the first time in old age. In addition to the older people who become poor, there are poor people who become old—5.0 to 7.2 million older people remain poor or near poor by government standards as of 1976.

In absolute numbers, more whites than blacks are elderly poor, but in 1980, proportional to the total black and white populations, almost three times more elderly blacks lived in poverty than elderly whites.

- Four out of five elderly minority women live with incomes below $2,000 per year.
- In rural areas, 86.5 percent of minority women have substandard housing versus 30 percent to 40 percent of white women in rural areas.
- Blacks tend to have more people dependent on them.
- Of all elderly female blacks living alone, two-thirds are officially classified as poor and 78 percent are at least near poor.

Older people are still hit by inflation (despite its decreasing rate since the early 1980s) as many live on fixed incomes and Social Security benefits. Although these are adjusted to the inflated dollar, they still do not absorb previous higher costs of living. In addition, most private pension plans are not indexed to inflation rates. Although in 1980 only one out of five men and one in twelve women 65 years of age and older worked, employment was the second largest source of income, accounting for 23 percent of the aggregate income of American elderly. Social Security income accounted for the greatest chunk of their income (38 percent), other retirement income and pensions made up 16 percent, and investments accounted for 19 percent. Together, these four sources provided 96 percent of the money income of the population 65 and older. In 1978, 91 percent of all married couples aged 65 + and 89 percent of individuals aged 65 + received income from Social Security (providing in most cases at least 50 percent of their income) and most recipients had at least one additional source of income.

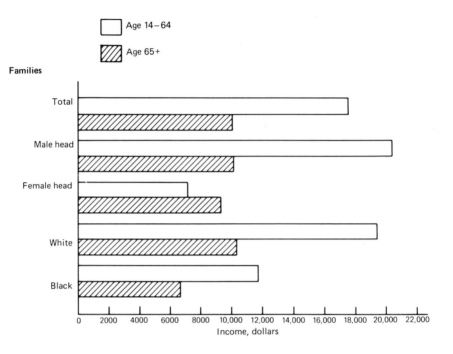

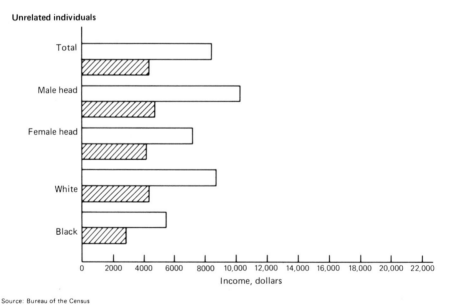

Source: Bureau of the Census

Figure 3.2. Median money income in 1978 by age and family status. Source: *Chartbook on Aging in America*, 1981 White House Conference on Aging, p. 53.

Some Notes on Social Security as a Major Source of Income. Social Security handicaps those who continue to work for wages by a work penalty, though there is no reduction in benefits for those who receive additional income up to any amount from stock dividends and bond interest or from insurance annuities or rents. Between 1967 and 1972, Congress has voted four across-the-board increases in Social Security benefits. During this period, average monthly benefits rose by 90 percent, resulting in a more than 50 percent increase in purchasing power. Since 1975, annual increases in Social Security have been tied to the Consumer Price Index, and thus gains in purchasing power have been negligible. At the end of 1980, the average monthly payment for a retired single worker was $341, and for a married couple, $513. Since Social Security constitutes only 38 percent of the total aggregate income of retirees, much of their income still remains unprotected against inflation.

In August 1984, the U.S. Congress unanimously approved measures to redress some long-ignored injustices borne mostly by women. It passed a bill that guarantees pensions for homemakers whose employed spouses die before retirement age, and lets working mothers keep their retirement-plan credits if they leave their jobs to raise families. It is expected that further liberalizations for women are likely to occur before the end of this decade.

Widows and widowers who come together for companionship frequently dare not marry because if they were a legal couple, their Social Security payments would be reduced. Husbands and wives are treated as separate taxable units though not as separate recipients of benefits after retirement, which can cause them to pay much more into Social Security yet possibly receive less on retirement than would a retired man whose wife had not worked.

On Retirement for Federal Employees. It is estimated that retired federal employees receive a total pension income from both public and private sources of one-quarter to one-half or less of their average preretirement earnings. Two-thirds receive less than $300 per month annuity, with two-thirds of these receiving barely enough to survive and one-half receiving less than $200 per month.

As with private pensions, the vesting rights (cash equity or nonforfeitable right to future benefits) of federal employees are still minimal. If one leaves government employment after service of up to one year, one receives a refund of one's contribution; for between one and five years, a refund plus interest computed at the rate of 3 percent compounded annually. To be eligible for an annuity, one must remain with the government for many years. Thus it is psychologically difficult for middle-aged persons who have ten or fifteen years but not the twenty-five or thirty years necessary for maximal retirement benefits.

The older woman is the poorest in society today. Under the federal retirement system, the survivor of a retiree gets only 55 percent of the retirement benefits received before the retiree's death. The 1972 change in the Social Security law (increase of spouse's Social Security benefits from 82.5 percent to 100 percent) meant that nearly 3.8 million persons (widows and dependent widowers) would receive an additional $1.1 billion in benefits. In actual dollar amounts, benefits to widows were increased $18 per month, from $138 in 1972 to $156 in 1973.

The Employment Retirement Income Security Act (ERISA) of 1975 affords participants and their beneficiaries federal protection through requirements directed to participation, vesting, funding, reporting, and disclosure. There is agreement that the rights of pension participants have been strengthened through ERISA, though delay and burdensome regulations have often weakened the actual impact of the legislative intent, and efforts to improve ERISA's implementation are necessary.

Expenditures and Assets

According to the U.S. Department of Labor's retired urban couple's intermediate budget, the total of $10,226 (approximately $852 for the month) for the year 1981 allowed for the needs listed in Table 3.7.

Of the single older citizens, 40 percent have total assets of less than $1,000. This includes an individual's total accumulated savings in real or personal property minus any debts. This net value is different from annual income, which may be larger than or only a fraction of total assets. Such assets as a home are often not easily converted to cash.

Employment

The working elderly make up 2.6 percent[18] of the total work force in the United States while they represent 11.6 percent of the total population and a greater percentage of the total adult population. More than 2.9 million (11 percent) of our older people were working in 1983. Slightly more than 19 percent of the older men (1.9 million) and about 8 percent of the older women (1.1 million) are in the labor force.[19]

Education

As succeeding age groups with more schooling reach 65, the older population shows a steadily rising level of educational attainment. In 1979, half our older Americans had not completed two years of high school, and the median for the 25–64 age group was high school graduation. About 2.1 million or 9 percent of older people were functionally illiterate, having had no schooling or less than five years of it. About 8 percent were college graduates (see Table 3.8).

Although the older population as a whole has experienced substantial gains in educational status, significant differences exist among racial groupings. For example, in 1979 one-third of whites aged 75 and older were high school graduates, while only 13 percent of blacks and 10 percent of Hispanics were so classified—and more

Table 3.7. Distribution of Expenditures

	Yearly	Monthly (approx.)
Food	$2,898	$242
Housing	3,393	283
Transportation	1,073	89
Clothing	409	34
Personal care	290	24
Medical care	1,091	91
Other family consumption	457	38
Other items	615	51

dramatically, more than one-half of 75 + Hispanics and four out of every ten blacks have had fewer than five years of schooling, while only one out of ten whites falls in this category.

Along with the "graying of the population" has come the "graying of the classroom." "Adult educational opportunities have expanded considerably during the last ten years, and older Americans have responded by returning to the classroom in increasing numbers."[20]

Housing and Living Arrangements

A trend in the 1970s toward independent living has resulted in a substantial increase in the number of households headed by persons 65 +. In 1980, approximately 16

Table 3.8. Years of School Completed, 1960–1980[*]

	Percent Completing		
	4 years of high school or more	1 year of college or more	4 years of college or more
1960			
Total population, 25 years and over	41.0	16.4	7.6
Persons 65 years and over	19.1	9.2	3.7
1970			
Total population, 25 years and over	55.2	21.2	11.0
Persons 65 years and over	28.3	12.6	6.3
1980			
Total population, 25 years and over	68.7	31.9	17.0
Persons 65 years and over	40.7	16.7	8.5

SOURCE: *Data Track 9*, American Council of Life Insurance, 1850 K Street, N.W., Washington, D.C. 20006, p. 13.

* Data source: U.S. Bureau of the Census, *Current Population Reports*. Series P-20, No. 363 and *U.S. Census of Population*, 1980, PC(1)1D.

million, or one-fifth, of all American households were headed by persons 65 +. One factor contributing to this trend has been an increase in single-person households, particularly those made up of widows and other older women who choose to live alone. Data from 1976 show that more than seven out of every ten household heads who are 65 + own their own homes, 84 percent of which are mortgage free. Even mortgage-free homes incur high costs for elderly homeowners, however. Taxes and utilities require older homeowners to spend a greater proportion of their income on housing. The same holds true for older renters whose incomes are lower than younger renters. Table 3.9 shows a breakdown of statistics on 1980 living arrangements for the 65 + noninstitutional population.

In 1980, 83 percent of older men but only 57 percent of older women lived in family settings; the others lived alone or with nonrelatives, except for the less than one in twenty who lived in an institution (which jumps to one in five in the group 85 and over). About three-quarters of the older men lived in families that included the wife, but only 38 percent of the older women lived in families that included the husband. Four out of ten older women lived alone. Almost four times as many older women lived alone or with nonrelatives than did older men.

Place of Residence

In 1980, a somewhat smaller population of older than of younger persons lived in metropolitan areas (64 percent versus 68 percent). Within the metropolitan areas,

Table 3.9. Living Arrangements of the 65 + Noninstitutional Population, 1980
(Numbers in thousands)

Age and living arrangements	Male		Female	
	Number	Percent	Number	Percent
65 +:				
Total	9,783	100.0	13,960	100.0
Living with spouse	7,389	75.5	5,311	38.0
Living with other relative	727	7.4	2,660	19.1
Living alone or with nonrelative	1,667	17.0	5,989	42.9
65–74:				
Total	6,549	100.0	8,549	100.0
Living with spouse	5,199	79.4	4,114	48.1
Living with other relative	426	6.5	1,243	14.5
Living alone or with nonrelative	924	14.1	3,192	37.3
75 +:				
Total	3,234	100.0	5,411	100.0
Living with spouse	2,190	67.7	1,197	22.1
Living with other relative	301	9.3	1,147	26.2
Living alone or with nonrelative	743	23.0	2,797	51.7

SOURCE: *Every Ninth American.*

however, more than half of older people (53 percent) lived in the suburbs due to the "aging" of the suburbs.

These figures are based on the total population; patterns for white and black elderly differ fundamentally. Older blacks are much more concentrated in metropolitan areas than are whites and more than 75 percent of the older blacks in metropolitan areas live in the central city.[21]

In a March 1980 household survey, 21 percent or almost 5 million of the persons then 65 and over reported that they had moved from one residence to another in the five-year period since 1975. Some 57 percent moved within the same county, 22 percent moved to a different county in the same state, and 20 percent moved across a state line. The extent of interstate movement seems larger because such migration tends to flow mainly toward Florida, Arizona, and Nevada. Although differing on proportions, older movers follow a pattern quite similar to that of movers of all ages.

"Despite more than thirty years of Federal promises, and some notable achievements, decent affordable housing still eludes many of the nation's elderly."[22] Recommendations of the 1981 Mini-Conference on Housing for the elderly stressed:

- greater help for homeowners against rising costs
- increased protection for renters against displacement
- expanded construction of assisted units for the poor
- broader choices of housing types and services for the frail elderly
- greater information about programs and services for all

Transportation

Transportation, providing means for mobility, is a major factor in providing meaning and preventing isolation for elders. In a 1981 report by Louis Harris and Associates, 14 percent of the nation's 65 + population surveyed expressed that "getting transportation to stores, to doctors, to places of recreation, and so forth" was a "very serious problem" for them. Inadequate transportation is especially serious for those elders who reside in the suburbs or rural areas where community services may be accessible only to those with automobiles. In urban areas, too, elderly are often fearful of public transportation or may live too far from the nearest transportation to avail themselves of it.

Health Status of Older Persons

In a 1979 survey by the National Center for Health Statistics, over two-thirds of the noninstitutionalized population interviewed reported their health good or excellent as compared with "others of their own age." A little more than 22 percent reported their health as fair and almost 9 percent reported their health as poor. Minority group members, residents of the South, residents of nonmetropolitan areas, and persons with low incomes were more likely to report themselves in poor health. Counting the approximately 5 percent of elders who live in institutions as being in poor health, a total of about one-seventh of older people consider themselves in poor health.

Chronic conditions are more prevalent among older persons than younger. In 1979, 45 percent of older persons reported limitations in their major activity (working or keeping house) due to such conditions.

The utilization of hospitals increases significantly with advancing age. The hospitalization rate for persons 65+ is 2.5 times greater than that for younger persons. In addition to a higher incidence of hospital admissions, older people stay in the hospital longer than younger persons and account for a disproportionate percentage of total surgical procedures. Hospitalization rates among older persons have shown a dramatic increase since the enactment of Medicare. It is important to note, however, that most persons 65+ are *not* hospitalized in any given year: Data from the 1979 Health Interview Survey reveal that fewer than two of every ten persons 65+ were hospitalized in the previous year as compared with one in ten in the under 65 population. Likewise, use of physician services increases with age, but persons 65+ have fewer dental visits than younger persons. It is estimated that, like the population as a whole, between 15 percent and 25 percent of all persons 65+ may have significant symptoms of mental illness, especially depression. However, older people use mental health services at about half the rate of the general population.

The nursing home population of the United States has increased markedly during the last two decades. From 1963 to 1977 the number grew from 505,000 to 1.3 million, an increase of 150 percent. The 1977 figure, it must be noted however, represents less than 5 percent of the elderly population. The likelihood of nursing home residence climbs with age to more than one out of every five persons in the 85+ category. More than 70 percent of nursing home residents are women, and whites represent 93 percent of the 65+ residents.

Death Rates and Causes

Heart disease, stroke, and cancer caused 75 percent of the deaths of people over 65 in 1978 as they did in 1965. As Table 3.10 indicates, however, diseases of the heart are the primary cause of death among people of all ages.

Involvement in the Community

The vast majority of older Americans are active, involved members of society. This is well illustrated by several facts:

• The elderly are better represented at the voting booth than any other group of the population.

Table 3.10. Selected Major Causes of Death in 1978, All Ages and Age Groups over 45

Cause	All ages	45–54	55–64	65–74	75–84	85 +
Number (thousand):						
All causes	1,928	141	293	452	497	324
Major cardiovascular diseases:						
Total	966	51	128	233	304	227
Diseases of the heart	730	44	108	184	221	156
Cerebrovascular diseases	176	6	15	36	63	50
Arteriosclerosis	29	*	1	4	10	14
Other	32	1	4	9	10	6
Malignant neoplasms	397	43	91	120	90	32
Influenza and pneumonia	58	2	5	10	18	19
Diabetes mellitus	34	2	6	10	10	5
Accidents	106	9	10	9	9	6
Suicides	27	4	4	3	2	(*)
All other	340	29	49	69	65	36
Percent distribution:						
All causes	100.0	100.0	100.0	100.0	100.0	100.0
Major cardiovascular diseases:						
Total	50.1	36.6	43.9	51.5	61.1	70.0
Diseases of the heart	37.8	30.9	36.8	40.7	44.4	48.2
Cerebrovascular diseases	9.1	4.5	5.2	8.0	12.7	15.5
Arteriosclerosis	1.5	.2	.3	.8	2.0	4.3
Other	1.7	1.0	1.6	2.0	2.0	2.0
Malignant neoplasms	20.6	30.2	31.2	26.5	18.0	9.9
Influenza and pneumonia	3.0	1.6	1.7	2.2	3.6	5.7
Diabetes mellitus	1.8	1.6	1.9	2.1	2.0	1.4
Accidents	5.5	6.5	3.3	2.0	1.8	1.9
Suicides	1.4	2.8	1.3	.6	.3	.1
All other	17.6	20.7	16.7	15.2	13.2	11.0

SOURCE: *Every Ninth American*, p. 15.
* Less than 500.

- A 1981 survey by Louis Harris and Associates found that 22 percent of the elderly in the United States are currently engaged in volunteer work and another 10 percent who do not now volunteer are interested in doing so.[23]
- Persons 65 + are the heaviest subscribers to daily newspapers and have the highest rates of regular TV news viewership of any age group in the population.

International Statistics on Aging

In 1980, the world's 60 + people numbered about 442 million, an increase of over 150 million since 1970. By 2000, the total number may reach 620 million, and by the year 2025, it is expected to reach nearly 1.1 billion.[24]

According to the United Nations projections, the proportion of the population aged 60 and over in more developed regions will grow from 11 percent in 1950 to over 22 percent in 2025. In parallel, less developed countries will see the percentage of older people in their populations increase from an average of 7 percent in 1950 to over 11 percent by 2025. Disaggregation of the estimates to the national level reveals that in some cases, such as in China, this proportion will be as high as 19 percent by 2025, just 3 percentage points under that estimated for North America.

In absolute terms, the numbers of persons aged 60 and over in more developed countries will nearly double between 1975 and 2025, rising from 166 million to 315 million people. In contrast, during the same time period the numbers of older persons in developing regions will more than quadruple, increasing from 180 million to 806 million people and thus accounting for over 70 percent of the world population aged 60 or older. The differential increase in numbers of persons aged 80 and over will be even more marked. During the 1975–2025 period, the size of this age group will double in developed regions, shifting from 19 million to 44 million people. Less developed regions will have to provide for 67 million people aged 80 or over in 2025, five times more very old persons than they have now.

Over the next three decades there will continue to be an increase in the absolute and relative size of the aging population in all regions and most countries of the world. This trend will accelerate in the majority of less developed countries. If the trend toward lowered birth rates continues, the more developed countries will have even greater proportions of their populations in the old-age category.[25]

There are more women than men in the more advanced years. With increasing industrialization and urbanization throughout the world there is the related phenomenon of mass migrations of young and better educated segments of rural populations to cities. The elderly are often left behind, increasing their numbers disproportionately in rural areas and depriving them of traditional resources and social support, particularly of younger family members. The number of persons age 75 and over and 85 and over, especially in more developed countries, is increasing more rapidly than that of any other age group of 60 or over. For these people of more advanced age, the provision of health and social services, institutional care, and continued income maintenance become critical issues.

Life Expectancy

Although life expectancy is increasing, and despite the fact that today's elderly are physiologically younger at advanced stages than their counterparts a century ago, there has been a trend toward earlier retirement from the labor force. To clarify needs of those who have not yet reached 65 in regard to their preparation for new social roles and identities, some examination of their numbers and proportion in the population is required.

A number of industrialized and urbanized countries have achieved a life expectancy of more than 75 years for women and more than 70 years for men. However, for the less developed countries the average life expectancy at birth is far lower, slightly less than 50 years, in some less than 40 years, for both men and women. These countries will, on the average, increase life expectancy by 16 years by the year 2000.

Tomorrow's Older People in the United States

A profile of older people in the year 2000 must be undertaken cautiously for unexpected trends could change predictions radically. Yet it seems likely that the future older person will differ from today's by being better educated, having a higher income, and probably experiencing better health. With the trend to early retirement and a probability that life expectancy will increase, tomorrow's older people could spend as much as a third of their life in "retirement."

Estimates now range from 23 million to 45 million for the number of persons aged 65 and older by the year 2000. The most common prognostication, however, is around 35 million[26]—8 million more than there are today. Today most older Americans are younger than 75. Moreover, only 2.5 million, about 9 percent of older Americans, are 85 or older. By 2000, there is likely to be a larger percentage of aged persons at the upper end of the age spectrum. Nearly 50 percent of older Americans, or 17 million persons, will be over the age of 75.

Most older persons are women, and this trend is expected to accelerate in the years ahead. Today there are approximately 150 women 65 and over for every 100 men. By 2000, this ratio is expected to increase to 155 for every 100. Two contrasting viewpoints emerge with regard to life expectancy. One school of thought maintains that life expectancy for adults who reach age 65 will not be much higher than it is today—approximately 13 years for men, 16 years for women, and 15 years on the average. Others contend, however, that if there are major breakthroughs in cancer, stroke, heart disease, and ailments associated with advancing age, it is conceivable that the average life expectancy at age 65 might be increased to 31 years—more than double what it is today. A third group now holds that changing life-styles of people, different nutrition, exercise, reduction of stress, and improved ecological factors could improve health more significantly and thus lengthen life.

Rising prices will continue to pose a major problem for persons living on fixed incomes. Even with a moderate increase in the cost of living, prices may be expected to rise by 50 percent during a typical period of retirement. While persons 65 and older constituted 17 percent of all voters who went to the polls in 1980, with an expanding population and an increased life expectancy, they may account for 20 to 25 percent of all votes in future elections. As Clark Tibbitts points out,

> there are positive roles for aging people, through which they can make valuable contributions to society. This point of view calls for a new concept of aging—a concept that gives recognition to the positive as well as the negative aspects of maturation.[27]

We do not know yet what these roles are. A combination of demographic factors, technological changes, and economic as well as political forces will create new conditions for roles to be developed and eventually validated. But it demands a vision and a perspective of the young, the middle-aged, and the old in concert to move toward such a conception.

> It is possible that, in the future, we will know enough about the biochemistry of aging to intervene in the aging process directly, by altering body chemistry through some treatment, as well as indirectly, through improved diet and health care. We may attain this knowledge in the foreseeable future, perhaps within the next 30 to 50 years. Some research in slowing down the aging process in lower forms of animal life has been promising. This new knowledge would mean that, by the year 2000, extra years of healthy life (if the intervention does not add healthy years, it is of little value) may be added to life expectancy. If so, some social questions emerge: What will happen to mandatory retirement in the sixties? What population increases will ensue, and what impact will they have? What will result from the increase in five-generation families? What will be the political implications of a much larger population percentage over 65?[28]

The demographic data presented here tell a story about our aging population and indicate their status, present conditions and future possibilities. These data provide a foundation for the social worker, a perspective, and an epidemiological orientation.

References

1. Adapted from: *Every Ninth American* (1982 Edition). An Analysis for the Chairman of the Select Committee on Aging, House of Representatives, 97th Congress, 2nd Session, July 1982.
2. Ibid.
3. *Chartbook on Aging in America*, 1981 White House Conference on Aging.
4. *Facts About Older Americans, 1977.* U.S. Department of Health, Education and Welfare, Office of Human Development Administration on Aging, National Clearing House on Aging, DHEW Publ. No. (OHD) 78-20006. Washington, D.C.: U.S. Government Printing Office, 1977.
5. *Every Ninth American* (1982 Edition), op. cit.
6. Robert N. Butler and Myrna I. Lewis, *Aging and Mental Health*, 3rd ed. (St. Louis, Mo.: C. V. Mosby and Sons, 1983).
7. Ibid.
8. Ibid.
9. M. Block, "Exiled Americans: The Plight of Indian Aged in the U.S.," in D. Gelfand and A. Kutzik (eds.), *Ethnicity and Aging* (New York: Springer, 1979).
10. Ibid.
11. Butler and Lewis, op. cit.
12. Lowell D. Holmes, *Other Cultures, Elder Years: An Introduction to Cultural Gerontology* (Minneapolis: Burgess Publishing Co., 1983), pp. 147–151.
13. Ibid.
14. *Chartbook on Aging in America*, op. cit.

15. *Families: Aging and Changing.* Hearing Before the Select Committee on Aging, House of Representatives, 96th Congress, 2nd Session, Nov. 24, 1980, San Diego, Calif. (Washington, D.C.: United States Government Printing Office, 1981), p. 1.
16. *Chartbook on Aging in America,* op. cit.
17. *Every Ninth American* (1982 Edition), op. cit.
18. 1983 Bureau of Labor Statistics.
19. *Developments in Aging, 1982: Vol. 1.* A Report of the Special Committee on Aging, U.S. Senate, p. 1.
20. *Chartbook on Aging in America,* op. cit., p. 130.
21. *Every Ninth American* (1982 Edition), op. cit.
22. *1981 White House Conference on Aging Mini-Conference on Housing for the Elderly,* June 1981 (Washington, D.C.: United States Government Printing Office, 1981), p. 3.
23. *Aging in the Eighties: America in Transition.* A Study for the NCOA, Inc., by Louis Harris and Associates, Inc., 1981.
24. *Bulletin on Aging,* Social Development Branch, United Nations Secretariat, vol. VI, no. 1 (1981), p. 9.
25. *The Aging: Trends and Policies* (New York: United Nations, 1975).
26. Herman B. Brotman, "Summary Table A: Middle Series Projections, All Ages and 65 +, By Race and Sex, 1982–2050 (Numbers in Thousands)," November 1982.
27. Clark Tibbitts in *Handbook of Social Gerontology* (Chicago: University of Chicago Press, 1959), p. 127.
28. Richard Kalish, *Late Adulthood: Perspectives on Human Development* (Monterey, Calif.: Brooks/Cole, 1975), p. 120.

4

Context and Framework for Social Work Practice

Societal Matrix

The societal matrix of social work is the environment that gives rise to its existence. All fields of human endeavor have been and continue to be responses to environment and also influences that affect environment. The Judeo-Christian religions have long held that humans are apart from nature, that nature is created for our use. The consequences of such a view have led to a rather intensive and extensive exploitation of our ecosystem with little concern about environmental pollution. When humans are seen as part of nature, the conditions of the ecosystem are included in our conception of the environment and the consequences involve potential action.

The resulting human conduct and interaction occur in an arena that is characterized by the four major phenomena of space and territory, time, matter and material resources, and people. These phenomena influence and shape the manifestations of nature in their myriad ways, and are also influenced and shaped by them. The precise extent and exact proportion of their interplay are at the heart of the scientific inquiry of yesterday, today, and tomorrow. Territory, material resources, and population throughout time give rise to a culture that is essentially "a system of beliefs, values and expressive symbols which govern [our] relations to [our fellow beings] and to [our physical] environment."[1]

Culture has several segments. The social structure of a social order, one such segment, comes into being through a set of ideas that define the rights and obligations of the positions people occupy in groups. Technology, another segment, represents the application of the knowledge of nature to empirical ends, ends attainable by humans. Technology, therefore, is always instrumental to a goal; and goals are influenced, if not shaped, by beliefs and values that have emerged throughout time. All social life arises from attempts to respond to the demands of the physical and cultural environment and to solve the problems of existence and survival that are shared by all people, everywhere, throughout all times.

The elemental drive to survive in a physical and cultural milieu on the one hand and the desire to find a purpose and meaning for survival on the other have led to attempts to devise solutions for specific times and places circumscribed by culture. Every society has to solve problems in order to exist and survive in the physical and cultural environment. This requires the performance of a series of functions. How these universal functional problems are solved and how these requisite functions are performed are conditioned by the physical and cultural environment and by the passage of time, history, and traditions. Five major functions can be enumerated: (1) providing for the existential needs of the population, (2) allocating of resources and property rights, (3) maintaining order with justice, (4) assuring continuity and socialization, and (5) creating social integration through participation.[2]

People's Needs and Society's Imperatives

Inherent in the existence of people and society is a dichotomous condition. Society must solve certain problems to ensure its continued existence and fulfill its needs or imperatives. People must also solve certain problems to ensure both their existence in the social matrix and also the fulfillment of their own needs and strivings — which frequently are not in harmony with those of their society. A person's symbiotic relationship with the society and the variance of one's needs from those of society produce tensions, stresses, and strains. Abraham Maslow's hierarchy of needs postulates that higher types of human needs can be gratified only after lower types have been gratified. At the bottom he places physiological and safety needs, moving upward to needs for love and belonging; further up to those for esteem, achievement, and recognition; then to self-actualization; and finally, to the needs to know and understand.[3] We encounter a number of needs that correspond, in some measure, to societal imperatives, although no theoretical hierarchical system has been developed for those as Maslow has done for human needs.

The particular demands made upon people at various stages of life have been referred to as the developmental tasks of infancy, childhood, adolescence, young adulthood, middle age, later years, and old age.[4] There is always a certain degree of disequilibrium between societal demands and a person's ability to cope with them, despite one's "training" for them during the socialization process. People who manage better than others are said to be functioning better socially. In times of accelerated cultural, technical, and social change, when there is less stability and tranquility, tensions usually increase and people generally find it harder to cope. Coping with varying and complicated demands at particular stages in the life cycle are not the only concerns for people. Their variety of needs may not be fulfilled in a satisfactory way or at a satisfactory time.

When physiological, safety, and esteem needs have been reasonably well met, people are ready to find gratification in self-actualization and in understanding the world and their own existence in it; to take part in enjoying the gifts of life and nature; to enhance the quality of living for themselves and for their family, peers, and friends; to engage responsibly and creatively to improve the lives of others in their Faustian endeavor. We are, therefore, concerned not only with social functioning, but also with personal fulfillment. People today must learn to actualize themselves not only as members of their own culture and society, but also as members of a world society and a culture of all people. This is only a vision today, but to strive toward its achievement is worthy of our best efforts. To assure people of all ages a maximum of security and the opportunity to function to the best of their ability and to attain personal fulfillment as participants in the world requires a number of social mechanisms and arrangements.

Social Mechanisms

Two major mechanisms by which society can develop a social security system designed to assure optimal existential conditions for all people are social policies and social practices. Realizing one's maximum potential and achieving existential fulfillment go beyond the level of experiencing a secure economic existence. Personal fulfillment is the opportunity to experience maximum growth as a participating member of society from youth through old age. It is predicated on assured economic security and on social security, which is the floor upon which the ladder toward personal and social fulfillment of people can be erected.

Both mechanisms are concerned with social functioning and the "interventions and regulations of an otherwise random social system."[5] They operate on a macro level and are designed to "promote the welfare of the whole population through a system of laws, programs and services."[6] According to Alvin L. Schorr, a social policy is a "course of action with respect to selected social phenomena governing social relationships and the distribution of resources within a society."[7] As such, it functions as a societal institution primarily concerned with social provisions for the population. Social insurances, health insurances, unemployment programs, and care for the sick and the disabled at every age are manifestations and features of a social policy. In several countries, there has been a broadening of this conception to extend across the range of all types of social and health services and all governmental intervention in the private market.[8] Increasingly, all economic policy is seen as part of social policy, and distribution of income and resources is viewed as germane to social policy.[9]

Within this context, social policy is designed to build a social security system for the total population. The extent of a society's social policy and its resulting laws, programs, and services are conditioned by social philosophy, value commitment, history, tradition, and a host of other variables. Recently, people who make social policy in a number of countries have expressed interest in the goals of human fulfillment, including educational policy as part of social policy.[10] Autonomous domains and efforts to maintain tight boundaries in social systems are still powerful enough, though, to thwart such inclusive efforts at the present time. Social policies have increasingly come to be seen as pillars of "social security"[11] in western and eastern Europe, if not yet in the United States, where there does not exist a comprehensive statement of national goals or a social policy encompassing such goals, though the "crisis of the welfare state" is a phenomenon of the mid-1980s in all major industrialized countries.

Social and Societal Policy

The tasks of social policy in societies go beyond the present ones. Social policy should eventually become societal policy, which influences various societal functions in order to create conditions so that people can find creative fulfillment and self-realization as social participants. Societal policy would indeed become the frame of reference that guarantees not only existential social security but also personal fulfillment. The goals of such societal policy should be primarily directed toward changing the structures (e.g., social institutions) to make them more responsive to changing human needs at various stages of the life cycle within a societal context, and toward changing sociocultural values and norms that are inimical to healthy growth and development, and therefore inhibit full-range human fulfillment through social participation for all ages.

Such goals can be achieved through appropriate and knowledgeable interventive planning methods, which are predicated upon a problem-solving approach.

> This mode of intervention in social problems rests on the assumption that their causes lie not in individual dysfunction but in system dysfunction and the inability of the community to provide the basic necessities of food, clothing, shelter; protection against disease, disaster and war; requisite social necessities of social power distribution, social communication, social control, and common value systems.[12]

> Social-problem solving originates in a recognition on the part of an individual or a group that there is a disjunction between an existing social situation (e.g., higher rates of infant mortality or poor health among elderly) and an ideal state or standard (the elimination of differences in such rates that are attributable to age, gender or race). The recognition of a gap between present reality and some valued future state provides the impetus for initiating activities that are managed by an individual or group who have been mandated or who have assumed the responsibility for planning.[13]

Social work is one field of practice that has carved out a domain to deal with problems that people encounter with regard to their social functioning, and beyond that to enhance human fulfillment and self-realization through active social participation. Social work is one of the social practice mechanisms that intervenes in order to mediate tensions between society's imperatives and a person's needs, wants, and expectations.

The Practice Continuum

A central goal of social work is to enable people to improve their social functioning, that is, to carry out their social roles in a way that is consistent with their ego capacities.[14] A major focus has been on socially assisting people to cope with life situations and conditions that present difficulties. Bartlett has taken this central idea and has elaborated it by stating that social work attempts to strike a balance between the demands of the social environment and people's coping efforts through working with them singly, in small groups, or in social organizations, either directly or through collaborative action.[15]

Treatment has been a key aspect of this type of social work, despite the fact that American social work has a long-standing tradition of social reform efforts that have concentrated on intervention to make social institutions more responsive to the needs of people rather than expect people to adhere and conform to unresponsive social systems. This type of intervention has moved closer to social policy (and even to societal policy), and there is agreement that a link between these two major modes of intervention is essential although they represent only one side of a coin, one aspect of a continuum.

Treatment of disturbed relationships among people, the procurement of financial aid through supplementary income, and support during periods of crisis and stress belong to the segment of ameliorative services on the malfunctioning end of the continuum of social functioning and human fulfillment. But people have "normal" problems of living as well. To meet the daily tasks of human existence in complex societies, to face up to the demands of being a child in school or a worker in a factory, of retirement in later years or death in old age are all normal events that can become crises under a certain confluence of variables.

At the other end of the continuum are the functions of growth and development and the enhancement of personal fulfillment, to be part of the world in a creative way, to be active in improving the human and social conditions for self and others, to continue to learn in order to know and understand oneself and one's fellow human beings, to realize one's own potential and to help realize the potential of others. From a person's malfunctioning we move via normal functioning to optimal functioning; and from amelioration of troublesome conditions and their treatment we move through deliberate, change-oriented action toward development and enhancement of the person in his social world. As Falck defines social work, its central focus is management of membership through planned helping and rational activities.[16]

In the late 1970s Carol Germain and Alex Gitterman developed *The Life Model of Social Work Practice*, which is based on an ecological perspective.[17] Attention is directed to the transactional processes of adaptation, stress, and coping, and the need for particular environmental supports for the release of the human potential. Humans adapt by changing themselves, changing environments, or moving to new environments. The *life model of practice* places emphasis on the *transactions* between people and environments; the social work function is to assist people to achieve a better match between their needs and situational, environmental conditions and qualities.

People at any age have to manage certain life-tasks that arise out of such transactions. These occur in these reciprocally related areas of living and may result in a variety of problems, coping difficulties, and/or stress.

1. Life transitions (e.g., developmental tasks as people grow older), status and role changes (e.g., retirement), specific crisis situations (e.g., loss of a spouse).
2. Environmental situational conditions (physical and social) that can include changes in housing (e.g., placement in a long-term care institution), natural crises or disasters (e.g., fires or floods), dealing with bureaucratic organizations (e.g., handling claims for Social Insurance and/or Medicaid, or negotiating the myriad arrays of the "aging network").
3. Patterns of interpersonal relationships and communications, such as difficulties in family relationships; problems with peers; disturbances in communications with kin, friends, public officials, functionaries, physicians, social workers, etc.

Figure 4.1 attempts to portray the "life model" and its relationship to social work intervention processes.[18]

As Getzel and Mellor point out, "The social worker's historical concern with human beings at the point of interface with the environment has special utility for work with the elderly. The environment that fits the changing needs of older persons contributes to their enhanced autonomy, competence and self-esteem. A bio-psycho-social conception of human beings is crucial in helping the aged. Assessment for social work intervention with or on behalf of the elderly involves a sophisticated understanding of life-long development, human aging and those particular health, social and economic conditions that individually and cumulatively challenge the elderly's adaptive and creative capacities."[19]

Components of Practice

The following framework is used to delineate social work analytically as a field of practice on a continuum within a societal matrix. The five components of social work practice with the elderly—as with any age group—are values, purposes and goals, sanctions, knowledge, and its intervention process.[20]

Values

All practice is guided by values, or "preferred stances of behavior." It may be more appropriate to speak of *valuations* rather than *values* since these imply an immutable universality that is based on "an objectivism that has no basis in logic and tends to concede much confusion."[21] Valuations are subjective reactions to the property of real values, always changing in accord with changing cultural environmental conditions of people.[22]

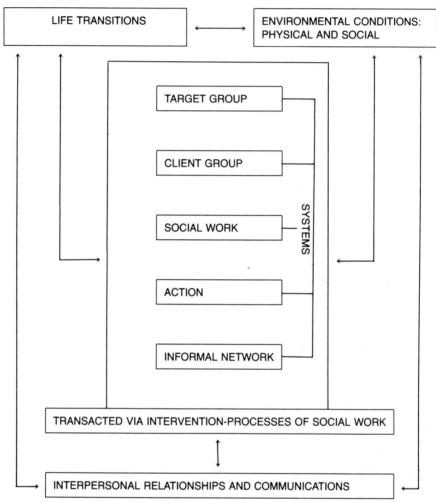

Figure 4.1. Representation of "Life-Model" and Intervention Processes of Social Work. Figure reprinted from and translated by Louis Lowy, *Sozialarbeit/Sozialpädagogik als Wissenschaft im angloamerikanischen und deutschsprachigen Raum* (West Germany: Lambertus-Verlag, 1983), p. 87.

At least five categories of valuations have been identified: human nature, people's relationship to other people in society, society in relation to people, the process of knowing, and the process of helping (mutual aid). Under each category a series of values can be subsumed on a high level of abstraction, which in turn must be operationalized in the crucible of practice. Conflicting valuations and inconsistent beliefs abound in every society and in social work as well.

Purpose and Goals

Three major purposes and goals of social work span the continuum from treatment to development: the curative and ameliorative, the preventive, and the promotional and enhancing. The curative, treatment-oriented goals have been accepted as a major province of social work. Intra- and interpersonal tensions and stress conditions, role conflicts, deviant behavior, and age-connected isolation of people have been traditional problem areas for social work intervention. Thoughts about public health and a raised public consciousness about social problems have moved social work toward prevention. This calls for attention to large-scale social problems and commitment to action to deal with such persistent problems as poverty, drug dependency, and alcoholism, and problems connected with the process of growing older and the position of the elderly in society. The war on poverty in 1964 led to the conception and execution of community action programs that have had a marked influence upon social work, including work with the aged.

Commitments to the third goal, to promote and enhance the quality of life, is of more recent origin. In the past, this goal was mostly expressed in the fields of recreation and informal and adult education rather than in the field of social work.[23] The developmental orientation, which increasingly tends to become part of the goals and practice of social work, especially in the developing countries of the world, seeks to create conditions for people that allow them to fulfill themselves optimally, find their place in tomorrow's world, and participate constructively and actively in the society as part of a larger world order. Fundamentally, this aspect of social work is oriented toward learning; it is the second and cultural part of the continuum.

Sanctions

Social work, like any other field, is not practiced in a vacuum. It is given sanction by society, which extends its degrees of legal authority for the implementation of its purposes in a variety of service agencies and by nonagency affiliated, autonomous social workers in private practice. When we view society as dynamic and ever-changing, this view accommodates conflicting forces and claims; when we view it as static and harmonious, this view preserves a status quo.

Sanctioning by society does not imply an establishment orientation or a commitment to adjustment functions to ensure conformity to the predominant cultural norms or adaptation at any price to prevailing social structures. It rather implies that social work is a force for the social integration of people and for a personalization that enables people to develop their own responses to societal expectations, with commensurate effects upon the social and cultural milieu. Thus social integration also means adaptation of the environment to the needs of the individual. It is an axiom of social work practice that when societal imperatives clash with the needs, desires, aspirations, and wishes of people, one accepts such conflict as natural and inherent in the work.

Work with the aged is similarly sanctioned. Settings and auspices vary considerably, and depending on the purpose and orientation of the programs and services offered, the consumers may be clients, patients, members, partners, constituents, or citizens. Patients and clients usually receive curative and ameliorative services. Other consumers are usually involved in action or development programs designed to enhance the well-being of individuals, families, groups, and organizations. Sanctions cover types of programs or services; organizational, personal, financial, and administrative structures through which the programs or services are offered; delivery of programs and services by matching them with the needs of people; provision for planning; and the creation and improvement of programs and services when needed.

Knowledge

Social work practice is based upon knowledge derived from a variety of disciplines — biology, psychology, sociology, social psychology, psychiatry, anthropology, law, theology, etc. It is also derived from systematized practice theory and accumulated practice wisdom that has emerged in the course of social work activities over the years. In addition, social welfare policies, programs, and services represent a matrix of knowledge areas that are requisite for every social worker. When we speak of knowledge, we need to differentiate among what is definitely known (empirically verified), what is tentatively known (in a hypothetical state), what is assumed to be known, and what is as yet unknown and based on beliefs. Social work practice is thus predicated upon knowledge in varying states. If application by practitioners results in ready and efficient performance, we speak of such technical expertness as *skills*.

The Intervention Process

Intervention is the "action of the practitioner which is directed to some part of the social system or social process with the intention of inducing a change in it."[24] Intervention aims at making a difference in outcome and in the course of events. It is guided by a constellation of values, purposes, and knowledge, and is based upon legal or institutional sanctions. It is justified on the basis of creative altruism. Social work has historically and declaratively shown regard for and devotion to the interests of others through service. Creativity is a necessary condition for effective service to other people.

Intervention has historically involved social work methods of casework, group work, and community organization. In the United States, the development of these three methods has been almost synonymous with the development of social work practice itself. These methods have different historical roots and therefore differ in development emphasis and focus. It is fundamental that each method contributes to a more inclusive and encompassing approach that includes relevant knowledge and values as well as techniques.[25] "Interventive acts and techniques are means to an end and are significant only when the end is defined in terms of social work purposes and values and the situation is accurately understood through the use of social work knowledge. It is through the conscious action of the social worker, who selects what is relevant for the particular situation before him or her that the appropriate knowledge and values become integrated with intervention."[26]

This type of thinking opened up a segmented practice orientation that makes it increasingly possible to rearrange the knowledge and attendant methodological skills gained from casework, group work, and community organization. New interventive repertoires resulted and the ingredients of the social work methods can be used for the widened purposes of social work and applied to the total purpose continuum. This includes treatment, when social functioning is impaired; action, to prevent problems that impinge on social functioning; and development, to enhance social functioning and allow for maximum self-realization for responsible and creative social participation. This last is the realization of the responsible and creative social dimensions of human existence.

The emergence of the "life model" has contributed significantly to these newer conceptualizations, the "discovery" of formal and informal networks,[27] and the contributions by "Agogik," originated by Benne, Bennis, and Chin[28] in the United States and known here as "the planning of change" model. This was refined by van Beugen in the Netherlands[29] and further elaborated by European social workers in the 1970s. Change can be designed, planned, and implemented, though in its implementation the results of these changes demand new adaptations, new designs, new plans, and new implementations. It is a cybernetic rather than a linear process.

There are five dimensions in the intervention process: specific targets of intervention, specific goals for intervention deduced from the general purposes of social work, steps in the intervention process, activities of the intervener (including modalities, methods, and techniques), and the roles of the intervener primarily as enabler, broker, advocate, expert, as well as therapist and teacher. Having outlined the major framework, let us now proceed with a more detailed discussion of these five components as they relate to social work practice with the aged.

References

1. Harold L. Wilensky and Charles N. Lebeaux, *Industrial Society and Social Welfare* (New York: Russell Sage Foundation, 1958), p. 342. A second, revised edition is available in paperback (New York: Free Press, 1966).
2. Adapted from the works of Talcott Parsons, *The Social System* (New York: Free Press, 1951); Kingsley Davis, *Human Society* (New York: Macmillan, 1949); Roland L. Warren, *The Community in America* (Skokie, Ill.: Rand McNally, 1963).

3. Abraham Maslow, *Motivation and Personality* (New York: Saunders, 1954).
4. Erik H. Erikson, *Childhood and Society* (New York: Norton, 1950); "Identity and the Life Cycle," *Papers by Erik H. Erikson* (New York: International Universities Press, 1959).
5. Alvin L. Schorr and Edward C. Baumheier, "Social Policy," *Encyclopedia of Social Work* (New York: NASW, 1971), p. 1362.
6. Ibid.
7. Ibid.
8. Ibid.
9. United Nations Reports, *1970 Report on the World Social Situation*, Social Development Division, Department of Economic and Social Affairs, United Nations, New York.
10. T. H. Marshall, *Social Policy in the Twentieth Century*, 2nd ed. (London: Hutchinson, 1967).
11. "The Changing Role of Social Welfare" in *National Social Service Systems: A Comparative Study* (Washington, D.C.: Division of International Activities, HEW, September 1970), chap. 2, pp. 3–6.
12. Alvin Schorr and Edward Baumheier, op. cit., p. 1370.
13. Robert Perlman, "Social Planning and Community Organization: Approaches," *Encyclopedia of Social Work* (1970), p. 1338.
14. Werner Boehm, *Curriculum Study of the Council on Social Work Education*, vol. I (New York, 1959).
15. Harriet M. Bartlett, *The Common Base of Social Work Practice* (New York: NASW, 1970).
16. Hans S. Falck, "The Membership Model of Social Work," *Social Work*, no. 29, 1984, pp. 155–160.
17. Carol B. Germain and Alex Gitterman, *The Life Model of Social Work Practice* (New York: Columbia University Press, 1980).
18. Louis Lowy, *Sozialarbeit/Sozialpädagogik als Wissenschaft im angloamerikanischen und deutschsprachigen Raum* (West Germany: Lambertus-Verlag, 1983), p. 87.
19. George Getzel and M. Joanne Mellor, "Introduction: Overview of Gerontological Social Work in Long Term Care," *Journal of Gerontological Social Work*, vol. 5, no. 1/2, 1982.
20. "Working Definition of Social Work Practice," as amended in Harriet M. Bartlett, op. cit., pp. 51–61.
21. Gunnar Myrdal, at the 14th International Conference of Social Welfare, Helsinki, 1968.
22. J. M. Bochenski, "Der Wert," in *Wege zum Philosophischen Denken* (Freiburg i. Br.: Herder Buecherei, 1959).
23. Louis Lowy, *Adult Education and Group Work* (New York: Whiteside and William R. Morrow, 1955).
24. Harriet M. Bartlett, op. cit., p. 161.
25. Harriet M. Bartlett, op. cit., p. 164.
26. Ibid.
27. Alice Collins and Diane Pancoast, *Natural Helping Networks* (New York: NASW, 1976).
28. K. Benne, W. Bennis, and R. Chin, *The Planning of Change* (New York: Holt, Rinehart, & Winston, 1969).
29. M. van Beugen, *Agogische Intervention* (Freiburg i. Br.: Lambertus, 1972).

5

Values as Context
for Work
with the Aging

Social work is a normative profession and values have a significant impact on its practice.[1] Values are defined as "conceptions of preferred and admirable things or characteristics of people"[2] and "preferred stances of thinking, feeling and doing."[3] They affect the people toward whom practice is directed, as well as the quality of social work.

Major Social Work Values

Throughout social work's history in North America two values have dominated its practice: the worth, dignity, and uniqueness of the individual and the right to self-determination by individuals, groups, or constituents in a community. This does not suggest that other values have been ignored, such as the reciprocal responsibility of people and society. What it does suggest, however, is a predominance of these two values in the thinking, feeling, and doing of social workers in the practice of the English-speaking world.

In the following excerpts from Beulah Compton and Burt Galaway's book *Social Work Processes*, these two major values are discussed within the context of social work practice in general.

RESPECT FOR THE DIGNITY AND UNIQUENESS OF THE INDIVIDUAL[4]

One of the central value premises which has been consistently accepted and supported by the social work profession is that each person is a unique individual with an inherent dignity which is to be respected. People are sufficient ends in and of themselves and are not to be treated as objects or means to some other ends. And each individual is unique; diversity and variety are to be welcomed and encouraged. Paul Tillich, a theologian who has directed attention to the philosophy of social work, refers to the uniqueness of every individual and situation as man's existential nature which he sees social work as promoting.[5] William Gordon derived his matching concept of the social work function from the basic notion that the social work profession does not attempt to move either the environment or the person towards some ideal model but rather strives to establish linkages between individuals and their environment allowing for the widest possible diversity of both people and environment.[6]

But what are some of the implications of this principle for social work practice? How can the premise that every individual is unique and has the right to be treated with respect and dignity be applied in concrete specific social work situations? The potential for operationalizing the value premise will be considered in two areas—sensitivity on the part of the social workers to messages they are giving to others about themselves and, secondly, the issue of whether or not classification procedures detract from individualization.

Social psychologists have established the position that people's image of themselves develops largely out of their communication with others. Specifically, people build and incorporate their own self-image from the messages they receive from other people about themselves. Further, people who feel good about themselves, see themselves as persons of worth, and have a sense of their own strength and capability, tend to be happier and have the ability to deal constructively and appropriately with their environment. Given these positions, social workers and other professionals intervening in the lives of people are well advised to be constantly sensitive to the messages they are extending to others about the worth of that person. Do we, in the little things we do, communicate to the other person that he is a unique individual to be highly prized? What, for example, is the message communicated when we safeguard time and provide a client with a specific time to be seen as opposed to a catch me on a catch can basis for visits?

Do appointments in advance communicate to the client a higher sense of respect than unannounced visits or hurriedly arranged telephone appointments? And, speaking of telephoning, how about the all too frequently overlooked return call? What message does the client get from the worker in terms of the client's worth when the worker does not have the courtesy or good sense to promptly return telephone calls? How about the ability to listen to the client, to secure from the individual his account of his situation, and to avoid [prior] judgments. And does not privacy both in terms of how we conduct the interviews and how we treat the material gained from interviews communicate something to the client about the esteem in which we hold him? The workers, attempting to operationalize the premise of individual uniqueness and dignity, may find it useful to repeatedly inquire of themselves, "What does this action on my part communicate to the clients about my perception of their personhood?" . . . keeping in mind that our behaviors probably communicate much more effectively than our words.

Another thorny problem confronting the social worker attempting to operationalize the value premise of individual uniqueness and dignity, is the issue of striking a balance between the need to classify and the responsibility to respond to persons as individuals. Classification here refers to the need to generalize beyond individuals and to organize phenomena on the basis of common characteristics. This process is essential in order to make sense out of a mass of raw data and is an essential part of the process of knowledge building. When the phenomena we are dealing with are people, however, there is an inherent danger in classification; we may start responding to people as objects placed in a particular category rather than as individuals.

The pitfalls of this process are being documented in a growing body of literature from the labeling perspective of the sociology of deviance field.[7] Not only does labeling or classification lead to distortion of individual differences, but, as labeling theorists and their supporting research are noting, a person labeled deviant, those doing the labeling, and the surrounding audience frequently respond to the deviant on the basis of the label rather than the individual characteristics. This creates conditions for development of a self-fulfilling prophecy in which the person becomes what he has been labeled.[8] Current efforts, for example, to divert youth out of the juvenile justice system are recognition of the position that just the process of labeling a youngster delinquent may contribute pressure towards additional delinquencies. Hans Toch states the problem succinctly:

Playing the classification game in the abstract, as is done in Universities, is a joyful, exhilarating experience, harmless and inconsequential. Classifying people in life is a grim business which channelizes destinies and determines fate. A man becomes a category, he is processed as a category, plays his assigned role, lives up to the implications. Labeled irrational, he acts crazy; catalogued dangerous he becomes dangerous or he stays behind bars.[9]

Dr. Karl Menninger, a noted psychiatrist, has reacted with strong words to the 1968 publication of a revised set of diagnostic (i.e., labeling) categories for psychiatry:

A committee of our worldly national body has just (1968) published a manual containing a full description of all the bewitchments to which all human flesh is heir to, with the proper names for each one, the minute suborder and subspecies listed and a code number for the computer. The colleagues who prepared this witch's hammer manual are worthy fellows— earnest, honest, hard-working, simplistic; they were taught to believe that these horrible things exist, these things with Greek names and Arabic numerals. And if a patient shows the stigmata, should he not be given the label and the number? To me this is not only the revival of medieval nonsense and superstition; it is a piece of social immorality.[10]

Social workers who are sometimes prone to adopt psychiatric terms and classifications might pay special heed to Menninger's concern.

But isn't some classification necessary? Or, are we to agree with [Elizabeth] Salomon's position that there is an inherent conflict between the needs of science to order and classify and the humanism of social work?[11] Toch suggests that "the point of concern rests in any labels that lead to sorting or disposition."[12] Toch takes the position that the labeling is necessary, for thinking or theory building is not particularly helpful in making dispositional decisions about people; concern should occur when decisions about what is going to happen to people are based upon the individual's having previously been placed in a particular category. And yet it is precisely at this point that classification appears to be most useful. Generally classifications come into play at the time when professionals are attempting to assess or diagnose a situation and then serve as a guide in selecting appropriate procedures for dealing with the problem.

Labeling older persons as "the aged" or "senior citizens" or even "golden-agers" without taking into account the uniqueness of each older person can only lead to a reinforcement of stereotypes (as will be pointed out later) and increase prevailing myths and thereby deny the older person the psychosocial perspective which social work applies to members of other age groups.

CLIENT SELF-DETERMINATION

The principle of client self-determination derives logically from the belief in the innate dignity of the person. If people possess an inherent dignity, then it follows that they should be permitted to become what they wish—insofar as possible, to determine their own life style. The belief in client self-determination clearly implies that people should be permitted to make decisions for themselves and carries with it the rather clear assumption that most of the time these decisions will be responsible . . . in the sense that people . . . will, for the most part, make decisions which are consistent with the welfare of the community. The social work stance has generally been to couple the concept of client self-determination with that of responsibility for the total community and to attempt to work out a balance between the two. Barring some clear cut indication of danger to others, however, the social workers in their day-to-day contacts with clients will generally attempt to maximize opportunities for client self-determination.

Inherent in the concept of client self-determination is the idea of alternatives. Self-determination implies decisions or the making of choices between one course of action contrasted with other courses of action. If there is only one course of action, how can there be self-determination? The client has no choice and thus no opportunity to be self-determining. Much of social work activity with clients might be thought of as a quest for alternatives in order to expand the client's opportunities for self-determination. The quest for alternatives may take many forms—helping the client develop new alternatives and resources within the environment or helping the client find and develop new ways to respond to . . . [the] environment. Thus, interventive activity may focus on removing blockages within the environment which are limiting the client's opportunities or [on] helping the client remove [inner] blockages that are limiting [the] ability to see alternative courses of action. [People] whose range of responses to [their] environment is limited by [their] own stereotyped and patterned behavior [are] as much lacking in opportunity for self-determination as the ghetto client confronted with [a] lack of environmental opportunities for choice. The principle of client self-determination, thus, will lead the social worker in the direction of developing alternatives where the client can in fact [make the decisions] implied in the concept of self-determination. . . .

This is one of the areas in which the social work profession may differ markedly from other professions. One generally goes to other professionals for expert advice, . . . expecting to be told what in the view of the professional is the best for the client. One expects the doctor to diagnose and to recommend a specific course of treatment or for the lawyer to tell us what action we should take in dealing with a legal problem. In both of these situations, of course, there is an element of self-determination inasmuch as the patient or client must ultimately make a decision as to whether or not to follow the expert's advice. In most dealings with professionals in our culture, the decision-making authority of the client is largely overshadowed by the expertise of the professional and, to a large extent, limited to the decision of whether or not to accept the professional's advice. But [this is] not so with the social work profession.

The expertise of the social worker lies less in the substantive areas of knowing what is best for the client[s] and more in the process area of assisting the client[s] in developing alternatives for themselves, making a decision amongst those alternatives, and then implementing the decision. To assume that one knows what is best for clients runs the very grave risk of developing what Matthew Dumont refers to as a rescue fantasy:

The most destructive thing in psychotherapy is a "rescue fantasy" in the therapist—a feeling that the therapist is the divinely sent agent to pull a tormented soul from the pit of suffering and adversity and put him back on the road to happiness and glory. A major reason this fantasy is so destructive is that it carries the conviction that the patient will be saved only through and by the therapist. When such a conviction is communicated to the patient, verbally or otherwise, he has no choice other than to rebel and leave or become even more helpless, dependent, and sick.[13]

It is sometimes frustrating for [new or even experienced workers] to come to grips with the reality that [they] cannot be full of all wisdom [and] masterfully assume and resolve the client's problems. A certain humility is necessary to recognize that the client is the chief problem solver. This is not to deny that the worker plays a major part in assisting the client through the process, [at times serving] rather forcefully as the client's agent. Does the foregoing suggest that the social worker [is never to] offer an opinion or . . . make suggestions? Emphatically, no. Just as the extreme of taking over and making decisions for the client is to be avoided so is the extreme of never sharing with the client our own viewpoint. Such action denies clients the benefit of our viewpoint and may effectively deny clients alternatives that they may wish to consider in [making] their own decision[s].

Long ago, Charlotte Towle recognized this danger[:] "The social worker's devotion to the idea that every individual has a right to be self-determining does not rule out our valid concern with directing people's attention to the most desirable alternative."[14] Workers have obligations to share with clients [their] own thinking, perhaps [their] own experiences, not as a way of directing the client's life but rather as an additional source of information and input for [making decisions]. It is imperative, however, that [this be] recognized as input to be considered and not as edict to be followed. Schwartz offers some very helpful suggestions in this regard.[15] [He] suggests that the worker does have a responsibility for making a contribution of data to the client [including] facts, ideas, and value concepts. . . . Schwartz argues that it is important to make clear that the worker is offering only part of the total available social experience; indeed, the worker is not the fountainhead of all knowledge. [He] suggests that the data contributed should be clearly related to the purpose of work with the client and [that] while opinions are important data, they should be clearly labeled as opinions and not represented as facts.

Client self-determination does not imply [no] worker . . . participation; the skill, and indeed the mark of a successful practitioner, lies in the [practitioner's] ability to share [his or her] knowledge and thinking without imposing [a personal]

viewpoint . . . leaving the client free to accept or reject the worker's view. . . .
One other aspect of self-determination requires emphasis. Some workers confuse
client self-determination and worker self-determination. Workers, in taking on a
professional responsibility, agree, tacitly at least, to limit their own self-determination
on the behalf of clients. The National Association of Social Workers Code of
Ethics clearly limits worker self-determination, especially within the seventh clause:
"I practice social work within the recognized knowledge and competence of the
profession." When . . . communication styles or dress styles [of workers] are an-
tagonistic to clients or to others who may influence clients, [the workers'] professional
responsibility calls for forfeiting . . . their own self-determination on the behalf
of their clients.[16]

Implications for Working with the Elderly

In our industrialized, youth-oriented society, the elderly have been accorded relatively
little respect or opportunity for self-determination. The core of attitudes, values,
beliefs, stereotypes, and myths that have shaped society's policy and the behavior
of many professionals, including social workers, toward this age group points to
the importance of separating values from knowledge. Knowledge is based on verifiable
data; values are based on belief, on what is felt to be true rather than proven to
be true. Knowledge about the aging process is incomplete, and what is available
has not been adequately disseminated throughout the professions and the society.

We tend to base our attitudes on the values and beliefs society holds and to
treat these beliefs and values as if they were knowledge. This leads to misperceptions,
lack of understanding, and lack of commitment to devote financial, technological,
and human resources to the elderly population. Like all of us, older people tend
to incorporate society's values about themselves as true, and thus they come to
embody many of the negative images that society portrays of aging. The same holds
true for women, many of whom have tended to accept themselves as the lesser of
the sexes.

We live in a highly urbanized, industrialized, technological society that emphasizes
productivity and technical skills. Those who can contribute productively and skillfully
to the economy are highly valued; those who no longer can or are no longer allowed
to are not valued. Predominant value orientations of materialistic individualism,
residues of a Calvinistic work ethic, and the equation of youthfulness with beauty,
progress, and adventure leave the elderly in a vulnerable and devalued position.
We are dealing with a set of attitudes that are shaped by these predominant value
orientations throughout society.

Ethical Issues

Medical crises, diminishing resources, and rapidly advancing medical technology
mean that today's social workers in health-care settings confront ethical dilemmas
on a daily basis.[17] In addition, society in general and physicians in particular are

currently in the position of deciding whether to direct their resources and energies toward the young and middle-aged and away from the elderly.[18] Such a decision is likely to come into play in cases of medical emergencies, when many health professionals are willing to say "This person has lived a full life; let him/her die in peace."[19] Physicians are often unaware of life expectancy data. For example, they may not realize that an 86-year-old women is expected to live more than five years longer. Furthermore, operating under the medical "degree of benefit rationale," physicians may allocate less care to elderly patients because the older the patients, the less likely it is that they will benefit "as much" (i.e., as long) as a younger person.[20] It is often up to social workers to see to it that age alone is not invoked as a rationale for not providing intensive care, surgery, or other treatment modalities. The ethical demand is clear for the social worker to advocate for the elderly client in such situations.

Medical researchers often "use" patients who are elderly, poor, and/or unable to verbalize or are terminally ill (and thus are especially vulnerable) to test experimental technology or as research subjects.[21,22] All too often, the ethical requirements of informed consent are not fulfilled in securing a patient's agreement to participate in the research. These requirements, as specified by Ratzan, are as follows:

- The research subject must freely consent to participate.
- The subject must be mentally competent.
- The subject must be informed of all the likely consequences of the research or experimentation, including risks, benefits, discomforts, and compensation.
- The elderly subject's actual understanding of the experiment must be accurate and complete to the satisfaction of the researcher, institutional review board, or other monitor.[23]

Complicating matters, even when explanations of research procedures appear thorough and volunteers appear to understand, this comprehension may not be complete and in addition, critical details may be forgotten at a later date.[24] The concept of informed consent is important for social workers because of the profession's commitment to individual autonomy and to facilitating reasoned decision-making.[25] The art of social work practice, upholding the principle of autonomy or self-determination, entails helping the person develop the potential for choice in informed consent by sharing accurate information and assuring that all ethical requirements are met before an elderly patient participates in experimental research.

Informed consent also applies to general medical care in doctors' offices, health centers, clinics, and hospitals. The fear and dependency fostered by illness can reduce an individual's ability to make reasoned decisions. In these situations, the social worker can do a great deal to assure that the elderly patient is given the opportunity to develop a truly informed consent to treatment. Physicians all to often usurp the older patient's right to informed consent under the guise of acting in his or her "best interests." Such a violation occurs when, under the principle of beneficence, the professional's concepts of benefits and harms differ from those of the patient, and the professional's judgment prevails because he or she feels that he or she knows better. Often, the professional may substitute the judgment of a family member for that of the patient in deciding whether to engage in treatment of a particular type. There are dangers in such assignment of responsibility, however, because the great stress felt by family members, often manifested as anger, depression, grief, and conflict with other family members, may render them less than competent to decide such matters.[26]

Informed consent is relevant to hospital discharge decisions and discharge planning as well. Inherent in the concept of self-determination is the idea that there are alternatives available from which individuals can choose, free from undue influence or coercion. In discharge planning, the patient most often has to be discharged to the first available bed, regardless of its convenience or suitability. This procedure hardly implies free reasoned choice from among alternatives—even less when the decision must be made more quickly, under the influence and/or coercion of utilization review boards. A patient's rights are violated when that patient is discharged from the hospital when medically ready but without emotional and social preparation and complete understanding of the reasoning behind the discharge. Patients' rights are also violated when they are discharged to a facility that will not provide reasonable continuity of care.[27]

Harry Moody has detailed ethical dilemmas that are inherent in long-term care for the elderly:

- Is it right to systematically mislabel clients in order to help them qualify for eligibility for services provided on the basis of "need"? For which clients and under which circumstances?
- Does one have an obligation to report cases of abuse, neglect, or mistreatment of patients in nursing homes? To inform higher officials or go to the press with the information?
- Is it proper to restrict admission to a given nursing home according to a patient's race or religion? According to their prior or current monetary contribution to the home?
- Is it proper for professionals to receive gifts from patients' families? From patients themselves?
- Should staff members intervene to encourage a patient to make a specific decision in favor of a treatment plan or in favor of participating or not participating in a clinical research program?[28]

He then presented the following useful steps for negotiating these dilemmas:

Source of the Problem. Is the issue we confront one that originates in long-term care settings themselves, or does it arise from some other factor—advanced old age, mental frailty, chronic illness, or terminal disease?

Ethical Dilemma or Practical Problem? Is the issue we confront a genuine ethical dilemma or is it rather a problem of implementation? In other words, are we unclear about what *is* the right thing to do or simply unable to carry out a solution?

Professional Perspective. How is the ethical issue framed by our perspective of professional practice (the view of social work in contrast to nursing, medicine, etc.)? How does a professional perspective help (or hinder) the clarification of empirical and normative features of the situation?

Level of Action. What is the appropriate level of social action where ethical dilemmas appear and find resolution? Is it at the policy level, the professional practice level, or the level of individual beliefs and values?

Ethical Theory. How can ethical theories help clarify the dilemma and its range of possible resolutions? Is it a matter of basic human *rights*, of *utility*, of individual *virtue*, or of *social justice?*[29]

Abramson recommends negotiating an ethical dilemma by "separating it into smaller, more manageable components":[30]

- identifying the decision-making sequence
- differentiating the technical from the ethical and value components
- considering the various alternatives and options at each stage
- analyzing the value and ethical issues connected to each alternative

Then the social worker can evaluate the options and eventually choose a course of action.

One way to deal with issues of ethics in health-care settings is to establish a bill of rights for patients. For starters, such a bill might include

- considerate and respectful care
- complete current information related to diagnosis and treatment
- informed consent prior to start of any procedure and/or treatment
- the right to refuse treatment
- the right to privacy
- confidentiality of all medical records
- a reasonable response to any request for services
- the right to refuse participation in research or experimentation with new technology
- a full explanation of the bill of rights

Rights specific to nursing home patients have been identified and include the following:

- the basic liberties guaranteed by Federal and State constitutions (such as protection from arbitrary usurption of liberty and property, the right to vote, and the freedom of religion)
- protection from arbitrary transfer or discharge
- freedom from mental and/or physical abuse including excessive and/or unauthorized physical constraints
- privacy for spousal visits and opportunities for spouses to share rooms
- treatment with consideration, respect, and full recognition of personal dignity and individuality

It is important that any bill of rights be published throughout each medical facility, given in writing and explained orally to each patient. In addition, direct care staff as well as administrative staff must be trained in carrying out the rights specified by the document and provision must be made for routine training of new staff persons. Training must stress that any institution tends inherently to abridge rights unless they are vigorously protected and must emphasize the need to beware of staff carrying out actions facilely, "for a patient's own good," that are contrary to that patient's rights.[31] Such training is, again, plainly an appropriate and desirable activity for social workers to undertake.

Health professionals, acting out of laziness or ignorance, are apt to make undifferentiated diagnoses of elderly patients as chronically brain damaged, neglecting to determine the degree of disability, reversibility, and progressiveness of the patients' disorders. The National Institute on Aging suggests, in fact, that 10 percent to 20 percent of the elderly diagnosed with mental impairments have "pseudo-senility"— that is, reversible conditions caused by drug interactions, malnutrition, fever, traumatic relocation, etc. Medical professionals and courts must be made aware of the definitional, conceptual, and methodological complexities that senility raises for gerontologists, and the role of such education is an auspicious one for social workers to take on. Again, it must be stressed that the facile assumption of incompetence in many elderly patients often reflects only a lack of the professional energy, interest, or imagination needed to communicate with persons of mental activity that is deemed "abnormal."[32]

Faced with patients who are not, for whatever reason, self-determining, the principle of autonomy requires the course of action that has the greatest possibility of facilitating or restoring autonomy, or the least possibility of precluding it. The principle of autonomy, as no surprise to social workers, is difficult to employ because of the diversity of patients' cultural and educational backgrounds and complex health problems. However, it can be argued that the elderly have "more" right to equitable treatment in health care since health, life, and autonomy are more precious to the elderly than to any other group in our society for the simple reason that they have less time in which to enjoy these gifts.[33] In another sense, however, we must avoid special treatment of the elderly solely on the basis of their age; in order to avoid imposing our will on frail elderly persons we must treat them as equal fellow members of the community, for only in this way can we help preserve their moral dignity and respect for themselves.[34]

A Sampling of Stereotypes and Myths

Opinions, thinking and behavior often stem from hackneyed or conventional expressions and modes of thought. Many of us are willing to accept folkloristic assumptions and unsubstantiated thought patterns, in part or on the whole, and tend to respond in our behavior accordingly. This is particularly true with regard to the aged. There is a tendency to classify older people into one homogeneous group, amorphous, undifferentiated, and impersonal, which runs counter to the major value of uniqueness of the person. The older individual [loses his or her identity] as a person. . . . Many of us are still suffering from a belief in stereotypes about old age and the aged; and most aged people, in turn, are the victims of these stereotypes. This perhaps has become one of the major problems of old age; there is a social-psychological dictum which tells us that people behave according to the way in which they are expected to behave.

The basic assumption of ageism is that a person's chronological age is correlated to his or her ability to perform specific types of activity. Here are some of these stereotypes:

1. "Older people are senile." This implies deterioration and cannot be measured accurately or chronologically. It has more to do with how one feels and acts. Senility, which means the physical and mental infirmities of old age, is often confused with senescence, the state or quality of growing old or aging. The fact remains that most older people are not senile and are not in their "second childhood."

2. "Older people look alike." This implies they all have such characteristics as wrinkled skin and gray, thin hair; that they are deaf, lame, untidy, bent over; that they have shaking head and hands and great difficulty with their speech, and are unlovely and unlovable. The truth is that there are wide individual and chronological variations in the physical aspects of aging.

3. "Older people think and act alike." The implication here is that they all tend to be irritable, sad, opinionated, forgetful, slow, inactive. We know that different people, regardless of age, have different capabilities and desires.

4. "Older people are not reliable or dependable." This implies they are incapable of assuming responsibility or carrying out an assignment. Some older people never relinquish their responsibilities and some go successfully from one assignment to another. For example, many older workers are more dependable than younger ones.

5. "Older people grow even more alike as they grow older." This could mean that old people are impossible to tell apart. The truth is that older people grow to be more and more like themselves as they age. They do not lose individual differences.

6. "Older people cannot learn anything new." Again, individual differences such as physical and mental health, previous learning experiences, intelligence, background, and personality are important factors that must be taken into consideration as well as motivation and interest. Learning processes can change for older people. It may take longer to absorb material, but the material may be retained better and longer. In some areas, the rate of learning may even increase in older people.

7. Some additional stereotypes: older people are chronically ill, dependent people; they are supported by public welfare and live either in housing projects, nursing homes, or homes for the aged; they are friendless, abandoned by their children, live in the past, and have nothing left to do but wait for death. Needless to say, these are not true for most older adults.

Consequences of Stereotyped Attitudes in Working with the Aged

The community, with its biases, tends to relegate needs and problems of the aged to second- or third-rate status. Therefore, most programs for the elderly in agencies and institutions are fragmented and isolated. The training of professional staff to work with the aged is not widespread or, as yet, particularly encouraged in schools of medicine, dentistry, public health, social work, etc. Overprotectiveness still seems to be a prevalent pattern in providing services to the elderly in the community and in institutions. Many institutions such as nursing homes, homes for the aged, and extended care facilities tend to cater to the elderly condescendingly, as though they were childish, helpless, and ever-dependent.

> Those who work with the elderly are often inclined to fit their personal experiences with their own aging parents and/or relatives into their work with elderly clients or patients and treat them as if they were their own parents or relatives. Young worker[s] may not yet be clear about [their] relationship with [their] parents [or about feelings involved, for example, in] severing dependency ties [with them. They] may then act inconsistently or with hostility toward another older adult. . . . Guilt feelings about . . . relationships[s] with . . . parents or grandparents may be a major reason for workers to do too much for an older person and add to this individual's feelings of dependency and helplessness.
>
> There often is a lack of understanding and knowledge of the aged, their problems, and the process of aging. Since more is known about the aged who have serious problems and pathology, we tend to forget about the great majority who are functioning "normally" without help. This reinforces pessimistic and negative views on aging. For these reasons [workers] with the aged must examine [their] own feelings concerning [their own] personal aging. Social workers may be hand-icapped by their feelings about aging, sickness, dying, and death [and by] personal emotional stress[es due to] unresolved . . . conflicts.[35]

Shura Saul, in *Aging—An Album of People Growing Old*, elaborates on these stereotypes and identifies them as myths—many of which can be refuted by facts and evidence culled from a number of studies.

Tranquility Myth

> Old age is a time of relative peace and tranquility when people can relax and enjoy the fruits of their labor after the storms of life have passed. This is also known as the "myth of the golden years" or "the harvest years."
>
> This extreme overlooks *the reality* that old age is a time of substantial stresses, especially those related to poverty, illness, and isolation. Often it is *these stresses* that produce the depression, anxiety, paranoia, and psychosomatic illnesses commonly associated with older patients and ascribed, in a stereotyped manner, to the aging process. . . .

Inevitability Myth

> An older person thinks and moves slowly. He does not think of himself as well as he used to nor as creatively. He is bound to himself and to his past and can neither change nor grow. He can neither learn well nor swiftly, and even if he could . . . he would not wish to. Tied to his personal traditions and growing conservatism, he dislikes innovations. . . . Not only can he not move forward, but he often moves backward, he enters a second childhood. . . . He becomes irritable and cantankerous, yet shallow and enfeebled. He lives in his past. He is behind the times. He is aimless of mind, wandering, reminiscing, and garrulous.

Indeed, he is a study in decline; . . . the picture of mental and physical failure. He has lost and cannot replace friends, spouse, job, status, power, influence, income. He is often stricken by diseases. . . . His body shrinks and so too does the flow of blood to his brain. . . . Enfeebled, uninteresting, he awaits his death, a burden to society, to his family, and to himself. . . .

. . . This "overdrawn picture" implies a number of preconceptions, for example, that all older people are similar, that aging involves various irreversible illnesses (mental or physical), a "fixed" state of mind, and shrinking capacities, and that an aged person is ipso facto rigid, unchangeable, sterile, and dependent.

Illness Myth

Aging is viewed primarily as a degenerative biological process and aging is synonymous with illness and disease. The evidence shows that most older people are not ill—although there is some degree of a physical slowdown. Many illnesses are treatable and can be controlled. Individuals react to illness idiosyncratically, and many compensate with mental and spiritual growth.

Senility Myth

The tautological saying goes: "All old people have brain damage because they are old." In fact, most do not have brain damage at all and do not act like children. Senility is an imprecise label that can be used to justify little or no social work intervention or assistance. It denies the person's dignity and worth and therefore counters one of the major values of social work.

Psychological and Psychiatric Myths

"Inevitabilities" [such] as memory loss, the inability to learn or perform new tasks, and a lack of capacity for self-help, decision-making, or problem solving [do not agree with the] realities, as presented by a number of psychologists . . . that chronological aging alone does not account for such changes but, instead, that they are connected with a number of other life circumstances. The interrelationship of psychological and physical health is important. . . .

Myth [of] Brain Damage: . . .

All people have damage to the brain as a consequence of aging.

Reality:

"Senility" is not inevitable. Two conditions, cerebral arteriosclerosis and senile brain disease, create brain conditions, as in younger people. Neither brain damage nor aging account for the occurrence of [all] mental conditions among older people.

Myth [of] Unresponsive-to-Therapy:

Older people are not treatable because their mental conditions are irreversible. Their mental disorders are primarily physical and, therefore, beyond the scope of psychiatric treatment.

Reality:

Many mental and emotional disorders affecting older people can be treated. To a notable extent, they are reversible. Under reasonably good circumstances, more older psychiatric patients improve or recover than fail to react to psychotherapy. Older people in group therapy also respond positively.

Furthermore, we are advised that a senile pattern of brain deterioration does not commonly accompany advancing age; when it does occur, it is likely to be pathological rather than a normal concomitant of growing old.

Myth of Asexuality or Sexual Senility

[There is a belief] that older persons become asexual persons, have no interest in sex, have no sexual needs, desires, or ability to function as sexual beings. Masters and Johnson's studies have amassed evidence to the contrary. In addition, if the elderly are found to be sexually active in any way, society points an accusing, damning finger at them, as if their behavior were abnormal.[36]

Myth of Unproductivity and Family Dissolution

The facts indicate that many older people have been forced into unproductivity through mandatory retirement policies. This is another case of blaming the victim. When given opportunities, older people make use of them. They desire relationships and maintain their interest in the world around them. The disengagement theory of Cummings and Henry has probably stirred up more controversy than any other sociological theory. It has been misunderstood, misperceived, and misquoted.

The idea that most families ship their older members off to institutions and therefore show that they don't care is not supported by the facts. Only 5 percent of all the elderly are in institutions at any one time; many live with or near their families. Because of lack of community resources (such as day care) many people are forced out of their homes, but not because the family wishes to be rid of the older member.

Part of their myth is the notion of a role reversal or a second childhood. Margaret Blenkner refutes this, speaking of adults developing "filial maturity"—an ability to handle the dependency needs of the parent. She convincingly argues that whatever the level of dependency one cannot blot out sixty and more years of living experience and claim that the older person is a child.[37]

Aging and Ageism

Using the work of Kluckhohn, Mead, and their followers, Margaret Clark states that Americans place high values on achievement, success, movement, activities, work, aggressiveness, acquisition of money, individualism, competence, mastery, progress, and orientation to the future—values particularly dominant during the period just prior to World War II when our elderly were then in the prime of life:

The individualistic, competitive, aggressive, future-oriented, acquisitive and success-oriented American of 25 years ago—and who rigidly clings to those values—is today's best prospect for geriatric psychiatry. . . . Those . . . who have been able to effect a shift in values in later life seem to be meeting the problems of aging today with less damage to body and mind.[38]

Against Ageism

Robert Butler coined the term *ageism* and defined it as follows:

> [It is] a process of systematic stereotyping of and discrimination against people because they are old, just as racism and sexism accomplish this with skin color and gender. Old people are categorized as senile, rigid in thought and manner, old-fashioned in morality and skills. . . . Ageism allows the younger generations to see older people as different from themselves; thus they subtly cease to identify with their elders as human beings.[39]

It is very important to improve popular knowledge about aging: currently, most young and middle-aged Americans, guided by stereotypes, avoid contact with elders and thus are without role models for their own aging.

Simone de Beauvoir in *The Coming of Age* wrote:

> We are told that retirement is a time of freedom and leisure: poets have sung "the delights of reaching port." These are shameless lies. Leisure does not open up new possibilities for the retired man; just when he is at last set free from compulsion and restraint, the means of making use of his liberty are taken from him. He is condemned to stagnate in boredom and loneliness, a mere throw-out.[40]

Frank Nuessel described the American "language of ageism," which reinforces stereotypes and fosters age segregation.[41] He illustrates that few favorable expressions exist to allude to the elderly, and that most terms referring to aging and the elderly are derogatory and demeaning, depicting the elderly as possessing largely undesirable traits. Such linguistic bias is clear evidence of the deep-rooted nature of institutional ageism in our society. Nuessel further points out that many ageist expressions are also sexist: "old biddy, granny, hag, witch, battle axe, old maid, and little old lady." However, many refer to men as well: *old codger, old coot, old geezer, old goat,* and *dirty old man.* General terms include *old crank, old fart, old fogey, old fool,* and *fuddy-duddy: decrepit, doddering, rickety, obsolete, old-fashioned, cantankerous, toothless, feeble-minded,* and *eccentric;* and *declining years, second childhood, over the hill, twilight years, geritol generation,* and *golden age.*

The Gray Panthers, the American Association of Retired Persons, and the National Council on the Aging are now monitoring the media's use of ageist images. Nuessel suggests a preventive measure as well—the development of a manual of guidelines for the media. Several studies have been done on the extent of ageism fostered by the media. It has been documented that the elderly (and especially older women) are underrepresented on television, that negative dialogue concerning the elderly greatly exceeds positive dialogue, that elderly characters on television play comic rather than serious roles, and that the mean age of elderly characters is below the mean age of the elderly population. The situation would seem somewhat better for newspapers. In a study of the *New York Times* and another paper for the years 1970 and 1978, content analyses revealed that most stories presented neutral images (neither positive nor negative) of elders, that positive images outnumbered negative images two to one, that significantly more elders are depicted in active than passive roles and that this ratio seems to be improving with time, that most stories covered individual events rather than issues, and in general, there has been poor coverage of "aging" in general. The author suggests that gerontologists hold workshops and seminars for journalists to educate them about aging, and social workers could conceivably take on this new role.

The myth that old is ugly and worthless is changing, though slowly. Groups have formed all over the country to combat the age discrimination that permeates our society. The fight against mandatory retirement is just one issue of a movement that is shattering conventional attitudes toward growing old. (On April 7, 1978, President Carter signed into law legislation that raised the legal mandatory retirement age to 70 for most employees.) The movement against ageism offers a new set of values that affirm the energy, creativity, and wisdom of older people. The fight is being led by a Philadelphia-based group called the Gray Panthers. Maggie Kuhn, at 70 +, and five of her colleagues founded the Panthers when they experienced forced retirement in 1970. They had been active in protesting the war in Southeast Asia, police violence against students and others, and governmental corruption. Suddenly out of work, they sought a new vehicle through which they could address social issues.

The Gray Panthers believe that the 22 million people in the United States who are 65 or older constitute one of the country's largest resources of human skill and experience, yet this resource is generally wasted because of our society's bias against old people. The Panthers challenge ageism against both young and old. They believe that old people have the responsibility and the freedom to seek a better life, not just for themselves, but for all society. Most important, the Gray Panthers believe that old and young have much to gain from interaction with one another.

Erdman Palmore, in a 1982 analysis of over a hundred research studies that have used his "Facts on Aging Quiz" to test Americans' attitudes toward aging and the elderly, found that negative stereotypes and attitudes about the elderly are still widespread in this country. He estimates that one-fifth to one-third of the American population endorses "core" negative stereotypes of the elderly (i.e., sick, senile, weak, dogmatic, useless, poor, and unhappy) and that many more feel the same way but are uncomfortable admitting their prejudices when tested. On the positive side, however, he concludes that negative attitudes are not necessarily inherent and, though highly resistant to change, can be influenced through education and positive contacts with older persons. [42]

Growing, learning, and being involved in the lives of others is a life-long process that certainly doesn't end at 65. A sixty-fifth birthday doesn't make people altogether different creatures. They have the same problems, feelings, interests, and abilities that they had when they were younger.

The New Ageism

Richard Kalish in 1979 described another form of ageism that is pervasive in the United States and is perhaps more insidious because it is perpetrated as much by advocates of the elderly as by their adversaries. This particular form of ageism equates all elderly with the least capable, least healthy, least alert, and most dependent among them. A proliferation of new services is sought with vigor to improve the lot of these unfortunate beings without any awareness that these services may eventually reduce the freedom and decision-making ability of their recipients. The new ageism also blames society for treating the elderly poorly. Most importantly, ignoring the fact that the vast majority of the elderly function effectively on their own, proponents of the new ageism ignore the huge diversity in America's elderly population. This bias is based on two types of failure models — the incompetence model and the "geriactivist" model. The first is used to secure funding by pulling on the heart strings to provide for the "incompetent" elderly, while geriactivism prescribes activism as the only acceptable activity for the elderly, who are charged with the obligation to stand up for their rights or be relegated to a status of "part of the problem." Again, in both these models, the rich diversity among our elderly population is ignored and devalued.

Kalish identifies three groups who perpetuate the new ageism, knowingly or unknowingly:

- funding agencies that compete with other agencies by stressing the dire needs of the elderly
- gerontologists and geriatricians who need to keep their programs going and may place a high value on activism
- the media, which provides these two groups and others with "what they want to hear"

He proposes a new nonageist way to view aging, which he terms the "personal growth model." The basic premise behind this model is that it is indeed possible and perfectly natural for elders to continue to grow because

- With aging comes relief from earlier responsibilities, such as children and jobs.
- The elderly are often less concerned about others' opinions of them and feel freer to pursue interests that are truly "theirs."
- The elderly have more leisure time.
- There is a type of liberation in the knowledge of and comfort with the finality of death.

By refusing to define the elderly as victims, we eliminate the possibility that, in a circle of self-fulfilling prophecy, they will eventually fill the role that we prescribe for them. As social workers, our task is to facilitate personal growth by communicating to elderly clients that we have faith in their abilities, particularly their ability to make decisions, and that "we respect their ownership of their own bodies, time, and lives."[43]

The Harris Surveys

In 1974, Louis Harris and Associates, Inc., commissioned by the National Council on the Aging, Inc., conducted the first nationwide survey of the attitudes and perceptions younger and older Americans had about the nation's elderly. In 1981, in preparation for the White House Conference on Aging, NCoA commissioned Harris to conduct another nationwide survey, "Aging in the Eighties: America in Transition," updating their 1974 study. Close to 3,500 interviews were conducted in 1981 and three new areas were covered, reflecting current concerns—the economics of aging and retirement, Social Security and the role of government, and health and health care. *

Today, just as in 1974, the vast majority of the public—young and old alike— view older people as healthier and better educated than they were ten or twenty years ago. However, opinions of the elderly's economic situation have turned around: where 52 percent in 1974 believed that the elderly were then better off financially than they were ten to twenty years earlier, only 38 percent today feel that this is the case. Table 5.1 shows that although in every case those aged 18 to 64 overestimated the elderly's experience of serious problems, their ranking of these problems coincided with the elderly's actual experience. Thus, to an extent, there is a degree of reality in the perceptions of the general population. A gap between the myth and reality of aging continues to exist, however, especially with respect to health care. For example, 47 percent of respondents aged 18 to 64 and 40 percent of the elderly respondents themselves believe that poor health is a "very serious problem for most people over 65," despite the fact that only 21 percent of elderly respondents reported that poor health is indeed a very serious problem for them personally. Similarly, while only one in eleven older respondents actually experienced lack of sufficient medical care, 45 percent of the nonaged sample felt "not having enough medical care" is a very serious problem for most elderly people. Similarly, over one-half of the nonaged public nationwide believes that "getting transportation to stores, to doctors, to places of recreation" is a very serious problem for most older people, although only 14 percent of the elderly themselves experience lack of transportation as a very serious problem. Since 1974, there has been a marked reduction in the number of Americans who feel that the media present "a fair picture of what older people are like." Perhaps our population is now more wary of media-espoused stereotypes of the elderly.

Although 68 percent of the nonaged public nationwide and 50 percent of the elderly themselves believe that "not having enough money to live on is a very or somewhat serious problem for most people over 65," only 17 percent of elderly Americans report lack of money a very serious problem and 24 percent a somewhat serious problem. However, it must be realized that income, race, and sex determine very dramatically whether or not money is perceived as a problem: for lack of money as a very serious problem, the figures jump to 55 percent for low-income elderly blacks, 54 percent for elderly poor Hispanics, and 19 percent for women. Similarly, while over one-half of white elders are "getting by with a little extra" or "buying pretty much what they want" with their present income, 80 percent of elderly blacks, over 70 percent of elderly Hispanics, and 53 percent of elderly women "just about manage" or "can't make ends meet."

* *Aging in the Eighties: America in Transition.* A study for the National Council on the Aging, Inc. by Louis Harris and Associates, Inc. 1981.

One-third of the study's respondents have "hardly any confidence" in our Social Security system and this lack of confidence is most pronounced among younger adults. There is significant support for the idea that "Social Security taxes should be raised if necessary to provide adequate income for older people," and this support is most pronounced among the elderly themselves, while those in the highest income brackets are most opposed to the idea. Neither do Americans feel, according to this survey, that there should be any reduction in benefits currently provided under the system. They do, however, feel it would be appropriate for workers who do not currently pay into the system to do so (i.e., Federal employees), and/or for Federal monies such as income taxes to be used to support Social Security partially. According to the survey, many Americans today look toward government (and the children of the elderly) to "assume more responsibility than they have now for the elderly," while less than half as many state that the elderly themselves, their employers, or religious and charitable organizations should do so.

In today's climate of continued inflation and high concern regarding our Social Security system, Americans display stronger reactions to the issue of mandatory retirement than they did in 1974. Ninety percent of all age groups agree that "nobody should be forced to retire because of age if he or she wants to continue working and is still able to do the job," and nearly 80 percent of all age groups feel strongly about this issue. Similarly, Americans are now more strongly opposed to the idea that "older people should retire when they can to give younger people more of a chance on the job." However, it is the elderly themselves who have "bought into this argument" and feel that elderly should make way for the younger generation. Similarly, the vast majority of Americans feel that "most employers discriminate against older people and make it difficult for them to find work," yet the elderly themselves are somewhat less in agreement with this statement.

The majority of respondents felt that retired older Americans have too little influence in this country today. Forty-three percent felt that "most government programs to help the elderly should be available only to those older people who have little or no income," yet most respondents agreed that the government does have a role in health-care delivery to all older Americans, regardless of income level. Nearly 90 percent felt that "Medicare . . . should cover more health-care services provided at home," and respondents were nearly unanimous in their endorsement of a tax break to "families that provide health care at home for the elderly."

Myths and the Social Worker

As mentioned earlier, social workers have inherited many of the myths of society and have made them part of their own value system. For this reason many do not even consider work with the aged. Barresi and Brubaker tested clinical social workers' knowledge about aging. They found that professional social workers possessed only 18 percent more knowledge than might have occurred by chance alone, and that their inaccurate perceptions (largely occurring in the areas of demographics and sociology of aging) reflected a slight negative bias against the elderly.[44]

Table 5.1. "Very Serious" Problems: Personal Experience of the Elderly versus Public Expectations

Q: Now I'm going to read you some problems that other people have mentioned to us. For each, would you tell me whether it is a very serious problem, a somewhat serious problem, or hardly a problem at all for *you personally*.

Q: And how serious a problem would you say (READ EACH ITEM) is for most people over 65 these days—a very serious problem, a somewhat serious problem, or hardly a problem at all for most people over 65?

	1981			1974		
	Personal Experience	Public Expectation		Personal Experience	Public Expectation	
		"Very Serious" Problems Attributed to Most People over 65			"Very Serious" Problems Attributed to Most People over 65	
	"Very Serious" Problems Felt Personally by Public 65 and over	By Public 18–64	By Public 65 and over	"Very Serious" Problems Felt Personally by Public 65 and over	By Public 18–64	By Public 65 and over
Rank as Actual Very Serious Problem for 65 and over						

78

4	Not having enough money to live on	17%	68%	50%	15%	63%	59%
3	Poor health	21%	47%	40%	21%	50%	53%
6	Loneliness	13%	65%	45%	12%	61%	56%
10	Poor housing	5%	43%	30%	4%	35%	34%
2	Fear of crime	25%	74%	58%	23%	50%	51%
8	Not enough education	6%	21%	17%	8%	19%	25%
8	Not enough job opportunities	6%	51%	24%	5%	47%	32%
7	Not enough medical care	9%	45%	34%	10%	45%	36%
1	High cost of energy such as heating oil, gas, and electricity	42%	81%	72%	—*	—*	—*
5	Getting transportation to stores, to doctors, to places of recreation, and so forth	14%	58%	43%	—*	—*	—*

SOURCE: *Aging in the Eighties: America in Transition.* A study for the National Council on the Aging, Inc. by Louis Harris and Associates, Inc., 1981.

* Not asked.

The social worker's own set of beliefs is challenged as he or she works with older clients. For example, in an institutional setting, social workers play a key role in fighting agency myths about the older person. Issues involve custodial care, values, and the improvement of the quality of life in the institution. In trying to change the value system of the agency, the worker elicits the elderly patient's desires for more than just food, clothing, and shelter. The social worker must fight the feeling of helplessness and the prejudices that cause difficulties and problems. In defending a policy of having social workers on the staff of a nursing home, one defends the rights of the elderly to continue to have a life with meaning, options, and opportunity.

In summary, working with older people forces an examination of one's own feelings about the elderly, death, and dying; about one's respect for elderly clients; about allowing them the opportunity and ability to make choices; about perceiving the worker's role as more than just custodial; and about advocating change in attitudes and programs within the scope of the social agency. Out of the various value conflicts faced by social workers who are in contact with elderly clients in a family agency, institution, community organization or self-help group (such as the Gray Panthers), two have particular relevance: coming to terms with one's own filial maturity and facing the finiteness of life.

Filial Crisis and Filial Maturity

Margaret Blenkner coined the term *filial maturity* to describe a middle-aged developmental state.[45] The adult at around 40 or 50 years reaches a filial crisis when parents can no longer be looked upon as a rock of support in times of emotional trouble or economic stress and when parents themselves often need comfort, support, and affection from their offspring. Offspring need to be depended upon in times of stress or trouble for advice, nurturance, and tangible assistance. In a filial crisis, adult sons and daughters do not take on a parental role vis-à-vis the aging parent; rather they take on a filial role, indicating that they are dependable as far as the parent is concerned. The healthy resolution of this filial crisis leaves behind the rebellion against one's parents initiated during adolescence and often unresolved long after.

The middle-aged adult sees parents as other mature adults see them if he or she has made peace with them—as individuals with their own foibles, strengths, weaknesses, needs, and rights and with a life history all their own that made them the persons they are now—and were before their child was even born. Resolving the filial crisis provides an opportunity for adult children to prepare themselves for their own aging and the tasks and demands of their own old age. There can be no "role reversal" as many writers have postulated, because the older person can never become a child again. Life history has intervened to prevent a return to childhood, although this does not exclude the possibility of regressive behavior that may have childlike manifestations.

Adult children may need help in completing their emancipation from their parents so that they may be freer to help their parents cope with the tasks of aging and assume their role of filial responsibility. The middle-aged person has to perform a variety of roles and tasks. The major life tasks are mostly instrumental—for example, to achieve and succeed by some standard in work, business, profession, or vocation and to raise a family and be involved as a citizen of a community.

Affective or expressive tasks also have to be completed if one is to earn approbation in our society. To be successful in the eyes of the elderly parents and to vindicate the aspirations they had for their young places considerable stress upon adult children. They must succeed in marriage and raise children in accord with prevailing norms and values, a job that is difficult in a world where values are no longer the guideposts they once were in giving parents a sense of security. This demands an adaptation to new and untried values on uncharted roads. Eventually adult offspring must face a battle that many view as downhill—since our society views aging as biologically inevitable and underplays social, psychological, and spiritual factors.

Older parents are expected to grow old gracefully. Tasks of the later years are ill-defined and hardly instrumental, since the years of productivity are supposed to come to an end, and very often against the will of the elderly themselves who are forced into mandatory retirement. They are shunted and put on the sidelines, and in a society like ours, oriented toward success and achievement, this means loss of status and often loss of self-esteem. The feeling of being obsolete permeates much of this age group, which has to face a sense of rolelessness. Quite a few older people cope well, others less so; many look for substitute roles that are in tune with middle-class expectations of productivity. The decreasing instrumental tasks are traded off in a search for increasing affective tasks for which there are few precedents in the middle years of life. Older adults look for a meaning to their lives; they have to come to terms with what has been, rather than what is now and what is going to be. They wish to reflect on their life and what they have done with it.

The adult offspring of older adults are a reminder of their parents' successes, often the embodiment of their aspirations, and also witnesses to their failures. Grandchildren are visible links in the continuity of the generations. Being a grandparent is a phase in life whereby one can relive the memories of the early phase of one's own parenthood by observing the growth and development of grandchildren. Relieved from the immediate demanding tasks and conflicts of the roles of parenthood, grandparents can enjoy their grandchildren more than they enjoyed bringing up their own children.

Facing the Finiteness of Life

People seek support for themselves, a vindication and validation of what has been. To face the complex tasks of old age, they want to know they can depend on their own grown-up children without becoming burdensome to them. They want to maintain control and mastery over their own lives—which does not mean the right to control the life of the offspring. This is sometimes difficult for older persons to accept and even harder to practice. For older persons, the last and perhaps most difficult task is to prepare for their exit from this world with dignity and a degree of comfort. To face nonbeing and termination of life is hard to fathom for all of us. To come to terms with death and learn to accept it emotionally is probably the most difficult task of life.[46]

> Preparation for death involves a condition unknown in past or present experience, for one cannot truly imagine one's own nonexistence. Yet, strangely, although fear of death is part of human experience, old people tend to fear it less than the young do and often are more concerned about the death of those whom they love than about their own. Many can accept personal death with equanimity. In terminal illness it may even be welcomed as a released from pain and struggle. Reactions to death are closely related to a resolution of life's experiences and problems as well as a sense of one's contributions to others. Profound religious and philosophical convictions facilite acceptance.
>
> The process of working through one's feelings about death begin with a growing personal awareness of the eventual end of life and the implications of this for one's remaining time alive. For some people the process begins early; for others the physical signs of aging occur before the awareness is allowed to surface. Some few attempt to deny death to the very end. A resolution of feelings about death may be responsible for those elusive qualities, seen in various people, known as "wisdom" and "serenity."[47]

Guidelines for Practice

Social workers cannot be truly effective with older clients unless they come to terms with their own feelings about dying and death, particularly in a death-denying society. Gradually, nonbeing and the finiteness of life are being accepted as subjects for discussion, and the right to die with dignity is appearing on the agenda of our health and social policy. It is obvious by now that social work practice with the aging really tests the worker's belief in the worth, dignity, and uniqueness of older people in the face of a predominant value orientation that relegates the elderly to an inferior position in our society and deprives them of their identity by denying them a role.

In American society a person's identity is maintained through validated social roles. Allowing older persons to make choices based on available alternatives, helping create social alternatives to make options possible and self-determination a reality, allowing older people to determine for themselves where they want to go, when, and how—all these demand a faith in the ability and capacity of aging persons to choose and to handle the consequences of their choices. Such attitudes affirm the dignity and worth of the elderly in spite of the myths and stereotypes that society has perpetuated and that many a profession—including social work—has incorporated.

References

1. For a more elaborate discussion of social work values, see Max Siporin, *Introduction to Social Work Practice* (New York: Macmillan, 1974), chap. 5 and Appendix A; and A.

Pincus and A. Minahan, *Social Work Practice: Model and Method* (Itasca, Ill.: Peacock Publishing, 1973).

2. Max Siporin, *Introduction to Social Work Practice* (New York: Macmillan, 1974), p. 65.

3. Louis Lowy, *Function of Social Work in a Changing Society* (Boston: Milford House, 1974), p. 28.

4. Beulah Compton and Burt Galaway, *Social Work Processes* (Homewood, Ill.: Dorsey Press, 1975), pp. 105–113. Reprinted by permission.

5. Paul Tillich, "The Philosophy of Social Work," *Social Service Review*, vol. 26, no. 1 (March 1962), pp. 13–16, cited in Compton and Galaway, op. cit.

6. William Gordon, "Basic Constructs for an Integrated and Generative Conception of Social Work," in Gordon Hearn (ed.), *The General Systems Approach: Contributions Toward an Holistic Conception of Social Work*, edited by Gordon Hearn (New York: CSWE, 1969), p. 6, cited in Compton and Galaway, op. cit.

7. For an introduction to this perspectus, cited in Compton and Galaway, op. cit., see Earl Rubington and Martin S. Weinberg, *Deviance: The Interactionist Perspective* (New York: Macmillan, 1968); J. L. Simmons, *Deviants* (Berkeley: Glendessany Press, 1969).

8. Robert K. Merton, *Social Theory and Social Structure* (New York: Free Press, 1957), pp. 421–426, cited in Compton and Galaway, op. cit.

9. Hans Toch, "The Care and Feeding of Typologies and Labels," *Federal Probation*, vol. 34, no. 3 (September 1970), p. 15, cited in Compton and Galaway, op. cit.

10. *The Crime of Punishment* (New York: Viking Press, 1968), pp. 117–118, cited in Compton and Galaway, op. cit.

11. Elizabeth Salomon, "Humanistic Values," *Social Casework*, vol. 48, no. 1 (January 1967), pp. 26–32, cited in Compton and Galaway, op. cit.

12. Toch, op. cit., supra note 114, cited in Compton and Galaway, op. cit.

13. Matthew Dumont, *The Absurd Healer* (New York: Viking Press, 1968), p. 60, cited in Compton and Galaway, op. cit.

14. Charlotte Towle, *Common Human Needs* (New York: NASW, 1965), p. 26, cited in Compton and Galaway, op. cit.

15. William Schwartz, "The Social Worker," pp. 153–154, cited in Compton and Galaway, op. cit.

16. National Association of Social Workers, "Code of Ethics," *Encyclopedia of Social Work*, vol. II (New York: NASW, 1971), pp. 958–959. For further discussion see also Alan Keith-Lucas, "Ethics in Social Work," *Encyclopedia of Social Work*, vol. 1 (New York: NASW, 1971), pp. 324–328, cited in Compton and Galaway, op. cit.

17. Marcia Abramson, "Ethical Dilemmas for Social Workers in Discharge Planning," *Social Work in Health Care*, vol. 6, no. 4, Summer 1981, pp. 33–41.

18. Cary S. Kart, "In the Matter of Earle Spring: Some Thoughts on One Court's Approach to Senility," *The Gerontologist*, vol. 21, no. 4, 1981, pp. 417–423.

19. Philip E. Cryer "Decisions Regarding the Provision on Withholding of Therapy," in Natalie Abrams and Michael Buckner (eds.), *Medical Ethics: A Clinical Textbook and Reference for the Health Care Professions* (Cambridge: MIT Press, 1983), p. 351.

20. Sally Gadow, "Medicine, Ethics and the Elderly," *The Gerontologist*, vol. 20, no. 6, 1980, pp. 680–685.

21. Joan K. Parry, "Informed Consent: For Whose Benefit?," *Social Casework*, 1975.

22. Richard M. Ratzan, "Being Old Makes You Different: The Ethics of Research with Elderly Subjects" in Natalie Abrams and Michael Buckner (eds.), *Medical Ethics: A Clinical Textbook and Reference for the Health Care Professions* (Cambridge: MIT Press, 1983), pp. 519, 523.

23. Ibid.
24. Harvey A. Taub, "Informed Consent, Memory and Age," *The Gerontologist*, vol. 20, no. 6, 1980, pp. 686–690.
25. Parry, op. cit.
26. Kart, op. cit.
27. Abramson, op. cit.
28. Harry R. Moody, "Ethical Dilemmas in Long Term Care," *Gerontological Social Work Practice in Long Term Care* (New York: Haworth Press, 1983), pp. 97–111.
29. Ibid.
30. Abramson, op. cit.
31. Carole W. Soskis, "Teaching Nursing Home Staff About Patients' Rights," *The Gerontologist*, vol. 21, no. 4, 1981, pp. 424–430.
32. Gadow, op. cit.
33. Ibid.
34. B. J. Diggs, "The Ethics of Providing for the Economic Well-Being of the Aging," in Robert J. Havighurst and B. L. Neugarten (eds.), *Social Policy, Social Ethics and the Aging Society* (Chicago: University of Chicago Press, 1976), pp. 55–65.
35. Louis Lowy, *Training Manual for Human Service Technicians Working with Older People* (Boston: Boston University Press, 1968), p. 17.
36. Shura Saul, *Aging—An Album of People Growing Old* (New York: John Wiley, 1974), pp. 20–26. Reprinted by permission of John Wiley & Sons, Inc.
37. "Social Work and Family Relationships in Later Life" in E. Shanas and G. Streib (eds.), *Social Structure and the Family* (Englewood Cliffs, N.J.: Prentice-Hall, 1965), chap. 3.
38. "The Anthropology of Aging: A New Area for Studies of Culture and Personality," *The Gerontologist*, vol. 7, no. 1, 1967, pp. 55–64.
39. *Why Survive?* (New York: Harper & Row, 1975), p. 12.
40. New York: Putnam, 1972, p. 168.
41. Frank H. Neussel, "The Language of Ageism," *The Gerontologist*, vol. 22, no. 3, 1982, pp. 273–292.
42. Erdman B. Palmore, "Attitudes Toward the Aged: What We Know and Need to Know," *Research on Aging*, vol. 4, no. 3, September 1982, pp. 333–348.
43. Richard A. Kalish, "The New Ageism and the Failure Models: A Polemic," *The Gerontologist*, vol. 19, no. 4, 1979, pp. 398–402.
44. Charles Barresi and Timothy Brubaker, "Clinical Social Workers' Knowledge About Aging: Responses to the 'Facts on Aging Quiz,'" *Journal of Gerontological Social Work*, vol. 2, no. 2, Winter 1979, pp. 127–146.
45. "Social Work and Family Relationships in Later Life" in E. Shanas and G. Streib (eds.), *Social Structure and the Family* (Englewood Cliffs, N.J.: Prentice-Hall, 1965), p. 50.
46. L. Lowy, "Adult Children and Their Parents: Dependency or Dependability?," Excerpts from an address delivered at the Hebrew Rehabilitation Center for the Aged, Boston, Mass., 1975.
47. R. Butler and M. Lewis, *Aging and Mental Health* (St. Louis: Mosby, 1973), p. 35.

6

Goals for Work
with the Aging

The goals of social work stem from its value base. The following "Working Statement on the Purpose of Social Work" was developed by participants at the Second Meeting of NASW on Conceptual Frameworks in 1979.[1]

> The purpose of social work is to promote or restore a mutually beneficial interaction between individuals and society in order to improve the quality of life for everyone. Social workers hold the following beliefs:
>
> - The environment (social, physical, organizational) should provide the opportunity and resources for the maximum realization of the potential and aspirations of all individuals, and should provide for their common human needs and for the alleviation of distress and suffering.
> - Individuals should contribute as effectively as they can to their own well-being and to the social welfare of others in their immediate environment as well as to the collective society.
> - Transactions between individuals and others in their environment should enhance the dignity, individuality, and self-determination of everyone. People should be treated humanely and with justice.
>
> Clients of social workers may be an individual, a family, a group, a community, or an organization.

OBJECTIVES

Social workers focus on person-and-environment in interaction. To carry out their purpose, they work with people to achieve the following objectives:

- Help people enlarge their competence and increase their problem-solving and coping abilities.
- Help people obtain resources.
- Make organizations responsive to people.
- Facilitate interaction between individuals and others in their environment.
- Influence interactions between organizations and institutions.
- Influence social and environmental policy.

To achieve these objectives, social workers work with other people. At different times, the target of change varies — it may be the client, others in the environment, or both.

Individual Treatment and Political Action

There has long been discussion and sometimes controversy in the field of social work regarding which goals to emphasize within the realm of interactions of persons and the environment. Opinion has usually been divided along the lines of social work methods between caseworkers emphasizing treatment of the individual person and community organizers, whose goal is to change the environment (i.e., society) through political action. Clarke A. Chambers has written the following regarding this issue:[2]

> It has been suggested that there is no simple dichotomy between political action and individualized treatment as two broad alternative functions of social welfare work. Some critics lament the failure of social work as a profession to participate, aggressively and militantly, in the resolution of pressing social problems through political action. They cite a number of factors and forces that have worked, and do work, toward social passivity, toward service rather than toward action. . . . Care of the individual client, whatever [the] needs might be, has always been a central and legitimate function of social work. To provide assistance so that [clients and their families] could move away from need, and from dependence upon others, toward independence and self-direction has been for decades a fully accepted principle of welfare work. Care, and the removal of the causes of dependency, may require help in one or more of the following areas: financial support, provision of health or recreational services, vocational guidance, family counseling, cash relief, a lead to a new job, an insight into the sources of marital conflict, two weeks at a vacation camp, the placement of an illegitimate child, prolonged psychiatric sessions, or a new set of teeth.
>
> In any case, the focus of such work is [to help clients help themselves], to see [them] through a time of crisis when [their] own resources —financial or psychological—are inadequate for the demands made upon [them], to liberate [them] from dependency—and poverty is but one form of dependency—to enrich [their] life, to assist [them] in making satisfactory adjustments for [their] environment or in reconstructing it, insofar as this is possible. The means may be those of public assistance—aid to needy children, for example; or casework; or psychiatric counseling; or indeed group work, whose goals were defined by Clara Kaiser to include "furthering social and emotional growth of individuals through productive and meaningful group experience, [the] achievement of socially desirable group goals, [the] socialization of individuals and . . . improving the quality of social relationships."[3]

Here then are represented the service functions of social work: assistance to individuals in the context of existing circumstances—whatever the means utilized, whatever the special skills employed, whatever the subdivision of task. The stress—although not the exclusive emphasis—is upon assisting individual[s] to make a reasonably satisfactory adjustment to [their] environment. If once, in a more primitive age, these procedures involved only—or at least primarily—care and perhaps cure, if they amounted to patchwork amelioration—what some called scavenger work—those days have long since passed. The goals, over a period of time, became more comprehensive and more positive, though still focused on the individual['s] well-being [and] adjustment to life as it actually was. This is social work—especially in its casework phase—in its retail, client-centered, service-oriented aspects. If, over the past 40 to 50 years it was inspired more by St. Sigmund than St. Karl, so be it.

But traditionally, professional social work has had a responsibility to society and to public welfare, as well as to the individual client. Even those workers whose daily routine necessarily forced a nearly exclusive concern with the adjustment of [individuals] to the givens of [their] environment have rarely been unaware of the direct and overwhelming influence of the health of society upon the health of the client. Grace Coyle summed it up in her presidential address before the National Conference of Social Work at the end of the depression decade of the 1930s: "There is no reasonable doubt that poverty itself is responsible for increased illness, that unemployment breeds unemployability, that crowded housing undermines family life, that undernourished children will grow into incompetent workers."[4]

Social workers are scavengers, of course they are, said Sidney Hollander in 1937, and so are doctors; and both must move from amelioration to cure to prevention and finally to positive measures to assure physical and social health. Social work must struggle to lift burdens from those who suffer (so often through no failing of their own) and must seek also to correct "the basic maladjustments to which this wreckage bears witness."[5]

When the limits of personal assistance were reached, then social work had the obligation to promote measures, through political and social action, that would lighten the external handicaps and create opportunities for fuller and richer lives for all. Helen Hall put it in the specific terms with which settlement workers habitually dealt: It was acceptable casework method she said in 1936, to assist a torn and deprived family to get out of objectionable quarters for the sake both of health and morale. "But in the long run," she continued, "it is both poor casework and poor health work merely to move particular families and do nothing toward changing the conditions out of which you have taken them and into which others will move." Social workers must drum up support for housing reform, slum clearance and public housing, and must assist other groups to work effectively toward these ends. "Social action for social change and advance is inescapable," she concluded, "unless we are willing to drift along eternally patching up the consequences of social neglect and industrial breakdown."[6]

So over and over again, as social workers pressed up to the limits of what a given situation permitted in the way of adequate individual assistance, leaders from the profession pressed forward with proposals to break down those external limitations or to push them back. Effective service always required social action. Even though the temptation persisted to rely "upon methods of individual treatment without a companion concern and activities for corrective measures," Rudolph

Danstedt warned, social workers were forced to recognize that "family-centered social work services, psychiatric services, and programs for control and prevention of juvenile delinquency" were effective only in a society in which the evils of "squalor . . . idleness . . . ignorance . . . sickness . . . [and] want" had been rooted out.[7]

And so the two overlapping phases of social work continue to exist, not always harmoniously, but certainly in interdependence—the one focused on [individuals and their] welfare, strongly influenced by the psychological disciplines, introspective, dealing in personalized, retail services; the other concerned with reform, with reconstruction, informed primarily by the social sciences, extroverted, dealing in group or community or wholesale services. Professor Pumphrey recently suggested the terms "compassion" and "protection"—the former referring to "direct physical services" aimed at making "life in the immediate present better for the beneficiaries"; the latter moved by the desire for security or stability—of self or of community—and engaged in "institutionalized action designed to forestall the need for compassion."[8]

Differences of opinion have occurred regarding whether social work should be provided for everyone or only for special "problem populations" and about the knowledge and skill bases necessary for general social work practice as well as for work with these special populations. The basic values of social work can be seen as a continuum, from stances and beliefs about the individual to society's responsibilities and obligations to the individual. Social work professes to believe that the individual is the primary concern of this society and that it is society's responsibility to provide ways in which obstacles to self-realization can be overcome. To live up to these values, we must view our goals as spanning a continuum that includes the curative, preventive, promotional, and enhancing (as outlined in Chapter 4). This continuum is reflected in the orientation of the profession, the practice, and the approach of social workers in their daily encounters with the elderly.

The Goal Continuum

Goals are focused on ameliorating the debilitating, disabling, and crisis conditions that beset older persons in their daily living. An elderly widow may need emotional reassurance that her son is not estranged from her and that his prolonged silence is largely due to his preoccupation with problems in his own family; a client may need help in facing a hazardous operation or additional financial assistance through public welfare. Intervention, on the other end of the continuum, is directed toward enhancing the strengths of older people and developing their capacities toward self-actualization. Individuals encouraged to participate in the program of the senior center in their neighborhood may, for the first time in their lives, discover their talents in painting.

The continuum orientation avoids rigidity. Engaging older persons in organized action to influence legislation or programs benefiting them (1) helps them achieve a sense of importance and self-worth and (2) improves their living standard and possibly the standard of those who follow them. An example of this is action to reduce fares in public transportation. Cure, care, and restoration are preventive measures insofar as they prevent the conditions from becoming worse or interfering with a person's functioning. Also preventive is providing supportive measures so that the individual will be able to cope with a threatening situation.

An effective, regular transportation service, for example, that provides access to a social agency or a senior center prevents people from being helpless, lonely, or isolated. Related to this form of prevention is the goal of enhancement—the achievement of the highest possible level of physical and social well-being. To extend adult educational programs to embrace older persons and to ensure that such programs are physically accessible, financially feasible, and socially comfortable are ways to make a goal operational.

Abraham Monk discusses several rationales for affirming that social work does indeed have distinct and imperative goals in working with the elderly. First, he points out that workers can play a key role in assisting the elderly in integrating their life experiences and coming to terms with the meaning of their life and death. Second, he suggests that social workers can be instrumental in helping the older person and his or her family mediate intergenerational conflicts around allocation and availability of resources and in assuring that to the greatest degree possible, the older person "complete his or her natural life cycle, with its expectable flow and sense of continuity, without culturally imposed inhibiting restraints." In doing so, social workers must "facilitate full use of the macroenvironment by the older individual" and "improve the quality of the microenvironment and the stimulation found within it," creating a "life-enriching environment" that "(1) energizes the person through heightened sensory cues, (2) provides focal points for mental orientation and social congregation, and (3) gratifies the need for security and belonging" as well as a "prosthetic" environment in which supportive and personal services are supplied as integral elements.[9]

Monk also describes obstacles to social workers' participation in these spheres:

- Since in working with the elderly it is imperative for social workers to confront their own losses, aging, and death, many workers choose to avoid working with older adults.
- "Seeing only death in the older person's future,"[10] many people devalue elders and deny altogether the necessity for social work intervention with this group. Thus, social workers may wish to avoid bearing the stigma of working with such a stigmatized population.
- Social workers may rationalize their "gerontophobia" by assuring themselves and others that it is simply not cost-effective to treat a population with so little time in which to live and enjoy the benefits of services.
- Many social workers believe the widespread myth that "you can't teach an old dog new tricks," and thus avoid working with clients whom they presuppose are rigid and unable to negotiate change or achieve development.

As well, he points out pitfalls that social workers must watch for when working with the elderly:

- Younger workers are unlikely to have had any relationships other than superficial ones with older persons prior to practice. With such a dearth of reality-based impressions, they therefore must guard against depersonalizing older clients.
- Social workers acting as case managers for older clients must avoid assuming a "paternalistic stance" that would interfere with their basic goal of fostering self-determination. It must be realized that even well-intentioned "bombardment" of clients with services is likely to foster dependence.[11]

HELP PEOPLE ENLARGE THEIR COMPETENCE AND INCREASE
THEIR PROBLEM-SOLVING AND COPING ABILITIES

. . . Social workers in general seek to understand the meaning of aging, free from the distortions of stereotypical beliefs, through an examination of their own feelings about the process of growing old and a sense of life's value within its inevitable limits. . . .

. . . The principle of individualization and the concomitant avoidance of age-related biases are the cognitive and ethical foundations of practice. Social work intervention requires an understanding of each person's lifelong ways of coping. . . .

. . . Social workers identify and assess the extent and quality of an older person's remaining strengths. They strive to help the individual maximize the use of these strengths, even in the face of loss and progressive deterioration. . . .

. . . Treatment objectives aimed at enhancing the older person's coping skills must be realistically scaled down to the level of his or her remaining strengths. This should be done on the understanding that even micro-behavioral changes are positive indications of the outcome of the treatment. . . .

. . . Although an older individual may never regain his or her waning strength, it is the social worker's task to bolster the person's sense of personal integrity. . . .

HELP PEOPLE OBTAIN RESOURCES

. . . Older people are especially intimidated by complex eligibility requirements and the discouraging bureaucratic maze of existing services. In addition, because of value-related conflicts, a sense of pride, or fear of surrendering their personal autonomy, they often refuse services to which they are entitled. Social workers strive to understand the source of such culturally based considerations and personal anxieties that older clients experience regarding the receipt of services. They then attempt to build up the client's trust, facilitate access to services, and make sure that the client knows about and obtains the services to which he or she is entitled. . . .

. . . Because most older people have several chronic conditions, they may require services on a continuous basis. In such cases, social workers must focus on case management and coordination with the aim of linking older clients to services, monitoring the delivery of services, reassessing the individual client's condition and needs at regular intervals, and making sure that available services are combined to meet the particular needs of the client. . . .

. . . Social workers need to make sure that services are provided in a way that restricts rather than promotes the excess disability syndrome. Part of this effort means seeing that primary support networks are involved in concerted action aimed at preserving the older client's life-style and personal options.

MAKE ORGANIZATIONS RESPONSIVE TO PEOPLE

. . . A major task for social workers is to promote an awareness of who these clients are and what their specific service requirements may be. Workers within agencies must develop treatment modalities that take into account the cumulative losses undergone by older clients, the social, mental, and physical limitations that affect an older person's request for help, and the difficulty that many older people experience in making use of services. . . .

. . . Social workers must interpret for agencies the need to define service priorities in ways that are congruent with major geriatric needs. . . . Service systems should include an "early warning" component attuned to the major crises of old age. . . .

. . . Workers must also make sure that older people, like competent clients of all ages, remain the masters of their own destiny and are involved in making determinations concerning their own future. Service systems should provide older clients with alternative courses of action from which they can choose. Furthermore, these systems should be coordinated to form comprehensive networks with multiple points of entry and, when possible, "one-stop" stations or centers that provide multiple services. . . .

. . . Given the contradictory evidence about whether services are best provided in an age-integrated or age-segregated system, social workers should retain a flexible, open-minded attitude. It is likely that some services obtain better outcomes when they are offered in multigenerational situations but that others may be more effective when delivered to clients of one age group only. In either case, the preferences of clients should be consulted, but when a given course becomes inevitable, such as institutionalization in a long-term care facility, proper counseling and adequate preparation of the client should especially prevail.

FACILITATE INTERACTION BETWEEN INDIVIDUALS
AND OTHERS IN THEIR ENVIRONMENT

. . . As people grow older, members of their lifelong support systems—spouse, offspring, relatives, and friends—die or move away. Both the onset of widowhood, spelling the probability that loneliness will be a permanent part of life, and the individual's bombardment by repeated losses point to the need for intervention that is geared to the circumstances of bereavement and the client's potential for resocialization. . . .

. . . When helping to resocialize the bereaved client, social workers assist in the development of new support systems and facilitate the individual's adjustment and integration to new social contexts, such as self-help groups, multiservice centers, and lifelong learning programs. . . .

. . . To the same purpose, social workers facilitate instrumental and expressive interaction between individuals of different generations. . . .

. . . Resocialization is also a challenge for the aging . . . couple when the last of their offspring leave home. Social workers facilitate clients' adjustments and their search for meaning in a new family situation that they may never have experienced before. . . .

. . . Social workers are increasingly called on to provide relief to those who are middle-aged, most especially when these individuals find they can no longer attend to the needs of aging, ailing parents or grandparents. In such instances, workers facilitate the integration of a family's strengths and resources through formalized personal care services. . . .

. . . Ultimately, the activities of social workers enable older people to remain in their familiar environment for as long as possible and thus to retain a sense of competence and continuity in their relationship with the environment. Workers' efforts in this regard may call for enriching the environment with architectural and other supports and ensuring access to services. When it is no longer possible for the older person to remain in his or her home and neighborhood, it is incumbent on the social worker to help the person prepare for the impending transition to institutional care as carefully and smoothly as possible, thus avoiding the trauma of a sudden uprooting.

INFLUENCE INTERACTIONS BETWEEN
ORGANIZATIONS AND INSTITUTIONS

The practice guidelines relating to the objective of making organizations responsive to people are applicable to this objective as well.

INFLUENCE SOCIAL AND ENVIRONMENTAL POLICY

. . . Over (three) hundred federal programs that benefit the aged directly or indirectly have been generated in the last fifty years, but their apparent abundance is not a valid indication of their adequacy. Social workers must critically examine whether these programs are relevant and appropriate in light of the changing social, economic, and demographic conditions related to the aging. . . .

. . . As formulated in the program implementation stage, provisions for eligibility, program restrictions, and determinations of service priorities are at times inconsistent with the intent of legislation. Social workers critically examine whether there is continuity between programs and policies and assist in the improvement of needs assessment and the setting of priorities. . . .

. . . Most public funds for the aged are used to provide cash supports, and this overshadows the provision of services. Workers must . . . defin[e] the extent and nature of clients' needs related to such areas as housing, nutrition, physical and mental impairment, isolation, transportation, and employment. They may then assist in the formulation of . . . innovative policies. . . .

. . . Social workers must devise incentives such as tax abatements and exemptions, cash payments, and special demogrants to be given to families and communities for assuming a wider responsibility for older people.* In a similar

---

* A "demogrant" is a technical term used to describe flat payments to people in need, such as family allowances, without having to prove need. This term was introduced by Alvin Schorr with regard to children support payments.

vein, they can design and promote cooperative and communal living arrangements as well as opportunities for work that promote the self-sufficiency of the aging.[12]

Goals for Older Americans

While specific goals in practice are based on the particular person, group, situation, condition, background, needs, problems, etc. (see Chapters 10, 12, and 13), general goals along the continuum are guided by the Ten Objectives of Title I of the Older Americans Act as originally promulgated in 1965; to date, unfortunately, avenues toward the achievement of these goals have not been supported by adequate resources:

> The Congress declares the general responsibility of all units of Government toward older people in our society, the rights and privileges which all older people should enjoy and which should be provided by those who carry out the functions of the national, state, and local governments:
>
> 1. An adequate income in retirement in accordance with the American standard of living.
> 2. The best possible physical and mental health which science can make available without regard to economic status.
> 3. Suitable housing, independently selected, designed and located with reference to special needs and available at costs which older citizens can afford.
> 4. Full restorative services for those who require institutional care.
> 5. Opportunity for employment with no discriminatory personnel practices because of age.
> 6. Retirement in health, honor, dignity—after years of contribution to the economy.
> 7. Pursuit of meaningful activity within the widest range of civic, cultural, and recreational opportunities.
> 8. Efficient community services which provide social assistance in a coordinated manner and which are readily available when needed.
> 9. Immediate benefit from proven research knowledge which can sustain and improve health and happiness.
> 10. Freedom, independence, and the free exercise of individual initiative in planning and managing their own lives.

Participants, when surveyed following the 1981 White House Conference on Aging, ranked the following overall recommendations as the highest priorities for America:

- Preserve the financial integrity of the Social Security system as the foundation of economic security for all Americans through preserving current funding levels for Medicare and Medicaid, maintaining minimum and current benefit levels to current and future employees, granting cost-of-living increases at specific times, and by expanding coverage to all gainfully employed persons.
- Develop a national health policy guaranteeing full and comprehensive health services to all Americans. This plan shall include a long-term-care community-based health system and in the interim shall provide case management, in-home health, mental, and social services through expansion of Medicare and Medicaid.

The policy should maintain the maximum independence of the elderly and protect the rights of institutionalized elderly.

- Eliminate mandatory retirement and other forms of discrimination against older workers and call on employers to hire older workers utilizing flexible part-time, temporary, shared, or other schedules.
- Provide adequate rental assistance for low- and moderate-income elderly renters and continue the current 25 percent rent-to-income ratio for low-income housing.
- Expand home health and in-home services based on individual needs, make eligibility requirements more flexible, reimburse such services at local rates, simplify administrative requirements for such services, and provide tax incentives to families who provide care for dependent elderly members.
- Give the highest priority to use macroeconomic policies to stop inflation.

An Illustration from Practice

The following vignette is designed to illustrate the goal continuum:

Mr. F. is a man in his late sixties, black, separated from his family and living alone in a furnished apartment. He was referred to a social worker in a community agency outreach program by the manager of a housing unit for the elderly, where he had applied for an apartment. The manager was concerned because there was a long wait for an apartment and it seemed to her that the man appeared agitated over the wait and anxious to change his present living arrangements. The social worker first made contact with Mr. F. at the hot-lunch program run by the housing unit. In talking with Mr. F., the worker discovered that he had had a stroke approximately four months before the referral. Ever since the stroke, he had not felt well. He was afraid that the medication the hospital had prescribed for him was making him crazy and that he would end up in a "nut house." He also feared that his medical condition was deteriorating and that he might die. He had been estranged from his wife and family for many years and had no close relatives. With his permission, the worker contacted the hospital and discovered that the medical personnel considered the damage from the stroke minor. They felt that his concerns about the medication and his deterioration were irrational, and they had referred him to their psychiatric clinic; but he had refused to accept the referral.

The worker, as she began to get to know Mr. F., raised the issue of nursing home care—with much ambivalence and anxiety. Because Mr. F. was obviously uncomfortable and agitated, the worker felt that he should be seen by a psychiatrist and was able to help him to accept the referral to a community psychiatric clinic. This effort was also aided by the hospital social worker who acted as a liaison among the psychiatric clinic, the community worker, and Mr. F. The psychiatrist who examined Mr. F. thought that he should be in a nursing home and that someone should make the decision for him. He communicated this information to the hospital social worker but took no other action either in relation to Mr. F.'s intense agitation or in relation to helping achieve the recommended plan of nursing home care.

The following day, Mr. F. returned to the hospital, asked to see the hospital social worker, and requested that she take no action regarding putting him in a nursing home. A day later, the community social worker met him at the hot-lunch program where she generally contacted him. He was extremely agitated. He had hoped that the psychiatrist would "give him a needle to cool him down," and when the psychiatrist had done nothing to help him, he felt helpless and desperate. He told the worker that if something were not done to help him immediately, he would do away with himself. It was a Friday afternoon, and he did not feel that he could last over the weekend.

Since Mr. F. himself now wanted hospitalization and since his agitation was so marked and coupled with suicidal threats, the worker telephoned the psychiatric clinic of the hospital to find out whether they would see him on an emergency basis for possible admission. The psychiatric clinic told her that it would not be possible for them to see him. She then called the hospital. The hospital social worker contacted the psychiatrist who had seen Mr. F., and he arranged to have him admitted to another hospital, a small private psychiatric hospital of which he was the director. Mr. F. spent a few weeks at this hospital, where he was given medication and physical care. He did improve somewhat during this time and was discharged to a small, good-quality, but all-white nursing home. At first, Mr. F. was greatly disturbed because he was the only black person in the nursing home. Later, he adjusted although he said that he had not made any friends there.

The community worker and her supervisor thought that there had been substantial mishandling of this situation by the hospital and that a protest should be registered both in relation to this patient and because of their general concern about the care, or lack of it, for the elderly. A visit was made to the hospital and a complaint was registered with the director of social services. Special attempts were made to find a racially mixed home for Mr. F., and the director confirmed that it was hospital policy that no patient be refused emergency admission. She suggested that if such a thing were to happen again, the person communicating such a decision should be identified so that definitive action could be taken. Unfortunately, the name of the person in the psychiatric clinic who had refused to have Mr. F. seen was unknown.

Evaluation of the Practice Illustration

The case of Mr. F. illustrates both treatment and prevention through outreach. If the community social worker had not been present at the housing unit, this man would not have been referred to the community agency unless and until he was in an even greater state of crisis than at the time of the initial referral. If the social worker had not reached out to him in an attempt to discover what lay behind his discomfort about his living arrangements, the connection between his concerns about his physical problems and his present living arrangements would not have become known. It is true that the worker was not able to prevent a crisis from occurring due to the hospital's poor handling of the situation. However, she did enable Mr. F. to accept the psychiatric care that he needed. If the community worker had become aware of the situation at an earlier point, she might even have helped prevent institutionalization. As it was, she prevented more intense ongoing suffering and perhaps suicide.

This situation illustrates a curative approach in relation to securing adequate care for Mr. F. and a preventive stance in relation to the lack of concern regarding the availability of adequate mental health facilities and the lack of outreach to the elderly from these facilities. A general orientation to goals will affect the specific goals for older people, whether they are individuals or members of families, peer groups, community organizations, or citizens action groups. Interventive activities by the social worker (discussed in later chapters) call for specific goals on a proper assessment of problems to be solved and needs to be met.

References

1. "Working Statement of the Purpose of Social Work," *Social Work*, January 1981, p. 6.
2. "A Historical Perspective on Political Action vs. Individualized Treatment," in P. E. Weinberger (ed.), *Perspectives on Social Welfare*, 2nd ed. (New York: Macmillan, 1974), pp. 89–92.
3. Clara Kaiser, "Group Work Education in the Last Decade," in Harleigh B. Trecker (ed.), *Group Work: Foundations and Frontiers* (New York: Associated Press, 1955), pp. 355–356 (reprinted from *The Group*, June 1953). Many social workers have wrestled with these issues. Particularly illuminating are Bertram M. Beck's "Shaping America's Social Welfare Policy," in Alfred J. Kahn (ed.), *Issues in American Social Work* (New York: Columbia University Press, 1959), pp. 191–218; and Donald S. Howard's "Social Work and Social Reform," in Cora Kasius (ed.), *New Directions in Social Work* (New York: Harper & Row, 1954), pp. 159–174. Nathan F. Cohen's *Social Work in the American Tradition* (New York: Dryden Press, 1958) is a work to which social welfare historians are indebted.
4. Grace L. Coyle, "Social Work at the Turn of the Decade," *Proceedings of the Conference* (1940), pp. 12–33.
5. Sidney Hollander, "A Layman Takes Stock of Public and Private Agency Functions," *Proceedings of the Conference* (1937), p. 190.
6. Helen Hall, "The Consequences of Social Action for the Group Work Agency," *Proceedings of the Conference* (1936), pp. 235, 237.
7. Rudolph T. Danstedt, "An Assessment of Social Action" (New York: Columbia University Press for National Conference on Social Welfare, 1958), pp. 203–204.
8. The two terms Pumphrey clearly sets forth are overlapping and intertwined functions, and both involve mixed motives. "In compassion the benefactor identifies with and seeks to alleviate the present pain which another person feels; in protection [benefactors guard] against painful consequences to [themselves], [their] group, or [their] community in the future." Pumphrey also notes the tendency of the compassionate response to lead to action designed to eliminate "the need for the sort of service" which compassion institutionalized has offered. Ralph E. Pumphrey, "Compassion and Protection: Dual Motivations in Social Welfare," *Social Service Review*, vol. 33, no. 1 (March 1959), pp. 21–29.

9. Abraham Monk, "Social Work with the Aged: Principles of Practice," *Social Work*, January 1981, pp. 61–68.

10. Ibid.

11. Ibid.

12. Ibid.

Sanctions
and Auspices
of Practice

Three aspects of social work practice with the aging provide the backdrop and the matrix for fulfilling the functions and carrying out the tasks that are commensurate with the values and goals of the profession: (1) the sources of sanctions for programs and services, (2) the types and organization of such programs and services, and (3) the financing of such programs and services. This chapter discusses these three elements.

All of society's sanctions for social work practice are based on social policies that are shaped by a complex interplay of values, knowledge, and power constellations.

> Our social policies toward aging have moved toward selective assumption of societal responsibility and away from reliance upon exclusive kin or filial responsibility, toward acceptance of rightful entitlement of benefits rather than dependency upon charitable supports that are stigmatized, and toward more institutional services geared to meet individual requirements rather then residual, undifferentiated services.[1]

Three major events and four national units have been instrumental in directing America's policymakers toward the field of aging and in mobilizing interest and engagement on the part of the profession and individual social workers. The three events were the first White House Conference on Aging in 1961, with its official report, *The Nation and Its Older People*; the second in 1971, on the theme *Toward a National Policy on Aging*; and the third in 1981, on the theme *The Aging Society: Challenge and Opportunity*. The four national units are (1) the Federal Council on Aging, an independent unit that reports to the Congress on how it coordinates policymaking related to the elderly; (2) the Administration on Aging, Executive

Department for Affairs of the Elderly, U.S. Department of Health and Human Services; (3) in the legislative branch, the Special Committee on Aging, with a number of subcommittees, first established in the U.S. Senate in 1965; and (4) the Select Committee on Aging of the House of Representatives. House and Senate committees and subcommittees with jurisdiction over elder affairs are depicted in Figures 7.1 and 7.2.

As stated in the Working Definition discussed earlier, "social work is not practiced in a vacuum or at the choice of its practitioners alone. Thus there is a social responsibility inherent in the practitioner's role for the way in which services are rendered. The authority and the power of the practitioner and what [he or she] represents to the clients and group members derive from one or a combination of three sources: governmental agencies or their subdivisions; voluntary incorporated agencies; the organized profession."[2] One of the main sources that give sanction, the aging population itself, is omitted in this typology but is discussed later.

Sources of Sanctions for Programs and Services

The Organized Elderly Population

In Chapter 3, a demographic profile of the elderly clearly demonstrates the steady and substantial growth of the elderly population in the United States. The status of older people as a political issue in contemporary American society is due in large part to the emergence of groups of organized elderly. Although such groups date back to the 1930s, the last twenty-five years have seen an amazing growth in the number, stability, and influence of senior citizen organizations. There are six major national organizations:

- American Association of Retired Persons
- Asociacion Nacional Pro Personas Mayores
- Gray Panthers
- National Association of Retired Federal Employees
- National Caucus and Center on the Black Aged
- National Council of Senior Citizens

As well as other more specialized national groups such as the National Citizens Coalition for Nursing Home Reform, many state and local senior groups have developed that are unaffiliated with a national group and that have state or local orientations and character.

> These groups may or may not have formal membership and their activities cover a variety of areas including recreation, social life, education, social services, and political activities. Occasionally they are made up of retirees of a particular vocation or religion.
>
> If politically active, these local groups usually are concerned with such issues as local utility rates, public transportation, local property tax relief, rent control

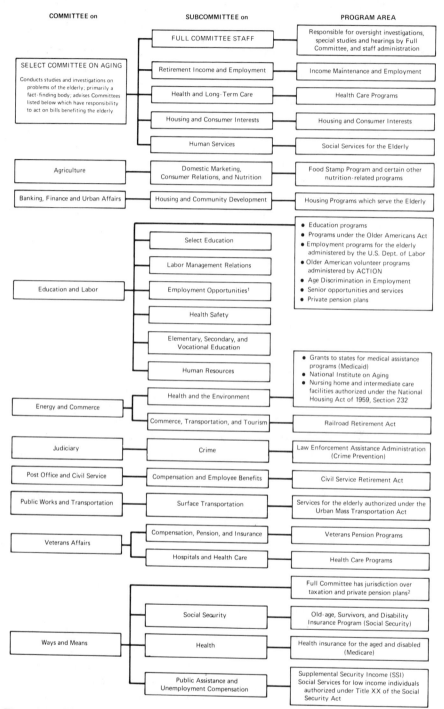

Figure 7.1. House committees and subcommittees with jurisdiction over areas related to the elderly. Source: *Federal Programs Benefiting the Elderly.* A Reference Guide by the Select Committee on Aging, House of Representatives, 98th Congress, First Session, Revised Edition (U.S. Government Printing Office, Washington, D.C., 1983), p. 60.

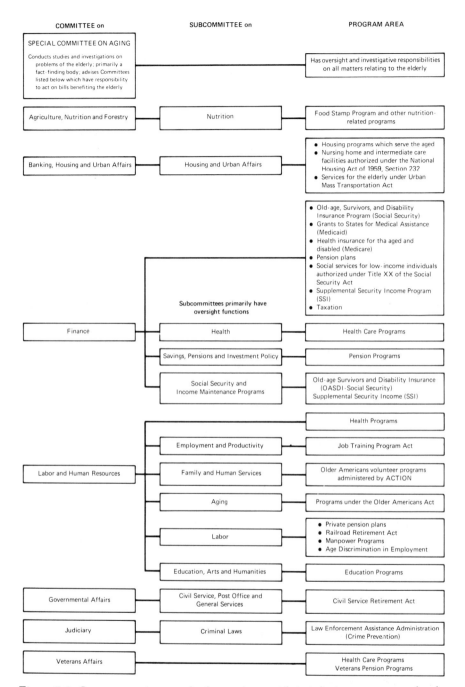

Figure 7.2. Senate committees and subcommittees with jurisdiction over areas related to the elderly. Source: *Federal Programs Benefiting the Elderly*, p. 61.

and local housing conditions, consumer fraud, or availability of community services. . . . In addition to belonging to national, state, and local organizations of the elderly, older persons also exert influence through membership on advisory councils. To ensure the voice of older persons in the Older Americans Act planning and programs, the Act mandates the establishment of advisory committees on aging at the national, state, and area agency levels. At the federal level, this requirement is effected through the establishment of the Federal Council on Aging. . . . At the state and area agency levels, councils . . . at least [one-half of which are] elderly consumers function as the policy-making boards for the state and area agencies on aging. Generally, municipal offices on aging not specifically covered by the Older Americans Act also establish advisory bodies with the majority representation reserved for older persons.[3]

Governmental Auspices

The two most important national laws affecting the aged are the Social Security Act, with numerous amendments since its passage in 1935, and the Older Americans Act of 1965 and its amendments of 1967, 1969, 1972, 1973, 1974, 1975, 1977, 1978 and again in 1984, which spawned the increase of the planning, legislation, and provider and professional agencies first labeled by Arthur Flemming, former Commissioner of the Administration on Aging, the *aging network*.

Summary of the Older Americans Act

The Older Americans Act was initially passed in 1965; it establishes program objectives and funding to plan, administer, and provide services to meet the special needs of citizens 60 years of age and older (except where the age limit is 55 for community service employment).

The 1978 amendments realign the act into six titles, in contrast to the previous nine. Titles I and II remain substantially unchanged under these amendments, with some new provisions that strengthen the role of the Administration on Aging. Title III consolidates and extends the provisions for social services, senior centers, and nutrition services, previously contained under the old Titles III, V, and VII, which have been repealed. Title IV contains all provisions for evaluation, research and demonstration, and training project grants. Title V (senior employment) replaces the old Title IX (senior employment) and VI provides for services to Native American tribes.

Title I includes a "Declaration of Objectives," calling for the availability of coordinated, comprehensive programs that include a full range of health, education, and social services for all older citizens who need them. Special priority is given to "the elderly with the greatest economic and social need." Under this title, federal assistance is provided for the planning and operation of such programs developed through a partnership of older citizens, community agencies, and state and local governments.

Title II outlines the structure and role of the federal Administration on Aging (AoA) in the Department of Health, Education and Welfare (DHEW)—now the Department of Health and Human Services (DHHS)—which has overall responsibility for administering programs established under this act and for overseeing and participating in the development of all federal policies and programs affecting the elderly. It provides a clearinghouse for all "information related to the needs and interests of older persons," and a Federal Council on Aging to advise the president and the AoA on all federal policies and programs for older Americans.

Title III is the principal source of funding for state and county governments planning for and providing services under this act. This expanded Title III provides for the planning and development of a "comprehensive and coordinated service system," authorizing funding and providing for one administrative structure of three key service areas: social services (formerly addressed by the old Title III); senior centers (formerly provided under the old Title V); and nutrition services (previously addressed by the old Title VII). A primary goal of these service systems is to maintain maximum independence of the elderly through the provision of support services with supplemental self-care.

State governments are allocated funds according to the number of persons aged 60 or older in the state as a proportion of all older Americans. Under the 1978 amendments, no state receives less than the sum received in fiscal year 1978. However, states will be required to increase their allocations to rural areas by 5 percent.

One state agency must be designated by each state to receive these funds and to develop and administer a state plan for the provision of services to the aging. The state agencies, in turn, must designate area agencies on aging (AAAs) to develop and administer local-area plans for "planning and service" areas. Area plans form the basis for the development of state plans, both of which must be prepared on a three-year basis, with annual adjustments as needed.

Local planning and service areas are flexibly defined; currently, an area can be any unit of general-purpose local government with a population of 100,000 or more. Other units of such size and areas adjacent may also be included to form a "regional planning and service area," when it can improve program administration. Area agencies may be any public or private nonprofit agency or organization, including an office of city or county government that has been appropriately designated for such planning.

Locally elected officials are to participate along with older individuals and the general public on advisory councils, established by each AoA to assist in planning. All the following social services may be funded under this title: health, continuing education, welfare, informational, recreational, homemaker, counseling, referral, services to reach other social services including nutrition and housing, repair and renovation of housing, services to prevent institutionalization, legal services, financial counseling, preventive health, career counseling, state ombudsman, and services for the disabled. In addition, funding is available for altering, renovating, and in some cases acquiring facilities for use as multipurpose senior centers. Funds may also be used for assisting in the operation of such facilities, including outreach. A state ombudsman program, begun as a demonstration program under the act in the past, is now required in each state.

During the fiscal years 1979 and 1980, to facilitate administrative consolidation of nutrition programs with other social service programs, areas could seek to use up to 20 percent of nutrition-service allotments for supportive services directly related to the delivery of congregate or home-delivered meals, including recreational activities, information and referral, and health and welfare counseling. (In such areas as Alaska, up to 50 percent can be used to allay unusually high costs.)

State allotments to AAAs are to be determined by a formula reflecting the geographic distribution of individuals aged 60 and older. Each state is required to publicize the formula it develops for review and comment. Federal money may be used to pay for up to 75 percent of the AAAs' cost of administering area plans and up to 90 percent of the costs of services. In fiscal year 1981, the sharing of costs for services shifted from 90 percent federal and 10 percent state and local to 85 percent federal and 15 percent state and local, with the states responsible for bearing the whole cost of the 5 percent decrease in federal funds for these services. A maximum of 8.5 percent of Title III funding may be used to cover expenses of administering area plans.

Each area is required to allot at least 50 percent of its social service dollars to three priority areas: access services (transportation, outreach, and information and referral); in-home services (homemaker/home-health aide, visiting/telephone reassurance, and chore maintenance); and legal services. If these services are already sufficient to meet the need, this allocation may be reduced. Area plans are also to designate, "where feasible," a focal point for the provision of these services. "Special consideration" should be given to the use of multipurpose senior centers for this purpose.

Title IV provides for the funding of evaluation, training, research, and demonstration efforts to be conducted by state and local governments and other public and private organizations, as follows:

1. Training programs for recruitment and for employment in programs for the aging. Under the 1978 amendments, special courses addressing the needs of rural providers are to be funded.
2. Research-and-development projects for determining elderly needs for service, for developing and evaluating new ways of addressing these needs (such as problems in the delivery of transportation services), and for the coordination of services by revising existing federal transportation programs for the elderly. Also addressed is the need to study comparative costs, problems, and needs for service delivery in urban and rural areas.
3. Demonstration projects to improve or expand social or nutrition services. Priority is given to funding of rural AAAs for addressing special needs of the rural elderly, including alternative health-care delivery systems, advocacy, outreach,

and transportation services. Special consideration is also given to projects that address special housing needs (including renovation and repair) and property-tax relief; needs for continuing education and preretirement education; needs of physically and mentally impaired older individuals for services such as special transportation and escort, homemaker, home health, and shopping; needs for alternatives to institutionalization through day care and funding through state Title XIX and XX allocations; and needs of the rural elderly.

4. Demonstration projects in several states were established to coordinate social services for homebound elderly, blind, and disabled.

5. Comprehensive, coordinated long-term care system projects, for the development of systems emphasizing assessment, care planning, referral mechanism, and alternatives to institutionalization.

6. Legal services demonstration projects to expand or improve the delivery of legal services to the elderly.

7. Model projects to relieve high utility and home-heating costs, with special consideration given to programs providing fuel or utility services to low-income elderly at reduced rates.

8. Multipurpose senior-center insurance revolving fund, providing insurance on mortgages (including advances on mortgages during acquisition, alteration, renovation, and construction). Mortgages that include the cost of equipment used in the operation of a new center are also to be insured. Annual interest grants may also be awarded for the acquisition, alteration, renovation, or construction of senior-center facilities.

9. Gerontology-center grants for establishing or supporting, in public and private nonprofit agencies, organizations for training, research, and program development, notably for long-term care and national-policy study centers.

Title V (previously Title IX) authorizes the Department of Labor to provide grants to fund part-time community-service jobs for unemployed, low-income people (defined under the 1978 amendments as persons with incomes up to 125 percent of the poverty level) aged 55 years and older. Under this title, grants are available to two categories of contractors—(1) states and (2) public and private nonprofit agencies and organizations. Preference in the second category is given to national organizations that have a "proven ability" in providing such services to older persons under similar programs.

Jobs are extended to a greater number of individuals, and states are given larger roles in the program than previously. Spending authorizations for this title were $350 million for fiscal year 1979, $400 million for fiscal year 1980, $450 million for fiscal year 1981, $277 million for 1982, $297 million for 1983, and $318 million for 1984, which shows a substantial decrease in the last three years. States are allocated 55 percent of the increase over fiscal year 1978 funding levels and national organizations, or "contractors," 45 percent. Allocations within states may be evaluated for the distribution between rural and urban areas. To improve coordination between state agencies on aging and nation contractors, all employment projects conducted under this title must be reported to the state office on aging thirty days before the project is undertaken for review and comment.

Provision is also made to assist workers in the transition to private employment in community-service jobs. Traditionally, such jobs have included assisting policemen and social workers; repairing homes of the poor and elderly; and assisting in senior centers, nursing homes, hospitals, schools, and many other public and private agencies. Technical assistance to help prime sponsors, businesses, and other organizations to create job opportunities through work sharing and other experimental methods is also provided for.

Title VI makes possible the development of social services, including nutritional services, for Native American tribes. Eligible tribal organizations must represent at least seventy-five individuals aged 60 and older. Grants made under this title will cover all costs of service delivery.

The White House Conference of 1981 was authorized to develop recommendations for further research and action in the field of aging. Representatives of federal, state, and local governments, professionals, and citizens were invited to participate and did so.

The Domestic Volunteer Service Act of 1973 was amended, extending for three years the Retired Senior Volunteer Program (RSVP), Foster Grandparent Program, and Senior Companions and Health Aides (the "National Older Americans Volunteer Programs"), which are operated under ACTION, the domestic equivalent of the Peace Corps Program that is organized as a federal volunteer service agency. Elderly individuals with incomes up to 125 percent of the poverty level are eligible to be considered for the Foster Grandparent or Senior Companion programs.

The Age Discrimination Act has been strengthened with several new amendments. The provisions for enforcement now apply, with certain exceptions, to all age discrimination in programs using federal funds. Previously, this law was limited in its application to instances of "unreasonable" discrimination. In addition, these amendments provide individuals with the right to initiate action in claiming age discrimination, after administrative remedies have been exhausted.

Administratively, the act has also been strengthened, by giving DHHS the authority to review and approve related regulations written by other federal agencies. All federal agencies will also be required to report to DHHS on compliance with this law in all federally funded programs, including those administered locally.

After a long delay, regulations to implement the Titles of the Older Americans Act Amendments of 1978 were issued in March 1980 and the stage was set to test the ramifications of these new provisions.

In 1984 the Older Americans Act was amended again and another three-year authorization was passed.

In addition, Title VII, Personal Health Education Training, has been enacted to provide funding for the dissemination of health information and for educating and training of older as well as younger persons in maintaining and preserving "good health." It is too early, at this stage, to know what the implications of Title VII are in general, and for social work in particular.

Recently, Rep. Ike Andrews, D-N.C., called the Older Americans Act "one of the best cures yet discovered for the health-sapping loneliness, depression, and isolation which too often accompany us into out later years."

However, major issues remain unresolved, such as (1) the organizational status of the AoA (to be directly related to the Secretary of DHHS rather than located within the Office of the Assistant Secretary for Human Development Services; (2) targeting specific services for specific aging population groups; (3) short- and long-term care and its relationship to the aging network; (4) more emphasis on research and training; (5) utilization of research results.

The Older Americans Act has resulted in the establishment of a nationwide network of agencies concerned with the elderly. At the federal level, the Administration on Aging, through regional offices, disburses the funds provided by the Older Americans Act and administers, monitors, and evaluates the programs of the various states. In turn, there is in each state a designated state unit on aging, which looks after the various community programs through a budgetary and planning review process. At the community level, designated area agencies on aging are responsible for the coordination of services and community resources.

In varying ways at the different levels of government, three basic strategies are engaged in the administration of the Older Americans Act. The first of these centers on the provision of services necessary to meet the objectives of the act. The Older Americans Act provides for services, and also encourages the development of resources in other segments of government for the benefit of the elderly. A second strategy is the linking of people with services; this can include the provision of technical assistance by one agency to another to provide more effective services, the provision of information by an agency to an individual about available services and referral to appropriate providers, and the location of individuals in the community unaware of and in need of services. Finally, there is the strategy of advocacy through which agencies look after the rights and interests of the elderly population. This may take several forms, including developing legislation, monitoring programs administered by other governmental agencies to see that the elderly are receiving their proportionate share of the benefits, ensuring that the rights of the elderly are not violated, and allowing the elderly full participation in the decision process that will influence their lives. The largest single source of other federal funding is from Title XX of the Social Security Act (now a block grant). These funds pay for the social services that are within the jurisdiction of a state agency and also provide funds for training of personnel.[4]

Social Security Program

Social Security benefits are the single most important source of income for the largest number of older people in all industrial societies. Everywhere such income is strictly transfer: it is earned by the young workers but is allocated to the elderly no longer at work—and the young provide for the old in the expectation that they will be provided for in turn.

Originally established in 1935 under the Social Security Act (Title II), the major income program of social insurance is financed through compulsory contributions from employers, employees, and the self-employed. The program initially offered only retirement benefits for industrial and commercial workers but was subsequently expanded to include disability insurance and benefits for the survivors and dependents of the insured workers. Coverage has been extended to include most of the following: self-employed persons; state and local government employees; employees of charitable, educational, and religious organizations; members of the armed forces; household employees; and farm workers. Today, nine out of ten workers are earning social security coverage; nearly one out of every seven American citizens receives monthly social security benefits. The social security program touches almost every American family in some way.

Although other programs, including Medicare, Medicaid, and supplemental security income, have been established under the Social Security Act, the term *social security* popularly refers only to the Old Age, Survivors and Disability Insurance program (OASDI). Table 7.1 includes only the OASDI program, which is administered entirely by the federal government through the Social Security Administration (SSA) and its approximately 1,300 branch offices.[5]

Beginning in 1935 with the passage of the Social Security Act, Congress in a piecemeal fashion has enacted over 150 programs aimed at improving the status and conditions of older persons. These programs, spread among thirty-five federal agencies and often not well publicized or explained, are frequently more bewildering than helpful to older persons. Social workers must have a good grasp of the structure and workings of the aging network in order to intervene effectively with older clients. The elements of this aging network are discussed below.

Congress acted in 1983 to restore financial solvency to the Social Security program and end four years of bitter partisan debate over the future of the program. The Social Security Amendments of 1983, signed by President Reagan as Public Law 98-21 on April 20, 1983, eliminated projected short- and long-term deficits in the OASDI programs. Congress left unresolved for the moment the future of the Medicare program, whose hospital insurance (HI) trust fund faces a far more serious financing deficit over the remainder of this decade. The 1983 amendments improved financing of OASDI by $166 billion between 1983 and 1990, and eliminated a projected seventy-five-year deficit of 2.10 percent of taxable payroll.

The most significant achievement of the 1983 amendments was that the Congress acted quickly and decisively to restore solvency in a manner that reaffirmed the existing structure of Social Security and was generally accepted as reasonable and fair. The bipartisan consensus achieved by the National Commission on Social Security Reform and its rapid enactment augurs reasonably well that Medicare's financing crisis can be handled.

Federal Level: Administration on Aging. The Administration on Aging (AoA) is located in the United States Department of Health and Human Services. AoA is responsible for providing coordination among federal agencies that have or could have programs benefiting the elderly; it serves as the federal government's chief advocate for the elderly and allocates funds for programs authorized under the Older Americans Act. The AoA is ultimately responsible for enforcing service priorities and allocation standards established by Congress for programs of the AoA.

In addition to allocating funds to state and area agencies and monitoring the use of those funds, the AoA, through the Office of the Commissioner on Aging, is authorized to fund directly model projects designed "to promote the well-being of older persons." These model projects often lead to an expansion of the basic programs administered by the state and area agencies. For example, many of the legal services for the elderly programs that have been sponsored by state and area agencies on aging were based on model projects funded out of money from model or demonstration projects. Thus, legal service is now commonly funded by state and area agencies on aging out of Title III monies.

The relationship between AoA and the regional, state, and area levels of the bureaucracy is constantly evolving. However, the present relationship as established by the 1973 amendments is as follows: AoA grants funds to state and area agencies on the basis of a plan developed by the state and approved by the regional office. The state plan identifies the program objectives to be accomplished during the coming year and sets forth plans of action to achieve these objectives. For the most part, the state acts as a conduit of funds to the area agencies, which in turn award grants or contracts to the direct providers of service. By 1981, the AoA programs were fully implemented, with 10 regional offices, 57 state and territorial offices on aging, and 665 area agencies.

State Agency. The state office on aging is the focal point in the state on behalf of elderly people. As the overall planner, coordinator, and evaluator of programs designed to serve the elderly, it is a key agency in the network on aging. State offices on aging are currently undergoing a transitional phase organizationally.

The experience of the existing agencies on aging demonstrates that no single location or approach is absolutely essential to assure a strong aging unit with power to affect state budget, programs, and policy related to older persons. In practice, cabinet-level departments, separate commissions and offices, and units located within larger agencies have all proven to be effective advocates for the elderly.

Thus, while the agency's location will not guarantee access to policymakers, the higher the location, the harder it is to deny this access.

A high location for the aging agency in state government is an important factor with respect to achieving the goals of intragovernmental prestige and power, high status within the aging community, increased budget levels, and the ability to influence the governor, legislature, and other department heads in a meaningful way.

The commission through its director, or the department or division through its commissioner, director, or chief, administers the programs funded by both the federal and state treasuries. How much the state allocates to the elderly, how much the AoA provides, and the extent to which other sources of federally funded

Table 7.1. Aging Network Schema for Orientation via Illustrations

Level	Public	Private—Nonsectarian and Sectarian

Federal National	Executive:
	    Federal Council on Aging
	    Federal agencies and
	        departments (e.g.,
	        HHS-AoA)
	    NIA (National Institute of
	        Aging), NIMH
	        (National Institute of
	        Mental Health)
	Legislative:
	    Senate Committee on
	        Aging
	    House Committee on Aging
	    Other Senate and House
	        committees
		National Council on
		    Aging
		American Association
		    of Homes for
		    Aging and others
		Units of national
		    organization
		Religious organizations
		    (e.g., Unitarian-
		    Universalists,
		    Aging Services of
		    Reform Jewish
		    Congregations of
		    America)

State	Executive:
	    Governor's Council
	    57 State Units on Aging
	        (e.g., Department of
	        Elder Affairs in
	        Massachusetts)
	    Other state departments
	Legislative:
	    Senate committees on
	        elderly
	    House committees on
	        elderly (e.g., Human
	        Services and Elderly
	        Affairs)
	Area-agencies on aging in the
	    U.S. (665)
		State associations of
		    units on aging
		Home care
		    corporations
		Religious organizations
		    and their units
		    on aging

Local	City Commission on Affairs of
	    Elderly in Springfield *or*
	Commission of Elders of the
	    Municipality (e.g., Elderly
	    Commission of Miami,
	    Florida)
	Array of social and health,
	    housing, access
	    (transportation) agencies
		Multiservice centers
		Councils on aging,
		    senior clubs
		Array of social and
		    health service
		    agencies
		    (counseling,
		    educational,
		    long-term day
		    centers, family
		    agencies)

SOURCE: Louis Lowy.

Aging Organizations	Professional Organizations
Gray Panthers	Gerontological Society of
American Association	America
of Retired Persons	American Geriatrics Society
National Council of	American Public Health
Senior Citizens	Association—Unit on
National Center for	Aging
Black Aged	NASW (National
Other national aging	Association of Social
organizations	Workers)—Task Force
	on Aging
	Other national
	organizations
State Association of	State chapters or regional
Older Americans	societies (e.g.,
State chapter of aging	directors of homes for
organizations	the aging)
Self-help groups	Northeastern
Mutual-aid groups	Gerontological Society
	Western Gerontology
	Society
	Professional organizations in
	other regions, counties,
	states
Local units of advocacy	Local chapters or groupings
and aging service	of professional
organizations	organizations,
(e.g., health	settlement house units
councils, retired	Volunteer organizations
executives)	Universities, Colleges
Self-help groups (e.g.,	Gerontology centers or
Alzheimers	Institutes
support groups)	

programs are tapped depends to a large part on the skill, creativity, and concern of the professional staff employed to work on problems of the aging.

Because the state plan is the key to the type of program funded in the state under the Older Americans Act, it is important that the input of older persons be considered in the formulation of the plan. Citizen participation in the formulation of the state plan is required in two ways. First, the state agency must have an advisory council with older persons constituting at least 50 percent of its membership. Second, no state plan may be adopted unless hearings are held and testimony given.

Area Agencies. The 1973 amendments to the Older Americans Act mandate the establishment of a national network of area agencies on aging. These area agencies, which may be either public or private nonprofit agencies, are charged with the continuing process of planning services for older persons, coordinating the actual delivery of needed services, tapping unused or underutilized resources, and developing new resources. Out of the firsthand experience of coordinating such services and developing new resources, the area agency develops a plan, refines the plan based upon the results of public hearings, and submits the plan to the state for approval. The plans of area agencies in turn become part of the state master plan submitted to AoA.

The majority of the now 665 operating area agencies are located within city or county governments or within regional councils of government. Each must have an advisory council, one-half of whose members must be elderly persons.

Local Offices on Aging. In addition to the agencies on aging functioning at a local level, towns or cities may also have offices on aging attached to the mayor's office, local councils, or commissions on aging. Once again, an organizational pattern emerges similar to that on the state level. The mayor appoints either a commissioner on aging who is a professional administrator of aging programs or a commission on aging composed of providers of services to the elderly, elderly consumers, and other interested citizens. If the latter method is used, the effectiveness of the commission will in part be determined by the amount of money provided. Although a commission composed of part-time volunteers may be able to establish policy, paid professional staff are necessary to administer programs. Once again, the definition of the role of the commission or the commissioner depends to a large extent on the importance attached to the needs and rights of elderly citizens by the community.

To receive funding under the Older Americans Act, the projects of these towns or city offices must compete with other proposed projects for a Title III grant award and must be approved by the area agencies. However, some local agencies offer programs exclusively funded by other federal and state programs and by local appropriations.

At all levels, many private organizations and agencies provide special projects for senior citizens. Especially well known are the multipurpose senior centers that have been organized all over the country. Senior centers provide recreational, nutritional, and health programs for their membership. Some centers are well funded and administered by large staffs of professionals who provide information and services related to health, housing, legal matters, nutrition, and counseling. Others spring up on an ad hoc basis and gradually become sufficiently funded and structured so that they can employ the services of a small professional staff. Some of these provide only a nutrition program; others offer a whole panoply of services. All senior centers serve to bring older people together and to provide them fellowship and sociability.

Voluntary Agency Auspices

Voluntary social service agencies, supported by individual donations, private foundations, private charitable organizations such as the United Way Fund as well as from government grants and contracts, provide a variety of services to older people. These services, which vary tremendously from locality to locality, range from social case work, job training, counseling, and preretirement education to meals on wheels, transportation, foster care placement, health care, and information and referral. Such agencies also may perform an advocacy function in the community on behalf of older persons and/or give free space, staff assistance, financial, and other support to organizations for the elderly, or may engage in education and research activities for professionals in the field. The following are some of the major national voluntary agencies:

- The National Council on the Aging, Inc.
- The Gerontological Society of America
- The American Geriatrics Society
- The Urban Elderly Coalition
- The National Association of State Units on Aging
- National Association of Area Agencies on Aging
- National Association of Homes for the Aging
- Association for Gerontology in Higher Education
- American Association of Retired Persons
- American Nursing Home Association
- American Occupational Therapy Association
- American Public Welfare Association
- Gray Panthers
- Institute for Retired Professionals, The New School of Social Research
- Institutes of Lifetime Learning
- International Federation on Aging
- International Senior Citizens Association, Inc.
- National Association of Retired Federal Employees
- National Association of Social Workers
- National Caucus on the Black Aged
- National Center on Black Aged
- National Council of Health Care Services

- National Council for Homemaker Services
- National Council of Senior Citizens
- National Retired Teachers Association
- National Tenants Organization, Inc.
- Retired Professional Action Group

In addition, professional associations such as the American Medical Association, the American Bar Association, and the National Association of Social Workers have committees or groups focusing primarily on issues affecting the elderly. Finally, there are in many cities local organizations of professionals serving the elderly. In Washington, for example, VOICE (Voluntary Organizations in Concern for the Elderly) joins social service professionals, leaders of senior organizations, clergy, community organizers, and gerontologists for monthly meetings on issues affecting the city's elderly.[6]

The Organized Profession

In the field of aging, many persons who administer programs or provide services are designated as professionals. The term *professional in aging* is used frequently as an umbrella to cover paid professionals and volunteers who work with older persons or deal with their concerns on a daily basis, such as social workers, home health aides and homemakers, recreational workers, visiting nurses, and employment and preretirement counselors.

These people work in a variety of settings—for example, institutions, including nursing homes, mental institutions, retirement homes, public housing for the elderly; foster care homes; hospices; universities; hospitals and clinics; adult day-care centers; and community centers and homes for the elderly in their own communities and neighborhoods. Some people work in senior centers, as community organizers, or as staff for organizations. Still others, including program administrators, city planners, social service and health planners, gerontologists, lawyers, and legislators, are involved with program and policy development in the field of aging. Social workers recognize that there are boundary and domain issues, and the question of what constitutes a social work professional is by no means neatly resolved. The organized profession (in contrast to professionals) that sanctions practice consists of professional organizations such as the National Association of Social Workers, the Association of Black Social Workers, and the Association of Social Workers in Private Practice.

The Council on Social Work Education is the overall accrediting body for graduate and undergraduate social work programs and as such is a major sanctioning agent for all training and education, including work with the elderly. The Gerontological Society of America, founded in 1945, is the major professional organization dedicated to research, service, and education in the field of gerontology throughout the United States. It exerts considerable influence on all professional groups engaged in gerontological endeavors and can therefore be considered of major importance for social work as well. In addition, there are the Association for Gerontology in Higher Education and the National Committee for Gerontology in Social Work Education which developed a one-year project in 1983, funded by AoA—to strengthen social work curricula in the field of aging, under the leadership of Robert L. Schneider.

Types and Organizations of Programs and Services

Social workers are called upon to perform a brokerage function, or as the United Nations definition states it, to assume "liaison activities," by linking people at varying stages and levels of need with the array of programs and services in a community that can be utilized, mobilized, linked, and fused so that the elderly can indeed benefit from them. We also refer to this function today as "networking" and "case-management." Social workers must possess a knowledge of community resources if they are to be of assistance to clients, groups, or organizations. The conversion of this knowledge into the effective delivery of services is what social workers must know how to do if they are to meet one of the societal demands incumbent upon them, to carry out social work functions.

It is essential for the social worker to be aware of existing resources, that is, to know what programs and services in a community or geographic area can be utilized to meet the specific needs of older people and solve the problems that have arisen because such needs have gone unmet. A corollary is the knowledge of what necessary community resources are lacking and how to go about getting these resources developed.

Responses to the following four questions from Neil Gilbert and Harry Specht's analytic framework can yield the underpinning for this know-how skill.

1. What are the nature and types of programs and services to be offered?
2. What are the bases of allocations of programs and services to elderly people?
3. How are the programs and services to be delivered to or obtained by the people who need them?
4. How are these programs and services to be financed and by whom?[7]

To illustrate, let us say that four widows who live alone and at times feel lonely don't like to eat alone, don't pay much attention to food preparation and eating, and consequently, don't get an adequate diet. Due to the high cost of food rich in protein, they can't afford to buy it. They begin to suffer from the effects of malnutrition. The social worker faces the questions mentioned above, worded to suit this specific situation.

1. What types of nutritional (food) programs for the elderly exist in this community? What is the nature of these programs? Do they offer a service to counteract the aloneness of these people? Do they answer to the special needs of these individuals? Of others in similar situations?
2. If a program and a service exist, who is eligible to take advantage? What are the criteria? Are these particular people eligible? Are others in similar circumstances

eligible? If not, what can be done to make them eligible? Should eligibility be increased and widened?

3. If eligibility is established, how can the people and the food program be brought together? How can resistances be overcome? How can people be mobilized to obtain the food? How can geographical access be facilitated? How can psychological access be promoted? How can financial assistance be provided to allow them to buy protein-rich food? How can medical services be brought in to counteract the incipient effects of malnutrition? What steps are needed to ensure social contacts in a nutritional site? Whom does the social worker contact to achieve this goal?

4. Who pays for these services? Will the agencies involved underwrite these programs financially? Can other financial resources be mobilized to ensure continued delivery of these services on more than a limited-time basis?

The following criteria should be applied in judging the adequacy of program and service delivery:

1. Availability—the relationship of the volume and type of existing services (and resources) to volume and type of clients' needs; includes adequacy of health personnel, facilities, and specialized programs.
2. Accessibility—relationship between location of supply and location of clients. This includes client transportation resources, travel time, distance, and travel cost.
3. Accommodation—relationship between the way services are organized to accept clients, their ability to accommodate to these factors, and their perception of whether services are appropriate.
4. Affordability—the relationship of prices of services to clients' income, ability to pay, and type and extent of their existing health insurance.
5. Acceptability—relationship of clients' and providers' attitudes about each other's personal and practical characteristics.[8]

Major Federal Programs Benefiting the Elderly

Know-how skills demand an ability to put together packages of services (i.e., service integration), such as transportation, financial assistance, food preparation, group services, and short-term counseling. One hundred thirty-two major federal programs that directly benefit older people and an additional 200 + programs that indirectly benefit the elderly have been identified.[9] These programs are administered by at least nine executive departments and more than twelve independent governmental agencies.

Analytic Schema of Needs, Problems, and Provisions

The analytic schema shown in Table 7.2 suggests the interface of the needs of people with the biological, psychological, and sociological processes of aging. The interfaces reveal problems when the needs with which individuals and society must contend are not met adequately. They point to the types of social provisions or benefits—policies, laws, programs, and services—that can or should emerge to satisfy these needs or to cope with existing or incipient problems.

Housing Needs and the Elderly: An Illustration

Since it would be impossible to describe and analyze all the need areas and social welfare programs for the aging in this text, housing needs are used as an illustration in the discussion that follows.[10]

> Adequate housing facilities are necessary for everyone; however, the basic needs in housing for older people are somewhat different from the needs of a growing younger family. With smaller incomes and poorer health, older people require less room in their homes. Smaller size and efficient arrangements are important considerations which have to include proximity to and availability of public transportation and access to shopping facilities, recreation, church, and cultural centers so that the older person can remain active in the community. . . . Many modern American homes and apartments [are] not appropriate dwelling units for older persons. Adequate housing . . . means . . . units . . . older persons . . . can afford [that meet their] special physical needs and [are] designed to avoid isolation. . . . Since older people are not a homogeneous group, they need a variety of housing types from which to choose depending on their health, life experience, income expectations, and personality. . . .

> TYPES OF LIVING ARRANGEMENTS

> We can differentiate at least five types of living arrangements: (1) people living at home, either in their own household, with relatives, with others, or under a boarding house or foster arrangements; (2) housing units specially constructed for the elderly, either as a part of the general housing development or as a segregated housing facility under public or private auspices; (3) institutional or congregate group-care arrangements, which would include homes for the aged, nursing homes, hospitals, and so on; (4) sheltered housing with a panoply of services available; and (5) retirement centers. It has been estimated that 69 percent of the elderly live in their own apartments or homes, 25 percent [live] in other people's homes, 21 percent live with relatives, 4 percent [live] with other people, and 4 to 5 percent [are] in institutions. One out of four older persons lives alone. Living at home is not without difficulties. This is true where there is a couple living together or a surviving spouse.

> For older couples, who have raised families and through them have resolved many of their differences, it may come as a shock to realize how irritating these differences can become when only two people are involved. Living with one's children may have satisfactions but it also has its problems if the arrangement is an involuntary one. Generations do not easily adjust to one another, especially when over a span of years their roles are changed. When the third generation arrives, many of the difficulties in the child-rearing process may be reactivated; it is not easy for a parent who has reared one generation to refrain from imposing lessons upon the next generation. But, many older people who live in their own homes often find it quite difficult to maintain them.

Table 7.2. Analytic Schema of Needs, Problems, Provisions

Human Needs	Special Factors Associated with Aging			Problems of Aged	Laws		
	Biological	Psychological	Social		Federal	State	Local
Biological and physiological Food, nutrition, eating Sex Clothing Housing							
Economic Income							
Health Physical Mental Care and safety							
Psychological Love, response, security Usefulness, new experiences Sense of identity and status							
Social Interactional role and interpersonal relationships Family Peer groups Nonpeer groups Interactions with Organizations Social Institutions							
Activities Occupation (work) Mobility							
Leisure Recreative							
Cultural Information, knowledge Aesthetics Play							
Political Legal status, protection Participation, involvement in affairs of community and state							
Spiritual (religious) Meaning of existence Relating to unknown (including death)							

The left margin is labeled PRIMARY NEEDS (spanning Biological and physiological, Economic, Health) and SECONDARY NEEDS (spanning Psychological through Spiritual).

SOURCE: Louis Lowy, "Social Welfare and the Aging," in Marion Spencer and Josephine Dorr (eds.), *Understanding the Aging* (Englewood Cliffs, N.J.: Prentice-Hall, 1975). Credit for the original idea is to go to the Projects Division of the Gerontological Society Social Welfare Committee, which developed the framework for the identification and organization of the content, *Working with Older People—Guides to Practice*, vol. 4, 1970.

Provisions										Future	
Programs					Services					Policies Needed	Laws, Programs, and Services Needed
Government			Nongovernment		Government			Nongovernment			
Federal	State	Local	Nonsectarian	Sectarian	Federal	State	Local	Nonsectarian	Sectarian		

Many of the aged live [alone] in rooming houses, usually in one of the blighted sections of the city and/or usually shunted off from contact with others. Their sense of isolation and aloneness is aggravated by the problem of living alone in rooming houses that are sometimes maintained by absentee landlords. It has been recognized that for older people to live alone successfully and in dignity, it is essential to have a battery of health and social services available which are easily accessible to them. Some of these include home health care and assistance, friendly visiting, homemaker and chore services, home-delivered meals, sometimes called meals-on-wheels service, transport, information services so that . . . older person[s are] enabled to function, if physically and mentally possible, in [their] own home.

Unfortunately, these services are not found in all parts of the country and very few of these services are well coordinated even in those communities that have them. They are a great help in making life easier and more comfortable for those whose physical conditions make it difficult or impossible [for them] to care completely for themselves. Older people living alone need a battery of professional services such as visiting nurses, social workers, medical aides, and others.

CURRENT POLICY

. . . The 1961 White House Conference recommended more housing of every type so that the elderly would have a wide range of choices, . . . easy mobility from one type of housing to another, and proper planning of units from the point of view of design and placement within the community mainstream. The 1971 conference was even more insistent when it stated that a national policy on housing for the elderly must have a high priority and must embrace not only shelter but services of quality that . . . span . . . independent living in and outside of institutions as a right.

The 1981 White House Conference on Aging, in addition to calling for a reaffirmation of the 1949 housing act's goal of "a decent home and suitable living environment" for all elderly families, made several detailed recommendations:

* Home equity conversion
* Shared housing
* Weatherization and other federal energy-assistance programs
* Protection of elderly from "condominiumization"
* Construction of at least 200,000 new housing units each year for elderly housing
* Continuation of HUD Section 8 and 202 programs for housing assistance
* Rental assistance to the elderly, and continuing to count out-of-pocket medical expenses as a deduction from income for purposes of application for such assistance
* Concentration of efforts to develop housing for poor and minority elderly residing in rural areas
* Inclusion of Native Americans in all sections of proposed housing legislation and insurance that all such elderly have the opportunity for suitable housing constructed in a manner and location of their choice at an affordable cost
* Continuation of federal mortgage insurance
* Emphasis on security and crime prevention in age-integrated and elderly housing

- Modification of HUD regulations to allow two persons not related by marriage to be eligible for apartments in subsidized housing
- Support of rent control
- Basing standards for construction of elderly housing on established gerontological research regarding physical and social needs of elderly
- Encouragement of construction of elderly housing as near as possible to the normal activities of the community
- Expansion of congregate housing as an option for the elderly
- Government provision of tax incentives to families that provide for housing needs of elderly members of families
- Support for the establishment of cooperative housing

Although present Housing and Urban Development (HUD) programs have shown some progress toward implementing these recommendations, the record is far from impressive.

What is particularly lacking is a definitive public policy which advances goals that are based on the following research evidence with regard to housing for older people: (1) Older people prefer independent living and economic supports are required to permit options. (2) Governmental and voluntary programs are needed to provide suitable housing and to facilitate relocation. (3) Housing for older persons should be supportive in its provisions of services and in architectural design to meet their physical and social deficits and needs. (4) Service systems and transportation should be designed so as to make health and welfare services accessible. . . .

TYPES OF LAWS, PROGRAMS, AND SERVICES

The Housing Acts of 1949, 1954, 1968, 1970, 1974 and 1976, and the Demonstration Cities and the Metropolitan Development Act of 1966 (Model Cities) have been the basic laws upon which programs for elderly housing were developed. The United States Department of Housing and Urban Development now administers over 20 [currently 35] programs dealing directly or indirectly with the housing needs of the elderly. Such programs include low-rent public housing, rent supplements, mortgage insurance, and long-term loan programs. In addition, state and local housing programs and neighborhood housing development programs in many states and communities have been in operation to attempt to cope with the housing problems of the elderly. Many communities have begun to take advantage of these programs and have developed special housing projects with a battery of medical, recreational, educational, and social services attached to the housing projects themselves. It was recognized that one of the most important features in housing for the elderly is to have available a series of services easily accessible to the residents.

In several communities across the country, provisions have been made to arrange for a network of health, social, and recreational services in order to maintain older people in their own homes as long as possible and to avoid institutionalization in congregate care facilities unless absolutely necessary. As of 1972, the Department of Elderly Affairs in Massachusetts, in accordance with its policy to find alternatives to unnecessary institutionalization, provides services directly to the elderly population through home care and nutrition services. Home care is offered through a network of 27 locally based non-profit organizations called Home Care Corporations. Under the supervision of the Department, they plan, develop, and implement at least homemaking and chore services, transportation, information and referral, and case management.[11]

They may also offer legal assistance, employment counseling, housing assistance, and nutrition.

On April 23, 1984, during site visits and a hearing in Boston, witnesses told the Aging Committee that the cost of independence for older Americans in public housing is often loneliness, ill health and loss of dignity.

"The problem isn't in the intent of our federal housing policy," Chairman Heinz said, "but the extent to which it's applied." He noted that there are only 1.2 million units available, when 3.4 million households qualify for assistance. More importantly, according to Heinz, the Congress "simply hasn't addressed the growing need for services of a population that is 'aging in place' in federal housing."

One of the sites the Senator and Boston Mayor Ray Flynn visited—Annapolis House—is not unusual in that 63 percent of the tenants are over 70 years of age. Without any onsite provision for health care, meals, transportation or social programs, Annapolis House and other projects like it, are in danger of becoming "nursing homes without services," Heinz said.

Under Secretary of the Department of Housing and Urban Development (HUD), Philip Abrams, told the Committee that HUD is expecting a final report on its 63 Congregate Housing Services Program (CHSP) demonstration projects by the end of 1984. Under this congressionally authorized project, HUD provided 3 to 5 year grants to public housing authorities and nonprofit 202 sponsors for meals for frail elderly and non-elderly handicapped residents. The objectives of the CHSP program are to prevent premature institutionalization; to encourage the improvement of support service delivery; and to fill the gaps in existing service delivery.

Secretary Abrams also said HUD was exploring other new housing alternatives for older Americans, including retirement service centers and life-care facilities.

In his statement, Raymond J. Struyk of the Urban Institute offered two approaches for helping the low-income elderly obtain the housing and services they most need. First, Struyk discussed the option of an "independent living voucher program." The voucher would entitle a frail elderly person or couple to occupy a rental unit in a congregate living facility—a housing project providing independent living with necessary, nonmedical support services. The second approach, aimed at elderly homeowners, is the housing voucher. With this second voucher, a person in a state which permits provision of supportive services at home rather than in an institution, could pay for such services.

Senator Heinz announced the Independent Living for Older Americans Act, legislation designed to provide "safe, decent and supported shelter for America's aged." His bill, cosponsored by Senator Dodd (D-CT), would expand current housing policy to provide full supported shelter for older Americans and minimize the need for unnecessary and costly institutionalization. Specifically, the Act would:

- Require the Federal Commissioner of Aging to initiate a national training program in elderly housing and services.
- Require the Commissioner to undertake a comprehensive study of policy options for promoting independent living for the low-income frail elderly.
- Require the Commissioner to undertake demonstrations of market rate congregate living developments for the moderate-income elderly.

The bill will be introduced later.[12]

Programs that are of existential significance to older people and have to be known by social workers include programs to provide financial assistance; programs to maintain or improve health conditions, including mental health on an acute and long-term care basis; programs to enhance participation in daily life, including housing, nutrition, and personal care; programs to assist in problem-solving and support as well as in facilitating access.

Because the number of these programs is so large, they will not be enumerated here. They can be found in *Social Policies and Programs on Aging* (Lowy), in *Federal Programs Benefiting the Elderly*, in Gelfand's *The Aging Network*, Kutza's *The Benefits of Old Age*, and many, many others.

Every year, the Special Committee on Aging of the United States Senate publishes a volume and appendices in "Developments in Aging" that contain federal policies related to aging throughout the term of Congress. It can be obtained by writing directly to the Special Committee on Aging, U.S. Senate, Washington, D.C.

In an earlier work, the author developed the typology of programs and services for the elderly that is presented below.[13]

A typology developed along a vertical dimension addresses itself to the structural axis, while a horizontal dimension relates to the content axis.

VERTICAL DIMENSION

1. Services to aged living in the community and to those living in congregate facilities.
2. Services which are age-integrated versus those which are age-segregated; i.e., services which are offered to older persons as part of an overall system of services to the total population versus services offered exclusively to older people.
3. Categorical versus comprehensive services. In the former, the service will be given to meet a specific need or to alleviate a specific problem, e.g., to provide a medical service or to offer a recreational program. In the latter, services are provided across-the-board, meeting a variety of needs jointly; e.g., an approach which attempts to cope with health, social, legal and recreational needs together.
4. Social utilities and social interventive programs and services. Services provided as a social utility (Kahn, 1965)[14] are benefits which are automatically available to all older persons. They are provisions to maintain the family, group, and community life considered vital and include public facilities (such as parks, libraries, beaches) to be used as one pleases, and developmental provisions available automatically to support needs and requirements of individuals in a

given social status or circumstance. Income security, housing arrangements, physical and mental services are included here. The user of a social utility comes as a claimant who determines whether or not he [or she] needs the service. Services that are interventive in nature are individualized attempts to improve social interaction where it is problematical or to relieve stress, change behavior that may be deemed deviant, [or] reduce disabilities or other impairments—physical, economic, social, cultural. The user of such services is either a client or a patient. Several of these types of services have also been referred to as "supplementary" or "special." They are required by older people who have particular problems at a particular time or . . . are necessitated by personal or social conditions (or both) which are more permanent or lasting and which frequently lead to institutionalization in a congregate care facility.

Within such facilities different types of ancillary, supplementary or special "interventive" services are being developed geared to the differential needs or problems of older people. A person who is more "autonomous" and self-sufficient obviously requires a different mode of care from a person who is "anomic" and highly dependent upon physical support.

In fact, we have seen examples of a continuum of services for older people in several European countries. Such a continuum provides services to an aged person in his home, in a day center, in outpatient clinics and in a congregate care facility according to the needs of the person at a particular time. Return to his [or her] home with appropriate backup services after discharge from a nursing home or [hospital] rehabilitation center . . . becomes much more feasible if such a continuum of services exists.

5. Services exist under governmental and nongovernmental, sectarian and nonsectarian auspices. Recently in the United States, many tax-supported institutions have subcontracted with voluntary agencies and they, in turn, receive governmental grants. Differing relationships to constituencies and governing bodies can be traced to these developments. Whether services are designed in or for a neighborhood, a locality, a region, or a state has further implications for design and delivery of such services.

As shown in Table [7.3], the vertical typological dimension suggests paradigms which are useful devices to delineate structural models of services. Therefore, we may have a uniservice social utility model (e.g., income security program), a uniservice social interventive model (e.g., counseling), a multiservice social utility (e.g., comprehensive social, recreational and health services in a housing unit for older persons) and a multiservice social interventive model, such as comprehensive medical care in the home after hospitalization. Additional illustrations will come to mind and other combinations can easily be arranged.

Table 7.3.

	Categories of Service	
Approach to Service	Social Utility	Social Intervention
Uniservice	————	————
Multiservice	————	————

Table 7.4.

Setting	Approach to Service	Categories of Service	
		Social Utility	Social Intervention
Community-based aged	Uniservice	———	———
	Multiservice	———	———
Institutionalized aged	Uniservice	———	———
	Multiservice	———	———

Dimensions of "community-based aged" and "institutionalized aged" can be diagrammed and related to uni- and multiservice approaches according to categories of services (see Table [7.4]).

HORIZONTAL DIMENSION

Running through the vertical structure is a horizontal dimension which encompasses the nature and content of services. An organizing principle most in accord with the aforementioned assumptions is the concept of "human needs" which are specifically related to the conditions of aging—biological, psychological, and sociological. Each "human need" is influenced and conditioned by the processes of aging, e.g., food needs change with age. In addition to meeting human needs, every society must meet certain functional prerequisites in order to operate as a viable social system. Since functional requirements for a society and concerns to meet the needs of its population are in a state of quasi-stationary equilibrium (Lewin, 1947),[15] discrepancies exist between meeting the human needs of its population and fulfilling societal prerequisites. This is particularly evident in the organization of services and programs to the aging population in the United States and several other countries around the world.

There are several possible [categories] under which to list the various "human needs." Substantial literature is available (Murray, 1949,[16] Maslow, 1954,[17] McClelland, 1951,[18] etc.). Maslow's hierarchical scheme of relative prepotency is useful here: (1) physiological needs; (2) safety needs; (3) love and belonging needs; (4) esteem needs (achievement and recognition); (5) self-actualization; and (6) desire to know and understand.

This author classified services according to the following areas of needs: food, clothing, shelter, sexual, psychological-emotional-spiritual, health, economic, social, cultural, political. No hierarchical order of priority is suggested in this enumeration, although Maslow's framework may be interlaced here possibly yielding a useful theoretical typological system. A model for understanding the organizational structure of programs and services for the elderly was also delineated. This model is presented here.[19]

Etzioni (1961)[20] and Gouldner (1959)[21] delineate two models of viewing organizations as prototypes but agree that both models have to be taken into consideration in the analysis of organizations. A goal perspective (or rational model in the Max Weber tradition) emphasizes the bureaucratic aspects of an organization and places its resources—material and human—at the behest of goal accomplishment. The result is a goal-oriented agency with minor attention to human costs. Efficiency is the leitmotif. We have learned, however, that human beings are not only material and technical resources, but people with their own needs who can and do affect the achievement of an organization's goal. Even if we were to disregard a humanistic ethos, the rational approach may in the end be nonefficient when it ignores the limits of rationality of [people] and the inefficiency of a purely goal-oriented approach. [22]

In contrast, the natural-system model asks the questions: how can the existing human resources be marshalled toward a better functioning of the social system? How do social relations enhance or impede the achievement of the organization's goal? Fundamental to the natural-systems model is the fact that parts are interrelated. It allows for an integrative holistic approach to an organization's development and assessment. Any services to a population—including the aging—must take into consideration the extent to which the functional imperatives of the organizational systems are being met. In other words, to what degree does an organization that provides services to the aging meet its economic functions, its socialization functions, its social concern functions, its social-participation and mutual-support functions? At the same time, it must look at the human needs which the service is designed to meet and which become, therefore, the major raison d'être for the organization.

Invariably, an organization runs the danger of goal displacement. This means that the energies consumed by the organization for maintaining itself as a system are greater than the energies available for accomplishing the goals for which it has been designed in the first place. This is complicated enough when applied to one organization providing a service; it becomes even more complex when this is multiplied in the linkage of several services through a network of interagency coordination.

Linkage of service through "exchange" of "people to be served," "persons with specialized skill to give the service" and "supporting resources" (equipment, funds, etc.) on a unilateral or on a reciprocal basis has been found to be one avenue to effect such coordination. [23] Other avenues, such as organization from the top down with authority originating in a central organization, are more prevalent in other countries of the world than in the United States.

Having briefly looked at service organizations from both perspectives, we are now ready to list a series of dimensions or variables which are useful in the analysis of organization:

1. Doctrine essentially is a theme or a philosophy that should guide the goals (objectives) and functions of the organization. Doctrine is a reflection of social policy toward the aged population which is based on conception of human needs, values held, priorities ranked, etc. Specifically, each organization offering a service to older people must examine what its philosophy is toward the people it serves, toward the people who provide services, the human needs it attempts to meet, and the way it plans to meet those needs. Only an articulated philosophy will be useful doctrine to serve as guidepost and repository for subsequent action.

2. Leadership is a most elusive concept. It can be viewed as a position or role as well as a quality of the role incumbent. What is the nature and quality of the leadership executed and to what extent does it emanate from the guiding doctrine? In whom is it vested? Is it shared with the producers and consumers

of services? To what extent is it oriented toward policy and administration? Does leadership thrust the organization towards innovative paths, or is it fixed on the system-maintenance level? Is it doing enough to risk conflict with the community to show up new avenues in delivering services or in pioneering a new type of service? What mechanisms are available to assess leadership, to change it and to spread it? I would agree with Selznick (1957)[24] that creative leadership is a crucial variable in the design and delivery of services in any organization; the lower the priority of the service is perceived in a community (e.g., the aged in our country), the more important becomes a dynamic commitment to the leadership to promote services and to impress the community with its essentiality.

3. Program is the translation of doctrine and leadership into concrete action expressed through the type of services rendered. Relative consistency with doctrine, philosophy, goal, and leadership must be examined. To what extent does the program meet the goals? What mechanisms can best keep it in accord with changing social needs for which the services have been designed and thereby minimize goal displacement? Does the actual program meet criteria of adequacy and equity?

4. Resources include financial, physical, technological, and human resources. Adequacy in relation to goals, and program operation of each resource singularly and in relation to others must be an important concern of every organization and its leadership. How can each resource be further developed and augmented? Too often, existing resources become a fixed boundary for programs, despite the affirmation that a human need exists which is not being met. Leadership [and] ingenuity and creativity [are] related not only to better utilization but also to maximization of the resource pie (Selznick, 1957).[25]

Since most services are rendered through people, recruitment, deployment, and development [through] education and training are tasks which demand major attention. Differentiation of tasks and appropriate use of professionals, technicians, and indigenous personnel are functions which may not only lead to a more rational deployment of people, but may also contribute to greater satisfaction of those who provide services and of those who receive them. Older people are as rich a resource in service delivery as in service dissemination.

5. Internal structure is concerned with the actual operation and administration of the organization, the distribution of roles, authority patterns, decision-making apparatus, and communication systems as they affect the capacity of the organization to carry out its program. How [do] administrative personnel policy and financial structure affect the ultimate delivery of service? How is power distributed and how does this distribution affect its use in the pursuit of the goals of the agency? To what extent does bureaucratic structure shape service with regard to older people, many of whom are quite unaccustomed to bureaucratic organization? While the essential characteristics of bureaucracy are designed to facilitate the giving of service in as impartial [a] manner as possible, they frequently tend to have the opposite effect on people who come in contact with bureaucracies. The impact of an impersonal system on those working in it and on those served by it has been analyzed by Merton (1940),[26] who indicates how this impersonality tends to develop routinization, overconformity, and reliance on red tape in those who participate in such organization. Although countertendencies to bureaucratization are noted by Bennis (1965),[27]

who predicts a more organic-adaptive approach to problem solving and a more humanizing, if not stress-free, quality of operation, they are by no means as evident in practice as some theorists hold.

Doctrine, leadership, programs, and resources are correlated with the workings of an internal structure. The "natural model" view holds that the internal structure yields data as to the constraints and expansion of services based on the way the organization mobilizes its human resources and then to meet its own needs or the needs of the people it serves. The internal structure must adapt to the requirements of the program rather than the other way around if a service organization upholds the doctrine that meeting human needs and alleviating problems are its major concerns.

COMPREHENSIVENESS, CONTINUITY, AND COORDINATION

In complex industrialized countries it is becoming increasingly rare that only one type of service is needed at any one time; in fact, everywhere . . . different types of services are needed concurrently. An older person who has been discharged from a hospital is likely to require a home-nursing service, a homemaker service, meals-on-wheels, and, in all probability, a friendly visitor to alleviate feelings of fear, apprehensiveness, and estrangement from others in his or her immediate surroundings.

Continuity, comprehensiveness, and coordination, the three "C's," are criteria in the development and evaluation of a network of services answering to the needs of a "whole person" and through a holistic approach will counteract a prevailing practice of fragmentation and discontinuity.

Several types of multiservice approaches have been tried out in many communities in the United States. Multiservice centers offering a series of health, legal, information-referral, counseling, recreational and educational services under one roof or, at least closely linked in geographic proximity, have sprung up in various parts of this country and have [met with] success, as perceived by the aged consumers and as evaluated by various research organizations (Epstein, 1964).[28] A number of such coordinated and linked service arrangements have been initiated in housing units for older persons based on the assumption that service should be offered and provided close to the residence of older persons.

DELIVERY OF SERVICES

The phrase "delivery of services" tends to imply a unilateral transfer of a commodity from a producer to a consumer. Not only does this suggest a one-way process, but it artificially isolates one phase of what is actually a dynamic and continuous process. Richan (1968)[29] distinguishes the meaning of "delivery" in relation to "social utilities" and "social interventions" and suggests three related, but separable, meanings of the term: (1) linkage, or the process of connecting potential users with services, (2) direct provision or the process in which the service is actually utilized, (3) service development, the process of assessing the existence of a needed resource. It is this writer's contention that all three processes demand attention in constructing a model for service delivery to older people.

Three major dimensions are suggested to construct models for service delivery.

1. Mode of delivery: technological/human
2. Orientation of delivery: outreach to persons vs. only upon demand by persons.
3. Timing of delivery: regular (routinized) vs. nonregular (nonroutine)

Technological modes, for example, refer to the use of mail-delivered checks to provide income payments in contrast to the use of personnel to provide post-retirement counseling. An outreach orientation does not wait until an older person asks for help but acts on the basis of presumptive need. This is closely related to a regularized system of delivery which institutionalizes the rendering of services, e.g., regular medical check-ups every three months for aged people in [housing for] senior citizens.

The illustrative paradigm shown in Table [7.5] is proposed as a device to schematize possible models of delivery of services for community-based aged on one dimension; regular vs. nonregular timing.

Three analytic concepts permeate all models and processes: . . .

1. Social utilities (financial services, medical care, housing facilities, etc.) and social interventive services (counseling, homemaking, group treatment, etc.) must be available when people need them as claimants, as clients, or as patients, possibly 24 hours a day, 7 days a week. They must be in existence and organized in a comprehensive, coordinated way on a continuous basis, so that older people can utilize them when they are required.
2. Such services must be accessible where the aged need them, in geographic proximity to their place of residence, whether in the community or in congregate care facilities. In addition, accessibility demands that services which are provided not be "hampered by elaborate control procedures, especially at the point of entry" (Richan, op. cit.). These procedures discourage people from using these services especially when they fall into the category of "social intervention," e.g., retirement counseling.

Table 7.5.

Timing of Delivery	Approach to Service	Categories of Service	
		Social Utility	Social Intervention
Regular, routinized	Uniservice	——	——
		——	——
	Multiservice	Recreational, educational, social services available every day	Comprehensive homemaker and friendly visiting for one year
Nonregular, nonroutinized	Uniservice	Recreational services, sporadically	Grief counseling, sporadically
	Multiservice	Recreational and educational services, sporadically	Grief counseling and supplementary financial aid, sporadically

3. Availability and accessibility do not guarantee that existing services are utilized. Experiences with Medicare and Hearings conducted by the United States Senate (1966)[30] confirm the reluctance of older people in particular to avail themselves of services. Lack of information is only one of the reasons given. Other reasons point to lack of acceptability of such services on the part of many aged persons. Apart from our social insurance programs, most services have not achieved the status of social utilities. As a consequence, these services remain heavily stigmatized. Pride and a sense of dignity prevent many people—young and old— from applying for public assistance or from requesting a homemaker service. Related to the problem of stigmatization are the problems of red tape; they experience difficulties in negotiating an impersonal "system," which is predicated on the assumption that people have to reach out to the dispensers of service rather than have them reach out to the people. Closely related to this aspect is the nature of the quality of services.

What mechanisms are available to make services available, accessible, and acceptable? This is a vital, but complicated question. In many instances we need a fundamental reshaping of organizational structures. The "natural model" approach is most useful here since it formulates the kind of questions which can provide impetus for constructive changes: How can the organization be structured to increase the likelihood that it achieves its goals? How can maximum use of existing resources be utilized to serve the "consumer" most efficiently and effectively? A beginning can be made in one part of the system, e.g., an agency may redeploy its staff and make it mobile and thereby affect other units of service as well. It can begin to institute an active outreach program, based on the experiences of Medicare Alert and the subsequently reported Project FIND (United States Senate, 1968).[31] It can initiate a meeting of older people in the community to get them engaged in developing a service of self-help and to act as advisors to its own operation. It can involve users of the service in policymaking and in service delivery. The reciprocal utilizations of [the] producer, dispenser, and consumer of services holds . . . great promise [for] a more equitable and beneficent service delivery approach.

PLANNING OF SERVICES

Since it is unlikely and unrealistic to expect that we will be able to develop a comprehensive, coordinated and continuous service delivery system which meets all the criteria mentioned, it is obvious that priorities have to be established. Unfortunately, we do not have the kinds of social planning mechanisms in this country which allow for judicious decision making in setting priorities. . . . But we will not be able to develop model services unless we pay attention to the development of such machinery. . . . This planning function requires commitment of financial, technological, and human resources to do the job, which means enunciating clear goals, harnessing of support behind these goals, and stated willingness to be held accountable for achieving these goals. Widespread involvement of the potential and actual consumers of services, i.e., the older people, conjointly with the younger segment of our population in this process is imperative.

Planning must be based on data made available through computers and through expert witnesses of older people as well as of professionals and subprofessionals; it must project the needs of the older population of tomorrow, rather than be tempted to base its plans on a static conception of today. . . . Those who will assume central functions in planning will need to be skilled in collecting data and projecting services into the immediate and long-range future. Decision-making bodies will have to be enabled to agree on goals and sort out priorities. . . . Mediating activities will be required to reconcile differing viewpoints of different segments of the population (old and young) and some positions will be advanced and advocated which are likely to be in conflict with those of others.

Financing of Programs and Services

There are basically two major sources to finance programs and services for the elderly: (1) public sources, or tax funds, and (2) private sources, or philanthropic funds. A mixture of the two has emerged as a prevalent mode of funding social programs and services in the United States today—that is, a combination of the tax monies allocated to private organizations and agencies under "purchase of service" or other types of contract arrangements, and the private dollars used to supplement publicly financed programs.

The Three Major Public Funding Sources in 1984

The Older Americans Act of 1965. As amended in 1967, 1969, 1972, 1973, 1974, 1975, 1977, 1978, and 1984, the Older Americans Act allocates funds to each state agency on aging for social service grants. To summarize information presented earlier, the titles of the Act in 1984 are as follows:

- Title I—Declaration of Objectives (definitions)
- Title II—Administration on Aging; Federal Council on the Aging
- Title III, Parts A and B—Grants for Support Services and Senior Centers; Part C—Nutrition Services: Congregate Meals and Home-delivered Meals
- Title IV, Part A—Training; Part B—Research and Development; Part C—Discretionary Projects and Programs; Part E—Multidisciplinary Centers of Gerontology
- Title V—Senior Community Services Employment Programs
- Title VI—Grants to Indian Tribes
- Title VII—Personal Health Education/Training

Related acts (among others):

- Energy Conservation and Production Act of 1977
- Age Discrimination in Employment Act, 1967 and 1978
- Public Health Service Act
- Medicaid
- The Library Services and Construction Act
- National Commission on Libraries and Information Science Act
- Higher Education Act of 1965
- Adult Education Act

- Housing and Community Development Acts of 1974 and 1976
- Economic Opportunity Act of 1964, as amended
- Rehabilitation Act of 1973

Revenue Sharing. Federal funds are allocated to state and local governments, which have broad discretion in their use. Revenue sharing provides federal aid to state and local governments to deal with community problems at a local level. States may spend revenue-sharing money for virtually any purpose. Local governments are required to spend the funds within certain very broad categories: (1) any capital expenditure permitted by state and local law, and (2) operating and maintenance expenses for environmental protection, financial administration, health, libraries, public safety, public transportation, recreation, and social services for the poor and aged. (Revenue-sharing monies may not be used as matching funds to obtain federal grant-in-aid money.)

Title XX, now Social Services Block Grant. This is a federally assisted state program in which grants are made to states to provide or purchase a variety of social services for needy adults within certain eligibility limits. It succeeded the original Title XX (Social Services title of the Social Security Act) in 1974. It is currently administered by DHHS.

The goals are

1. To help people become or remain economically self-supporting.
2. To help people become or remain self-sufficient (able to care for themselves).
3. To protect children and adults who cannot protect themselves from abuse, neglect, and exploitation and to help families stay together.
4. To prevent and reduce inappropriate institutional care as much as possible by making home and community services available.
5. To arrange for appropriate placement and services in an institution when this is in an individual's best interest.

The welfare department or other designated agency must put together a Comprehensive Annual Services Plan (CASP), showing the services to be offered, what goals they will meet, and how much will be spent for each service. States must publish these plans and make them available to citizens.

In an effort to "streamline" federal programs, Congress in fiscal year 1982 eliminated several programs benefiting the elderly and consolidated many other programs under new or existing block grant programs, including Title XX. The Community Mental Health Centers program and the National Clearinghouse on Aging were eliminated, while the High Blood Pressure Control Program, the Home Health Services and Training Grant Program, the Preventive Health Service, and Grants for Health Education were all combined into the newly formed Preventive Health and Health Services Block Grant Program. Under such block grant programs, each geographic region and special interest group is forced to compete for funding; one cannot help but worry about the fate of the smaller, less powerful areas and groups.

Private Sources

The possibility of obtaining private support from such sources as local philanthropic and welfare funds must be assessed on a community basis. Major agencies include United Way, with over 2,000 local organizations, and foundations, over 100 of which have indicated an interest in providing funds for programs and services for the aging.

It is the mixture of public and private funding sources that provides most of the financial underpinning of services and programs affecting the elderly today. Most likely, this mix will continue to be the main avenue of fiscal support in the future. The current political climate encourages expanded exploitation of the private sector's resources and state responsibility and reduction of public, especially federal involvement in programs and services.

References

1. Abraham Monk, *Social Work*, vol. XVI, no. 3 (July 1971), p. 102.
2. "Working Definition of Social Work Practice," *Social Work*, vol. 3, no. 2 (April 1958).
3. *The Law and Aging Manual* (sponsored by the National Council of Senior Citizens, Inc., July 1976), pp. 10–11.
4. Louis Lowy, *Social Policies and Programs on Aging*, (Lexington, Mass.: Lexington Books, D.C. Heath & Co., 1983), pp. 36–41.
5. Ibid., pp. 48–51.
6. *Law and Aging*, op. cit., p. 12.
7. *Dimensions of Social Welfare Policy* (Englewood Cliffs, N.J.: Prentice-Hall, 1974).
8. P. Perchansky, and T. W. Thomas, "The Concept of Access: Definition and Relationship to Consumer Satisfaction," *Medical Care*, vol. 19, no. 2 (February 1981), pp. 127–140.
9. *Federal Programs Benefiting the Elderly*. A Reference Guide by the Select Committee on Aging, House of Representatives, 98th Congress, First Session, Revised Edition (Washington, D.C.: U.S. Government Printing Office, 1983).
10. Louis Lowy, "Social Welfare and the Aging" in *Understanding Aging*, M. Spencer and J. Dorr, eds. [Englewood Cliffs, N.J.: (Appleton-Century-Crofts), 1975], pp. 147–155.
11. Ibid.
12. United States Senate, Special Committee on Aging.
13. Louis Lowy, "Models for Organization of Services to the Aging," *Aging and Human Development*, vol. 1, no. 1 (Farmingdale, N.Y.: Baywood Publishing Company, 1970), pp. 21–35.
14. Alfred Kahn, "New Policies and Service Models: The Next Phase," *American Journal of Orthopsychiatry*, vol. 35, no. 4 (July 1965), p. 658.
15. Kurt Lewin, "Frontiers in Group Dynamics," *Human Relations*, vol. 1 (1947), pp. 5–41.
16. Henry Murray, *Explorations in Personality* (New York: Oxford University Press, 1949).
17. Abraham H. Maslow, *Motivation and Personality* (New York: Harper & Row, 1954).
18. David C. McClelland, *Personality* (New York: Dryden Press, 1951).
19. Lowy, "Models for Organization of Services to the Aging."
20. Amitai Etzioni, *Complex Organizations: A Sociological Reader* (New York: Holt, Rinehart, & Winston, 1961).

21. Alvin A. Gouldner, "Organizational Analysis," in Robert Merton (ed.), *Sociology Today* (1959), pp. 400–428.
22. W. Roethlisberger and W. J. Dickson, *Management and the Worker* (Cambridge, Mass.: Harvard University Press, 1939); and others.
23. Sol Levine and P. E. White, "Exchange as a Conceptual Framework for the Study of Interorganizational Relationship," *Administrative Science Quarterly*, vol. 3 (March 1961), pp. 583–601.
24. Philip Selznick, "Leadership in Administration," *Leadership and Administration* (New York: Harper & Row, 1957), pp. 142–152.
25. Ibid.
26. Robert Merton, "Bureaucratic Structure and Personality," *Social Forces*, vol. 8 (May 1940), pp. 560–568.
27. Warren Bennis, "Beyond Bureaucracy," *Trans-action*, vol. 8 (May 1968), pp. 560–568.
28. Bernard D. Epstein, *Medical Care Program for the Elderly in a Housing Project, Public Health Reports*, vol. 79, no. 11 (1964), pp. 1005–1014.
29. Willard C. Richan, "The Responsibilities of the Social Work Profession" (mimeographed, 1968).
30. U.S. Senate, 89th Congress, 2nd Session, *Needs for Services Revealed by Operation Medicare Alert*, report by Subcommittee on Federal, State, and Community Services to the Special Committee on Aging (Committee Print, October 1966).
31. U.S. Senate Resolution 223, "Developments in Aging," report of the Special Committee on Aging (March 15, 1968).

8

Knowledge Required
for Working
with the Aged

Sources of Knowledge

Effective social work with the elderly necessitates minimally a solid knowledge base in the following areas, each of which functions as an interactive system in clients' lives: the biology and physiology of aging, the psychology of aging, the sociology and political/economic aspects of aging. Failure to consider any one of these arenas puts the worker at a disadvantage, whether he or she is engaged in casework, group work, community organization, or management and planning. For example, historical events such as the Great Depression, World Wars I and II, and the consequences of slavery may have profound implications for understanding the psychological, biological, and/or social state of today's elderly client.

There is a burgeoning literature dealing with each of these sectors of gerontological knowledge. There are other aspects of knowledge as well, e.g., economic, political, historical, anthropological, religious, but space does not permit even a cursory discussion here. It should be stressed, however, that the state of the art is at times tentative and much of the accumulated knowledge is accompanied by caveats disclaiming universality, validity, or reliability. Thus, it is important for social workers to keep abreast of recent developments in gerontology. This can be accomplished by reading current journal articles, books, newsletters, and reports (many of which are available at university libraries and/or gerontology centers); attendance at workshops, conferences, and/or courses; and keen attention to the media for recent developments in aging.

Social workers will be called upon to develop their own data base(s) for specific purposes. For example, they may be asked to carry out a needs assessment for purposes of clarifying the scope of target populations for proposed programs and services, or to evaluate the appropriateness, effectiveness, and adequacy of existing programs and services. Social workers must design and conduct their own gerontological research. Because they are aware of the multiplicity of factors in an older person's life, they have much to contribute in the way of appropriate, realistic, and comprehensive research efforts. One veteran gerontological researcher commented, "Social workers know what questions to ask."

Biological and Physiological Knowledge

Aging processes and changes in various bodily systems affect the physical and social functioning of people in their later years. Social workers must be aware of biological and physiological effects, since changes in personality and behavior are often due to organic dysfunctions that will affect the approaches, methods, and techniques that are used. There are many theories, and much research is going on to explain the aging process. Florence Vickery distinguishes between primary aging, the decline of functional abilities, and secondary aging, which results from diseases and trauma. [1] In old age there is an increased loss of vigor after each illness. The primary aging process takes place in cells that are controlled by DNA, the genetic material. Three kinds of genetic effects may be the causes of the aging process:

1. Missing or incorrect genetic sequence in DNA, genes that cause low resistance to disease
2. Genes, originally beneficial, that produce harmful changes as byproducts of normal function
3. A lessening of genes that influence cell longevity

Social workers should be aware of eight physiological systems that can be differentiated:

1. Skeletal and muscular systems
2. Circulatory system
3. Endocrine system
4. Respiratory system
5. Nervous system
6. The senses (sight, hearing, touch, taste, and smell)
7. Digestive system
8. Reproductive system and sexuality

Psychological Knowledge

Among the cognitive, affective, and behavioral learning patterns and various theories of personality, particular emphasis is placed here upon developmental theories. They have major relevance for social work practice. Difficulties with developmental tasks are one aspect of the problem. However, as mentioned earlier, the roots of the social problem of aging lie in a perceived or actual disjunction between the individual pace of aging and the uniform social context within which Americans and most population groups in Western countries grow old.

The social worker must be aware of and understand the psychological changes related to cognition, perception, psychomotor performance, and learning. In addition, aspects of affect and emotion, notably attitudes and interest, need to be understood. There are many texts available that discuss in detail these materials; these will be referred to at the end of this chapter.

Theories of Personality

A number of personality theories have emerged in gerontology. John Mogey distinguishes three types of theories: (1) descriptive, covering a wide gamut of phenomena; (2) analytical, using variables to build a model that generates a description of what happens or is predicted to happen in a particular situation; (3) constructive, constructing an ideal from empirical data or practice experiences; after such data are sorted they are categorized in such a way that they become useful typologies for guiding practitioners. This represents the utility of theory for the social worker.[2] The following represent major theories today:

- Disengagement Theory
- Activity Theory
- Sub-Culture Theory
- Life Satisfaction Theory
- Psychoanalytic Theory
- Continuity Theory
- Exchange Theory
- Stratification Theory
- Social Breakdown Theory
- Developmental Theory

Many texts and articles review and analyze these theories and need not be repeated here. However, since in this author's view the developmental theory is particularly compatible with social workers and has special relevance for the profession, it will be briefly discussed here. Margaret Blenkner has stated the concepts of developmental theory succinctly:

> The concept of development is fundamentally a biological notion. It has to do with the process [of] a living system [—a process that] is sequential, cumulative, and irreversible. It is not, however, a simple unfolding of preexistent organic mechanisms but a complex interaction of genetics and milieu, constitution and life experience. Together they shape the individual organism which throughout its life span is always in the process of becoming . . . what it becomes in the end, limited by its nature. What the limits of that nature are . . . in a sense [is] the subject of the behavioral sciences.

Development proceeds in stages which overlap; the transition from one stage to the next is more gradual than the events that signal the stage. Thus adolescence is a stage; menstruation the event that signals it in the human female. In a different context, "disengagement" can be thought of as a developmental stage and retirement the signaling event. In either case, something new is emerging which is unlike that which has gone before although not independent of it. Change—to be labeled developmental—must be cumulative, but it must also "eventuate in modes of organization not previously manifested in the history of the developing system." . . . Developmental change is irreversible. "A child who has once learned to talk can never be returned to the state of one who has never talked" and—one might add—[a person] once become adult can never again be child, though in senile decay he [or she] lie once more a-babbling. In a truly developmental view of the human life span, the characteristic properties emerging in successive stages cannot be wholly described in terms of earlier behavior or earlier influences but must be viewed in their own developmental context: the stage that is becoming.

Despite this attribute of "becomingness," developmental theory does not rest on a teleological view of nature. It does not assume the operation of purpose or final cause; it merely specifies that a sequence of changes, to be considered developmental, must contribute to the generation of properties or qualities which though now in the individual are characteristic of the species. . . .

Of the various ego psychologists with whom social workers are familiar, [Erik] Erikson offers the best starting-off point for considering the second half of life. Erikson's conception of the life cycle is a truly developmental one, and he has been called the first of the psychoanalytic theorists to carry us beyond the stage of genital maturity. Erikson himself, speaks of the "epigenetic principle," whereby "each item of the healthy personality . . . is systematically related to all others, and they all depend on the proper development in the proper sequence of each item and each exists in some form before 'its' decisive and critical time normally arrives."[3]

Developmental Stages. Erikson conceived of eight distinct stages in the human life cycle. He posed his stages in terms of crises or tasks, successful solution of which lead to health, failure to pathology. The sequence he held to be universal; the typical solution to be dependent on the particular society of which the person is a member. These stages are basic trust versus basic mistrust; autonomy versus shame and doubt; initiative versus guilt; industry versus inferiority; identity versus identity diffusion; intimacy versus self-absorption; generativity versus stagnation and, finally, integrity versus despair. Erikson's description of the healthy resolution of the last great developmental crisis, "the fruit of the seven stages," is as follows:

I know no better word for it than integrity. . . . It is the acceptance of one's own and only life cycle and of the people who have become significant to it as something that had to be and that, by necessity, permitted of no substitutions. It thus means a different love of one's parents, free of the wish that they should have been different, and acceptance of the fact that one's life is one's own responsibility. It is a sense of comradeship with men and women of distant times and of different pursuits, who have created orders and objects and savings conveying human dignity and love.

Although aware of the relativity of all the various life styles which have given meaning to human striving, the possessor[s] of integrity [are] ready to defend the dignity of [their] own life style against all physical and economic threats. For [they know] that an individual life is the accidental coincidence of but one life cycle with but one segment of history; and that for [each individual] all human integrity stands and falls with the one style of integrity of which he [or she] partakes.[4]

Developmental Tasks. Robert Peck expands this last developmental crisis and poses the following developmental tasks:

1. Ego-differentiation versus work role preoccupation: Am I a worthwhile person only insofar as I can do a full-time job? Or because of the kind of person I am? The person faces this most graphically upon retirement from work. The task involves an ability to redefine one's worth in other ways, to arrive at a sense of "who-ness" rather than a sense of "what-ness," to redefine oneself in terms of "being" rather than of "doing."
2. Body transcendence versus body preoccupation: This requires a redefinition of happiness and comfort if one is to handle the decline in physical powers, the lowered resistance to illness, lessened recuperative powers, and the increase in physical discomfort that later life brings on. Those who fail at mastery become overly preoccupied with their physical decline, are full of anxiety and even narcissism, and may be prone to somatization.
3. Ego transcendence versus ego preoccupation: This task involves coping with the prospect and meaning of death—"the night of the ego." Success may be measured in terms of one's inner state of contentment or stress and one's constructive or stress-inducing impact on others.[5]

According to Peck to master such tasks is "to achieve the ability to live so fully, so generously, so unselfishly that the prospect of personal death looks and feels less important than the secure knowledge that one has built . . . a broader future for one's children and one's society than one ego could ever encompass."[6] These tasks provide a framework for understanding what faces elderly people in order to help a client or a group toward mastery and a successful old age. Blenkner affirms that the developmental theory provides the best handle for social workers in helping their clients.

Adaptive Developmental Tasks. Margaret Clark and Barbara Anderson used a sociological and anthropological frame of reference in outlining five adaptive developmental tasks which they regard as challenges facing an older person:[7]

1. Admit that aging involves limitations. Age does limit certain physical and mental abilities. Being able to admit this and not deny it is a key. Those who deny that age brings changes neither adapt their activities nor find new ones; some continue to try to look young, others become sick, for it is easier to be sick than to be "old."
2. Change physical activities and social roles. Once people accept limitations,

they must make accommodations to changing capacities—get assistance with homemaking, change their workload, move to a smaller apartment, etc.

3. Find new ways to fulfill one's needs. When old problems or their solutions change, new means to meet one's physical, emotional, and economic needs must be found, such as substitutes for work, assuring one's income, and new friends, interests, and activities. Several studies indicate that failure in this task is a major and most frequent cause of maladaption to successful aging. Mastery of this adaptive task relies heavily on society's meeting its responsibilities to elderly people and making options available.

4. Develop new criteria for self-evaluation. The older person must be able to feel a sense of worth and satisfaction from other than work-related roles. This is difficult in our work-oriented industrialized society, which places little value on leisure, play, and recreation and provides few roles for retired workers.

5. Establish new values and goals for one's life. Older adults must find a positive acceptance of new values within their social milieu. Success involves cultivating satisfying relations with others and receiving positive feedback from them.

As can be discerned, Clark and Anderson's adaptive tasks show many similarities to Peck's developmental tasks. In an earlier work, I made the point that the developmental approach is a preventive and life-enhancing one rather than a curative one. I cited the following necessary tasks for the later years:

1. Redefinition of social identities with development of new social goals in an associational context
2. Linkage of past and present to the future with regard to family, peers, associations, services, and community
3. Adjustment to physical and mental changes
4. Development of new self-image transcending societal expectations of behavior of older people
5. Development of sense of integrity—a profound concern for system, order, and meaning of human existence.[8]

Orientation to Aging. Sheldon Tobin states that changes in orientation to processes of aging begin before the losses of aging begin. This would enforce the developmental rather than the reactive approach to personality. As people age, they prepare for coping with the following crises:

1. Internal and external bodily changes
2. Loss of status
3. Loss of significant people
4. Modification of range of available roles or activities
5. Whatever it means to face death[9]*

* More recent studies in developmental theories include those of Marjorie Fiske Lowenthal, Robert Jay Lifton, Robert and Pauline Sears, Richard Vaillant, Richard Lazarus, and Klaus Riegel. Stress and coping with life's tasks continue to be major themes in many of these studies that promise to add new dimensions and insights to understanding human development during the middle and later years.

Qualities Associated with Successful Aging

Clark and Anderson's five adaptive tasks emerged from their in-depth anthropological study of several hundred well-adjusted and poorly adjusted old people living in the San Francisco area. They observed several qualities that seem closely associated with successful adjustment to age.

1. Attitude toward life: well-adjusted elderly change the attitudes they held during middle age. The poorly adjusted hold competitive, overly ambitious, jealous attitudes as opposed to the self-acceptance, cooperation, and more appropriate levels of aspiration of the more successfully adjusted aged.
2. Personal independence: The well-adjusted want independence due to pride and desire not to burden their children and others. But they are also aware of their limitations and that striving for total independence is not realistic. The poorly adjusted want independence for defensive reasons; they are motivated by fear rather than a sense of autonomy.
3. Social acceptance: The well-adjusted try to achieve this by congeniality—by being interesting to others; the poorly adjusted seek acceptance through achievement and feeling superior to others.
4. Resilience: Well-adjusted people can handle losses and illness and bounce back. They are able to distinguish changeable from unchangeable situations. Underlying this is a basic acceptance of the realities of life. Poorly adjusted elderly are compelled to solve every difficulty; they take each defeat personally.
5. Patience: People in their seventies are better adjusted than those in their sixties because it takes time to adapt. Apparently, men adjust more easily than women.

In 1962, Susan Reichard et al. identified five categories of older persons based on their response to the aging process:[10]

1. Mature type—free from conflict, accepting of themselves, no regrets for the past
2. Rocking-chair type—passive, welcoming a chance to rest and be free of responsibility
3. Armored type—having a highly developed set of defenses to protect themselves against the anxieties of aging
4. Angry type—blaming others, unable to accept their aging status
5. Self-haters—blaming themselves, seeing life as disappointing

In a second study project, Bernice Neugarten and her associates not only categorized personality types, but related these types and role activities to life satisfaction. As a result, the following typology has emerged:[11]

1. *Integrated* or able to cope with inner impulses and outer reality
   - Fully involved and functioning in many social roles, *or*
   - Engaged in focusing on fewer areas, *or*
   - Disengaged, withdrawn, and preferring the simple life

2. *Defended*
   - Holding on or maintaining a high level of interaction to resist what one feels is decay, *or*
   - Constricted, with low life satisfaction, having withdrawn in order to cope
3. *Passive-dependent*
   - Dependent, with mid-levels of life satisfaction, low interaction, and gratification from depending on others, *or*
   - Apathetic, immobilized and unable to structure the world to gratify one's needs
4. *Unintegrated*
   - Disorganized, anomic, and withdrawn from the world

Neugarten makes a concluding statement relative to the studies:

> . . . There is no single pattern by which people grow old. . . . Older persons, like younger ones, will choose the combinations of activities that offer them the most ego involvement and that are the most resonant with their long-established value patterns and self-concepts. Aging is not a leveler of individual differences, except, perhaps, at the very end of life.[12]

The Filial Crisis as a Task. The filial crisis occurs in one's forties and fifties, when parents are no longer a source of strength and support for children but may in fact turn to their children for support. Blenkner refutes the oft-cited notion of a role-reversal, in which the father becomes the child and vice versa; she feels it is a pathological not a healthy development. Blenkner writes as follows:[13]

> Successful accomplishment of the filial task, or performance of the filial role, promotes filial maturity which has its own gratifications, different from those of genital maturity, and leads into and prepares for successful accomplishment of the developmental tasks of old age—the last of which is to die.

The child's ability to see his parents from a mature perspective, as individuals with needs, limitations, and life histories, is the keystone to filial maturity. It is a way to prepare for one's own old age, and it is a stage in the developmental process.

Life Review as a Task. Robert N. Butler and Myrna Lewis, whose work is identified with the concept and process of life review, state it as follows:

> The tendency of the elderly toward self-reflection and reminiscence used to be thought of as indicating a loss of recent memory and therefore a sign of aging. However, in 1961 one of us [Robert N. Butler] postulated that reminiscence in the aged was part of a normal life review process brought about by realization of approaching dissolution and death. It is characterized by the progressive return to consciousness of past experiences and particularly the resurgence of unresolved conflicts which can be looked at again and reintegrated. If the reintegration is successful, it can give new significance and meaning to one's life and prepare one for death, by mitigating fear and anxiety.

This is a process that is believed to occur universally in all persons in the final years of their lives, although they may not be totally aware of it and may in part defend themselves from realizing its presence. It is spontaneous, unselective, and seen in other age groups as well (adolescence, middle age); but the intensity and emphasis on putting one's life in order are most striking in old age. In late life people have a particularly vivid imagination and memory for the past and can recall with sudden and remarkable clarity early life events. There is renewed ability to [freely] associate and bring up material from the unconscious. Individuals realize that their own personal myth of invulnerability and immortality can no longer be maintained. All of this results in reassessment of life, which brings depression, acceptance, or satisfaction.

The life review can occur in a mild form through mild nostalgia, mild regret, a tendency to reminisce, story-telling, and the like. Often the person will give his life story to anyone who will listen. At other times it is conducted in monologue without another person hearing it. It is in many ways similar to the psychotherapeutic situation in which a person is reviewing his life in order to understand his present situation.

One of the greatest difficulties for younger persons (including mental health personnel) is to listen thoughtfully to the reminiscences of older people. We have been taught that this nostalgia represents living in the past and a preoccupation with self and that it is generally boring, meaningless, and time consuming. Yet as a natural healing process it represents one of the underlying human capacities upon which all psychotherapy depends. The life review as a necessary and healthy process should be recognized in daily life as well as used in the mental health care of older people.[14]

Dying and Death as a Crisis and Task. All mortals have to face what Erikson calls the "night of the ego." It is the final and most awesome crisis of all human beings. Kübler-Ross pioneered in the study and the care of the dying. She identified five stages that mark the normal road to dying, at least for those who are conscious and whose time permits them to face this last human crisis: denial and isolation; anger; bargaining (attempts to postpone death); depression; and acceptance. Some comments on these stages clarify further:

> Not every person goes through each stage in the sequence presented, and people may move back and forth between stages or may even be in two stages simultaneously. In the final stage, . . . dying people come to accept impending death; [they have] made peace with [themselves] and with others and [are] ready to die. In many ways, [they are] almost completely disengaged from everyone and everything except very close family members (perhaps only spouse and children, or even only spouse) and one or two friends and the hospital staff who, during their final days, are vitally important people to them. Although these stages have received considerable recognition, other writers have proposed other stages or have denied that any one sequence of stages is seen in more than a small proportion of the dying.[15]

Many issues concerning death and dying are especially meaningful for the elderly. Butler and Lewis write:

There are medicolegal considerations that go beyond psychotherapeutic efforts with the dying. Technical knowledge has made it possible to preserve life in persons who would have died in the past—and in the absence of apparent sentience—by artificial support of circulation, respiration, and nutrition.

Who is to make the decision to allow someone to die? Mental health personnel may be called upon to help make such a decision. The doctor[s] may have moral concerns or be fearful about future litigation. Malpractice suits have skyrocketed. [Their] training is appropriately directed toward the prolongation of life and it may be wise indeed for society to sustain that commitment in the medical profession.

The mental health specialist can help by individual or collective discussions with all pertinent participants: the [patient], if feasible, the family, the doctor, the clergyman, the lawyer, even business colleagues. One must check to see if the individual's house is in order and if appropriate arrangements have been made in the interest of [such] person[s], [their] family, and the "natural objects of [their] affection." [They] may *need* or desire to live only to complete certain personal and tax arrangements. Some persons and their families may want to sustain life until after a [grandchild] is born, for example, or a favored grandchild has married.

Mental health workers' contributions should be in the nature of fact-finding— as to both the practical and the emotional aspects of the situation. The family should not be put into the difficult position of finally deciding, for the doctor[s] [have] the ultimate responsibility. They must decide not to force-feed by tube or needle. But [their] decision and [their] conscience must derive from hard data, in the context of moral and legal situations.[16]

The right to die involves major moral, ethical, and legal concerns. In the fall of 1976, California was the first state in the nation to declare a legal right to die. The legislature adopted this as a legal right and the governor signed the bill. Butler and Lewis explain the debate:

. . .Many others however, feel it is impossible to predict death, that persons have recovered from comas, that tampering with death is sacrilegious, or that death itself is such an insult and tragedy that any compliance with it is inhumane. Thus we hear debate over the "right to die with dignity."[17]

Social workers will be increasingly drawn into this debate and will have to make decisions and learn to live with the consequences. Human worth and dignity is extended to include death as part of life, and dying with dignity is to be accorded a value commensurate to that of living with dignity. A noted psychiatrist has listed seven questions that all people can try to answer for themselves in order to come a little closer to feeling what the elderly feel as they confront death:

1. If you faced death in the near future, what would matter most?
2. If you were very old, what would your most crucial problems be? How would you go about solving them?
3. If death were inevitable, what circumstances would make it acceptable?
4. If you were very old, how might you live most effectively and with least damage to your ideals and standards?

5. What can anyone do to prepare for his [or her] own death, or for that of someone very close?
6. What conditions and events might make you feel that you were better off dead? When would you take steps to die?
7. In old age, everyone must rely upon others. When this point arrives, what kind of people would you like to deal with?[18]

Psychiatric Disorders

It is important for social workers to have some rudimentary understanding of the various psychiatric disorders in order to sharpen diagnostic skills. Butler and Lewis discuss a number of categories in their book *Aging and Mental Health.*[19]

Sociological Knowledge

Recognizing the influence of social and situational factors on the biological and psychological conditions of aging, we must concern ourselves more specifically with position and role changes, notably family and peer roles, and with a relatively new role in the third part of life—that of the retiree. Position in the social structure affects the personality. People are influenced by family, work associations, and social groupings of peers and colleagues. There is considerable variety among the norms and aspirations of people, as they are grouped in different classes along loosely structured class lines. Views of the aged and aging among different religious, ethnic, and cultural subgroups influence people who reach old age.

The social roles of persons in given positions in society specify their rights and responsibilities, what is expected of them, and what they can expect in return from others in society. For older people there are a series of role changes. Family roles and peer and friendship relationships undergo significant changes; these will be discussed in Chapter 11. Being old may cause people to lose eligibility for positions that they value. Age is a prime criterion of eligibility for entry into and maintenance of the more desirable positions in an industrialized, technological society. In addition, as persons enter the third part of the life cycle, they find out that role prescriptions have changed. No longer is the "script" the same as it was before entry into the stage of old age.

The Role of Retiree

Retirement has come to be practically synonymous with aging. It represents a major status and role change in an older person's life, whether it comes voluntarily or as a result of mandatory retirement policies. Many studies have evaluated the reasons, effects, and impact of retirement, often with conflicting results. In our industrialized, work-oriented society, retirement represents a major loss for the older adult and presents itself as a major change with which one must cope. Retirement over the last century is a phenomenon that has been gaining ground rapidly.

In his discussion of retirement, Atchley states:

> In 75 years, retirement in the United States changed from a rare and novel social pattern to a practically universal institution. Retirement can be viewed in several ways—as a process, as an event, as a social role, or as a phase of life. It can be viewed as both a cause and an effect. It is a complex social pattern that touches the lives of almost everyone. Consequently, knowing about retirement is just as important to a comprehensive knowledge of social humans as knowing about adolescence, middle age, an occupational career, or any other phase of the life cycle.[20]

In tracing the evolution of retirement, Atchley contends that it is a phenomenon of industrial society, and he analyzes the contrasts between primitive rural cultures and modernized, urbanized nations. He suggests that industrialization has allowed people to live long enough to contribute their necessary work in the society's economy, with several years left in their life span. Increased knowledge concerning nutrition and sanitation has significantly reduced the death rate, especially infant mortality, permitting a much larger portion of the population to survive into old age.

The author quotes data from sociological surveys by Donald Cowgill and Lewelyn Holmes in 1972 indicating that older persons in less modernized nations are transferred to less strenuous activities that are advisory or supervisory in nature. In these societies, older people have tended to retain power through control over land and its use or through religious beliefs that traditionally have placed elders in the strongest position to influence the supernatural. In rural primitive cultures, when only the fittest survived to become old, the old were an elite who shared economic and political advantage and possessed essential knowledge about the workings of the society. With the advent of industrialization, Atchley maintains, persons from all walks of life survived in large numbers to become old, and there were not enough honorary positions to go around. Industrialization reduced the power of older people by divorcing management from ownership and putting a lower premium on experience. He believes that as the scientific revolution changed our ideas about the supernatural, it eliminated the role of elders as bridges to previous generations. Atchley concludes:

> For these reasons, the stage was set for the development of retirement in the maturing industrial society. . . . The economy was productive enough to support a sizable number of adults without jobs. In capitalist societies, there was incentive to restrict the size of the labor force. The decline in the birth rate meant a smaller proportion of children drawing on the economic surplus. The rise of the national state and the labor union had made it possible for part of the economic surplus to be diverted to support people not in the labor force. This made pension systems possible. The rationalization of labor, the decline of entrepreneurship, and the rise of the secular city meant that it was not always possible nor necessarily desirable for the individual to hold a job into old age. And this made it possible for people to begin to accept without guilt the concept of retirement as an *earned* right.[21]

Ewalt Busse distinguishes between economic and social retirement: Economic retirement occurs when the person actually stops working and begins collecting his or her pension. Social retirement is the time when persons realize they are no longer involved in the work role with which they have come to identify. Busse underlines the "crisis" that often does occur for the retiree. "Retirement is regarded as an achievement in principle but dreaded as a crisis when it actually occurs."[22] Atchley speaks of retirement as a process beginning when a person recognizes that some day he or she will retire and ending when the person actually leaves. In between are gradual stages of preparation, attitude changes, conditions leading toward retirement, and the adjustment period. Atchley writes:

> After the event, be it formalized or not, the individual is expected to assume the role of "retired person." In gerontology there has been a long and loud debate over the nature of the retirement role; and, in fact, over whether such a role even exists. Part of the confusion stems from the fact that various definitions of *social role* are possible.
>
> Most people would agree that there is a position, *retired person*, that . . . individual[s] [enter when they leave their job] under given circumstances. The disagreement comes when an attempt is made to specify the *role* associated with that position. A social role can mean either (1) what is *expected* of any person in a given position, (2) what *most people do* in a given position, or (3) what *a particular person does* in a given position. . . .
>
> The greatest disagreement centers around the nature of the cultural expectations concerning retirement behavior. Some people say that there are no rules to tell [people] what [they] should do in retirement. Others hold that there are plenty of rules; they are simply on a different dimension than those associated with work.
>
> Work roles are usually instrumental—that is, the rules specify actions to be done. [Workers] must be in a certain place at a certain time and perform certain functions while [they] are there. In addition, [they] often belong to various organizations as a result of [their] job: union, professional association, and so on. The most significant expectation the retiree faces is that he [or she] will drop not only [the] work role but work-related roles as well. Thus, the retirement role is largely a set of norms governing the types of roles an individual can legitimately play.
>
> There is no specific activity expected of a retired person just as there is no specific activity expected of a child. The expectations exist purely as a set of rules specifying how an individual should occupy himself.[23]

Preparation for Retirement.   Although it has repeatedly been found that a counseling program for potential retirees is beneficial, fewer than 30 percent of all companies help their workers prepare in any way, and fewer than 10 percent provide comprehensive programs. Counseling programs can provide the important function of immediately preparing and exposing the worker to the facts of retirement income as well as introducing a gradual transition to increasing time in roles outside the work role.[24]*

*In April 1978 a new law governing mandatory retirement policies in the United States was adopted. In several states legislation has been introduced to eliminate mandatory retirement altogether, in the private sector as well. In October 1984 the governor of Massachusetts signed the elimination of mandatory retirement into law.

Impact of Retirement. There are conflicting results from studies done on the impact of retirement on individuals. For most, retirement is a process, and retirees and their spouses experience it differently at different points in time. Manney summarizes this aspect:

> At any one time, a majority of older people probably would say they experience retirement in one of two ways: either as a state of unsatisfying idleness which they resent, or as an enjoyable respite from a lifetime of work. The majority seem to accept it; most workers retire voluntarily, and at least a third of these do so precisely to devote more time to leisure. Given assurance of an adequate retirement income, most older workers would probably gladly retire, even if they have been highly competitive work-oriented people. Another important factor in successful adjustment to retirement is the presence of retired friends to help make full-time leisure an acceptable way of life.
>
> A smaller number of retirees never manage to find sufficient rewards in leisure to replace the satisfactions they had from work. They do not feel justified in deriving satisfaction from leisure because they have never perceived leisure as a legitimate way to spend one's time. These individuals retire involuntarily and reluctantly, and, not surprisingly, quickly become bored and discontented. Many of these retirees eventually withdraw into a disgruntled apathy.
>
> This latter image of retirement is rather widely held among the young. Active, competitive, success-oriented young people feel that retirement *must* be traumatic because it so directly violates the doctrine of the American work ethic. There is a certain amount of truth to this view; probably few older workers retire with perfect aplomb, entirely free of tension between their new state of leisure and the memory of the satisfactions and habits of four or five decades of work. The urbanization and industrialization of our society has largely separated . . . work from . . . family and community. The identity [adults have] historically had as [members] of a viable community [they] now receive from [their] career. The wage system has replaced the economic function of the family and community. . . . Work replaces [the] old links to the traditional political and family systems. Severing that key link to work must be traumatic, for work has isolated [the person] and made his [or her] relationship to society an individualistic one.
>
> However, at the same time, retirement has been established as a *right* for all workers. In 1935, the Social Security system established a right to a retirement income, and in succeeding years the popular view has grown that workers deserve a period of leisure after years of productive contribution to the economy.
>
> Retirement is an ambiguous, problematic institution which Americans can justifiably experience and perceive in many ways. The view that older workers deserve leisure—at least partly at public expense—after a lifetime of work is a widely held popular belief. However, retirement also contains the suggestion that the older worker has grown incompetent, cannot meet the demands of competitive industry, and should be eased out when his [or her] most productive years are over.[25]

The Social Worker's Knowledge of Retirement. Social work's involvement in the retirement process and in shaping leisure programs as well as in shaping retirement policies and leisure policies is a significant frontier that needs to be addressed by the profession. Activities and functions by social workers in these arenas are understood and recognized. A full utilization of social work skills need not wait.

It would appear that the importance of the right to support in one's old age as outlined in the Social Security Act has obscured some other crucial areas, such as providing older adults with new, different, and more meaningful roles to fill the retirement years, so that retiring from the work force does not bring with it such a traumatic loss. Society values full involvement in work and perceives negative connotations about leisure, regarding it as useless time. Viewing an older person's contributions as valuable and thus counteracting the prevailing myths and stereotypes are keystones to providing outlets and options for the older adult who is unable to remain in the work force. For those who want to remain in the work force and are capable of doing so, necessary adjustments should be made, such as giving older workers more time to perform certain tasks.

Another point often neglected is the effect of retirement on women. It has generally been assumed that the male experiences the greatest impact. In the past this was largely true, but more and more women are entering the labor market, and making careers an important part of their life. In addition, when a woman has been home by herself, retirement of the husband requires a shift in the roles of the marriage since the couple may now be spending more time together.

Knowledge References

Because of the vast literature relevant to the knowledge base of gerontology that exists today (and is likely to exist tomorrow), selected sources of gerontological knowledge for *social workers* are enumerated here. Many more are listed in *Gerontology: A Cross-National List of Significant Works* (University of Michigan, Institute of Gerontology, 1982); indexed in the computerized scan collection maintained by the National Gerontological Resource Center of AARP (American Association of Retired Persons) in Washington, D.C.; and listed with citations in the quarterly *Current Literature on Aging*, which is published by the National Council on the Aging, Inc., Washington, D.C.

Journals

Aging, U.S. Department of Health and Human Services
Aging International, International Federation on Aging
Clinical Gerontologist, Haworth Press
Generations, Western Gerontological Society
The Gerontologist, Gerontological Society of America
Journal of Clinical and Experimental Gerontology, Marcel Dekker Journals
Journal of Geriatric Psychiatry, Boston Society for Gerontologic Psychiatry
The Journal of Gerontology, Gerontological Society of America
The Journal of Gerontological Social Work, Haworth Press
International Journal of Aging and Human Development, Baywood Publishing Company
Perspective on Aging, National Council on the Aging, Inc.

Pride Institute Journal of Long Term Home Health Care, St. Vincent's Hospital, New York City, New York
Research on Aging, Sage Publications, Inc.

Newsletters

Age Pages, two-page summaries of information on specific topics related to aging, National Institute on Aging
Aging Reports, U.S. Senate Special Committee on Aging
Aging Services News, biweekly report of legislative developments
Bifocal (Bar Associations in Focus on Aging and the Law), American Bar Association
Human Values and Aging, Brookdale Center on Aging, Hunter College
Newsletter, House of Representatives Select Committee on Aging
Network, Gray Panthers
Older Americans Reports, weekly report of legislative developments

Books

Robert Atchley, *Social Forces in Later Life*
Robert Binstock and Ethel Shanas, *Handbook of Aging and the Social Sciences*
James Birren et al., *Handbook of Aging and Mental Health*
Butler and Lewis, *Aging and Mental Health*
Eisdorfer and Lawton, *The Psychology of Adult Development and Aging*
J. Caroll Estes, *The Aging Enterprise*
Beth B. Hess and Elizabeth Markson, *Aging and Old Age: An Introduction to Social Gerontology*
Rosalie Karp, *Assessment of the Elderly*
Elizabeth Kutza, *The Benefits of Old Age: Social Welfare Policy for the Elderly*
Louis Lowy, *Social Policies and Programs on Aging*
Mace and Rabino, *The 36-Hour Day*
Ron C. Manuel (ed.), *Minority Aging: Sociological and Social Psychological Issues*
Elizabeth W. Markson (ed.), *Older Women: Issues and Prospects*
Anne Munly, *The Hospice Alternative: A New Context for Dying*
Eloise Rathbone-McLeod, *Isolated Elders*
Murgura, Schultz, Markides and Janson, *Ethnicity and Aging: A Bibliography*
Silverstone and Burack-Weiss, *Social Work Practice with the Frail Elderly and Their Families: The Auxiliary Model*
Silverstone and Hyman, *You and Your Aging Parent*
Steinberg and Carter, *Case Management and the Elderly*

Reports

Care Reports, *1982–83 Chartbook of Federal Programs on Aging*
NCoA, *Aging in the Eighties: America in Transition*, reprints and hearing reports of the Senate Special Committee on Aging and the House Select Committee on Aging

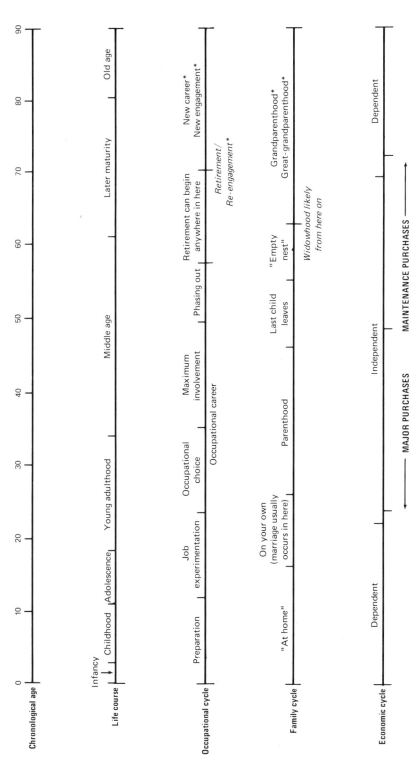

Figure 8.1. Relations among age, life cycle, occupational cycle, and family cycle. (These relationships fluctuate widely for specific individuals and for various social categories such as ethnic groups or social classes.) Robert C. Atchley, *The Social Forces in Later Life,* 3rd. ed. (Belmont, Calif.: Wadsworth Publishing, 1975), p. 91. Asterisks represent additions by the present author.

The Life-Cycle Perspective

What we think we know about aging today—even in its most tentative form—has to be set against a historical canvas. We are intersecting at a historical moment, and behavior of older people is to be understood in terms of historical, cultural, and social conditions that affect behavior and that in turn influences these conditions. We have selected a developmental point of view, a life-cycle perspective.

> This life cycle perspective on aging is important for two reasons, one rather obvious, the other more subtle. The obvious reason is that the conceptual separation of old age from past life, and the social segregation of older people, are outstanding conceptual and social errors. The strengths and weaknesses older people possess do not arise spontaneously at age 65, and older people do not possess the same characteristics from age 65 until death. Life is a continuum which constantly changes. No stage in life, no age category, can be adequately understood apart from the others.
>
> The more subtle point is an extension of this idea. If we can understand the old . . . by studying . . . youth, we can also understand the young . . . by studying [their] anticipation of one day becoming old. [A person] does not live only as a plant or animal does, in an orderly one-way progression from one stage to the next. [A person] anticipates events to come and decides his [or her] next step with a distant end in mind. French novelist Benoîte Groult captures this idea in a phrase: "Youth comes to an end, and behaves aggressively because it is struggling against the image of old age." Thus, the life cycle proceeds in two directions. Later events are explained by antecedent events; antecedent events may also be explained by anticipated later events.
>
> In this perspective, our society's largely negative images of old age suddenly take on new importance, not just for old people, but for all the younger people who are aging in the face of these images. Negative images are not likely to encourage us to plan intelligently while young, so we may enjoy old age's unique positive qualities. Rather, we are more likely to grow old in a way that fulfills our pessimistic expectations.[26]

It is this ever-moving cycle of life, the timeless march of generations, that provides the perspective within which the elderly have a place that is already validated (see Figure 8.1).

References

1. Florence Vickery, *Creative Programming for Older Adults* (New York: Association Press, 1972), p. 60.
2. John Mogey and L. Lowy, *Theory and Practice in Social Work* (Boston University Council on Gerontology, 1966).
3. Margaret Blenkner, "Developmental Considerations and the Older Client," in J. E. Birren (ed.), *Relations of Development and Aging* (Springfield, Ill.: Charles C. Thomas, 1964), pp. 247–266.
4. Erik Erikson, "Identity and the Life Cycle," *Psychological Issues*, New York, 1959, p. 53.

5. Robert Peck, "Psychological Developments in the Second Half of Life," in Joe Anderson (ed.), *Psychological Aspects of Aging* (Washington, D.C.: APA, 1956), pp. 42–53.

6. Ibid., p. 268.

7. Clark and Anderson, op. cit.

8. Louis Lowy, "Meeting Needs of Older Adults on a Differential Basis," *Social Group Work with Older People* (NASW, 1963).

9. Sheldon Tobin, "Basic Needs of All Older People," *Planning Welfare Services for Older People* (Publication of Training Workshop by Public Welfare Association of New York, 1965), p. 5.

10. Susan Reichard, F. Livson, and P. G. Petersen, *Aging and Personality, A Study of Older Men* (New York: John Wiley and Sons, Inc., 1962).

11. B. L. Neugarten, S. Tobin, and R. J. Havighurst, "Personality and Patterns of Aging," in B. L. Neugarten (ed.), *Middle Age and Aging* (University of Chicago Press, 1968).

12. B. L. Neugarten, "Personality and the Aging Process," *The Gerontologist*, vol. 12, pt. 1 (Spring 1972), p. 13.

13. M. Blenkner, "Social Work and Family Relationships in Later Life," in E. Shanes and Gordon Streib (eds.), *Social Structure and the Family* (Englewood Cliffs, N.J.: Prentice-Hall, 1965).

14. Robert N. Butler and Myra Lewis, *Aging and Mental Health* (St. Louis: Mosby, 1973), p. 43. By permission of the C. V. Mosby Co.

15. Avery Weisman, *On Dying and Denying* (New York: Behavioral Publications, 1972), p. 137.

16. Butler and Lewis, op. cit., p. 259.

17. Ibid.

18. Richard Kalish, *Late Adulthood: Perspective on Human Development* (Monterey, Calif.: Brooks/Cole, 1975), p. 94. Copyright © 1975 by Wadsworth Publishing Company, Inc. Reprinted by permission of the publisher, Brooks/Cole Publishing Company, Monterey, California.

19. Butler and Lewis, op. cit., p. 50 ff.

20. R. C. Atchley, *The Sociology of Retirement* (New York: Halsted Press, 1976), p. 158.

21. Ibid., p. 158.

22. *Behavior and Adaptation in Late Life* (Boston: Little Brown, 1969), p. 100.

23. Robert C. Atchley, *The Social Forces in Later Life: An Introduction to Social Gerontology*, 1st edition (Belmont, Calif.: Wadsworth, 1972), pp. 67–68.

24. Ibid.

25. James D. Manney, Jr., *Aging in American Society* (Wayne State, Detroit: Institute of Gerontology, University of Michigan, 1974), pp. 81–82.

26. Manney, op. cit., p. 12.

9

The Intervention Process
of Social Work

This chapter introduces the interventive actions of the social worker engaged in working with older people. Based on the framework discussed in Chapter 4, five analytic dimensions are outlined and the process-action approach of practice, patterned after the problem-solving model of Beulah Compton and Burt Galaway, is introduced. Subsequent chapters elaborate this social work practice approach for individuals, families, groups, and community organizations since distinctive characteristics are required in working with people on these different levels.

Five Analytic Dimensions

As discussed in Chapter 4, social workers have to conceive of five dimensions as they prepare to engage in practice—targets, goals, steps, activities, and roles.

Definition of Targets of Intervention. The worker is concerned with a variety of older persons in different situational contexts—individuals, family and/or peer group members, and members of organizations, clubs, church groups, and other community affiliates.

Specification of Goals. Spanning a continuum from a treatment orientation to an action and developmental focus, social workers refine their goals, determining what are to be the intended outcomes of the intervention and how unintended outcomes can be harnessed for the "good and welfare" of the person-in-the-situation. As was pointed out before, goals are the result of an amalgam of the values, the assessment of the condition or problem to be dealt with, and the combined judgments of worker and elderly person.

Carrying out the Steps in the Interventive Process. Whether older people are individuals, family or group members in a client or patient status, or constituents of community organizations, the social worker and older people engage and work together toward accomplishing agreed-upon goals. It is expected that this process be planned and carried out systematically, taking into account feedback and building the results of such feedback into the pursuit of the goals, which may be amended because of the process that is unfolding. That is why this process follows a cybernetic design rather than a linear model.

Activities of the Social Worker. In specifying goals, determining the nature of the condition or problem, and carrying out the steps of the interventive process, the social worker utilizes a series of modalities, such as the following: formal and informal interviews; group meetings; neighborhood or community organization activities; tenants' meetings; conferences involving co-workers, agency staffs, or community representatives in interagency or interdepartmental meetings of an organization; and members of the informal network, such as family, friends, peers, and colleagues.

The social worker applies a variety of techniques or skills such as psychological support, information giving, interpretation, clarification, development of insights, creation and use of groups and organizational structures, use of program media and tools, mobilization, counseling, teaching, and management of human, material, and technical resources.

Roles of the Social Worker. In carrying out these activities, workers assume a variety of professional roles, primarily three: enabler, broker, and advocate. As enablers they make it possible for older persons or groups of elderly to help themselves utilize their motivation, capacities, and strengths to optimum advantage. As brokers they negotiate and provide a liaison among social institutions, organizations, agencies, and older people in need of services of any kind (social, health, consumer, legal, etc.). As advocates social workers speak up for the rights of the elderly and negotiate their access to services; at the same time they assist people to speak up for themselves to demand the quality of programs and services to which they are entitled as a social benefit.

These three primary roles are performed in judicious interplay. At times one role receives greater emphasis than another. A social worker in an adult education program may want to stress the enabling role, while as a counselor to an older woman, the worker may assume the broker role and bring the woman into contact with the RSVP (Retired Seniors Volunteer Program). In a community action program the social worker may act as advocate and also act to enable the group to achieve its goal, such as reduced fares for transportation.

Three additional roles utilized by social workers are those of therapist, teacher, and expert.

Process-Action Model

Compton and Galaway have developed a problem-solving model for social work practice.

> The model rests upon the belief that effective movement toward purposive change, or altering something that one wishes to alter, rests upon the ability of [workers] to engage in rational, goal-directed thinking and to divide [their] activities into sequential steps, each characterized by some broad goal of its own which must be accomplished before one can successfully complete the succeeding phase. The achievement of such interim goals depends upon active worker-client participation and there must be agreement between these partners that the goals have been achieved before one can move on to complete the following stages.[1]

These authors acknowledge that they are not the first or the only persons to have called this way of conceptualizing practice a problem-solving model. The term was probably first used by Helen Harris Perlman. They explain the model and the nature of the problem-solving process as follows:

> [This model] does not in any way deny the irrational and instinctive characteristics of [people] but it accepts the findings of social scientists studying the mental hospital that even the most regressed psychotic patients are at least as responsive to changing external reality as to their timeless internal fantasies, that altering reality alters ways of coping, and that given a chance to participate in making decisions that affected their lives, inmates generally did so in a responsible manner and with constructive results for all concerned—professionals as well as themselves. This model further accepts the view that social work processes are not a set of techniques by which [experts,] who [understand] what "is really wrong" [seek in their] wisdom to improve, enlighten, plan for, or manipulate a recipient in his [or her] ignorance or in his [or her] emotional need. Rather it is seen as an attempt by one human being with specialized knowledge and training and a way of working to establish a genuinely meaningful, democratic, and collaborative relationship with another person or persons in order to put his [or her] special knowledge and skills at the second person's or group's disposal for such use as [the person or group chooses] to make of it. It recognizes that decisions about what individuals and groups of individuals should be, have, want, and do are decisions that involve values, and in this area [one] is a "legitimate expert for [oneself] and no [one] is a legitimate expert for others." This approach rests upon the assumption that the given in [all] human being[s] is [their] desire to be active in [their] life—to exercise meaningful control of [themselves] toward [their] own purposes. . . .
>
> The problem-solving process itself, in and of itself, is the process by which worker and client decide what the problem or question is that they wish to work on, what is the desired outcome of this work, how to conceptualize what it is that results in the persistence of the problem in spite of the fact that the client system wants something changed or altered, the procedures to be undertaken to change

the situation, the specific actions that are to be undertaken to implement the procedures, and how these have worked out.

For the worker, the use of [this process] involves considerable skill, and the cultivated capacity to keep a clear head as well as an understanding heart. However, it gives the worker no specific guides to specific procedures. It does not promise that if one does this type of thinking and exploring one will come out with *the* (or with *this*) answer. It rather promises that one must do this type of thinking and exploring, consciously and knowingly, in relatively this order if one wants to increase the probability of coming out with *an effective answer* that is in the direction of the client's goals. What the answer is, specifically, will depend upon what the question is, specifically, what the client wants, specifically, and what worker and client can bring to the process in terms of knowledge, understanding, resources, and capacity for action together.[2]

Since a process is inherent in this problem-solving model, the element of time takes on a key function. It is the passage of time and its use by the worker that gives the model a particular quality and character. It is, therefore, in a series of phases that the problem-solving process unfolds and allows us to differentiate a number of stages. The process-action model utilized here is an adaptation of the Compton-Galaway problem-solving model. This author is indebted to their creative contributions, which made it possible to arrive at a more systematic approach in the presentation of social work practice with the elderly.

In the flow of engagements between a social worker and older people, four major sequences can be differentiated: entry, defining the task, working on the task, and termination of the task. This plan and approach has been underlying much of the work of the Boston University Group Work Theory Committee begun in 1959 under the leadership of Saul Bernstein and continued under the leadership of James Garland and Ralph Kolodny. (The members of the Committee were Robert Chin, Louise A. Frey, James A. Garland, Hubert E. Jones, Ralph Kolodny, Louis Lowy, and Marguerite Meyer.) Two publications, *Explorations in Group Work* and *Further Explorations in Group Work* resulted (both have been translated into German and other languages and constitute much of the core of social work practice and teaching in German-speaking countries). The work done by this committee led to the conceptualization of a developmental model of social group work based on phase theory.

Entry includes the following spiral-like processes: Contacting and providing access to available services, maximizing motivation of elderly and minimizing their resistance to the use of services, establishing an initial helping relationship that results in the formulation of a service contract between the parties, and arriving at a time frame. Defining the task consists of maintaining the helping relationship established, and defining the situation and conditions that postulate a need, a problem to be solved, or a condition to be improved. This process of assessment brings into sharper focus more specific goals for the subsequent encounters and moves toward task formulation. This phase ends with a plan regarding how to work on the task. Working on the task demands the use of the strengths of the elderly client; the use of the resources of family members, peers in the immediate surroundings of the elderly person, or the community; and use of the professional self and the skills of the social worker. A diverse number of such skills and techniques are selected to facilitate this process, and the social worker assumes the roles of enabling, brokering and advocating as well as the roles of the activist and expert in a variety of ways as the situation and the tasks demand their deployment. Termination of the task encompasses terminating relationships, possible further referrals or transfer to other helping sources, and evaluation of outcome. Evaluation, however, is a continuing process that permeates all phases and yields feedback for input throughout this process.

Phases of the Process-Action Model

Entry Phase

According to Compton and Galaway, people who accept help (1) have to have faced the fact that there is something in their situation that they want changed and that they cannot change by themselves; (2) must be willing to discuss the problem with another person; (3) must accord that other person at least a limited right to tell them what to do or to do things for them; (4) must be willing to change themselves or their situation or, at the very least, to go along with changes that others make in their situation.[3]

There are basically two types of clients: the voluntary one who comes of his or her own accord and the involuntary one for whom the worker initiated the contact and set up the appointment. Regarding the issue of resistance among the elderly in seeking help, many have difficulty accepting help because they have ambivalent feelings about dependence and independence and they have feelings of failure, or because they are often isolated people who feel lonely, helpless, or hopeless. The many physical and emotional losses that have occurred in their lifetime frequently engender a sense of futility, and they may be denying, avoiding, or hedging the fact that they have a problem.

To help motivate older people, the social worker recognizes that they can change, utilizes their strength, and helps them perform some action to feel useful and worthwhile and to achieve a sense of mastery, a sense of the future, and a sense of dignity. In preparation for the first contact, the worker needs to collect data. There are some key principles to keep in mind for this. The client system is the primary source of information; the data selected should be related to the problem at issue; workers should not collect data they are unwilling to share with the client. Finally, workers must obtain the client's permission to use these data.

Defining the Problem. The primary jobs are seeking to understand and asking the necessary questions in order to conceptualize the problem and establish a common ground to work from—one that both worker and client understand as the starting point for intervention. *Partialization* is the separating out of the specific problems to be focused on. It is important to note that the problem may lie with another "system," and not with the client at all. *Goal setting* gives the problem-solving process its purpose. It is important to separate the problem from the goal, in order for each to be seen separately. There are differing types and dimensions of goals; interim goals are part of the ultimate or optimal goal. As a result of discussions about the problem and the goals to be set, the worker and client arrive at a preliminary contract prior to concluding a more definitive service contract.

Functional Relationship. The most important resource social workers have is their professional functional relationship with the people and groups of people with whom they work in the furtherance of goals. Many social work writers have attempted to express the nature of the professional functional relationship.[4] Allen Pincus and Ann Minahan list three common elements: purpose, commitment to the need of the "client-system," and objectivity and self-awareness on the part of the worker:

> A relationship can be thought of as an affective bond between the worker and other systems operating within a major posture or atmosphere of collaboration, bargaining, or conflict. . . .
>   Although social workers form different types of relationships with different systems, there are common elements in all professional relationships that make them different from personal relationships.[5]

Compton and Galaway phrase it this way:

> The relationship comes out of the interactive communication about difficulties. It grows and develops out of purposive work. The relationship as an affective, experiential interaction should develop as necessary to the task. It is not necessarily pleasant or friendly; sometimes the problem is worked out in reaction and anger. . . . But a relationship will grow whenever one person demonstrates to another by . . . actions and . . . words that he [or she] respects the other, has concern for and cares what happens to [the other], is willing to listen and to act helpfully. This is the kind of relationship on which help is based and it cannot be manufactured.
>   The fact that the relationship develops out of purposive work means that it has motion and direction and emergent characteristics. It grows, develops, and changes, and when the purpose has been achieved it enters a stage of termination. The time structure is another variable which directly affects the nature and rate of the development of the relationship. Whether time limits are imposed on the process arbitrarily by outside forces or . . . imposed as necessary for task accomplishment, they have a deep affect on the emergent quality of the relationship.[6]

Compton and Galaway elaborate the three aforementioned components and identify seven essential elements of the helping relationship: (1) concern for others, (2) commitment and obligation, (3) acceptance and expectation, (4) empathy, (5) genuineness, (6) authority, and (7) power. These elements are used in different ways by social workers and modified by the effect of the following eight variables:

1. The purpose of the relationship.
2. The role of the worker and the role of the other in interaction.
3. The position of the worker in terms of agency and job.
4. The position of the others with whom the social worker is in interaction.
5. The goal toward which the social worker is directing his [or her] activity. (Note that in the helping relationship the worker and client share a goal but this may not be true in other social work relationships involving advocacy or conflict.)
6. The goal toward which the other person is directing his [or her] activity.
7. The form of communication. (In the helping relationship the form of communication between worker and client is usually verbal, but in other relationships other forms may be principally utilized, such as letters or reports, etc.)
8. The forms of intervention to be utilized by the worker.[7]

Both worker and client bring to the professional relationship past experiences, physical and emotional states, anxiety about the relationship, expectations, perceptions of others in the relationship, and various social and environmental factors. There is a burden on workers to be aware of what they bring and to discipline and control such factors in the interest of the client and the tasks to be accomplished.

Older people have had many types of relationships with many types of people in their lifetime. The degree, extent, and scope of these relationships are varied based on personalities, situations, conditions, locations, time, etc. Older people have had a number of functional, professional relationships with officials in bureaucracies, employers, and professionals, notably physicians, nurses, and social workers. These past experiences will influence the nature and quality of the functional relationship that comes into being and is sustained in the course of the social work encounter.

Arriving at a Service Contract

In social work, a contract is defined as follows by Compton and Galaway: "[It is] the explicit agreement between [the] worker and the client concerning the target problems, the goals, and the strategies of social work intervention, and the roles and tasks of the participants. Its major features are mutual agreement, differential participation in the interventive process, reciprocal accountability and explicitness. In practice these features are closely related.[8] Compton and Galaway develop this further:

> Mutual assessment and decision making [are] at the very heart of the development of the contract. Worker and client, in the contact phase, have identified a beginning place [and] set some initial goals and collected some data and done some exploration together related to identified problem and goal. Now they are faced with putting [these] data together to determine [the answers to the following questions:] what is the nature of the problem, what does the client want done about it (a reworking of goal), and how are they going to do it[?] This process involves the ordering and organizing of the information, intuitions and knowledge that client and worker

bring so that the pieces come together into some pattern that seems to make sense, at least in the here and now, in explaining the nature of the problem and in relating it to the "doing" about the problem. In this process there should be movement from what is observed, inferred or deduced, based on knowledge and experience, to some conclusive explanation of what we make of it, and from there to what the client wants and how it can be implemented. Such assessments cannot evolve from one person's head, nor from the simple addition of one item to another but rather from the combination of these data in relevant ways. It evolves from viewing the relationships of these elements to one another as they (client and worker) appraise them and the situation, and from the assessment of their total significance to the client in the light of what he [or she] wants from the process. At its best, this process involves both client and worker in assembling and ordering all information and in making judgments as to the meaning of this for their work together.[9]

The eventual decision to use help leads to the contract. Throughout the process of exploration, older clients become aware of the quality of the relationship being made available to them. The social worker demonstrates an ability to respect these people and to value their feelings, and has made clear the agency expectations that they will participate in helping themselves. The older people discover that even though they may have learned no new facts about their problem, they now see it in a somewhat different perspective. They have a sense of comfort in having shared their burden, and they take some measure of reassurance from the fact that they can do something about their situation. They also have some feeling of accomplishment in having taken the first step toward a solution. Some of these feelings have been experienced rather than talked about and represent the nonverbal components of the agreement.

Exploration is thus supportive as individuals anticipate future help, having seen the social worker's commitment as a professional person to helping them, combined with the individuals' desire to be helped with a specified problem. Still unknown are what the future ramifications of that problem may prove to be, the precise goal to be achieved in regard to it, and the exact length of time it will take to accomplish it. Although the specific nature of the helping process is still unknown, enough of it has been experienced to be reassuring. Also supportive to the client is information about the practical details of help, the time and length of appointments, the place of meeting, and any fee required.

The contract is the culmination of the initial exploratory period and enables clients to participate in a plan to use help in a way that substantiates their own decision for help and thereby implements their use of it. The contract may culminate initial exploration but it does not terminate it. Receiving help is a much too complex human experience to believe that the making of a contract resolves the ambivalences or the resistances to working on it. Exploration goes on throughout, and greater understanding of a problem may require a revised contract.

There are many older people who did not originally request help but who are receiving it. The agency may have reached out to these people. For example, it is common practice in hospitals to search out those patients with special needs in order to assign them to groups. Less usual is the approach in a ward group in which the aim is to intervene in the ongoing daily group processes in order to guide them toward therapeutic ends or at least to prevent them from being antitherapeutic. In these instances, the population may not feel a pressing need for help with problems of group living and may not want it after it is offered. In a nursing home, the residents may not be permitted a choice about participation, or they may be so disoriented that they seem unable to make a choice.

Despite these obstacles, exploration proceeds and the contract, with its verbal and nonverbal elements, is eventually achieved. When a contract has been concluded and this is firmly perceived by the person or the group, the first sequence is completed.

Defining the Task

Building on the functional relationship that has been developed so far and working at maintaining it leads to further assessment (or diagnosis) of the condition or problem to be dealt with. The purpose of this process is not to come up with an answer in labels or categories, but to order the worker's understanding of the person, the situation, and the problem for purposes of defining goals and actions. Factors in the client system—whether this be person, family, group, organization, or community—need to be studied, evaluated, and assessed in order to determine what to do about the condition or problem. Compton and Galaway designed the useful outline below. It is a practical guide for encompassing relevant data and its form should be perceived as a sensitizing device, not a checklist.

FACTORS TO BE CONSIDERED IN STUDY AND ASSESSMENT[10]

I.   The individual
   A. Physical and intellectual factors
      1. Presence of physical illness and/or disability
      2. Appearance and energy level
      3. Current and potential levels of intellectual functioning
      4. How [individual] sees [own] world [and] translates [surrounding events]—perceptual abilities
      5. Cause and effect reasoning—ability to focus
   B. Socioeconomic factors
      1. Economic factors—level of income, adequacy of subsistence, and way this affects life-style, sense of adequacy, self-worth
      2. Employment and attitudes about it
      3. Racial, cultural, and ethnic identification—sense of identity and belonging
      4. Religious identification and linkage to significant value systems, norms, and practices
   C. Personal values and goals
      1. Presence or absence of congruence between values and their expression in action—meaning to individual
      2. Congruence between individual's values and goals and the immediate systems with which he [or she] interacts

   3. Congruence between individual's values and practitioner's—meaning of this for interventive process
   D. Adaptive functioning and response to present involvement
      1. Manner in which he [or she] presents self to others—grooming, appearance, posture
      2. Emotional tone and changing levels
      3. Style of communication—verbal and nonverbal—level of ability to express appropriate emotion [and] follow train of thought, factors of dissonance, confusion, uncertainty
      4. Symptoms or symptomatic behavior
      5. Quality of relationship individual seeks to establish—direction, purposes, and uses of such patterns for individual
      6. Perception of self
      7. Social roles that are assumed or ascribed—competency with which these roles are fulfilled
      8. Relational behavior
         a. Capacity for intimacy
         b. Dependency—independency balance
         c. Power and control conflicts
         d. Exploitiveness
         e. Openness
   E. Developmental factors
      1. Role performance equated with life stage
      2. How developmental experiences have been interpreted and used
      3. How individual has dealt with past conflicts, tasks, and problems
      4. Uniqueness of present problem in life experience
II. The family
   A. The family as a social system
      1. The family as a responsive and contributing unit within a network of other social units
         a. Family boundaries—permeability or rigidity
         b. Nature of input from other social units
         c. Extent to which family fits into the cultural mold and expectations of larger system
         d. Degree to which family is considered deviant
      2. Roles and status of family members
         a. Formal roles and role performance (father, child, etc.)
         b. Informal roles and role performance (scapegoat, controller, follower, decision maker)
         c. Degree of family agreement on assignment of roles and their performance
         d. Interrelationship of various roles—degree of "fit" within total family
      3. Family rules
         a. Family rules that foster stability and maintenance
         b. Family rules that foster maladaption
         c. Conformation of rules to family's life-style
         d. How rules are modified—respect for difference
      4. Communication network
         a. Way family communicates and provides information to members

        b. Channels of communication—who speaks to whom

        c. Quality of messages—clarity or ambiguity

   B. Developmental stage of the family

     1. Chronological stage of family

     2. Problems and adaptations of transition

     3. Shifts in role responsibility over time

     4. Ways and means of problem solving at earlier stages

   C. Subsystems operating within the family

     1. Function of family alliances in family stability

     2. Conflict or support of other family subsystems and family as a whole

   D. Physical and emotional needs

     1. At what level . . . family meet[s] essential physical needs

     2. At what level . . . family meet[s] social and emotional needs

     3. Resources within family to meet the above needs

     4. Disparities between individual needs and family's willingness or ability to meet them

   E. Goals, values, and aspirations

     1. Extent family values are articulated and understood by all members

     2. [Whether] they reflect resignation or compromise

     3. Extent to which family will permit pursuit of individual goals and values

   F. Socioeconomic factors

III. Small groups

   A. Functional characteristics

     1. How group came to be

        a. Natural group

        b. Formed by outside intervention

     2. Group's objectives

        a. Affiliative, friendship, and social groups—mutuality and satisfaction derived from positive social interaction, tendency to avoid conflict and stress identification

        b. Task-oriented groups—created to achieve specific ends or resolve certain problems, emphasis on substantive rather than affective content

        c. Personal change groups—emphasis on psychological and social content, dynamics of interpersonal behavior

        d. Role enhancement and developmental groups—recreational, educational, and interest clusters, emphasis on rewards and gratifications of participation, observation, learning, and improved performance

     3. How group relates to contiguous groups—how it perceives itself and is perceived as conforming or differing from outside values

   B. Structural factors

     1. How the members are selected and new members gain entry

     2. Personality of individual members

        a. Needs, motivation, personality patterns

        b. Homogeneity, heterogeneity

        c. Age of members

        d. Factors of sex, social status, culture (see these entries under individual and family) in relation to function and purpose

       e. Subgroups, their reason for being and purpose served

       f. Nature and locus of authority and control

          1. How leadership roles develop

          2. How decisions are made

  C. Interactional factors

     1. Norms, values, beliefs, guiding values

     2. Quality, depth, and nature of relationships

       a. Formal or informal

       b. Cooperative or competitive

       c. Freedom or constraint

     3. Degree to which members experience a sense of interdependence as expressed in individual commitments to the group's purposes, norms, and goals

IV. Organizations

  A. The organization as a system with a mandate

     1. Organizational task—mission within the social structure

       a. Clarity with which task is stated

       b. How task is perceived by organization's members

     2. Individual and group roles relevant to the task

       a. . . . Persons who have the responsibility of carrying out the mandate of the organization

       b. Elements and parameters of their roles

       c. Congruence between expected role behaviors and how these roles are seen by bearer and others

       d. [Whether] roles [are] assumed, delegated, earned, or appointed

     3. Location of organization within system of organizations

       a. Population group designed to serve

       b. Kind of problem for which it is accountable

       c. Isolation from or cohesion with other organizations

       d. Quality of interorganizational communication

       e. Way organization manages input from other systems

  B. Culture of the organization

     1. Style with which organization operates

       a. Governing beliefs of members

       b. Expectations and attitudes of members

       c. Theories that govern and guide organizational action

     2. Modes of interaction with external groups or within

       a. Formal or informal

       b. Deference to authority—hierarchical

       c. Ritual

       d. Channels of communication

     3. Organization's technologies—resources, methods, and procedures of task in implementation

       a. Jargon

       b. Routine and protocol

       c. Accepted and approved modes of communication

  C. Competence of the organization

     1. Availability and adequacy of funds, physical plant, equipment

     2. Scope of authority vis-à-vis the community

3. Special status, force, and control in relation to larger community
4. Merit of guiding policies, flexibility, and responsiveness
5. Efficiency of internal decision-making process
6. Level of morale, spirit of commitment of members
7. Degree to which above factors combine to make the organization more than the sum of its parts

V. Community
   A. The community as a social system
      1. Community's organizations, institutions, and groups which affect existing condition and how they are linked with each other
      2. Location of the problem and units related to it
      3. Units that can be engaged to deal with problem—their stake in change, how accessible they are
      4. How . . . change in any one part [will] affect other units
   B. The community as an organic entity
      1. Attitudes toward social control and conformity
      2. Opportunities for social mobility
      3. How community defines success or failure
      4. Beginning appraisal of power structure and how it exercises controls
      5. How power is achieved in the community
      6. How . . . prevailing problems [are] identified and by whom
      7. Beliefs held about causes of social problems
      8. How community labels the victims of social problems
      9. Problem-solving capacity and resources . . .
   C. Intercommunity structures and processes
   D. Relationships and negotiations within governmental and nongovernmental sectors

The culmination of the assessment process is the recognition of where the problem resides and who and where the target of intervention really is. The problem may be defined as residing within the client; outside, but experienced by the client; or in the nature of the client's situation. Consequently, the target of any change may or may not be the person at all. For example, the targets may be family members that put pressure on the person who needs relief from these pressures. Or the target may be the kitchen staff of a nursing home that prepares unsavory meals and contributes to dissatisfaction, annoyance, and low morale among the residents. The assessment may result in recognition that the target of intervention should be the local transportation system and not the participants of a day center for older adults since the inadequate bus routing prevents older people from getting to the day center in reasonable comfort. After client and worker have jointly defined the problem to be worked on (this may or may not be the same as the presented problem), the next decision is to define goals: what is to be done now?

Goal Formulation. Goals should be sufficiently specific and concrete to be measurable. Only in this way will the client and worker be able to know whether the goals are accomplished, and only with the establishment of measurable goals can the profession of social work establish its accountability. Broadly stated goals such as "helping the client feel better" are meaningless. Another major consideration in goal setting is to set goals for which there is a reasonable chance of attainment.

Worker and client in establishing goals should, of course, consider variables such as degree of interest of the client in obtaining the goal, abilities of the client, and the resources available to the client in the community. Once goals meet these criteria a determination must be made of the appropriate type of service, assistance, or appraisal. Goal formulation is a process that is informed by feedback mechanisms and responds to changing signals, cues, and conditions. Compton and Galaway have discussed this:

> With a mutually agreed-upon definition of the problem and a mutually agreed-upon solution, the task remains of planning a way to move from problem to solution. The development of an intervention plan consists of decisions, again jointly made by the client and worker, as to the steps which will be taken to solve the problem—to reach the goals. The steps in the process of making this decision markedly parallel those used in defining the problem and arriving at the goals. The worker will first discover from the client what steps the client would like to take in terms of reaching the solution and what steps the client expects the worker to take. Likewise, the worker must establish what is expected of the client as well as what the worker expects to do to accomplish the goals, and again, any difference in these expectations must be negotiated and resolved so that the client and worker are both clear as to the steps each is taking to move from problem to solution. . . .
>
> There are four important limitations on worker activity which the responsible worker must consider. These are time, skill, ethics, and agency function. Time constraints on a worker are a reality factor that must always be considered in entering into a contract. Workers cannot responsibly commit themselves to activities which are beyond the time they have available; conversely, a client can reasonably expect worker[s] to do what [they say they] will do. . . . Poor quality service is provided when workers make commitments that they cannot complete, and, conversely, frequent contacts between worker and client do not necessarily imply a high quality service.
>
> The worker should not enter a contract that calls for worker activity that exceeds the skills of the worker. Part of a professional responsibility is to be aware of one's own strengths and weaknesses. When a client requires a specialized skill such as counseling or bargaining with a large bureaucracy, which a particular worker does not possess, then the negotiated plan must include involvement of another resource to assist with this aspect of the intervention.
>
> Workers should avoid involvement in intervention plans that commit them to unethical behavior. An obvious example would be the securing of economic resources through illegal means. . . .
>
> The work between worker and client is always limited by the function of any agency in which the worker is involved. This is an unfortunate limitation and relates to the tendency to organize social services in this country around functional specializations rather than the provision of generic services. Workers can be alert to defining agency function broadly and, when necessary, should certainly consider the possibility of requesting exceptions to agency function or attempting to work within their agency to secure a broader definition of function.[11]

After agreeing upon the goals to be reached, both parties are ready to work on the task.

Working on the Task

Working on the task demands the use of the strengths and capacities of the older people; the use of human resources in their immediate environment, such as family, friends, peers, neighbors, etc.; the use of community resources, that is, benefits, programs, and services; and the use of the social worker's self, his or her abilities, know-how, contacts—in other words the translation of the social worker's knowledge into skills and techniques.

During the development of the three major social work methods in their historical context, various techniques and skills were identified, studied, and exercised. In Chapters 10, 11, 12, and 13, the application of these techniques and skills in working with individual older persons with families and with members of groups and organizations will be described, discussed, and illustrated through case materials taken from practice.

Workers' activities can also be conceptualized in terms of their roles—the behaviors a client system expects of workers in performance of their functions and also the worker's expectations for his or her own activities.

> Interventive roles constitute behaviors in which the worker is expected to engage to accomplish the goals specified in the contract; the concept of interventive roles is broad enough to encompass both the client's behavioral expectations of the worker as well as the worker's expectations of him/herself. Differences in these areas, of course, must have been resolved as a result of the contracting process.[12]

Six roles will be identified here: enabler, broker, advocate, therapist, teacher, and expert.

Role of Enabler.

> The worker enacts the enabler role when intervention activities are directed towards assisting the clients to find the coping strengths and resources within themselves to produce the change necessary for accomplishing objectives of the service contract. The major distinguishing element of the enabler role is that change comes about primarily because of client efforts; responsibility of the worker is to facilitate (or enable) the client to accomplish a defined change. . . . The enabler role can also be used to help clients find ways of altering their own environment. The distinguishing feature, again, is that the client effects the change with the worker performing a supporting or enabling function to the client.[13]

The worker who assists a group of elderly neighborhood residents in thinking through the need for a new day care center, identifying factors that must be considered in establishing a center, and planning the steps that might be taken to provide the service will be serving as an enabler to a community group. The worker who helps a group identify sources of conflict within the group and influences that are blocking the group from moving toward its defined goals and then discovering ways of dealing with these influences will be serving as an enabler in relation to the group.

Teaching is one important aspect of the enabling role. Frequently workers will provide clients with information necessary to decision making; in some situations providing information may be all that is required for a client to accomplish defined goals. Giving information must be clearly distinguished, however, from giving advice. Giving information implies supplying the client with data, input, or knowledge which the client is free to use or not use on [his or her] own behalf; giving advice implies a *should* quality and carries the clear connotation that the worker knows what is best for the client. . . . Encouraging verbalization, providing for ventilation of feelings, examining the pattern of relationships, offering encouragement and reassurance, modeling behavior, engaging in logical discussion, and rational decision making are all avenues by which the enabler role might be enacted.

Role of Broker.

The worker serves as a [link] between the client and other community resources. The activities of the worker are directed towards making connections between the client and the community in order to accomplish the objectives specified in the service contract; effectively serving as a broker, of course, requires a broad knowledge of community resources as well as knowledge of the operating procedures of other agencies so that effective connections can be made.[14]

The worker who arranges for an older person to be accepted in a training program to assist other older people or work for improved housing functions is a broker if the activities involve connecting the person to other community resources. Workers who bring in specialized resources to groups—such as outside experts who discuss the latest Medicare provisions—are functioning as brokers in the sense that they are serving as links between their client (or group) and additional community resources. When working with a community group, such as the Gray Panthers, the worker can assist them by identifying sources of funding that can aid the organization in moving toward its goals. The common element is making a referral in order to connect the client to another resource. Referral is a basic part of the enactment of the broker role; frequently, assisting a client to find and use a needed resource is the most important service a worker can provide.

Role of Advocate.

Advocacy is a concept which social work has borrowed from the legal profession. The advocate becomes a spokesman for the client by presenting and arguing the client's cause when this is necessary to accomplish the objectives of the contract. . . . The advocate is not neutral but, just as in law, is a partisan spokesman for his [or her] client. The advocate will engage in arguing, debating, articulation of the client's interest, bargaining, negotiating, and manipulation of the environment on behalf of the client.[15]

Case advocacy assumes a partisan stance on behalf of a person or a group of people who cannot negotiate their demands alone, find redress for grievances, or cut through bureaucratic red tape. Group or class advocacy emphasizes the creation and support of neighborhood and direct-action groups representing the interests of the disadvantaged. Such advocacy is of especial interest for the community organizer and can be meaningfully employed in a variety of agencies. Paul Terrell writes:

> The advocate of this type can also play an important role within the system of municipal governmental bodies; and a variety of specific roles can be enumerated for those working on a community level for government bodies or in community action programs. First of all, the advocate can act as a general spokesman for the disadvantaged community and their representatives in his [or her] day-to-day contacts with public officials and community influentials. The advocate represents such local groups in those councils to which they do not have access. The advocate will consistently demand from those operating within the blinders of their own organization's necessities the consideration of the needs of the disadvantaged.
>
> Secondly, as a result of his [or her] own access to the views, plans, and informational resources of the establishment, the advocate is well equipped to provide local action groups with relevant knowledge. Thirdly, the advocate, on the basis of his [or her] training and expertise, can use such knowledge . . . to offer advice concerning effective methods of action for local groups. Knowing of vulnerable institutional practices and the spots of maximum weakness in municipal plans and proposals, he [or she] often is able to suggest the most efficacious forms for direct action or other forms of pressure. Fourthly, the advocate as professional can offer a wide range of specialized assistance to local community organizations. He [or she] can help them "objectify" their views, present the considerations their adversaries consider paramount, fill in gaps in their information, and clarify distorted views or unfeasible plans or goals.
>
> Next, the advocate can attempt to create countervailing pressures to public or private activity not in the interest of the disadvantaged [and] can help to create organizations in those instances where the need is great and action is possible. Sixthly, the advocate can do contingency planning so as to capitalize on crises. Violence and confrontation often create a mood in which advantageous social change can be effected. In the time of confusion and enthusiasm for change immediately following such crises, the advocate must be prepared with detailed proposals for change.
>
> A range of professions other than that of social work can act as advocates in a variety of circumstances. Most obviously, lawyers can perform the role. In addition, city planners can be of assistance, especially to groups involved in disputes with urban renewal agencies. As a number of professional persons become increasingly interested in the connections between social dysfunctions, and progressively more concerned with the needs of the disadvantaged, a form of coalitionism [among] politicians, lawyers, planners, mental health specialists, and social workers is developing within our communities.[16]

This type of advocacy role comes closer to the activist role in which social workers will assume leadership for a particular cause of the elderly and proclaim a partisan position, for example, vis-à-vis the Gray Panthers. There is considerable controversy within social work as to the appropriateness of this role. As stated by Terrell:

> This possibility creates the danger of falling into the temptation of serving as a client's spokesman without a clear contract with the client to do so. A lawyer does not become a spokesman for a client until a client has retained the attorney and fully authorized his services, so likewise the social work advocates should take great efforts to be sure they have an explicit contract with the client prior to engaging in these types of advocacy activities.[17]

Role of Therapist. Therapeutic interventions are geared toward intrapersonal adaptations; changes come into play when social workers decide that treatment of mental and/or emotional impairments is called for and that specialized individual and/or group counseling skills are required. This function of the social worker straddles a borderline between social work and psychotherapy. Increasing attention is being paid to further elaboration and delineation of this role. Notably, the works by R. Butler and M. Lewis[18] and by J. E. Birren and R. B. Sloane[19] have provided impetus and guidelines to deal with this function.

Role of Teacher. Teaching is a ubiquitous function of social workers. They perform educational functions when they instruct older persons in cognitive, affective, and motoric learning tasks;[20] when they teach family members in case management functions and provide information on community resources and entitlements for their older parents in partnership with social agencies;[21] when they train human service providers (including social workers), teach courses and institutes, and conduct conferences on aging and the aged in educational and professional organizations and institutions.

Role of Expert. As a trained, knowledgeable professional, the social worker offers his or her skills, expertise, and body of knowledge in order to influence others in support of a social policy or to convince decision makers of the importance of particular programs. Social workers in this role give expert testimony before congressional committees or act as advisors to governmental agencies, such as legislative committees on the federal or state levels, and to mayors and governors in city halls and state houses.

Evaluation. Each of the roles discussed might be used to reach the same objectives, leaving the worker and client free to consider alternative approaches. Additionally, the roles may be used in conjunction with each other in reaching the same objectives. During all these activities evaluation is part of the social worker's efforts. Compton and Galaway write:

> First, evaluation efforts are an essential part of the service to clients. The worker working with an older person, family, group, or organization of elderly to achieve some defined goals has a responsibility to engage the client or members in regular evaluative efforts to determine if their activities are producing the desired results.

Second, workers have a responsibility to cooperate and assist in the more formal evaluations of agency programs and policies; line level practitioners may not be called upon to give leadership to these formal evaluation efforts but their assistance and cooperation is essential if program evaluation is to be conducted. Both types of evaluations—the worker's continuous evaluation with the client and formal program evaluation—should create feedback for the worker to integrate into practice. . . .

Client and worker are continuously involved in a process of ongoing evaluation of their actual experiences. Their evaluation may indicate a need to redefine the problem (or define an entirely new problem), to reassess objectives (or develop new objectives), or to alter the intervention plan. . . . The opportunity to change problem definition, goals, and intervention plan does not, however, remove from the worker the responsibility to be sure that these changes are mutually negotiated with the client and to be sure that any intervention activities are undertaken on the basis of a clearly specific service contract. Experience with interventive activities may indicate a need for change in the contract but changes in contracts cannot be made unilaterately, and because experience may indicate a need for changing a contract does not mean that intervention should continue in the absence of such a contractual agreement.[22]

Termination Phase

When the joint activities of social worker and clients (or constituents) have achieved mutually agreed-upon goals, or when one of the parties concludes the service, the encounter, and the relationship of client with agency and worker, the termination phase, is at hand. As Compton and Galaway state it, "There are three endings— referral, transfer and termination."

Referral. Referral comes into play whenever "a client or a service instigator requests an involvement in a situation that falls outside the parameters of an agency's defined services, or whenever we define a problem as beyond our expertise or our agency's parameters of service."[23] Responsibility *does not* end with the referral. Social workers must assume responsibility for the results of their judgments and actions when making a referral. A worker must recognize that asking for help from others is not simple for older people, and the time of referral is a vulnerable period; clients are open to suggestions and ready to work, but they can become easily discouraged if they experience no movement. The more threatening the problem, the less prone is the person to go somewhere else again and rehash it. Referral involves not only sending the person to another agency, but also follow-up— making sure the client got there and is receiving the necessary service.

Transfer. Transfer is referral to another worker, usually in the same agency, and quite often due to a worker's departure from the job. The worker needs to be aware of his or her own feelings regarding transfer; transfer is more effective if plenty of time is allowed for it and if it is gradual. Older clients especially may have feelings of desertion and be angry about being pushed around. They should be given the opportunity to discuss these feelings. The new worker must recognize these feelings and go very slowly in the initial meetings.

Terminating the Relationship. In evaluating the movement toward accomplishment of the goals, worker and client (individual or groups of people) may come to the conclusion that they have reached the end of their activities. Either the goal is accomplished—for example, a telephone reassurance service has been provided or counseling has resulted in more harmonious family relationships—or achievement of the goal eludes both partners. In the first instance, a degree of satisfaction may accompany the ending; in the second, a sense of incompleteness, coupled with a feeling of frustration, may be part of the ending. In any event, an ending involves terminating a relationship. Obviously it does make a difference whether the relationship was of short duration and invested with low intensity of feelings or whether it stretched over a couple of weeks or even months and was invested with high intensity of feelings.

What is important is that termination of a service in most instances means giving up a relationship, as social services generally are rendered by human beings; and giving up a relationship entails a loss. For older persons this constitutes one more loss, in addition to those losses that they have experienced already. "Grief as a result of loss is a predominate factor in aging. Loss of the marital partner or other significant and loved people (including a social worker) can be profound, particularly since it is difficult in later life to find any kind of substitute for such losses."[24]

Reaction to this may be denial, regression, anger. The worker must allow for these feelings to come through and be available as a target for these feelings, even as a scapegoat and also as a person who engages in an objective evaluation process with the client. The tasks in termination are (1) working out the conflict (for worker and client) between the acknowledgment of improvement and goal on the one hand and the movement away from help on the other, (2) working out the fear of losing the relationship and the support of the concerned person, (3) examining the social work experience and recognizing the program needs for accomplishing goals, (4) considering how these experiences can be transferred to other problems as they may come along, (5) examining what is involved in stabilizing the gains made so far, and (6) clarifying the worker's and agency's continuing position vis-à-vis present and future expectations and needs by the client.

Empathy. While empathy is a key quality of any helping relationship at any stage, it is of particular importance at the termination stage. Empathy is the capacity to enter into the feelings and experiences of another, knowing what he or she feels and experiences, without losing oneself in the process. Being a helping person means making an active effort to put yourself in the perceptual frame of the other person, using the understanding to help without losing your own perspective. Allan Keith-Lucas lucidly differentiates among pity, sympathy, and empathy:

Consider three reactions to someone who has told us that he strongly dislikes his wife. The *sympathetic person* would say, "Oh, I know exactly how you feel. I can't bear mine, either." The two of them would comfort each other but nothing would come of it. The *pitying person* would commiserate but add that he [or she] was most happily married. Why didn't the other come to dinner sometime and see what married life could be like? This, in most cases, would only increase the frustration of the unhappy husband and help him to put his problem further outside himself, on to his wife or his lack of good fortune. The *empathetic person* might say something like, "That must be terribly difficult for you. What do you think might possibly help?" And only the empathetic person, of the three, would have said anything that would lead to some change in the situation.[25]

Thus empathy towards the person who mourns the loss of the relationship demands a capacity for grieving without morbidity and without losing oneself in guilt. This is why recapitulation and review of what has gone on before are essential activities on the part of social workers when they engage in the process of termination. To arrive at a meaningful judgment as to the manner in which the social work encounter has been conducted is the consummate task of both partners at this phase.

An Illustration of Workers' Roles

Mrs. O., an Irish Catholic woman in her early seventies, was referred by a housing manager to a worker at a public assistance agency for help with some concrete needs such as a hearing aid and new glasses and for an evaluation regarding preventive intervention. The manager who had referred her to the agency was concerned about a drinking problem, her relationship with her son, and about possible problems in her perception of reality. The manager reported that Mrs. O. had one son who was an alcoholic and who came to see her demanding money, which she gave him even though she had very little. Mrs. O. had been separated from her husband for a number of years; he had died three months before the referral. She also had another son and a daughter with whom she had contact and a sister who visited occasionally. The rest of the family would become angry with her when she aided the alcoholic son, however, and during these times, would decrease their contact with her.

Contact

When Mrs. O. was first introduced to the worker at the housing project by the manager, she agreed to an appointment but stated that she was going out and would let them know when she returned. She did not do so, but the worker happened to see her return. The worker, therefore, went to her apartment, but the woman said she could not see the worker at that time because she had had a drink at dinner and had to sleep it off. They made an appointment for the following week, and the woman did not avoid the worker this time. In fact, when the worker explained that Mrs. O. did not have to see her if she did not want to the woman indicated a desire to speak with the worker. The woman's greatest concern centered around a buzzing in her ears that bothered her to such an extent that she did not feel like seeing anyone. She was reluctant to cook for herself since she had found roaches in her apartment. She was also concerned about her alcoholic son and her own drinking.

The son would encourage her to drink when he came, and she would do so and then feel sick. This, plus his requests for money and his disturbances when he arrived at the apartment drunk, made her angry with him; and yet she felt that she needed to take care of him. She also shared some bizarre thoughts about events that she thought caused her difficulties, even though in reality they had no connection with her problems. The worker located a hot-meal program, which the client considered; she encouraged her to put a telephone in her apartment and attempted to enable her to visit a medical clinic (with home service) in her apartment building. Within a few weeks, she seemed to improve considerably.

After regular contact of a few months she was able to go out and enjoy people more; she was drinking less and was less bothered by the buzzing in her ears. Shortly thereafter she could take action in relation to her alcoholic son by obtaining a restraining order keeping him out of the building when he was drunk. The worker was also able to help her obtain a television set to keep her company and help her remain oriented to reality. Although she was frightened of it at first, she grew to like it, and it did help with keeping her mind off the buzzing in her ears and other unpleasant and unrealistic thoughts.

She admitted that loneliness was her main problem. Although this was intensified by her hearing problem, she could not accept a hearing aid. When her family discovered that she was no longer subject to unexpected visits from her alcoholic son when he was drinking, they began to visit her more often. After a few months of contact, the client did follow through on an appointment with an outpatient facility for a medical investigation of her hearing problem. She had a considerable amount of wax taken out of one ear and this stopped the buzzing and improved her hearing somewhat. She also finally followed through on an appointment to a hospital eye clinic and was able to obtain new glasses.

By the end of the contact, she functioned at a much better level. She had obtained concrete help and achieved a more frequent and meaningful contact with her family, and she was able to participate in the social activities in the housing project. The worker remained in touch with the housing manager and spoke on Mrs. O.'s behalf to him, pointing out to him Mrs. O.'s progress and urging him to look after her from time to time.

Discussion of the Illustration

This case illustrates the way in which an elderly person is to be perceived as a unique individual with the right to her own self-determination in a dignified manner. The worker recognizes this by allowing her to decide which services she wishes to accept and at what pace. At the same time, the worker reaches out in order to help her accept the service offered without being frightened. The worker draws on the client's strengths in connection with her relationship with her family, her common sense, and her desire to feel more comfortable. The worker then uses these strengths to help the client achieve a restored equilibrium through ameliorating some of her debilitating conditions and through helping her to provide satisfying and growth-enhancing experiences that promote self-actualization and prevent further deterioration.

The worker performs mainly the role of broker among the client, her family, and the health-care agencies. In the role of enabler, an essential part of the enabling function centered on using the relationship between the worker and the client and by being a consistent, caring listener who eventually could help the client sort out the realities of her situation. The degree of improvement is striking and so is the client's ability to maintain this improvement and to operate more independently by the end of the contact. The worker worked as an advocate vis-à-vis the housing manager, though the enabler and broker roles were more evident in this situation.

References

1. Beulah Compton and Burt Galaway, *Social Work Processes* (Homewood, Ill.: Dorset Press, 1975), p. 234. Reprinted by permission.
2. Ibid., pp. 238, 239.
3. Ibid., p. 239.
4. See the following works: Helen Harris Perlman, *Social Casework: A Problem-Solving Process* (Chicago: University of Chicago Press, 1957), pp. 65–66; Florence Hollis, *Casework: A Psychosocial Therapy*, 2nd ed. (New York: Random House, 1972), pp. 228–244; Ruth Elizabeth Smalley, *Social Work Processes* (New York: Columbia University Press, 1967), p. 29; Grace L. Coyle, *Group Work with American Youth* (New York: Harper & Row, 1948), p. 91; Gisela Konopka, *Social Group Work: A Helping Process* (Englewood Cliffs, N.J.: Prentice-Hall, 1963), pp. 107–118; Margaret E. Hartford, *Groups in Social Work* (New York: Columbia University Press, 1971), p. 194; Helen Northern, *Social Work With Groups* (New York: Columbia University Press, 1969), pp. 53–58; Allan Keith-Lucas, *The Giving and Taking of Help* (University of North Carolina Press, 1972), p. 47.
5. Allen Pincus and Ann Monahan, *Social Work Practice* (Itasca, Ill.: F. E. Peacock, 1973), p. 69.
6. Compton and Galaway, op. cit., pp. 146–147.
7. Yvonne L. Fraley, "A Role Model for Practice," *Social Service Review*, vol. 43, no. 2 (June 1969), p. 144.
8. Compton and Galaway, op. cit., p. 329.
9. Ibid., p. 330.
10. Ibid., pp. 245–246, 247, 248, 249, 251.
11. Ibid., p. 388.
12. Ibid., pp. 339–340.
13. Ibid., p. 343.
14. Ibid., p. 342.

15. Ibid., pp. 344–345.

16. Paul Terrell, "The Social Worker as Radical: Roles of Advocacy," in Paul E. Weinberger (ed.), *Perspectives on Social Welfare* (New York: Macmillan, 1974), p. 337.

17. Ibid.

18. Robert Butler and Myrna Lewis, *Aging and Mental Health*, (St. Louis: Mosby, 1973).

19. James E. Birren and R. Bruce Sloane (eds.), *Handbook of Mental Health and Aging*, (Englewood Cliffs, N.J.: Prentice-Hall, 1980).

20. Louis Lowy, "Continuing Education in the Later Years: Learning in the Third Age," in *Gerontology and Geriatrics Education*, vol. 4(2), winter 1983/84 (New York: The Haworth Press).

21. Marsha M. Seltzer, Kathryn Simmons, Joann Ivry, Leon Litchfield, "Agency-Family Partnerships: Case-management of Services for the Elderly" in *Journal of Gerontological Social Work*, vol. 7, no. 4 (The Haworth Press, Inc., 1984), pp. 57–74.

22. Compton and Galaway, op. cit., p. 382.

23. Ibid., pp. 422–423.

24. Butler and Lewis, op. cit., p. 36.

25. Allan Keith-Lucas, *The Giving and Taking of Help* (University of North Carolina Press, 1971), pp. 80–81.

Working with Individual Older Persons: The Process-Action Model Applied*

This chapter has been structured on the basis of the process-action model described in Chapter 9. A brief description of each of the parts of this process and some of the major issues involved is followed by case examples from which are drawn the principles of working with individual older persons. Following the process-action model is an abbreviated section on institutionalization and the special issues this raises. Most of the case illustrations are drawn from experience in working with older people residing in the community. Many of the principles, however, can be applied to situations in a number of congregate residential settings.

Entry Phase

Contacts that initiate referrals and the initial personal contact with the older person, referred to as intake or initial interview in many social agencies, are processes that can mark both the beginning and the end of the entry phase. The manner through which an elderly person comes to the attention of an agency will of necessity influence the way in which the worker will approach the person and the situation. Before the specifics of the first interview are discussed, a few considerations regarding the background of the entry situation need mention.

The agency must have a policy regarding the type of elderly people it serves and the services it offers. There are various ways an agency may establish a contact

* At least four-fifths of this chapter was contributed by Ellen Orlen, Assistant Professor of Social Work, Boston University, although this author takes full responsibility for all of its contents.

with individuals. They may come to the agency on their own, another agency may refer them, a family member or other individual may initiate the referral, or the agency may find people through an outreach program. An outreach program is the result of a policy that encourages agency contact with the community to stimulate the use of its service.

Outreach is most often done with elderly people by contact with nutrition sites; public housing projects; golden-age clubs; drop-in centers; hospitals; Social Security, Supplemental Social Security, and Medicaid offices; police departments; churches; and visiting nurse associations. Contact is also made by spending time where elderly people congregate—senior centers, cafeterias, parks, rooming houses, and small apartment buildings. The purpose of outreach is prevention, and much prevention can be accomplished by finding people in these settings before crises bring them to the agency.

If the person is referred by another agency or individual, it is important to obtain adequate information about the reason for referral, the referring person's prior contact with the elderly person, any relevant history, identifying characteristics of the elderly person and other important individuals in his or her environment, and any other pertinent information. It is essential that the elderly person be informed of the referral, give his or her permission for it, and be clear about its purpose prior to the first contact with the agency. If this is not done, confusion, wasted effort, and the alienation of the client and others may occur.

Many of the general principles related to initial interviews apply to elderly people. From the start, the purpose of the interview must influence the way in which it is structured. If the agency has initiated the contact, an honest explanation of the agency's purpose in contacting the client is the most important place to begin. This will help the client become less anxious about the motives of the agency and about the future course of the contact. If the client initiates the contact, it is best to allow him or her to begin with a statement of the problem as he or she sees it. This gives the person a chance to express what is uppermost in his or her mind, affording some immediate relief and helping the worker learn important information regarding the person and the situation by listening and observing.[1]

Helpful Techniques

The following techniques, as described by Florence Hollis, can be helpful both during the initial interview and later in the contact with an individual.[2] (1) Support or sustainment includes empathic listening; evidence of interest and concern; acceptance; reassurance; recognition of abilities, accomplishments, and strengths; encouragement; and sometimes concrete acts that demonstrate caring. (2) In direct influence or advice giving, three precautions are suggested. Workers should be fairly certain that they know the best plan for the client, that the suggestion is offered out of the client's need rather than the worker's own need, and that the client continues to be encouraged to make his or her own decisions after the worker has outlined several alternatives and their consequences, as far as can be determined.

Given these precautions, the direct-influence technique can be useful with very anxious or depressed clients, with clients whose personalities are such that they are unable to make decisions, or with clients who make decisions that are not in accord with reality. (3) Frequently employed during the entry phase is the exploration-description-ventilation technique. This process consists of interaction between the client, who shares facts and feelings, and the worker, who encourages and elicits the client's expression of the facts and the feelings related to him or her by exploring the issues associated with the situation.

Special Considerations

Most elderly people have been brought up to address adults as Mr. and Mrs. except for close family, friends, and children. It is, therefore, a sign of respect that the elderly person be addressed by Mr. or Mrs. unless he or she indicates preference for another title.[3] Many elderly people, particularly as they get into their seventies and eighties, suffer from visual or auditory sensory deprivation. In such situations, it is important for the worker to speak clearly and concisely, to be willing to repeat as many times as necessary, and to be patient while the elderly person attempts to understand him or her.[4] The pace of an elderly person is often slower and the worker needs to adjust to this. Due to the factors just mentioned, nonverbal communication takes on greater significance than when working with younger people. Elderly people who have had multiple losses with few replacements often have a great need for affection. If the elderly person expresses affection to the worker, it should be accepted, and judicious, well-timed physical contact or touching on the part of the worker can be a most meaningful way, sometimes the only way, of communicating.[5]

The worker should begin with the client's request since it is often the key to other needs that the client is not aware of or cannot express. It is important to look beyond the concrete request in order to give elderly clients a chance to utilize fully the services of the worker without having these services imposed on them.[6] The usual ambivalence present at the beginning of the social work relationship is sometimes intensified for the older person, who often struggles with maintaining as much independence for as long as possible as a means of coping with the problems and the losses experienced during the aging process.[7] This need to maintain independence becomes threatened when the elderly person faces the need for help in relation to his or her functioning, thus making it more difficult to engage with a worker in the helping process.

Another common occurrence both during the entry phase and throughout the contact with an individual elderly person is the expression of reminiscence. If one does not understand the significance of this activity, it is apt to be viewed as a digression and/or a sign of a deteriorating mind.[8] One study that explored the relationship of reminiscence to depression in a group of elderly people found that it had adaptive significance in regard to maintaining self-esteem, engaging in life review, resolving grief, and reacting to stress.[9] Reminiscence, therefore, provides a vehicle in the worker-client relationship for diagnostic judgment and is also a therapeutic tool.[10]

It is well to bear in mind that additional considerations are essential in protective service referrals. (This is discussed more fully later.) In many protective service situations, the client has not requested help nor does he or she see that there is a need for help. This means that the worker may be representing the authority of the mental health department, and if this is the case, it is necessary to be honest about the purpose of the contact while at the same time presenting oneself in as nonthreatening a manner as possible. It is often useful in such situations to try to relate to any concern that the client raises and to attempt to help him or her feel as much a participant in the process as possible. If the person is physically ill or suffering physical discomfort, it is helpful to begin by focusing on this and on what can be done to alleviate it. If a trusting relationship can be established between worker and client, this can help to facilitate the steps necessary to provide the appropriate type of care.

It is important to be as explicit as possible during the entry phase. Therefore, if the situation warrants a longer contact, either for the purpose of defining the task or for working on the problem, the approximate time frame should be spelled out and an explanation of what will take place during it and at the end of it should be given. It is also important to clarify any financial issues during the entry phase, such as a fee, if applicable, or information related to third-party payment by insurance, contract, or the like. Often, people are referred to an agency on an individual basis and there is need for other methods of intervention—group, advocacy, etc. It is well to keep this in mind at the point of entry so that one can be open to the various systems impinging on the individual as one moves into the phase of defining the task.

The following cases are illustrative of some of the issues involved in relation to the entry process.

Case Number 1: Mrs. J.

Mrs. J., a Jamaican widow in her late sixties, was referred to an outreach social worker from a family agency because she was living alone and presumed isolated. She was also referred for a communication problem due to a hearing impairment. She had come to this country several years before in order to take care of her youngest son's children while he attended college and his wife worked. At first, she lived with her son and his wife. Mrs. J. had been a widow since her own children were quite young. While the children were growing up, she had worked as a maid and had struggled to educate all six of them. Most of them had left Jamaica in order to better themselves educationally and economically, though only one child was in the United States at the time of contact. Mrs. J. had had hypertension for many years and had been hospitalized for a mild stroke a couple of years prior to the referral. At the time of the referral, she was on medication for this condition and was often too ill with headaches and dizzy spells to go out.

In addition, she had suffered a hearing loss that could be helped only partly by a hearing aid (which was broken), and because of this hearing impairment and her Jamaican dialect, she had great difficulty in communicating with people.

The worker first directed her efforts toward establishing a relationship and toward helping Mrs. J. to repair her hearing aid. From the beginning, she talked with the worker about the son with whom she had lived. Mrs. J. had left their home without warning because she was uncomfortable living there. She and her daughter-in-law did not feel positively toward one another and she blamed her daughter-in-law for turning her son against her. She felt that her son did not visit her often enough and that he did not show her enough attention. Shortly after she had left their home, she suffered a stroke.

The worker was able to obtain Mrs. J.'s permission to talk with her son and his wife in order to clarify the reality of the situation from the couple's point of view and also to try to help each of them to understand the other's point of view a little better. Contact with the son and his wife revealed that they cared very much about Mrs. J., but felt unable to meet her needs on a day-to-day basis due to the pressure of their own lives. The son was intent on making a good impression in his job, worked odd hours, and traveled a great deal. His wife was working, going to school part-time, and caring for their small children. The son was attempting to fulfill the high standards his mother had set for him. This, along with their other responsibilities, prevented them from spending much time with Mrs. J. They, in turn, felt very guilty about this and anxious about her health, which they knew was being aggravated by the problems in their relationship. Mrs. J., on the other hand, felt rejected by them and found it difficult to adjust to the fact that they were not treating her in the same way that would have been possible and accepted had they all remained in Jamaica.

The worker spent most of the rest of the contact trying to help the couple and Mrs. J. understand each other's perspective and trying to improve communication between them. She did so by showing each of them how they exacerbated the situation in small ways. For example, instead of setting overt limits and explaining them, the son would not call or visit at all when he felt that his mother was too demanding. She, in turn, would make him extremely uncomfortable about his lack of attention each time she saw him, rather than trying to understand his pressures and appreciating the efforts he did make. Mutual interpretation did help ease the relationship somewhat, though improvement was limited by the fact that the son would not agree to meet together with the worker and his mother to discuss the issues.

It was discovered by the time of termination that Mrs. J. did indeed have a number of friends with whom she had long-standing relationships and who did offer support emotionally. Her physical condition had improved slightly and she and her son were able to communicate on a somewhat better basis.

Discussion of the Case. This is an example of the way in which a limited contact with a social worker through outreach enhanced an elderly person's strengths and enabled her to continue on her own on a more comfortable and surer basis.

Basically, the picture this client presents is one of strength. She had raised a family on her own, worked hard, and achieved mutually satisfying relationships with a number of people. Even following the rift with her son and the stroke, she was able to function primarily on her own. The most important combination of facts in this case is the juxtaposition of the client's physical illness and emotional upset. The relationship of emotional factors to physical illness in the elderly cannot be overemphasized.[11] Thus, easing the emotional components in the relationship with the son served a preventive role regarding Mrs. J.'s physical health. Without the worker's ready availability on an outreach basis, this preventive work could not have been done.

The second important factor in this situation is the influence of two cultures in conflict and the effect of this conflict on the individuals involved. Mrs. J. wanted her children to be middle-class and American. By doing so, she did not understand the nuclear family style or the work ethic that they were being urged to adopt. She somehow expected them to become middle-class and American and still retain the same loyalty and attention to her that she would have received in Jamaica— a loyalty that results from the informality of marriage relationships[12] and the respect of children for parents and elders among the nonwhite population in Jamaica.[13] The culture conflict as well as the racial attitudes in the United States made it difficult for the son to be comfortable engaging with a white social worker in joint sessions with his mother to address the very issues that would expose him and his wife. The exposure of these issues would then have interfered with the life-style he had worked so hard to achieve under immensely difficult circumstances.

Case Number 2: Mrs. I.

Mrs. I. was referred to a community service agency by a bank employee with whom she had had contact. He felt that she was in a crisis, and he did not know what to do for her. The agency worker found that Mrs. I., a white woman in her seventies, was divorced, living alone in an apartment, and had no family. She appeared dirty and unkempt and talked at length to the worker about various needs—about her enormous gas and electric bills, a broken window, too many stairs to her apartment, a medical checkup, lost Social Security checks, insufficient funds, and her need for new clothes. She had recently been hospitalized at a local private mental hospital for a suicide attempt that she claimed was a frame-up. She had apparently phoned a friend during an attack related to a heart condition. The friend phoned the police who found her with a plastic bag over her head. She said that she was told to breathe into a paper bag when experiencing these attacks and was all out of paper bags. She was not sure why her friend had called the police. She felt that the hospital had treated her against her will and had kept her "doped up" and submissive. She said that they had planned to put her in an expensive nursing home partly owned by one of the doctors. She managed to assert her rights, however, and to be discharged. She ordinarily did not leave her apartment because of her illness, but she had hired college girls to help her with her shopping and cleaning.

Discussion of the Case. At the time of the first contact or at the point of entry, the worker must make decisions and draw tentative conclusions quickly on the basis of limited information. In this situation, the client was asking for help with a large number of items, most of them concrete, and at the same time, she was relating information that indicated that she might very well need help with problems related to her ability to function. Of necessity, the worker would have to begin with the concrete needs that the client presented, at least insofar as possible. Much information would be clearer if the worker could have contacted the private mental hospital involved; however, any request to do so at the beginning of the relationship might prevent the client from trusting the worker. At a later point, after a trusting relationship had been established and some concrete needs met, if it still seemed important, the worker might be able to gain permission from the client for this contact. It is easy in a situation such as this to become anxious and to take precipitous action prematurely. It does not appear from the little that we know about her that the woman was actively suicidal; therefore, jumping into a protective role might jeopardize any trust the client had and, in fact, might preclude a chance to help in the future due to the client's withdrawal from the relationship. One could speculate that the client might reach out in a crisis toward a person she trusted as she had done with her friend. If the social worker fulfilled such an expectation, it might have then enabled him or her to offer the client critical help. Alternatively, the contact with a caring person, such as with the worker who had helped satisfy concrete needs, might help the client feel less hopeless for a time and thus avoid another crisis until more was learned about the situation and the appropriate intervention procedures were determined.

Defining the Task

Defining the task involves assessment and leads to concluding a service contract; it is the second phase in the process-action model. Here again, as in the entry phase, many of the basic principles in working with any individual hold true with special considerations added related to older people. Any elderly individual who is about to engage in an assessment process about himself or herself has the right and the responsibility to know the purpose of the process and something about the way in which the information given will be helpful to the task at hand. It is to be hoped that an exchange will have taken place during the entry phase between worker and client clarifying these aspects. Nonetheless, it will probably be necessary to repeat the information at various times during the entire process and to elaborate on various points as things progress. If a worker begins to elicit a great many facts and feelings without the purpose being clear to the elderly person, the effect of the experience is demeaning and frightening and could well be perceived as an attack on the person's integrity and independence.

Of necessity, one must begin with gathering as much information as possible about the problem. It is useful to know how long the problem has existed, what previous attempts there have been to deal with it, how successful they were, and how the person has coped with stressful situations in the past. The history of the person in relation to the problem is important. Any additional history that the person deems important, along with an exploration of the feelings that are expressed in connection with both the problem and the history, can be very helpful.

Information related to the person's present capacity to function is often important. This information includes the state of the person's capacity to function intellectually and emotionally, his or her capacity for judgment, and the way he or she relates to others. It also includes the state of the person's physical health and the degree of mobility present. The number of losses the person has experienced and the type of losses, along with the type of supports and strengths available to the person, help to augment the picture. The person's ethnic background and socioeconomic status and any religious influence are additional facts to learn. An assessment of the systems involved in the problem—those within the person and those related to the family and the community—need consideration in order to determine where the most appropriate type of intervention can be employed.

When the evaluation of the situation is complete enough to define the problem, the worker and the older person should be at a point where agreement on the appropriate tasks for both flows naturally from the assessment process. Final negotiation of the contract—taking into account the tasks to be accomplished, the time frame, the people involved, the methods to be employed, and specific goals—marks the ending of this phase. This step is often difficult with certain groups of elderly persons. Some lack the educational background that would enable them to understand the role of the social worker. Some fear becoming dependent, perceive themselves as powerless, or are not accustomed to being encouraged to be a participant in such a process rather than a recipient of service. Some need to deny the existence or severity of the problem or lack faith that anything or anyone can help change things substantially.

In spite of these obstacles, it is vital that the worker make every effort to carry out this part of the process carefully. Some aids in doing so are persistence, patience, repetition, consistent offering of suggestions without railroading, and the use of the relationship with the client and of others, such as family, to help with the interpretation. It is also helpful to be honest about what is possible and what is not, have faith that one can help, demonstrate reliability, follow through, and perform some act of filling even some small concrete needs or requests.

In working with the elderly individual, there is often extensive need for contact with collaterals. The elderly person is involved in a network of social systems that he or she may find difficult to negotiate; workers are in the position of deciding how many of the systems involved they need to contact and to what extent. First and foremost, the worker should never contact any collateral person or agency without the client's permission, unless it has been established that the client is definitely mentally incapable of giving permission for such contact and that the contact is essential to his or her well-being. The worker should also encourage the client to negotiate the system insofar as he or she possibly can; frequently, the worker can increase the elderly person's capacity to do so.

No information should be shared with any collateral person or agency without permission from the elderly person, and the information obtained from collateral sources should be shared with the client insofar as possible. Workers may find that they are called upon to interpret their role and to act as advocates in behalf of the elderly person. Sometimes advocacy is confined to issues related only to an individual client. At times, however, the issue may be larger than the individual person and may need to be followed through on a broader level. Collateral contacts can be extremely useful and even crucial but should be undertaken with caution and care. Once the task has been clearly defined, the worker is ready to move on to working on the task.

The following cases are illustrative of some of the issues involved in defining the task.

Case Number 3: Miss M.

Miss M., an 80-year-old single woman, was referred to a community service agency by the visiting nurse association because she was having difficulty caring for herself. She was living alone in an apartment, with no close relatives. She did have one nephew in a neighboring town but he did not become involved until much later in the contact. She had lost all confidence in performing daily activities, particularly cooking. She would call a neighbor every five minutes asking if she was cooking the right thing and if she was cooking correctly. She was so distraught that she could not even make the smallest decision. She could not decide what to eat on a given day, whether to take her pills, etc.

She was assigned to a social worker from a community agency who was doing outreach in the area. After seeing the degree of her discomfort, the worker felt that the woman should be evaluated by a psychiatrist for possible medication and an assessment as to whether she could safely remain in the community. She finally agreed to be seen at the local clinic by a psychiatrist. He felt that she needed to be in a day-care program and suggested one at the local mental hospital. It was difficult for the woman to accept this idea because she was afraid of being crazy and of being institutionalized. The worker was able to help her to accept the plan not only by discussing her fears and the realities of the program at considerable length, but also by accompanying her to the day-care program for the first few days.

The day-care program enabled the woman to function in her own apartment more adequately for a number of months. At the end of that time, however, the hospital began looking for another form of care because they were equipped to give this kind of care only on a short-term basis. The day-care program was not geared primarily to older people. Since there were no day-care programs for the elderly operating in the community at that time, the only alternative seemed to be a semi-custodial arrangement. A particular boarding home was chosen that furnished meals, socialization, and supervision. It allowed the residents freedom and provided companionship for residents who were not severely physically ill.

During the time the client had been going to the day-care program, she had expressed her unhappiness during the weekends when she was alone. It was difficult for her to give up the apartment where she had lived for a number of years but she finally agreed to move into the boarding home and did adjust well to this setting. Her nephew became involved toward the end of this process and did take some responsibility in trying to choose the particular boarding home selected for her.

Discussion of the Case. This case illustrates the difficulties inherent in trying to help set a service contract with an elderly person who is all alone and whose problems involve self-care. Early in this situation, it was necessary to involve a collateral resource, the psychiatrist. Fortunately, the client was willing to see him. Although the client was very unhappy and could not function adequately, she would not have been able to accept the care that she needed if the social worker had not taken the following actions: (1) spent considerable time establishing a relationship with the client in order to engender trust, (2) effectively helped the woman sort out her feelings about the plan, and (3) arranged to accompany her by taxi to the day-care program at an early morning hour for a few days and remained with her during the first few hours of her attendance at the program.

This last action allayed the client's fears and enabled her to mobilize the energy needed eventually to attend the program on her own. It is an example of the importance of flexibility and commitment in working with the elderly. If the client had not had a satisfactory experience with the day-care program at first, it is likely that she would have had more difficulty in accepting the semicustodial arrangement that was ultimately necessary. The lack of any day-care program for the elderly, either in the hospital or in the community, which would have enabled the woman to remain in her own home longer, definitely raises advocacy issues. There is room for advocacy in relation to the mental hospital, which would be a natural resource for the type of longer-term day care needed, and in relation to the community as a whole, where work toward establishing day-care programs for the elderly might be undertaken.

Case Number 4: Mr. W.

A social worker from a social agency came into contact with Mr. W. through an outreach program in his community. Mr. W., a man in his early seventies, was separated from his wife, lived alone, and had recently moved to a new apartment. He had come to the United States from Italy as a young boy and had left school early to go to work. His initial requests were in terms of concrete needs such as glasses and special shoes. The worker's willingness to help with the concrete needs and her offer of additional service in relation to the "nervousness" he mentioned led to a discussion of his feelings of loss in relation to his retirement and in relation to an experience with a woman who had been important to him in the recent past.

He then shared feelings concerning his children and former wife. He spoke of the fact that his wife had been mentally ill and that this had made for great hardships for him and the children. His concern about his relationship to the woman who had recently been of importance to him seemed related not only to the loss of the woman as a person but also to his capacity to perform sexually since this had been an issue between them. He had had some prostate problems and wondered if there was a connection between these problems and his periodic impotence.

With his permission, the worker verified with the hospital that the type of prostate surgery that had been performed would not interfere with the client's sexual functioning. She tried to help him understand the relationship between sex and emotions and also the variations in sexual response that came with age and that do not necessarily indicate the loss of capacity for sexual functioning at all. As the client shared the pain of his past life and the loneliness of his present situation, he became uncomfortable and began to withdraw. What he wanted most was a new relationship with a woman.

Discussion of the difficulties he had had in his relationships with women, a painful process, did not seem to offer him any clarification regarding his unsuccessful and unsatisfactory experiences. The worker and client therefore agreed that she would see him only on an irregular basis when he requested it. This decision was based on their mutual recognition that the life review was painful and not constructive, the concrete needs had been met, and the client's wish for a new relationship must wait for opportunity. The client did, in fact, call on the social worker when he had a transient upsetting experience. By the time the worker terminated, he had met a woman and made some friends and he was feeling much more content.

Discussion of the Case. This case illustrates how an initial request for concrete items such as glasses and shoes allows for the establishment of a relationship that enables the client to express feelings. The client and the worker can then decide together to explore the feelings for clarification of meaning and to determine whether intervention is indicated and mutually agreeable. The initial emotional issue was the client's loneliness. He shared this by talking of his losses regarding his wife and children, his job, and his recent unsatisfactory relationship with a woman. Exploration of this loneliness revealed his concern about his sexual functioning. The worker's action in clarifying the medical reality and in educating the client regarding normal sexual functioning at his age was a simple but effective way of dealing with some of the feelings expressed.

The worker respected the client's wishes to refrain from pursuing a life review and its relationship to his present difficulties with women since it was painful for him and since he did not seem to anticipate that this process would provide constructive results. The worker wisely encouraged the client to contact her when he felt it necessary. Interestingly enough, the second time he called on the worker for help, he did so when he had had an emotionally upsetting personal experience, a step he would have been unable to take unless he had understood clearly the worker's function. The worker was able to help the client with his feelings about his sexual functioning and also to allow him to terminate when he chose to do so. Subsequently, this enabled the client to ask for help without fear that the worker would pursue a discussion of painful feelings beyond his wishes.

Excerpts from First Interview.

> The worker told Mr. W. that she could help him in two different ways—with doctor's appointments and orthopedic shoes, but also with other problems he might have, such as the nervousness he had mentioned earlier [illustrates clarification of roles as broker and counselor]. Mr. W. answered that he would like that okay [responsive with some hesitation]. The worker then asked when he first remembered being nervous [start of exploration and history taking]. Mr. W. answered that when he was in his sixties and had his eye operation, he couldn't see well and had to quit his job. He was nervous before that but more so afterwards. He had tried another job, but it was too difficult [shares one important loss].
>
> The worker then asked how old he was. Mr. W. answered 74. The worker commented that he had been retired for a number of years. He responded affirmatively. The worker then commented that this could be difficult [empathized, enabling client to go further]. Mr. W. continued that it was difficult and lonely. He then added, to be truthful, that he had had an affair with a woman. He excused himself for being forward, then went on to say that when they were together he had some trouble—which he was still having. Then he had the prostate operation, and then, well, he finally had an erection because he really cared for her; but he guessed she got tired of waiting for him so she had gotten married. He wished her happiness but he thought she was no good. She had been married a few times. When he met her she had few clothes; he bought her pretty clothes but she finally left.
>
> He was obviously still upset about this and had tears in his eyes as he spoke [discussion of the first loss leads to expression of additional losses and to concern about bodily functioning]. The worker responded by saying that it was difficult to lose someone, and lonely, and added that Mr. W. had had to retire earlier than he wanted to after having worked all his life [worker reflects feelings]. Mr. W. responded by saying that he tried to keep busy. He hoped to meet people in the housing project where he lived [defends against pain, tries to think of the positives].

Excerpts from Interview Regarding Decision Not to Continue Worker-Client Contact on Regular Basis.

> The worker asked Mr. W. if it [was] okay to discuss what they were going to do with their relationship. Mr. W. answered that it was. The worker explained that social workers can help in many ways. One was to help with concrete needs, making phone calls and finding out information and the like, which she had done for him; another was to help people talk about emotional problems that trouble them. The worker explained that everyone has emotional problems and for some people it helps to discuss them with a social worker. The worker said that she and Mr. W. had talked a lot about some of his problems and it seemed to her that

talking had caused him a lot of pain [explanation of role and acknowledgement of painful discussion]. Mr. W. answered affirmatively.

The worker went on to say that she found him to be a strong, intelligent man. She added that of course these problems would hurt but he was still functioning and doing okay which showed his strength [supports strengths]. Mr. W. responded with tears in his eyes that he still felt bad over his wife and children and their bad upbringing. He added that it was so hard for him [recapitulation of previous painful concerns]. The worker responded by saying that he had done the best he could under the circumstances [allays guilt]. She added that they did not have to discuss the past [permission to refocus] and they could talk of the future and the present. She asked him what he would like to talk about [engages client in decision making].

Mr. W. responded that he was lonely and wanted someone to talk with, have dinner with, etc. The worker explained that this was a normal, understandable wish, but that this was not her role and unfortunately she did not have someone for him [he had previously asked her to find him someone]. The worker concluded by summing up the agreement about the future relationship. She had promised to give him information in relation to a concrete request, and she would call him or see him to give him the information. Following this, they would not see each other on a regular basis; but he would call her if he needed help either with concrete needs or emotional concerns [supports wishes but sets appropriate limits, redefines role, and renegotiates contract].

Case Number 5: Mrs. E.

Mrs. E. was referred to an outreach worker of a social agency for evaluation and possible follow-up by her homemaker, who was planning to be away for several weeks and was concerned about how Mrs. E. would manage during that time. She had been diagnosed as having chronic psychosis for which she had been hospitalized several times. However, at the time of the referral, she was functioning adequately with the help of the homemaker in her own apartment. The worker visited the client at her home prior to the homemaker's absence. Mrs. E. was receptive to the contact with the worker but suspicious of her motive in coming. She perceived herself as being able to care for herself and saw all her problems as related to the things others did to her. During the homemaker's absence, the worker visited the client, who seemed to function adequately in spite of considerable bizarre ideation. The client did not seem to want the worker to come except on a friendly visitor basis.

Upon the homemaker's return, the worker stopped visiting and offered to be available as needed to either the client or the homemaker. A few months later, the client again came to the worker's attention because she was asking for money at the hot-lunch program, claiming that she did not have any money or any food. The worker again checked with the homemaker who confirmed that she was still shopping for the client and that the client seemed to have enough money and seemed to be eating. Contact revealed that the client was, in fact, more upset than usual since she had had words with the only one of her children who visited her and the child had stopped visiting. The worker contacted the child, who was pleased to have someone with whom to discuss the situation. The child wished to visit but was frightened of what responsibility he might have to take and became angry when his mother was angry with him. He was happy to resume visiting again with some support from the worker, and the client returned to her previous capacity to function.

Discussion of the Case. This case illustrates some of the factors necessary to make an assessment of a situation and the usefulness of availability through outreach. Although it was obvious that the client had serious long-standing mental illness, the worker focused mainly on the client's ability to function at a level maximal for her and at which she had been able to maintain herself in the community for some time. The worker evaluated the actual level of functioning and took into consideration that the homemaker might be feeling concerned in relation to her anticipated absence from the client, even for a short period, since she knew that the client was dependent on her.

The worker concluded that the client was functioning at her optimal level and could not really use intervention at the time of the first request, particularly when she demonstrated that she could endure the homemaker's absence without incident. At the time of the second referral, a different assessment was made, however, based on the fact that the client was acting differently from her usual behavior and based on the speculation that the client's actions symbolized her feeling of a lack of nurturing. Further investigation revealed the difficulty with her son, which did seem to be related to her current behavior. It is important to emphasize that the availability of the worker, who was geographically nearby, made it easier for her to become involved for brief periods as a consultant, a broker between the generations, and a supporter to the client under stress.

Working on Tasks Related to Problems of Physical Illness

Working on the task usually covers a period of time that begins after the service contract has been concluded and the goals have been defined and set forth, and continues until the beginning of the termination process. In work with an individual, this phase is often referred to as *treatment.* Three main issues stand out when one thinks of the impact of illness on an individual: threats to oneself or one's body image, dependence-independence conflicts, and dealing with the anger and anxiety evoked by the experience.[14]

Threats to Oneself or One's Body Image. Actual bodily changes, impairment of bodily functions, or loss of body parts may cause people to feel attacked, less attractive, out of control, concerned about future damage to the body and/or unworthy of the love and attention of others. General considerations in handling these reactions include the following: obtaining knowledge of the person's past weaknesses, strengths, and capacity to function, particularly patterns of coping with stress; helping people express fears and concerns about their body, realistic or otherwise; clarifying the medical realities so that the person can base actions and reactions on facts and on a true understanding of the implications of these facts; drawing on previous strengths and coping patterns by reminding people of their ability to manage stress in the past and the manner in which this has been done; mustering all useful and appropriate environmental supports—medical, financial, family, community, home health aids, etc.—and making use of experimental relaxation techniques that can alleviate stress.

All the above are true for all people suffering from physical illness. Specific characteristics may result from frequent chronic illness meshed with the physiology of the aging process itself, fewer environmental supports due to past losses related to age, and the more prolonged experiences of the elderly in responding to life stresses. If the person has a longstanding unrealistic perception of his or her body, this of course influences reactions to illness related to body image. One would need to know what this original distortion was and to what it was related before dealing with it in relation to the specific pathology involved.

Dependence–Independence Conflict. Most adults wish to remain independent as long as they can and to as great an extent as possible; however, during illness this general wish for independence is in conflict with a wish to be taken care of, since illness tends to make people feel less competent and more dependent. In attempting to help a person in such a situation, one needs to gather information regarding the degree of dependency present prior to the illness in order to set a realistic goal regarding the degree of independence possible for this particular person. Appropriate dependency may be necessary for a time, and it is important to help the person see the necessity for this.

This temporary period of dependency helps people gather strength for the future independence they desire. Drawing on clients' memory of their previous capacity for independent functioning may enable them to take the risk of greater independence when this is appropriate. Providing environmental supports will enable the greatest degree of independence; they are therefore a valuable aid in this situation.

Of special concern to the elderly are fears that they will become unproductive, will burden their children, will become totally dependent, and will be eventually institutionalized. If the client has a history of being unusually dependent, it is necessary to set limits from the beginning. Often a chronically dependent and demanding person will respond to firm realistic limits when they are combined with regular, consistent care and attention that is freely offered before it is requested. This cuts down on on the intensity and number of frantic attempts to become inappropriately dependent.

Anger and Anxiety. Some people will express their emotions fairly directly by talking about them, while others will express them indirectly through behavior or symptomatology. One needs to understand the meaning of people's conversation and behavior in order to identify what emotions they are expressing. For example, withdrawal may signify anxiety or anger or both. To identify which specific emotions are troubling people, it is necessary to help them communicate their feelings — directly or indirectly. As details of the reaction are accumulated and emotions are explored, further detail is elicited, emotional expression is encouraged, and permission is given to share it within the security of the relationship, which provides for control when necessary. The particular emotions with which the client is struggling then become clearer, and the client is afforded relief through this emotional expression.

Reflecting the feelings expressed directly or indirectly and making generalizations are also useful techniques. In dealing with these emotions, the elderly display particular characteristics: more entrenched patterns of defense established over a lifetime; a greater need to rely on medical personnel because of chronic and recurring illness and, therefore, a reluctance to antagonize them; and a greater tendency to be concerned about proper behavior in relation to society's expectations. If the person has a history of poor impulse control and inappropriate expression of anger, this may be intensified as the person grows older.

In such cases, learning to control anger and limit its expression may be the worker's goal for the client. This is best done through consistent, regular nurturing in combination with the setting of limits that are explained in an open and rational manner. Likewise, if excessive anxiety has been the history, limit setting rather than elicitation of feelings may be the better method.

The following case illustrates the issues of threats to body image and the anger evoked by an amputation. It is also an example of the termination phase of the helping process.

Case Number 6: Mrs. Z.

Mrs. Z., a widow in her seventies, was referred to a community service agency for counseling. She had recently returned to her apartment after an amputation of both legs due to circulatory problems. The client was living alone. Married children and siblings living in the vicinity were involved and supportive. A social worker from the agency visited the woman regularly for five months and worked with her in relation to her adjustment to the amputations. This adjustment was related to a number of areas of her life: resocialization, self-care, living arrangements, and her self-image. The client knew that the worker was leaving in a few weeks. The portions of the interview that follow illustrate how the worker deals with the client in relation to her physical handicap and in relation to the termination process. The worker had provided services as enabler and counselor in relation to the physical handicap, and as advocate and broker in helping to secure a change of apartment.

Excerpts from Termination Interview.

Mrs. Z. handed the worker a gift which she said was an expression of her appreciation for what the worker had done for her. The worker asked Mrs. Z. to tell her what she had done for her and Mrs. Z. began to cry gently. [Question elicits feeling as well as a review of their work together.] Mrs. Z. said that she had been very depressed when the worker came, and didn't know how she could live. She said that the worker helped her feel better about herself, for she was so ashamed of the way she looked, and that now she was not ashamed and even went out, and that every day she would go out to more places. The worker responded that she was glad to have been able to help Mrs. Z., but she did not want to underemphasize Mrs. Z.'s role in helping herself [supports client's strengths].

. . . The worker asked whether Mrs. Z. realized that the worker would be leaving soon. Mrs. Z. replied gruffly that she did not want to talk about it. The worker commented that she thought Mrs. Z. sounded a little angry with her for leaving. [Worker indirectly reflects feeling that client is expressing.] Mrs. Z. retorted angrily that she was not angry, that she would get over it. [Client denies feeling but shows even more of her underlying emotions in the way she denies them.] The worker then suggested that she thought Mrs. Z. was just a bit angry with her and told Mrs. Z. that if she wanted to show it by crying or raging at her that it was okay. Mrs. Z. did start crying and the worker found herself beginning to cry with her. Mrs. Z. put her arms around the worker and for a moment or two they both cried.

The worker told Mrs. Z. that she would miss her, too. . . . Mrs. Z. suddenly became sad, and the worker asked her what it was. Mrs. Z. said that sometimes she looks at other people and envies them for their legs. She then said that it was so hard to be brave. The worker agreed that it must be so hard for her and told Mrs. Z. that she admired her courage. The worker then asked Mrs. Z. to tell her what it feels like when she envies others. Mrs. Z. replied that she wishes that she could walk and get around on her own but she knows that she can't and that she has to accept the situation and try harder. The worker then asked Mrs. Z. if it made her angry, and added that it was all right if she wanted to scream, that she would understand and not let her get out of control [permission for expression of feeling and reassurance that the situation would remain within limits].

Mrs. Z. answered that she wanted only to cry and to have someone listen to her as the worker was doing. The worker told her to cry, to go ahead, and Mrs. Z.'s body shook with sobs. [The worker thought that Mrs. Z. was also expressing hidden emotions about the worker's leaving.] Mrs. Z. then began to relax and soon she was smiling again. . . . Again, Mrs. Z. assured the worker that she would be all right. The worker asked her if she were also trying to reassure herself. She answered that she was and the worker told her that she had confidence that Mrs. Z. would be all right. [Workers explores anxiety and offers support at the same time.]

Discussion of the Case. The client has been struggling with her altered body image, how that relates to her value as a person, and how other people react to her as a result. The worker has used the techniques of exploration, ventilation, support, and reflection of feeling in addressing the related issues. One of the controversial portions of the interview is the worker's loss of emotional control (she cried) and the physical contact. It is true that the worker's temporary and minimal loss of control could frighten and burden the client. In this case, however, the incident had the effect of allowing the client to offer the worker something (she wanted to say thank you) and of showing Mrs. Z. her own strength and the degree of the worker's investment.

Physical contact can be very meaningful to elderly persons, who are often deprived of the normal means of emotional expression through touching due to their isolation and/or loss of important relationships. One must use caution and understand the ramifications of what the experience can mean within the context of their relationship. The worker's gentle persistence in eliciting the feeling related to termination was most important in enabling the client to deal with it—and her immediate relief was striking. It should be mentioned that an elderly person is subject to illnesses exacerbated or triggered by emotional stress in much the same way as a younger person, although the affected bodily areas are sometimes different.[15]

Case Number 7: Mrs. P.

Mrs. P. was a woman in her late sixties, divorced, and living alone. She had adult children living in a neighboring state who kept in contact and visited, and other more distant relatives in neighboring towns whom she saw occasionally. She had worked as a teacher and later as a housemother and had injured her arm and her back as a result of an accident several months earlier just before she was about to start a new job. She was living in a high-risk area of the inner city and although she was somewhat uncomfortable and ashamed of living there, her relatives made her feel even more so. Her arm and her back, which she had fractured in the accident, were healing well and with good progress, yet she was feeling very incapacitated and much less able to do things for herself or engage in activities that she enjoyed previously. She was referred to a social worker from a home care agency for help in obtaining a homemaker and for emotional support.

Summary of Contact and Discussion of the Case. Mrs. P. was most receptive to the worker who visited her at home. She presented her problems as physical, emphasizing her need for household help; she also expressed her desire to work and be involved in activities, while at the same time showing some hesitancy and concern about becoming involved. By the time of the second visit, Mrs. P. had been rehospitalized for difficulty in walking related to her back problems. The worker was struck by the degree of Mrs. P.'s pleasure with the care she was getting in the hospital when the worker visited her there. When she returned home a few weeks later, a homemaker was obtained. She found it difficult to manage on her own at home, even with the homemaker, especially in the area of "not being cared for."

This became a central theme throughout the rest of the contact and was one of the areas in which she was able to gain insight in relation to her underlying feelings. Another major issue that she brought up at this time was the decision about whether or not to stay in her apartment. Since her family disapproved of the location, this reinforced her feelings of discomfort about being there. However, there were many positives in the situation in terms of the cost of the apartment and in terms of the relationships with her neighbors, which kept becoming more solid; therefore, this raised a conflict for her and she kept changing her mind about whether to move. This also became a theme throughout the rest of the contact and was also one of the areas in which she was able to gain insight in relation to her underlying feelings.

By the time of the fifth visit, Mrs. P. had been hospitalized again, this time also because of her back problems. She did not seem pleased; in fact, she was depressed because the doctor had said her back condition was chronic, although she knew the X rays had not shown any difference from before. This realization seemed to trigger her feelings about previous losses, particularly the loss of her husband. At this time, she also expressed the realization that she needed a push to become more active.

This led to a discussion of the loss of mobility in her arm, what adjustments she could make to the loss, and how to continue to function. She was not able to face the permanence of the loss of mobility and therefore was not able to look at what she could do in a compensatory manner. This too became a theme throughout the rest of the contact and was another area in which she was able to gain insight in relation to her underlying feelings. She was finally able to face her limitations and use help to make the most of what mobility she had.

Subsequent visits seemed to follow a pattern of alternate denial and acceptance of the connection between her back symptoms and emotional factors. When she was feeling better physically and/or when she felt pushed too much by the worker, Mrs. P. withdrew and denied the connection. When she was physically ill with back pain, she seemed to see the connection more easily. She was enabled to do so by telling the worker what she was experiencing physically and what had happened that upset her emotionally. The worker then reflected back to Mrs. P. the link between the physical symptoms and the emotionally upsetting experiences that she had shared with the worker, thus helping her to connect the two. Following these visits, she was also able to see the relationship between her emotions and the symptoms, even when she was feeling better physically, and was also able to feel better physically more consistently.

When she did have "flare-ups," they were milder and of shorter duration and did not require hospitalization or medical intervention. She also acknowledged that she had achieved a more positive perception of herself as a person following this period. In addition, she became more optimistic about her physical progress and less anxious about recurrences. She began to be much more active, became involved in a political organization for the elderly, and began to make more friends. During the course of the contacts with the worker, it became clear that one of the emotions that most often caused a return of her back symptoms was unexpressed anger. She acknowledged that she had always held in her anger, and she began to be able to see how this had affected her.

She not only began to be able to see the connection between her emotions and her symptoms, but she also began to express her anger more readily. She was better able to do so because she now allowed herself to be aware of her anger and thought enough of herself to feel justified in expressing it. At one point, she expressed the fear of being crazy because her emotions did at times interfere with her physical functioning. The worker was able to reassure her that she was not crazy and that this happened to many people. At another point, she stated that she felt stupid because she had allowed her emotions to affect her physically. Again, the worker was able to reassure her that she was not at all stupid and that people are not able to control their reactions without knowledge of their emotions and the relationship of these emotions to their physical functioning.

The worker helped her understand that the process of linking the two consciously would have to be initiated by someone other than herself, since the relationship of her emotions to her symptoms was not conscious to begin with. Although the client felt much better able to understand herself and to manage, she did remain a bit anxious at the time of termination about carrying on entirely on her own. A short, focused contact would help her solidify the gains she had made, and she was therefore transferred to another worker in the agency for a short period.

The following excerpts from selected interviews over a period of time illustrate the flow of worker-client interaction in the case of Mrs. P.

Excerpts from First (Home) Interview.

> Mrs. P. said her doctor felt she should now make more effort to get out. She said she would like to find some work, but felt handicapped by her injury. Worker asked what kind of work Mrs. P. had done in the past. She explained that she had taught school many years ago. She had then married, eventually divorced, and obtained employment as a housemother in various private schools. She had enjoyed this work and was preparing to start a new job at a school when her accident occurred. Worker asked if she could still teach and she said she would like additional income but felt it would be very difficult to find any employment while she still had frequent physical therapy and medical visits.
>
> Worker then suggested volunteer work at schools or hospitals, and Mrs. P. said she would have to think about it. Worker also asked if Mrs. P. was involved in any activities with her neighbors and she said she was not [since] there were few people who shared her interests. Worker again commented on Mrs. P.'s talent in arts and crafts and asked if she would be interested in running a class for others in the neighborhood who might be interested. She said she might be interested in something like that but would have to have supplies.

Discussion of Excerpts. The client presents her dilemma—namely, that her doctor would like her to be more active and she does not feel able to do so. As the worker tries to explore alternative types of activities with her, the client keeps finding obstacles that will prevent her from engaging in what activity is suggested. This type of response implies that she is not ready to invest energy in any activity, even though she feels that she should because the doctor and the worker are suggesting them. When this occurs, it is necessary to look beyond the reality reasons offered as obstacles and try to find what underlies her difficulty in becoming involved. One of the themes in the obstacles presented by the client is her feeling of being handicapped. The logical place to begin is with these feelings about her injury and how it limits her.

Excerpts from Second (Hospital) Interview.

> Mrs. P. was not sure when she would return home, but was determined to stay until the cure was complete. . . . Her children had been to visit since her hospitalization. They did not like her apartment and wanted her to move. They were willing to subsidize her, but she would rather have stayed within her own budget limits. When asked specifically what she did not like about the apartment, Mrs. P. mentioned people who congregated in the lobby. She agreed that she would probably not mind those in the lobby if the neighborhood were better. She then went on to tell how good the neighbors had been to her before her recent hospitalization. They came in and stayed with her for hours and helped her when the ambulance came. Worker and client then discussed her exploring housing in another [specific] community. She seemed quite enthused since it was a community where she had friends.

Discussion of Excerpts. Mrs. P.'s first statement is the first indication of her expression of the conflict between being taken care of, which necessitates remaining sick, and going home and being independent, which necessitates getting better but being alone and uncared for. She then goes on to illustrate her ambivalence about moving. One begins to get the impression that she would not be too unhappy to stay where she was if her family approved of her residence.

Excerpts from Sixth (Home) Interview.

> Worker found Mrs. P. in excellent spirits and very proud of the fact that she had gotten out of bed, prepared her breakfast, and was now getting ready to go to the hairdresser. . . . Worker then brought up the subject of how Mrs. P. saw the worker's purpose in visiting her. She mentioned that she had originally come to see Mrs. P. because of her feelings of depression and her desire for relocation and that since that time they had touched briefly on her loneliness and illness as well. She wondered whether these were the issues that Mrs. P. recognized and wished to work on further.
>
> Mrs. P. stated that she had been lonely and depressed, but did not want to dwell on these subjects. She said the feelings were fleeting and she recognized that she had to overcome them herself. She now felt she had to be more outgoing. . . . Worker stated that Mrs. P. also said she would like the worker's continued help with relocation although the worker believed that Mrs. P. continued to have ambivalent feelings about moving since she spoke with great pride about the marvelous security that existed in the building.
>
> . . . In regard to her arm and back injury, Mrs. P. then said she was interested in pursuing the suggestion that she receive occupational therapy as she felt she had to learn more about managing her household chores within her physical limitations. She agreed that she was much less apprehensive than after her first

hospital discharge and credited this to having received more explicit information from her present physician. She was also given, at the time of discharge, sleeping pills and a muscle relaxant that, unlike her first hospital discharge, gave her a feeling of continuity with her doctor and an indication that the doctor was still caring for her.

Discussion of Excerpts. This is a most interesting interview in many respects. To begin with, Mrs. P. has made marked physical improvement and not only is she happy about this but she is pushing herself to become more active and is actually involved in more activity such as going to the hairdresser. Since she is feeling better and functioning better mentally and physically, she seems reluctant to go any further with the exploration of the issues bothering her at this time. The worker respects her pace and does not push her to go on until she is ready.

What is also significant is that not only is Mrs. P. better physically and mentally, but she is now able to face the chronicity of her back and arm injuries. While in the hospital (second interview), she was depressed over this, but she has now been able to adjust to the reality and is able to accept what occupational therapy can do for her, which she could not do as recently as at the previous interview. A final important gain she has made is the capacity to accept bringing some of the comforts of the hospital into her home that she was not able to do before.

The factors that enabled her to make these gains included the support from the relationship with the worker; the worker's gentle pushing to help her look at the reality of her condition and the options she did have; and the worker's efforts to help her become aware of the way in which she handled her reactions to her physical limitations and the options available. The doctor's willingness to share more fully the information about her condition and to help her with arranging for the "hospital comforts" at home and the regularity of a homemaker were additional important factors in the gains she was able to make.

Excerpts from Thirteenth (Home) Interview.

Mrs. P. had experienced a flare-up of her back [problem] and felt it was purely physical, attributing it to a new exercise. Worker agreed that this episode could have been caused by the exercise but wondered if Mrs. P. felt that emotional causes had no bearing on or relationship to her back problems at all. At first Mrs. P. said that she could not see the connection. The worker reminded her of their discussion about her feelings of anger and she said that she thought the discussion had been very meaningful and very helpful to her; but she still seemed reluctant to accept the concept of emotional causes. Worker asked if Mrs. P. thought that it meant she was "crazy." Mrs. P. agreed that to her it carried that implication.

They then had a lengthy discussion about emotional effects and psychosomatic illnesses in general, and the worker stressed that in no way did she wish to convey the idea that she thought Mrs. P. was crazy. This obviously made Mrs. P. more comfortable and she seemed accepting of the concepts they had been discussing. Worker then reviewed their goals for Mrs. P.—to help her face her disability, learn to adapt to her limitations, plan for the future realistically, etc. Worker told her that at times she though she had made her angry. Mrs. P. interrupted to state that she understood and was in complete agreement with the things the worker was trying to help her with. She commented on how grateful she was, not only for the help she had received from the worker but also for the homemaker and the transportation being provided for her.

In regard to the worker's saying she thought she had made Mrs. P. angry at times, Mrs. P. denied this had ever happened and wondered why the worker thought she should have been angry. The worker explained that at times she thought she had touched on subjects which were painful to Mrs. P.; that under those circumstances she [the worker] would have felt angry and she sensed that Mrs. P. had been also. Worker also said that other times she felt that she had pushed her perhaps further than she cared to go. Mrs. P. again denied anger, agreed that the worker might have pushed her, but gave the impression that she considered this to be both beneficial and necessary as she described herself as one who needed to be pushed in order to make progress. . . .

Worker then asked if she had discussed her condition with the therapist. She said that she had and was told that she would never gain full use of her arm or hand although she would see some improvement. Worker asked how she had felt when told this by the therapist, and she said that she could accept it [because] she had suspected the truth about her arm for quite some time. She did discuss with the occupational therapist some areas in which she was having difficulty and was shown ways to overcome some problems and was encouraged to keep trying.

Discussion of Excerpts. There are three important issues in this interview. The first is Mrs. P.'s concern that having psychosomatic symptoms may mean that she is crazy. The worker's explanation and reassurance here are most important tools in facilitating progress. The second is Mrs. P.'s anger at the worker for having made her feel uncomfortable in the process of helping her uncover her feelings. The client is so quick to deny this that it is evident that she has been struggling with this and that it may have even been the cause of her recent back flare-up, although this does not come out in the interview.

Even though the client is not able to acknowledge her anger at the worker, the fact that the worker raises it with her and gives her permission to express it and feel it and the fact that the worker shares with her the information that it is a normal reaction serve to relieve the client and ease the relationship. The third issue is Mrs. P.'s eventual acceptance of never having complete recovery of motion in her arm. She had been unable to accept this as recently as the last interview. Here again, the worker enabled her to make progress, and it is so subtle that in this case she has not even connected the progress with the cause. It is not important that she do so.

Excerpts from Twenty-first (Home) Interview.

Mrs. P. was in excellent spirits and served tea. She and worker chatted about superficial matters for most of the interview, but Mrs. P. did say that she had told her physical therapist she was dissatisfied with her progress and the therapist was contacting her doctor to discuss other exercises. Mrs. P. was annoyed with her condition and was very pleased that she was able to express this, indicating to the worker that this was how she had urged her to act.

Discussion of Excerpts. Mrs P. is dealing with termination with the worker by having a ritual—serving tea; she has never served the worker anything before. She also expresses dissatisfaction with her progress, and she recapitulates their work together by demonstrating how well she is expressing her anger rather than holding it in and showing somatic symptoms.

Excerpts from Twenty-second (Home) Interview.

Mrs. P. was again depressed about her physical progress at the time of this interview. Worker said that she felt her general concern about her physical condition was not a recent feeling and wondered what had happened in her life recently to cause this depression. At first, [Mrs. P.] could think of nothing, and then she said her homemaker had not come on Friday afternoon and had not notified her that she would not be coming until mid-afternoon. Worker asked what the homemaker's not coming had meant to Mrs. P. She said she had been very disappointed and had been unable to do some marketing she had planned to do. . . . Worker said that Mrs. P.'s disappointment was certainly understandable and wondered what else the homemaker represented.

When Mrs. P. could not think of anything else, the worker asked whether when the homemaker did not arrive and Mrs. P. had to alter her plans she was reminded of her physical limitations and her dependency on another person (the homemaker) and whether this, in turn, led to her discouragement and depression. She agreed. . . . Mrs. P. then said that her children were coming for Mother's Day and almost immediately followed this statement with one about her dislike and dissatisfaction with her housing. There was a recapitulation of the discussion of the link between Mrs. P.'s children's reaction to her housing and her feelings about it, and again she seemed surprised to learn this but did eventually concede that perhaps there was some validity to the idea. . . .

Worker then discussed with Mrs. P. the possibility of her continuing with someone from the agency, which she had previously indicated she would be interested in doing. Worker explained that she had been exploring possibilities within the agency and had found a worker with whom she hoped Mrs. P. would continue. Mrs. P. questioned the worker's educational background and was somewhat reluctant but willing to try it. She gave the worker a small gift and a card. As the worker was leaving, Mrs. P. said that she really appreciated the worker's help in "sorting out" what was going on within her and wondered whether another person would also be able to help her. Worker assured her that she was not unique (which Mrs. P. disclaimed) and pointed out how much of the work Mrs. P. had done herself and could do in the future, especially since she now seemed so much more aware of the process.

Discussion of Excerpts. In this final interview, Mrs. P. again expresses her unhappiness about losing the worker by expressing depression about her physical progress. When the worker explores this with her, she talks through the temporary loss of the homemaker and about her feelings of loss regarding the worker and her dependence on the worker. There is another recapitulation of her ambivalence about the apartment, one of the early issues in the contact, and a discussion of her anxiety about the new worker. Worker gives her credit for doing the major part of the work in understanding herself and also points out to her how useful her new found knowledge will be to her. Mrs. P.'s gift is her way of saying thank you to the worker and is again part of the termination ritual.

Working on Tasks Related to Problems of Terminal Illness

The stages that most terminal patients go through according to Elizabeth Kübler-Ross are by now familiar to many people who work with the dying: denial and isolation, anger, bargaining, depression, and acceptance.[16] A summary of the highlights of each of these stages and their implications for working with the terminally ill person is presented below in order to trigger an awareness of some of the major issues in this area.

During the denial and isolation period, it is recommended that one allow terminally ill persons to deny the severity of their illness as long as it is comfortable for them to do so. Clues to the person's wish to deny include changing the subject quickly to one other than the illness and a tendency to be casual toward the discussion of the illness. Most people have a tendency to move back and forth between denying and accepting the reality. The best approach is to allow this by carefully listening to the conversation and watching the actions that seem to convey the person's perspective of the moment. During the period when anger predominates, the relationship of the sick person with the family and with those providing service can become very difficult since the anger is often expressed in an irrational fashion at anyone in the environment. Ample opportunity for ventilation with someone who is able to accept this anger is needed during this stage.

During the bargaining period, the terminally ill person makes attempts to delay the inevitable. Helping with the expression of guilt that the person feels both in relation to past misdeeds and in relation to impending death is important during this stage. Clergy can often be helpful with this. Bodily deterioration, coupled with the loss of one's ability to function in a job or at home, often precipitates the depression stage. Two types of depressions can occur. One is related to the present or to recent losses such as body disfigurement. The other is related to impending losses and to the final separation through death from loved ones. Reassurance regarding the sick person's self-worth will often help with the first type of depression. Acceptance of feelings and the presence of a caring person, without false reassurance regarding recovery, may help the second type of depression. Physical contact is also often meaningful in response to the second type of depression.

The final stage of acceptance is marked by an absence of feelings. At this time, people may need to be undisturbed by events outside of themselves. Nonverbal communication is even more important during this stage and the presence of an important person can offer the most reassurance, although a great many visitors does not. Some terminally ill people never reach this final acceptance stage, or not until very close to the end, and must struggle all the way through.

The importance of dealing with one's own feelings in relation to working with a terminally ill person cannot be overemphasized. A study that examined the attitudes and feelings of workers with terminally ill patients found that they tended to develop three types of coping mechanisms to deal with the strain. The first was a tendency to defend themselves against the disturbing content of their work by intellectualizing, by attacking the administration of their agency and the medical profession for shortcomings in dealing with the dying, and by avoiding positive feelings toward the dying clients and contact with the client's family after death.

The second manner of coping consisted of a struggle to understand and deal with the feelings evoked. These workers were able to recognize their reactions but had not yet learned to handle them as well as they would have liked. The third manner of coping was marked by the workers' ability to integrate work with the dying patient with themselves personally and philosophically. These workers were aware of the effect of the pain and were able not only to understand and to deal with their feelings but to find replenishment from both their work and their personal lives as well.[17]

The issues for an elderly person who is terminally ill are not appreciably different from those for a younger person. One possible exception is the elderly person who is quite old and has come to terms with his or her own mortality. For this person, death may seem somewhat less of a deprivation than for a younger person. An additional phenomenon that is worth noting is the tendency of elderly people to prepare for their own death often long before they become terminally ill or die.[18] This is a natural developmental task that should be supported by the worker rather than being viewed as morbid or abnormal.

The following case is illustrative of work with a terminally ill older person.

Case Number 8: Miss T.

Miss T., age 77, a single Irish Catholic woman, was living alone in an apartment at the time of referral. Her only relatives were a niece and a married sister living out of state. The sister came to visit periodically. Two sisters had died of cancer. At least one had died in a nursing home, where the client felt the nursing staff had been unkind to her. Both sisters and the client had had colostomies. The client had terminal cancer, and although she had not been told directly, she seemed to know it. Initially she was referred to a family service agency by the visiting nurse association, for depression, loneliness, confusion, unresolved issues regarding the colostomy, a possible drinking problem, and bizarre sexual fantasies such as her claim that she was sleeping with her doctor.

The client's initial perception of the social worker assigned to her was related to her experiences with the visiting nurses. She wanted the worker to give her an enema since the nurses would not give them to her as often as she wished. The nurses felt that it was better for her not to have them too frequently. The client viewed her colostomy as "that dirty thing" and described it as such. She also commented frequently on how clean her sisters were with their colostomies. Once the worker had made it clear that she was not a nurse and could not give the client an enema, the client asked if the worker could take her to the bank. The worker clarified that she was there to help with problems related to the client's medical situational, perhaps to obtain a homemaker or to help her get someone to go with her to the bank.

The client was then able to share some feelings and voiced her concern about the fact that there were only three left in her family. When the worker reflected this concern, the client talked of her will and burial arrangements and of preparing for death. She expressed regret over the surgery, concern over managing to care for her colostomy, and shared her ambivalence over the possibility of nursing home care. She was fearful that nursing home personnel would be unkind to her as they had been to one of her sisters. She preferred to live with her niece but the niece did not feel able to care for her. The client then began to mourn over her past losses, siblings and parents; she expressed feelings of being uncared for, unlovable, and unattractive and expressed her fear of death in a nursing home.

As she began to work through her feelings regarding going to a nursing home, she struggled with the reality that her niece would not take her. This was hard for her to accept. Approximately six weeks after the worker started to see the client, the client's sister arrived to stay for a while and help out. The sister was quite helpful and was able to sustain the client at home for a little longer. There was friction between them and worker's role shifted as she tried to help them with this, individually and together. The sources of conflict between the sister and the client were the client's drinking and the sister's "bossiness." Over the Christmas holidays, both the sister and the worker were absent, and there was a marked physical and emotional deterioration on the part of the client. She became disoriented and did not cook or eat properly, and she did not reintegrate as well as would be hoped when both returned.

Finally, the client felt ready for a nursing home. The worker located the home, took the client there for a visit, and went with her when she was admitted. Again, the worker's role shifted. This time the primary focus was related to the client's adjustment to the home. The worker also helped by dealing with the nursing home personnel. In addition, the worker encouraged the sister to deal with her guilt, anxiety, and anticipatory grief. The client was at first withdrawn and disoriented. Then she became restless and dissatisfied. Finally, she again became withdrawn, and shortly thereafter she died.

Discussion of the Case. One of the first pieces of information that comes out is the fact that the client's two sisters died of a similar illness after having had similar surgery. Knowledge of the manner of their deaths is of course going to produce intense anxiety in the client. If she thinks about the situation, she inevitably must realize that she has the same disease, has had the same surgery, is not doing well, and will eventually have the same fate as they have had. In spite of this, she has not been officially told by the doctor that she does have cancer and is not doing well, and therefore, though underneath she knows the reality, it is easy for her to vacillate between belief and disbelief, a common reaction even when the person has been told directly.[19]

The client's preoccupation with the dirtness of her colostomy shows that she infers that she is a dirty person, that others will not want to be with her and take care of her, and that somehow she deserves her fate. In contrast, she sees her sister as being clean and undeserving of suffering and death. Implied in this conception is the primitive idea that if terrible things happen to us, we are being punished for something.[20] The client has a drinking problem and some bizarre sexual fantasies. She may feel that she is being punished for either or both of these things or for other "sins" in the past.

In addition, we learn a second piece of information—that one sister had to be cared for in a nursing home and a very unsatisfactory one at that. The client obviously feels guilty about this, even though objectively there was probably very little that she could have done about it. This raises all kinds of horrors in her own mind about being in a nursing home herself, reinforces her ambivalence about going to a home, and may also serve as a source of concern that she is being punished for having allowed her sister to endure the nursing home experience.

The referral itself raises many interesting issues. There are many areas delineated as problems, and the worker must decide what the total picture means, how the problems are connected, which ones need addressing, and in what order. One could speculate that the client has been lonely for some time, from the history of drinking and also perhaps from the bizarre sexual fantasies. The primary issues that need addressing immediately are her feelings regarding the colostomy and her illness, what these reactions mean in terms of helping her plan for her future, and an assessment as to how much the confusion interferes with her functioning and her ability to plan for her own care.

Although fairly early in the contact the evidence of her confusion is obvious in such responses as her perceiving the social worker as a nurse, she is not so confused as to be unable to deal with her feelings about her illness and eventually to plan for her own care. She does need some supervision and some encouragement to eat properly, which could be furnished by a homemaker, but due to the delay in the doctor's willingness to authorize this and in the sister's arrival, a homemaker does not materialize. As so frequently occurs, once the worker shows a willingness to help with the concrete requests, even by acting as a liaison in obtaining the necessary concrete service, the client then seems able to share meaningful emotional material.

The client has indeed suffered multiple losses and in dealing with her own approaching death, the grief in relation to these losses becomes reactivated.[21] In mourning again over her lost relatives, especially the sister who died in the nursing home, she is helped by the worker to express not only her sense of loss but also her guilt, which in turn then helps her to face her own deterioration and ultimate death. This and the exploration of reality in relation to the unavailability of the niece both help her accept the necessity of eventual nursing home care. This is eased somewhat by the arrival of the sister, who does care for her for a short period.

While the sister is there, the worker need no longer play as nurturing a role with the client as before; and it is natural for the focus to shift to the relationship between the sisters. The fact that the Christmas absence of the worker and the sister produces such marked deterioration is both a sign of the degree of the spread of the disease as well as evidence of the marked integration of the body with the emotions, especially in elderly and ill people.[22] Perhaps the degree of deterioration also helps the client to accept the necessity of nursing home care.

It is important to be aware of the way the worker offers enabling support by accompanying the client to the nursing home for the visit and the admission and by playing a large part in selecting it. As the client withdraws, the worker puts more energy into dealing with the nursing home personnel so that they will not withdraw from the client, and into helping the sister deal with the impending grief. One must be careful during this period not to withdraw oneself from the client as a result of feelings that the client's withdrawal and impending death evoke.

Excerpts from Early Interviews Illustrating Client's Reaction
to Terminal Illness and Related Practice Techniques.

> The client stated that she had been next door all day having a crying jag. The worker responded by repeating the words crying jag and asking what had made her so upset. The client continued by saying that she didn't know. It was a strange thing to her. She had gone in to see the nurse and she was talking to the nurse about her illness and the doctor and her niece, and suddenly she got to thinking about her sister and the next thing she knew she was crying. She added that she wondered if the worker knew she hadn't cried about anybody since her mother had died. The worker asked why she supposed she was crying about her sister now rather than when she actually died. [Worker elicits more feeling through exploration and at the same time tries to clarify the real reason why the client could not grieve for her sister at the time of her death.] The client answered that she did not know. She supposed it was because her sister was so sick. The worker continued to explore and elicit feeling by reflecting that it was difficult to feel sad at the time she actually died. The client responded positively and went on to express more grief by saying that the worker was right. Her sister was such a beautiful person! It was such a shame she had to get an illness like this. She was such a clean person and always kept herself looking wonderful, never smelled at all. [Client is emphasizing sister's worth in terms of cleanliness, implying that the sister was a better person than she and inferring that the sister should not have been punished by dying.]
> The worker then attempted to clarify historical information related to the client's mother's death and to find out what was different about the grief in that situation. She asked the client if she cried right at the time of her mother's death. The client responded positively and continued to speak of many other losses. She said she cried at the time of her mother's death and that she wasn't the only one

who died—she had had a lot of her family die. Her father had died of an accident working on the railroad. They couldn't even open the casket because of the way he had been killed. Her mother had died 30 years after her father. He had been such a wonderful companion to her mother. Her brother had died in Ireland. . . . Then there was her sister Marion. She had gone in for surgery and three months later she was dead. Her sister Milly had managed to last quite a few years after her surgery, but after she went into the home, she died. The worker realized that the fact that the client's sister had died in a nursing home might have much meaning, and she reflected the statement in order to elicit more information and feeling.

She said she didn't know that the client's sister had lived in a nursing home and asked if that was before she had gone into the hospital. The client answered the worker, expressing more feeling, which finally led her to the crux of the issue that was bothering her. She said the sister had gone to the nursing home after the hospital, and added that it had been awful. Her niece and she had had a fight with the nursing home people the very day that the sister had died. . . . She added that no one told them, but from the way her sister talked about her illness— she didn't want to talk about it, but she thought this sister had the same thing that her other sister had and that she herself had. (When she said this, her eyes looked a bit misty and her hands stroked her swollen, lumpy belly.)

She then asked why this had to happen to her. Why her? Why not her niece or somebody else? Why had this happened to her? She asked the worker to look at how awful she looked. She stood up and indicated her belly with the big lump on the right hand side. She wondered what people thought. The worker responded with some support and a gentle push toward what she felt was the client's main concern. She said she didn't know that it looked bad. When the client had a dress on it didn't show that much. She then added that she did not think that this was really what the client was concerned about. She asked if the client wondered what people really thought was wrong with her. The client answered emphatically that she did. The worker continued by saying she did not think that they noticed very much and what was more important was what the client herself thought was wrong with her. The client responded with some denial by saying she did not know what was wrong with her. She added that something was happening to her but she didn't know.

Working on Tasks Related to Problems of Grief

Multiple losses for the elderly serve to strengthen their capacity for enduring stress and at the same time make them more vulnerable to successive losses. This means that elderly persons may tend to continue to function with amazing strength through a series of losses that are cumulatively taking a silent toll; then, with seemingly suddenness at the point of an additional loss that they find is just one too many, they may become seriously ill, deteriorate markedly in their capacity to function, or even die. The losses often cannot be prevented, but the knowledge that they are indeed taking their toll can help social workers reach out in offering supportive services and educating families and the elderly themselves regarding supportive measures.

Preventive supportive measures primarily offer elderly persons a chance to share their feelings of loss, their anxiety about the future, and any anger they have. The regular nurturing relationship with a social worker, which helps the elderly person sort out the issues and build in the necessary concrete environmental supports (from homemaker to legal help), can provide a cushion for future losses that will enable the elderly person to function independently for a longer period. It is with this as a backdrop that one can begin to look at working with the elderly person in relation to grief.

According to Erich Lindemann, acute grief includes the following symptoms: physical sensations, depersonalization, guilt, irritability with others, fear of losing control or insanity, and incorporation of the lost person (the last is a sign of abnormal grief but can be borderline).[23] Methods and activities that can be helpful in working with a person in relation to an acute grief reaction include the following: listening; the presence of a known, trusted person; education regarding normal grief; reassurance about the person's reactions; elicitation of the specific emotions that the person is feeling, such as anxiety, guilt, anger and sadness; repetition of feelings and their expression; a reliving of the trauma (how it happened); idealization of the lost person by the grieving person; and encouragement of rituals related to death. These help in the expression of grief and in the alleviation of guilt.

After the person has experienced as much acute grieving as he or she can tolerate, encouragement to make new investments in people and things can be helpful. If the social worker has helped with the acute grief reaction, even if the person is much better, the loss of the worker will often recapitulate the grief as all new losses are apt to do. This does not need to be totally negative, for it may allow more of the original grief to get worked through in the process of the termination.

A note of caution in working with the elderly regarding grief should be considered. Some old losses that have been buried for a period of time may not lend themselves to helpful intervention with an older person, for they may stir up too much that is extremely painful and cannot be resolved. Elderly people can be most helpful in determining when this is the case if they are allowed to regulate the degree to which old losses are raised and dealt with and control or shut off the process when it becomes too painful, frightening, and/or unproductive. (Refer to Case Number 4 mentioned under Defining the Task.)

It is also necessary to know the signs of abnormal grief so that a person may be referred for more intensive help if indicated. Signs of abnormal grief include delay of the reaction; distorted reactions or altered patterns, such as not feeling the loss; adopting symptoms of the illness of the deceased person; psychosomatic illnesses; substantial alteration in relationships to friends and/or relatives; furious hostility against a specific person; wooden and formal activity; lack of reattachments; irrational spending and the like; and agitated depression marked by insomnia, restlessness, and bitter self-accusation (in this last instance the person may be or become suicidal).[24]

The following case is illustrative of a grief reaction and how to deal with it.

Case Number 9: Mrs. B.

Mrs. B., a 65-year-old widow living alone, came to a family service agency with an original request for help in finding an apartment. The client had lived in her apartment for 29 years. Her husband had died four years before. Approximately two months prior to the request, a handbag snatching had frightened her; two days later, she had fallen and broken her arm. She wanted to move because the experience made her afraid to live in the neighborhood. She was originally seen in reference to her request for help in finding an apartment.

Exploration of this request, however, resulted in a decision not to move since the type of apartment available within her income was not what she wanted. At this point, she began to share her feelings of loneliness with the worker. During the next several months, she was asked to join a socialization group at the agency. She did so and enjoyed it a great deal. The group did not last for many sessions and several months later she again returned to the agency requesting help in finding an apartment. It was soon determined that she was still not ready to move, and contact began to focus on the loss of her husband and how this had affected her life.

Excerpts from Interview Illustrating Grief Process and Worker's Handling of It.

Mrs. B. stated that she was just looking at all the things she had in her house and thinking she would really need someone to help her if she moved. She couldn't do it by herself. If her husband were there, it would be different. . . . She felt in a rut. . . . She thought it was all due to her husband's death. She asked the worker to look at his picture. She went on to say she thought he was a wonderful man. The worker replied that it was a nice picture and that they both looked very happy [reflects feeling]. Mrs. B. replied that they were very happy. She added that it was not the same now that he wasn't there. The worker commented that she guessed it must be pretty lonely [continues to reflect feeling, encouraging more expression of it]. Mrs. B. replied that lonely was not the word for it.

She went on to say that he had died right there on the couch the worker was sitting on. The worker asked if it really was right there. Mrs. B. answered that he was lying there one night and told her to get someone to help him. She didn't know who to call. She called the doctor and told him her husband was all white and there was no pulse, and the doctor had told her he was dead. She guessed she had been hysterical. The ambulance had come, and he was dead already when they got there. The worker asked where Mrs. B. was when they took him in the ambulance. Mrs. B. answered that she was with him and that she knew that he was gone. The worker asked Mrs. B. what the worst thing was that she could remember about his death. She answered that the worst thing was that he was fine one minute and that the next minute he was gone. . . .

The worker asked Mrs. B. what her husband actually died of. Mrs. B. told the worker he died of a stroke. . . . She said that he had just gone to the doctor and that the doctor hadn't said anything unusual. She then added that she hadn't been the same since a recent virus either. . . . She said that she thought she had had a stroke too when she felt so bad . . . that her eyes were black and her skin color not too good. It had always been so good. She looked so white when she had the flu. The worker asked if that had really disturbed her. Mrs. B. answered that it was the color of death. The worker asked if Mrs. B.'s husband had looked that color when he was lying there, when he had the attack. Mrs. B. answered that it was and that it was a sallow color and that it had been horrible. She said that the color was like death. . . .

She said that it was the suddennes of it. He had been okay one minute and the next he was gone. She knew that he was gone. She had had such a good life with him. He had been such a good man (crying). She said she shouldn't think about him so much. It couldn't bring him back. She shouldn't think about him. The worker asked why, was it because it was too painful. Mrs. B. said that was the reason and she didn't want to brood [over] him. The worker told Mrs. B. that she said the word *brood* as though it were horrible to think about about her husband and to miss him [giving permission for grieving]. Mrs. B. replied that she couldn't bring him back (crying).

The worker asked Mrs. B. if she didn't think it was good to express her feelings about a loss like this. Mrs. B. answered by saying that many men died younger than he [defends against the expression of grief]. The worker answered that she knew that but that he wasn't just any man, he was her man [reinforcing the reality and gently pricking the defense]. Mrs. B. answered (crying) that she knew, but that it was not good to think so much him and to brood all the time. The worker replied that everybody was sad when they lost someone; some people got depressed right after the loss; others later; others never expressed their feelings. She suggested that maybe it would be good for Mrs. B. to be able to express her feelings. Mrs. B. replied that she had cried for two weeks after he had left. But it only really bothered her after she had the virus.

Discussion of Excerpts. Client begins with an expression of her difficulty in moving and reveals that what is really making it hard for her to move are her feelings over the loss of her husband. Worker, realizing this, encourages her to express her feelings to see if allowing her to grieve more fully will help her feel more comfortable and more able to do what she wants to do. It becomes apparent that one of the worst things about her husband's death was its suddenness. It also becomes apparent that her most recent reactivation of discomfort in relation to the loss of her husband was triggered by her own acute physical illness. The illness reminded her of her husband's death, particularly the suddenness of it, and frightened her, since she associated herself with him and worried that she might suffer the same fate. This association reactivated her unresolved grief in relation to the loss of her husband and further immobilized her by anxiety and depression. It is quite common for the grieving person to identify with the lost person.[25]

Working on Tasks Related to Sexual Problems

Sexual problems are common at all ages, and older adults are no exception. Problems for this age group are apt to be intensified due to a number of factors. Our older adults grew up during a period when sex was not discussed, when encouragement of sexual feeling was suppressed, and when sexual education was minimal. This has led to a degree of inhibition that will probably not exist for the next generation of elderly. Another important environmental factor is the negative attitude of society toward sexuality in older people, an attitude that many older people have incorporated. Society's attitude has also resulted in a lack of provision for any physical contact in institutions, where there is no opportunity for privacy, where men and women, even husbands and wives, are separated geographically, and where any behavior associated with sexuality either between residents or between residents and staff is not tolerated.[26]

In addition to these external difficulties, physical illness, fear of orgasmic failure, loss of a spouse or partner, a negative perception of one's aging body, and other emotional factors that deflect available energy or influence one's perception of oneself can also interfere with sexual functioning. Marital problems, long-standing or recent, and/or boredom with the particular sexual relationship are also commonly found among older people with sexual problems.[27] These factors call for special consideration of sexuality in dealing with an elderly individual. If there is a possibility that sexuality is an issue, it is valuable, initially, to give permission for its discussion, thus enabling the person to raise issues related to sexuality freely and without fear of condemnation or ridicule.

It is important to be cautious in evoking sexual feeling if the person has little hope of finding a suitable partner. Sharing educational information regarding sexual functioning in older people, the varied forms of sexual satisfaction, and the source of society's taboos can be useful only if the person is emotionally ready to listen. Cooperation with medical resources in clarifying medical restrictions on sexual behavior, if any, can be reassuring to the older person who might be frightened and reluctant to ask. Addressing emotional factors that are inhibiting satisfaction can be quite successful. This is also true of marital counseling. If the elderly person or persons are in an institution, it may be necessary to play an advocate role to improve conditions and attitudes in the institution.

The following case illustrates how a social worker can be helpful to an older person or couple in relation to sexual issues.

Case Number 10: Mr. and Mrs. A.

Mr. A. was in his late seventies, and Mrs. A. was in her middle sixties. This was a second marriage for both, and the length of the marriage was approximately ten years. The marriage had been mutually compatible prior to the husband's illness, and the sexual relationship had been satisfactory. Mr. A. was diagnosed as having severe heart disease and had been physically deteriorating for approximately two years. His physical deterioration resulted in lessened mobility, frequent hospitalizations, and diminished capacity for sexual functioning. Mrs. A. refused to have intercourse with him and was repulsed by his ejaculations which she described as diseased and green in color. He was unable to achieve orgasm and became more demanding of her sexually as she began to refuse him. He then began to accuse her of being involved sexually with other men.

Discussion of the Case. This case is illustrative of a sexual problem based on a marital problem that can occur with elderly couples. That is, the marital balance is interfered with by one partner's physical deterioration combined with the other partner's resentment of the necessity of caring for the spouse plus the spouse's diminished sexual capacity. This can be intensified if it is a second marriage, due to the couple's possible lesser investment in each other. Both may be less sure of the other's affection than if they had spent many years together. In this case, the spouse's illness also served to threaten the wife's defenses against her anxiety about her own aging, since it caused her to perceive her husband as old.

She did not want to think of herself as being married to an old man and therefore as being old or becoming old herself. The husband's increased sexual desire was a result of his inability to perform sexually and was also related to his need to deny his aging, his illness, and the concomitant threat to his masculinity. Therefore, the more Mrs. A. rejected him, the more he pursued her and the more he pursued her, the more she rejected him. The pursuit heightened her fears of succumbing to this "old" man and the degree of his intense need frightened her as she perceived it more and more as an attack and an aggression. He accused her of other liaisons as a defense against the realization that he was no longer worthy of her affection.

The hospital social worker visited the couple regularly at home as part of an outpatient team program seeing the couple together and seeing each person individually. (Individual appointments with the wife were held in the office.) The wife was encouraged to ventilate her feelings of resentment at the burden of caring for her husband and at his unreasonable demands and accusations. The social worker attempted to help her see what he was going through on an emotional basis as well. Mrs. A. was also encouraged to grieve for the loss of the kind of man he was when she had married him. Mr. A. was encouraged to ventilate his feelings of being uncared for and unappreciated by his wife. He too was encouraged to mourn the loss of his physical capacities, and the worker attempted to help him understand some of his wife's frustration and disappointment also.

Environmental resources were used so that Mrs. A. had some time each week to get out of the house while provisions were made to have someone stay with Mr. A. Sessions with the couple together revolved around improving communication between them, supporting what remaining positive feeling still existed between them, and structuring with them some guidelines for what they could reasonably expect from one another. The husband's paranoia decreased as did his demands for intercourse. The wife was able to resume being more affectionate and caring, and the marital balance was at least partially and temporarily restored.

Working on Tasks Related to Problems of Self-Care

Situations that are brought to the attention of social agencies quite frequently involve the elderly person's capacity for self-care. Referrals are often based on behavior that calls attention to the elderly person through its effect on others. The behavior may consist of one or a combination of the following: confusion over finances, suspiciousness related to finances resulting in nonpayment of bills, neglect of adequate standards of cleanliness regarding the body and/or the home, neglect of proper nutrition, wandering, misuse of fire-hazardous materials (such as stove, cigarettes), noisy behavior, and refusal to follow medical advice. Such behavior may have already led to problems, or it may during the contact with the social agency lead to problems with the following results: eviction; cancellation of heating fuel, gas supplies, electricity, or water; vermin; malnutrition; robbery, assault, accident, or fire; serious illness; and even death.

Since these situations cause consternation among people in the elderly person's environment and since there is often serious risk of life and health involved, social workers tend to have strong emotional reactions to dealing with them. Workers are often torn between doing what will help the elderly person remain satisfied and what society, pragmatism, and precaution dictate as solutions to the problems. Workers who decide to assume responsibility need to be clear where they stand on the issues and need to be comfortable with their stand in order to retain as much objectivity as possible.

In working with the elderly person under such circumstances, it is desirable to involve family as quickly as possible; if there is no one in the family willing to assume responsibility, close friends will sometimes provide help or information, or act as liaisons. A solid medical and psychiatric workup is essential for understanding the cause of the impairment of functioning and for establishing whether medical treatment will help. A positive liaison relationship with medical personnel is useful. If the worker is convinced from the start that the behavior of such clients is not injurious or hazardous to themselves or others, it is important to support their rights to their own individual life-style. In such cases, it often becomes the job of the social worker to educate others and to be an advocate with others in relation to allowing these elderly people to live the way they see fit.

An exploration of financial resources is often necessary, and a relationship of trust most easily makes this possible. Legal precautions and aids may involve conservators, guardians, and a clarification of legal liability and the elderly person's civil rights. Community environmental supports may enable a person to remain at home for a more extended period—for example, hot meals, homemakers, chore services, visiting nurses, and telephone reassurance services. Some of the problem-causing behavior may be diminished by addressing the person's depression, anxiety, and other related emotional issues. The worker's honesty, reassurance, and respect for the person's wishes insofar as possible, plus exploring and taking action on immediate concerns, no matter how insignificant they may seem, can open up the relationship and enable the elderly person to accept the services needed.

If institutionalization becomes absolutely necessary, the social worker must play a meaningful role in helping with the transition. Helping the elderly person accept the necessity for the change may involve dealing with the anxiety related to the change, with the fear that there is only deterioration and death ahead, and with the realization that there will be multiple losses involving possessions, independence, and relationships with familiar people. If the elderly person is sufficiently intact, grieving can be an important preparatory process.

Even when this is not the case, the elderly person can often understand more of what is happening than one would expect and can express more emotion in relation to it, even indirectly, if encouraged to do so. Helping any family members with the guilt feelings and helping to choose a suitable institution are indispensable in such situations. It is important to remember that changes tend to exacerbate deterioration in people with organic brain damage. Therefore, taking more time in the beginning to think through a plan is a better idea than acting precipitously and having to change the plan.

The following cases illustrate a variety of situations related to the issue of self-care.

Case Number 11: Mr. P.

Mr. P., and 82-year-old widower, was referred to a family service agency by the housing manager of a public housing project for the elderly. He was in the process of moving into the project when the manager noticed that he had been wearing the same dirty clothes during several contacts over a period of several days. The manager visited Mr. P.'s old apartment and decided that because of the condition of his belongings and his appearance, Mr. P. might not be capable of keeping himself and his apartment tidy enough to avoid attracting vermin, to avoid the wrath of his neighbors, and to prevent the deterioration of his health. The situation, based on the manager's experience, could cause eventual eviction, and to prevent this, she referred Mr. P. to a worker from a social agency. She hoped he could be helped to accept the necessary supports to maintain himself in his apartment.

Excerpts from First Interview.

> The worker began by telling Mr. P. that her name was Mary Brown. She wrote it on a piece of paper in big letters and he repeated it. She told Mr. P. that the manager asked her to see him and help him move in. She said she was a social worker and that she was going to work with him to help him get settled. She reminded him that the manager had told him that he had to keep very clean to live in the apartment. Mr. P. replied that he would keep clean if that was what they wanted. The worker added that the manager was very serious. The manager was planning to check on him once a week to see how he was doing and the worker said that she would be his friend and try to check on him too. She told him she did not work for the housing authority, but that she was a social worker. She told him he did not have to be afraid of her and that she was going to try to help him but that they would have to work hard together.
>
> Mr. P. replied that the worker should not be afraid of him either. He had been a fighter, but he wouldn't hit her. (They both laughed.) The worker added that Mr. P. would have to wash his clothes. She asked him if he saw all the dirt on his sweater and asked how long he had had the sweater on. He said for about three months. He then added that he didn't care, that his wife used to take care

of him like a baby, that he didn't always live like a pig. (His eyes filled up.) The worker said that she knew that it must be very hard for him without his wife and asked him how long he had been alone. He said that it had been about a year and that she had died on Christmas Eve. The worker then asked Mr. P. how long he had been married. Mr. P. replied that they had been married for 59 years; with the tears streaming down his face, he added that 59 years was not long enough. . . .

The worker later went on to say that she would come and see Mr. P. every week and that they could talk more about his wife. She added that sometimes it is really good to have someone to talk to and that it might make him feel happier. Mr. P. stated that he would never be happy again, never. The worker suggested that perhaps moving would make him feel better. She said he had a nice apartment and suggested that his old apartment must remind him of his wife a lot. Mr. P. pointed to the window and asked the worker if she saw the hill. He said he had been in the neighborhood all his life, . . . had moved there when he was eight or nine, . . . they used to slide down that hill in the winter. . . . He told the worker to look at all the clothes he had and took her over and opened the closet to show her that his clothes were clean but old and faded.

She replied that Mr. P. did have some nice clothes and that they now had to get him to wear them. Mr. P. offered to change his shirt three times a day if that was what they wanted, and he smiled as he said this. The worker replied that he did not have to go overboard. One a day would be good. Mr. P. asked if they had washing machines in the project. . . . At a later point, he said he didn't care if he moved or not. The worker said that she thought it would be a good change for him. Besides, she added, he couldn't stay where he was because they were tearing it down. She added that this was a good apartment with a good view; he could look out at the hill and remember some of the fun he had sliding when he was a boy—and it was good to remember the fun times. Mr. P. added that he would like to do that. There was a place across the street for dressmaking that belonged to his cousin. . . .

Later, he said that he was okay by himself and that he could take care of himself. The worker replied that she was sure he would do fine but that she was going to try to help him. She said she wanted to come and see him again next week. She asked if she could see him on Thursday or Friday. He replied that he would prefer Friday, if he remembered. Tuesdays and Thursdays were too much the same, and he got them mixed up; but Wednesdays and Fridays were better. . . . The worker told Mr. P. she was going to write the date down and leave it on his counter to remind him. Mr. P. asked her what would happen if he forgot, adding that he sometimes did forget. The worker said she was leaving the note right there to remind him and that she would call him up to make sure.

Discussion of Excerpts. Although a major issue in this situation is the worker's approach and activity during the first interview of the entry phase, the case is also an excellent example of how a protective service is handled while working on the task. The worker's use of authority (in this case the authority of the housing project) can raise questions. One needs to decide before even getting involved in such a situation whether it is appropriate to do so and whether the agency has the means to deal with this type of issue. Some agencies and social workers would feel they should not get involved because they would be taking on the housing authority's "dirty work" and interfering with the client's civil rights.

Depending on the judgment of the housing manager, this man may or may not be capable of caring for himself; and if he is capable of caring for himself, the social worker's intervention may very well be an infringement of civil rights. On the other hand, if the man is not capable of caring for himself (at least without some supports) and the social worker does not intervene, the man may end up being evicted and having to be institutionalized. Some social workers and agencies will at least do an evaluation before going ahead, in the hope that some preventive work can be done.

The social worker began by telling the client her name and writing it down in big letters. Since the client was hard of hearing and undoubtedly also had some impairment of vision due to his age, this was a good way of making sure the client knew who she was (reality orientation). It would also have been desirable if she had included the name of the agency. She immediately stated the reason she had been asked to see the client, making certain the client understood the purpose of the contact and enabling him to avoid confusion and concern. The worker was careful to separate herself from the housing authority in spite of the fact that she acknowledged the connection between them. Being new and inexperienced in this area, she emphasized the authority a bit too much. Very early during this first contact it became clear that the client was not taking care of himself, partly because he was still grieving over his wife's death.

The worker responded to the client's major present concern regarding the loss of his wife, and thus showed her concern for him as a person. She tried to show him how she might help him, both in terms of taking care of himself and by talking with him about his loneliness and grief. She tried to offer him some hope in relation to the new apartment, and he responded by reminiscing about his childhood in the neighborhood. She later referred to this reminiscence when encouraging him regarding the move, thus reinforcing his positive memory and association with the neighborhood. By the end of this interview, the client was already responding by offering his willingness to try to clean up for her. It would also have been helpful to discuss his wish for independence supportively. Evidence of possible organic brain impairment in the form of memory loss is evident from his concern over the date of their next appointment. Worker uses reality devices to help him with this.

Case Number 12: Mrs. J.

Mrs. J. was an 84-year-old white woman who was separated from her husband and living alone in her own apartment at the time of referral. She had no children, and her closest relative was a cousin who resided out of state. There was no legal separation but her husband had been out of the home for at least five years. It was unclear whether there had been contact between them during that time because client's reporting was unreliable and the husband could not be reached. Client was referred to a family agency by the visiting nurse association because she was having difficulty maintaining herself in the community due to poor financial management and her irrational suspicions of others. The visiting nurse association had also made a referral to have hot meals delivered and had contacted the local mental health center. The client had lived in the same area for many years.

As the contact progressed, the following information emerged: The client was receiving Social Security but was not currently eligible for Supplemental Social Security because of a modest bank account that was higher than the allowed amount of savings. Phone service had been disconnected for several months because of nonpayment. The client claimed that she did this because her husband came to the home and used the phone. She also had overdue gas and electric notices. She stated that her husband came and took her bank books and stole her money so that she could not pay her bills.

She had a $300 oil bill that she would not pay because she said that other people in her building were stealing her oil. She was therefore heating her apartment by turning on the gas jets full blast and leaving the oven running twenty-four hours a day. She had been a very active church member until several months before and had many close friends from the church and her neighborhood. However, she was spending her time in the house except for shopping. Without a telephone she could not speak with her friends and no one was coming to visit her. She had lost interest in the church and had succeeded in isolating herself.

She had been treated on an emergency basis at the local hospital for bruises from a fall that occurred in her kitchen. They had referred her to the visiting nurse association for follow-up because she had been brought to the hospital by the police several times before. They had been summoned by the client and also by a neighbor who had seen her wandering around the neighborhood in her nightgown at night. The hospital stated that her diagnosis included heart murmur, degeneration of the spine, and senile dementia with paranoid gestures. She was frequently confused and disoriented as to time, place, and person and showed evidence of memory loss. However, at other times she was quite lucid and appeared aware of her inability to manage or make important decisions.

Discussion of the Case. This type of protective service referral is often brought to the attention of a social agency. It presents difficult problems and requires resources that the community often does not have. From the description, it is obvious that this client cannot manage on her own. She needs substantial supports to control her finances and to obtain the necessities of life without jeopardizing herself or others. The client has just a little over the savings allowed to be eligible for Supplemental Social Security, and this prevents her from obtaining any protective service from the local welfare department. In addition, no one has the right to force her to pay for the things she needs unless she is declared mentally incompetent; and she cannot be declared mentally incompetent unless someone files with the court a petition against her for incompetency.

Mental health facilities do not generally do this nor do private social agencies. Legal aid and legal assistance organizations, which are set up to help poor people with legal problems, generally refuse to take such action because they perceive their responsibility as protecting civil rights rather than taking them away even when the person may be in danger if left alone. Thus there is often no responsible community agency that will take action to establish a conservator for an elderly person even when it may be in that person's best interest and even when it may enable the person to remain in the community for a longer period. This is indeed a gross injustice to the elderly. There have been a few agencies that have assumed such responsibility on an experimental basis with positive results, and their action needs desperately to be replicated.[28]

Working on Tasks Related to Intergenerational Issues

Most older people prefer to maintain their independence as long as possible and when this is no longer possible, they expect to turn to their children. The children expect this to happen.[29] Many older people do not wish to be dependent and they often do not need to be for a good part of their aging years. However, they do expect to have someone they can depend on, and they need this at times of illness and other crises.[30] Most adult children grapple with a change in their relationship with their aging parents during their own middle age. At this time, they must face the fact that rather than looking to their aging parents for strength and support, they are being called upon to lend their strength and support to the parents themselves. By so doing, they not only enhance the lives of their parents, but they also begin to prepare themselves for their own aging process. This is a normal, maturational, developmental task to achieve filial maturity.[31]

Whether or not it is desirable for older people to live with one of their children when they have difficulty managing on their own depends to a large extent on the history of the relationship. If the dependence-independence conflicts have been successfully resolved, both individually and between parent and child, and if the relationship is basically a positive one, living together will tend to be more workable; at times, the worker can help resolve past conflicts in a manner that will enable joint living.[32] At other times, however, the relationship is such that they should not live together. In these instances, however, the worker may be able to help them to resolve some issues between them in order to improve the quality of the interaction while maintaining separate households. The worker may also help them to accept this arrangement comfortably.[33] Contact with parent and child individually or together is a useful and flexible tool.

The following case is illustrative of the type of work that can be done with an older parent and a young adult child. This is a variation of the middle-aged child and aged parent combination more commonly found.

Case Number 13: Mrs. I.

Mrs. I. was in her early sixties, separated, and of Irish Catholic background. She came to a family counseling agency in relation to problems about her single daughter, Mimi, who was in her early twenties. Mrs. I. also had a married daughter, Sue.

Mimi had been living at home until approximately one year before. She left the area to live in another state but returned and had been living with her mother for the last few months. Mrs. I. was concerned because Mimi had been having sexual relations with her boyfriend without being married. She also felt guilty for calling Mimi a prostitute when she found out about this and for threatening to throw her out of the house. She feared her increasing loss of control over her daughter, which left her no important role for herself, and she worried that Mimi would move out and she would lose her.

She was lonely and concerned about her own aging. She was depressed and had trouble getting up in the morning. She asked for help, however, in terms of concrete needs and activities for herself and because of Mimi. She said Mimi needed help, was depressed, and was not eating right. Mrs. I. also felt guilty because she had pushed Mimi into seeing this particular boy at a time when Mimi was not dating and Mrs. I. was worried that she would not get married. Mrs. I. had been the middle child of nine children. Her father had been very strict, and her mother worn out from having so many children. Her father had beaten the girls for secretly meeting boys. She left home at an early age because of the family situation and decided that she did not want so many children. She did not marry until she was in her early thirties. Her husband started to drink and to beat her fairly early in the marriage.

She thought having children might help but it had not. She said she had a "nervous breakdown" when her younger child was about a year old and that she had been treated with oral medication by her obstetrician. She described another "nervous breakdown" about a year and a half before coming to the agency. At this time she was seen in an outpatient mental health facility. Mrs. I. separated from her husband when the children were small. He saw them for the first few years after the separation. She had not had a relationship with a man since the separation from her husband. She was concerned that Mimi should not make the same mistakes she had made. She was much preoccupied with her fantasies about the frequency of Mimi's sexual experiences with her boyfriend, feeling certain that they spent all their time in bed.

Contact. Mrs. I. was assigned to a social worker who saw her at the agency alone and together with Mimi for a number of sessions. The worker also saw Mimi alone. Shortly after Mrs. I. started seeing the worker, she and Mimi had an argument and Mimi moved out. This had apparently happened a few times before, but this time Mrs. I. refused to call her because she knew her boyfriend was with her. She was able to share with the worker her feeling of being left out by Mimi and her boyfriend, and with the worker's help, realized that this must have been the way her husband had felt when the children were born. She also missed going shopping with Mimi. She expressed concern about what Mimi would tell the worker about her.

In her first individual interview, Mimi was able to share with the worker her anger and guilt about her mother. She wanted to be able to communicate with her mother but felt that her mother did not allow her to do so. She was pessimistic about anything helping the situation, but was willing to try. In the first joint interview, Mrs. I. reiterated her concern about Mimi's sexual relationship with her boyfriend, and Mimi shared her feelings about how difficult it had been for her growing up because her mother was always sick and always telling her that she was dying. Mrs. I. expressed her guilt about the demands that she had made on Mimi, and Mimi, with the aid of the worker, helped Mrs. I. see some of the positive things she had given Mimi. Mimi voiced concern that her mother was more interested in her married sister than in her.

Shortly thereafter Mimi returned home. Immediately there began to be more friction between them over the same issues. During the next few sessions, Mrs. I. began to struggle with the realization that Mimi was "growing up," as she put it, and that it was natural for Mimi to want to be on her own. At the same time, she blamed her married daughter for forcing Mimi to leave. She also continued to express her guilt about her own marital failure and what connection this might have with Mimi's present actions. In the early joint sessions between Mimi and Mrs. I., Mrs. I. would withdraw or laugh inappropriately when Mimi expressed anger at her. Mrs. I. would deny her anger at Mimi. The one emotion she could express was despair and she did so by crying. It became clear that part of Mrs. I.'s concern about Mimi's marital status was related to her own girlhood fear of not getting married.

Mimi was only able to see the situation in terms of her mother's need to change. After a few joint sessions, Mimi moved out again. This time, however, she decided to move into her own apartment, and to do so permanently rather than just moving impulsively and temporarily only for a few days. During these sessions they were both able to see that the key issue between them was an inability to communicate. Mimi was able to show Mrs. I. that her situation was different from Mrs. I.'s experience at her age. In fact, she did have a good job and therefore did not need marriage for financial security. Mrs. I. finally accepted at least this part of the argument. As Mimi prepared to move, Mrs. I. tried to accept it. She offered to buy her a sofa, which pleased Mimi very much. She was able to talk of her own loneliness and her future.

As the time grew closer, Mrs. I. made it more difficult for Mimi by crying as Mimi began to move her things and by threatening to cancel the order for the couch. Mimi began to realize that she would have to do for herself many things that her mother had done for her. This helped her realize what a loss it was for her mother, who likewise would not have Mimi to do things for her. As the joint sessions continued, Mrs. I. was able to share with Mimi the fact that she felt badly about saying things that hurt her. She explained that she was so angry at the time that she could not help herself, but would feel terrible about it afterwards. Mimi was able to share with Mrs. I. how difficult it was to be totally responsible for her mother.

During the worker's absence over Christmas vacation, the situation again became explosive between them. They agreed that they had missed the joint sessions, which allowed them not only to blow off steam at each other but to understand the other's point of view as well. Both tended to downplay their positive contacts together and needed the worker to help them see these as positive. During this period, the worker helped them express their concern over how painful the treatment process was and also helped them feel hopeful about the outcome. During this period, the married sister began to try to undermine the relationship between Mimi and Mrs. I. As Mimi looked at the situation with the worker, they came to the conclusion that Sue had previously felt secure knowing that Mimi was at home taking care of mother. Sue was threatened by Mimi's new relationship with her mother, which allowed her more freedom, thus placing new responsibility on Sue to share obligations to mother.

As Sue adjusted to this new shift and assumed more responsibility about spending time with her mother, this further eased the relationship between Mimi and her mother. Mrs. I. continued to grieve over the loss of Mimi, but she began to accept her being out of the home and even her relationship with her boyfriend, though still insisting that she should marry him. As time went on, Mrs. I. and Mimi would fight over little things, but Mrs. I. began to try to accept Mimi's life-style. At this point, Mimi seemed to need help in becoming accustomed to the new relationship. They were saving their fighting for the joint sessions in the office and were getting along fairly well on the outside. Mimi was feeling very torn between her obligations to her mother and her boyfriend, who seemed jealous of her continuing interest in her mother. During these later joint sessions, Mrs. I. began to be able to express her anger much more directly than previously.

Termination was difficult for both of them, but more so for Mrs. I., who had fewer important people remaining in her life. She was able to review how she had changed and grown, though there was some regression, both on Mrs. I.'s part and in the relationship with Mimi. This was relatively short-lived however. Mrs. I. was able to express her feelings of loss regarding both the worker and her daughter and her thoughts about how they were intertwined for her. She reworked some old losses during the termination process—in particular, the loss of the psychiatrist she had seen at the mental health center. Both Mrs. I. and Mimi were able to express anger at the worker for not magically helping the situation more than she had. In a final joint interview, Mimi was able to tell Mrs. I. what kind of behavior alienated her, showing her that she did not want to pull away but that Mrs. I. often forced her to do so. Mrs. I was able to acknowledge how hurtful she had been at times. Worker acknowledged how the relationship had changed, pointing out that they would continue to be angry with each other at times but that they might not be so engulfed by their angry feelings.

Discussion of the Case. This case illustrates a number of issues. The type of intergenerational conflict that took place between mother and daughter was actually more reminiscent of a conflict of a middle-aged parent and an adolescent child than of an elderly parent and an adult child. Nevertheless, this kind of situation is not uncommon for parents who have a child during their middle years and find themselves losing the child (often a last child) during a particularly vulnerable time (when they have just begun to age). Mrs. I.'s preoccupation with Mimi's sexuality could be interpreted as a reflection of her own struggle with sexuality since Mimi recreated for her some of the conflicts of her own adolescence. She had never been able to achieve a satisfying and enduring sexual relationship and therefore feared that the same fate would befall her daughter.

Her preoccupation with sexual fantasies about Mimi and her boyfriend expressed her anxiety and at the same time fulfilled her unconscious sexual wishes. The mother-daughter pattern of relating to each other, with Mrs. I. withdrawing and Mimi being explosive and then withdrawing physically and then returning, illustrates the means by which they expressed their ambivalence in the relationship. Mrs. I. needed Mimi as an important source of emotional fulfillment, yet she could not forgive her for acting in a way that she thought was unwise and that embarrassed her. Mimi wanted her freedom but was not quite strong enough to establish her complete independence.

She needed her mother and also felt an obligation to her. The worker's flexibility in seeing them individually and together as the situation warranted was a valuable tool. It offered them support and an opportunity for ventilation and confrontation with each other, with the worker acting as mediator and interpreter. The worker recognized Mrs. I.'s need to grieve for her daughter and her past losses and was able to allow her to do this during the process. In some ways, Mimi needed to grieve for the loss of her mother as she broke away and set off on her own—though this was more subtle.

The degree of change achieved is also important here. There was substantial change in the two parties' understanding of each other and in their ability to communicate—but the degree of change was far from total. One of the worker's tasks was to help the client recognize the changes and accept the limitations inherent in the situation. The steps of the termination process show up well in this situation. Termination involved a review of the process, the expression of anger, regression, a recapitulation of old losses, and expressed fear of the future— all in relation to the worker.

Termination Phase

The final phase of the process-action model is termination. Although many issues related to termination are similar for individuals of all ages, there are special considerations in relation to the elderly. An awareness of what the worker experiences will help in understanding and managing one's own feelings during termination and thus will enhance one's capacity for helping the client with the process. If worker and client terminate because their work together is really over and has been at least moderately successful, the separation, though still replete with feeling, is often easier for both; the worker can gain satisfaction from the task accomplished and the knowledge that the client has emerged from the process in improved circumstances. If the client terminates before the worker feels the task is finished, however, the worker often feels inadequate and/or guilty for not having been able to help the client remain.

If the worker feels the task is finished but the client either does not agree or wishes for an extended relationship, there must be an attempt made on the part of the worker to help the client understand the reasoning behind his or her decision. If this does not help, the worker may rethink the decision and try to find another way of supporting the client following termination; or the worker may give up trying to alleviate the situation, though often with some discomfort. If the agency policy is such that the worker feels pressured to terminate before the worker feels the client is ready, the worker must struggle not only with the usual emotions involved in termination but also with an added guilt toward the client and resentment toward the agency.

As the field of social work makes a closer examination of the length of treatment and puts greater emphasis on brief treatment, termination is becoming a more common issue—particularly in relation to the elderly, who often benefit from maintenance of some sort of relationship after the "focused" work is finished. Attempts are sometimes made to find substitute sources of maintenance, such as friendly visitors. Some agencies have used a team of two social workers, one with more training, usually an M.S.W., who assesses the situation, and one with less training, usually a social work assistant, who carries out some of the direct service tasks and plays a maintenance role. The worker with greater training is thus freed for making assessments of additional clients and for returning to a particular client during a crisis.[34]

If termination occurs because a worker leaves an agency, the experience may be both a positive and a negative one. Workers may leave for positive reasons, but the separation from clients and colleagues can be a painful one that stirs up feelings of loss related to previous personal separations. In order to deal with these feelings, workers often begin to withdraw their investment from the agency some time before the actual departure. The effect of termination on the client is the other side of the picture. The reaction of clients to termination will often be influenced by the worker's reaction and the way it communicates itself to them. Clients may be anxious about their ability to manage without being able to depend on the worker. They may feel deserted, angry, and/or relieved that the pain endured during the growth process is ending. They may need to deny their negative feelings or to leave the worker before the worker leaves them.[35]

If clients are to be transferred, they may be anxious about reengaging with another worker, and in some instances, may be unable to do so. They will often review the process they have been through with their former worker and may regress to an earlier and less effective level of functioning temporarily. With knowledge of how worker and client are apt to react to the termination process, the worker will be ready to deal with it and to help the client deal with it. One of the most important considerations is to enable clients to participate in the decision-making process. The worker should help the client express feelings about the separation and should be clear about which feelings are the client's and which are the worker's, keeping them distinct from one another. The worker should be aware of the client's past experience with loss, since this will help in understanding the implications of the separation. Each client should be individualized, and a plan of termination should be developed on the basis of each individual's needs. Careful consideration should be given to all aspects of the transfer to another worker.[36]

The main difference between termination with elderly clients and others is that most elderly clients have already experienced multiple losses and often have less opportunity for replacement of important relationships. This sometimes makes them stronger and better able to cope with loss than some younger people are, but it also makes them more vulnerable to repeated losses, which are cumulatively taking their toll.

The following case is illustrative of work with an elderly individual during the termination process.

Case Number 14: Mrs. A. G.

Mrs. A. G., a widow in her seventies, was living alone. She had just returned from hospitalization for a heart attack when she was referred to a family agency by a visiting aide for help in her relationship with her daughter. The daughter had removed many of her belongings from her mother's apartment during the mother's illness and had withdrawn somewhat from the relationship. The mother could not forgive her for what she had done, and every contact between them resulted in arguments and mutual accusations. Mrs. A. G. was seen by a worker for a few sessions and then assigned to a student social worker. The student worker saw her regularly for a period of eight months, during which time she helped her ventilate her angry feelings toward her daughter.

The worker contacted the daughter and clarified the situation from her point of view. She also helped the client sort out the realities of the experience and deal with her feelings about it. It became clear that neither the client nor her children could accept her illness. The primary reason for this was that her illness created limits regarding her mobility and prevented her from playing a nurturing role with the children as she had done in the past. Gradual acceptance of her physical limitations with the help of the worker enabled the client to be less angry and resentful of her children. This, in turn, produced a more positive response from them. The worker helped her achieve this by encouraging ventilation of her angry feelings and by helping her look both at her past achievements and at her continuing worth as a person.

Excerpts from Termination Interview Illustrating Some Techniques and Methods.

> Mrs. A. G. not only looked well on this day but she seemed relaxed and calm. There was no barrage of complaints that had to be gone through. . . . The worker suggested that she seemed to fully understand everything that had been going on for the past eight months. She wondered if Mrs. A. G. was as pleased with herself

as the worker was. Mrs. A. G. answered that she was pleased and that she felt okay. She said she would not let herself be the way she was as she did not want another heart attack. The worker asked her if she could think about the worker's role in her life through all this. She replied that the worker had been good to talk to. She added that she did not think she would have anyone else to talk to who would understand her. The worker told her she would try to get her a friendly visitor. Mrs. A. G. thought this would be good.

The worker told her that people sometimes became angry when an important person in their lives left them. She added that if the anger wasn't expressed in words it came out some other way and their bodies were affected. . . . The worker suggested at a later point that she thought Mrs. A. G. was angry with her for leaving and concerned about how she would manage once the worker had left. Mrs. A. G. stated that she was not angry, and then grabbed a newspaper out of the worker's hands, thinking it was hers. The worker explained that the paper was hers and pointed to Mrs. A. G.'s paper on the chair. The worker then told Mrs. A. G. that she thought that what she had done was an angry gesture.

Mrs. A. G. looked sheepish, but she calmed down and admitted that she was a little angry. The worker suggested that they talk about it some more, that if they could talk about how Mrs. A. G. felt, they could then face together the real issues that were troubling her. Mrs. A. G. said that it would be all right, and then started talking about her health, swollen arm, therapy, doctor, etc. The worker suggested that she did not like being in poor health. Mrs. A. G. agreed and said that it was very hard. She said that she used to be independent and able to do everything for herself. She used to be able to go out and to be with people. Now she was like an invalid, always tired, and had no energy to cook meals for her children and their families. Her grandchildren were too full of noise and she couldn't enjoy them. The worker agreed that giving up her independence had been a major loss in her life. She said that she was trying to adjust but it was hard. . . .

The worker encouraged Mrs. A. G. to think about the pluses in her life. . . . The worker then asked Mrs. A. G. if they could talk about her [the worker's] leaving. She said she knew that they had done so during the past month and that it had been hard. Mrs. A. G. agreed that it had been hard, but she said she thought she was going to manage without the worker. The worker replied that she was a strong woman. The worker said that Mrs. A. G. needed to build on her strengths to continue to feel better and to function at a higher level. The worker told her that she had gained a lot of insight into her behavior since they had been working together. Mrs. A. G. said that she thought so too. . . . For the first time in months she did not walk to the elevator with the worker, an obvious indication to the worker that she did not need to hang on to the worker as she had in the past.

Discussion of Excerpts. At the beginning of the interview the worker refers to the barrage of complaints that they usually had to get through. This had been a pattern in most of the early interviews. She would have to allow the client to ventilate, with support, all the things that were making her angry that particular week, before they could go on to addressing the issues. The lack of complaints in this interview indicates that the client does not need to act in this childish way and is calling on her strength to act appropriately and to manage in view of the worker's impending departure. Worker tries to link the client's anger with termination and tries to help her see that if she does not express it overtly, she may become ill as a result. At first, it is difficult for the client to acknowledge her anger but, when the worker points out to her something she has done that illustrates the anger, she does recognize it and feels free to acknowledge it. It is interesting to note that when the worker encourages her to express the anger further, it gets expressed in relation to the basic problem that has been the source of her trouble from the beginning—her health, particularly as related to the need for dependency. The worker helps her express her unhappiness in connection with the loss of her physical strength and then supports her emotional strength, which the client now is readily able to call forth. The separation is carried further when she no longer needs to accompany the worker to the elevator.

Case Management

Case management is a valuable and versatile approach to meeting the service needs of the home-bound elderly and other people with complex situations that place them at risk of institutionalization.[37] Social workers engaged in case management work primarily with older individuals on a one-to-one basis.[38] On a day-to-day basis, they are likely to be at their desks only occasionally, for paperwork and heavy telephone use; their time is spent largely in the field. Steinberg and Carter have described "the client pathway" along with intervention processes in the case management process. They have identified fourteen client-level functions that are served at the five stages of the case management process; a distillation is presented here.[39]

PHASE I: ENTRY

Functions

Case Finding, in order to reach all the people who need help in maximizing their strengths and in obtaining multiple services in a coordinated way in order to live in the least restrictive environment and to experience a maximum feasible quality of life.

Prescreening, in order to respond to those who most need and can benefit most from the case management service, without inappropriate referrals or excessive waiting time, and to save older people and their helpers from undergoing a partial induction experience or waiting period that may lead only to a referral to another agency.

Intake, in order to engage the client in a dignified way to assure that the nature of the case management service is understood, demonstrate that the personnel are competent and trustworthy, and involve the client in the service. In many case management programs, intake is accomplished when the worker knocks on the door and gains entry into the client's home for the first time. Intake should also involve learning the client's expectations of the service, assure the person or kin of rights of choice and control, assessing the relative urgency of the case, handling any existing emergencies, notifying other previously involved agencies, and arranging appointments for routine next steps.

PHASE II: ASSESSMENT FOR CARE PLANNING

Functions

Assessment, in order to understand the client as a whole person and be aware of all aspects of the client's situation that threaten everyday functioning and longer term well-being. The case manager, in assessing the strengths and needs of the client's situation, should first observe the client at home. The skilled clinician will also use informal interviewing techniques or a structured assessment tool to assess the feasibility of various courses of action. Areas to be covered include assessment of which problem places the client at greatest risk?; on which problem is the client most ready to work?; which solutions will best fit the client's values and beliefs?; and what can be expected from the client's natural support network? As well, the client's mental status should be evaluated. After beginning with the client as primary source of information, the worker may turn to family and friends, physician's reports, medical records, agency case records, etc., for supplementary information; however, any of these should be procured only with the permission of the client. It must be realized that it is often impossible to arrive at a fully comprehensive assessment on the first visit.

PHASE III: CASE GOAL SETTING AND SERVICE PLANNING

Functions

Goal Setting, in order to develop clear expectations about what is to be achieved through the case management service consistent with the aspirations and preferences of the client. Case goals . . . must be operationalized in terms of achievable objectives, which in turn are translated into action priorities. Case managers may need to negotiate conflicts between client, program, agency, family, or inter-agency goals. Workers should recommend different intensities of service not based solely on physical functioning but should also consider objectives related to the case goals. For example,

- If the main objective is to maximize the client's potential for self-care, the amount of service may be kept to a minimum.
- If an objective is to strengthen the care giving of the family or friends, the amount of service will be modulated to fill gaps in care.
- If an objective is to reduce depression in the client and among family members whose physical or emotional capacities are stretched to the limit in providing care, the amount of service will be increased to provide respite.

Determining, specifying, and providing such gradations in level of care requires good communication about case goals and objectives between workers of different agencies as well as among workers in the same agency.

Care Planning, in order to arrange an individualized package of services suitable to the client's needs and values. Sufficient time must be made available to search out options and to engage all relevant actors in the planning process. The care plan should specify:

- the desired outcomes or objectives
- what is to be done by the client; what is to be done by family, friends, or neighbors; what is to be done by the case manager; what is to be done by others within the agency; and what is to be obtained from other agencies (in what sequence, for what duration, how paid, whether additional specialized assessment if needed, what desired but not available)
- what events will trigger a new step in the plan, reassessment, or revised plan

Capacity Building, in order to maximize the potential of the client and of the client's informal support network to function independently and when necessary to obtain, coordinate, and monitor services on their own. This may involve holding "network" meetings of relatives or friends, counseling or teaching significant others how to care for the client, referring spouses or adult children to services they themselves might need, arranging for neighbors to be paid as caretakers, and most importantly, teaching the client how to take over the referral and monitoring functions of the case manager and discontinuing services where they are no longer needed.

PHASE IV: CARE-PLAN IMPLEMENTATION

Functions

Care-Plan Implementation, in order to assure that high-quality services are found and delivered quickly and smoothly and that the client is suitably utilizing the available services.

Working with Client and Natural Support Network, including giving information about services to come; modeling behaviors in how to secure services; providing support or sharing responsibililty for obtaining services; helping out with specific tasks for clients; confronting the client with how he or she may be exacerbating his/her own problems; engaging clients and others in monitoring services in the home; and preparing for reductions or termination of services.

Working with Service Providers, including informing agencies about the case manager's work with the client; purchasing services; encouraging providers; monitoring service delivery; mediating conflicts between providers or between client and provider; acting as advocate or ombudsman when necessary to obtain or correct service; correcting records to reflect actual performance of providers; identifying and reporting barriers to service delivery; troubleshooting with landlords, utilities, tax officials, zoning, and/or sanitation departments; and requesting progress reports from providers as needed.

Working within the Agency, including informing ancillary personnel as needed; reporting barriers created by agency policy or procedures; making and updating reports essential for case records, administration, or evaluation; and obtaining consultation if needed.

PHASE V: REVIEW AND EVALUATION OF STATUS

Functions

Reassessment, in order to keep current regarding the status of the client and the suitability of the current service plan. Reassessment may consist of a full replay of the original assessment process, a partial update of the conditions most central to case goals or a continuous cumulative, incremental process. Need for changes may be revealed through reassessment, including replacement of one service by another, modification of intensity of service, or termination of service. These changes may be necessary because costs may be deemed unjustified or the service may not assure maximum independence commensurate with the client's condition.

Termination, in order to phase out the case management service when it is no longer necessary for the well-being of the client. Reasons for termination include: the client him/herself terminates, the case goals have been achieved, a single service provider accepts comprehensive responsibility for the care; the client enters an extended care facility, hospice program, or dies; the client insists on services which the worker thinks will be counterproductive or refuses recommended service plans or in other ways is considered so uncooperative as to waste resources or risk the agency's credibility or liability; the presenting problem has been alleviated and the case manager thinks that the client or caretaker can carry responsibility for the service procurement and coordination tasks; and/or demands for services and scarce resources make it necessary to set priorities among clients and withdraw services from those who can still benefit but whose needs are less hazardous than others.

Maintaining Relationships with Former Clients, in order to remain accessible in the event that case management services are needed at a later time. In addition, this helps to reinforce client achievements; track program results; support the ongoing service provider, if any; and giving "drop-out" or service-rejecting clients a second chance.

Given the functions and activities involved, it is indeed advisable to revise the term "case management" and call it "care management" instead.

Racial and Ethnic Minorities

As pointed out by the National Institute on Aging, "the number of individuals with ethnic affiliations is greater than the word 'minority' might imply."[40] Their figures show that "40% of the entire U.S. population over age 65 in the 1980s will be black or first and second generation Americans belonging to various racial/ethnic subgroups."[41] One result of the 1971 and 1981 White House Conferences on Aging was the recognition of the heterogeneity of America's elderly. Along with the "emergence of the older woman in her own right emerged an awareness of issues central to specific ethnic and racial groups. Social workers must carry this awareness into their practice through developing a solid knowledge base about the specific ethnic and racial groups their clients represent. They must understand ethnic-cultural factors (i.e., social differentiation based on such cultural criteria as a sense of peoplehood; shared history; a common place of origin; language, dress, and food preferences; and participation in particular clubs or voluntary associations."[42] They must also grasp the effects of ethnic minority status (often low social class, discrimination, racism, and prejudice) on their clients, and how they have become part of their culture and behavior in an attempt to survive in an often hostile environment.

There is danger, however, in lumping all members of any one ethnic or racial group together and assuming that each shares characteristics assigned to that group. Minority clients need to be individualized, even when dominant cultural themes are recognized and appreciated, lest individual and cultural subgroup differences be obscured. Barbara Jones Morrison points out that "this will be assured when practitioners follow the basic social work precepts of starting where the client is and understanding his/her needs in relation to where he or she has been."[43] Although "Blacks and Hispanics have emerged as political entities to be reckoned with over the last two decades,"[44] there is a tendency in America, reflecting our assimilationist orientation, to view all white ethnics as having "similar traits, problems, and aspirations."[45]

Often, ethnic and racial affiliations are correlated immediately with consideration of problems and needs. Social workers must be careful not to fall into that trap: there are also considerable strengths that many minority persons bring to their adaptation to aging. For example, adopting a negative attitude, a white social worker might make an a priori assumption that black elders would not be receptive to the worker's services and programs because they are suspicious of the white bureaucratic process, have an aversion to paternalistic treatment, and/or refuse to partake of services offered by an agency located geographically outside their community. In adopting this attitude, the worker misses opportunities to make use of such resources as the black church, social organizations, and schools as places to perform outreach and disseminate information about his or her agency's services and programs.

Several writers have general suggestions for social workers in working with racial and ethnic minority elderly: [46,47,48,49]

- Workers must respect the elder's interactional style. This may mean spending more time in initial interviews so that the client has "sufficient time to look them over."
- Bureaucratic coolness in interpersonal exchange is likely to antagonize some minority elders, while addressing a black elder by his or her first name may be regarded as demeaning and disrespectful rather than informal and friendly. Workers must be sensitive to the fact that their presence in initial contacts will be evaluated by the client in terms of his or her prior experience with authority and power, and may reflect experience with discrimination and oppression.
- The worker–client relationship should reflect teaching and learning for both parties. Thus, the worker recognizes that the client has much to teach by virtue of his or her age and culturally based knowledge, balances the precarious power relationship involved in helping, and contributes to the client's sense of pride.
- Zuniga-Martinez stresses the importance of working with minority aged within their own homes, which serves as a "leveling factor in the relationship and allows the worker to observe how environmental and familial variables affect the client."
- Use of eye contact and nonverbal cues should be made with sensitivity to the client's cultural and individual preference.

- Workers should assess the extent to which their clients have become assimilated to the majority culture.
- In general, minority elderly prefer intimate types of service provision (i.e., needs met by self or family). However, care must be taken not to assume that this is the case for any individual client, for, as Adams found, ethnicity alone is *not* a good predictor of service preferences. It must be considered together with age, level of education, cohort effects, and "family member living status."
- In general, it is important for workers to be aware that Native American, Hispanic, and other ethnic elderly play influential roles in their families.
- Social workers can do much to improve minority elders' access to human services, which may be limited due to language and cultural barriers.

Barbara Jones Morrison has provided social workers working with elder ethnic and minority group members with some guidelines surrounding issues of nursing home placement and residence. She reminds us that minority elders are more at risk of institutionalization because their health is poorer than that of whites. She calls for social workers to provide "extra" outreach and support to minority family members who are contemplating institutionalization of an elder because in such contemplation they must struggle to resolve value conflicts against strong cultural prescriptions that they should care for their own. She cautions workers not to assume that either (1) all-white facilities provide better care or (2) all-non-white homes are better for black clients because such homes are culturally congruent.[50]

Social workers on the staff of a nursing home must assess the extent to which the facility is committed to ethnic factors and cultural congruence. Jenkins provides a useful conceptual and operational framework for such assessment, which should attend to three major dimensions: (1) attention to ethnic factors in program content, (2) matching versus mixing of staff and clientele in relation to race and ethnicity, and (3) the extent of ethnic minority input at the policymaking level.[51] Regarding programming, the worker should look for routine use of ethnic foods, culturally familiar music, art, dance, and recreation activities; celebration of holidays important to minority residents; whether staff is routinely educated regarding the importance of attention to cultural consistency in program planning; and church services allowing minority members to worship as they are accustomed to. According to reported client preference, staff should generally be mixed racially/ethnically to reflect a stance of integration and humanity, and "matched" when language barriers are involved. Toward these ends, workers should seek to sensitize staff and administrative personnel to the importance of considering the quality of care in sociocultural terms, on an individual basis. This may include in-service staff training consisting of both consciousness-raising and concrete suggestions. Workers should feel free to consult with organizations such as the National Caucus on Black Aged, the National Organization of Hispanic Elderly, and the National Indian Council on Aging and should, whenever possible, enlist family members and volunteers from the ethnic and racial minority communities to plan social and recreational activities that are culturally congruent.

The Frail Elderly

Silverstone and Burack-Weiss have proposed a new moded, the "Auxiliary Function Model," for social work practice with the frail elderly and their families.[52] They define frailty as either temporary or permanent, partial or total, occurring largely in the old-old, and as "the functional consequence of reliance on someone else to fulfill everyday tasks once handled independently." They contend that frailty evolves as "depletions arising from the aging process itself (a general slowing down, heightened sensory thresholds that diminish input from the environment, the weakening of intersystemic boundaries that undermine resilience) combine with external losses (ego sustaining relationships and roles) to confound attempts at mastery." Their "Auxiliary Function Model" provides a means of adaptation to battling with diminished resources in the form of the prosthetic boost of a supporting environment that includes significant others, with a goal of "replenishment of what was and conservation of what is." Like "an auxiliary lighting system triggered to action by failure of a permanent system and fading when power is restored," interventions of the Auxiliary Function Model "fill in for and bolster areas of depletion." The auxiliary function is carried out through the medium of a relationship; emotional bonding and attachment are seen to be vital, along with fulfilling instrumental needs. Thus, the frail elderly sustain a "sense of control and meaningful connection to the mainstream of life which makes survival worth the effort." The social worker may perform the auxiliary role alone, but more often, he or she assists significant others in assuming the role or shares the role with them. Establishing the client's trust in the worker, engaging him or her affectively (developing a therapeutic worker–client relationship), and possibly making concrete interventions during the process, the social worker undertakes a *study*, *assessment*, and *plan* on behalf of the client. This process is outlined below.[53]

OUTLINE OF STUDY, ASSESSMENT, AND PLAN
1. Study
   A. Overview
      1. Presenting problem and precipitating event
      2. Referral source
      3. Client profile (fact sheet)
         a. Age, sex, marital status, race, religion
         b. Family constellation
         c. Socioeconomic and cultural influences
         d. Environmental influences
      4. Client and family behavior in interview situation
      5. Professional contacts and consultation arranged
   B. Depletion and losses
      1. Primary: physical and mental
      2. Secondary: social and economic
   C. Current adaptation (restitution, compensation, and/or accommodation)
      1. Individual functioning
         a. Activities of daily living

        b. Problem-solving capacities
        c. Affective and interpersonal behaviors
     2. Environmental functioning
        a. Physical surroundings
        b. Family: resources and problem-solving capacity
        c. Service organizations
        d. Other informal resources
   D. Previous adaptation
     1. Developmental and situational crises
     2. Life-style
     3. Family exchange patterns
2. Assessment
   A. Summary of study
   B. Interpretation: reformulation of problem
3. Plan
   A. Long range objectives
   B. Short range goals
   C. Social work tasks

Disabled Elderly

Diminuition of the senses, physical dexterity, and cognitive abilities come with aging for many adults. In fact, some elderly persons become functionally disabled by these losses. Certain elderly persons, however, have dealt with disabilities *throughout* their entire lives. Elderly blind, physically handicapped, and retarded persons may have special needs and problems as they age, and gerontological social workers must become conversant with the issues of these populations. Each is discussed in turn below.

Developmentally Disabled Elderly. Seltzer and Seltzer comment that the elderly mentally retarded and their families are a recently identified subgroup requiring and receiving social work intervention.[54] Janicki et al. caution practitioners not to stereotype this group.[55] They remind us that older developmentally disabled persons are as diverse a group as are nonretarded older persons, and that the service needs of each are unique and must be met on an individual basis. Although many developmentally disabled persons enter into "aging" status earlier than most nondisabled adults (approximately mid-forties to mid-fifties), improved medical services and health care technologies have increased their life span. Seltzer and Seltzer estimate that there are roughly 1,100,000 to 1,400,000 retarded adults over 55 in the United States.[56] To ensure adequate services for this group, Janicki et al. argue that there is a need "both [to] improve the accessibility of generic aging services for developmentally disabled persons and to develop and maintain specialized services" that address their needs.[57] Most mentally retarded persons live in the community, either with relatives or friends, or alone. Contrary to popular belief, no more than 5 percent of the general mentally retarded population has even been institutionalized.[58]

Integrated case management is indicated with these clients because services most likely will have to be obtained from various agencies and possibly even different care systems. Special services may include providing supports to aging parents or other caretakers of the elderly retarded; guardianship and protective services; assistance with obtaining health care, transportation, and access to entitlement programs; client advocacy; attention to emotional needs; and provision of opportunities for socialization. Social workers with older mentally retarded clients should arrange for the provision of services and structuring of environments to maximize the maintenance of functional skill levels. As well, awareness of *potential* problems and anticipatory planning allows for provision of less traumatic interventions. For example, particularly urgent for many older retarded adults is the threat of having to leave their living situation through the aging or death of parents or caretakers, or through diminished ability to care for themselves. Social workers can assist their clients and clients' families achieve peace of mind by engaging in "permanency planning" with them, with the goal of "assuring as secure a lifestyle as possible for the elderly retarded person until he or she dies";[59] this can often include "1) residential security, 2) legal protection, and 3) financial security"[60] as well as working with client and family around issues of separation.

Blind or Visually Impaired Elderly. Most blind people in the United States are over age 65, yet the blind service system was designed and developed to meet the needs of young and employable adults,[61] and it can take up to six months for older adults to obtain rehabilitation services from blind system agencies. Visual problems and most eye diseases progress with age, and many elderly do not recognize visual impairment until it has progressed dramatically. Social workers can be instrumental in facilitating the early detection, diagnosis, and treatment of visual problems; in many cases, educating elder service providers can prevent blindness in clients. Social workers can pave the way for coordination between the elderly service and blind service networks as well.

Poor vision in old age need not be a catastrophe. Changes in the home environment and counseling can often enable the elderly blind or visually impaired person to function normally. Irving Dickman's excellent guidebook *Making Life More Livable*[62] details such adaptations, may of which are quite simple but may make all the difference in the world. Dickman informs us that "each type of vision impairment creates a different kind of seeing problem and that acuity scores are little help in determining the needs of a specific individual."[63] Workers should consider the amount and type of visual loss, what the home is like, and the individual's life-style. They should also make sure to involve the older person in deciding on adaptations to be made in the home and allow the client to reject suggestions for any reason. In working with older blind and visually impaired clients, social workers should remove hazards and obstacles from the home environment, e.g., assure that doors are not left ajar, cover dangerously slick floor coverings or secure protruding rug corners or edges, and provide optical aids, including task-oriented devices (such as needle threaders or large-size, large-print playing cards).

It is important to keep solutions as simple as possible, on the theory that the more complicated the solution, the less likely that it will be used. Workers must also take the time and effort necessary to train clients in making optimal use of adaptations, help to restore lost self-confidence to visually impaired elderly clients, and be sensitive to the immense energy it may take clients to get through the day maneuvering through an environment that, because it cannot be seen, is threatening. Social workers must also help clients to "widen their life space" and spectrum of activities, which may well have narrowed drastically because of visual loss. Finally, they should not neglect to counsel family, friends, and other service providers that impaired vision is not a sign of failing memory or reduced intelligence: such attitudes can needlessly rob people of dignity and even lead to unnecessary institutionalization.

Physically Handicapped Elderly. The physically handicapped elderly person, like the visually impaired elder, can benefit greatly from alterations or adaptations in his or her environment. For example, care should be taken to assure that the home is free of barriers. The social worker can facilitate such changes as installing ramps and widening doorways to accommodate wheelchairs, installing safety rails and higher toilets in bathrooms, or adjusting the level of knobs on cabinets. As well, the worker should help the older client to adjust functionally and psychologically to the changes.

Older physically handicapped persons, especially those who have been confined to a wheelchair for a long time, exhibit a higher rate of physical deterioration sooner than nondisabled adults. The social worker's role is to help these adults deal with increased disability as they age and to ensure their access to entitlements they require. It may actually be easier for older disabled persons to adjust to decreased functioning and increased dependence because they have had to deal with some degree of functional disability throughout life (Janicki, personal communication). The lifelong disabled person, then, may serve as a positive role model in support groups for newly disabled elders.

Hospice

The basic goals of the modern hospice are to allow the chronically ill patient to retain individuality and dignity and to experience maximum levels of comfort and mental clarity while sick and dying. The hospice replaces the American tradition of curing the patient at all costs (i.e., in acute care hospitals, the staff often ignores or avoids dying patients because they are perceived as failures) with caring for individuals and their families through easing physical, emotional, and spiritual pain. The basic components of hospice care are physician-directed services, care provision by an interdisciplinary team, pain control, around-the-clock services, and bereavement counseling. All components are aimed at providing a "comprehensive continuum of care for the patient and the family." Hospices focus on the patient and family as one unit. The hospice philosophy holds that if possible, the patient should remain at home surrounded by loved ones and possessions; if this is not possible, care is provided in a homelike in-patient setting. Hospice care may last for several days to several months; it averages about two weeks. Nina Millett, in *Hospice Care: Principles and Practice*, points out that the values, concepts, and goals of the hospice movement are highly consonant with those of the social work profession.[64] She details the rich and varied roles available to social workers in the modern hospice: providing direct service and advocacy to patients and families, collaboration and consultation, . . . education, and becoming involved in "policy and planning, research, and legislation."

In direct service with patients and families, social workers help their clients negotiate a "constant assault [of] losses of all types, both real and anticipated." These include the three major areas of loss—privacy, body image, and relationships—and may involve an infinite number of "little deaths." Patients also often face financial difficulties, fear and anxiety about the course of the disease, changes in communication patterns with spouse and other family members and friends, increased demands on others for care, sexual concerns, and feelings of worthlessness due to their inability to carry out familiar roles within the family. Social workers are trained to realize that all these problems necessarily compound existing problems and difficulties, which become exacerbated by the enormous strain imposed by terminal illness; workers can assure that all these factors are considered in all aspects of patient and family care. Direct service in a hospice setting requires competence in strategies of crisis intervention, short- and longer-term casework, patient advocacy, provision for concrete needs, and basic physical care procedures. As well, workers must be willing and able to work as an integral part of a team: in the hospice, teamwork "is more than a concept or an ideal—the interdisciplinary team must function as a cohesive unit." Formal team meetings are held weekly and informal conferences occur almost daily. Close teamwork provides a "mutual support system for staff members" as well as opportunities for revising care plans in response to "rapid changes in either the patient's physical condition or the emotional condition of family members." In the context of close teamwork, roles of staff members inevitably blur, especially in the home setting. Finally, Millett cautions that social workers choosing to work in the hospice must be able to handle large amounts of uncertainty and the rapid changes that are sure to occur in such areas as "physical condition of the patient, family members' emotional and physical health, and schedules."

Working with Individual Persons in Institutions

Services Related to the Application for Admission

Institutionalization produces a crucial change in the life of a person and his or her family. It precipitates multiple losses in relation to people, pride in possessions, and waning independence. People about to be institutionalized need help to express anger and grief, accept the situation, and make the best use of their ability to function throughout the process. At the beginning of the application procedure, they may be anxious and feel rejected by their family; the family, in turn, may feel guilty and ashamed, but at the same time, they may want the older person taken care of by others. The older person and the family should be helped to participate as fully as possible in the entire process.[65]

Counseling can help the person and the family decide whether long-term care is the most appropriate plan and choose specific facilities for this care if indicated. An assessment of the older person's physical and mental health as well as the level of his or her capacity to function is essential to the application process. Decisions involve the appropriateness of long-term care, what type of facility is most desirable, and plans for interim care. The establishment of goals for the person after admission to the institution is equally important. Screening to suit a particular older person to a particular facility should be based on the age, residence, health, and social requirements that justify the older person's need for this type of facility.[66]

If the person is refused, it is important to help him or her understand the reasons for refusal and the feelings this experience elicits. The person and the family also need help in finding other resources for counseling and care. If a person has to wait an extended period for admission it is helpful to keep in touch with the person and the family in order to help with stress during this time. When the person is actually admitted, it is important to help prepare him or her and the family for the move by reviewing the decision in favor of the institution, by reassessing the person's capacities to function, by planning a medical examination, and by reviewing financial plans. Residents and staff should also be prepared for the new arrival and a warm welcome should be provided.[67]

Ongoing Services after Admission

Information regarding available services and help in using them on a continuing basis should be readily available. The staff must help the person continue his or her ties with the community insofar as possible. The person should be helped to maintain previous roles or to find new ones. Additional areas that require help include information about and adjustment to important changes within the institution, relationship problems in and out of the institution, feelings related to bodily changes, behavior problems, adjusting to routines and accepting essential services, and personality changes. Family members are likely to need help with separation, anxiety, guilt, and concern over the person's condition and care. Collaboration with members of the staff of the institution and with collateral people in the community is an important part of the job of the social worker in an institution.[68] A final important role for the social worker is related to the dying resident and his or her family, and to the family after the death of the resident. (For more information in relation to working with the terminally ill and with grief, refer to the earlier sections under Working on the Task.)

The following example is illustrative of social work with an elderly person in an institutional setting.

Case Number 15: Mr. W.

Mr. W. was a black man in his middle sixties, separated from his wife and children. He had grown up in the South and had worked mostly at unskilled jobs, moving around a great deal and coming north in the hope of improving his economic situation. He had a heart condition, circulatory problems, and cataracts. At the time of referral, he was in a nursing home because of his physical problems. He was referred to an outreach social worker from a community agency because of his withdrawn behavior and his refusal to agree to the amputation of a leg, which had been recommended because of his circulatory problems. He had a history of heavy drinking, but this was not a current issue at the time of the referral. He was unhappy in the nursing home, spoke often about leaving, and had a history of having been admitted to a number of nursing homes over a period of years, staying for a limited period, and then leaving. He wore two or three layers of clothing at a time and wrapped his belongings in several layers of napkins.

At the beginning of the contact with the worker, he seemed withdrawn and would not even engage in conversation until the worker had performed concrete services for him, such as buying him cigarettes with his money or filling his water pitcher for him. His initial conversation was extremely superficial and distant, and once he began talking, he could talk in this manner incessantly. Gradually, he began to reminisce about his early life, then to share his anger at some of the people in the nursing home, even at the worker. He began to leave his room occasionally after considerable encouragement and reassurance from the worker. Eventually, he began to talk about his fears regarding the amputation of his leg. He also could acknowledge some of the good things that happened to him in the nursing home. Thus, there began to be progress in a number of areas.

Discussion of the Case. This vignette is an example of the work that can be done in an institutional setting, either by a social worker from within the institution or from the outside. This man might never have been seen by a social worker were it not for outreach, unless a social worker in the nursing home had had the time, the skill, and the commitment to perform a similar outreach function. This situation illustrates the need to respond to seemingly unimportant concrete requests by a client to establish a caring relationship that will permit further involvement.

With this man's history of frequent unsatisfactory institutionalizations and the degree of his withdrawal, it is important to note the degree of his potential for involvement with the social work relationship and his potential for movement in becoming more engaged in his environment. The withdrawal manifested by the way he dressed himself and the way he covered his belongings is a protective defense against what he sees as a hostile, dangerous environment. There may very well be pathological problems at work here. However, it is essential to be aware of some of the factors operating within the institutional environment that may be intensifying the need for this type of functioning. Such factors are impersonalization, confinement, exposure to more deteriorated patients, isolation from familiar people and places, and the knowledge that most patients who enter never come out. *

References

1. Annette Garrett, *Interviewing: Its Principles and Methods* (New York: Family Welfare Association of America, 1950), p. 28.
2. Florence Hollis, *Casework: A Psychological Therapy* (New York: Random House, 1972), pp. 89, 90–94, 96–97, 98, 103–104.
3. Butler and Lewis, op. cit., p. 138.
4. C. Paul Brearley, *Social Work: Aging and Society* (London: Routledge & Kegan Paul, 1975), pp. 54–59.
5. Butler and Lewis, op. cit., p. 140; and Brearley, op. cit., pp. 56–58.
6. Brearley, op. cit., p. 8.
7. Alvin I. Goldfarb, "Psychodynamics and the Three-Generation Family," in Ethel Shanas and Gordon F. Streib (eds.), *Social Structure and the Family* (Englewood Cliffs, N.J.: Prentice-Hall, 1965), p. 37.
8. Allen Pincus, "Reminiscence in Aging and Its Implications for Social Work Practice," reprinted from *Social Work*, vol. 15 (July 1970), pp. 47–53 (Washington, D.C.: NASW, 1970), p. 3.
9. Arthur W. McMahon and Paul Rhudick, Jr., "Reminiscing—Adaptational Significance in the Aged," *Archives of General Psychiatry*, vol. 10 (March 1964), pp. 292–298, as cited in A. Pincus, op. cit., pp. 2–4.
10. Allen Pincus, op. cit., pp. 5–6.
11. Robert Butler and Myrna Lewis, *Aging and Mental Health* (St. Louis: Mosby, 1973), pp. 63–64.
12. Fernando Henriques, *Family and Colour in Jamaica* (London: Eyre and Spottiswoode, 1953), pp. 106–107.
13. W. J. Gardner, *A History of Jamaica from Its Discovery by Christopher Columbus to the Year 1972* (London: Frank Cass, 1971), p. 183.
14. Charlotte Babcock, "Inner Stress in Illness and Disability," in Howard J. Parad and Roger R. Miller (eds.), *Ego-Oriented Casework* (New York: Family Service Association of America, 1963), pp. 45–64.
15. Ibid.
16. Elizabeth Kübler-Ross, *On Death and Dying* (New York: Macmillan, 1964), pp. 38–137.
17. Anne Tull, "The Stresses of Clinical Social Work with the Terminally Ill," *Smith College Studies in Social Work*, vol. XLV, no. 2 (February 1975), pp. 137–158.
18. Robert Peck, "Psychological Developments in the Second Half of Life," in John E. Anderson (ed.), *Psychological Aspects of Aging* (Washington, D.C.: APA, 1956), p. 48.
19. Kübler-Ross, op. cit., p. 41.

* For further reading on working with older persons in institutions, see Elaine Brody's *Social Work Guide for Long-Term Care Facilities* (Rockville, Md: NIMH Publications, 1974). Subsequently expanded into a book: Elaine Brody, *Social Work in Long Term Care.*

20. Ibid., p. 32.
21. Arthur C. Carr, "A Lifetime of Preparation for Bereavement," *Archives of the Foundation of Thanatology* (New York: The Foundation of Thanatology, 1969), pp. 14–18.
22. Butler and Lewis, op. cit., pp. 63–64.
23. Erich Lindemann, "Symptomatology and Management of Acute Grief," *American Journal of Psychiatry*, September 1944, pp. 141–148.
24. Ibid.
25. K. Abraham (1924), "A Short Study of the Development of the Libido Viewed in the Light of Mental Disorders," *Selected Papers on Psychoanalysis*, vol. 1 (New York: Basic Books, 1954), pp. 418–501, cited in Ralph J. Kahana, "Grief and Depression," *Journal of Geriatric Psychiatry*, vol. VII, no. 1 (1974), p. 28.
26. Irene Mortenson Burnside, "Sexuality and Aging," in I. M. Burnside (ed.), *Sexuality and Aging* (University of Southern California Press, 1975), pp. 42–53.
27. Alexander Runciman, "Problems Older Clients Present in Counseling about Sexuality," in I. M. Burnside, op. cit., pp. 54–56.
28. Leon D. Fisher and Jeffrey R. Solomon, "Guardianship: A Protective Service Program for the Aged," *Social Casework*, December 1974, pp. 618–621.
29. Ethel Shanas, *The Health of Older People: A Social Survey* (Cambridge, Mass.: Harvard University Press, 1962), as cited in M. Blenkner, "Social Work and Family Relationships in Later Life with Some Thoughts on Filial Maturity," in Ethel Shanas and Gordon F. Steib, eds., *Social Structure and the Family* (Englewood Cliffs, N.J.: Prentice-Hall, 1965), p. 48.
30. M. Blenkner, op. cit., pp. 57–58.
31. Ibid.
32. Jean M. Leach, "The Intergenerational Approach in Casework with the Aging," *Social Casework*, vol. XLV, no. 3 (March 1964), pp. 144–149.
33. Ibid., pp. 146–148.
34. Marcella Farrar and Mary L. Hemmy, "Use of Nonprofessional Staff in Work with the Aged," pp. 1–7, reprinted from *Social Work*, vol. 8 (July 1963), pp. 44–50.
35. Sidney Z. Moss and Miriam S. Moss, "When a Caseworker Leaves an Agency: The Impact on Workers and Client," *Social Casework* (July 1967), pp. 433–437.
36. Ibid.
37. Raymond M. Steinberg and Genevieve W. Carter, *Case Management and the Elderly* (Lexington, Mass.: Lexington Books, 1983), pp. 1–32.
38. Ibid.
39. Ibid., p. 222–234.
40. National Institute on Aging, *Age Page* (Bethesda, Maryland, 1980).
41. Ibid.
42. Carol S. Holzberg, "Ethnicity and Aging: Rejoinder to a Comment by Kyriakos S. Markides," *The Gerontologist*, vol. 22, no. 6 (1982), pp. 471–472.
43. Barbara Jones Morrison, "Sociocultural Dimensions: Nursing Homes and the Minority Aged," *Journal of Gerontological Social Work*, vol. 5, nos. 1/2 (fall/winter 1982), pp. 127–145.
44. Kyriakos S. Markides, "Ethnicity and Aging: A Comment," *The Gerontologist*, vol. 22, no. 6 (1982), pp. 467–470.
45. Ibid.
46. Maria Zuniga-Martinez, "Social Treatment with the Minority Elderly," in R. L. McNeely and John L. Colen (eds.), *Aging in Minority Groups* (Beverly Hills, Calif.: Sage Publications, 1983), pp. 260–269.

47. Ruppert A. Dowling and Elaine J. Copeland, "Services for the Black Elderly: National or Local Problem?" *Journal of Gerontological Social Work*, vol. 2(4), summer 1980, pp. 289–303.

48. Melvin Delgado, "Politics among Elderly Hispanics," *Journal of Gerontological Social Work*, vol. 6, no. 1 (September 1983), p. 95.

49. James P. Adams, Jr., "Service Arrangements Preferred by Minority Elderly: A Cross-Cultural Survey," *Journal of Gerontological Social Work*, vol. 3(2) (winter 1980), pp. 39–57.

50. Morrison, op. cit.

51. Shirley Jenkins, *The Ethnic Dilemma in Social Services* (New York: Free Press, 1981), pp. 43–74.

52. This quotation and those following are from Barbara Silverstone and Ann Burack-Weiss, *Social Work Practice with the Frail Elderly and their Families: The Auxiliary Function Model*, (Springfield, Ill.: Charles C Thomas Publishers, 1983), pp. 10, 12, 13, 14, 15, 16, 18.

53. Ibid, p.

54. Marsha Mailick Seltzer and Gary B. Seltzer, "The Elderly Mentally Retarded: A Group in Need of Services," *Journal of Gerontological Social Work*, in press.

55. Matthew Janicki et al., "Service Needs among Older Developmentally Disabled Persons" in M. P. Janicki and H. M. Wisniewski, (eds.), *Aging and Developmental Disabilities: Issues and Approaches* (Baltimore: Paul H. Brooks Publishing Co., in press).

56. Seltzer and Seltzer, op. cit.

57. Janicki et al., op. cit.

58. Seltzer and Seltzer, op. cit.

59. Ibid.

60. Ibid.

61. Robert J. Wineburg, "The Elderly Blind in Nursing Homes: The Need for a Coordinated In-Service Training Policy," *Journal of Gerontological Social Work*, vol. 4(3/4) (spring/summer 1982), pp. 67–81.

62. Irving R. Dickman, *Making Life More Livable* (New York: American Foundation for the Blind, 1983).

63. Ibid.

64. Nina Millet, "Hospice: A New Horizon for Social Work," in Charles A. Corr and Donna M. Corr (eds.), *Hospice Care: Principles and Practice* (New York: Springer Publishing, 1983), pp. 135–147.

65. Elaine M. Brody. *A Social Work Guide for Long-Term Care Facilities* (Rockville, Md.: NIMH, 1974), pp. 73–74.

66. Ibid., pp. 77–79.

67. Ibid., pp. 83, 84, 87–89.

68. Ibid., pp. 99, 100, 120–121.

Working with Families

Aluma K. Motenko
Adjunct Assistant Professor
Boston University School of Social Work

Whom Are We Talking About?

The older person's family consists primarily of his or her adult children, their own nuclear families, and the older person's spouse. A minority who have never married, are childless, or are divorced without adult children rely more heavily on siblings and other relatives and friends.

Most older people have living children—four of every five elders have children.[1] Of those who have children, half have one or two and half have three or more.[2] Three-and-four-generation families are commonplace today: 94 percent of elders with children are also grandparents and 46 percent are great-grandparents.[3]

These adult children of the elderly have been called the "sandwich generation";[4] there is even a special term for the female children—"women in the middle."[5] These terms refer to the responsibilities of the adult child for dependents at both ends of the age spectrum. They have responsibilities for their own children and grandchildren as well as for their parents and grandparents. Adult children are "in the middle" not only with respect to their age but also with respect to multiple generations who place competing demands on their time and energy. In addition to traditional roles as wives, homemakers, mothers, and grandmothers, women are now, for the first time in history, also engaged in roles as care-giving daughters and daughters-in-law. Balancing these multiple responsibilities is an important task for the family to deal with.

While adult children are an important component of the family system of the older person, the elder's spouse is the most important family tie. Spouses depend on each other for emotional gratification, household management and care during illness. Today, older married couples are living together independently for longer periods of time due to the increasing lifespans of men and women and improvements in health care. Butler and Lewis estimate conservatively that older couples have an average of thirteen years together, after their children have established separate households, or one third of their entire married life.[6] Since women outlive men by an average of seven years, the majority of older women live their later years as widows. Approximately two of every three older men are married and living with their wives, while only one of every three older women is married and living with her husband.[7] (These statistics apply primarily to white, middle-class older persons; see Chapter 3.)

Are Older People Separated from Their Families?

Older people have not been abandoned by their families. On the contrary, they are well integrated into a kinship system of strong filial bonds. Strong positive relationships are common both between older people and between the older person and immediate or extended family members. These relationships are based upon mutual love and affection manifested through concern and care, rather than upon fears of disinheritance. Filial responsibility is also a strong factor in the bond between family members. Many stereotypes about the decline of intergenerational solidarity in modern society are unfounded.[8, 9]

The close involvement of the elderly with their families is expressed by frequent contact, interdependence, and care provided during crises. Most older people see their children at least once every week if they live in geographic proximity. Among elders with children, three-fourths of those interviewed by Ethel Shanas had seen at least one of their children during the previous week.[10] Other relatives also maintain regular contact with the elderly. One-third of the elderly see a relative other than a child, grandchild, or sibling at least once a week.[11] Older people who live alone are just as likely as those who live in larger households to see their children several times per week. Older people who live alone are not necessarily isolated and vulnerable. Half of the elderly who have children and live alone are within ten minutes' distance of a child.[12] To be old does not mean to be socially isolated. Social isolation is more commonly caused by health, income, personality, and adaptation patterns established throughout the life course than by age or relationship with kin.[13]

The family relationships of older persons are maintained through a system of interdependence and exchange of goods and services. Help is provided across the generations by older persons receiving as well as giving help. The majority of elders help their children and grandchildren, and the majority of older people also receive help from their children.[14] The kind of help received from children is similar to that given to sons and daughters—help with home repairs, housework, babysitting, care in illness, and various gifts. The ability of older persons to give as well as receive within the family network is an important contribution to the maintenance of the self-esteem of the elder.

Strong filial bonds persist when the illness of the older person progresses to the point that the elder is no longer able to reciprocate the help provided to him or her. When an older person becomes severely incapacitated and requires intensive care, family members willingly provide the care. Families do not abandon their disabled elderly, as is popularly thought. In fact, families sacrifice their personal, financial, physical, and emotional resources to maintain older persons in the community and avoid or delay institutionalization. Studies show that despite the hardships and worries incurred in caring for disabled elderly family members at home, the majority of family care-givers report that their relationships with their elders remained stable during the care-giving period. Over 90 percent still preferred maintaining the ill older person at home after one year rather than seeking institutional care.[15,16]

Social workers must dismiss the stereotype that families reject the aged and that isolation is an inevitable concomitant of old age. The facts reveal that families maintain close contact and intimate relationships with their elders. Families provide older persons with a wide variety of services and can be counted on in times of crises and illness. The social isolation of the elderly from their families is a myth, indeed; when it does occur it is due to factors other than the supposed emotional alienation from the family.

Who Is the Client?

We should not automatically assume that the older person is the client. The role of older persons as providers as well as recipients of services necessitates assessment by the social worker of who the client is.

There is a strong tendency among social workers and other professionals to view older people as recipients of services. Contrary to this view, the elderly are an important source of support to spouses, children, grandchildren, siblings, and other extended kin. At one level, the client may be the older spouse or adult child who is experiencing difficulty in the role of care-giver. At another level, the family unit may be the client, in the complex relationships and mutual reciprocity involved in giving and receiving help, or the older person may be the client either as a recipient or as a provider of services.

The social worker, aware of the interdependence of family members and the role of elders as providers as well as recipients of services, will critically assess the client group or individual for intervention, and address the needs of the total family—the caregivers as well as the elderly.

During the process of assessing who the client is, one group may emerge as the primary client while others take a secondary place. Alternatively, the social worker may assess multiple groups of primary clients and work with each individually or assess the family as the client and work with the family as an interacting system.

Responding to the needs of the family as an interdependent unit strengthens the capacity of the family to give care.

What Is the Nature of the Family? Why Is the Family Important?

The family is defined here as a group of individuals who are related by blood or marriage. The nuclear family is part of the extended family. The nuclear family is defined as a married pair with dependent children and an independent household.[17] Nuclear family members are bound to the extended family by voluntary ties of affection or duty. The extended family includes persons related by blood or marriage beyond the members of the immediate family, such as siblings, cousins, and in-laws.

The modified extended family is considered the normative pattern of family relationships in the United States today. This pattern involves, for all but the very sick, separate households connected by voluntary ties. Each member of the family is part of a highly integrated network of social relations and mutual assistance. Supportive relationships function from one generation to another as well as from one nuclear family to another. Although an older person may live alone, he or she is a part of this complex system of support called the modified extended family.

The modified extended family is viewed as a dynamic rather than a static system. New members or more distant relatives may be added as the need arises for information, services, or help from these relatives.[18] Matilda White Riley has pointed out that family relationships today are never fixed—they are created and recreated by family members throughout their lives.[19] Furthermore, individuals control their relationships by selecting and activating the relationships they deem most significant. As individuals age and change, new family relationships develop to accommodate new needs in response to changed interests or activities marked by stages in the life cycle. Social workers must be aware of the dynamic nature of family relationships in order to maximize the functioning of the family. Clients not making appropriate use of available kin can be encouraged to exercise their autonomy in developing new relationships or terminating old ones as the need arises.

In addition to other functions, the family serves as the primary source of emotional support for its members. It fulfills the individual's need for security and maintains the person's self-esteem as a valued and loved member of the family. The family provides the individual with his or her self-concept as a significant human being. Maintenance of family ties contributes to the enhancement of the personal growth of family members. When an individual experiences emotional stress, support for change and for the productive resolution of the crisis can often come from family members.

The concept of "intimacy at a distance" is used to describe the desired relationship between older persons and their families.[20] Elders wish to maintain their independence and physical distance in terms of their own households and life-styles, while engaging in mutual assistance and support of their family members. The family persists as the primary source of emotional and instrumental support, although relationships are continually growing, changing, and adapting to new demands. The dynamic nature of these relationships allows them to support the changing needs of the elderly, the adult children, and the other members of the family network, as well as continuing to fulfill important basic needs.

What Does the Family Provide?

Families provide the majority of care to the elderly, by far outstripping the amount and type of care provided by professionals and paid help. The family is the primary source of care. Professional care is an adjunct to that provided by the informal network of the family. Family networks are generally able to respond to the needs of older people and to carry out a wide variety of helping behaviors.

The types of family members actively caring for the elderly can vary considerably, depending on the marital status of the older person and the number and sex of his or her children. When a spouse is living, he or she will most likely be the primary care-giver. If the older person is widowed or divorced and has living children, they will be the primary care-givers. When neither spouse nor children are available, a more distant relative will be designated as the primary care-giver. A female relative will usually be designated before a male; if the older person has a son and a daughter, the daughter will, in most cases, perform the primary care-giving tasks. Wives, daughters, sisters, and nieces predominate over their male counterparts. Elderly wives (helped by daughters) are the predominant care-givers for disabled husbands, while adult daughters (and to a lesser extent, daughters-in-law) usually have the responsibility for widowed older people.[21] The typical spouse who is the care-giver is most often a wife in her seventies, in fair to poor health herself, who provides care to a severely impaired husband. The individuals most turned to for help in a health crisis are women in middle age.[22] This is usually a married adult daughter who is herself a mother of children and frequently is also a grandmother. Lang and Brody have found that two characteristics of middle-aged daughters are associated with higher care-giving responsibilities: shared households and greater ages of the daughter.[23] In general, older people who are severely impaired live with their families and are cared for by their daughters. Daughters who are fifty years of age and over have more parent-care responsibilities than daughters in their forties. The typical late middle-aged daughter holds concurrent obligations to nuclear family members and to employment outside the home. These facts suggest that, in addition to spouse care-givers, older middle-aged daughters one of whose parents lives with the family represent a vulnerable group.

Providing care within a shared household is the minority pattern of care-giving among nonspouse care-givers.[24] When this does occur, it is usually in response to deteriorating health and functional status of the older person. It is most prevalent among care-givers who are lower-income and neither married nor employed outside the home.[25] The reduced availability of financial and emotional resources associated with low-income, single, unemployed persons suggests that isolation can result from intensive care-giving involvement, which can lead to individuals becoming a risk to themselves, to their families and to the community.

Care-giving most often involves a broad range of services requiring an extensive time commitment. It is less common to provide concentrated help in one or two areas. Emotional support is the most universal care-giving activity and is considered by older people to be the most important type of help provided.[26] At the same time it is the most difficult task for many care-givers, especially for adult children.[27] Regular and ongoing communication with the older person is a central characteristic of the family support network. Care-givers regularly discuss the elder's problems with him or her. Care-givers have considerable knowledge about the functional deficits and changing needs of the older person.[28] They are also informed about other individuals and formal agencies assisting the older person. Care-giving involving communication and emotional support is a natural outgrowth of existing emotional involvement between an older person and his or her family. Morris, Sherwood, and Gutkin attest to the resiliency of the informal support network of the elderly.[29] At least one key family helper can deal with the older person's problems and helping network while exhibiting the capacity to respond to new and unfolding needs of the frail elder. Resiliency is a critical variable in successfully monitoring the older person's welfare and responding to inevitable changes in health and functional status.

Spouses are the most involved in care-giving tasks, in time and range of tasks performed. Adult children are second only to spouses. Other relatives have less frequent contact than adult children and spouses and fewer task involvements.

The majority of care-givers provide direct assistance with activities of daily living. Horowitz and Dobrof differentiate among three levels of care-giving involvement.[30] The basic level and least intensive type of involvement is help with shopping and errands, providing escort and transportation, and financial management; this level of support is provided by the majority of care-givers across all kin categories. A second level of support is in-home assistance consisting of help with homemaking and meal assistance. The majority of spouses and adult children provide in-home assistance, which is labor-intensive work requiring considerable time commitment. The most intensive level of assistance is personal and health care and, as the most intimate assistance, it is most likely to be rendered by the family members closest to the older person.

The care provided to the elderly by family members is extensive. The more severe the impairment of the older person, the greater the family's contribution. Family support systems appear to have a great deal of response capability to deal with severe reductions in the functional capacities of vulnerable elderly. The majority of family members believe that it is appropriate for them to provide the help they are currently providing.[31] Large numbers of key helpers are doing more things for their older relative for longer periods of time than they had originally expected.[32] Sager reports that families are doing more than professionals think they could or should.[33] Intensive care-giving is not without its costs to the care-giver, the nuclear family, and the extended family, and the stresses and strains associated with care-giving may increase the vulnerability of the care-givers themselves.[34]

Sociodemographic Trends and Care-giving

Changing sociodemographic patterns have had a dramatic impact on the family lives of Americans. The large increase in the number of older people in the population, the aging of the adult daughters who are the care-givers, and the decreased number of adult children available to provide care have all created unprecedented and uncharted patterns of parent-care activities.

The proportion of dependent elderly in the population is increasing. Older people in the upper ranges of the age spectrum are the fastest-growing segment of the older population. These older people are most likely to be physically and emotionally frail and require support by others (see Chapter 3).

A second demographic fact impinges upon the family's care-giving capacity. As the life span increases and elders are living well into their eighties, their children are also entering old age. Adult daughters, who are principally called upon to help their parents, are likely to be in middle age or early old age themselves. These adult children are beginning to experience such age-related changes as lower energy levels, the onset of chronic ailments, and the social role and psychological losses of retirement and widowhood.

While the frailest elders are ever-increasing and the middle-aged care-givers are getting older, the pool of family members available to provide support is also decreasing. The falling birth rate has resulted in fewer children left to care for a rapidly expanding number of frail old people. As a result, middle-aged daughters are caught in a demographic bind: they are increasingly likely to have at least one parent who survives into old age, fewer siblings with whom to share care-giving responsibilities, and a lowered capacity with which to undertake these responsibilities.

Brody has characterized the phenomenon among women in midlife resulting from these sociodemographic patterns as the "refilling of empty nests."[35] At a time when middle-aged daughters and sons are beginning their own retirement years and adjusting to the empty nest created by the independence of their own children, they experience a refilling of their nest. Their parents unexpectedly require their aid, often thwarting their plans for retirement and desires to spend more time together as a couple.

The refilling of the empty nest is an unprecedented shift in patterns of help during the family's life cycle. While the dependencies of children are expected, accepted, and provided for by the family and society, the dependencies of the old are not expected (they occur with greater variability and irregularity), are harder to accept, and have not yet been provided for.[36] Normative expectations, behaviors, and standards have not yet been developed for assisting families in dealing with the frailties of the elderly.

Social Policy and the Family

Current health and social policy is biased toward institutional care over community and home-care services. This policy leaves families without social and economic support in their care-giving tasks. Of public funds for the elderly, 90 percent is channeled to institutional care—which serves only 5 percent of the older population.[37] Since the major providers of long-term care services are the families of older persons, these families are meeting the chronic care needs of their elderly members through their own personal, emotional, financial, and physical resources, without concerted help from publically funded programs.

Within the past decade, federal health, rehabilitative, and welfare agencies have implicitly followed policies of reversing the trend of providing care to the elderly and chronically ill in isolated, highly bureaucratized, and impersonal institutions.[38] This emerging reliance of a conservative federal administration on the family serves the political purposes of cutting public outlays for long-term care. The ability of the family to provide service support for frail elderly is being promoted with primary emphasis on the public dollar. It is less a recognition of the social importance of the interaction of older persons with family members than the perpetuation of a new myth. The myth of adult children neglecting and abandoning their parents may be giving way to a new myth extolling the opposite notion—that the family alone can provide the needed chronic care.

Clearly what is needed is a policy of appropriate public services to back up the care family members are willing and capable of providing. Formal services do not supplant the informal services provided by the family; they support them and allow the family to continue providing care. Families do not expect any other provider to give more help than they themselves do. While adult children do not want to shoulder the entire burden of dependent parents' care, they also don't want to shift that entire burden onto another provider. Families want to maintain a central role but not be the sole source of help.[39] To support care-givers is the desired role of long-term care policy. Prolonged lack of community and in-home support may likely result in a breakdown of the family support network and consequently to unnecessary and even more costly institutional placement of the elderly.

Stress in Care-giving

The stress inherent in care-giving has already become apparent through the preceeding discussion of the helping patterns of the family and demographic trends. Providing an older person with emotional support, help with household tasks, and personal care involves complex psychological and social adjustments for the care-giver. Stress is generated through the adjustment to increased physical and emotional demands when you are getting older yourself, feeling a personal reduction in energy level, and have few family members with which to share the burden.

It is not surprising that family members who provide direct services to their elders experience the most strain in care-giving. Those who provide the most labor-intensive tasks have greater care-giving strain than individuals who provide fewer hours of care per week. Spouses who care for severely disabled older persons and daughters who share their households with parents experience the most strain. Lack of freedom is a frequent complaint. Often care-givers are so overwhelmed with the tasks of providing help that they have no time or energy for other activities. Their curtailment of activities leads to confinement in the home with the sick older person. This isolation leads to daily impatience and irritation concerning care-giving, which conjures up feelings of resentment, anger, and frustration. Lack of freedom is also felt in the long run; because of their involvement and commitment to caring for a parent or spouse, care-givers face difficulties in making long-range plans, such as moves, retirement plans, or vacations.

Care-givers who do not provide all the required help directly but are able to share service-provision with formal agency support are not as overburdened with the responsibilities of meeting the continual needs of the older person. Using formal home-delivered and community-based services allows the care-giver to shift from providing more labor-intensive instrumental tasks to providing increased affective support. The ability to engage in social and psychological support to an older person adds meaning to the care-giving experience[40] in addition to decreasing the physical work load, all of which reduces the stress of caregiving.

Time limitations are felt by all care-givers. The impact is felt first in personal and family time, then in time with friends, and last in work time. The most stressful component of care-giving is the psychological and emotional involvement with the older person. Physical and financial demands are also present but cause less stress than emotional demands. Personal strains caused by decreased daily and long-term freedom, lack of privacy, and constant irritation and frustration are strongly associated with having a dependent elderly parent or spouse. These strains involve a sense of physical and emotional fatigue and a feeling of not being able to satisfy the elder no matter what one does.[41]

Guilt and negative feelings emanating from the care-giving experience are stress-producing emotions that can be diminished by close feelings of attachment. A care-giver's fears of his or her own aging often contribute to negative attitudes about care-giving and to increased stress. Accepting the physical decline of the older person can be difficult. Other care-givers are beset with worry and guilt both about the older person and about their own care-giving abilities and responses. These guilt and negative feelings can be diminished through social work intervention, as will be described later in this chapter.

Stress in care-giving often leads to the entry phase of the social work relationship. Stress can immobilize the effective coping and care-giving capacity of the family support network. The overburdened family becomes helpless and searches for a source of relief. At this point the family system is stripped of resources and is unable to continue coping with care-giving tasks. At such a progressive state of family breakdown, the social worker must provide leadership in fulfilling functions that the family is no longer able to assume.

We do not want a stressful family situation to develop to this point. Rather, preventive intervention is desired at an earlier point, when social work intervention can build upon the strengths and resources of the family support network in order to improve its functioning. Work with family members to lessen stress and introduce appropriate formal service support, such as respite care or homemaker assistance, can relieve the care-giver burden and maintain the ability of the family to continue caring for the older person. The social worker's task as enabler is appropriate in aiding the family maintenance of coping mechanisms, developing opportunities to avoid social isolation, and allowing existing supports and networks to remain intact. The social worker should be cognizant of the need to encourage the informal network to function effectively as well as the need to step in where informal supports are unavailable and remedy such gaps with formal services.

Social Work Intervention: Entry Phase

In the entry phase—the initial diagnosis of the functioning of the older person—the primary care-giver and the family support network is made. The client is defined and the immediate tasks to be worked on are discussed in the process of establishing the contract.

Assessing the psychosocial needs and the functioning of each unit in the family system is a complex and difficult task. It requires expert knowledge of expectable behavior in old age[42] as well as knowledge of the unique behavior of the individuals concerned. This behavior is often observed at the point of initial contact with the social worker, when fatigue, anger, and fear on the part of the family are evident.[43] Fatigue is commonly experienced at the point of initial contact by family members who have unsuccessfully attempted to handle the problem independently before seeking professional help. The family now finds itself in a crisis situation, overwhelmed by the stress of care-giving over an extended period, by a sudden deterioration in the older person's condition, and/or by a change in other circumstances of the family.[44] Anger can accompany fatigue caused by repeated failures and inability to cope. The fear experienced by family members at the first meeting is the result of apprehension of meeting the social worker, who is a stranger. The family may also be fearful of discussing personal problems or uncovering the past.

The dynamics of the interrelationships among family members are the product of a long history, predating the initial contact by over half a century.[45] Many of the accustomed roles, alliances, and communication patterns are recalled when the family is reunited in planning for an older person.[46] Some of these are positive patterns; others, however, can evoke negative feelings of previous painful exchanges. Such reminders of past unpleasant experiences can create barriers to successful communication and exchange in anticipation of meeting with the social worker. Fear may also be caused by family members viewing the social worker as a judge of their behavior, responsibility, and devotion to the elder. They may view the social worker as someone who will find fault or place new burdens on them.

Understanding that fears, fatigue, and anger will often be both latent and manifest at the point of initial contact can help the social worker begin to separate behaviors generated by a crisis situation from the normal coping patterns of the family members. Distinguishing between functional and dysfunctional coping patterns of behavior in a crisis is a crucial factor in the ability of the social worker to assess the strength of exhibited coping patterns. Such assessment is a prerequisite to determining whether the family is able to manage with only some assistance or whether the social worker needs to fulfill more extensive functions that the family is incapable of managing.

The assessment of the older person and of the interrelationship of the family members is a time-consuming process involving the mutual and reciprocal[47] communication of all the parties involved—which always includes the older person. The attainment of care-giving goals can be reached only through mutual and reciprocal understanding and commitment to those goals. It is therefore important to involve all members in this process from the start. Goals that are set by family members with assistance from the social worker are likely to result in care-giving tasks that meet the needs of the elder as well as the care-givers.

As stated by Barbara Silverstone and Ann Burack-Weiss, "no matter how impaired the older person . . . he or she is capable of some degree of involvement. In most cases the elder can participate far more than expected if given time and patience on the part of the worker. We must never forget that it is the elder who must live out the consequences of any actions taken."[48] Not involving the elder in communications regarding the case plan or failing to elicit his or her preferences is an abrogation of the elder's rights to maintain control over his or her life as long as possible. We must never lose sight of the primary goal in any care plan—namely, to promote the elder's independence and ability to do without assistance as much as possible for as long as possible. Promoting the maximum independence of the older person begins at the point of initial contact and continues through the process of developing the case plan. Sharing the case plan and its implementation is an ongoing process requiring the social worker to repeat, simplify, and clarify goals and tasks so that all parties understand and agree to the plan developed.[49] Only involvement of the elder and family members, through mutuality and reciprocity, can result in their benefit through social work intervention.

The social worker should not expect the process of assessment and the development of the care plan to proceed without conflict: "Intergenerational conflict is essential for a healthy discharge of the normal tensions that exist among family members."[50] The issue for the social worker is not whether the relationships among family members is conflictual: loving, caring family members of different generations must express conflict to maintain their relationship. This conflict, however, should result in a clearing of the air and improved understanding among the members. It must serve constructive purposes. When conflict is destructive and serves to widen the gulf between family members, a third party is needed. A social worker can help families channel conflict toward constructive purposes, resulting in improved understanding and respect.[51]

An appropriate care plan must involve assessment of three aspects of family functioning: (1) the older person, (2) the primary care-giver, and (3) the relationship between the older person and the care-giver. An older person can fall into one of the following situations:

- someone who can manage alone and knows it
- someone who can manage alone but thinks he or she cannot
- someone who cannot manage alone and knows it
- someone who cannot manage alone but thinks he or she can[52]

The older person who can manage alone and knows it, as well as the older person who cannot manage alone and knows it are the simplest with whom to develop a care plan. The older person in these situations can be of great help to the social worker and family in communicating the limits of his or her abilities. In the situation of older persons who can manage alone but think they cannot or older persons who cannot manage alone but think they can, the social worker and family have a more difficult task in assessing the elder's functional capacity and in working through the discrepancy between the older person's perception of his or her ability and actual capacity.

Assessment of the care-giver involves determining the individual's capacity to provide the care required, given the care-giver's physical and mental health status; competing commitments, such as employment, spouse, children, and important social and recreational activities; and desire to care for the older person. Assessment of the relationship between the older person and the care-giver concerns the determination of the nature of the relationship. Is is positive or negative, too much or too little? Is respite care needed for the older person and/or the care-giver so that they may get some relief from household or care-giving tasks to rest or pursue other interests and avoid social isolation? Upon completing the initial diagnosis of the functioning of the various components of the familial support system and defining the target client, the social worker and family are ready to define the tasks and establish a contract.

Defining and Working on the Task

The overriding goal of the social worker in guiding the family toward defining the tasks to be worked on is to minimize the strain of care-giving and unproductive tension in the relationship between the older person and the family. In doing so the social worker is maximizing the maintenance of healthy support functions and forestalling further breakdown of the family network. Seven tasks of the family will be discussed here: (1) care-management, (2) balancing responsibilities, (3) coping with guilt, (4) achieving filial maturity, (5) adjusting to the disruption of the marital relationship, (6) helping older parents plan for the future without interfering, and (7) deciding to institutionalize the older person. The particular task for the family will be followed by a discussion of the parallel task for the social worker.

Task One: Care-management

Care-management (often referred to as "case-management") is the function of coordinating and linking the individual with services. Family members commonly assess the functioning of the older person, assess the service options available, arrange for the provision of services, and monitor the implementation of the treatment plan. Care-management, usually considered the task of the social worker, is considered here as the primary task of the family, which can require varying types and degrees of social work assistance. The more disabled the older person and severe the breakdown of the family network, the greater the necessity for the social worker to step in and take over care-managment functions.

The first step in care-management is assessment of the older person. The family evaluates the strengths and resources of the elder, by observing the older person's behavior and capacity to maintain activities of daily living. Family members are often the first to notice decline or change in functioning during the course of interacting and communicating with their older parent or spouse. Maintaining adequate communication with the older person is a crucial factor in the ability of family members to assess the functioning of the older person appropriately. Families who have a close, warm relationship, visit frequently, and engage in activities together will be better able to see real changes and have fuller knowledge of the elder's daily patterns and preferences than families who are not as close physically and emotionally. Families who are only able to speak on the telephone because they live far away from their parent will have the benefit of hearing the older person's perceptions of conditions but not of observing the older person in his or her own environment. Things may, in fact, be either worse or better than they seem from information that can be gotten through telephone conversations.

Focusing on the strengths and resources of the older person rather than on his or her weaknesses and deficits should not imply that the negative is not important to ascertain. It is equally if not more important, however, to maintain awareness of the positives that remain despite advancing disability. Reinforcing strengths over weaknesses helps older persons maintain independence through compensating for the things they cannot do so that they can concentrate on what they can do. For example, an older person who can no longer clean house and drive to the market to shop can have someone take him or her shopping and clean the house so that the older person can continue to prepare meals and maintain the household, if this is desired.

Assessment of service options and development of a treatment plan often go hand in hand: the nature of the services available will influence the compensations that must be made in the plan to meet the needs of the older person. The goal of the treatment plan is to "normalize" the older person's routine within the bounds determined by the individual's impairment, allowing the older person as much responsibility for him- or herself as possible. The routine should provide a daily structure for the older person's activities. At the same time it should satisfy the elder's need for creativity, to offset tedious routines.

Although too much responsibility and stimulation is to be avoided, too little is just as harmful. The family member must be extremely careful not to fall into a paternalistic mode. To assess the older person's need for services is not to take over or overroutinize. Families must continually keep in mind the purpose of care-management—to help older persons maintain as much control over their lives as possible by compensating for what they cannot do. It is better to increase services as the need arises than initially to provide more services than are necessary. The treatment plan must be carefully developed so that essential help is provided without taking over for the older person what the individual can do alone. Minimizing older persons' responsibility for themselves damages an essential aspect of their self-esteem and fosters premature dependence, which can accelerate the onset of disability unnecessarily.

Assessment of service options requires knowledge of service system options and reimbursement mechanisms. The older person's functional capacity with the right amount and type of service must be appropriately watched to ensure that the service alleviates excessive demands and allows maximum positive functioning of the individual. Once options are evaluated and a plan is developed utilizing the most appropriate available service options, the family must manage the implementation of the plan.

Constant monitoring of the older person's response to the treatment plan is required. This involves supervising the prescribed treatment and the workers who provide it. The family must monitor the course of the older person's condition and evaluate the significance of changes that occur. Often advocacy with medical and other health and social service professionals will be necessary as needs arise. Finally, families must anticipate needs for future assistance and services so that action can be taken when and if changes occur and the treatment plan must be altered.

The care-managment task requires the family care-giver to be both objective and subjective at the same time. The objective—"What does mother need? What is best for mother? What can mother do for herself?"—must be welded with the subjective—"What *should* I do for mother? What *can* I do for mother?" It is very difficult for a family member to separate emotional attachment with their spouse or parent from an objective professional assessment of the individual's needs. The objective and subjective requirements of care-management are difficult during the best of times. The difficulties in attaining these goals are exacerbated during crises and family breakdowns. Social work assistance is required to help the family successfully complete the care-management tasks.

Social workers can be more objective than family members. They can help families differentiate the objective from the subjective. Social workers possess knowledge that family members do not have, and can appropriately assess the family's capacity to provide help. Their knowledge of and experience with formal services and reimbursement mechanisms allows social workers to assess service options that will meet the family's needs. In addition to meeting the needs of the older person, the worker can discuss services as tools to be used by the care-giver in maintaining significant ongoing activities.[53] However, a worker's knowledge of the older person's strengths and resources cannot be surpassed by the family's ability to know the elder through relationships that span many years. Together with the family, the social worker can combine the strengths of the family's knowledge with his or her own professional viewpoint to develop a comprehensive and accurate assessment of the older person and a treatment plan.

The social worker must allow the informal supporters, the family, to identify unmet needs as they develop and provide the necessary support services. Just as the family must be careful not to be paternalistic and overmanage the older person, so too must the social worker be continually cognizant of not usurping the assessment and monitoring functions of the family.[54] The social worker should monitor the ability of the family and the formal services to meet the needs of the elder. The social worker need not be too hasty to step in, lest the family not be given an adequate chance to mobilize its resources. On the other side of the coin, however, the social worker must not allow family breakdown to advance too far. If the family is incapable of providing the support necessary, it is the social worker's task to provide leadership and compensate for an informal system that is not working. The social worker can cause the breakdown of the informal system if he or she overmanages the case. Social workers can also cause breakdown by not stepping, when unavailable.

The social worker's task in care-management is critical in helping the family to provide appropriate care to the older person. The care-management task is the overriding immediate concern of the family. Maintaining stable care-management functions must be resolved satisfactorily before other issues can be attended to.

Task Two: Balancing Responsibilities

In the care-management task, the family care-giver and social worker focus on meeting the needs of the older person. Often, the needs of the care-giver are ignored in the process and the capacity of the family to provide care is not adequately tapped. In fact, caring for the older person is but one of the responsibilities of the care-giver. Family care-givers must balance their responsibility to the older person with responsibility to their own family and the responsibility to themselves in order not to neglect sustaining aspects of their own lives.

It is extremely difficult to balance personal needs with care-giving responsibilities. Helping the older person maintain maximum functional independence and dignity, considering the older person's opinions and preferences, providing the needed care, maintaining an intimate relationship with the older person, and assuming actual and potential financial costs all impose a heavy burden on the care-giver. Care-givers also have a responsibility to themselves to maintain important aspects of their life-styles. Daily interaction with others (social network) and contact with select persons who give support and assistance to each other (support system) are central markers of self-esteem and self-worth. Neglecting this critical aspect of life through devotion to caring for an older person can result in social isolation and depression. Depressed care-givers benefit neither themselves nor the older person.

Care-givers must readjust their personal routines each time the older person's routine is changed. The care-giver's routine must compensate for the emotional drain from heavy responsibility for the older person by allowing for personal time. Care-givers must avoid severe drain on their physical as well as mental health. Sometimes, disruption of sleep due to caring for an older person at night is a problem that must be handled.

In addition to readjustment of person routine. is the need to readjust perspective on the family's future plans. Family vacations, career goals, living situations, and retirement plans often must be changed due to increased responsibility for an older person. Adjusting and coping with an uncertain future is stressful. Lack of adjustment to personal routine and lack of family planning to allow for respite and time to maintain social supports and social networks can lead to abuse of the older person.

Care-giving daughters and sons carry additional responsibilities for their own nuclear families. They must balance care-giving and responsibility for self with responsibilities to other family members. They must devote time and energy to family activities and to communication with their spouses and children. Maintaining the nuclear family as an effective decision-making group over a long period of time can contribute much to reducing the strain of the care-giving commitment on the part of the family. Since the consequences of deciding to care for an older family member affect the adult child's spouse and children, involvement of all the family members in the care-giving decision will increase everyone's understanding of the consequences of the decision and reduce the conflict that the added responsibility can create. Family members should ask themselves: "How does this change my life as an individual and our lives together as a family? What are we giving up? What are we gaining? How will I accommodate this change in my life-style? What can I do to help? What will my role be?"

The social worker can help the care-giver and the family increase their awareness of the involvement of all the family members in making the care-giving relationship a successful one for everyone involved. Everyone needs to be actively involved in caring for an older person. A joint decision to care for the older person followed by cooperative assistance with care-giving tasks and other household responsibilities can reduce the burden on the primary care-giver and consequently the strain on the family as a whole. Continued periodic family discussions can help readjust perspectives and needs and provide a forum for discussing problems and feelings.

The social worker can help the family view change as a natural progression of the life cycle. The maturity of the individuals who make up the family goes hand in hand with the maturity of family life as a whole. Growing and changing always necessitate making adjustments for new activities. The social worker's assistance is often required in the restructuring of daily activities within the life-style of the individual and the family unit so that the care-giver does not become overburdened. The social worker's perspective and expertise can help family members guard against isolation by maintaining social network contacts and social supports. Respite activities help families balance their responsibilities to themselves as individuals, to other family members, and to the older person. Not only does balancing responsibilities reduce strain on the individual and the family, it also contributes to the maintenance of family stability. The social interaction among the members of the family can be enhanced through the appropriate balancing of responsibilities and the opening up of communication among the family members who are affected by the care-giving decision.

Task Three: Coping with Guilt

Guilt is the result or the catalyst of many uncomfortable feelings from the past and present.[55] Facing up to your feelings is an important first step toward coping with guilt. Unrecognized or unresolved feelings can have a profound effect on family relationships. These feelings can foster a negative relationship between older spouses and between adult children and their older parents. Negative feelings and behavior can hinder or block attempts to be helpful to an older person and can lead family members to make unwise and inappropriate care-giving decisions for the older person. Unresolved feelings can be very painful—sometimes really oppressive— for adult children and spouses.[56] Understanding, accepting, and attempting to resolve these feelings can improve the well-being of all family members and lead to a more positive relationship between care-giver and elder.

Feelings toward your parent and/or spouse are complex and often involve a number of extreme opposites that appear simultaneously: "I love my mother and want to help her, but I hate the way she makes me feel so guilty." Silverstone and Hyman state that strong feelings of love, compassion, tenderness, and respect are likely to be accompanied by sadness as spouses and children realize that their aging loved ones are no longer the people they used to be and that death is coming closer every day.[57] Silverstone and Hyman examine several common feelings among family members—love, compassion, respect, tenderness, sadness and anger, hostility, shame, contempt, fear, jealousy, and sexual feelings. They stress that while love and affection are often at the root of a helping relationship, some relationships stem only from respect and concern—not love.[58] A son's lack of real affection may be painful to him, but may not diminish his feelings of responsibility for his parents' welfare and concern about their problems. Love is not an essential base for a care-giving relationship.

Silverstone and Hyman posit that the comfortable feelings of love and tenderness as well as the uncomfortable feelings of fear, anxiety, anger, hostility, and contempt are associated with close ties and are often most intense between persons most closely attached to each other.[59] They affirm that some children/spouses live in fear of their parents/spouses even when the parents/spouses are weak, helpless, or terminally ill. The children/spouses can be afraid of disapproval, of losing love, of death, of the irrevocable loss of the older person, or of losing an inheritance. Silverstone and Hyman define anger as a transitory feeling that can become hostility in its chronic state.[60] Contempt is defined as the way a person feels toward someone he or she considers worthless or immoral. Few relationships are free from these negative feelings, but Silverstone and Hyman alert us to the fact that occasional flare-ups can solidify into permanent attitudes that can greatly complicate a family relationship.

The sexual feelings of children toward their parents can arouse competition with one parent for the affection of the other parent. These feelings of jealousy and competitiveness, if unresolved, may last a lifetime and result in the inability of adult children to admit that their parents have sexual needs.[61] Emotional conflict in care-givers can also be stirred by feelings of shame. Shame is described by Silverstone and Hyman as shame for yourself that you do not do enough for your parents or shame for your parent or spouse's personal failings.[62] Adult children and spouses may feel that if they were better people, they would do more for their elders. When we are ashamed of our parents, it is usually because we fear that their shortcomings will reflect badly on us in the eyes of other people whose opinions we value.

Care-givers' fears of their own aging and their inability to accept their parents' old age can cause anger and increase the burden of guilt. Horowitz and Dobrof found that the more anxiety a family member has about growing older, the more negatively the care-giving experience is perceived.[63] Denial of the aging process and the wish to avoid the painful experience of witnessing the decline of a loved one's capabilities create a lot of anxiety around caring for the older person. Care-givers may try to avoid confrontation with what causes anger and guilt rather than concerning themselves with helping the older person. The care-giver exhibits anger and avoidance rather than the understanding, concern, and loving attention that the older person needs.

Witnessing the pain and decline of an older person is a reminder of their mortality and of our own mortality. It is natural to experience anger and anxiety at the realization that we are "losing" a loved one—that a part of them we cherish is no longer there, whether that be a mental or physical capacity. Negative feelings toward an older person are a natural reaction toward change. A gradual or sudden deterioration in physical or mental health status is a change that at first we would like not to accept. We may hope that it isn't true or will reverse itself. Eventually, our ability to face up to negative feelings toward an older person—whether they be caused by fear of aging, shame, jealousy and competitiveness, or other fears—determine whether we can resolve our guilt and accept the situation.

Resolving our guilt is complicated not only by the multiple negative and contrasting feelings we may have for an older person. Unrealistic societal expectations can cause distress, role conflict, and strain in the relationship between the older person and the family members.[64] Societal expectations of filial obligation are strong, but norms for meeting these expectations, to support care-givers, have yet to evolve. Family members who feel that they are unable to meet the older person's needs often feel that they are not doing enough to help the older person and that they should do more. An expectation that families should meet the needs of their members whatever the cost to themselves may be unrealistic. Care-givers' perceptions that they are not meeting their personal norms or societal norms regarding proper filial behavior are likely to be accompanied by feelings of guilt. To the extent that care-giving competes with other vocational, parental, marital, and social obligations, the care-giver experiences role conflict. Role conflict can lead to resentment of care-giving responsibilities. Resentment and guilt can foster filial distress, which can in turn strain the existing relationship. Scharlach found that the more a daughter believes that she doesn't do enough for her aging mother, or that what she does exceeds what she feels realistically able to do, the more dissatisfaction she will experience and the less she will enjoy her relationship with her mother. The mother's benefit from the relationship is also lessened as the daughter's dissatisfaction increases.[65]

The social worker must examine expectations with the care-giver to resolve guilt over unrealistic societal or personal expectations. Helping the care-giver examine negative feelings toward the older person can lead to coping with guilt and developing or maintaining a mutually satisfying relationship with the older person. Working with the family to establish a good relationship will decrease emphasis on expectations that increase guilt feelings and the care-giving burden, and improve satisfaction with the relationship.[66] Mutually satisfying relationships, in which each party gives to and gains from the other, result in less conflict. Help given through a satisfying relationship is more constructive and beneficial for the older person as well as the care-giver. Establishing a good relationship not only relieves guilt and improves care-giving abilities but also increases feelings of closeness with the older person, satisfaction with the relationship, and ultimately the well-being of the care-giver, the older person, and all who interact with and depend upon them.

Task Four: Achieving Filial Maturity

Achieving filial maturity is a task concerning the relationship between adult children and their older parents. Coping with the relationship between spouses will be discussed in Task Five—adjusting to the disruption of the marital relationship. Filial maturity is a middle-age developmental state that results from successful resolution of a "filial crisis."[67] A filial crisis occurs when past relationships with parents are no longer operable or appropriate. This occurs when aging parents require the assistance and support of their adult children. The offspring must now be available so that their parents can depend on them. Adults' perception of their parents as well as established patterns of interchange may be radically altered by the realization that they can no longer depend on their fathers for advice and financial help and that now their father needs to depend on them. Parents can no longer be viewed as a source of strong emotional support. The tables have turned: where once they provided support to their children, they now look to their children for affection, comfort, companionship, and security, as well as financial and household assistance.

In order to be dependable, adult children must resolve the filial crisis and enable themselves to provide support to their parents. A healthy resolution of the filial crisis leaves behind the rebellion against one's parents initiated during adolescence and often unresolved long after[68] as well as the perception that one's parents are pillars of strength to be turned to whenever needed. Now your parents are seen as individuals with strengths and weaknesses, achievements and failures as well as physical and mental attributes and deficits. You need to assess your parents and to reassess your relationship with them. Old patterns of interaction need to be broken and new ones established. In the process of crisis resolution, adult children see their parents as individuals in their own right outside of the role of parent, with all of its nurturing requirements.

Reconciling your past relationships with your parent—as a child, a young adult, and then a mature adult—with the present and future is a difficult process. Can you accept your parent's old age and adjust to the emotional and/or physical changes? Even if you do accept emotional and physical changes, you must then accept the likelihood of a progressive downward course of your parent's condition. Adjusting to an uncertain future is an unsettling prospect.

Can you accept the fact that your parents may no longer be able to provide you with the support for which you have looked to them in the past? You must now provide support to them. Can you accept this new role without feeling or becoming overburdened? You must also compensate for the loss, reduction, or change in the physical and emotional intimacy you once had.

Do you like your aging parents? Silverstone and Hyman point out that older people have a right to adequate care, having their needs met, their security maintained, their pain diminished, and their loneliness alleviated.[69] They have no right to expect to be liked just because they are old—even by their own children. Children should separate their feelings toward their parents from their feelings regarding their parents' conditions. If you know that you love your parents but have negative feelings toward their failing health, then you can separate your fears of your parents' dependency on you from your love and can simplify the task of coping with the changes in your parent's condition and the impact that will have on your relationship. You will realize that your denial or your desire not to see them is a result of difficulty in adjusting to their physical and mental condition and does not occur because you hate them. You hate their condition—not them.

Lowy posits that successful resolution of the filial crisis provides adult children with the opportunity to confront their own mortality and their own aging.[70] They can begin to prepare themselves for their later years and to cope with their own developmental tasks.

The social worker can assist adult children to see their relationship with their parents as a dynamic one bounded by mortality. While a daughter must work through the stages and changes she went through in her life-long relationship with her mother, she must reach a new understanding of yet another stage in their relationship when different needs of the mother and the adult child must be met.

The realization that her mother will not live forever may provide the impetus for a daughter to assess her feelings and either come to terms with her existing relationship with her mother or decide that she is now able to change her attitude toward her mother. Often, an adult daughter needs assistance to emancipate herself from past "daughter" roles so that she can freely help her mother now that assistance is needed.

This new stage of care-giving will not last forever. In a sense, it culminates a child and parent's relationship since birth. The quality of the relationship often continues into old age. If the relationship was close and intimate, the child will continue to be warm and affectionate. On the other hand, if the relationship was cool and conflictual it may continue to be so. The social worker can help adult children continue to express their feelings toward their parents despite the parents' decreased or changed abilities to reciprocate.

The social worker can help sons and daughters see their relationship with their parents as a dynamic interaction of two parties. Both parties contribute to the relationship. Either party's actions can deteriorate or improve the relationship as well as maintain the status quo. Conflict and rebellion of the past can be resolved, and improved understanding and interaction can result. On the other hand, an amicable relationship can deteriorate if a child fails to respond to the changing needs of the parent. Care-giving can bring an adult child and parent closer together. Providing assistance to a parent can become a positive focus of the relationship. It may allow a daughter and her father to see each other more often and have more to say to each other. The father may allow his daughter to do more things for him now, which can bring them closer together. On the other hand, care-giving can worsen a relationship. A daughter who is unable to achieve filial maturity may resent her father's requests for assistance and deny his need for support. The daughter's inability to resolve her conflicts can result in negative feelings and behavior of the father, which can then lead to more negative feelings on the part of the daughter. Care-giving may also have no effect on the relationship. A devoted daughter may remain one, while a cool relationship between daughter and father may be maintained by both sides until the father's death.

Task Five: Adjusting to the Disruption of the Marital Relationship

Loss of functional and mental capacity or deterioration in abilities of a spouse radically alters the relationship between a husband and wife. Marital roles and relationships are disrupted and new levels of functioning must be established.

Previous roles of active partners in a marriage give way to the new roles of caretaker and patient. The disruption is a dramatic role-shift in long-established patterns of relating both to each other as husband and wife and to the outside world as a couple. Activities that were shared, household tasks assumed by the spouse who is now incapacitated, and major aspects of their life together are now no longer possible. The spouse who becomes the care-giver experiences a loss of emotional support from his or her partner, along with increased responsibilities. Care-giving spouses must alter their life-styles to attend to new duties. Often, this results in discontinuing previous activities to focus on care-giving. Reduced social networks and social supports can lead to unhappiness and anger over the added burden and depression. Pain and loneliness is often experienced by the care-giver at the loss of role and satisfying life together. Often, financial stress accompanies illness when a spouse can no longer work and has high medical and long-term care expenses. Successful coping with the disruption in the marital relationship may not result in anger and depression. At best, it is a tremendous adjustment over time to adapt to a new life-style and learn new skills needed for household tasks previously accomplished by the spouse, as well as new skill for care-giving tasks.

The tasks required to resolve the "marital crisis" are similar to those essential for reaching filial maturity. Past relationships must be reconciled with the present and future. A care-giving spouse must adjust to an uncertain future and confront the likelihood of a progressive downward course. He or she must accept the fact that his or her spouse can no longer provide the kind of support he or she once did. He or she must now provide the support. The care-giving spouse will have to separate his or her feelings regarding his or her spouse's condition from his or her feelings toward him or her as a person and partner.

They must balance instrumental and affective care-giving roles so as not to be drained through constant caring tasks but have enough energy to take time to talk to his or her spouse, share experiences, and maintain the type of emotional involvement that existed before. The care-giving spouse must cope with his or her spouse's upsetting behaviors that are the result of illness and deterioration.

Wives who maintain their husbands at home as well as those who place their husbands in institutional care must adjust to the disruption of the marital relationship. Wives who care for their husbands at home must take on care-management tasks and balance responsibility for themselves with responsibility for their spouses. They often are anxious about their own health and must be careful not to engage in care-giving tasks at the expense of their own health. It is difficult to take care of yourself when so much of your time and energy is devoted to caring for your spouse. Wives whose husbands are institutionalized must continue to monitor their husband's functioning and to balance responsibilities, even though they do not supply the majority of the day-to-day care their husbands require. While it may be easier for them to care for their own health, they may have guilt at their inability to care for their husbands. They may also experience increased pain and loneliness at the separation from their husbands. Institutional placement often marks a final separation between husband and wife that brings to an end all wishes of return to a former life-style. The stark reality of a husband's absence is extremely difficult to adjust to. More difficult than coping with physical illness or loss of functional ability is the loss of mental functioning. Coping with such loss involves specific problems that can require twenty-four-hour supervision, and behaviors that are difficult to understand and control, not the least of which is the heartbreaking reality that your once vigorous, intelligent husband is no longer fully cognizant of where he is or who you are. This last is particularly difficult to resolve in cases of Alzheimer's disease.

The social worker should respond to the care-giving spouse as to a person in crisis. The separation of a couple by the advent of illness and mental impairment has the significance of a lingering death.[71] The social worker should help a wife go through the grieving process for her husband, which involves various stages of acceptance in which coping mechanisms are used to handle anxiety until a new level of functioning can be attained. Adult children and friends should be involved in supporting the parents. The presence of a confidant who provides a stable and intimate relationship over time can act as a buffer against the loss of roles and decreased social interaction.[72] The role of the social worker is to respond to care-givers under stress by seeing them as individuals in crisis. No matter what the unique characteristics of the individual's problem, he or she is seeking to reestablish a sense of balance in life in an attempt to adjust to the disruption of the marital relationship.[73]

Task Six: Helping Older Parents Plan for the Future without Interfering

Helping older parents plan for the future without interfering with successful life-styles is a delicate task of forming a partnership with parents. Attempts at developing a partnership can help adult children as well as older people prepare themselves for the day when they cannot manage on their own.

The notion of mutual reciprocity is key in the concept of a partnership. Adult children can gather information, suggest alternatives, raise cautious warnings, and express concerns. Parents may gather their own information and/or depend on their children. They may have strong positive or negative opinions about the available options that they should fully explore. Adult children can aid in this exploration and help parents assess what might be most appropriate. They may challenge a parent's decision and discuss it openly if all are willing. They cannot, however, make the decision for their parents. Older parents, as do all individuals, have the right and need for independence and maintenance of control over their destinies. The need for mastery and autonomy is especially important for older persons as they experience material, social, physical, and mental losses.[74] The older person should make the final decision.

The most effective help adult children can give to parents who are still healthy is preventive. Planning along with them to avoid tragedy in the future is best accomplished by open, respectful, relaxed discussion.[75] Sometimes children think they know what is best for father but father disagrees. Father has the right to live the way he is comfortable and happy provided he is not in danger of harming himself or others. If it appears that the older person is in danger or not able to manage without assistance, a social work assessment is necessary to help adult children evaluate the degree of independence desirable. Overprotection or under-protection of adult parents can best be avoided by proper social work assessment and assistance.

Adult children are not only assisting their parents by working at a partnership, they are also preparing *themselves* emotionally, socially, and financially to be available when the time comes that their parents will require their assistance. Careful anticipation of future crises by all concerned can offset the shock, grief, disruption, and guilt that accompany such crises.[76] Silverstone and Hyman suggest that future planning focus on the parents' health, their social world, and their finances. The family can discuss the possibility of catastrophic illness and physical incapacity that would leave the older person unable to care for him- or herself independently. It is difficult to contemplate these possibilities and even more difficult to broach the subject with your parents. Some parents bring up the subject and find that their children cannot discuss it with them. Nothing is lost by exploring options, becoming familiar with community agencies and services, anticipating future problems, and making a tentative plan of action. As aptly stated by these authors, plans are like insurance. They may never need to be activated if your parents are spared a disabling illness. If an illness or deterioration does occur, you will not have to go through the additional heartache of being caught unprepared, not knowing what to do, and having to resort to quick solutions that may be less than satisfactory.

Advance planning should include consideration of friends, family, and meaningful social groups that can be relied on in the future for affection and companionship as well as help with chores, transportation, and small emergencies.[77] Attention should be paid to the appropriateness of the older person's housing both as to space available and as to proximity to shopping, medical care, recreational activities, religious organizations, and public transportation. Maintaining meaningful social activities is very important to the future well-being of your parents.

Finally, advance planning includes a discussion of the parent's financial situation. While some parents may be reluctant to discuss their financial situation because of a sizable inheritance or because they have so little, others will have no problem being as open about this area of their lives as they are about other aspects. Children can help point out pitfalls ahead that the older person may not have considered. They can help find out what financial assistance is available to older people in the area and what their parents may qualify for. A child can explore health insurance with the parents to be sure both that they know how much will be covered by an acute or long-term illness and that they will have the funds to cope with the cost of a serious illness.

Preparation does not, however, imply that changes should be imposed. Adult children should be careful to offer quiet support of their parents' life-styles. A life-style for an adult child need not correspond with the life-style of the parent. Children must provide help that will meet the parents' needs rather than their own. The ideal is to encourage life-styles that will allow the older person autonomy and personal growth until the very end of life. Adult children can work toward these goals by promoting the elder's capability and willingness for self-help. They can help parents find ways of learning and growing to meet needs both before and during the period of decline.

The social worker, by helping a daughter maximize her preparedness while minimizing her interference in her parents' life-style, can aid the daughter to maintain herself as a source of emotional support and inspiration to her parents in helping to fulfill their hopes, dreams, ambitions, and new goals and horizons. Adult children should be helped to understand that they are not responsible for their parents. They are responsible for themselves, their marriages, and their children. They are responsible for being a source of support to their parents. Assisting parents does not give them the right to take control away from parents. Aging and illness do not require that older people give up control over their lives. In understanding that increasing disability of older people is a major worry of families, social workers can help adult children cope with their worries through planning and exploring options so that they are prepared individually and as an interdependent family. The social worker can help the adult child maximize reciprocity in the fulfillment of filial responsibility so as to minimize the guilt and burden in the relationship.

Task Seven: Deciding to Institutionalize the Older Person

Institutionalization, one solution to the problem of caring for an incapacitated older person, brings with it latent emotions and life tasks. Some older persons interpret entering a nursing home as rejection by their spouse and children.[78] They have not reconciled their functional deficits, their inability to remain in their present living situation, and the need for change in their lives. For others, however, nursing home placement is the result of a mutual family decision to secure the best possible living situation and care for the older person.[79] Yet other families' decisions involve some feelings of being rejected on the part of the older person, some guilt on the part of the spouse and/or children, and denial of the need for change. Most of the time, deciding to institutionalize a parent or spouse is a painful, soul-searching process that is the result of attempts to manage in the community and/or a health crisis.

Feelings of rejection can be diminished by social workers and family members extending their efforts to maintaining continuing meaningful ties with older persons in an institution, showing them that they are not abandoned. Open appraisal of the institution and exploration of options prior to placement can improve the family and older person's ability to accept the decision as a necessary or even positive step in dealing with the situation. Sound appraisal of the institution means a realistic evaluation of the positives and negatives of the physical, social, and medical conditions. Matching the older person's needs with the type of institution is important. An active, alert, energetic, ambulatory older person would be better placed in a home in an urban neighborhood near stores, schools, and cultural activities than in a suburban home in a picturesque setting isolated from stimulating community activities. As in *Task Six*—helping older parents plan for the future— locating an appropriate long-term care institution involves assessment of the older persons' health, their social world, and their finances, as well as their personality and life-style preferences and available options. Attempts to place older persons in an institution that allows them to maintain as many aspects of their previous lives as possible and be as much a part of the mainstream of the community will ease the adjustment of the older persons and preserve their well-being.

The varied life circumstances that bring people to institutions have differential effects on the relative abilities of individuals to accept the decision in a positive light. Older persons who choose to enter an institution will make more attempts to adapt than will those who had the decision made for them or are disoriented or confused. Those who have time and opportunity to consider alternatives prior to making the decision can view the decision as a compromise based on analysis of options and needs. In contrast, elders who are transferred quickly and without warning from another institution, such as an acute care hospital, will have a more difficult time adjusting to a situation that is beyond their control.

Because of hopeful anticipation of return to an independent, familiar lifestyle, some older persons and families who view the placement as temporary may maintain more of a positive outlook than those who see it as permanent. On the other hand, others may view the temporary placement as a negative setback, rejecting all aspects of institutional life and not trying to socialize with others in the facility. Such elders may view a temporary placement more negatively than those who perceive it as permanent and resign themselves to making the best of their situation.

The poorer the health of the institutionalized elders and the more severe their physical, emotional, and intellectual impairments, the more likely it is that they will enter an institution with greater medical and social support. The greater the care supplied by the institution, the less the control the older person can exercise over daily schedules and activities. In general, the more control older persons can maintain over their lives, the more positive their outlook on life will be and the easier their adjustment to institutional life.

Research on the sociodemographic characteristics of institutionalized elders reveals that they have fewer family supports and are older than noninstitutionalized elders.[80,81] Older people who never married or are widowed are more likely to be institutionalized than are their married counterparts with living spouses. Older persons in institutions are three times more likely to be single and twice as likely to be widowed than those outside.[82] Elders with family support enter at a later age than those without. Whereas only 5 percent of those 65 and older are institutionalized, one of every eight persons 80 and older is institutionalized.[83] Advanced age and lack of family support options play a large role in the decision to institutionalize an older person. In addition, the paucity of appropriate long-term care options in the community (including a range of home care alternatives) aggravate these decision-making processes by forcing inappropriate choices, and thereby create unnecessary family tensions.

Whatever the life circumstances and sociodemographic characteristics of the older person, the decision to enter an institution is always an acknowledgement of diminished capacity to care for oneself.[84] Adjusting to this reality requires the help of family and social workers to counteract the propensity for withdrawal, passivity, and depression brought on by feelings of loss.

The realization that the older person must become more dependent on others for activities of daily living is difficult for the family members in the community to integrate into their image of the person as well as for the elder to incorporate into his or her self-image. If family is available, they are often depleted of resources and energy through having tried to care for the older person at home. When family is unavailable, the older person is often exhausted and frustrated by trying to manage on his or her own against declining capabilities and difficult odds. Institutionalization can relieve the difficulty experienced by individuals and families who have gone through failures in managing with the loss of functional capacity. Social workers can help older persons and families adjust to institutionalization and reach a new equilibrium through understanding that the decision reflects a relief from burdensome and unsuccessful situations as well as acknowledging the uncomfortable realization of the older person's diminished capacity for self-care and independent life-style.

The decision to institutionalize an older person can mark the termination of a social work relationship. It can also be the beginning of a new contract between the social worker and the client requiring selection of an appropriate placement and adjustment of the family and the older person to a new way of life.

Termination

Termination of a social work relationship with elders and their families occurs when the contracted tasks are completed and both the older person and the family have achieved a new level of functioning independently and as a unit. When new problems and situations arise that the social worker can or should not handle, the client should be referred to resources appropriate to these new problems or situations.

Termination of the relationship can also occur because of the death of the older person. Too often, the death of the elder inappropriately signifies the end of services to families.[85] The surviving family needs continued social work assistance in working through their loss. Grieving is affected by the nature of the death, the length of the illness, the openness of communication within the family, and the degree to which the older person was a central emotional force in the family.

Whatever the cause of termination, a successful social work relationship will always leave the family with the comforting knowledge that they have someone to turn to in the future. The professional relationship developed by working together remains an invaluable resource for the family.

The following case illustrations are presented to exemplify the points made and to relate practice to the theoretical material offered.

Case Illustrations

These five illustrations deal with the seven tasks of family work enumerated previously.

Case Number 1: Mr. and Mrs. F. (Task: Balancing Responsibilities) *

Mr. F., an 80-year-old, retired Polish steelworker, had been treated at Shady Hill Long Term Care and Rehabilitation Center following a fracture of his right hip. He had been rehabilitated to functional independence at a wheelchair level. Ambulation training had not been possible because of a long-standing arthritic condition.

Prior to admission six months ago, Mr. and Mrs. F. had been enjoying their retirement. Various social and recreational activities filled their day. During the early months of Mr. F.'s admission, Mrs. F. visited daily and indicated to the social worker and to the other members of the treatment team her intention to take Mr. F. home when he could "walk and dress himself." When it became evident to the team that Mr. F. would not be able to walk and would be confined to a wheelchair, but could be independent in the wheelchair, Mrs. F. became evasive about taking him home, claiming that she was worried about her own health. She had mild diabetes that did not appear to interfere with her activie, independent life-style.

During the following month Mrs. F. began to visit less frequently. Mr. F. became increasingly depressed and withdrawn, although he continued to maintain his functional ability through physical and recreational therapy. At this point he no longer required rehabilitation service. A discharge plan had to be made. The social worker began to discuss nuring home placement with Mr. F. The social worker made repeated attempts to include Mrs. F. in these discussions but Mrs. F. declined.

The social worker continued to reach out to Mrs. F., supporting her concerns about her own health. Mrs. F. began to share with the social worker worries that were based on her husband's previous patterns of depending on her to take care of him. She repeatedly said, "I can manage to take care of myself. But if I have to take care of him I will get sick, and then who will take care of me?" The social worker's focus with Mrs. F. shifted from discussions of Mr. F.'s condition to an exploration of possible options to relieve Mrs. F. of the extra responsibilities she would have in taking care of both her husband and herself.

At this point Mrs. F. agreed to participate in a meeting with her husband and the social worker to discuss a home discharge plan. They discussed a number of service options that were available to the F.s in their own home. Mrs. F. agreed that she would try to bring her husband home with homemaker service, home health aid service, visiting nurse care, transportation for medical appointments for both Mr. and Mrs. F., and meals-on-wheels service. In-home services would allow Mrs. F. to continue participating in the local garden club and visiting with her sister, who lived around the corner and with whom she had always had a close relationship. Mr. F. could entertain his friends at home while his wife was out. Mr. and Mrs. F. were able to return to some of the recreational and social patterns established before Mr. F.'s illness.

* Acknowledgment is made to Trudy Zimmerman, Assistant Clinical Professor, Boston University School of Social Work, for supplying this illustration.

Case Number 2: Mr. and Mrs. T. (Tasks: Adjusting to Disruption of Marital Relationship and Deciding to Institutionalize)*

Mr. and Mrs. T. were very devoted to each other. They spent a lot of time each day enjoying activities together. They shared many interests and responsibilities. Mr. T. took care of most of the financial and household management tasks.

Mr. T. developed Alzheimer's disease. Mrs. T. maintained him at home for two years. She provided her husband's personal care, which consisted of dressing, bathing, and grooming. She also accompanied him whenever he left the house, although he was able to walk without assistance. Mr. T. was able to feed himself. He did, however require supervision. Mrs. T., in addition to caring for all of Mr. T.'s personal needs, had to learn to take on the household responsibilities her husband had previously held.

Mr. T. fell on the ice the second winter of the onset of his disease. He fractured his leg, and required surgery and recuperation with rehabilitation at a long-term care facility. After his surgery Mr. T.'s thinking became more confused. He needed constant supervision. Initially, he had trouble understanding how to use the walker he now needed. After several months of therapy Mr. T.'s leg healed and he succeeded in learning to use the walker adequately. Mrs. T. took him home.

Homemaker and home health aid services were provided to the T.s. Mr. T. would try to get out of bed at night and required constant supervision to prevent accidents. One night he fell out of bed and fractured his wrist. He returned to the long-term care facility. Mrs. T. decided that she could no longer take care of her husband at home.

Social work assessment revealed that Mrs. T. had tried to engage Mr. T.'s 45-year-old daughter from a former marriage to take on more responsibilities for the care of her father. The daughter told the social worker, "My stepmother will tell you that she was doing all the work, but when he was waking up in the middle of the night, she always called me to come over and help her out." Mr. T.'s daughter was doing all the shopping and meal preparation for her parents. She lived in the same town, but worked full-time and had three children of her own still at home as well as her husband to attend to. She was having difficulty managing to provide the help that she was already giving to her parents, let alone taking on additional responsibilities. It became evident to the social worker that Mrs. T.'s decision not to care for her husband at home any longer was reached only after attempts to provide the care herself, with the assistance of her husband's daughter, the homemaker, and home health aid services, had proved insufficient. The constant supervision he required during the day and night was just too much for her to cope with. Discussions regarding the care that Mr. T. required took place with the social worker and Mr. and Mrs. T. Mr. T. could not, however, actively participate due to the severity of his impairment.

---

* Acknowledgment is made to Trudy Zimmerman, Assistant Clinical Professor, Boston University School of Social Work, for supplying this illustration.

Three months after Mr. T.'s return to the facility, Mrs. T. made an appointment to see the social worker for assistance in locating new housing. Through exploration of the T.s' living situation, the social worker learned that the couple had been renting a small but comfortable house for the past ten years; now the owner of the house had decided to sell. While Mrs. T. had the option to remain a tenant, she had decided that this was an opportune time to move to a small apartment: "What do I need all that room for now?" The social worker met with Mrs. T. several times over the next few weeks to explore what such a move would mean to Mrs. T. It was her assessment that giving up the home the couple had shared was a necessary step in the process of working through the loss of her husband as an active participating partner in the marriage. Having a small apartment more suited to her own needs symbolized her new life without her husband. Assuring herself that the move would be a positive step in Mrs. T.'s adjustment to living alone, the social worker referred Mrs. T. to a community caseworker specializing in housing. The worker helped Mrs. T. apply for elderly housing and negotiate the system. She was approved for a small apartment.

Mrs. T. continued to visit Mr. T. but began to cut down the visits from every day to every other day. She had made some new friends in the building and had joined the building's social activities club. The hospital social worker maintained ongoing supportive contact with Mrs. T. through the adjustment phase.

Case Number 3: Mrs. G. (Tasks: Achieving Filial Maturity and Coping with Guilt) *

Mrs. G. had been visiting a cousin in Arizona when she suffered two strokes that left her with some residual weakness in her leg and cognitive and perceptual deficits. Her two daughters encouraged her to return to her home in Chicago so that they could be nearby to provide support and assistance. Mrs. G.'s income was too high for Medicaid eligibility and other home services, but too low to pay privately for all the services she required. As a result, she returned to Chicago with some visiting nurse and home health aid services. She depended on her daughters for her meals and shopping.

The assistance her daughters provided was less consistent than she had hoped. Cognitive and perceptual impairments from the strokes had left her with poor judgment, diminished recent memory, and problems in sequencing activities. On a number of occasions, the visiting nurse observed her forgetting to turn off the stove and leaving the water running in the tub. After several months of managing marginally in this manner, Mrs. G. suffered more small strokes. She then required acute hospitalization until she was stabilized, followed by a stay at a long-term care facility for rehabilitation.

At the long-term care facility Mrs. G. was evaluated by the members of the rehabilitation team, who found new impairments in the area of problem-solving

* Acknowledgment is made to Trudy Zimmerman, Assistant Clinical Professor, Boston University School of Social Work, for supplying this illustration.

skills, attention span, and spatial perception. Mrs. G., although able to walk, seemed confused and not fully aware of her surroundings much of the time. The rehabilitation team and the community providers had serious concerns about Mrs. G.'s ability to function safely at home under her previous arrangement.

A family-team conference was called by the social worker so that various options could be considered. It was apparent that the daughters had not communicated with each other before the family meeting and had not approached their mother about plans. They refused to consider any plan that necessitated a change in the previous arrangement. They maintained that their mother would do fine once she returned to the familiar surroundings of her home. When the staff pointed out Mrs. G.'s memory deficits, the daughters replied, "She only remembers the things that are important to her. She has a selective memory now and has always had one." The social worker made the assessment that the family was not yet ready to accept Mrs. G.'s need for much more care. They could not accept the changes in their mother's condition and abilities and the consequent adjustments they would have to make in their relationship with her. They denied that she hadn't been doing fine before. They couldn't tolerate not seeing their mother as the powerful and capable lady she had always been. The concerns of the team and the doctor's prediction that Mrs. G. would most likely have additional small strokes and would suffer from further loss of functioning were unheeded by the daughters.

It was Mrs. G.'s wish to go home. The daughters refused to consider institutional care for Mrs. G., claiming that "she doesn't need it." They did agree that their mother could benefit from more consistent monitoring by community providers. Mrs. G.'s daughters offered to pay for a homemaker twice a week. They didn't think she needed it but agreed to do it to appease the social worker. The family also agreed to allow the team to evaluate Mrs. G.'s apartment and make recommendations for adaptive equipment in order to make her home a safer environment.

After Mrs. G. returned home, the social worker called the family weekly. She usually spoke to one of Mrs. G.'s daughters, the homemaker, or Mrs. G. The social worker also arranged that the visiting nurse would call her to discuss any concerns that might materialize in the future. In this way, the social worker could be alerted to problems as they arose with the aim of stepping in to avert a crisis from developing.

Case Number 4: Mr. and Mrs. C. (Task: Planning for the Future)

Fred and Sue felt burdened. Although they had wanted his parents to move back to Worcester so that they could help the older couple, they had questions and doubts about his parents' ability to manage on their own given their health problems and apparent frailty. Fred at times was at a loss in trying to figure out how to help his parents; he was resentful that most of the responsibility fell to him rather than to his brothers, and looked to the social worker to share the burden. Fred visited his parents every day and helped them with their shopping, laundry, and financial management. According to Fred, Mr. C. had begun losing his vision fifteen years ago and gradually became very dependent on Mrs. C. to handle household affairs.

Mr. C. was frustrated with his wife's recent inability to continue in the role she had once filled. Now she preferred to sit at home and took little interest in cleaning, cooking, or going out to do the shopping or for recreational purposes, all of which left Mr. C. with household responsibilities that he neither wanted nor was fully able to handle, given his vision impairment. He attributed her change to "laziness."

Fred and Sue requested information about recreational programs for Mrs. C. and were concerned about her loss of memory and health complaints. They wondered whether Mr. and Mrs. C. could manage to care for themselves without extensive support from the younger couple. Fred was angry at his father: he felt that no matter what assistance he provided, his father was not satisfied. He struggled with the question of how best to help his parents in the face of his father's long-standing need for independence. Fred and Sue discussed the possibility of nursing home placement with his parents, who were quite opposed to the idea. With the worker's assistance the family arranged for a homemaker and meals-on-wheels.

In an interval of eight months, as Mr. and Mrs. C. became more aware of their limitations, Fred and his wife were able to convince Mr. and Mrs. C. to apply for admission to a nursing home. However, as the couple continued to deteriorate, Fred called the social worker asking for help in maintaining his parents in elderly housing during the waiting period for nursing home placement. At this point, the daughter-in-law became the primary collateral contact.

The following issues were addressed: (1) provision of health aid services to Mrs. C., (2) increased homemaking help, and (3) the introduction to Mrs. C. of a volunteer to walk with her during the week.

Mr. C. felt less guilty about his wife's appearance and inactivity, the son and daughter-in-law were bolstered in the interim waiting period, and the couple felt less hostile to one another.

Case Number 5: Mr. S. (Task: Care Management) *

Mr. S., a 70-year-old widower, lived in elderly housing, where he had many friends. He owned a car and liked to help others with their shopping and errands. He was close to a woman in the building; they shared meals and provided regular companionship for each other.

Recently Mr. S. had been calling the police and pulling the emergency cord in his apartment, claiming that intruders with animals were attempting to break in. He regularly went to the management office asking for his locks to be changed. The management office had threatened to evict him if his daughter wouldn't make him stop his "outbursts." Joyce, Mrs. S.'s daughter, contacted a social worker for assistance in dealing with her father's paranoia and recurring hallucinations. Joyce had always respected her father's need for independence and deferred to his wishes.

* Acknowledgment is made to Rose Ann Ariel, Social Worker, and Joann Ivry, Director, Services to the Elderly, Jewish Family and Children's Services, Boston, Mass., for providing this illustration.

He had a strong, outgoing personality and was also stubborn and easily angered. Since his wife's death from cancer eight years ago, he had little regard for the medical profession, and had repeatedly thwarted his daughter's efforts to take him for a physical exam.

It was difficult for Joyce to accept the fact that her father was having visual hallucinations, since he had never been sick before this. She wanted to believe that burglars were really trying to break into her father's apartment. Initially, the social worker helped Joyce arrange for neurological and psychiatric exams for her father, which was difficult because of Mr. S.'s strong hostility toward physicians. Mr. S. was diagnosed as having Alzheimer's disease in its early stages. The hospital's recommendations included taking medication to control the hallucinations, restricting Mr. S.'s driving, and moving to a level IV nursing home so that he could be supervised. Medication therapy was begun.

Although Joyce realized that Mr. S. should not continue driving, she was reluctant to tell him. Joyce stated, "Every time we speak, he makes me feel like a little girl." She felt guilty, angry, and trapped by the situation. Finally, she told Mr S. that she was taking the car and giving it to her son. Mr. S. was upset and frustrated because he still didn't comprehend why the doctors were saying he could no longer drive, though it had been explained to him many times.

In a matter of weeks, Joyce was able to arrange a weekly homemaker, a home health aid three times a week, and a friendly visitor. Mr. S. was able to accept the homemaker. However, because he felt that the home health aide and friendly visitor were babysitters, he became rude and antagonizing to them. Joyce then decided to discharge both. Joyce also arranged for Mr. S. to take transportation to a daily hot-lunch program. Mr. S. did begin attending the program regularly although he refused to take the transportation even in poor weather. He preferred to walk, in order to maintain some of his former independence.

Throughout all these attempts to provide services, Joyce felt angry and manipulated. These emotions created tensions in her own unstable marital life. She felt that her father was stubborn, demanding, and deliberately selfish. The social worker helped Joyce cope with the deterioration in her father's health. It had been difficult for Joyce to accept the changes in her father's personality, life-style, and functional capacity and to adjust her relationship with him to accommodate these changes. Where before she deferred to him, she now had to be more assertive in helping him make decisions concerning his life. His loss of independence and his depression caused her great sadness and upset. She now spoke with her father twice a day to check that he had taken his medication. She visited several times a week and helped him with his food shopping and laundry. Although he was managing, his physical condition was becoming weaker.

Joyce would have liked to take a several-day vacation with her family, but was fearful of leaving her father because of her daily calls to remind him to take the medication and her calls to make the reservation for him at the hot-lunch program. He frequently called her with so-called emergencies that brought her across town to help him. She felt torn by her desire to help her father, yet angry and resentful that she was carrying the sole responsibility for him. Soon a social family agency she contacted arranged a back-up service for her to get emotional support and counseling to deal with her anger and resentment. The social worker in that agency now had become involved in working with Joyce as a client, so that she could better perform her role as an informal caregiver. The formal and informal systems got linked.

References

1. Robert N. Butler and Myrna I. Lewis, Aging and Mental Health: Positive Psychosocial and Biomedical Approaches (St. Louis: C. V. Mosby, 1982).
2. Ethel Shanas, "Older People and Their Families: The New Pioneers," Journal of Marriage and the Family 36 (1980), pp. 9–15.
3. Ibid.
4. Dorothy Miller, "The Sandwich Generation: Adult Children of the Aging," Social Work 26 (1981), pp. 410–423.
5. Elaine M. Brody, "'Women in the Middle' and Family Help to Older People," The Gerontologist 21, 5 (1981), pp. 471–480.
6. Butler and Lewis, op. cit.
7. Shanas, op. cit.
8. V. L. Bengston and J. Treas, "The Changing Family Context of Aging and Mental Health," in J. E. Birren and R. B. Sloan (eds.), Handbook of Mental Health and Aging, (Englewood Cliffs, N.J.: Prentice Hall, 1978).
9. Barbara Silverstone and Sarah Miller, "Isolation in the Aged: Individual Dynamics, Community and Family Involvement," Journal of Geriatric Psychiatry 13, 1 (1980), pp. 27–47.
10. Shanas, op. cit.
11. Ibid.
12. Ethel Shanas, "Social Myth as Hypothesis: The Case of the Family Relations of Older People," The Gerontologist 19, 1 (1979), pp. 3–9.
13. Silverstone and Miller, op. cit.
14. Shanas, "Older People and Their Families," op. cit.
15. Mary Adams, Mary Ann Caston, and Benjamin G. Davis, A Neglected Dimension in Home Care of Elderly Disabled Persons: Effect on Responsible Family Members. Paper presented at the 32nd annual scientific meeting of the Gerontological Society, Washington, D.C., November 1979.
16. Dwight L. Frankfather, Michael Smith, and Francis G. Caro, Family Care of the Elderly: Public Initiatives and Private Obligations (Lexington, Mass.: Lexington Books, 1981).
17. Butler and Lewis, op. cit.
18. Shanas, "Social Myth", op. cit.
19. Matilda White Riley, "The Family in an Aging Society: A Matrix of Latent Relationships," Journal of Family Issues 4, 3 (1983), pp. 439–454.
20. Leopold Rosenmayr and Eva Kockeis, "Propositions for a Sociological Theory of Aging and the Family," International Social Science Journal 15 (1963), pp. 410–426.
21. Abigail Lang and Elaine Brody, "Characteristics of Middle-aged Daughters and Help to Their Elderly Mothers," Journal of Marriage and the Family 39 (1983), pp. 193–202.
22. Ibid.

23. Ibid.
24. Amy Horowitz and Rose Dobrof, *The Role of Families in Providing Long Term Care to the Frail and Chronically Ill Elderly Living in the Community.* Methodological Report, Health Care Financing Administration, August 1982.
25. Ibid.
26. Ibid.
27. Ibid.
28. John N. Morris and Sylvia Sherwood, "Informal Support Resources for Vulnerable Elderly Persons: Can They Be Counted On, Why Do They Work?" *International Journal of Aging and Human Development* 18(2) (1984), pp. 81–98.
29. John N. Morris, Sylvia Sherwood, and Claire E. Gutkin, *Meeting the Needs of the Impaired Elderly: The Power and Resiliency of the Informal Support System.* Technical report, Hebrew Rehabilitation Center for the Aged, Boston, Mass., 1981.
30. Horowitz and Dobrof, op. cit.
31. Morris and Sherwood, op. cit.
32. Ibid.
33. Alan Sager, *Planning Home Care with the Elderly: Patient and Family and Professional Views of an Alternative to Institutionalization* (Cambridge, Mass.: Ballinger, 1983).
34. Aluma Motenko, *Family Support for the Elderly: What Price Glory?* Paper presented at the 35th annual scientific meeting of the Gerontological Society of America, 1982, Boston, Mass.
35. Lang and Brody, op. cit.
36. Ibid.
37. Robert Morris, "Identifying Problems in Long Term Care," in James Callahan and Stanley Wallack (eds.), *Reforming the Long Term Care System* (Lexington, Mass.: Lexington Books, 1981).
38. Ethel Shanas and Marvin Sussman, "The Family in Later Life: Social Structure and Social Policy," in Robert Fogel et al. (eds.), *Aging: Stability and Change in the Family* (New York: Academic Press, 1981).
39. Victor Cicirelli, *Helping Elderly Parents: The Role of Adult Children.* (Boston, Mass.: Auburn House, 1981).
40. Patricia Archbold, "Impact of Parent-Caring on Women," *Family Relations* 32 (1983), pp. 39–45.
41. Cicirelli, op. cit.
42. Abraham Monk, "Social Work with the Aged: Principles of Practice," *Social Work* 26 (January 1981), pp. 61–68.
43. Barbara Silverstone and Ann Burack-Weiss, *Social Work Practice with the Frail Elderly and their Families: The Auxiliary Function Model,* (Springfield, Ill.: Charles C. Thomas, 1983), pp. 222–224.
44. Ibid.
45. Ibid.
46. Ibib.
47. Ibid.
48. Ibid.
49. Ibid.
50. Louis Lowy, "The Older Generation: What is Due, What is Owed," *Social Casework* 64, 6 (1983), pp. 64–66.
51. Ibid.
52. Barbara Silverstone and Helen Kandel Hyman, *You and Your Aging Parent: The Modern*

Family's Guide to Emotional, Physical and Financial Problems (New York: Pantheon Books, 1976).

53. George Getzel, "Social Work with Family Caregivers to the Aged," *Social Casework* 62, 4 (1981), pp. 201–209.
54. Morris and Sherwood, op. cit.
55. Silverstone and Hyman, op. cit.
56. Ibid.
57. Ibid.
58. Ibid.
59. Ibid.
60. Ibid.
61. Ibid.
62. Ibid.
63. Horowitz and Dobrof, op. cit.
64. Andrew E. Scharlach, *Relief of Role Strain Among Women with Aging Mothers.* Paper presented at the 36th annual meeting of the Gerontological Society of America, San Francisco, November 1983.
65. Ibid.
66. Ibid.
67. Margaret Blenkner, "Social Work and Family Relationships in Later Life with Some Thoughts on Filial Maturity," in E. Shanas and G. Streib (eds.), *Social Structure and the Family Generational Relations* (Englewood Cliffs, N.J.: Prentice-Hall, 1965).
68. Lowy, op. cit.
69. Silverstone and Hyman, op. cit.
70. Lowy, op. cit.
71. Rose Locker, "Institutionalized Elderly: Understanding and Helping Couples," *Journal of Gerontological Social Work* 3, 4 (1981), pp. 37–49.
72. M. F. Lowenthal and C. Haven, "Interaction and Adaptation: Intimacy as a Critical Variable" in Bernice L. Neugarten (ed.), *Middle Age and Aging* (Chicago: University of Chicago Press, 1968), pp. 220–234.
73. Elise Martini Beaulieu and Judith Karpinski, "Group Treatment of Elderly with Ill Spouses," *Social Casework* 64, 3 (1981), pp. 22–26.
74. Lowy, op. cit.
75. Silverstone and Hyman, op. cit.
76. Ibid.
77. Ibid.
78. Blenkner, op. cit.
79. Rose Dobrof and Eugene Litwak, *Maintenance of Family Ties of Long-Term Care Patients: Theory and Guide to Practice*, DHEW Publication, Number (ADM) 79–400, 1977 and 1979.
80. Shanas, "Social Myth", op. cit.
81. Sylvia Sherwood and John N. Morris, *Alternative Paths to Long Term Care.* Final Report to the Administration on Aging, June 1982.
82. Shanas, "Social Myth", op. cit.
83. Ibid.
84. Renee Solomon, "Serving Families of the Institutionalized Aged: The Four Crises" in George S. Getzel and Joanne M. Mellor (eds.), *Gerontological Social Work Practice in Long Term Care*, (New York: Haworth Press, 1983).
85. Ibid.

Working with Groups
of Older Persons

Our discussion of working with groups of older persons will follow the steps of the process-action model. Reviews of groups in institutional and community settings will be presented, as well as groups for minority elderly and elderly women. We shall begin with a brief look at different types of groups and the impact of different settings upon group work. Carol Meyer has written:

> The need for group services in this field is particularly clear because older people require peer support to sustain their ego image and self-confidence and to anchor them in times of swift transition and social discrimination. Use of groups to accomplish such tasks in a society that is alien to the needs of the aged population seems logical and humanitarian. Because loss of relationships, status, and community characterize the later phases of aging, the social isolation of older people becomes a salient issue for the social worker. Formed groups led by sensitive, energetic young social workers can bridge the gaps of loneliness and segregation that so often accompany old age.[1]

Settings

Older adult groups operate in a variety of settings under a variety of auspices — in multiservice centers, adult day health centers, senior centers, community centers, settlement houses, nursing homes, homes for the aged, hospitals, rehabilitation centers, churches, family service associations, veterans facilities, and so on. Many agencies operate group programs that meet many needs to varying degrees with varying success. The question must be raised, however, of whether these programs can be classified as social group work. *

Harriet Bartlett's constellation concept may be useful here:

> Social work practice, like the practice of all professions, is recognized by a constellation of value, purpose, sanction, knowledge and method. No part alone is characteristic of social work practice nor is any part described here unique to social work. It is the particular content and configuration of this constellation which makes it social work practice and distinguishes it from the practice of other professions. [2]

In other words, in social group work practice, the services provided must be under auspices with social work orientation and the practice must be under the direction of a social group worker. (This does not mean that specific aspects of service cannot be carried out by volunteers, untrained leaders, etc.) The setting in which social group work is practiced determines and influences many variables of the group work process. As Helen Phillips wrote:

> Clarity about agency function and ability to use it both for direction and selection of the worker's effort and for a stable point from which process emanates are essential to social group work skill. [3]

In working with the aged, as with any other group of people, social group workers adapt their services to the nature of the setting, utilizing its opportunities within its limits to achieve their goals with group members. To be able to use the inherent social structure and culture of a setting for beneficial activity is one of the outstanding contributions of the social worker among the helping professions. "The problems manifested by older people depend upon the balance between reality pressures and the person's usable resources—economic, emotional, social and physical." [4] The nature of the setting influences the way group programs are carried out as much as the auspices determine the goals and methods of the service. Social workers in a hospital or residential treatment center take into account such constellations as the ward and the presence of doctors, nurses, and other members of the treatment team, and attempt to utilize these environmental components in the helping process.

In a home for the aged, a nursing home, or a public housing project, to cite just a few examples, the nature of the setting, its social structure and normative patterns, and its organizational hierarchies and behavior will influence social work practice. It is to be noted that we have just begun to understand this dimension of the profession, and social science material on organizational theory and organizational behavior will have a good deal of bearing upon professional activity. While these group services utilize existing settings, it is also necessary to look into the use of groups in family service agencies. Many family service agencies utilize family groups for diagnostic and treatment purposes and integrate group work

---

* See Irene M. Burnside, *Working with the Elderly: Group Process and Techniques* (1978) for discussions of group psychotherapy with older people and elaboration of therapeutic group work practice.

knowledge and skill into their service programs. Harold B. Sharkey provides a good illustration of how a family agency makes use of the group as a modality to carry out its service function:

> The group has decided advantages in serving aged persons, especially those needing additional stimulation to widen their social and emotional experiences. . . . The content and purpose of groups can vary from one end of an extensive continuum—emphasis on clarification of attitude, examination of distortions in family relations, and maladaptive behavior—to, at the other end of the continuum, a primarily structured, cultural, and socializing experience.
>
> The department on Services to the Aged has participated in a limited way in the agency's family life education program. Informal talks to a variety of aged groups in community settings offering group services have been geared toward topics of general interest dealing with parent-child relationships, preparation for second marriages, and the like. The question periods that follow bring forth stimulating responses and discussion. Such meetings have additional value in that they serve to introduce the agency to a group that is generally reluctant to initiate applications for help. Experience indicates that during the two- to three-week period following the meeting, a number of individual applications are received from these groups, though stimulation of these applications is not at all the intent of the group educational service. . . .
>
> Services to the Aged has found at least two types of groups helpful. One is the formal, treatment-oriented group conducted by a [social] worker following or supplementing individual contact for some clients, the only medium of help for others. The other type is the quasi-social group. The agency can take forceful measures and initiative in bringing together into a small group individual clients whose depression and isolation have inhibited their social contact. The group should be mixed and should take turns meeting in individual homes, with simple refreshments served.
>
> Despite initial pressure by the worker and the clients' early wavering, once having established social contact, the clients will enjoy the experience and will look forward to future meetings. Although group services are still in the early stages, positive signs are emerging. For example, it has been noted that some people have begun to socialize with each other outside the regular meetings; one very timid man has openly expressed his desire to remarry, and the group is becoming more actively involved in planning for itself, although it continues to regard the worker as the expert, authoritative consultant.[5]

Some questions that can guide the social worker in assessing the impact of a setting are as follows:

1. What are the policies of the agency or organization with regard to the use of groups? Would administrative as well as direct-care staff willingly sanction social group work programs?
2. How do these policies affect the formation and operation of groups? For example, are there any rules and regulations that enhance or impede these processes? What types of facility exist that make group programs feasible and successful?

3. Are organizational structure and climate conducive to conducting group work, including such factors as schedules of other services offered and timing of nursing shifts at the setting?
4. Is there financial support to carry out group programs?
5. Would development of transportation services necessary to run the group be feasible?

Types of Groups

In social group work the dichotomy of task versus growth orientation has long permeated typological classification. While such dichotomy has been useful in its simplicity, it has not captured the subtleties and differentiations that exist in practice. A more sophisticated attempt was made by James Garland, who presents the following typology:

1. RECAPITULATION AND RESTITUTION

This type [is] most closely related to classical, psychoanalytically oriented insight groups. . . . [Such groups imply] high commitment to overall personal change on the part of the client; a reasonably intact ego and system of controls over impulsive behavior; long-term involvement. . . . Dynamics include processes such as: catharsis; therapeutic regression; high transference, both individual and group; and reenactment on an affective and/or action basis of significant emotional and relational states, especially those having their genesis in early childhood and/or present, intimate personal situations. The interactional assumption is of comprehensive involvement of all aspects of the personality with few attempts, at least in the beginning phases of the group, to be "social," "nice," or "cooperative." The stance of the worker/therapist is most likely to be permissive, non-directive, and non-self-disclosing. Some contra-indications for involvement in these kinds of groups are poor impulse control, problems with reality testing, psychotic character structure, and low motivation for change.

2. SUPPORT AND STABILIZATION

This model, probably most similar to the kind of group and individual work practiced historically in social agencies, involves attention to the ego and adaptive capacities of the client. It is most suited for: persons who, for whatever reason, have not contracted for major personality reorganization; persons with fragile character structure who cannot bear the intensity, stress, and complexity of type 1; persons who are experiencing life crises such as divorce, bereavement, economic instability and the like; and persons whose life circumstances are unsupportive, stress-producing or unstable. . . . [Examples are] persons subject to economic, racial or sexual discrimination and persons experiencing dehumanizing effects of large institutional life. Dynamics include: moderate transference; some regression in service of the ego; and clarification of present group process and affect (as compared to interpretation of genetic material). The interactional process may involve skill building, on the level of articulation and formation of concepts, concrete activity skills, and semididactic learning of negotiation and other social competencies. On the interpersonal level, the use of group support, cooperative activity and cohesion are more likely to occur earlier in the group than in the first type. The worker is more likely to be active, at times instructive, an initiator of verbal and activity structure, and, as above, more likely to operate more exclusively in the realm of clarification and response to derivative material.

3. GROWTH AND EDUCATION

This type, most familiar in traditional . . . [group service] agencies, is applicable to persons who are experiencing major life developmental challenges or transitions, or persons who, because of isolating, regressive, or stagnating influences over a long period of time, are at a point of needing to relearn or to learn for the first time certain kinds of developmental skills and competencies. This latter group might include, for example, persons who have been hospitalized in psychiatric institutions for many years, or . . . [people] who, for a variety of reasons, in their adult years are making major changes in life role and functioning. The growth group might, from a programmatic point of view, reflect a variety of styles. Most important is the focus on the specific kinds of competencies or social skills to be learned or the general range of developmental tasks to be encountered and mastered. Thus, the format of experience may range from didactic classes for adults on how to negotiate a loan, concrete recreational experiences associated with the transition of a child into peer group living, discussion of interpersonal relationships as experienced by married couples; or reminiscences on the part of elders about the total meaning of life experience in the light of their present social, psychological, physical, and political situation. The role of the group worker in this setting is likely to be flexible and range from the reactive-reflective stance all the way over to becoming a teacher of specific skills or an enabler of an outside expert or members themselves to be teachers of skills. Group composition is more likely to be determined by mutual growth issues than specific character structure. . . . It is not uncommon for a melding of the growth and support approaches to take place in the case where there is a crisis intervention that is associated with a life stage transition.

4. TASK AND ACTION

The task/action group is most closely related to the committee, the grassroots community organization group, ward government in . . . [institutional] settings. . . . It deals with group productivity as a primary goal and focus, involvement of the individual participant as a member with a role rather than as a total person; and attention to getting work done, as compared to focus on individual development or social relationships. Where the task approach is applied to persons with special needs (e.g., psychiatric patients), the structured work orientation may serve both as a filter and a conduit for mediating interpersonal relationships. It may provide a safe vehicle, when adapted for those purposes, to be used in the interest of the therapeutic or growth needs of these vulnerable persons. It may be particularly relevant when adapted for therapeutic purposes for persons with limited ego capacities, impulse disorders, or cognitive deficits, and/or little power to affect their personal lives, or their environments, from a political standpoint. It may be advantageous in this last regard, for example, for . . . elderly clients to act in their own behalf with regard to their autonomy and/or power relationships to the general community.[6]

Catherine Papell and B. Rothman conceptualized three models (social, remedial, and reciprocal) in social group work.[7] The models capture essential similarities and differences of purpose and group type, and postulate commensurate interventive stances by the social worker. Let us relate these to working with the aged.

The Social Model

The first model assumes a unity between social action and individual psychological health. The assumption is that individuals need opportunity and assistance in revitalizing their drive toward others in a common cause and in converting self-seeking to social contribution. This orientation toward creating skilled citizenry and social consciousness combined with the comparative responsibility of the aged makes the social model seem most appropriate in working with the aged, with its developmental tasks in a changing social environment. According to Maurice R. Linden and R. Courtney's developmental theory, senescence is a period of concern for "order and system" and "reaffirmation of moral and ethical standards," and therefore, the citizen role—an orientation to serving the community—can assume a new emphasis for the aged.

The social goal model advances programs for the aged that go beyond playing a role of "benign protector and provider." These programs attempt to fill the social needs of the ego in its aging process. Group self-consciousness leads to self-esteem in the elderly and as the aged perceive common interests and goals and band together to achieve mutual purposes of a social and economic character, prestige will increase. Increasing group identification around social problems and community issues may lend importance to older people's problems of insecurity and force the social environment to be less hostile to the aged population. Based on the idea that each individual has the ability or potential to anticipate meaningful activity directed toward societal change, emphasis is on community interests rather than on purely individualistic needs. The worker looks for and encourages the development of indigenous leadership and acts mostly in the role of a consultant. In an earlier work, I made the following points:

> The social group worker can do his [or her] share by utilizing his [or her] skills in developing meaningful activities [that] go beyond purely recreational functions . . . and which—in the context of nonwork roles—are societally approved roles nevertheless.
>
> Centers for the aged might do well to avoid the term *recreation* in their name and to establish a connotation that [they] cover a whole range of services and opportunity, says Max Kaplan. For many older adults, the "playful" aspects of these program activities produce feelings of conflict, guilt, and hence anxiety. I don't believe it is an accident that day centers have a disproportionate number

of women as members. For many men the program has aspects of being "sinful wasteful play," and to consider these activities as substitutes for a work role is not quite in keeping with reality. There are work activities which day centers or other community programs can utilize. . . . Service projects [using] men's work skills [as] tailors, artisans, etc. . . . can cooperate with other community services or industries. At the same time there is room for recreational play activity, if it is considered as such and not necessarily as a substitute for work which the older person has not yet accepted.[8]

The Remedial Model

The remedial model establishes a treatment contract. The worker takes a central role in determining the group's goals and orientation. Members are seen in a more unhealthy than healthy light and the goals are to help each member "get well." The worker is seen as an expert who establishes treatment goals for each member. In this model the members are very dependent upon the worker—"the worker knows best!"—and interaction between group members and the worker is fostered rather than interaction between group members themselves.

Fritz Redl speaks of treatment in the following manner:

Treatment is a multidefined term. Whenever you talk of treatment you speak not of an educational polishing process but of an "unpacking" process. This process must be related to particular phases of individual therapy. The group worker must design group life to support the indivdiual therapy process and must also indicate to individual therapist[s] where [their] limits must be placed at any one time.[9]

This model's use in groups of older adults reinforces the view that aging is a decline; it emphasizes pathology rather than health. Although at times treatment may be appropriate, the worker has to be careful not to impose this model when members are in fact able to function autonomously and independently.

The Reciprocal Model

The reciprocal model attempts to serve both the individual and the group. It views them in symbiotic interaction and focuses on the encounter of people in a system of mutual aid. There are no a priori therapeutic ends and, therefore, no goals of desired outcomes. Group members engage in interpersonal relations for problem resolution. The goals of group members become defined during the group process. The worker, as part of the group, shares in this process and relates his or her goals to the continuously emerging needs of the group and its members. As workers influence and are influenced, their goals and those of the group interrelate and tend to become complementary.

The major goal of workers is the creation of conditions that allow for reciprocity and for engagement in an existential endeavor to fulfill human needs and aspirations. Consequently, they do not have any specific goals for members or group but emphasize the general goals of "searching out common ground between need and demands of members, challenging obstacles which obscure this common ground," and developing and building a contract among members and with members and worker to strengthen the group's goals and to help it move toward achievement within the limits of the contract. This model allows for a sense of both control and mastery and also gives the worker room to provide support and protection by taking into account some dependency needs.

A Developmental Model

The design of a developmental model from the faculty of the Boston University School of Social Work is a compromise among the reciprocal, social-goals, and remedial models. Their model looks at group life as a "microcosm of the world" whereby experiences of members can be transferred to other situations in their lives. "It emphasizes the dimensions of interpersonal closeness and distance and allows for gradual development of the individual to become a member with varying degrees of investments in the life of others. As a result, time processes become significant aspects of development which are marked as phases of group life with their own pace, as the goals of the group are based on the needs, aspirations and capabilities of its members and continue to satisfy these needs."[10] Goals are based on the stage of group development at which individuals are and on their interests, differential needs, and aspirations as group members experiencing reciprocal relations with others. The worker, who is both part of and apart from the group, formulates generalized goals for the group and its members and modifies them according to his or her diagnostic impressions as the group develops over time.

Group goals attempt to relate group experiences to the world of reality, preparing the members for better adaptation to their life situation on the one hand, and on the other, utilizing this strength toward changing social conditions and structures when they are no longer serviceable or functional. In this respect, it combines features of the remedial, reciprocal, and social-goals models. The specific goals of workers—the result of a continuous diagnostic process of the person in the situation and in a social milieu—propels them to adapt their goals to the changing conditions, directions, and goals of the group and to each member's changing needs, interests, expectations, and goals. Behavioral changes of people and interaction rather than task accomplishment for its own sake are primary concerns of the worker. "Essential to guiding this process is the social group worker who must not only have understanding of the needs of individuals, of group formation and group development processes, but must also have skill in lending support on the one hand and making demands on the other, in order to keep up the tensions of interpersonal stimulation and hence, offer continued growth potential in negotiating closeness and distance of people to satisfy differential needs of group members."[11]

Choosing a Model

The nature of setting—institution, golden age club, hot-lunch program, etc.— and the need of people at a particular time in a specific situation will determine which model is most appropriate. Groups may use different models at different stages—they are not mutually exclusive. Groups of older adults are found in many settings; essentially, the purpose and goals of the people in the setting will determine how the group moves along and what it can do for and to the individual person. The social worker must be sensitive to this and must be aware of the potential, the limits, the problems, and the opportunities inherent in group work.

Many approaches to group work are currently being used with older adults; each may be more or less suited to one or more of the above models:

- life review, oral history, and reminiscence groups
- family and couples groups, such as groups designed to support couples, one or both of whom have entered a nursing home, in adjusting to loss of traditional marital roles, depression, anxiety, financial strain, and reactivation of old family conflicts
- widow's and widower's support groups
- remotivation and reality orientation therapy groups
- music, art, and dance therapy groups
- women's consciousness-raising groups (Barrett, for example, found this type of group was more effective than either self-help or "confidante" groups in facilitating women's adjustment to widowhood)[12]
- psychodrama groups, which Kerry Paul Altman feels are useful in mitigating role reduction and facilitating role reengagement or substitution for elders[13]
- movement, exercise, or yoga groups, "focusing on sensory integration, eye-hand coordination, range of motion, increased lung capacity, endurance and strength," as well as social interaction[14]
- nutrition groups
- discussion groups that "promote a process which yields increased social interaction, improved reality orientation, self-esteem, and increased understanding of self and others" and that provide an easy format for newcomers to groupwork[15]
- traditional psychotherapy groups
- disability-specific treatment groups with increased social interaction as an important correlated goal
- mutual support groups
- life skills groups (i.e., for deinstitutionalized mental patients) to develop such faculties as verbal and noncommunication skills through such techniques as role play. As Nora Stabler writes, it can be a great deal less embarassing to relearn basic skills with other people who have the same problem[16]
- ethnic- or race-specific support groups
- special interest groups
- leisure time groups
- social action groups
- neighborhood groups

In 1981 Toseland, Sherman, and Bliven, for example, found that an approach based on the growth orientation, group process, discussion format, and less directive leadership style was more effective than a more structured and task-oriented approach for developing a mutual support group among the community elderly.[17]

Needs Met by Group Participation

In an earlier work, the author reviewed Howard McClusky's categorization of the differential needs of older persons on a minimal–optimal continuum. This categorization is useful to place needs on a hierarchical scale. How satisfaction of these needs may be facilitated at successive phases of social group work under the developmental model will be illustrated later.

Coping needs come into play in order to meet fundamental survival concerns through adapting to changes associated with the aging process[,] such as reductions in energy, and change[s] in the social position of older people which are likely to result in reductions of income, health and functional ability of social affiliations, status and relationships. At the same time there is an expansion of disposable time and a greater freedom from certain role obligations. Coping with such changes requires adaptation because unless these coping needs are met successfully, there is little power left with which to meet the additional human needs. Taking Maslow's hierarchical concept, we can assert that opportunities for meeting survival needs through successful coping mechanisms—individually or socially supplied—are basic to meeting all other needs.

Expressive needs designate those strivings associated with fulfilling oneself by engaging in activities for their own sake and not necessarily to acccomplish a task or reach a goal which can be designated as instrumental. In later years, notably with more disposable time available and fewer work-role demands placed upon people [men and women], expressive needs can find greater potentialities for outlets, provided they have not been stifled too much during the preceding periods of the life cycle. Talents and interests dormant or alive can be stimulated to make the later years more expressively productive rather than merely instrumentally productive.

Expression of contributory needs [is] predicated on the assumption that people want to give to others, to their families, their friends and neighbors, to their "community," however defined. The blend of self-interest and altruistic interest in human beings is always fascinating; the extent of this blend constitutes a significant dimension of the human personality. Older persons certainly have the same need to share and negotiate the blending of "self and other interests" as have younger people. In addition, however, they have accumulated many life experiences, some digested, some undigested, some fragmented, some integrated—but they have a reservoir of contributions to be tapped by others, in the service to others— whether young, middle-aged or old. This is what Butler refers to as the "elder function" in a society, the task to leave a legacy and to contribute thereby to the heritage of civilization.

We all need to exert some degree of influence on the factors impinging upon the conditions of our lives. Despite the impression that the degree of influence over our lives has appreciably diminished, we continue to strive to assert our powers of affecting the world we live in and it seems that without the illusion or reality of exerting some measure of influence, we would be unable even to meet our basic coping needs. As people grow older, their exertion of influence diminishes greatly, because they are relegated to inferior statuses, diminished positions of power in their social world as the results of ageist, discriminatory attitudes and practices in large parts of this world. And yet, as people grow older, they can exert influence over segments of their lives and their social world—individually and collectively—if they are consciously aware of the types of influences possible and if they associate with others, as the experiences of the "Gray Panthers" have quite effectively demonstrated. Older people want to continue to enjoy a sense of mastery and autonomy and exert some measure of control over certain aspects of their life-space, even those who are residents of total institutions.

All people at any stage in their lives need opportunities for expression of love and affection, for gratification of their ego-needs, for being assured that life has a purpose and meaning. At the later phases of the life cycle, this need seems even more pronounced than earlier where one is still more concerned with the todays and tomorrows than with the yesterdays, and when time to make up, time for restitution is diminishing. The need for transcendence rather than preoccupation with continued ego-involvement . . . appears to be a most profound need as one reaches the later years of one's life. What have I done with my life? (Erikson) Has it been invested with meaning? (Frankl) What legacy do I leave? (Butler) To age successfully, indeed, means to come to terms with body-transcendence and to achieve a "sense of integrity" when completing the only life cycle available to any of us.[18]

Major needs of older people are detailed individually in the following non-hierarchical framework.

Love and Affirmation

To a large extent, our needs to belong, be rooted, and be accepted are based on our relationships with those we love—family and friends. As people grow older, close family members and friends depart and leave the older person alone in a world of yesterday. In earlier years, the loss of a loved one was traumatic enough; however, the younger person could still overcome the loss by replacement. For the aged person, isolation and loneliness gradually become a reality that did not exist before. The new surrounding world seems cold, unconcerned, and strange.

Where are the roots for belonging? This sense of aloneness and being deprived of family and peers engenders a feeling of irrelevance, meaninglessness, and status anxiety unknown to the majority of younger people. It necessitates an emotional reorientation, for which many older people do not have so great a capacity, and also a new role adaptation, for example, as widower or widow, whose status and concomitant role definitions are at best ambiguous in our society. "Group associations can provide many opportunities to replace old friends with new ones, to substitute family ties with peer ties, to give new status and hence new relevance to one's existence."[19] Self-help groups, for example, can "enable the elderly to provide emotional support, encouragement, and practical help to one another in an atmosphere of commonality of interest and commonality of experiences."[20]

Usefulness

Usefulness in our society is measured in terms of work output; not being part of the work community places inevitable strains upon the older person. Compensations for this loss of status (and its concomitant feeling of uselessness) are not easy to come by. In our society cultural goals of achievement and success are highly venerated; the instrumentality for realizing these goals is found mostly through our economic system, that is, in business, in the trades or in the professions. For those who are no longer part of this "instrumentality," our society has not offered too many acceptable alternatives. To use Robert Merton's concept here, we might say that the discrepancy between the cultural goals and the institutionalized means is great indeed and therefore produces an anomic state for the aged. Can we develop "modes of adaptation" which avoid a "retreatism" and "rebellion"? Can we help older adults devise modes of "innovation" which are feasible, desirable, and meaningful to the aged and to the culture at large?

What type of group experiences can further this "mode of innovation"? How can older persons get a sense of achievement and success (our highly valued cultural goal) when the means used [such as artistic activity, games, and play] are frequently devalued? Aren't many older people ambivalent about these societally devalued means to achieve success? Could this not call for a two-pronged approach to the content of group experiences: (1) initially, to select "programs" which are valued in our society (economic activity, civic activity); (2) to interpret to old and young the potential and actual value of programs which are customarily referred to as "leisure-time activity."[21]

Frail elderly have little chance to develop reciprocal relationships since their role in dyadic relationships with care-givers is often dependent. Groups can serve as an antidote to such a harmful situation.[22] Further, a group can provide opportunities for frail elders to cope with and vent anxiety and fear regarding their growing dependency, thus freeing them to invest such "bound" energy in ways more productive for them as individuals and as a group.[23]

Growth through Learning

The older adult brings to the learning situation a greater volume of experiences (quanity) and more different kinds of experiences (quality) than young people or middle-aged adults do. A youngster's experience is derived from external sources. Older adults' experience is within themselves; it is what they have done. Their identity is defined in terms of what they have accomplished, how they have lived so far. By virtue of this definition of *self*, the person has a great investment in its value. Where a situation minimizes the worth of self, people are left with feelings that their experiences are rejected and that they are rejected as well. Because older people have rich experiences, techniques should tap their experiences and ability as learners; group discussions and group projects should be emphasized since participation and ego involvement ensures more learning.

Attempts have been made by adult educators to relate new concepts and broad generalizations to experiences drawn from the learner. Studies on the transfer of learning and the maintenance of behavioral change have indicated the desirability of another step: to include in the design of learning opportunities for experience so that learners can plan and rehearse how they will apply this learning to their day-to-day life. A major concept in androgological (adult education) practice is the "unfreezing experience," whereby learners are helped to look at themselves more objectively and to free their minds from preconceptions. Group work can help older people come to grips with new learning situations and take responsibility for their own learning through self-directed inquiry—to learn collaboratively, not competitively, and to learn by analyzing their own life experiences.

Status and Identity

Many older people in our society experience losses of status and social identities. In an earlier work, I arranged these identities under three headings—work identity, identity related to a change of family roles, and sexual identity.

> In a work-oriented society which values highly the Protestant ethic, an individual is expected to perform a work role. An individual occupies many statuses, but our society accords the highest status in the hierarchy to those individuals who participate in the work roles which society has defined fairly clearly. Each member is expected to occupy a work status and to perform the appropriate role in that status. The person's "who-ness" is determined by what a person does. . . . Work identity gives [people their] social identity.
>
> [Older adults who are] retired (whether by choice or by compulsion) find [themselves] out-of-step with society's expectations; . . . part of [their identity is lost; they are] no longer [producers]; at best [they are consumers] (often with limited means and hence not too useful as that either in the economic sense). Loss of work identity adds another dimension of trauma to the gradual isolation and aloneness mentioned above. Many of our interpersonal associations are found in the "world of work." The work group is a major impetus for creating peer associations, which often extend beyond the immediate work environment. It can be seen that retirement cuts people off from these associations and contributes toward creating feelings of isolation and loneliness.
>
> Emotional supports of parts of the family and work group have been withdrawn from many older people. Increased isolation and an ambiguous status, which produces status anxiety in an anomic social structure, feed into the older person's emotional problems. What types of group support are available . . . to give . . . a sense of status, a self-image of worthiness, of accomplishment? As Alvin J. Goldfarb writes: "In order to maintain [self-esteem, the mentally older adult] may crave appreciation, marks of affection, or reassurance that he [or she] has made an impression upon this world in his [or her] lifetime through his [or her] words, . . . deeds or . . . children. One or more of these proofs of achievement may be

especially important . . . if there is no longer opportunity . . . to maintain self-esteem through the continued performances of duties by wage earning or through service.[24]

Ego Integration and Gratification

In order to function as an "executive," the ego needs hope, needs a linkage of past, present, and future. Since the older person is faced with physical decline, a loss of social identity, a feeling of economic and social insecurity, the ego is less flexible and less able to adapt when adaptive tools are needed most, namely, during a period of transition and readaptation. . . . To preserve identity, old persons attempt to withdraw and exclude stimuli. They react by protecting the boundaries of the ego; by excluding stimuli (they see what they want to see, hear what they want to hear); by conserving their energy in avoiding new, unknown situations; by regressive behavior; and often by being excessively dependent in order to coerce love [while] at the same time bemoaning the dependence, fighting it.

Roughly, we can differentiate four basic modes of adaptation to stress situations: (1) fight, (2) flight, (3) pairing, and (4) dependency. Many older people use all four interchangeably, [as] expressed in aggressive, withdrawing, complying, and dependent behavior. While particular behavior manifestations depend upon the particular personality structure's response to the normal crisis of aging, we know from experience that the crisis of aging demands major adjustments for the person, especially in a society in which institutional means have not been too widely available.[25]

If structured well, the group becomes ego-supportive and can provide what the ego needs—hope and a sense of the future. Thus, it can help members to assess the present realistically, with the support of the members and the worker. To summarize, Jean Maxwell's statement as to the six opportunities that groups provide in meeting needs of older people serves eminently well:

1. Providing peer support
2. Renewing old friendships and replacing old friends with new ones
3. Developing new "identities" as a result of new statuses
4. Increasing the scope of belongingness beyond family—getting a sense of participating in community and home usefulness
5. Providing recognition and "status" and a sense of self-esteem
6. Helping define new expectation of behavior, hence developing new modes of functioning.[26]

Life Review

Furukawa and Shomaker, drawing on the work of Butler and Lewis, have written about the usefulness of group work in helping the elderly negotiate the developmental tasks of aging through life review and reminiscence:

The activities and processes used for the life review and reminiscent groups are quite similar. Each group attempts to allow elderly individuals to verbalize and share their experiences. Initially, when the tendency for older people to direct their thoughts to the past and to self-reflect was observed, it was believed to be an indication of loss of recent memory. However, a therapeutic quality emerged as the consequences of the life review process were scrutinized. Butler postulated that reminiscence was a normal part of life review evolving from the elder's realization of approaching dissolution and death. The process is characterized by a conscious effort to recall past experiences, and, in particular, unresolved conflicts are reexamined and reintegrated. The ability to reintegrate and find resolution to conflicts gives new significance and meaning to a person's life and eventual preparation for death by mitigating fear and anxiety.

Life review activities may include obtaining older person's extensive biographies from them and other family members. Some instruments useful in the life review process are family albums, scrapbooks, memorabilia, genealogies, and other re-membrances that may expedite reawakening of key memories and responses. The recalling activity is conducive to assisting the older family members summarize life's work and frequently, the process allows for shared feelings about parenting with their offspring. Hence, the goals and effects of life review are "expiation of guilt, resolution of intrapsychic conflicts, reconciliation of family relationship, transmission of knowledge and values to those who follow and renewal of ideas of citizenship and the responsibility for creating a meaningful life. In many respects, the life review process has a psychotherapeutic quality beneficial to the participants.

The reminiscing process is viewed as a developmental milestone that allows a person to gain an understanding about life. A reminiscing group is useful to older people because it offers an opportunity to share experiences with each other, to gain an insight of self and others, and to review historical events of the time. The sharing of memories often promotes a bonding among the participants, assists to reaffirm individual identity and personal worth, and reduces loneliness and isolation.

Reminiscing groups may be long- or short-term, formal or informal, and structured or spontaneous. Short-term groups have a limited number of participants, and topics are selected to meet the special needs of the participants. Generally, sessions for this group are held to less than ten weeks. Long-term reminiscing groups have a more formal structure, require a periodic assessment and review of their goals, and admit new members only upon individual group members' approval. A weekly meeting is also conducive to establishing a reminiscing group and provides an event that older people may anticipate on a regular basis. Spontaneous reminiscing groups are usually informal and often serve as entertainment with nostalgic qualities stimulated by special occasions. A democratic and open climate is necessary for sharing memories and is essential for all types of reminiscing groups.

The reasons for developing reminiscing groups for older people are to:

- form cohort affiliation
- enhance socialization
- exchange ideas
- augment interaction
- promote intergenerational understanding
- faciliate recreation
- expedite reality orientation and remotivation

- encourage therapeutic life review
- work toward self-actualization and creativity
- serve as a springboard for starting other types of groups.[27]

Entry Phase of the Process-Action Model in Working with Groups

The group has to come into being; it has to begin. This part of the process involves choosing group members and reaching out to individuals to become affilitated and to establish a contract.

Group Formation

Most older adults are ambivalent about joining a group. This is due in part to poor self-image, a fear of rejection by others in the group, and a reluctance to risk entering into intimate relationships in light of previous losses. Thus, in the beginning, it may be advisable to plan activities that place little demand on members, such as listening to a lecture or concert.[28]

When older people first come to the program they are generally passive participants, and activity is most often a threat rather than a challenge. The tendency is to develop personal relations on a superficial level with the substitution of fantasy for emotional participation. This is particularly true in the club program; meeting once a week produces a transient and necessarily superficial relationship. In the day center, open five days a week from 9 A.M. to 5 P.M. there is a living and participating experience, a way of life that has a considerable effect on the individual's capacity for developing satisfying social relationships and dynamic experiences. Harry Levine writes:

> In the day center, the older person moves slowly but surely toward active participation and social activity, first with one person and then in small groups, moving toward groups involving more members and finally with the center as a whole involving all of the members. Efforts are made to expand their interest and to increase their ability to carry some responsibility for developing their own program. We involve older persons in helping one another, but most important, we create a climate affecting the group so that it has warmth and is conducive to growth and expansion of the personality.
>
> The program is organized with the understanding of the capacity of the individual and within the capacity of the particular individual at this particular stage, so that the program tends to stimulate interest and involve the older person in constructive, meaningful, and at the same time, pleasurable activities. Often the older person who is part of a subgroup will need constant encouragement and repeated assurance to be able to continue attending and to move forward to a larger group. This encouragement provides the help he [or she] needs to be part of the group.[29]

Sebastian P. Tine speaks about the defenses against involvement:

Socially mature individual[s have] mastered the act of maintaining . . . personal integrity by being able to make wise choices in the selection of . . . involvements and commitments to others. The process of maturation . . . necessarily involves the ability to protect [oneself] from the dangers of overextending [oneself] in areas which may detract from the realization of [one's] most personal and familial goals. . . . When the individual reaches old age he [or she] has achieved a degree of mastery in this respect. . . . The varied defensive techniques [used] against involvement may have become unconscious in operation. The suggestion for involvement in social relationships may bring about automatic defensive maneuvers by the older adult. What was once a healthy process in earlier years may become a means of furthering one's own isolation. . . . This may explain the nonspecific resistance . . . older adults have to group participation.[30]

Criteria for forming groups include, for the pleasure- and utilitarian-minded members:

1. Relevance of the activity to the individual's stated interests
2. Relevance of the activity to worker's estimate of the individual's unconscious motivation
3. Place of the suggested group and the individual's pattern of attendance
4. Individual's level of developmental resources in relation to the requirements of the activity
5. Special staff goals for particular individuals.

And for members with particular problems:

1. Level of positive health
2. Degree of vision and hearing loss
3. Amount of affect shown in individual contacts with worker
4. Ability to handle interpersonal contacts as seen in individual's reaction to group situations
5. Attitude toward group experiences
6. Degree of independence
7. Income level
8. Number and quality of relationships with others—family, friends, etc.
9. Number and quality of present group affiliations.[31]

The importance of the worker's outreach efforts to potential new members of a group cannot be overemphasized. This is crucial if the worker is to overcome the difficulties described in starting a new group. Thus, the worker's approach has to be threefold: (1) to individualize the members and make accurate diagnoses of each member's stage of development vis-à-vis the tasks of aging; (2) to assess whether the group can meet the individual's needs; (3) to be able to use his or her skills to make the group work process enhance the individual's functioning as a member of the group. Whenever possible, requests to join the group should be honored.[32]

Initiating Person-to-Person Affiliations

Garland et al. comment on the preaffiliative stage of group development in the developmental model:

> The initial period of group association is one in which the members are becoming familiar with one another and the situation, and have not yet formed close ties. Relationships are [not] usually intimate and a good deal of use may be made of rather stereotypic activity as a means of getting acquainted and at the same time retaining some distance and protection. The group and the worker tend to be seen as reflections of other groups and leaders with which the individual has had contact in his [or her] social experience (as distinguished from family experience). Members' ambivalence toward involvement is reflected in their vacillating response to program activities and events. An on-again, off-again attitude toward such things as parallel versus interactive play, accepting versus not accepting, and responsibility versus avoidance in cleanup and planning [is] quite common. The basic struggle in this ambivalent, preaffiliative phase, when viewed in the light of the closeness dimension, is one of approach and avoidance. Whether the group's members elect officers and plan a month in advance at the first meeting or lurk outside the club room furtively peeking in the door, they are probably experiencing some kind of anxiety about becoming involved and are attempting to find ways within their framework of social experience to accomplish this process of exploration and affiliation.[33]

The frame of reference for members is a societal one, members identifying not with the group that is in the process of formation, but with those of previous experiences. This accounts for the initial difficulties many members have at first attempts in relating to others—they come to the group with a negative societal reference point and are quite resistant to extend themselves to others. Workers use skills in guiding members' early interactions with one another, helping them, in effect, learn resocialization techniques. Workers are seen as representatives of society's attitudes and norms, and thus the posture taken here is cultural, for they can help the group become an arena for identifying new self-images.

In working with older persons, exploration and assessment take into account the specific circumstances of the stress situation that aging produces, and the basic problems and/or developmental tasks that are indigenous to old age in our culture. Workers recognize that their diagnosis, or assessment, takes into account the following factors:

1. Overall needs and developmental tasks of older adults in our society
2. Function and structure of the agency and services provided for the older adult
3. Particular social and cultural milieu of the older adult; background, aspirations, norms, and values
4. Particular problem constellation of the older adult; which group for whose needs?
5. Particular personality of each person—as an individual and as a group member.

Based on a diagnosis, the group worker is in a position to determine what type of group meets what type of need and solves what type of problem, and what kinds of guided group interaction and program media are indicated to accomplish what kinds of goals. Opportunities may produce certain results, but we should be sure whether they are intended or just happened to occur.

Establishing a Contract

Furukawa and Shomaker feel that establishing a written or oral contract with group members at the outset serves to minimize issues that could become disruptive to the group process.[34] They suggest that the contract "provide clear guidelines for the group's meeting schedule, the obligations of the members individually and collectively," and that it include "expected number of members, whether attendance is mandatory, the purpose of the group, and how meetings and socialization will be structured," and most importantly, insurance of confidentiality among group members and leader(s). They feel such a contract is effective in ameliorating members' anxiety and thus frees energy for group process.

Needs Met at the Entry Phase

During the entry stage when a group formation process gets underway, vulnerable older persons are most likely to be most apprehensive[,] and psychological as well as physical distance are probably to be maintained at arms' lengths. To bring a few people together in greater physical proximity than heretofore is now the most important activity by the worker; people may not engage in interactional pursuits, [or] take much notice of each other at first, but repeated contact may foster a breakdown of physical space barriers and lead to a lessening of physical, if not psychological distance.

Their coping needs are being addressed, as are their needs to exert some influence over their own life space. To be near to somebody else may turn out to be useful to that "somebody else" and the older person has indeed contributed to others and even received from others, in turn.[35]

Illustration of Entry into a Group

The following vignette, which describes the first meeting of a group, illustrates the approach-avoidance issues faced by the social worker during the preaffiliative stage.

The Agency. The older adult service of city A has a long tradition of services for older people. Most clients came downtown into the agency until 1970, when outreach services started. The agency serves elderly in need of subsidized housing as well as those of moderate means. A trained social worker has her office in a housing project, where people can come to her with their problems at certain hours. She also maintains an office at the downtown agency. Another social worker was assigned to meet with a group in the lounge for the purpose of developing with them some group activities.

Group Members. There are sixteen group members, most over 65 years old, mainly women with a variety of ethnic backgrounds.

- Mrs. F. is Chinese. She lost her property in Mainland China. Two sons live in the United States. She speaks several languages, but is not adept in English.
- Mrs. V. feels responsible for the lounge. She opens it at 2 P.M. She is a very active black woman and likes all kinds of handicrafts.
- Miss L., Mrs. V.'s sister, is a friendly person and all the black women talk to her. She has poor eyesight.
- Miss M. has a physical disability and has been hospitalized several times.
- Miss G. suffers from arthritis and has to use a cane. She likes to remember the good times.
- Mrs. T. is in a wheelchair. She is the only one in the group who is younger than 65.
- Mrs. P. is quiet, rarely opens her mouth. She has difficulty with her dentures.
- Mrs. A. is very lively when she talks; she is more than 80 years old. She has poor eyesight and uses a cane.
- Mr. C. is a widower, former cook; he likes to play cards.
- Mrs. P. is a well-dressed woman about whom nothing is recorded.
- Miss R., Mrs. A.'s sister, is very quiet. They came together at the first meeting only.
- Mrs. R. came only for a short time to the first meeting. She is a black woman who just wanted to talk to Miss L.
- Mrs. E. had just moved in the day before the first group meeting. She has poor hearing and wears a hearing aid.
- Mrs. S. likes to make yarn poodles. She only came to the meeting to talk to Mrs. V. on this topic.
- Mrs. B. is a black woman who has a good sense of humor.
- Mrs. L. is black. She is always smiling, but rarely talks.

First Meeting.

Soon after 2 P.M., two women came into the lounge, and worker asked where they usually sat in this room. Worker was told that they mostly grouped in the middle of the room around the table. Worker thought it was a bit long, but did not like to alter it the first day, thinking they were used to it. The two women were talking about the article in the "militant" newpaper of the neighborhood. Miss M. said she thought a person living here had given wrong information. Worker asked if they would perhaps like to give better information to the same paper. But they did not answer the question, telling worker, "It will come out."

Gradually seven women arrived, and they and worker talked about the rainy weather, etc. At about 2:30 P.M., worker began to define her role. Worker told them she was from Germany, had taught there in a school of social work, and now is studying here. Then worker made clear that she was now coming once a week on Thursday afternoons for an hour or so to have a group meeting with them and that she could not come as often as their former worker had done. Worker asked them to introduce themselves and to write their names on a piece of paper, so that she could learn to know them better. They all did it, and Mrs. F. asked worker to write down her name for her. Worker wrote it and she translated it in Chinese letters. She had introduced herself as an "international woman." Worker asked if all the others were Americans and if they were from the city. Miss G. answered they were.

The group was interrupted by Mrs. A. coming from the outside, where it was still raining. Worker's neighbor was very polite, getting a comfortable chair for her and putting her on worker's side. Mrs. A. soon started to talk; she said she had bad eyes and bad legs (she was coming with her cane) and she could not do much in a group. Worker said, "We can talk about different subjects and perhaps tell what would be interesting to all of us.

Mrs. F. wanted to know something about Germany, and after having whispered with Mrs. T., who sat with her wheelchair at her side, they asked worker if her mother was still baking bread at home. Worker answered, "No, we were buying it at the bakery. Only for the weekend, my mother used to bake cakes and of course cookies, above all for Christmas." Some of the women said it was the same here; when they first came to America, they had to bake their bread themselves and then all these bakeries got started. They then said Germans were good housewives. Worker answered that in the time of her grandmother, they certainly were devoted to the house and their families, but already in her mother's generation some women started to have professions and now even more. But still many women stay at home during the years when their children are small, because there are only a few day-care facilities.

They then started to talk about the children here. It was Miss G. who started to say that they were in the streets until 10 or 11 o'clock at night and that this had not been possible when they themselves were young. Worker asked if the children were noisy. Mrs. A. said that they had been very dangerous to her when she was down to look for her mail. One day they had tried to get her purse. Some of the women told her to keep outside the corridor if there was a gang of children. Mrs. V. started to tell that once when she bought a cabbage a woman asked if she could hand her a cabbage too, and while she was trying to get it, the woman took some dollars out of her purse. "You cannot trust people any more these days," she said, and some of the tenants agreed.

Mrs. F. brought the talk back to Germany, asking worker if it was true that in Germany, before the time of Hitler, women had started to get into professions, then had to go back to their families, and what did worker think was better? Worker answered, "I was a child before Hitler's time and I do not really know if many women had professions there, but I know that Hitler wanted mothers to have many children and they had to stay at home if there was nobody to look after the children." Worker added that she thinks when a woman decides to have children, she has the task to give them a good home, and if she has no children or her children are teenagers, she should have a chance to find a good profession. But this was perhaps sometimes not easy to realize.

Miss M. said, "All this women's liberation is exaggerated, women can get good jobs here." Worker would have been interested to talk more about this, but they were interrupted. Mrs. F. had to leave because she had to see her doctor.

She tried to say worker's name when she said goodbye, but she had some difficulty with it. Mrs. T., in the wheelchair, said they had lived near each other for some time now. They used first names and often did not know last names. Worker answered that they could call her by her first name too. Soon after, a man, Mr. Ch., came into the lounge; they called him by his first name. They told him that they had a new group leader, whispering to worker that he could not see her. Worker was trying to find out what activities they would like to begin on the following Thursday. He said he liked to play cards and asked if worker could play whist. Worker answered, "I played it in England but was better at canasta." He did not know that game. Worker asked if the ladies were interested in playing cards, but they seemed to be indifferent. Mr. C. left soon after and worker again started to ask them what they would like to do.

Mrs. T. said she liked to cook. Worker joined in to ask if they could do it in the kitchen near the lounge. They said yes, but nobody wanted to do the work, above all to wash the dishes afterwards. Mrs. T. replied that she could sit with her chair in the kitchen and do the cooking, and she proposed to make crêpes (pancakes). The people then discussed what was needed for pancakes and what they could have with them: syrup, sausages, and coffee. "You will make the coffee, you make the best coffee," they said to Mrs. V. She was sitting on worker's right-hand side preparing white wool. Worker told her she was very quiet and asked what she thought about the idea. She answered, "I am just listening."

While they were talking about this, Mrs. R. came into the lounge in her raincoat and turned to Miss L. to talk to her. It was a bit disturbing for the rest of the group, but worker did not say anything about it since this was her first time with the group. It was already 3:30 P.M., and worker said she had to leave soon; perhaps they could make the pancakes in a fortnight, if somebody could bring the flour and everybody could contribute some money for the eggs. They did not come to a decision, and worker said they could decide this next Thursday and also asked them what else they would like to do next week.

As they did not come up with any plans, worker said it would be very interesting for her to know something about their life experiences, especially if they could think of a "funny story" from their lives that they could tell next Thursday. Miss L. said she had not had much fun in her life, but her sister said she could sing a song. Worker said yes, they could also contribute something else to entertain the group. Worker had already gotten up from her chair to say goodbye when Mrs. P. apologized for coming late, saying that she had tried to find matching shoes for the dress she intended to wear to her daughter's wedding the following week. Worker sat down again because she felt she should talk a bit to her. Mrs. P. said immediately she did not like to knit but to cook. So they told her about the plan to make pancakes. Then worker said she must really leave now (it was almost 4 P.M.) and she wished them a nice evening. "I hope to see you next week." Most of the people said they were looking forward to it.

Discussion of Illustration. This is a typical entry situation. The individuals entering the room are quite unsure what this venture is all about; they and the worker engage in small talk to feel each other out. The worker herself is apprehensive and feels uneasy. While the members had met before and knew one another, the worker is unknown to them. She has to deal with the approach-avoidance conflict. Introductions served to break the ice. The worker's background served as a ready topic of conversation; it was to the members an emotionally neutral subject, and her reference to her grandmother was to become a first link in the chain for building relationships. The next theme concerned the generation of children in the neighborhood and the members' concerns about their safety, a topic uppermost in the minds of many older persons in the city.

Testing of the worker proceeded, and the members informed her that referring to one another by first names had been a norm; this indicated already the existence of a common bond and pointed to the fact that they felt some sense of belonging. They were a group in the first stage of development, and the worker had to fit into it; she had to gain the trust of the members and adhere to the norms that were already accepted by them. There were attempts by the worker to move toward defining the task for both parties and to look for areas of agreement in order to set up a service contract. She was aware of the backlog of life experiences of the people and was sensitive to their concerns, trying to tap their strengths, resources, and skills (e.g., making pancakes and coffee).

Decision making as a group could not succeed as yet, since the approach-avoidance issue had not been resolved when the new worker entered the scene. Leaving the first meeting was more difficult for the worker than for the members; she finally managed it and built a bridge for the future: "See you next week." There was to be continuity; entry had been accomplished, and the stage was set for engaging to define the task for further work. The worker right from the outset perceived herself primarily to be in the role of enabler, which was also expected by group members.

Defining the Task

The worker and the group come to define their tasks together, both the goals the worker sets forth initially for the members-to-be and the group goals that develop as the aggregate becomes a group. "The task of working with the older adult is a resocialization process and since resocialization occurs in one's experience with [oneself] in relation to others, the opportunity for interaction is more prevalent in smaller groups."[36] It is the peer association needs that are primary, not the worker-member needs. As Susan Kubie and Gertrude Landau write, the *worker* becomes a bridge in guiding member-to-member relationships:

> The status of the group, the feeling of doing what is expected, the rewards which result—these provide the person (not the role) with a consciousness of what others think of him [or her]. A self-image is made possible which may be internalized and transferred to other groups. The interpersonal relationships of group members provide opportunities for members to develop a "social self" based on the reality of individual performance and achievement. It is the social worker's task to guide these relationships so that the performance and achievements are positive, realistic; [to] instill a sense of mastery . . . is especially important because the older person

has met "frustration of mastery" in the outside world. His [or her] services in the world of work are no longer needed, . . . past contributions [are] often forgotten.

This leads to another important factor, namely, resocialization. The older adult is faced with transitional status—an ambiguous role expectation and performance—because he [or she] is cut off from a previously enjoyed status in the community, in . . . work, family, and citizen-status roles, and not offered a new, well-defined status in return. Therefore, he [or she] harbors ambivalent or openly hostile feelings toward those who deprive him [or her] of . . . social positions. The negative traits often ascribed to reaction formation can be handled only "by a slow process of resocialization through satisfying interaction with a new community." A new social circle—the group—can be utilized in this process of resocialization as a "laboratory" for the older person to test out, . . . to get back a reflection of . . . acts with the help of an empathetic and understanding worker who helps avert overwhelming failure and shame, who is there to protect and guide, to enable and teach.[37]

Moving from Testing toward a Contract

Once the basic problem has been solved as to whether the group experience is potentially safe, rewarding, and worth a preliminary emotional investment, members begin to lock horns with the power and control issues of group life. The problems of status, ranking, communication, choice making, and influence come to the fore. There is a testing of the group worker and other members, and an attempt to define and formalize the relationships and to create a status hierarchy. Physical strength, aggressiveness, mental agility, and skill in whatever endeavors the group considers to be of high value must be discovered. Cliques form and alliances are made, at times for purposes of mutual protection. These may vary in size from two against the group to the total group against one. This latter situation sometimes arises out of the need of the group to protect itself from a very powerful and aggressive member, or from the psychic danger posed by a deviant or handicapped member. It is at this time that scapegoating first appears and, with it, an attempt to exclude individuals from membership.

> The relationship which appears to be most significant in connection with the power-control issue and which has the greatest effect on the nature and intensity of intragroup control dynamics is that between the worker and group. The worker has the ability to give or withhold in material or emotional terms, and this may include food, handicraft materials, a meeting room, extra time for meetings, or personal attention for individuals. His [or her] role as therapist, teacher, parent, or representative of agency, community or social class, however the group perceives him [or her] gives him [or her] a potential for influencing the affairs of the members that is at the same time comforting and overwhelming.[38]

The task-definition phase represents a most difficult and perhaps fearful part of the process of an older adult group. At a time of waning power (as sensed by individuals), entering into the process of testing the limits of individual members, the group, and the worker can be particularly frightening. During this phase, there are often power struggles among the members and with the worker. The dropout danger is very high; members become fearful of taking the risks involved in engaging in such a struggle. If a member becomes ill, and this often happens, the guilt associated with the group's activities during this phase can be overwhelming.

However, with skill, sensitivity, and willingness to be depended upon, workers can enable members to find more nonthreatening issues to catch onto as a means of testing limits and controls. They can help guide members to mastery of object relations so that the testing of each other leads not to rejection but to acceptance of differences in ideas and in roles taken in the group. Having tested each other, members and worker move toward concluding a contract. Both parties are ready to agree on the terms and to define the contractual relationship for further mutual engagement. The working agreement has been described by Louise A. Frey and Marguerite Meyer:

> The decision to become affiliated with the other people in the group is not just a matter of liking or disliking them. In a social work group, the struggle with accepting the stated purpose is tied in with the decision about future close association with the people. As the purpose grows clearer, the working agreement becomes firmer. The worker's behavior as he [or she] helps members through the initial stages of the group sets the framework of the working agreement. The worker articulates the specific terms of the agency service as applied in this group and elicits members' reactions and feelings, both behaviorally and verbally. The verbal adult group can be helped to verbalize; the nonverbal group may need worker's clarification of evident feelings and responses. The working agreement is established as group and worker recognize why they are together and what is expected of each in this relationship.
>
> The working agreement becomes a reference point throughout the group's life and is a dynamic force in accomplishing its objectives. This clear understanding of purposes is an important foundation for the development and maintenance of trust. Members should not be tricked into involvement under false pretenses if a helping relationship is to be established. The group which is not clear about its purposes or the working agreement can use this obscurity of purpose as a means of resisting deeper evaluation, greater self-awareness, and fuller responsibility. Handling such resistance is much more difficult for [workers] who [are] not sure [of their own] and the agency's goals. With those members in whom mistrust is a significant personality dynamic, the working agreement can be a source of reassurance and a damper on delusional ideas. To . . . "normal" [people], the working agreement expresses respect for [them] and helps [them] engage in a responsible way in the group experience.[39]

Needs Met by the "Power-Control Stage"

The social group worker is mindful of the opportunities and pitfalls, but also of the challenges to help assert the vulnerable, more isolated older person to come forth in a social encounter and learn to cope with power claims by others. Here are chances for meeting their needs for influencing others, for developing a sense of victory, of gaining a sense of autonomy, despite apparent waning powers, even a victory over the social worker in the office, or the nurse in the hospital, as one has practiced to assert one's powers over Mr. A or Mrs. B on the patient floor in a first gathering of the resident's group.

The "power and control" or "storming" stage is group development offers magnificent chances for testing, for trying out and trying on, for finding outlets for meeting coping, expressive, contributory and influence needs. This stage also provides people with an opportunity to release feelings which they otherwise would control to their disadvantage. Older persons who are afraid to get angry and are then immobilized by this fear have now a chance to observe others becoming angry and not being hurt by or punished for it. They are thus encouraged by the example of others via a mirror image to express this feeling instead of being thwarted by it. The example of others in the group who may be freer to express affection— being less fearful of rejection—may also help other elderly to experiment with expressive affection towards others more readily. This makes them more likely to receive more affection from others as well.[40]

Building on Early Group Solidarity

The group provides members with a sense of belonging that replaces previous affiliations and ties that have been broken. The group can become a family for the members, replacing what many have lost. This is characteristic of the third stage of development: intimacy. The group engages in interpersonal relationships; members begin to allow themselves a degree of dependency on the group, and a sense of solidarity develops.

> The third stage of development is characterized by intensification of personal involvement, more willingness to bring into the open feelings regarding club members and workers, and striving for satisfaction of dependency needs. Sibling [type of] rivalry tends to appear as well as overt comparisons of the group to family life. There is a growing ability to plan and carry out group projects, although this proficiency is affected as interpersonal conflicts arise. There is a growing awareness and mutual recognition of the significance of the group experience in terms of personality growth and change.[41]

Transference issues are most apparent here since the frame of reference is the family. The group becomes a substitute and replacement for losses that have been suffered. This stage is heavily loaded for an aged client, for it involves taking many risks to allow oneself to become intimate in the light of possible (and probable) additional loss. Here is an opportunity for taking a role in the group, for obtaining a new social identity. While the status as a peer member requires new adaptations to changing role expectations, older adults' life experiences have at least prepared them for such a role, which is not true of the status and role of a nonworker. The adjustment to a new world of leisure may be hard on those who have experienced greatest satisfaction in their work role, but it is no less hard on those who suddenly find themselves without resources to fill unoccupied time regardless of previous gratifications.

Informal groups have been used quite successfully to provide leisure activities, although the emphasis on the recreational and play aspects has overshadowed the essential task of developing a nonwork role. The social worker's use of the group as a medium to help individual older adults adapt to a nonwork role and to find meaningful substitute roles is a most essential task. An excerpt from a group meeting highlights these issues:

> Being surrounded by others "in the same boat" allows for a feeling of identification and allows for reassurance. The members in this meeting felt reassured that this task of "body transcendence vs. body preoccupation" (which was translated into terms the group could understand) was a universal one, and there was a feeling of comfort derived from the admission and sharing of painful feelings, fears, etc. The worker helped the group explore their feelings to ensure that the members would not resort to excessive denial, but rather would perceive the reality of their physical condition.
>
> The worker then moved the group toward relieving some of the anxiety over their condition by pointing out the value of the group's examination of health services to ensure adequate physical care. Thus, the use of relationship, the common bond between group members, was employed by the worker to disallow an early withdrawal from the developmental problem of "body preoccupation." Allowing members the opportunity to share their fears and concerns, providing mutual support, alleviates stress and anxiety that each member perceives to be his [or her] unique problem. . . . Simply letting it "off your chest" [often] relieves internal pressure that builds with . . . no outlet for expression.[42]

By setting goals for themselves, groups build a future into their experiences. By structuring a time orientation into the program and utilizing the techniques of support and clarification, a social worker can help group members reintegrate their past experience and, at the same time, direct their present efforts toward making a contribution to society. With the task defined, the group is ready to *work* on the task; a new stage is set.

Needs Met by the Intimacy Phase

When it happens that greater interpersonal closeness occurs over time as well as frequency of interpersonal encounters increas[ing], then the phase of intimacy does appear, the phase usually referred to as the establishment of a "real group," characterized by the appearance of feelings of solidarity and group bonds and by the shaping of norms. In my experiences, this occurs more rarely among vulnerable older persons and, perhaps more importantly, it is not so relevant whether it does occur at all. To be sure certain aspects of the "intimacy stage" that replay family dynamics and demonstrate psychosocial closeness may not get played out at all when this phase is not reached, such as investment in love and affection, ambivalences, likes and dislikes of members and emotional attachments with other peers and the establishment of norms, the do's and don't's of group life. Needs for greater ego-gratification and affective expression may not find fulfillment to the extent desired by many a social worker. However, the energy of personal investment with attendant multiple losses, abandonment and accumulated frustrations when norm violations take place, may be too high a price to pay for the rewards of achieving the intimacy stage of the group. On the other hand, some people in the group may indeed proceed towards this phase and reap ego gratifications beyond their fondest dreams. Herein lies the assessment skill of the worker: to recognize how far to support the vision by assessing the older person's strengths and adaptive capacities to meet the demands of this stage. The worker must allow him/herself to be tested and re-tested and based on the result of these tests, formulate a "service contract," spelling out clearer mutual expectations between the older persons, the group members and him/herself.

Of particular relevance here is "reminiscing"—not that reminiscing could not occur earlier in the group's development, but it is during the "intimacy stage" when reminiscing with other group members rather than merely with the worker is more frequent and can be utilized as a group rather than as a solo activity.

Much of the theoretical construct behind the value of reminiscing comes from Freud's discussion of the significance of early memories, both conscious and subconscious, as they influence later adaptations. In social group work, however, only conscious material should be dealt with, and the worker should avoid a consideration of the underlying causes of such behavior. As Pincus states:

> The worker's goal is to help the client make appropriate use of reminiscence. As always, the interventive plan should follow a careful assessment of the client's use of reminiscence. . . . Simple empathic listening is important, but workers must go beyond this. They should accept the client and sensitize the relevant others in the person's situation (e.g., the members in the group) to the importance and functions of reminiscing and the need to encourage it in appropriate situations.

And Ebersole states, "The major reason to encourage reminiscing among a group of aged people is to produce or enhance a cohort effect. . . . They have little desire to affiliate with their own age group if they view it as devalued, out of step with the mainstream of life, or inadequate." And further: "The second reason for group reminiscing with the aged is to increase opportunities for socialization by capitalizing on the exchange of early memories." In the early stages of group development the worker must be more active to insure that each participant is "assured of time to talk and efforts must be made to emphasize, by re-statement, any expression of feelings or concerns for other group members." If the group reaches "intimacy stage," the group members will tend to do this for one another.

I could add here a third reason for group reminiscing: to help older people in general, but frail elderly in particular, to meet ego-transcending needs. The linking of the past with present and future can be facilitated through the appropriate use of reminiscing. Care must be taken when the material of the conscious past is painful and when "life review" leads to bringing up hurts and griefs without being able to cope with them. This is why corrective interventions not only by the worker but also by other group members are so vital and why the "stage of intimacy" lends itself to deal with meeting ego-transcending needs.[43]

Illustration: From the Time of Entry to the Phase of Defining the Task

The following record demonstrates, among other things, the common needs that led to the formation of the group, the planning, and the technique of beginning the group. The record demonstrates the technique of communicating the worker's acceptance of the people, which is crucial in the process.

After acceptance has occurred, the social worker moves toward concluding a service contract to enable both parties—group members and social worker—to define the task and to start working on it.

A Family Service Agency with Group Services. In the early spring, a new group of clients was in the making. Wishing to experiment with older people in a group, the agency staff carefully selected a group of thirteen with some characteristics and needs in common. Reduced to living on Social Security income, in contrast to their former higher economic level, they had all come to the agency regarding environmental or medical problems with which they were helped. Workers in the department had been using casework to help with personal and family problems. The older people were either uninterested or had been unsuccessful in community groups of peers, and most of them tended to withdraw into a lonely existence. Taking into account the culturally accepted ways for older people to get acquainted, the staff held two teas in the spring, which clients understood as an opportunity to meet with the social worker and a few others who had been coming to the agency, and also to see the new quarters.

At the first tea, clients were enthusiastic and surprised at their ability to talk with one another. At the second tea, "the wallflowers of the first meeting became the stars of the second." As they moved into discussing common problems, the worker described and interpreted the group program, and they asked if they could begin a series in the fall. The series began in November, meeting every three weeks, a compromise with the ideal of weekly sessions. This was necessary because of their physical condition, medical appointments, and the great effort required in getting out at all. Taxis were provided for those who needed transportation.

The average attendance was six people. The agency was flexible regarding the verbalized needs of the group, such as the clients' desire to meet every three weeks, and also regarding needs anticipated or expressed through behavior, such as having a tea to introduce group to worker, agency, and each other. Worker's previous knowledge of individuals' tendency to withdraw and not participate in groups was useful. In the entry phase, approach-avoidance patterns were evident, and encouraged to remain evident by the worker.

Session 4, in December.

> The pattern of the group to arrive early continued. At first, either the worker or office secretary helped them hang up their coats, but they were soon doing this for themselves, assisting each other and chatting in an easy, friendly fashion. The secretary's planned function was preparing refreshments on the table in the meeting room, symbolizing in this way the interest of the total staff—a conscious support on the agency's part of the clients' identification with the agency. Mrs. W.'s description of her housing in a skid row neighborhood had a shock impact on the group. In discussions of living in homes for the elderly, she strongly objected to

application blanks that required personal information, resented turning herself over to matrons who run her life, and living closely with people who would be curious about her.

She brought out, in housing discussions, that she did not care to make friends because it obligates her; she had believed this all her life. Her lurid stories about people in her neighborhood and the dangers of going out finally drew some caustic questions from the group. "Why do you stay there then?" "You must really like it though you say you don't." In regard to applications with personal questions: "What's the trouble? Do you have something to hide?" Instead of openly resenting this, she apparently enjoyed the challenge and talked back. Her attendance, however, was spotty, with only an occasional note to the worker about an illness as her excuse for not coming. The realities of the housing problem were very difficult; conditions in low-rent areas are substandard.

Discussing this in the group obviously brought no solution for them. Mutual frustration and depression would get nowhere. Therefore, the worker purposefully described to the group the function of the parent agency in the community through service on committees for improving social conditions. This provided for them a link with the agency, with the worker in the role of spokesperson for the needs and preferences of these older people. Although not verbalized as such, they were dealing with an underlying developmental task: facing the end of life with the knowledge of having made a contribution to society. All group members then asked what the agency could do to alleviate their immediate problems in their homes.

The worker indicated that she could join with other individuals to see the housing manager and try to make immediate changes, such as repair of the furnace, water pipes, plaster on their walls, etc. She pointed out that she made this offer to them and they could accept or reject it. She further stipulated that they had to be willing to speak up and to support each other since a collective approach is more likely to yield results. After lengthy deliberations and discussion, the members accepted the "deal." Worker clarified mutual expectations, and they made an appointment to see the manager. Mrs. W. assumed a leadership role; the worker supported her and indicated that she would meet with them prior to seeing the manager and play out in advance what each person might do and say.

Discussion of the Session. The theme of housing runs like a thread throughout the meetings of the group. Here is a vital, existential need that is recognized by the worker, who knew that she had to meet the test successfully during the first stage of the group's life. The mutual task has been defined, with the worker taking a lead in describing the advocacy role of the agency and herself; there is a job to be done and group solidarity is essential to face the tasks. The worker conveys her understanding to them. The demand for concrete steps to alleviate a problem led to the task definition for group, individuals, and worker, culminating in a service contract. This was made possible by the worker's specification of an offer to assist but not to take over.

The long discussion that followed indicated that the members had realized that it was not the job of the worker to get anything for them, but that they had a responsibility to act for themselves and the worker was there to assist them in a difficult undertaking. The worker kept their sense of independence intact and used the esprit de corps of the group to move toward obtaining help. She used herself as a bridge based on the relationship established in phase one, and made explicit the differential participation of both parties in the interventive process. The focus of the worker's activities continued to be assisting individuals to solve problems, and to strengthen their egos in the process in order to meet the crises that would continue to arise in their lives.

Working on the Task

The stage of differentiation is one in which members begin to accept one another as distinct individuals, to see the social worker as a unique person, and to see this group experience as a unique experience from which each can find an acceptable intrapsychic equilibrium. As clarification of power relationships gave freedom for autonomy and intimacy, so clarification of and coming to terms with intimacy and mutual acceptances of personal needs brings the freedom and the ability to differentiate, and to evaluate relationships and events in the group on a reality basis. The identification of "what the group is for" seems almost to be the signal that differentiation is around the corner.

As the members consider the nature and meaning of the group, there is a tendency for them to reflect consciously on how it compares with the other groups and social situations with which they are acquainted. We have noticed how this process of comparison comes after intimate relationships have been entered into and as a culmination of a struggle over deviance and conformity, sibling [type of] rivalry and interdependence. We see emerging a new acceptance of individual differences and group permission for free expression in this regard. If interdependence has been accepted, there is also the emergence of a group system for mutual support for this individuality and, where needed, consistent controls when individual behavior becomes group-destructive.[44]

This stage allows the group its greatest opportunity for productivity and development. The group takes on its own viability, becoming an entity separate from the familial references of the previous stage. It is in this stage that the worker can best enable the group to make use of its own skills and capabilities, providing members with many opportunities for mastery of new roles. This does not imply that during previous stages such opportunities would not exist. The developmental model merely postulates an optimal condition and suggests that this model should provide a useful conceptual outline for the process and structure of a typical social work group.

The model is presented as a tool for practice to be used in conjunction with knowledge of individual and group psychology and management and programming techniques, and in the service of general social work values and goals. It is during this stage, when members have built their group, and worker and group have learned to work together on the task which they set out to accomplish, that the central core of social group work, the decision-making process, gets played out to the fullest.[45]

Decision Making: A Core Process

The special function of the decision-making process in social group work is to benefit group members, particularly older persons, by helping them come to terms with their needs for achievement, power, and control and with their feelings of mastery. The group as a whole is perceived as an instrument for meeting these and other needs and also for the experience of making choices, subordinating one's wishes and desires for the greater good, and transferring behavior thus learned to new situations. When group members have learned how to cope with alternatives and what is involved in making decisions, they should be helped to transfer this learning to a similar situation either in the same group or in a different group. Since social group work is concerned with the utilization of the decision-making process for purposes of helping individual members achieve goals for themselves — that is, meeting their own needs as well as contributing to achieving the goals of the group— it follows that enhancement of social functioning of individual group members is also a concern. Since social functioning is the sum of the roles performed by a person, group work, as a method of social work, is concerned with helping individual group members enhance the performance of their roles. Decision making is inherent in any social role which a person is called upon to perform.

> Decision making involves making proposals and securing agreement; it involves a power dimension, because some group members have to control others (and these others in turn have to allow themselves to be controlled) in order to get agreement on a decision. If all group members share a set of norms, it is easier to arrive at a decision; providing information as to the possible alternatives and their consequences is usually sufficient. If a group does not share common norms, the process of decision making becomes prolonged, since the activity of the group is directed toward securing common norms, toward assuming power, rather than toward making a specific decision. "Why do they take so long? Why can't they agree? Why do they talk around the subject instead of making a decision?" A group worker knows that his first task is to find out "where the group is," that is, whether the members have common norms and what these are, before the decision-making process can flow. It follows that the worker's task has to be directed toward helping a group resolve the struggle for common norms before he [or she] can help them in reaching decisions in a meaningful way.[46]

Inherent in the decision-making process is conflict, a group phenomenon characterized by tensions and filled with emotions. The following example from Kubie and Landau illustrates this:

> Mr. Falk had been active in politics all his life, as a worker in local party organizations, and at the center, [he] constantly referred to all the influential people he knew. When he had been nominated as sergeant-at-arms the year before, he had made a vehement campaign speech about law and order, and the discipline he would enforce if elected. He was elected and proceeded as he had promised, stirring up considerable resentment by his harsh methods. Not long after this he had a heart attack which kept him in the hospital and at home for several weeks. Mr. Falk often refers to this attack as "the time when my job here landed me in the hospital."

In his absence Mr. Wilman agreed to finish out his term of office and was then himself elected as sergeant-at-arms, and Mr. Falk became vice-president.

During the period of the new budget cuts, Mr. Falk rose during a birthday party program to make an inflammatory speech about the reduced allowances, claiming that they were due to the new political administration against whose election he had warned the membership. He said that although he himself was not a recipient he was "spending his life's blood" to work with those who would undo this hardship. The suggestion of a corrupt administration responsible for their budget reductions and the intimation that he knew influential people who could change these cuts was agitating and confusing to the already upset membership.

The worker reminded him that this was a birthday program and in that his speech was out of order, but that he could address the members at another time on this matter. He was acutely resentful and said that the staff was allied with the Department of Welfare and therefore unwilling to have the members' "good and welfare" discussed. He added that the members could run their own affairs, and need take no interference from staff. After this meeting there was much discussion in subgroups about his attitude. Some were only concerned about the suggestion of help through political influence, but others were resentful about his attitude toward staff. Most of such members had had longer experience than he of the role of staff, either as guiding and facilitating the activities of special groups, or as counselors to those with personal problems. A few said explicitly that if it were not for the mediating influence of staff, "everybody in this place would be at each other's throats."[47]

Many older adults in our society have become deprived of their decision-making functions, which is a most significant loss for many aged in our population. Their contributions are not readily sought, their own field for making choices is circumscribed, and their life field is shrinking. It follows that the area of making meaningful choices needs increased attention, to help maintain self-respect and to give a continued sense of self-worth. Too many group work experiences for the aged exist in a world of make-believe since the choices they are offered are not real and meaningful.

The world of older people has been contracting. Many status and role changes have occurred for them; they find themselves in nonwork roles, with their former group affiliations often dissolved and their circle of friends and acquaintances diminished. Thus, quite a few older people are faced with the task of resocialization. They have to establish new relationships with contemporaries and find new modes of adapting to the unaccustomed roles of being grandparents, retirees, etc. On the one hand, their choice opportunities are diminishing; on the other hand, they are expected to make choices among alternatives of which they have little knowledge.

One could say that the scope of choice opportunities increases during adolescence and decreases with senescence. The group worker has to be aware of these factors and offer older people realistic experiences in making choices so they can maintain previously learned skills in decision making and apply them to their new life situations. Older people may be helped a great deal by recognizing, for example, that their vote in a self-governing older adult group has significance, that they are able to influence the outcome of an election in their group. This may become a bridge to other ventures in decision making and can affect the future life and self-image of older people despite the fact that many previous choice alternatives have been curtailed. Kubie and Landau provide an illustration of a person's development in elected office.

> The third president, Mr. Mannheim . . . had come to the center some two years before his nomination, and though he [had] made exploratory visits to [see] some of the special activities, [he had not been] interested in joining any of them. He was then 73 years old, a tall, slender man, formerly a shoemaker by trade. He had an easy manner and a pleasant smile. He spoke English with a strong Jewish accent and a limited vocabulary. When he first came to the center, he had two sources of security, [unlike] most of the older members. He had excellent relationships with his children and grandchildren, and at that time still had money of his own. He therefore had not suffered the sense of defeat which others had experienced due to long years of isolation and because of receiving public assistance. He quickly made friends among many of the card players and was popular with the women.
>
> When he was elected, he took great pride in this distinction, but his limited ability to deal with discussion or opposition was patent. His manner was crude ("Who said you could talk? Sit down!"), yet this soon proved to be more a lack of polish than a drive for self-assertion. He had great personal security and therefore a flexibility in understanding and in tolerating differences—a flexibility which became clearer as he quickly learned more acceptable forms of speech and techniques of conducting meetings from the worker's example.
>
> He also felt a personal responsibility toward newcomers in welcoming them to the center and stressing "Here you can be happy without thinking of your race or color; it is here a real democracy!" He took over responsibilities for the daily management of the center. As the problem of caring for hats and coats became urgent, he helped build partitions in the cloakroom and made hatchecks out of the tops of Dixie cups. When finally cloakroom clerks and cleaners were secured, he made sure that furniture was moved and kitchen corners and window sills thoroughly scrubbed.
>
> When a retired barber came to the center, there was much discussion about having him offer a hair-cutting service to the members. This involved arranging for renewal of his license, towel service, supplies, a chair, tools, etc., and took some time. Mr. Mannheim became impatient and finally took action by discussing the matter with the president of the board of directors, explaining that as the two presidents who managed the center, they must push this matter through. At the end of Mr. Mannheim's first year in office, he came to the staff for data on the amounts of supplies used in refreshments and other statistics concerning the center, which he used in a report of his year in office. This was an innovation not followed by later presidents, but typical of his attitude while in office—that of a practical stewardship of center affairs.
>
> During his two years in office he became very attached to one of the women members and visited her daily. But he could not bring himself to decide on marriage because of his poor health, because his children were opposed, and finally because his savings were being steadily exhausted. The end of his presidency coincided with the end of his financial resources and he had to apply for Old Age Assistance.

This must have been a difficult adaptation because Mr. Mannheim formerly took great pleasure in sending treats of ice cream or candy to his particular group of friends. However, he made this adjustment in dignified silence.

Later his woman friend suddenly married someone else. This event required a more severe readjustment and he looked ill and wretched for some weeks. But today he has adjusted to this disappointment also. He has found a new activity in a discussion group for current events. Here his sound common sense and balanced viewpoint give him renewed status. He also serves on the executive committee, as do all former officers, [and is] chairman of the visiting committee.[48]

Methods and Techniques

Like any social workers, group workers use their relationship with the client to move toward helping objectives. Unlike caseworkers, however, they utilize group and program media as major tools to achieve their goals. Many an older person ventures toward new contacts, new activities, and new experiences over the bridge of his dependence on a staff worker. In a supportive relationship, the worker helps older people understand themselves better; through the worker as a symbol of society and community, they can gain a measure of acceptance by the very society that has deprived them of their previous status and role. The mutual support that members of a consciously guided group can give one another reinforces the strength of the individual member.

Through the many dimensions of group dynamics, the worker aiming at supportive treatment manipulates these processes to provide members with opportunities for mastery, achievement, and sublimation. The use of program media, discussion as well as activities, increases the confidence of individuals in their capacity to meet the stresses of their situation. Creative self-expression and limited catharsis through program media increase the individual's capacity to handle his or her emotions appropriately without excessive denial, repression, blockage of aggression, and ego constriction. The development of a democratic organizational form and the encouragement of the processes of decision making and conflict resolution express the worker's confidence.

> In relation to older adults their worker must take a larger measure of responsibility for process than is usual in younger age groups. That is, he [or she] must take a larger hand in shaping members' motivations and creating the group experience in which the individual may continue to grow and develop. The worker must not only be a helping person, but a person whose initiative, knowledge and relationships will serve to bolster the confidence of the older adult in trying out new experiences.[49]

Silverstone and Burack-Weiss point out ways in which groups with frail elderly may differ from other groups: there may be distracting entrances and exists that break the mood, sensory/cognitive deficits may result in nonsequitors and/or side conversations, attendance may fluctuate more than usual due to changeable weather and levels of health, and "work may progress slower than usual due to digression, reminiscence, and socialization."[50]

Supportive Techniques. The interpersonal relationships of group members provide opportunities for developing a social self based on the reality of individual performance and achievement. It is the worker's task to guide these relationships so that these performances and achievements are positive and realistic and can instill a sense of mastery; this is especially important since older people have met frustration of mastery in the outside world. Their services in the world of work are no longer needed, their past contributions probably forgotten.

The worker also uses support to increase self-confidence and help members achieve a better sense of reality. Such support can be provided in a variety of ways. One is through identification with the worker. It is important to recognize that older people often internalize society's perception of themselves as superfluous; the younger worker is often perceived as a symbolic representation of that society. Therefore, through acceptance and verbally expressing confidence in their worth and ability to perform the task, the worker may instill in the members a greater sense of confidence and guard against their falling prey to the self-fulfilling prophesy.

It is important for elderly persons to have someone they can lean on and accept as their leader, their authority. To them the worker personifies confidence and hope. Workers are people they can trust, who in turn are willing to trust them and help them engage in activities that satisfy their needs, which were unrecognized before. As time goes on, members learn to accept themselves much more and to rely on their own strengths and judgments. The worker has to wean them gradually and to instill a sense of self-reliance in them so that they can assume responsibility for themselves again and become less and less dependent on the worker.[51]

Reflection and Clarification of Issues. The worker allows time for reflection and clarification of the issues, ideas, and problems that members are interested in. This allows for the sharing of ideas and helps in building group solidarity. Members are given the opportunity to reflect upon their experiences, both as individuals and as group members. The following excerpt from a group meeting serves as an illustration:

> The group had succeeded in securing discounts from merchants, in designing the membership cards, and had recently begun to publicize the program. At this point few older persons had taken advantage of the discounts, and one member, Mr. J., began to seriously question the value of their efforts. "Here we have gotten all these discounts and no one wants to use them. Perhaps we did not get discounts that senior citizens want or need. The idea of a discount program is stupid anyway. Old people just don't know how to help themelves. We're silly to think we can help them. I want to do something else."
>
> At this point the worker told the group that they must realize that it takes a while for others to hear about a program and accept its value. She emphasized how well she thought they had achieved their goals so far and how useful this program had proven to be in other communities. She told them how pleased the director of the agency was with their progress and related to them her conversation with a senior citizen who had utilized the discounts and was quite excited about them. She then suggested [a] return to the question about how to better publicize

the discounts and restated her confidence that [they] would be successful. The group agreed that they should try to avoid becoming too easily frustrated and continue with the task.

This excerpt illustrates the techniques of discussion, reflection, clarification, and support. The worker, in utilizing clarification, attempts to help the members establish the "right" perspective and separate objective from subjective factors. In this example, it was essential that members recognize that others do not readily understand the benefits of new programs and that widespread recognition and praise for their work would not come immediately. The members also needed to come to grips with their fear of failure and uselessness, and recognize that an objective appraisal of their work would bring forth different conclusions from those based on subjective fear. Thus it appears evident that social group work can assist the aged in resolving the issue of "ego differentiation versus work role preoccupation."

Program Structuring.[52] Program is more than activities. It is the planning of activities and the interaction that takes place among individuals when they participate. Programs include recreational, educational, cultural, creative, artistic, and dramatic activities that respond to the interests, desires, motivations, and needs of older people in their many and varied individual expressions. Vickery speaks of activities not as ends in themselves but as "settings for interpersonal relationships among members that will produce feelings of approval and recognition."[53]

Mastery involves a person's capacity and successful use of resources in solving problems and in learning life's tasks and feeling adequate in regard to them. Programs should challenge the individual's capacity, provide resource help when needed, define life tasks at various points along the road of aging, and encourage their achievement. Thus an effective use of programming can supply the challenges and opportunities necessary to enable members to master the tasks of aging.

> In group work it is assumed that the group's process of planning program activities often is more important to the development of members than is the final product. With older adults, however, it is equally and sometimes more important to stress the value of a final product. Aging persons struggling to replace losses (family, home, work, friends, loss of control of functions of the body) may use program activities to gain neuromuscular control, intellectual stimulation, friendships, and work satisfactions.[54]

Examples of program topics of interest to older persons are the following:

1. Sexual concerns and related issues of courtship and marriage
2. Health and illness
3. Death of members and the collective supports the group can establish for their own deaths
4. Spiritual and religious concerns
5. Involvement of other family members and discussion of generational conflict.

In work with older adults where interaction patterns are limited, at least initially, and where decision making is difficult, group program planning and collective group execution form a basis for the interaction to occur through participation and [through people] having a sense of the program as their own. Skills and roles are mastered as [the] programs widen and the backgrounds of the individuals are dipped into, so that they can recapture a skill and make a contribution.[55]

To help older individuals resolve the issues involved in "ego transcendence versus ego preoccupation," the choice and use of program becomes a significant factor. The worker should develop a program whereby group members will have an opportunity to make a contribution to the society and express their concern for "order and system." Programs such as a discount project designed to improve the economic welfare of senior citizens and activities designed to expand health services enable group members to make a contribution to their community.

Anticipatory Guidance. The worker needs to be able to anticipate what feelings may emerge as a result of group discussion or activity and to handle them constructively for individuals and group. During reflection and clarification of issues and feelings, and in the process of structuring the program, the worker has already explored capacities of individual members. Workers must be sensitive to potential reactions, sensitivities, and emotionally laden areas and either go into them carefully and sensitively or initially avoid them until the group is ready.

Testing and Exploratory Methods. Group participation makes it possible to discover and guide the latent as well as the overt leadership potential of older people for socially useful purposes. Therefore, older adults' involvement in groups is most important if they are to achieve social changes that in the long run, will benefit not only themselves but the younger generation. The group becomes a laboratory for testing out and learning new roles. With the worker's support, members can teach one another, lead, or follow—whichever is most comfortable. The worker can interpret the meaning and actions of members as roles shift and members try out new roles.

Exploring losses and the meaning of past and present lives is a vital part of a group work encounter. It serves to relieve anxiety, establish common bonds, and develop trust and intimacy, and it both lets members get to know one another more deeply as individuals and prepare for their own deaths. Workers, however, must do more than enable the older person to make a contribution. They must be aware of the life-review process and its significance for helping an older individual prepare for death and assume his or her role as "perpetuator of culture." One cannot hope to transcend the limits of one's own ego if one is preoccupied with unresolved conflicts and experiences that need to be reintegrated. Therefore, the worker should allow time for reminiscence at the meetings.

Material for such *reminiscence* will often resolve around the problems and duties related to the project tasks of the group. For example, in one such group, a man began to discuss his past after reporting to the group that he had secured a discount for senior citizens from a local drugstore. "All my life I wanted to be a pharmacist, but I was too scared to talk to people. In fact, I did not like people. I was afraid to ask them the simplest questions, so I spent my whole life working in a factory." When another group member asked whether he still found people so frightening after working with them in the group, he replied that he liked working on the discount program, but still didn't think he liked people.

The social worker commented that it must have taken a lot of guts to choose to work with people now after avoiding them so long. She also asked if he had avoided people due to a lack of confidence in himself. A member suggested that perhaps he did not like himself. He replied that he never had much confidence and began to reminisce silently. This example illustrates the manner in which past experiences and conflicts are often brought up in a task group. The worker should not ignore this material, but rather use the technique of clarification to help the group member reintegrate these experiences and conflicts so that he or she can achieve ego transcendence. Only conscious material should be dealt with, and the worker should avoid a consideration of the underlying causes of such behavior. Some pertinent comments come from Allen Pincus:

> The worker's goal in treatment is to help the client make appropriate use of reminiscence. As always, the intervention plan should follow a careful assessment of the client's use of reminiscence. When societal norms have inhibited reminiscing, the worker can help the client to understand its value and help . . . overcome . . . reluctance to engage in this activity. This will prevent repression or denial of memories that in effect deny that his [or her] life had any meaning. Simple empathic listening is important, but [workers] must go beyond this. [They] should accept the client and sensitize the relevant others in [the person's] situation, whether family members or staff in a nursing home, to the importance and functions of reminiscing and the need to encourage it in appropriate situations.
>
> . . . It is one thing to acknowledge the validity and the substance of . . . memories, another to help [people] use these memories appropriately—that is, in situations in which they would not be rebuffed. Emphasis [is] therefore given to sharing these treasures with their grandchildren or the children of friends. One group decided to work on a project with the local public school wherein the members might serve as resource people in discussions of early modes of transportation in New York City [and in] talks about early communication media and the like. One group had so much fun reminiscing they decided to write a column in their club newspaper for the enjoyment of the total membership. One man became so stimulated by his memories that he started writing stories about his early work experiences, how he met his wife, the places they had lived, and so forth. He sent his writings to his grandchildren, whom he seldom saw because they lived some distance away.
>
> When there is avoidance or repression of reminiscing beyond that resulting from societal norms, the client can be helped to work these through in a supportive manner. The worker can question [elderly persons] about [their] past and help draw [them] out. [They] may be overwhelmed and experience difficulty in sorting out memories and integrating them into a self-concept. Here the worker's skills

in exploration, focusing, probing, and the like can help the client organize his [or her] thinking about the past. When reminiscing is excessive, morbid, and disorganized, the worker can use casework techniques to help the client focus on [better] memories. In addition, the worker can seek to increase opportunities for gratification in the client's current life situation and reduce situational stress.[56]

The joys and pleasures of happy events can find expression through the group, and rituals such as birthday parties and other recognition ceremonies assume an important place in group life and influence its emotional climate. Such rituals have often been part of programs in group services; however, their emotional significance in relation to group and members and to the older person's family and friends outside the group has not been sufficiently recognized or utilized to enhance the self-image of the aged person. Here is a chance to link the past with the present and the future.

Conflict Resolution. The worker should allow for conflicts to occur and should act to enable the group to resolve these conflicts. As with crisis intervention, when group crises occur the worker can help the group utilize the strengths and resources of the members to resolve their own conflicts. Forman speaks of the reluctance of workers to allow for conflict: "Discussion is encouraged, but argument is shied away from: democracy is preached, but the emotion of controversy is avoided. . . . In sum, comfortable and secure activities are dealt with, all of which have some value, but few of which serve to dissolve the stereotype of the uselessness of the aged."[57] Conflicts are essential to the group's existence and their solution is essential to its survival. Workers tend to avoid such situations for fear that older adults cannot handle them, due to health problems and emotional deterioration:

> Although judgment must be used in the selection of conflict solutions, the resolution of conflict is essential to the maintenance of group life and the resolution must be viewed as advantageous by the group. Allowing for conflict and pushing for change often taps the more passive dependencies of older adult members [and their desire] to have the worker do for the members, rather than members doing for themselves. [If] the worker [creates] a crisis [by] refusing to allow members to remain so dependent, argument and controversy follow, resulting in an image . . . that group members are capable of handling group tasks and could still be useful contributors. Of course, this presupposes that the worker has evaluated the group's readiness for this and its ability to handle a less dependent role. Just as work with older adults requires understanding and kindness, so does it require controversy and emotion. Older adult groups should not be [limited to] pleasantly mediated experiences that have little relationship to life; they should include the excitement, the emotion, and the controversy that make life meaningful.[58]

In many groups, the ability of the group to initiate its own discussions is often difficult. This can be attributed to a large degree to passivity and a few authoritarian individuals. Some groups express combativeness, others conformity. Determining this requires (1) understanding of the duration of group life, (2) cultural factors, and (3) the worker's capacity to tolerate differences.

Conflict . . . has to be set against the needs and problems of older people, such as body preoccupation, physical and mental loss, loss of work and sexual identity, reversal of family roles, fear of death, etc. Any reality occurrence in a group, such as death of a member, conflict with a son or daughter or a member, sickness, tends to become reflected in the total group, and each member tends to share in this experience vicariously. The group assumes its share of the problems of the aged as a whole.[59]

Opening up Channels of Communication. The decline in physical and mental processes is a very real problem in the aging process, particularly during its later stages—it is a universal crisis that must be resolved. The social worker must recognize that a certain degree of body preoccupation is a universal, normal reaction to the anxiety aroused by degenerative physical and mental processes. However, the worker can translate this preoccupation into healthy expression through skillful development of an appropriate group task. Since one should start where the group is, a task that grows out of concern over physical decline will be of interest to the group.

Groups can focus on issues surrounding the developmental tasks of aging, and the worker can help members rechannel their preoccupation with the body through a constructive activity, such as working on tasks that improve health services in the community. Members may then regard the environment as less threatening and begin to see that there is concern within the community (as well as realistic recognition) of the problems involved in any physical decline of the aged. By providing opportunities for the group to address such reality issues, the worker provides an experience that relates the members back to society as citizens and confirms the importance of their relationship to the community.

Relating Individualization within the Group to the Outside Community. The social worker with the group must be continuously aware of the individual's needs, interests, and concerns, and relate these to the group—while relating the group's concerns to the individual.

In our attempts to assess older persons as individuals or as members of groups, we have to be aware of the individual [and] at the same time, and with equal interest, we have to be aware of the groups, culture and society—the total scale—of which he [or she] is a part. [We also have to be aware of the] effects and consequences of [the] presence or absence [of older people] from a group, a culture or a society. A society without older persons or one in which their contributions are not recognized—one in which they are not counted as vital organs of the total organism and in which they are devaluated, isolated, left without social roles, without representation or status—is very much like a scale in which some note is missing, a handicapped instrument for the expression of total life.[60]

Contributing Ideas, Values, and Information. Decisions are based on facts and values, and the worker's role as resource person includes providing the information and values that are of significance in the decision-making process. While emotional and unconscious factors interfere with rational decision making, the worker has to be ready to supply useful information for cognitive choices.

The worker's skill in sorting out the group's values is important so that the members may become aware of the reasons for their choices. To give an example, a group of older adults wanted to plan a New Year's Eve party. When making this decision, they indicated that they thought this would not entail many preparations and the party could be planned with a minimum of "problems." They were getting quite worked up and started planning with a good deal of gusto. The worker knew that their adult children had traditionally relied on many of these group members to be their baby-sitters on New Year's Eve. He was aware that many of these grandparents had been ambivalent about this arrangement. Before they were to make a decision (which could have many consequences beyond the immediate party), the group members had to be provided with "information" in relation to the decision involved.

The worker remined the group members that in previous years they had been baby-sitters for their grandchildren and their own children were probably counting on their services again. He pointed out other alternatives for baby-sitting arrangements. These "facts" became part of the decision-making process. The worker also initiated discussions on values in our society, about relationships of parents and adult children and the reciprocal feelings involved in such relationships. This led to clarification of cognitive and emotional factors in this situation. The group members took these factors into account when they were helped to evaluate the attributes and consequences of their decision about a New Year's party. Before reaching a final decision, they met with their (adult) children as a group, utilizing the worker as a catalyst, and reviewed the total situation. Eventually they arrived at the decision to hold the party. This decision, however, was based on a conscious awareness of the premises for the decision, a sorting out of various alternatives and a cognitive awareness of the consequences of the decision. Finally, the children of the older adults were included in the decision making. This broadening of the client system—the older adults—by linking it with a tangential system—their children—led to better communication and enabled the older adults to become comfortable with the consequences of their choice. The worker as a resource person and catalyst was instrumental in this process.[61]

Needs Met by the Differentiation Phase

Once a "group" has become established at this stage of development, the invariable group processes get played out: Who is on top and who is at the bottom? Who is close and who is distant? Who is accepted and who is rejected? Who adheres to the emerging norms and who does not? What are the sanctions for this? Feelings of dependency (upon the worker and/or peers) and independence (from worker and peers) get expressed more markedly now. To what extent can the vulnerable, older person tolerate "closeness" and norm-adherence during this stage as appreciable tolerance of closeness and norm conformity is expected? Research and demonstration reports indicate considerable success in mental hospitals and old age homes in working with deteriorated senile people suffering from chronic brain syndrome, to bring them into contact and communication through various forms of group therapy, though not necessarily of social group work. Here the evidence is by no means in, though there is a body of practice–experience which confirms that hot-tempered exchanges, conflict-ridden argumentations provide many a "frail" older person with the essential juices to feel alive and to feel part of human interaction. Nowhere is this more essential than in institutional settings that value order and calm for organizational benefits over lively conflict and tension for continued human growth and vigor.[62]

Illustration of Working on the Task

In the following example, the roles and techniques of the worker have a particular effect on the group. The unique qualities of several key issues are related to the fact that the group meets in a nursing home.

Nursing Home, Patient Council Meeting, October 14. In attendance were: patients Jeane B., Joseph G., Harry C., Jerry M., Dorothy G., Mary K., Annie F., and the social worker. Following coffee, the social worker opened the meeting. The minutes were read by Mr. C., and after a discussion of the items, a motion was made to elect him permanent secretary. It was noted by some that although there were bulletin boards in various parts of the building, the notices were not always observed by all patients. The group wondered how patients who did not see the bulletin board on a regular basis could be made aware of what was going on. It was agreed that efforts would be made to keep all patients informed and that part of the function of the Patient Council would be to disseminate information on decisions reached at these meetings.

Harry C. raised the question of why it was necessary for him to take medicine for his heart when he had never done so before and wanted to know why the druggist was charging $8.25 for heart medicine. This provided the opportunity to discuss Medicare and Medicaid in detail and how all patients are free to choose their own druggist, pharmacist, and other medical or paramedical services. In discussing Medicare and its requirements, a detailed discussion of skilled nursing and other levels of care ensued. Harry C. mentioned that he had a sister in a private nursing home who "would like to come here, but our fees are too high." This led into a discussion of how a nursing home determines its costs, how they are directly related to the service provided, and it was fully recognized that not everyone required all the services available at the home.

Jeane B. responded to Harry C.'s comments by saying that if anyone wanted a "home away from home," this was the place. Immediately, a barrage of positive comments regarding the cleanliness of the building, the atmosphere provided by the staff, and the attitude of the staff ensued. The only negative comments made, which were prefaced with frequent apologies, related to the lack of cleanliness in one part of the second floor. The social worker took note of this and explained some of the problems. A further discussion was held about patients' attitudes and responsibilities in helping to keep the place clean and how frequently their anger towards family and illness can result in abuse of their immediate environment. It was brought out that this was their home and that although administrators had considerable responsibility to keep the home neat and clean, they had equal responsibility to the limit of their ability. For example, if they saw paper on the floor and were capable of picking it up, they should do so.

Annie F. raised a question of dining room schedule and the confusion that seems to take place near the elevator. She made some suggestions and it was agreed that the social worker would discuss this with the kitchen and see if better plans could be worked out. Several of the patients wondered whether those who were able could go out to eat in restaurants. We discussed the implications, and it was agreed that those who wanted to go and were willing to pay for themselves (meal and transportation) and could obtain medical approval would be eligible for such an excursion. The social worker was to investigate certain local restaurants and report back by the next meeting.

The social worker said that several other homes were interested in starting patient councils with this group's help. It was his opinion that the group should wait until after at least two or three more meetings, when it could share some experiences. The patients were excited about the idea of helping other homes start patient councils and more than happy to visit homes and help them get their councils started.

Another concern raised by a member of the Council was that her visitors were upset at the abusive language used by one disturbed patient. This led to a most interesting discussion as to how much to allow a patient to "abuse visitors," how much to expect visitors to tolerate, and how much responsibility those who are healthy and alert have to help visitors and patients understand the problems involved. It was agreed that the personnel at the home did have a certain responsibility to those patients who had been there quite some time and who might be a little disturbing at times. However, the group would move as quickly as possible to see that those who might be inconvenienced might understand the condition of the disturbing patient.

In this particular case, Miss R. from Social Service was able to report that she was working with the family towards plans for this patient and that perhaps the group could provide assistance to visitors in terms of a place to visit with their friends and also an understanding of the problems. In brief, the patients respected the fact that patients cannot just be removed without very serious consideration since all of them recognized that they at some point might be in the same position. Prior to closing the meeting, various questions were asked concerning policies of the home, etc. The next meeting was scheduled for December 15, at 9:30 A.M.

Discussion of the Illustration. The very formation of the group within the institution sanctions and promotes the independence of patients and their taking more control and responsibility. Examples of a number of ideas initiated by patients and operationalized are (1) happy hour on a regular basis; (2) participation in golden-age clubs and groups outside the nursing home; (3) planning and implementing programs, bus trips, Christmas party, etc.; and (4) airing complaints about the institution and working them out by going through appropriate channels with guidance from workers. The worker supported members and empathized with underlying fears, needs, and feelings. There was a need for social identity and status and a need to be useful to help others become involved. Concerning ego integration, life in an institution can become so routinized that sense of time, what day it is, etc., easily become lost. This can lead to "pseudo dementia" and confusion. This is why "reality-orientation" exercises (what day of the week is it? what month of the year are we in? etc.) have been so useful in working with people in institutions.

Group members, as part of an institution, realize the need for and importance of involving others, even in giving basic information of different activities offered.

They become a bridge of communication and resource for other patients. The fact that they have so little control over their home environment is brought out. The group is the first step in gaining some feeling of control. They grasp the feeling that they can have choices. The participants are involved and ready to work on the common tasks with the social worker, who contributes ideas, sorts out alternatives, and provides a sense of continuity and reasonable stability that allows for a degree of predictability—which is important for the ego development of the members.

Termination and Separation

The final stage of group development is that of separation. The group experience has been completed, and members may begin to move apart and find new resources for meeting social, recreational, and vocational needs. The process of termination in this stage may involve some regression and recapitulation, both spoken and acted out, of former group experiences and relationship patterns. In addition to permitting anxiety over separation and loss, the recapitulation serves an evaluating function, helping the group rethink and reassess the meaning and value of the total experience. If the group experience has made a significant impact on the group members, the assumption is that it now becomes the frame of reference for approaching new social, group, and familial situations.

The approach of group termination appears to set off a number of reactions, the diversity of which is reminiscent of the range of approach-avoidance maneuvers displayed in stage one. Anxiety that was experienced in earlier stages [over coming together] now is felt in relating to moving apart and breaking bonds that have been formed. Even where individual contacts among members or between members and worker antedate or continue subsequent to group association, there is a significant impact of finality that is evident in records and recollections of group terminations.[63]

The authors go on to list a number of reactions they observed in a group during the process of separation:

1. Denial is evidenced by members forgetting when the group would end.
2. Regression is manifested by the reappearance of individual and interpersonal conflicts and issues that had been resolved.
3. Recapitulation occurs in which earlier events, crises, and activities are relived. Reminiscing about the group also occurs.
4. Evaluation is undertaken—similar to the above review.
5. Flight behavior occurs that can be destructive or positive. In the former, there is denial of the positive side of the experience, with anger and rejecting behavior (e.g., missing meetings). In the latter, there is moving beyond the group to find new activities and new friends. Members substitute for what will soon be lost.

The worker's focus is to enable group members to separate, to help facilitate group evaluation, and to assist members to accept their ambivalence about termination. Termination for an elderly group member can be especially difficult to handle as it represents yet another loss in a long line of losses previously suffered. Elders look to the group to replace the losses of family, friends, and activity—and letting go and giving up again can be extremely difficult and painful. Workers have spoken of the reluctance of members to terminate a group experience, as well as their resignation about its ending. It seems to them that "everything" is ending. Could group termination highlight the individual's struggle at coping with a more final pending termination—that of death?

Termination can also mean experiencing a sense of accomplishment, learning a new set of skills, and getting the strength and courage to move on to other activities, whether these be another group, new friendships, or new community involvement. This is particularly important for the older person who has had little if any sense of another future to look forward to.

Needs Met by the Termination or Separation Phase

The final stage of group development is that of termination or separation. Many a group of older persons, particularly vulnerable older persons, may never reach a formal separation stage; they may, however, reach separation without ever going through an orderly process of any of the phases of group development. In fact, the likelihood that an aggregate of older persons will separate before becoming a fairly cohesive group is great, indeed. Peers move away from the neighborhood and join their families, some enter institutions (mostly permanently), others merely stop coming to the "group" and do not contribute to group building efforts, and others die. Separation and aloneness—if not loneliness—are frequent occurrences in the day-to-day lives of older people. And many have come to accept separation as a "normal loss." Here the social worker has to be particularly sensitive to avoid getting caught up in his/her own feelings, especially where the worker is much younger. The focus of the worker is to enable individuals to accept these losses without necessarily being able to replace them and yet, at the same time, to engage in grief work and to review earlier events, to recapitulate past experiences and to use reminiscing about relationships and events. When the aggregate has indeed become a group, then the support of others in doing grief work can be enlisted and separation losses become group rehearsals for future losses that are sure to occur. There we are dealing with "anticipatory grief work." Exiting from the social world is as much part of the total human experience as is entering into it. And it is during the termination episodes when the needs for ego-transcendence can be most fully realized, [since] here the person is faced obliquely, surreptitiously or openly with the quest as to the meaning of life. Whether an answer will be sought depends on the way in which the worker (and other group members) utilize this opportunity to come to terms with this existential question. The most vulnerable elderly, whether at home or in a nursing care facility, as well as the least vulnerable elderly, face this ultimate question. Here spiritual feelings can be tapped and placed in the service of the ego to relate to the world of which one is a part. The interpersonal encounter is the instrument through which this relating can occur when the worker and his/her "co-workers," i.e., group members, engage in activities that facilitate coming to terms with a person's own finiteness on this earth.[64]

Illustration of Termination of a Public-Housing Group

A group composed of residents of a new housing facility for the elderly had a task-oriented focus in which it planned a monthly activity for the entire building. Approximately ten months ago, the group began with eight members, four female and four male, ages ranging from 62 to 81. All members were on a fixed income, although two of the women had experienced the luxuries of middle- and upper-middle-class comforts in their earlier years. Education varied from some high school to beyond high school (dental hygienist training). Group members were generally active and self-sufficient. Two members were born outside the United States in Middle Eastern countries; one of the men was black. One woman was crippled from a childhood disease. Each of the men in the group had a history of alcoholism; two had difficulties during the life of the group.

> *Opening a Group Meeting, Late April. Present were Mr. G., Mrs. D., Mrs. T., Mr. R., and the social worker.* Mrs. T. was first to arrive. She said the others were downstairs in the lobby. Worker asked why, and she said they were waiting for her to come. No one has done this before, and worker explained that she had arrived early. She went and got Mrs. D., the only one besides herself who'd been waiting. Mr. R. then entered with his camera. He had film in it and wanted to practice a few shots. Worker told him that perhaps after the meeting they could do that. Mrs. D. and Mrs. T. then entered, followed by Mr. G. Everyone was happy to see him and told him so.
>
> Mr. R. began the meeting by asking, "What is a senior citizen?" He directed the question to the worker, but she threw it out to the group. Mrs. T. said it's when you're over 60. Mrs. D. said it's when you get benefits. Mr. R. said others get benefits. She said no they don't, provoking an argument. Mr. R. tried explaining that the disabled do, but Mrs. D. wasn't listening. The worker clarified for everyone that the blind and disabled get Social Security and other benefits too. Then worker asked the group what else happens when one becomes a senior citizen. Mrs. D. kept interrupting others and kept talking about the benefits (which she didn't think most people deserve).

Discussion of Illustration. This vignette brings out several issues. The worker had brought up termination the week before this meeting. Although participation and commitment to the group had varied, a few of the members were anticipating the meeting and expressing its importance to them. Although traces of an intimacy stage had begun to develop in the group, it was always mixed with much approach-avoidance. Gestures and signs of closeness are evident. Mrs. T. going to find Mrs. D., Mr. R. bringing his camera so he would have something tangible he could keep from the group, and finally, the bringing up of an issue of major concern to all—sharing feelings and thoughts on their identity and role in society. The worker purposely opened this up to the group to explore together.

> *Later in the meeting of April.* Worker asked the group if they'd like to have cheese and crackers. They said yes. Mr. G. offered to donate his can of corned beef spread and some salt-free crackers. Worker said that would be great. Worker asked Mr.

R. if he'd like to make some cupcakes or something. He said that the last time he made them, someone made a nasty comment. Mr. G. and Mrs. T. said they'd enjoyed his cupcakes. Mr. R. smiled and offered to bring a loaf of bread to the party. Worker accepted it and then pointed out to the group that if we had all these refreshments, we'd need people to work with the food. Mrs. T. said she would, then the others volunteered too.

Mrs. D. said sickly people shouldn't be allowed to work with food. Mrs. T. agreed that if someone had a cold, they shouldn't. Mrs. D. seemed to be making a reference to things other than colds. She said she didn't want to eat the food "they" prepared. Everyone (including worker) seemed annoyed. Worker said that if anyone felt not in good health on the fifteenth, he or she wouldn't work with the food. The others agreed to decide individually. Then Mrs. D. said they should have potato chips. Mrs. T. said they were too salty and many tenants had high blood pressure. Mrs. D. asked who. Mr. R. said he did.

When an argument erupted between Mr. R. and Mrs. D., worker asked them both to quiet down and said, "You two seem to be pretty angry today." Mrs. D. denied that she was angry; Mr. R. acknowledged the anger and said she was starting it. Mrs. D. turned to Mr. G. and asked if he thought she'd been argumentative. Mrs. T. withdrew from the discussion. Mr. R. and Mrs. D. continued to talk at the same time. Worker explained to them that when she stopped the conservation, they'd both been talking about two separate things—the visiting nurses who come on Wednesdays and the potato chips—and they hadn't been listening to each other. Mrs. D. said she was entitled to her opinions and she felt she should be honest. Mr. R. said this was a democracy and he was entitled too! Mrs. D. said she wasn't arguing. Worker said she hoped we could all be honest and share our feelings if there was something we were angry about. [Worker purposely generalized the statement, picking up on what Mrs. D. had said about being honest, but not directing anything specific at either of them.] Mr. G. and Mrs. T. hadn't said anything. There was a slight pause here, and Mrs. T. used the space to go back and pick up on talking about the refreshments. She seemed very uncomfortable during the conflict and needed to talk about something more neutral.

Discussion of Illustration. The members developed an identification with the group as more than just planners of a large activity. They were integrating their knowledge and awareness of their peers' needs (as well as their own) and relating this to their planning. The group provided the members with a feeling of status and identity. This is illustrated by individuals' volunteering to bring things from home to add to the activity and increase its chances of being a "success." The worker's skill had enabled her to guide the group in previous meetings, planning tasks that would almost guarantee success and personal reward for the group. This gave them a foundation so they could continue to build, experimenting with their own ideas and gaining the confidence needed for assuming responsibilities themselves. Eventually they would no longer need to rely on the worker as they had in the beginning to structure programs.

This worker learned that some dependence is necessary with the elderly before independence can occur. This vignette also illustrates how difficult it is when members have various ideas of the use and purpose of the group as well as variations in ego functioning. Some are more willing than others to risk themselves and relax defenses. In this case, the worker chose to comment on the behavior of the individuals and explore where the anger was coming from. One member recognized the anger while another denied it. Others became silent and withdrew from the interaction as the conflict increased. The worker tried to encourage expressions of feelings and anger but was aware of how threatening it became to the total group, so she didn't pursue it when the focus of the conversation changed.

Last meeting of the group with this worker in early May. Present were Mr. R., Mrs. D., Mrs. T., Mr. G., and the social worker. Worker told the group that she thought for our last meeting we could look at and evaluate the group and the activities over the past several months, both the good and bad points. Mr. R. felt the biggest problem was that people didn't show up enough. The others felt this was a problem also. Worker asked how we would change that. Mr. R. said we should get more people by going from door to door and asking them to join. Worker asked if he felt this would get the most people involved. He thought for a second and commented that many people don't care for activities. Worker explained that that's why we try to have different activities, because everyone is different and enjoys different things.

Worker asked the group what their thoughts were about the activities we had done. Worker said we should be critical, that we could learn from examining what we had done wrong and hopefully improve. Worker listed the activities the group had had. Everyone liked the penny sale the most. The group also said it enjoyed the plays and dancing. The parties were fun too. Worker asked if there were any activities they liked less or not at all. No one mentioned any. Worker asked if group had any suggestions in general about the way we prepared, set up, ran activities, etc. Mrs. D. suggested a dressmaking class. She said clothes were expensive and a lot of people might like to learn how to make their own.

Worker said it was good that we were thinking of new activities but we had to remember that our activities were for everyone in the building and some things we just couldn't do. Worker said that perhaps she'd want to start a class or talk to Mrs. S. about doing this. Worker used our Spanish class as an example, stating that it had been a great idea and we had tried to learn a little, but there was no one who could really teach us; thus we had been let down. Worker reaffirmed the importance of planning when we begin an activity, a group, etc. Mrs. T. said the worker had done a great job too, asked whether there was anything they could do to keep her there, and mentioned signing petitions. Worker thanked her for her thoughts and said leaving was very difficult after spending several months with them.

Mr. R. said he'd enjoyed the group and working with the worker. He wanted us to pose for a picture, which everyone did. Mrs. T. kissed worker goodbye and got teary-eyed. Mrs. D. began nervously talking about something else. Mrs. T. apologized for crying. Worker put her arm around her and told her it was okay to cry. She then got involved in the picture taking as they all did. Mrs. T. left after the pictures. Mr. R. and Mrs. D. remained and talked for a while. Worker thanked each of them individually for their gifts. Mrs. D. heard Mr. R. and worker talking and commented "He's a generous man." Worker turned to him and smiled and said he certainly was. As they left, they both squeezed the worker's hand.

Discussion of Last Meeting. There was an air of mourning that permeated the last meeting. Denial of feelings and regressive behavior became manifest. Issues that seemed resolved earlier reappeared. The members wanted to retain their social worker. Evaluation was initiated by the worker to allow for recapitulation, to help the group rethink and reassess the meaning of their experience. It was life review of the group—with a purpose. Group members were allowed to "mourn" and "grieve" and thus could be freed to move ahead again. The worker opened up these opportunities. The experience included finishing up, facing a loss, and acknowledging accomplishment; a bridge was built to walk across to a new beginning.

Excellent material on working with the elderly, particularly around the practice of group work and group treatment can be found in Irene Burnside's *Working with the Elderly: Group Process and Techniques* (2nd edition).[65] This book has excellent chapters on reality orientation, remotivation therapy, music therapy, dance movement therapy, family sculpting, self-help groups, and group psychotherapy. It also provides comprehensive references on resources, bibliographies, case studies, and learning exercises.

Working with Groups in an Institutional Setting

Although the overall principles of group work intervention as outlined in this chapter apply to institutionalization, an institution's effects upon both residents and staff present particular problems and issues for the social worker to deal with.

Institutions for the aged are heterogeneous. They include residences, nursing and convalescent homes, hospitals, and psychiatric facilities. Also, they differ in size, auspices, ownership, rates, and form of payments received. What role can social workers play in these institutions? Giordano and Giordano suggest that they become change agents. However, "to do this we must take a hard look at the institution. . . . How can the attitudes of staff members toward patients be changed? How can . . . activities that will motivate patients be instituted? What physical change can be implemented to make the institution more comfortable?"

In one way or another, social workers have been and are involved with the process of institutionalization and the institutionalized population. They have referred elderly persons to institutions. They have been utilized at intake to help the elderly adjust to institutional living and their new role in it. Within the institution, social workers perform many different functions and fill many positions. As caseworkers, they focus on . . . elderly individual[s] and are concerned with relationships between [them] and [their] family, other residents, and staff.

They also attempt to alleviate guilt feelings of the resident's family. Social workers are helpful to residents and staff alike in times of crisis—for example, when suicides or natural deaths occur. In addition, they are active in group work, recreation, resident councils, and in-service staff training. In some institutions, social workers are administrators or assistants [or] members of supervisory policy-making bodies, such as boards of directors; thus they indirectly or directly help determine the institution's focus and orientation[66]

Unique Aspects of Institutional Settings

In many institutional settings, such as homes for the aged and nursing homes, residents who enter have to relinquish independent living, probably for the remainder of their lives. The population tends to be made up of more infirm groups of individuals, both physically and mentally, than a comparable group of individuals living in the community. Often the environment they enter is sterile and depersonalized, and control of major areas of their lives has been taken away. The institution fosters dependency and engenders feelings of loss; the very nature of this setting helps reinforce the societal myths and stereotypes of the aged and aging process.[67]

Nelida Ferrarri, writing of some of the unique aspects of groups and individuals in an institutional setting, points out that individuals living in such a setting are already living as a group, "united not by their past experiences, but by a common presence of need and discomfort, of frustration and anxieties . . . together, but lonesome. They [have] solitude, but not privacy. They [are] alone, but without the chance to be with themselves. A group yes, but a lonely group, with its members unidentified in a big gray mass." She goes on to summarize life in such a setting:

> Group life in this setting was not satisfactory for most residents; . . . there were already subgroups with leaders and followers. . . . Residents' illnesses, loss of facilities and the ever-present attitude of "do for me rather than ask me to do" [challenged] the skill and patience of the group workers to develop meaningful programs rather than just program. . . . Under an apparent frozen surface were tensions, actions, emotions, loyalties, likes, and dislikes, but life was there and a need to find ways to use its energy constructively. . . . The residence body was structured separately from staff and board, and the communication between them was very poor. Residents [did] not trust the administration, which was seen both as protector and enemy; at first, worker [was] seen as member of the administration, and the residents tend[ed] to be suspicious. Communication with the outside community [was] broken, and there [was] social and individual dysfunction.[68]

Gisela Konopka delineated the functions of working with groups on the institutional team some time ago. She sees them as twofold: to help with the group living situation and to conduct treatment-oriented groups. Elaine Brody speaks to this, as follows:

> Complexities of institutional life need to be carefully considered before any group program can be effectively initiated: departmental independence, medical needs of residents and accompanying limitations, schedules of other services and activities, timetables of nursing shifts and schedules, conflicting perceptions of resident needs among staff, family, and residents. The zealous, albeit well-intentioned worker who attempts to bypass these institutional considerations and conduct his [or her]

own independent group will encounter conflict, or abandonment and isolation of his [or her] program from the rest of the institution. To be effective, group services in the institution must be understood and supported by all significant institutional elements.[69]

Roles Groups Can Play

Groups can play meaningful roles for residents within an institutional setting. They can, as in other areas, alleviate the isolation, loneliness, powerlessness, and anonymity that so many residents feel, especially cognitively impaired elders, who are often socially ostracized because of their memory loss and confusion.[70] Groups can give residents an opportunity to work through and resolve grief, mourning, and options for "replenishing the social losses" of old age and institutionalization (Silverstone and Burack-Weiss); promote a sense of belonging and self-identity in the unfamiliar setting; and provide stimulation and recreation.[71]

Groups can also have a spill-over effect beyond the immediate group experience. Herbert Shore wrote of the experiences residents had in activity groups: "What is vital is the experiences our residents acquire as a result of method not content. If this is true, and if (as we do) we provide our residents opportunities for decision making about their recreational life, then our residents can and should make decisions about every other aspect of their life."[72]

Groups in an institutional setting can provide an arena and opportunity to develop mastery in negotiating the environment of the institution. Individuals tend to feel very small, meek, and obedient in the face of the rather complex, frightening milieu in which they find themselves. In addition to efforts on the part of individuals, collective efforts, which are shared and supported by other members, can be uplifting. Thus, a small group can be a source of strength for facing the larger world, the institution. It can also become a training ground for members to learn from. Barring obstacles of multiple physical/mental impairment, fear of retributions, and inexperience, groups can also provide opportunities for social action and self-advocacy.[73]

Referring to the models proposed by Papell and Rothman, it appears that the reciprocal model is appropriate to this setting, since one of its key ideas is to mediate between the demands of a larger social system and the needs of the individual group members. The worker can help the group find that balance between individual needs and institutional requirements by focusing on the members' abilities to do things for themselves.

The group becomes a unit for satisfying mutual needs. The worker is not an authority figure representing the institution, but rather a mediator and, at times, an advocate. This model allows residents to achieve a sense of control and mastery of their individual tasks and to reconcile these with environmental concerns. Further, the peer support offered by group members may actually result in improved functioning of members.[74] The reciprocal model also gives the worker room to provide support and protection to individuals, taking into account their dependency needs. Gerald Euster points out that the function of groups in an institution is to bring staff and residents together. Towards this end, the tasks of the social worker are as follows:

1. Redefine staff and patient roles to ensure more active collaboration in constructing institutional activities.
2. Promote continuing effectiveness of the institution.
3. Use group meetings as a source of patient-patient, patient-staff, staff-patient, and staff-staff feedback and evaluation.
4. Search out potential and resources of residents.
5. Provide opportunities for patients to maintain contacts with the world outside the institution. [75]

Role of the Worker

In institutional settings, social workers often see people both formally in the units where residents live and casually in the daily routines of institutional life. Since workers form relationships with people before convening a group, group members already know them and seek their attention and allegiance, claiming them as "their" social worker. When group members see the social worker outside of regular meetings, they often attempt to discuss other individuals or particular happenings that have occurred.

Shore speaks of workers' attempts to use themselves consciously, even in casual conversations and in the halls and elevator, etc. The worker comes to know more of the total person by seeing group members in other interactions in the institution. "The importance of the individual relationship with every resident cannot be stressed enough. The relationship will have very intangible facets and will mean different things [at different times] but the worker remains a stable factor throughout."[76]

To maximize the benefits of such individual contact, the worker must attempt to establish a positive relationship with each member prior to the first meeting. To avoid a frustrating group life, the criteria for the group programs must be individualized and particularized to fit the needs of each person. The technique is to give individual support and encouragement; to help members overcome the "undifferentiation" of the mass, which they fear; and to recognize and accept their individualities and help them develop a personal, trusting relationship with the worker.

Elaine Brody emphasizes the importance of the work done prior to the first meeting.[77] Thinking, planning, and a careful determination of the purpose of the group should focus on matching the needs of group members with the purpose. In an institution, identification of members of a group often precedes the development of the purpose. Thus, a worker may be aware of many residents who seem to be demonstrating a particular need of one kind or another, and this may lead to the development of a group based on those needs.

Other tasks of the group worker in the institutional setting have been delineated by Silverstone and Burack-Weiss[78] and Miller and Solomon:[79]

- "Doing with" group members, providing support, and modeling behavior for future resident behavior and action.
- Avoiding overidentification with members' fears and despair without placing unrealistic demands on members.
- Identifying and creatively utilizing unimpaired areas of functioning of members. Each may contribute on one or more of several levels, including cognitively, emotionally or physically.
- Sensitively and patiently dealing with initial resistance born of fear of intrusion of privacy or of stirring up emotionally-laden issues.
- Working together with therapeutic, recreational, and other staff as valuable resources.
- Respecting long-term care residents' decisions not to share personal experiences because, unlike elders in the community, they can't retreat to privacy after group sessions.
- Avoiding the pitfall of elders' buying into the idea that the group leader, by virtue of being younger, is the "expert" and "knows what is best for them." Such an attitude makes it impossible for the group to develop as a creation of the members' own needs and desires.

Types of Groups

There are many types of groups in an institutional setting. Euster has provided a useful typology:[80]

    I.   Groups for self-management
        A. Patient or resident council
            1. Type of group: representative, elected, or revolving membership
            2. Size and composition
                a. Variations according to number and arrangement of living units and health of residents
                b. Meetings between departmental staff members and residents to strengthen representative composition of group
                c. One staff member as group adviser
                d. Membership generally not more than 15 persons
            3. Objectives
                a. Resident and staff collaboration in examining and solving daily living problems
                b. Review and development of institutional policy and procedures
                c. Modification of institutional appearance
                c. Development of resident leadership skills
                e. Group action for increased social responsibility
                f. Improvement of resident-staff relations
                g. Attainment of esprit de corps
        B. Groups based on living units
            1. Type of group: open to all members of unit; voluntary
            2. Size and composition

        a. Encouragement for all residents and staff on unit to meet

        b. Units generally not more than 20 residents

    3. Objectives

        a. Opening channels of communication (to and from resident council)

        b. Referral of problems concerning total institution to resident council

        c. Ventilation of problems of unit living

        d. Correction of distortions of information among residents and staff

        e. Provision of information

        f. Distribution to patients of social responsibility within their capacity

        g. Encouragement of leadership among patients

  C. Committee for planning activities

    1. Type of group: voluntary; formed by staff or representative (may be a committee of the council)

    2. Size and composition

        a. Dependent upon number and arrangement of living units and health of residents

        b. Group generally composed of fewer residents and staff than council

    3. Objectives

        a. Consideration of total leisure-time activity needs of residents

        b. Development of latent skills of residents for leadership in program activities

        c. Activation of group pressure toward increased resident participation in group and individual activities; organizations such as alumni club may be useful vehicles for engaging former patients as leaders in programming and for assuming responsibility for special events, friendly visiting, and other volunteer service to institution

II. Groups for special interests and skill mastery

  A. Hobby groups

    1. Type of group: open-ended to allow new members to enter and older members to leave as they develop skills for individual pursuits

    2. Size and composition: small enough so staff, residents, and resident leaders can offer individualized assistance to members

    3. Objectives

        a. Social interaction through sharing of hobbies and life experiences

        b. Acquisition or restoration of proficiency in an activity of individual interest

        c. Restoration of confidence and ability to complete tasks

  B. Groups for creative activities

    1. Type of group

        a. Voluntary or formed by staff to focus on particular patient interests or to search out common interests

        b. Possibly a time-limited group experience to provide incentive to members to participate more fully

    2. Size: between 10 and 15 members, to provide the atmosphere of club

    3. Objectives

        a. Group planning, development, and achievement

        b. Service to the institution (newspaper, decorating, special projects)

      c. Service to outside community (making toys, sewing for children's home, other volunteer services)

      d. Self-actualization and growth through learning and expanding skills (cooking, gardening, crafts)

C. Enrichment groups

  1. Type of group

      a. Voluntary or formed by staff and patients to focus on particular patient interests or to search out common interests

      b. Always open to permit new membership; families permitted to participate in selected activities

  2. Size: between 10 and 15 members, in order to maximize involvement

  3. Objectives

      a. Reorientation to world through discussion of current events and community and world issues

      b. Restoration of interest in trips using community resources

      c. Cultivation of restorative interests (exercise, games, adult education)

      d. Increasing understanding of psychological and physical aspects of aging

      e. Increasing understanding of concepts of rehabilitation, restoration, and self-help.

Admission to an institution is often a very traumatic event to the potential resident, one that is accompanied by feelings of loneliness, overwhelming loss, and general anxiety. Orientation groups for such new residents may serve to alert them and their families quickly to role expectations, institutional objectives, and the total range of services offered. Groups can also open channels of communication, correct distorted conceptions of institutional objectives, and set the stage for future group activity and problem solving. They may also serve to counter the depersonalized, anonymous feeling of the institution and provide the newcomer with a smaller, warmer, safer place to express the fears and anxieties that individuals experience during this crisis in their lives.

> Verbalizing problems was the first step toward understanding and resolving them; the group provided a channel for release of tensions and hostilities; as it was okay to "complain," sources of the complaint could be explored; the group provided mutual support for common problems that members were facing. It helped new residents perceive more clearly their own problems; relationship with the social worker made it possible to accept help; the group alerted the rest of the institutional staff to individual needs and problems and it provided reassurance to the new resident that he or she could indeed function and make his or her way in this new community.[81]

There is a particular need for group affiliation for those residents who are not the average participants in activities, who are isolated, withdrawn, or do not fit into the everyday activity and social milieu of the residential community. The focus here is not on a hobby or an activity of some kind, but on creating a place for residents to help one another cope with their environment and learn what it means to relate to others. The purposes of such a group are to build self-esteem, to engender feelings that can lead to greater participation in other activities and greater affiliation with others in the home, and to establish rewarding interpersonal relationships.

Working with such a group calls for great skill. One must bring in objective, factual, and dispassionate materials to avoid having such an aggregate of residents become too threatening. Individuals should be allowed to remain at the preaffiliative stage as long as possible, keeping social distance from others and building a bridge through the worker.[82]

Kubie and Landau conclude their book by noting the value of group work:

> Older person[s venture] toward new contacts, new activities, new experiences over the bridge of [their] dependence on a staff worker. . . . As [people gain] assurance in the community [they bring] personal troubles to [the worker] for help. . . . In short, . . . security . . . is revived by [the worker's] acceptance of [them] and . . . from this personal acceptance, [they] can move on to further growth and new adaptations.[83]

Group Work with Minority Elderly

Hisashi Hirayama has written on the utility of and unique considerations in group work with minority elderly:

> Groups appear to be a particularly useful tool for work with the minority aged for several reasons. First, similar to other elderly persons, the minority aged have needs to associate and share their thoughts, feelings, and past and present experiences with people of similar backgrounds. Second, they have needs to share their ethnic and cultural heritages with their cohorts as well as with younger generations. Third, their ethnic identity and natural consensus-seeking group behaviors may lend themselves to the formation and operation of groups.
>
> It is not sufficient for social workers to work with the elderly solely in formally organized groups. It is particularly important to extend interventions and working relationships to the elderly's microenvironments, strengthening support systems at home and in the neighborhood. To do so, workers must develop an understanding of the particular minority community in question, including its values, patterns of interpersonal relationships, problem-solving mechanisms, and [operation of] support systems. . . . Without this knowledge, the worker may act contrary to the interests of clients by unintentionally disrupting, rather than strengthening, whatever informal support systems exist. Numerous opportunities to use existing natural groups, such as families, extended families, or informal neighborhood groups of the elderly, tend to be overlooked as valuable mediums for service delivery. Thus it is important for workers to learn to use various techniques of working with intergenerational groups of grandparents, grandchildren, extended family groups, and others.
>
> . . . The minority elderly may be classified into three different groups based on their patterns of service utilization:

1. The first group . . . comprise[s] . . . those who can benefit from group services at neighborhood centers, health clinics, social clubs, congregate dining programs, and various other forms of day programs. These individuals tend to be physically, mentally, and socially capable of taking advantage of the available services and can enjoy new relationships and developmental group programs.

2. The second group . . . comprise[s] . . . those who are prevented from benefiting from the available programs because of access factors. Lack of transportation, a language barrier, a physical handicap, poor health, illegal immigration status, or cultural traits all are factors that may discourage participation. This group's activities and support systems are pretty much centered on their neighborhood, for example, visiting friends, neighbors, family members, and nearby stores.

3. The third group involves those who are institutionalized in such places as nursing homes, mental institutions, and boarding homes. The contrast between a home environment and that of a nursing home unquestionably poses problems for all who must stay in a home, but to the minority aged it usually poses special problems because of cultural and/or language barriers. Residents often become isolated and withdrawn as they are unable to cope with a variety of unfamiliar institutional and interpersonal demands. . . .

[One advantage of groups for minorities in community based settings is that] information related to the availability of services and how and what to do to obtain them may be dispensed in groups. Misconceptions about eligibilities and value conflicts and resistance to approaching agencies may be resolved in group processes. Importantly, facilitation of a mutual aid system among members encourages their individual self-determination.

There are certain unique psychosocial and cultural traits of the minority aged that the worker must be aware of when he or she attempts to work with the elderly in groups. By and large, the effectiveness of group work depends upon the amount of sensitive attention the worker is capable of giving in group process to these unique traits. Consequently, the success of the worker's influences and activities is related directly to his or her knowledge and acceptance of a given culture, its formal and informal systems, and its norms. . . .

The social worker must be clear as to the purpose he or she intends to achieve through the group and should remember that he or she is trying to form and develop a group with people who are fearful, skeptical, suspicious, and reluctant about participating in a group. Particularly during the developmental stage of groups, members need a good deal of direction, encouragement, and stimulation from the worker. . . .

Solomon proposes empowerment as a goal of social work practice with minority persons. Empowerment is "a process whereby persons who belong to a stigmatized social category throughout their lives can be assisted to develop an increase skills in the exercise of interpersonal influence and the performance of valued social roles." . . .Empowerment in group process enables members to maintain or enhance their self-esteem. It motivates use of their skills, individual resources, and group resources in the effort to achieve self- as well as group determined goals. She identifies two roles for practitioners that are consistent with self-determination and, consequently, enhancement of self-esteem. These are the "resource consultant" and "sensitizer" roles.

The resource consultant role is defined as one who links clients to resources in a manner that improves their problem-solving capacities. This role is considered to be much broader than that of a resource dispenser who merely delivers tangible resources to clients. . . .

. . . The sensitizer is defined as one whose "role behaviors are designed to assist the client gain self-knowledge necessary for him to solve his problem or problems. . . ."[84]

References

1. Carol H. Meyer, "Introduction—the Field of Aging: A Prototype of Social Work Practice," in "Social Work with the Aging," collection of articles selected from *Social Work* (New York: NASW, 1975), p. 5.
2. Harriet Bartlett, in "Working Definition of Social Work Practice," *Social Work*, vol. 3, no. 2 (April 1958).
3. Helen U. Phillips, *Essentials of Group Work Skills* (New York: Association Press, 1957), p. 51.
4. Sebastian Tine, P. Deutschberger, and K. Hastings, "Generic and Specific in Social Group Work Practice with the Aging," in *Social Work with Groups* (New York: NASW, 1960), p. 17.
5. Harold B. Sharkey, "Sustaining the Aged in the Community," *Social Work*, vol. 7 (January 1962), p. 22.
6. James A. Garland, "The Relationship Between Social Group Work and Group Therapy: Can a Group Therapist be a Social Group Worker, Too?" Paper presented at the fifth annual Symposium on Social Work with Groups, Detroit, Michigan, October 21, 1983.
7. Catherine Papell and B. Rothman, "Social Group Work Models: Possession and Heritage," *Journal of Education for Social Work*, no. 2 (Fall 1966), pp. 66–78.
8. Louis Lowy, "Meeting the Needs of the Aged on a Differential Basis," in *Social Group Work with Older People* (New York: NASW, 1963), p. 68.
9. Fritz Redl, in G. Konopka, *Social Group Work: A Helping Process* (Englewood, N.J.: Prentice-Hall, 1963), p. 268.
10. Louis Lowy, "Social Group Work with Vulnerable Older Persons: A Theoretical Perspective," *Social Work with Groups*, vol. 5, no. 2, (summer 1982), (New York: Haworth Press, 1983), p. 25.
11. Ibid.
12. Carol J. Barrett, "Effectiveness of Widow's Groups in Facilitating Change," *Journal of Consulting and Clinical Psychology*, vol. 46, no. 1 (1978) pp. 20–31.
13. Kerry Paul Altman, "Psychodrama with the Institutionalized Elderly: A Method for Role Re-engagement," *Journal of Group Psychotherapy, Psychodrama and Sociometry*, vol. 36, no. 3 (fall 1983) pp. 87–95.
14. Nora Stabler, "The Use of Groups in Day Centers for Older Adults," *Social Work with Groups*, vol. 4 (3/4) (fall/winter 1981) pp. 49–58.
15. Ibid.
16. Ibid.
17. Ron Toseland, Edmund Sherman, and Stephen Bliven, "The Comparative Effectiveness of Two Group Work Approaches for the Development of Mutual Support Groups among the Elderly," *Social Work with Groups*, vol. 4 (1/2) (spring/summer 1981) pp. 137–153.
18. Lowy, "Social Group Work with Vulnerable Older Persons," op. cit., p. 22.

19. Lowy, "Meeting the Needs," op. cit., p. 70.
20. Toseland, Sherman, and Bliven, op. cit.
21. Lowy, "Meeting the Needs," op. cit., p. 71.
22. Barbara Silverstone and Ann Burack-Weiss, *Social Work Practice with the Frail Elderly and Their Families: The Auxiliary Function Model* (Springfield, Ill.: Charles C Thomas Publishers, 1983).
23. Ibid.
24. Lowy, "Meeting the Needs," op. cit., pp. 72–73.
25. Louis Lowy, "The Group in Social Work with the Aged," *Social Work*, vol. 7 (October 1962), p. 45.
26. Jean Maxwell, *Centers for Older People* (Washington, D.C.: NCOA, 1966), p. 5.
27. Chiyoko Furukawa and Dianna Shomaker, *Community Health Services for the Aged* (Rockville, Md.: Aspen Systems Corp., 1982), pp. 225–242.
28. Silverstone and Burack-Weiss, op. cit.
29. Harry Levine, "Day Centers for Older People" (New York: Department of Public Welfare, 1952).
30. Sebastian Tine, "Process and Criteria for Grouping," in *Social Group Work with Older People* (New York: NASW, 1963), pp. 6–7.
31. Ibid, p. 14.
32. Furukawa and Shomaker, op. cit., pp. 64–65.
33. James Garland, Ralph Kolodny, and Hubert Jones, "A Model in Stages of Development of Social Group Work Groups," in Saul Bernstein (ed.), *Explorations in Group Work* (Boston: Boston University School of Social Work, 1962), p. 21.
34. Furukawa and Shomaker, op. cit.
35. Lowy, "Social Group Work with Vulnerable Older Persons," op. cit., p. 25.
36. Morris Levin, "Selected Implications for Social Group Work Practice with Older Adults," in *Social Group Work with Older People* (New York: NASW, 1963), p. 40.
37. Susan Kubie and Gertrude Landau, *Group Work with the Aged* (New York: International Universities Press, 1954), p. 209.
38. Garland et al., op. cit., p. 30.
39. Louis Frey and Marguerite Meyer, "Exploration and Working Agreement in Two Social Work Methods," in Saul Bernstein (ed.), *Explorations in Group Work*, op. cit., p. 15.
40. Lowy, "Social Group Work with Vulnerable Older Persons," op. cit., p. 26.
41. Garland et al., op. cit., p. 34.
42. Jennifer Burns and D. Miller, "Ego Development of Older Adults through Social Group Work." Unpublished Paper, Boston University, 1970, p. 4.
43. Lowy, "Social Group Work with Vulnerable Older Persons," op. cit., p. 27.
44. Garland et al., op. cit.
45. Gertrude Wilson and Gladys Ryland in their book *Social Group Work Practice* (Boston: Houghton Mifflin, 1949), refer to the decision-making process as the "central core of social group work" (p. 66).
46. Lowy, "Decision Making and Group Work," in Saul Bernstein (ed.), *Explorations in Group Work*, op. cit., pp. 84–85.
47. Kubie and Landau, op. cit., p. 41.
48. Kubie and Landau, op. cit., pp. 38–39.
49. Tine, "Process and Criteria for Grouping," op. cit., p. 19.
50. Silverstone and Burack-Weiss, op. cit.
51. Louis Lowy, *Adult Education and Group Work* (New York: Whiteside, 1955).

52. For an extensive discussion of program in social group work, see Gertrude Wilson and Gladys Ryland, *Social Group Work Practice: The Creative Use of the Social Process* (Boston: Houghton Mifflin, 1949); and Ruth R. Middleman, *The Non-Verbal Method in Working with Groups* (New York: Association Press, 1968). See also Edwin A. Crist, "The Retired Stamp Collector: Economic and Other Functions of a Systematized Leisure Activity," in Arnold M. Rose and Warren A. Peterson (eds.), *Older People and Their Social World* (Philadelphia: Davis, 1965), pp. 93–112.

53. Florence Vickery, *Creative Programming for Older Adults* (New York: Association Press, 1972), p. 222.

54. M. Levin, op. cit., p. 11.

55. Ibid.

56. Allen Pincus, "Reminiscence in Aging and Its Implications for Social Work Practice," *Social Work*, vol. 15 (July 1970), p. 52 (Andrew Dibner has done considerable work in relation to reminiscing of the elderly. See *Understanding Aging*, eds. Marian G. Spencer and Caroline J. Dorr (New York: Appleton-Century Crofts), 1975), pp. 67–90.

57. Mark Forman, "Conflict, Controversy and Confrontation in Group Work with Older Adults," *Social Work*, vol. 12, no. 1 (January 1967), p. 81.

58. Ibid., pp. 82–83.

59. Louis Lowy, "'Roadblocks' in Social Group Work Practice," *The Gerontologist*, vol. 7, no. 2, pt. I (June 1967), p. 112.

60. Nelida Ferrari, "Assessment of Individuals in Groups of Older Adults" in *Social Group Work With Older People* (New York: NASW, 1963), p. 4.

61. Lowy, "Decision Making," op. cit., pp. 100–101.

62. Lowy, "Social Group Work with Vulnerable Older Persons," op. cit., p. 28.

63. Garland et al., op. cit., p. 41.

64. Lowy, "Social Group Work with Vulnerable Older Persons," op. cit., p. 29.

65. Irene Burnside, *Working with the Elderly: Group Process and Techniques*, 2nd ed. (Monterey, Calif.: Wadsworth, 1984).

66. J. J. Kosberg, "The Nursing Home: A Social Work Paradox," *Social Work*, vol. 18 (March 1973), p. 104.

67. Erving Goffman's classic statement in *Asylums* (Chicago: Aldine, 1959) is most apropos for these types of institutions as well.

68. Ferrari, op. cit.

69. E. Brody, *A Social Work Guide for Long Term Care Facilities* (Washington, D.C.: Department of HEW, U.S. Government Publications 1975), p. 126.

70. Stabler, op. cit.

71. Ibid.

72. Herbert Shore, "Social Groups in a Home for the Aged." Unpublished paper, at Gerontological Society of America.

73. Silverstone and Burack-Weiss, op. cit.

74. Ibid.

75. Gerald Euster, "A System of Groups in Institutions for the Aged," *Social Casework*, vol. 52 (October 1971), p. 523.

76. Shore, op. cit., p. 16.

77. Brody, op. cit.

78. Silverstone and Burack-Weiss, op. cit.

79. Irving Miller and Renee Solomon, "The Development of Group Services for the Elderly", *Journal of Gerontological Social Work*, vol. 2, no. 3, spring 1980, pp. 241–257.
80. Euster, op. cit., pp. 523–529.
81. Shura Saul, Richard Segal, and Ezra Saul, "The Use of the Small Group in Orienting New Residents to a Home for the Aged." Unpublished paper, 1975.
82. N. Feil, "Group Therapy in a Home for the Aged," *The Gerontologist*, vol. 7, no. 3 (September 1967).
83. Kubie and Landau, op. cit., p. 209.
84. Hisashi Hirayama, "Group Services for the Minority Aged," in R. L. McNeely and John L. Colen (eds.), *Aging in Minority Groups* (Beverly Hills, Calif.: Sage Publications, 1983), pp. 270–280.

13

Community Organizing
with Older Persons

This chapter outlines community organization practice with older adults following the process-action model.

Ralph Kramer and Harry Specht define community organization as follows:

> Community organization refers to various methods of intervention whereby a professional change agent helps a community action system composed of individuals, groups, or organizations to engage in planned collective action in order to deal with social problems within a democratic system of values. It is concerned with programs aimed at social change, with primary reference to environmental conditions and social institutions. It involves two major and interrelated concerns: (1) the processes of working with an action system, which include planning and organizing, identifying problem areas, diagnosing causes, and formulating solutions; and (2) developing strategies and mobilizing the resources necessary to effect action.[1]

This definition includes, on the one hand, working with an action system and mobilizing the resources needed to produce change and, on the other hand, diagnostic and planning tasks.

Community Organizing as Problem Solving

Robert Perlman and Arnold Gurin contend that it is through a problem-solving process that the aims, purposes, or goals of community organizational efforts can be accomplished. In a model analogous to the model described in Compton and Galaway, they detail the problem-solving process as follows:

340

- Defining the problem that is to be addressed or solved
- Building a structure or communications system for addressing it
- Examining and selecting, from among alternative solutions, policies and lines of action
- Taking the action necessary to implement the chosen policy in programmatic form
- Revision of the above decisions and actions in the light of continuous monitoring, evaluation, and feedback[2]

Two kinds of complementary activities have to be carried out by the practitioner in the various phases of this process: interactional tasks and analytical tasks. In Table 13.1, these two tasks are related to the phases of the problem-solving model. To anchor these abstract concepts Perlman and Gurin maintain that the organizational context breathes life into the actual practice of community organization and also shapes its operation.

> We have found three kinds of organizations that are distinguished by the central function associated with each, by their structure or form, and by the typical problems and tasks they present to practitioners in community organization and social planning. The three contexts of practice that constitute our framework are (1) working with voluntary associations, (2) community work with service agencies, and (3) interorganizational planning.
> Voluntary associations cover a wide variety of groups and organizations based on a membership whose common interest is in achieving some change or improvement in social arrangements, institutions, or relationships. A service agency is a formal bureaucratic organization that has as its central purpose the provision of a service to a designated target population. Planning and allocating organizations are networks of formal organizations whose function is the determination of how to organize and deploy resources to deal with social problems.
> Each of the contexts contains within it distinct purposes, ideologies, and other factors that determine the approaches and activities that are undertaken. The commonality in practice, to the extent that it exists within each of the contexts, derives from the practitioner's central task. Thus, his [or her] basic job in working with voluntary associations is to build and develop the association and to help increase its effectiveness in obtaining its objectives, whatever they may be. The task in the service agency is conducting relationships between the service system and the community in which it is based, which includes the clientele that it serves. Finally, the practitioner in allocating and planning organizations is responsible for the articulation of needs and resources through an interorganizational system.[3]

Voluntary associations in the field of aging include self-help organizations, such as local neighborhood groups of elderly, and self-help and action organizations, such as the Gray Panthers, the Legislative Council of Older Americans, etc. They may be local or area-, state-, or nationwide in scope and reach. Service agencies provide services to, for, and by the elderly, such as councils on aging, home care corporations, health councils, national councils of senior citizens, etc. Planning

Table 13.1. Analytical and Interactional Tasks during Phases of Problem Solving

	Analytical Tasks	Interactional Tasks
1. Defining problems	Preliminary studying; describing the problematic aspects of a situation; conceptualizing the system of relevant actors; assessing what opportunities and limits are set both by the organization employing the practitioner and by other actors	Eliciting and receiving information, grievances, and preferences from those experiencing the problem and from other sources
2. Building structure	Determining the nature of the practitioner's relationship to various actors; deciding on types of structures to be developed; choosing people for roles as experts, communicators, influencers, and the like	Establishing formal and informal communication lines; recruiting people into the selected structures and roles and obtaining their commitments to address the problem
3. Formulating policy	Analyzing past efforts to deal with the problem; developing alternative goals and strategies and assessing their possible consequences and feasibility; selecting one or more for recommendations to decision makers	Communicating alternative goals and strategies to selected actors; promoting their expression of preferences and testing acceptance of various alternatives; assisting decision makers to choose
4. Implementing plans	Specifying what tasks need to be performed to achieve agreed-upon goals—by whom, when, and with what resources and procedures	Presenting requirements to decision makers; overcoming resistances and obtaining commitments to the program; marshaling resources and putting procedures into operation
5. Monitoring	Designing system for collecting information on operations; analyzing feedback data and specifying adjustments needed and/or new problems that require planning and action	Obtaining information from relevant actors based on their experience; communicating findings and recommendations and preparing actors for new round of decisions to be made

SOURCE: Robert Perlman and Arnold Gurin, *Community Organization and Social Planning* (New York: Wiley, 1971), p. 62. Reprinted by permission of John Wiley & Sons, Inc.

and allocating organizations span municipal commissions on the elderly, area agencies on aging, state-wide units (offices) of aging, the national administrations on aging, etc. (See Chapter 7.)

There are overlaps among volunteer and service organizations and also among planning and allocation groups. For example, the National Council of Senior Citizens is a self-help action organization that also provides services to its membership and gets involved in planning and allocation functions. Perlman and Gurin write:

> Planning and allocating organizations assign resources and program responsibilities to service agencies. Some planning bodies seek voluntary contributions to finance their work; others are creatures of legislatures. In both instances they must relate to voluntary groups that have interests in the problems being addressed. Service agencies study the needs that they are designed to meet, evaluate performance in relation to need, and propose changes in function, program content, and resources. The service agency may carry out these tasks directly or through a planning organization. Increasingly the agency must also relate to the pressures of voluntary groups.
>
> A voluntary association can act as a generator of proposals directed to service agencies or to planning and allocating organizations. Its functions include the formulation of goals, the organization of people to advance goals, the development of proposals, and the mobilization of resources to support programs. It is also within its province to seek modifications in programs, to resist programs that are inimical to its interests, and finally, to seek the removal and replacement of services that are deemed undesirable.
>
> The interrelationships among the three contexts of practice are circular and interactive. Modifications may originate anywhere in the system and the interactions are reciprocal among all the contexts. They may be visualized as follows:

Planning Organizations   Service Agencies

Voluntary Associations

[Nevertheless the context is important, since the practitioner is] guided by the structure, aims, and operating procedures of the organization that pays the bill.[4]

Problem Solving through the Process-Action Model

Let us briefly take the five phases and relate them to the task of the social worker engaged in organizing practice.

Defining the Problem (Entry)

The first issue that arises at the point of problem identification is whether to accept a current formulation as provided by an existing service, organization, profession, or interest group or whether to define the problem in more "objective" terms, based on a body of data that will somehow describe the condition more adequately and therefore presumably provide a better guide for intervention. The planner is frequently enmeshed from the outset in a variety of prejudgments and constraints that stem from the auspices under which he [or she] is operating and various other factors. The theoretical model is nevertheless useful in defining some of the tasks that need to be performed, since the planning process necessarily rests on an appraisal of the situation that is to be affected. The exercise of appraising the problem with as much freedom from predefinition as possible provides an opportunity to consider a range of alternatives in addition to those that may already exist in the minds of relevant actors.

A related issue is the question of boundaries. On the one hand, the planner seeks to understand the problem in its broadest dimensions in order to consider all of the factors that may be relevant to his [or her] work in the later stages of policy development and program implementation. The kind of information that is brought into view and the way it is organized have an important effect on subsequent decisions.[5]

When asked, the residents in a particular neighborhood may say the problem of the elderly is that they have nothing to do. Yet in ordinary conversation, they constantly may talk about how many people have been robbed or jumped in the streets and how the elderly are afraid to go out of their doors. The worker must be alert to both points and make a decision about what it is that people are most concerned with. How do nonresidents, merchants, professionals, etc., see the problem? Can points of view be reconciled? What problems can be worked on? The problem must be of concern to people in the area; the closer to home the problem, the more likely people are to be concerned. Is the problem a crisis or not?

In defining the issue, a list of problems confronting a community needs to be compiled. The following list may serve as a starting point:

1. Income Adequacy
   Social Security benefits
   Regulation of pension funds on federal and state levels
   Public and private assistance payments
   Property-tax relief
   Cost-of-living adjustment
   Appropriate adjustments for handicapped
   Guaranteed annual income
2. Nutrition Needs
   Nutrition counseling and education
   Food stamp assistance
   Congregate eating facilities
   Cooperative food buying/meal planning for better money management
   Access to food markets, food service, and eating places
   Availability of home-delivered meals
   Special cultural, ethnic, and economic action related to nutrition

3. Health Maintenance
   Application of preventive-care concepts
   Health education
   Payments for eyeglasses, drugs, dentures, hearing aids, and protheses
   National health insurance
   Low-cost or discount prescription service
   Multiphasic health-screening opportunities
   Mental health counseling and services
   Accident prevention
   Utilization and coordination of community resources
   Survey of health problems for older persons
   Rehabilitation facilities
   Crisis intervention
   Delivery of homemaking and nursing services
4. Health Facilities
   Rehabilitation centers
   Nursing-home standards
   Mental institutions
   Day-care centers
5. Consumer Interest
   Insurance abuse
   Exploitation (fraud, quackery, overpricing, dishonest advertising, price-setting, unsafe products)
   Air and water pollution
   Medicare and Medicaid abuses
   Government regulations
   Legal services
   Deceptive sales practices (door-to-door, installment)
   Markets within walking distance
6. Employment
   Age discrimination
   Job opportunities
   Strengthened security of private pensions
   Public service employment programs
7. Transportation
   Subsidized local transit systems for service to elderly
   Reduced fares or free transportation
   Special transportation resources
   Rural problems
   Research and information
   Strategies for new programs
   Special state transportation departments
8. Housing
   Initiating low-income housing

Reduction of rents and rent control
Relocation of displaced persons
Housing-code enforcement
Housing assistance
Housing design and environment
Architectural barriers
Loans and grants for home rehabilitation
9. Security
Community protective measures to assure safety
10. Legal Services
Asserting legal rights of the poor
Defense against legal actions initiated by the government, landlords, or businesses
Quality of government services
Veterans' benefits and disability benefits
Changing food regulations
Availability of legal assistance
State-wide legal services
11. Legislative Changes
Knowledge and understanding of legislative processes
Acquaintance with government spending and revenue sharing
Registering and voting
Contact with local, county, and state representatives
Collecting data on voting records
Educating community on issues
Visible participation in demonstrations
Planning strategies
Positions on advisory committees of public and private agencies
12. Recreation
Increases to state and localities for recreational programs

The worker must narrow problems down to a few and must assess conditions for organizing: population, ethnicity, religion, educational background, political organizations, interest groups, institutions in area, how people see worker, etc. Then the worker must assess which of the above have bearing in a particular situation.

Workers must be able to use their assessment skills, relating to the conditions that prevail in a community group or organization (see Chapter 9 for assessment outline). They must arrive at a "diagnostic stance" to determine the nature of the problem to be solved. The worker's skills in the entry functions as spelled out in previous chapters apply here as well.

Building Structure while Defining the Task

A skilled, analytical process of exploration should be directed toward an evaluation of the state of thinking in the field about the general problem, the areas of consensus and disagreement, and the degree to which potential participants in the venture are being propelled toward change. Out of such an analysis, there begins to emerge a picture of the issues that are involved in a choice of structure.

For example, if exploration indicates broad consensus on the purposes that different parties wish to pursue, but differences as to what measures will be most effective, the structure can be weighted toward maximizing expertness in problem solving. If, on the other hand, there are wide differences concerning values, purposes, and goals, there is a prior task of finding a mechanism that can achieve an agreed-on direction with sufficient legitimation to exercise influence on the problem being attacked.

The traditional model of bringing the contending parties together so that they may find agreement is not the only way of achieving that purpose. Indeed, it may often be the wrong way. Another [way] is to gather together a more homogeneous grouping that is agreed on a goal and that undertakes to influence others to change their practices in order to achieve that selected goal. Most of the literature on community organization and planning has dealt with structure from one of the following perspectives: consensus, cooptation, or centrally planned change.

Consensus refers to the traditional "council" model, criticized in the literature on the ground that "participation of all" leads primarily to trade-offs and the protection of the status quo. Cooptation is associated with the type of structure in which representatives of a minority view or interest are included within an organizational framework dominated by others but render[ing] legitimacy to the latter's purposes. This was the way in which the inclusion of representatives of the poor on antipoverty boards was frequently characterized. "Tokenism" would be the popular term for a structure making for cooptation of less influential groups.

The third approach to structure focuses on the problem of achieving change through the mobilization of influence. A central planner—individual, group, or organization—with a purpose to fulfill organizes a structure designed to maximize [the] opportunity to achieve that purpose. . . . It should be noted first, however, that the approaches to structure that have been mentioned do not exhaust the possibilities and that other factors of equal importance to the practitioner have not been dealt with adequately in the existing literature.

For example, a practitioner is frequently faced, in the early stages of the development of a project, with an inadequate level of existing interest in the issue or need that he [or she] is mandated to address. His [or her] target is not (or not yet) the conquest of resistance to change, but [conquest of] the kind of apathy that stems from lack of knowledge or concern about the problem. The purpose of the initial organizational efforts in such a situation is basically educational—to expose potential participants in the project to the problem situation in a way that may arouse interest and concern. Study committees frequently serve this type of educational purpose rather than being directed primarily to the discovery of new information.[6]

While defining the task, social workers in such situations are engaged in either attaching themselves to an existing structure or to creating one if none exists. In any event, a worker must make use of his or her relationship capacities and skills with individuals and group members to help them direct their efforts and energies towards their goal accomplishment through the use of resources that either exist or that need to be created.

Formulating Policy, Responsibility, and Goals

Deciding what needs to be done (goal-formulation) is the next task. Policy formation takes its point of departure from general statements of goals and values and leads into more specific program measures. It is an operational statement of a goal or goals. Some of the essential properties of a policy are continuity over time (subject, of course, to change); institutionalization in the form of law or regulation or statement of principle; and most importantly, provision of an explicit guide to future actions.

> Because policy involves . . . ends and means, it cannot be viewed only as a technical function. Policy formation is a process of making choices, as indeed is all of planning. The choices at the level of policy are, however, in a large measure choices of "values" in the sense that they determine the purposes that are to be served and the benefits to be sought.[7]

Once the contract has been established and the task is defined, the worker engages in communicating alternative goals and strategies to those who are involved in a community organizational effort. Are the goals of the community group compatible with those of the worker? The worker's goals and community goals may be to improve the physical conditions of a neighborhood. The worker may have an intermediate goal of bringing together two ethnic groups, while one of the ethnic groups may be seeking to drive the other one out of the neighborhood. This incompatibility in goals would make it difficult if not impossible for the worker to work with the group.

Implementing Plans (Working on the Task)

To what extent can the policies formulated be implemented and the goals be reached? Desirability and feasibility of objectives need to be in balance. Here we move toward working on the task and carrying out the plans to achieve the goals agreed upon and specified. Perlman and Gurin refer to this phase as programming:

> Programming involves the detailed spelling out of implementing actions to carry out broad policies related to a goal. It is essentially a logistical type of activity, guided by considerations of effectiveness and efficiency in seeking a result. Like any logistical enterprise, programming involves the mobilization of resources and their delivery to where they are needed. The following are the major elements to be considered:
>
> 1. Content of the jobs: . . . the specifics that need to be done—activities, programs, services; [the] sequence and quantities; [the] physical arrangements
> 2. Resources: what is required to do the various pieces of work—capital facilities, manpower . . . qualifications, and funds; where those resources are now located, who controls them, how they can be mobilized
> 3. Feasibility: availability or nonavailability of resources; changes needed in order to achieve the objectives in policies; distribution of resources, creation of new resources, and the like; existence of acceptance or resistance; strategies for achieving necessary changes (conflict, negotiation, bargaining, and so on).[8]

In practice this action phase of community work is present in all previous phases. It involves the use and blending of a variety of activities, techniques, methods, and mechanical tasks. With the elderly, the use of these devices must be geared to their speed and ability to accept them. The elderly often take longer to do things, but they just as often have more time in which to do them.

Workers' Methods and Techniques

Again, let us use this phase of the process of organizing a community to elaborate methods, techniques, and skills deployed by the social worker.[9]

Relating. A worker must establish empathetic, genuinely understanding contacts with individuals and organizations—an atmosphere in which people feel free to talk with the worker and with each other. He or she must accept people as they are at their own level and with their own idiosyncracies; recognize individual capabilities and limitations; and help people make use of their capabilities in relation to the tasks at hand.

Motivating. People must be encouraged and sustained in working at the task at hand. They must feel that what they are doing will benefit themselves and others in their community, and have a sense that they are involved and that their ideas are important, though not necessarily always accepted by others.

Communicating. People must understand what has been done, what is being done, and what is going to be done. Face-to-face communication takes place between individuals or in groups. Sometimes things are said but not "taken in" by others. Workers must make every effort to clarify what has been said and make sure it has been understood by themselves and others. Mass communication is quite necessary during community work. A newsletter is usually effective, but newspapers, radio, and TV can be deployed to communicate activities to the broader community. All mass communicating should cover necessary facts and be as concise and readable as possible. Workers must keep many lines of communication open.

Helping. This is done in two main ways: First, in relation to the task at hand and second, in relation to other problems found with individuals or families. In relation to the task at hand, the worker should assist people carrying out their assigned tasks in the organization. In relation to individual and family problems, the worker should help people get to appropriate health or social services through referral.

Interviewing. This is used in talking with individuals to gather information about them, their community, or their organizations. Listening and making a person feel comfortable during the interview and observing rules of confidentiality are vital ingredients. An interview may take place anywhere: in an office, in a restaurant, on the street, or in the home.

Coordinating. Various actions and/or events taking place should support or at least not be in conflict with each other. The worker may act as a focal point for coordination or may help an organization member act as a coordinator. Once made, plans should be followed as closely as possible, but in case of change, all involved persons should be notified as to the nature and consequences of change. All events or activities taking place should be reported to all involved people.

Referring to Resources. Members of an organization or group will need information about and from a variety of community resources. Therefore, the worker must be familiar with available resources and also should make group or organization members aware of them. Many a person may need assistance to get to resources and assurance that it has been obtained. Although workers should focus on the task at hand, they should not ignore individual or family problems that appear.

Individualizing. More times than not, it is necessary to work closely with individuals to help them perform tasks more efficiently. Either the worker or individual may initiate such an approach. Individuals should be allowed to discuss feelings about their performance with worker, and the worker should support the person's strengths.

Timing. Doing things at the most opportune time is often crucial. The worker must be alert to the best moment for action, be aware of the time needed to make changes, know the capabilities of groups and organization members, and know when they are ready to take action.

Enabling. The general direction in community work is to help people to do for themselves. For this reason the worker has to be sensitive to people's ability to perform tasks, and must allow them also to fail sometimes.

Directing, Guiding, and Leading. There are times when it is necessary to tell a group or person what needs to be done and how to do it. In this instance workers assume a more leading role; they make facts available, suggest alternative actions that might be taken, help persons or organizations assess possible consequences of each action, and make direct suggestions for action. They encourage organization members to take on leadership where they are capable and help organization members develop leadership ability through training.

Anticipating. The worker must be alert to any changes that might take place in situations and must anticipate alternative reactions of people and be prepared to deal with each alternative.

Setting the Stage. At times it will be necessary to set the stage for a meeting between the people and someone in a position to help them. The worker should let the people or organization know what he or she is going to do; contact the person or agency and give them details about the group and what is needed; and have organization members make appointments with persons or agencies where possible.

Strategies

The use of planned strategies is based on four variables:

1. An analysis of community power factors
2. The group or organization's resources (size, energy, skills, values, external allies)
3. Current social and political organizational climate; values, norms, and group and political-action mores
4. Application of three basic interventive stances (consensus, negotiation, contest) as related to the situational factors in a community organization enterprise.

Table 13.2 attempts to order these factors and interventive stances. It is based primarily on work by Roland Warren. As with casework and group work, the community organizer performs a series of roles, the major four being enabler, broker, advocate, and expert. Regardless of how many roles workers take on to be effective, they approach the job of organizing with a consistent point of view or philosophy of community action. If they are to help people help themselves, community organizers' deepest conviction is that they will not dominate the organization. The ultimate responsibility for policy decisions rests with the people. The organizer accepts explicitly the right of self-determination for the individual, the group, and the community. It is the foundation upon which all action is based.

Monitoring and Feedback (Terminating)

Evaluating information and feeding it back to guide action applies to the problem-solving process in two ways. First, this describes a continuous activity that permeates the problem-solving processes we have been describing, that is, problem formulation, the building of structure, policy choice, and program implementation. Second, evaluation applies to the action outcome or end product of the total process.

With respect to the first meaning, we have indicated that interaction with various actors in a problem-solving situation turns up at every step new information on the problem itself and on perceptions and preferences concerning the problem. This is used, for example, to "correct" or modify earlier decisions about structure or the most appropriate policy to be adopted. It also means that the definition of the problem changes as the process goes on, that people's views adapt themselves to one another as they interact, and that solutions tend to be a choice among alternatives each of which represents some gains and some losses. Morris and Binstock make a contribution to this in their discussion of feasibility, which calls for the adaptation and modification of goals in response to resistance encountered.

The more popularly understood meaning of evaluation, however, applies to the monitoring of operations that takes place as a result of a problem-solving or planning process. Data are obtained on outcome and effectiveness and are used to make decisions on continuing, discontinuing, or modifying the policy or program

Table 13.2. Basic Interventive Stances

Correlated Factors	Consensus (Collaboration)	Negotiation (Campaign)	Contest (Disruption)
1. Goals of group or organization:			
a. Mobility	Individual mobility		Group mobility
b. Degree of agreement among parties	High agreement (consensus)	Medium agreement (difference)	Low agreement (dissensus)
2. Perception of proposed change	Rearrangement of resources	Redistribution of resources	Change in status relationships
3. Issue salience	Low, especially to target	Significant importance	High, to both parties
4. Power relationships	Little difference or irrelevant	Significant differences or limited relevance	Great difference
5. Power concentration in community	Low concentration	Moderate concentration	High concentration
6. Coalition capability	Low capability	Limited capability	High capability
7. Worker roles, in order of importance	First enabler Second expert-broker Third advocate	First expert-broker Second advocate Third enabler	First advocate Second expert-broker Third enabler
8. Characteristic tactics	Joint problem-solving, information gathering, discussion; mutual agreement	Education, persuasion, bargaining, compromise; arbitration	Maximum direct pressure through disruption, coercion, power coalitions, norm violations, civil disobedience

SOURCE: Roland Warren, "Types of Purposive Social Change at the Community Level," *Papers in Social Welfare* (Walthan, Mass.: Brandeis University, 1965).

under scrutiny. Analytical and interactional issues merge here. The technology of scientific evaluation or research drawn from the social sciences needs to be adapted to operating situations and often resistances are encountered to the methodology of the evaluator. When evaluation takes place after a policy or program has been in effect for some time, the judgments that are made concerning its effectiveness—the unanticipated consequences that followed its implementation—provide material for a new round of problem formulation and planning.[10]

Termination of the task and of the interactional relationships herald in the final phase. When the task is fulfilled, interpersonal separation may still produce problems, although probably to a lesser extent than when the goal had not been accomplished. The group may cease to exist for one of the following reasons:

1. Purposes have been achieved: success!
2. Group has been absorbed by another group with similar goals.
3. Group has been destroyed by external pressures and/or internal disruptive forces.
4. Group has gradually faded away to a point of ineffectiveness or disappearance due to frustration with goal-achievement efforts, competition from other groups, lack of significant meaning for members.

Community Action

To move a group of aged toward effective action, the social worker needs not only to provide strategies and techniques for action, but to instill a new sense of confidence and dignity among them. Workers must convince the elderly that in spite of years of possible disappointment, something can be done. Their enthusiasm sets an example. By listening patiently, empathizing compassionately, and offering words of encouragement—simply by being genuinely concerned—the worker dispels the feelings of dread, despair, and impotence that haunt many of the aged population.

The worker's first task is to create a relationship of trust between him- or herself and the individual. The organizer knows that elderly people are often not as receptive to new faces as are young people. To build a positive, meaningful relationship requires even more time. Community organizers must strive to be consistent, honest, and above all, patient. They must be careful not to impose their values on the aging individual; they must be quick to observe but slow to judge. They must be aware that it is difficult for many older persons to accept aid from strangers.

Before the elderly can open themselves to an outsider, there must be an implicit trust. The myriad losses of friends, family, mobility, and finances have added up creating a sense of powerlessness. Many despair that their time has come and that there is nothing anyone can do to help them. Another problem arises among the elderly who become poor only in their later years. Aged individuals who have been self-sufficient for so many years resent the fact that suddenly they must depend on others for aid.

Individuals are the building blocks with which the community social worker constructs the organization. The association will be no better than the quantity and quality of participation that it receives from its constituents in the community. For this reason alone, the organizer must be able to move the elderly as individuals to find a new life in community action. However, while the organizer is working with individual people, the primary focus of the community organizer must be broader than the individual. Concern is with mobilizing the resources of an entire community. Thus, tasks are oriented primarily toward activation of all forces in the area to join in collective action.

For example, the Back Bay Aging Concerns Committee: Young and Old United, a community action group in Boston, is an effective network of people of all ages representing religious groups, corporations, professions, commerce, and neighborhoods working together to serve older persons in Boston's neighborhoods. Its goals are:

- to help meet the needs which many people face as they grow older. . .
- to provide older people opportunities to serve others through active participation in their community. . .
- to break down the barriers of age and urban isolation. . .
- to enable as many residents as possible to be contributors to, not casualties of, life in Boston. . .

The Hebrew Home for the Aged in Riverdale, New York, spawned the Riverdale Neighborhood Network, a system for swapping services by and for elderly residents of this community. Two hundred delegates (one-half professionals representing agencies and one-half elderly residents of Riverdale) attended a conference in 1981 that resulted in development and publishing of the "Skills and Service Swapping Yellow Pages." Barter arrangements continue to develop through use of this network. For example, "College students studying foreign languages are being matched with residents of a home for the aged who speak the same language. This gives the student an opportunity to improve conversational language skills and at the same time learn about the life-style and customs of the older person, while the resident is placed in the prestigious position of teaching and sharing."[11]

Unraveling Interactional Tasks

The interactional tasks presented below put the problem-solving process of the process-action model in perspective with regard to the elderly. Much of this material is excerpted and adapted from John M. Haynes and Joel Serkin's "Community Action and the Elderly Poor."[12]

Awakening Discontent and a Desire for Change in the Community. Discontent cannot be artificially induced. Dissatisfaction often lies dormant and the worker's role is to release this repressed sentiment by listening patiently and posing questions skillfully. Gradually, people become conscious of repressed discontent. Workers prompt the community to look at itself honestly and to ask questions. They free the elderly to talk about their problems, and in the process, they create a community that is conscious of problems. The organizer pays close attention to the discrepancy between what people say the problems are and what people actually talk about as problems. For example, in rural communities, elderly persons may say there are inadequate health facilities, while the problem they talk about is a lack of transportation to the county hospital.

The aged will seek to organize when they perceive that they are not condemned to live in the past. The role of the social worker is to help the elderly recognize, release, and vocalize their latent discontent. They arouse the community to the possibility of change. They do not deceive them into believing that change will come rapidly or without effort because they know that unrealistic expectations will result in eventual frustration and disappointment.

Converting the Desire for Change into a Desire to Organize. General dissatisfaction must be focused upon specific issues. This is the "unfreezing" activity. The release of negative feelings by the elderly at the outset should be viewed as a constructive sign. Discontent with today will provide the motivation to organize for tomorrow. However, if feelings of dissatisfaction are aroused and not subsequently channeled properly, the end product will be disastrous. Although people have a will to work for change, if they are not provided with intelligent direction, there will be no forward movement. When community discontent is stimulated but not translated into action, the elderly sink into apathy.

The worker enables the aged to see that their dissatisfaction is the result of concrete problems and that these problems are susceptible to change through organization. After cultivating a base of support, community organizers assert that the community must gather. They invite the participants. The group is ad hoc. The organizer may decide that an existing neighborhood organization (church, fraternity, or club) that already has the allegiance of the elderly should sponsor the meeting. It is essential that all groups have access to the meeting and that there be an opportunity for maximum involvement on the part of all parties.

The meeting's purpose is to plan a program for action. The community representatives must define goals and devise a strategy to implement the goals. Organizers will occupy an important position at the first session. They must be careful not to impose their will on the meeting, yet they cannot abdicate their responsibilities in the decision-making process. They are guides, arbiters, mentors. They offer direction, but assure that the participants are involved in the planning process. Organizers set the tone of a meeting. They conduct the meeting at a level that is comfortable for the constituents.

Locating and Involving Leaders. Obviously, not every elderly person in the community can be involved on a day-to-day basis in the decision making of an organization. Nevertheless, all individuals in the community must feel that they are represented in the leadership of the organization if they are to have allegiance to the organization. This means that the worker must be able to locate indigenous leaders who are identified with and accepted by the major formal and informal groups in the community. Having located them, the worker must then get them involved in the organization. Formal groups include schools, churches, social agencies, and unions. Informal groups include street blocks, housing projects, coffee klatches, etc.

Identifying formal groups is relatively easy. For example, contact with local church groups can help identify leaders. Of course, in identifying groups, the worker must understand not only the nature of the organizations but also the value that the elderly place upon the group. Thus, a church may be a high-value organization to an elderly person, while a labor union (unless it has activities for retired members) is likely to have a lower value. The organizer should concentrate on higher-value organizations. However, formal groups are not likely to provide many contacts among the elderly since many no longer participate in formal organizations in the community. Therefore, the community organizer must concentrate on reaching informal groups of elderly persons.

In dealing with community service agencies, the community organizer must be an effective advocate for the elderly. Welfare and social agencies have a wide constituency. Most other sections of the community are more articulate and more highly organized than the elderly. Therefore, their needs tend to be met first by the agency. Community organizers, as advocates, must constantly strive to represent the elderly before these agencies to see that the needs of their constituency are met.

Obviously, workers cannot do all of this alone. Therefore, their role is to open the doors of the formal organizations and agencies to the leaders of groups in the community to achieve the ultimate goal of community participation by the elderly.

Focusing on Broad Issues. Bringing together elderly people for action can be achieved only on the basis of issues that are broadly based and that are most likely to affect and involve the greatest number of all people in the community. Issues that form the central focus of the organization must appeal directly to a base of support within the constituency. The strength of the organization rests on common problems that concern the major groups that make up the potential membership. The organization has value only if it meets the needs of its constituency. Conversely, if the members do not feel that the organization accurately defines and meets their needs, their interest in it will wane and finally die.

The worker's role is to emphasize common goals. Individuals will come to the organization expecting to satisfy a variety of needs. So, community organizers must first understand what the elderly expect to get from the organization before they can accurately define the common goals. Once aware of the reasons individuals are attracted to a group, the community organizer is able to help the group identify their common needs. The organization will not act effectively until all accept each other, feel secure, and open up. The organizer must foster group interaction. This is done through understanding the motivations of the individuals and being empathetic to their needs. From empathy flows acceptance.

Once the individual is accepted, the organization becomes a part of the individual's life. In the process, the individual comes to understand that his or her problems are not unique; rather, they are shared by other members of the group and can be resolved through group action.

Workers keep a broad focus on the issues. They must be able to maintain a perspective of the entire elderly community. Just as individuals come to the organization with specific needs that can be resolved through the group, so they bring specific problems that are immediately shared by the entire group. The social worker's role is to bring diverse elements together, clarify issues, enlarge areas of common concern, and establish processes whereby the elderly community can make collective decisions. This process is particularly difficult for elderly people, who may become preoccupied with small details and lose sight of the broad perspective.

Training for Leadership. The natural tendency—especially among those elderly who lack confidence—is to get the organizer to provide answers or solutions for them. However, the social worker engaged in community organization must resist this temptation, as must the social worker with individuals or small groups. A worker must make people understand why he or she cannot do their jobs for them. If the organization is to prosper beyond the activity of the worker, new leadership must be developed and expanded. In the early stages, the tendency will be for local leaders to check back on everything they do in an attempt to find the right answer, the simple solution. Social workers should not give the answer, even if they have one; rather, they should provide data, suggest alternatives, relate prior experiences, and through group discussion seek clarification of the goal and the tactic (as discussed in the preceding chapter on group work).

Just as nothing succeeds like success, failure breeds despondency. Workers must be constantly aware of the immediate abilities of the emerging leaders. In assigning tasks, they must be careful to choose tasks unsophisticated enough to be carried out with reasonable certainty of success. People learn more quickly from success. With each successful accomplishment comes the confidence and the desire to handle other tasks. Gradually, community organizers will increase the amount of responsibility delegated until indigenous leaders are prepared to assume tasks that originally fell on workers' shoulders. Workers should view their role as basically phasing out their own involvement in the execution of day-to-day policies, freeing themselves to play their true role of expanding the organization into other areas.

Involving the Community at the Grass-Roots Level. The rank-and-file elderly must themselves take an active part in planning and implementing the programs. The community must feel that it is an integral part of the organization and that the organization is part of it. By employing many of the elderly in local volunteer positions, the worker closes the gap between the personal needs and the amount of available services. In the process of discovering self-worth, the elderly individual gains renewed self-confidence. This reawakening of individuals makes them even more effective people, reinforces their relationship to the organization that provided this new life, and provides the organizer with new recruits.

Operations. The social worker must develop a pace of operations for the organization consistent with the capabilities of the community. A pace for growth that is comfortable for everyone involved cannot be too fast. Workers cannot give the participants too much to do or tasks that are too difficult, or participants will soon become discouraged. On the other hand, failure to provide activities will be equally discouraging as members will feel that the organization is not going anywhere.

Workers seek to create a rhythm of development that is based on an ever-growing series of victories. They should ensure that projects are small enough to be undertaken and completed in a reasonable span of time.

Rate of Development. The social worker maintains a relatively even rate of development of the groups within the organization. No organization is stronger than it parts. If certain groups are disorganized or apathetic, their disaffection will temper the enthusiasm of the other groups. Petty rivalries will develop within the organization as the disorganized groups' leaders become jealous of the success of the other groups. As the leaders of the apathetic groups continue to participate in the organization, they must seek rationalizations for their failures. These rationalizations could affect the other groups, since the organization will spend much time and energy arguing about the reasons for the failures of the few rather than the success of the majority.

Elderly people especially may tend to become discouraged when they see other people ahead of them. Many have seen failures, so that too much success on the part of one section of the organization might reinforce the feeling of failure of another, to the detriment of the total organization. Skillful workers turn the potentially failing situation into a learning situation for all. Taking the problems to the entire organization for discussion and solution strengthens the entire fabric of the organization, reinforces the cooperative nature of the venture, and brings problems out into the open, where they can be shared by everybody rather than festering off on the side.

Identifying the Organization with Cultural Traditions of the Community. The worker recognizes the importance of ritual in the lives of the elderly. Many elderly are immigrants who maintain close ties with the festivals and customs of their country of origin. The aged are often strongly affiliated with religious traditions. In rural communities, the elderly are often the most active participants in local celebrations. It is the worker's role to adjust the organization's character so that it becomes an integral part of the life of the community.

Community organizers remember that the purpose of the organization is to raise the quality of life for the elderly. They know that the organization must be enmeshed with the cultural traditions of the community. Life is more than food and shelter. The organization's program must accommodate the spiritual as well as the physical needs of the members. The elderly will be as anxious for their organization to participate in the local festival as to be involved in social action. The organizer must recognize this need and not discourage activities that do not appear to deliver immediate dividends to the organization.

Communications. The social worker must develop effective lines of communication within the association and between the association and the rest of the community. Communications with the association depend on an honest interrelationship among the leaders as well as between the leaders and rank and file. The community organizer is primarily concerned with the relationship among the leaders, for they are the first-line decision makers. To facilitate communication among the leaders, the community organizer creates a climate in which all members are free to express themselves. All must feel that their contributions are valued.

In this respect, organizers must be especially careful not to show favoritism to any one individual or idea. A feeling of trust between them and each individual and among all the individuals must be engendered. In such an atmosphere, the elderly will be freed from anxiety of censure and be willing to express their true feelings. They will not be afraid to express points of view with which they may feel the organizer or their peers disagree. Only in such an atmosphere will an honest and vital dialogue occur.

Communications with the rank and file should be handled primarily by indigenous leaders. The individual, isolated and frustrated, will trust the leaders, for they speak his or her language. Leaders are able to translate the decisions of the organization into terms that the rank and file can understand and relate to. At the same time, leaders become conduits for passing information up the line, thereby keeping the organization responsive to the needs of the rank-and-file elderly. Nothing can substitute for face-to-face communication. This line of communication serves several functions: it keeps the elderly community informed of the organization's activities and makes them part of the organization; it also reinforces leaders' position with their constituency by keeping them up to date and involved.

Another source of communications with the rank and file is a newsletter. A newsletter not only speaks to the elderly but is a means of keeping the community at large informed about the organization's activities. In addition to reporting on plans and progress, a newsletter should deal in personal items. It should be a vehicle for group recognition of individuals active in the organization. By discussing personal events, the newsletter expresses the organization's concern for the individual. The elderly must be involved in the planning and production of the newsletter. Community organizers must avoid contributing too heavily or concentrating on well-polished articles and slick layouts. Their contribution is to advise others how to do it. It is the members who must get the satisfaction out of the final product.

The organization will often become involved in projects that demand the support of outside groups. An effective means of linking the organization with the community at large is a speakers' bureau in which the elderly are directly involved. They are trained to speak publicly for the organization, and they visit and speak at other neighborhood organizations, taking the message of the elderly to the community at large. A speakers' bureau serves as a means of communications; it builds confidence in the individuals who participate and draws them closer to the organization.

Should the organization have the occasion to use the mass media, the community organizer should encourage the individual rank and file to express themselves. Workers must overcome the initial tendency to present the most articulate and polished front to the world. Uninvolved elderly are more likely to be "turned on" by a peer speaking in their behalf than by a younger, more dynamic, but also more remote community worker.

The Resident Council

Jessica Getzel recently discussed the role of the social worker and the ideals, formation, and operation of resident councils in nursing homes. She sees the resident council as a means of empowering nursing home residents, "even the most otherwise defiant and challenging . . . [of whom] may become desperate out of his/her dependency for care as personal power ebbs."[13] A resident council serves, thus, two purposes: "as a vehicle for residents to exercise their rights and protect their interests by participating fully in the decisions and tasks which affect their everyday lives"[14] and as a powerful therapeutic tool for restoring residents' feelings of control of their lives and for fostering closeness and socialization among members.

A resident council must have the administration's full sanction and encouragement and be willing to allow autonomy to members and officers, or else the council will only "add to residents' actual and perceived dependency on the institution . . . for residents have limited energy to devote to a charade." If the resident council is successful, it fosters healthier relationships between residents, administration, and staff members in several ways: "staff begin to perceive residents as more independent and capable; the council gives positive expression to positive changes of staff and administration make on residents' behalf; it serves a 'mediating function' which William Schwartz sees as 'acknowledging that residents, staff and administration ultimately need one another to do their tasks and that obstacles naturally develop which interfere with symbiotic strivings."[15]

In establishing a resident council, the social worker must be aware of these pitfalls: (1) the election of officers frequently opens up a contest among residents for prestige and power, two resources in short supply in a nursing home; (2) residents may fear that participation in the council will antagonize staff; and (3) members may fear illness or death of a member or leader of the council.[16]

Getzel sets some guidelines for social workers in setting up and operating a resident council:

- The structure of the council should be clearly developed and interpreted to residents.
- Sharing responsibilities among members gives recognition to the possibility of illness and incapacitation of a particular member.
- It is important to allow council members to dip into their own organizational experience and have the time. . . [to] make decisions.
- Administrators should be invited as advisory [members] rather than as the powerful adversary.
- Floors with less functional members may address their concerns more fully by special less structured sub-committees.
- Residents, with staff support, write their own memoranda and reports, and have regular appointments with the administration.
- Honest discussion with residents about limitations is vital.
- In the event of a death of a key member, members must be allowed to grieve ritually and openly in the Committee meeting.

- As the resident council solidifies, opportunities to link residents' activities to their families and outside community groups should take place.
- Families should be kept apprised of the activities of the Resident Council and should be encouraged to use it.[17]

Action of a Resident Council: An Illustration

Long-Term Care Facility. The east wing of the 300-bed residential facility in this case is a community of a few couples, one woman, and the rest men. The residents were asked to organize a Resident Council and a social worker met with it. Last spring, there was a mounting sense of dissatisfaction, a comparatively high level of anxiety, and complaints. A few major events had been unsettling to the residents. One couple had lost their favorite son through a heart attack; this event was threatening to other residents. The wife's depression and her need for intense care seemed to be contagious. Another factor was the unstable health of a community leader. In answer to the complaints and the anxiety, a meeting of the Resident Council was announced. The meeting would be a way of looking at common concerns rather than individual situations.

May 4: First Meeting.

The meeting was opened with the recognition of growing unrest and with the suggestion by the social worker that everybody might want to share their concerns. Immediately there was a rush of people who wanted to air their individual woes. The council listened to several stories that generally reflected a feeling of not being cared for and not feeling secure. People mentioned that without enough help they could die alone. With each story the common experience was pointed out. Of course, the residents pursued their problems individually and felt no sense of a collective ability to deal with any of them.

After several stories, feelings of both support and anger mounted, and the question became "what can be done?" The strongest reaction was "go to the director, straight to the top." When worker asked who would like to go the response was, "You of course—we can't do that, no one would listen to us." The worker suggested that everybody try to define the problem and look at several different ways of approaching it and then decide. The problem was defined as insufficient medical and nursing care. The worker pointed out that she was there to help, but not to do for them what they could do better for themselves.

This was met with a great deal of anger and further discussion of how helpless they felt. In looking at how effective it would be to see the director with a problem of this nature, the worker raised the question of who else they might approach first. Someone suggested that Dr. F. was a boss and a "head man." The worker raised the possibility of discussing the problem with the floor internist. The response was that the well ones could cope and did not need to talk with him, and the sick ones had more at stake and feared he would be angry and not take care of them.

After discussing *who* to go to, the council talked about *how* to proceed. Alternatives included having a committee speak for the whole group, having one representative, and having the worker speak for them, which was the overwhelming choice. The meeting was closed with a review of the problem and the various possible whos and hows to resolve it and the agreement that everyone would think about it for a week and use community meetings to find some solution. The next meeting was to be held the following week.

May 11: Second Meeting.

One resident opened the meeting with accusations and anger: "No one pays attention to me. I can't even get a bath. No one will even talk to me!" Another resident countered that he got help whenever he needed it by asking to see the doctor and added, "You have to speak up for yourself." This led to discussion of different types of residents, especially the complainers "who wear out the staff" and make it hard for real troubles to get attention. One resident defended the doctor, telling how wonderful he was and told others only to ask if they really needed him.

The discussion centered on the anger aroused because the doctor was not available when needed and not visible to the floor, since he made rounds during lunchtime or suppertime. The council turned to the who and how of the approach, looking at the possibility of direct two-way discussion. The residents said, "There's more help on other wings," and "we don't count because we are not sick enough," etc., and added, "The doctor is God and we can't question him." They suggested that the easiest way was for Dr. F. to schedule specific hours so the residents "don't have to beg or sit around and wait all day."

With future exploration and discussion, the social worker tried to get them to see that there were different expectations among the residents about care, that a greater need was experienced when someone felt ill, and that not seeing the doctor could make them feel uneasy. The worker pointed out the need for appropriate use of the doctor's time. The resolution of the who and how was that the fairest approach would be a direct and reasonable discussion with Dr. F., where they could express concerns and, one hoped, come to a working agreement. A great amount of support from the social worker was required so the meeting with the doctor would be a rational, mature discussion and not a confrontation of uncontrolled anger.

The meeting closed with one resident sharing a positive experience that occurred since the last meeting. He was not getting satisfaction about a clinic appointment and had decided to speak up for himself. He had gone to the doctor's office, waited, and requested service. The doctor had made the referral to the clinic and the resident's problem was relieved. He shared this experience as evidence that he felt good after he pursued service and had found the doctor most helpful. He suggested that if he was successful as an individual, certainly the whole group had a chance.

May 22: Third Meeting.

Dr. F. spoke for several minutes about self-concern and health as people grow older, the recent concerns of many people on the east wing. He talked about different kinds of physical problems, some of which can be changed, but many of which are not amenable to cure and require endurance. Dr. F. noted that his job as a doctor was to help where possible, but that he was not able to heal all or change every painful condition. He explained that doctors were not God and that he did not have all the answers. He explained his very busy schedule and said that at times he might forget something but that he wanted to be reminded.

The residents seemed somewhat relieved by his openness and relaxed attitude. A few went into personal incidents and stories, but a general concern about his visibility was expressed. Dialogue continued around scheduling, finding an appropriate doctor, a private doctor versus a wing doctor, how to use the nurse for referral, the need of residents to understand results of tests, etc. Dr. F. told the group that he did care; he was not mean, but they needed to trust his judgment. He needed this!

The meeting concluded with Dr. F.'s explanation that his practice would be very busy for the next two months and his time on the wing would vary by the week. By September 15, his schedule would be different and his rounds would be made at the same time on most days. Until then, he agreed to post a list of his expected times for each day of the week and invited anyone who felt an appropriate complaint to ask to see him individually. He told the nurse not to screen out any requests.

June 1: Fourth Meeting.

Dissatisfaction had been expressed in earlier meetings about insufficient staffing of aides and orderlies. An issue that was particularly pressing was a need for more baths. Many of the residents had waited three or four weeks to get one. The director of nurses arrived and began to explain the recruitment problem of getting people to work with elderly—that her budget had limitations, that when many of her staff called in sick she had to set priorities, and that the other wings need more assistance, because this unit could get along with less help because they were independent and smart and could understand her problems.

Then the residents began to tell their feelings. Their concerns included waiting at night for an answer to the bell (one staff member for 80 residents). Also, no one came on time for the afternoon shift, so they could not get 4 P.M. medicals on time; the shower was too powerful so they couldn't use it alone; the two staff members who know them best were often given the same weekend off; and they felt all alone on weekends, at which time, even if they were sick, they could just as well die since they were told to "wait until Monday!" Their biggest concern was a weekly bath: "You people wash the floors and walls, but not us."

One resident suggested helping each other, but was overwhelmingly put down since he had suggested that people were self-centered and lazy; the other residents responded that they only wished they were as well as he was and then they'd like to help too. One resident challenged the director of nurses; he suggested that if she had a limited budget she should ask for more. When told recruitment was the real issue, the resident suggested that perhaps the pay was too low to attract staff. The meeting ended with an announcement that two experienced summer workers that they knew and liked would be returning in three weeks for the summer.

July 7: A Month Later.

> At this meeting, members learned to support each other and express a common position. The meeting was called to announce the plans for a mass cleaning project that would dismantle every room in order to fight cockroaches. The worker shared the specific instructions given to staff by the cleaning department. The east wing was scheduled for cleaning on Friday. The cleaning required twenty-four hours of disruption. Residents became very angry and hostile because this procedure was scheduled to interfere with the Sabbath. They shouted, "Why don't they let us decide anything" and "they don't even ask what time would be good," and as the anger rose, "We will refuse to let them into our rooms." The worker asked, "What can we do about this that is reasonable?"
>
> The residents suggested that the worker communicate their feelings. Since time was of the essence, the worker excused herself from the meeting and called the cleaning department on the spot to explain the predicament. The residents agreed to be cooperative and helpful in this distasteful and dreaded operation if it were scheduled for a reasonable day. The worker was able to negotiate the change with the cleaners. The residents felt greatly relieved and satisfied that their voices had been heard. They also found that negotiation does not have to be made in anger, but that reasonable, mature dialogue can resolve matters of conflict. They were more willing to be cooperative and less upset with the whole cleaning process and they requested printed, specific instructions so they would be sure to do their best.

Discussion of Illustration. The agency set up a self-governing action group to allow ventilation of feelings. Residents had a vehicle in the residents' council for expressing their anger and resentment. The social worker involved the members in the definition of the problem and elicited and received information about their grievances. A formal communication structure was established, and group processes began to develop that were utilized by the worker to effect changes. After the goals for action to be undertaken had been established, a series of strategies—negotiating, campaign, and contest stances—were proposed, with an opportunity for residents to test preferences and consequences. The worker was able to present different viewpoints and rallied the members around.

Other staff members were brought in to present their stories and to listen to the argument of the residents and be affected by their feelings and their points of view. Once a solution had become generally accepted, the worker was able to negotiate an agreement and reap a victory for the members. They, in turn, were willing to honor their part of the bargain and reaffirm the service contract with the social worker. They also experienced a sense of self-worth, of participating in decision making that affected them, and of being listened to and helped with their problem. The worker, acting largely in the roles of advocate and broker, used her skills as a spokesperson on behalf of the residents who could not articulate their wishes and demands. She also was an action strategist and used both the resources of the institutional community and resources of the residents, including their ego strengths and their expressed feelings.

She was able to balance the needs of the residents with the desire of the agency for conditions that were relatively free from conflict. She used appropriate timing and considered the readiness of colleagues to engage in a rational dialogue. Work with this resident council illustrates how the continuum of social work practice makes use of the goal model (described in the previous chapter, in the section on working with groups) and extends it to work with a community of residents in a long-term care facility. In comparison to the patient council's group meetings discussed above, the activities of this resident council were primarily directed toward bringing about changes in the institution, the residents' community, rather than toward alleviating stress conditions for the patients and helping them cope with their problems and the integration of their egos.

Political Involvement, Attitudes and Power of Older Adults

An older person can participate in a variety of political activities, ranging from passive to increasingly active modalities. Milbrath presented a hierarchy of political involvement along such a continuum, beginning with "spectator activities," such as voting, discussion and opinion leadership, and using buttons or stickers; progressing to "transitional activities" (petitioning political leaders, making monetary contributions, and attending political meetings); and finally "gladiatorial" participation, which he defines as campaigning, active party membership, soliciting political funds, protesting, demonstrating, and office seeking and holding.[18] Torres-Gill identifies three factors necessary for people of any age to become motivated for political activity: (1) "First, a person must feel that he or she is a member of society with a personal stake in the political system; (2) A person must have a sense of efficacy; he or she must feel that his or her actions will make a difference; (3) An individual must have access to the political system he or she wishes to participate in—hence, he or she must be physically capable, competent, and legally qualified to vote."[19] Herein lie avenues for the intervention of social workers: to promote development of each of these necessary elements for each of their older clients. This may include assuring transportation, encouraging clients to act on their own behalf, and working toward their developing a sense that such participation will indeed make a difference. Torres-Gill asserts that for the minority elder, these three factors take on additional significance and proposes strategies for involving and organizing minority elders:

(1) Identify the existing groups, service clubs, and organizations and individuals who work with seniors. In every community there are existing organizations and individuals who have developed credibility and provide leadership based on long years of association with minority seniors. Generally, the church, senior citizen clubs, and local grass-roots organizations are best suited for this role;

(2) Identify the established politicians and organizations, not necessarily part of the local community, who can contribute to the needs of the communities. Again, every local area, whether a city, county, or region, will have politicians and organizations who can bring in money, resources, and legislation beneficial

to seniors. It will be important, particularly in certain states, to involve state and congressional legislators, city councilmen and county officials if substantive accomplishments are to occur for minority seniors;

(3) Link the existing groups in the local communities with established politicians and organizations. By linking these two entities it becomes possible to identify specific areas around which seniors can mobilize and around which established politicians can develop constituencies. Many local politicians will have already garnered their senior citizen support. However, this does not always guarantee that they will have provided actual resources or support to the seniors which can be measured in increased funds, better legislation or programs. Often, it takes a "broker," possibly a professional, practitioner, or local organizer, to bring them together and continually prod, monitor, and otherwise assure that follow-up and continuity occur;

(4) Stay with these efforts for extended periods of time. It is critical that individuals not mobilize and generate enthusiasm and then leave quickly. This will generate ill will and a feeling of being used, which in turn will make it more difficult to organize later. Individuals and organizations who seek to mobilize seniors must be prepared to immerse themselves in these communities and stay for extended periods;

(5) Concentrate on visible and substantive short-term gains while working on long-run issues. In most communities, few if any minority seniors are present on local boards, commissions, and advisory groups. These positions, while ceremonial at times, can become important and effective if filled by articulate seniors from the local community. They provide positions of leadership and visibility for the local communities and can be accomplished quickly[,] thus providing concrete accomplishments from which long-term efforts can follow;

(6) Create linkages with nonminority aging organizations. Many local communities will have important and politically powerful senior organizations which, in all likelihood, will not contain minority seniors. To the extent these groups (generally middle-class white retirees) are willing to be supportive, important allies will be formed. Create opportunities such as forums, receptions, and meetings whereby minority and nonminority senior leaders will interact and develop mutual trust;

(7) Conduct workshops and sessions which provide training and orientation for seniors who may not be fully aware of the issues important to the larger community. Often, minority seniors who are leaders in their communities will not have had the opportunity to understand the large issues affecting the entire community. In order for them to be knowledgeable, competent, and effective in larger nonminority settings, it is important to conduct training and orientation sessions.[20]

Several myths persist regarding the political behavior and attitudes of older people despite evidence to the contrary. Take for example the belief that people "disengage" from politics as they become older. Researchers have found that the small fall-off in political participation that does occur as people approach middle and old age is actually a function of socioeconomic characteristics, especially level of education and income, and does *not* reflect increasing age.[21] Similarly, Norval Glenn challenges the widely held notion that people become more conservative as they grow older. He asserts that researchers have only just begun to tackle the complicated methodological and definitional issues involved in this area. He also points out that cohort effects are probably responsible for the fact that while older persons appear to be somewhat more conservative than younger adults, they have become less conservative in recent decades (just as younger adults have).[22]

Because of the social, economic, geographic, and ethnic heterogeneity of the older population, the political behaviors and attitudes of aged voters, as well as their partisan alignments, are diverse. As Campbell expresses it:

> . . .because each age cohort includes people who differ profoundly in many important conditions of life it is not likely that any group will be very homogenous in its attitudes. The evidence which national surveys provide us does in fact demonstrate that attitudinal differences between age groups are far less impressive than those within age groups.[23]

Weaver has found evidence, however, that the elderly may function as a united "political community" in areas where direct economic interest is involved. He found that the elderly, *as a coherent group*, are "more in favor of liberal reformist, or interventionist alternatives" to controlling health care costs, "than younger adults."[24] He did not find such block-like posture, however, in issues less directly related to economic interests. On issues such as the Vietnam War, abortion, and racial integration, positions varied in accordance with "traditional demographic partisan and ideological lines."[25]

One group of elderly residents of "adults only" communities in Arizona organized and succeeded in enacting state legislation that made it illegal for property in "adults only" communities to be rented or sold to persons with children. Hudson points out that these elders may very well have been doing themselves political harm by isolating themselves from younger neighbors who might well be "sympathetic to and supportive of the aspirations of older persons either neutral or hostile to them."[26] One very powerful social action group, the Gray Panthers, has taken particular advantage of the common interests of younger and older people. Its ethos and activities are described below.

Intergenerational Social Action: The Gray Panthers

No organization can illustrate better than the Gray Panthers how grass-roots involvement and social-action commitment can bring about feelings of personal dignity, self-worth, and control over one's destiny, and also a sense of goal accomplishment for a large group of people. The following is part of their *Statement of Purpose*: "We are a group of people—old and young—drawn together by deeply felt common concerns for human liberation and social change."[27]

The *Gray Panthers* believe that the young and old are allied on several fronts: both groups are afflicted destructively with powerlessness and alienation, and both are set apart as useless since they do not contribute to the nation's economy through participation in the labor market. Further, both age groups "have difficulty making those who hold power and control take them seriously." The goal of the Gray Panthers is to utilize the "vast storehouse of intelligence, skills, wisdom, creativity, idealism and energy" of young and old, "providing opportunities for each to work together on issues reflecting broad public interests." It is felt that the groups "complement . . . each other by sharing different insights and experiences." Importantly, "through interaction, the young benefit from the experiences and wisdom of the old and begin to view aging not as a problem to be avoided until age 65, but as an experience to be integrated into the total life span."[28]

The people affiliated with the Gray Panthers are committed to the creation of a society wherein all people are able to fulfill their highest potential and the value and the needs of all are recognized. To these ends they have dedicated their energies and resources. In an effort to avoid creating yet another entrenched bureaucracy, the Gray Panthers developed a relatively informal, flexible structure, with shared leadership and decision-making responsibilities. The group is built on a "network" principle, involving relationships among individuals and groups of people. The movement has concentrated on the problems of age discrimination and age stereotyping and the relationship of ageism to racism, sexism, and other oppressive, dehumanizing forces within our society. Their first meetings in the summer of 1970 were used as an opportunity to exchange ideas and strategies for social action and to provide the mutual support they needed for the various projects in which they were engaged.

The group grew to 100 retired men and women by the end of the first year. They began to reach out to college students, to support them in their opposition to the war and the draft. Meetings over these mutual concerns were held at a Quaker retirement center and then at a nearby college. Out of these came an organization of old and young with a common desire for social justice, especially to deal with economic and social needs of young and old adults and with ending the war in Vietnam.

In the summer of 1972, a national steering committee with representation from all parts of the United States was formed because bimonthly meetings no longer sufficed for the growing membership. Funding for the group has come almost exclusively from friends and supporters' small contributions, from church groups, and from speakers' honoraria.

On December 1, 1973, the Gray Panthers joined forces with the Retired Professional Action Group, which had been organized as one of Ralph Nader's public citizen groups. This merger formalized the working relationship that the two groups already had since they began in the late sixties to utilize the talents, skills, and experiences of older people. Both groups attracted a nationwide constituency of old and young people. Both groups worked on such issues as the rights of patients in nursing homes, the regulation and reform of private pension systems, the elimination of age discrimination, and the training of older people for public-interest work.

One of the issues of Ralph Nader's group was an investigation of the hearing-aid industry. A report was prepared showing how many companies were defrauding citizens with hearing problems, especially older people. The Gray Panthers took over this issue and worked on actions that could be taken in correcting the situation.

As a result, many states have enacted legislation in an attempt to control and provide guidelines for the hearing-aid industry. Growing out of research that Ralph Nader developed regarding nursing homes has been the preparation of the extensive *Citizens' Guide for Nursing Home Reform*.

History was made at the first national convention, October 9 to 12, 1975. At this convention, delegates adopted the following goals:

> We are Gray Panthers, the people who celebrate growing up and growing old. We are all ages—old, young, and middle. We deny that aging is a toilsome treadmill grinding to a tragic halt as the years pile up. We affirm aging as a life-spanning process of growth and development from birth to death. Old age is an integral part of the whole, bringing fulfillment and self-actualization.
>
> Our goal is to break down the stereotype of aging as withdrawal and decline, and to reform the lopsided economic system empowered by highly concentrated centers of monopoly wealth which denies human values and fails to provide opportunities for human growth. We seek new priorities in which every woman, man, and child may have room to develop and mature as free human beings able to cope in dignity with life's gifts and demands from the womb to the tomb. We seek economic and political empowerment of the old, the young, the poor, the handicapped, and Americans of various ethnic backgrounds who are disinherited. We seek the same for the disinherited in all the world.
>
> We demand responsible government—government that makes people the first priority, and does not begin to think about corporate benefits until there is a good roof over every person's head, good food on every person's table, universal and adequate health care, education for freedom and dignity open to all regardless of age, race, or status, and a job for everyone who is able to work.
>
> All of these values are interdependent. For instance, where, how, and at what cost people are sheltered within walls and under roofs help determine their family development and stability, their mental and physical health, their relationship to education, jobs, and buying, their ethnic freedom and opportunities, and their ability to live in harmony with their neighbors. Housing, and these related values are closely related to the process of growing up and growing old with wholeness, jobs, and a creative spirit. Human values and economic values are closely intertwined.[29]

The national movement has worked on consciousness-raising research and action programs, with emphasis on sensitizing and training programs aimed at eliminating ageism. For example, its Media Watch Task Force has monitored radio, television, and print advertising's depiction of the elderly and has succeeded in adding "age" to race and sex as an area in which the National Association of Broadcasters agreed to become more sensitive. As well, the group has advocated radical changes in our national health care system and worked for patients' rights and nursing home care. At present, national-level task forces exist on health, housing, and media watch. In addition, the Gray Panthers are represented at the United Nations.

Depending on the strengths and the developmental history of such groups as the Gray Panthers, the social worker who is involved in an advisory and catalytic capacity should perform tasks that make them effective as community action groups.

By forming coalitions to advance the causes of the elderly, social workers can contribute their knowledge and expertise about aging and the special needs of older persons; they can participate in research efforts that deliver important data. Most important, they should lend their visible support. In this way, the social worker becomes a partner—not just a deliverer of services—in the struggle to eradicate ageism and age segregation and its concomitant consequences of social and cultural injustice.

Several excellent guides and manuals exist that may be used by social workers in organizing older adults:

The Silver Lobby: A Guide to Advocacy for Older Persons, Clinton Hess and Paul Kerschner, Ethel Percy Andrus Gerontology Center, University of Southern California, 1978

Washington State's Approach to Senior Citizen Advocacy, State of Washington, Department of Social and Health Services, Bureau of Aging, 1979

The Gray Panthers Manual, Vol. 1: Organizing, The Gray Panthers, Philadelphia, Pa., 1980

Rape and Older Women: A Guide to Prevention and Protection (particularly the chapter entitled "Community Organizing for the Purpose of Crime Reduction"), Linda Davis and Elaine Brody, NIMH, Washington, D.C. 1981.

As social workers should stay abreast of the content and magnitude of political and social issues affecting America's elderly, several publications may be of help:

Collation, Journal of the National Citizen's Coalition for Nursing Home Reform, Washington, D.C., 20005

Older American Reports and *Aging Service News*, weekly reports of nationwide developments including congressional action affecting older Americans. Capitol Publications, Inc., 1300 North 17th Street, Arlington, Va. 22209

Gray Panther Network: Age and Youth in Action, Philadelphia, Pa., 19104.

Community Planning

Problem solving in the community will focus on major social problems that will be faced by the elderly today and tomorrow.

> The practitioner serves as expert, fact finder, and analyst, and as a program implementer and facilitator. . . . Clientele is made up of consumers or recipients of services. [Both] consensus [and] conflict may be employed as . . . strateg[ies]. A basic assumption is that change can be brought about through rational decision making.[30]

Planning organizations—local, regional, state, and national agencies under governmental as well as nongovernmental auspices—employ social workers (although not in large numbers) to carry out planning functions that basically involve coordination, allocation of resources, and innovation.

A dominant feature of all these settings is that organizing and planning take place through interorganizational relationships. Many important practice issues revolve around the type of dependence and the degree of interdependence that exist among the units involved. A critical question is the distribution of power or authority in decision making and implementation. Although planners have some leeway in devising structures for interaction, to a great extent the focal points of power are fixed in an interorganizational situation, and this constitutes an important constraint.[31]

Several efforts were made recently to counteract this constraint. First, the Gerontological Society of America, through its research fellowship program and in conjunction with the State of Illinois Department of Public Health, sponsored the development of the Union County Illinois Elderly Health Advocacy Group. The group, seeking to reinforce social power and decision-making levels of elderly citizens, involved elderly consumers (51 percent) and service providers as collaborative participants and equal members committed to the goals of health services planning, review, evaluation, and change. The project was based on a consensus model of community planning and adhered to established group structure and process dimensions. Judging from the positive community response to the project, Phyllis Ehrlich, the project director, postulates that the model is a viable alternative to conventional health care planning.

A second project, also aimed at lessening the elderly's sense of powerlessness to affect their own destinies, developed in Miami and has now been existence for eight years, successfully surviving budget cuts and staff reductions without losing members. Beginning with community organization of elderly residents of a selected target area, the "Neighborhood Family" project has evolved into a group of approximately 350 members, living within ten blocks of each other, interacting as a kinship group in terms of keeping watch over each other's welfare. In so doing, they also became the indigenous governing body of their own multipurpose mental health clinic, which simultaneously constitute the geriatric service unit of the comprehensive community mental health center.

An Example of Community Planning

In the following example of a community planning effort, the design, development, and operation of a health and community service for the elderly in a housing project demanded that the social work practitioner serve as an expert, a fact finder, an analyst, a program implementor, and a facilitator. The situation taxed the worker's skills and functioning as a community planner.

Preparation of the Plan. For many years, the Older Adult Board of the Committee of Inner City Settlements had been concerned with the planning and implementation of comprehensive services to meet the needs of older people living within and outside of public housing developments. Their concern and commitment grew out of their work with the elderly in the Greenville Homes development, opened in December 1950. No social, recreational, or health services had been provided in this housing project of 600 units.

A social worker assigned to Greenville Homes soon discovered that many elderly had special needs that were not being met. A new requirement made it necessary to identify elderly people in need of services before organizing services to meet those needs. (This resembled the model employed in the late 1950s and early 1960s in work with multiproblem families.) The limitations of this requirement necessitated reorganization by the planners. For example, originally unidisciplinary groups met together—caseworkers, group workers, and neighborhood organizers—to help plan and facilitate a program. There were problems of communication and periodic time-consuming case conferences. The limited impact of these efforts on income maintenance, health care, housing, employment, and training programs was rarely perceived.

It should be noted that the employment of outreach workers for the elderly was not an experiment unrelated to experience, conventional wisdom, and research. From June 1961 through December 1962, Inner City Settlements had a subcontract with the Housing Development Authority to relocate certain residents before construction began. In 1963, Inner City Settlements expanded their outreach program in the neighborhood. When redevelopment plans began, the Housing Development Authority arranged that a new, low-rent public housing development for the elderly would be included to accommodate the displaced people. Thus in 1966, the social worker, who was director of older adult services of Inner City Settlements, initiated a meeting with the Housing Development Authority to discuss the possibility of implementing a project to demonstrate the value of comprehensive community health, recreational, and social services within the housing project itself. It would make services centrally identifiable and easily accessible when residents needed them and would include older people living in the neighborhood as well. Certain participating community agencies and institutions agreed to contribute staff services and supplies to the planned delivery system, including the family service and counseling agency, University Hospital and its outreach health service and division of psychiatry, the visiting nurse association, the state department of public welfare, a women's club, and Inner City Settlements.

The Housing Development Authority was depending on community agencies to provide health and welfare services and was receptive to their interest and concern. The planning committee was invited to review the architectural designs and to suggest the type of facilities and space necessary to provide comprehensive services on the site as well as modifications to the design in general. The physical arrangement of the housing development included two seven-story buildings that were joined by a landscaped terrace on the second floor level. The buildings overlooked a central ground-level plaza. The Housing Development Authority, after lengthy negotiations with the planning committee, agreed to make available a community room that opened onto the terrace and to design two rooms on the second floor for use as health and social service quarters.

The community room or recreation room, was spacious and had a bank of large windows on three sides. It was attractively furnished by the Housing Development Authority and included a small library with current magazines, a piano, a television set, and a sewing machine. It also had a small but well-furnished kitchen. Next door to the recreation room was a laundry room with washers and dryers.

In 1966, a proposal was drafted by the director of older adult services. It was submitted by Inner City Settlements and approved by the planning committee to the Administration on Aging of the Department of Health, Education, and Welfare in Washington, D.C. As a demonstration grant, it contained the following program assumptions:

1. A coordinated, comprehensive and continuous system of health and community services can be delivered to older residents in a housing project; services can contribute to the prevention of deterioration and breakdown of the aged people before crisis occurs.
2. A continuous coordinated and comprehensive service system is useful as a model which can be adapted and included in the initial planning and design of housing for the elderly anywhere in the country.
3. A variety of community and health services can collaborate effectively in planning, designing, and delivering such a system of services to older residents; such collaboration will result in more efficient and better distribution of limited resources of agencies and institutions.
4. Coordinated efforts can reduce such problems often associated with older people as social isolation and physical and mental breakdown.
5. Many older people can contribute to the planning, designing, and carrying out of services and thereby remain involved in community life.
6. This type of program will provide needed training opportunities for professional, technical, and auxiliary personnel in direct work with the aged as well as the opportunity for such personnel to learn to function as members of multidisciplinary teams in a coordinated community program.

Public funding, however, was not forthcoming: the application was rejected. The social work planner persuaded the participating agencies to adopt an alternative plan since the proposed services were vitally needed by the older people in the area. The plan for implementing the service system was developed by the planning committee with leadership provided by the social work planner. Commitments were made by these agencies to redeploy their own staff to operate services in the housing project. In this manner, costs of the services were absorbed in the budgets of the respective agencies. This was crucial to the development of the project. It meant, however, a limitation of the proposed services until a time when expansion would be feasible. In April of 1968, the housing units were completed and open for occupancy, with a number of services available on site.

Operation of the Plan. Initially the limited number of services available when the housing units opened for occupancy included the social work staff provided by Inner City Settlements to coordinate the project and develop group, community, and recreational programs. In addition, the family service and counseling agency provided a full-time social worker on site, a part-time social work assistant, and students from a local school of social work who did their field work practice there. The visiting nurse association assigned one of its nurses on a part-time basis as an initial step in developing the health component. The nurse assigned had served this area of the city for more than twenty years and had known or cared for many of the residents during that time. During the first two years of operation, the major lack in the project's services was a fully developed medical component.

In the spring of 1970, the new chief of health services at University Hospital offered a health screening program for all residents in public housing and for those elderly in private housing participating in other phases of the project program. Approximately 50 percent of those eligible responded, with findings that resulted in further preventive or corrective treatment or continued follow-up observation. Since then, a clinic has been set up and is in operation two days a week. It is available to all elderly persons. Dental and psychiatric consultant services has been secured to round out the health unit. Arrangements have been made with a local pharmacist to pick up prescriptions and deliver medicines. The social services component is another significant part of the program. The social worker maintains a case load of about 50 percent of the 125 elderly residents in the public housing unit and 10 percent of the 100 residents in the private housing sector.

In line with the objectives of the total program, social service assistance includes any supportive service that the residents need in order to function better to maintain themselves or to help them through a crisis. Services have included casework counseling, the provision of homemakers, working with a newly discovered diabetic toward acceptance of the illness, and shopping for groceries for a temporarily ill client. However, the major thrust of social service has proved to be crisis intervention, and most situations involve a health problem—physical, mental, or both. The visiting nurse provides health care to patients in the housing project who are part of her regular case load. She also screens the patients who are to see the doctor and assists him during clinic hours. Social worker, physician, and nurse work closely together, and there is continual referring and conferring among them.

The Aid-a-Friend Program of the neighborhood women's club accepts referrals of residents in need of a friend and also provides transportation to pick up and deliver surplus food items to residents twice monthly. A resident council staffed by a community social worker meets monthly and deals with issues of direct concern to the residents, such as safety, security, housing comforts, adaptation to and integration with the surrounding community, lack of supervision of small children in the area, and problems that arise largely because of living in close proximity with one another. A community room is open daily under the supervision of two elderly residents affiliated with Elderly Volunteers, a local service group; they are paid a nominal salary by this agency.

A variety of activities is offered—health information programs, nutritional demonstrations, crafts, music, movies, socials, and programs for special occasions that include dinners and parties. These activities are carried on with group leaders, holiday dinners are prepared and served entirely by residents, and continuous attempts are being made to strengthen existing leadership and to develop new leaders. In the role of coordinator, the social worker of the project is vital in linking the various services and in monitoring the delivery. The worker arranges for conferences and meetings between project and community resources and also serves as staff and liaison person to the policy board.

The policy board, staffed by the director of older adult services, is composed of board members and executives of the participating agencies. It meets regularly to review the project, develop guidelines, and evaluate its operation. Although initial attempts to involve representation from the residents on the board had not been overly successful (they thought it placed them in an authoritative role that estranged them from their peers), they have recently agreed to participate in groups of two or three on a rotating basis. So far, this arrangement has worked out and their presumed fear has been proven groundless. New indigenous leadership is being groomed and the residents themselves assume increasing responsibility for the direction of the project.

The program, now in its tenth year of operation, was evaluated by a local university by means of a subcontract. This evaluation requirement was built into the design of the project. The report concluded as follows:

> The original objectives have been met and a comprehensive coordinated health, social, and community service delivery system is workable and can contribute to maintaining older people in their homes. When such services are provided, they are heavily used by the residents and for the most part, residents hold positive attitudes toward the service delivery system. This model of a service delivery system can be established through the combined efforts of existing public and voluntary agencies. Such programs, however, cannot be implemented on any significant scale without additional funding from public sources. This type of program has proved successful in early identification of problems of the elderly and, therefore, has strong potential as a program in prevention. *

Social planning, social policy formulation, and administration are closely interrelated. With the advent of more programs and services for older people by government and nongovernment agencies, social workers have moved into planning, policymaking and administrative positions that test their skills on the macro level of practice. The role of social work and workers in developing and implementing social policy for the aged is discussed in the next chapter. This role transcends the more circumscribed focus of direct social work intervention on the community level and moves into a larger arena of the macro system.

References

1. Ralph Kramer and Harry Specht (eds.), *Readings in Community Organization Practice* (Englewood Cliffs, N.J.: Prentice-Hall, 1969), pp. 8–9.
2. Robert Perlman and Arnold Gurin, *Community Organization and Social Planning* (New York: Wiley, 1971), p. 61. Reprinted by permission of John Wiley & Sons, Inc.

* United South End Settlements of Boston, Mass. Report of the Older Adult Committee, 1972.

3. Ibid., pp. 76–77.
4. Ibid., pp. 82–83.
5. Ibid., p. 63.
6. Ibid., p. 68.
7. Ibid., p. 70.
8. Ibid., p. 73.
9. Louis Lowy, *Training Manual* (Boston: Boston University Press, 1968), pp. 180–191.
10. Perlman and Gurin, op. cit., pp. 74–75.
11. Hebrew Home for the Aged, Riverdale, N.Y.: Brochure, 1982.
12. John M. Haynes and Joel Serkin, *Community Organization Planning and Resources for the Older Poor*, Technical Assistance Monograph, no. 1 (Washington, D.C.: NCoA, 1968).
13. Jessica Getzel, "Resident Councils and Social Action," *Gerontological Social Work Practice In Long Term Care* (New York: Haworth Press, 1983), p. 179–185.
14. Barbara Silverstone, *Establishing Resident Councils*, New York Federation of Protestant Welfare Agencies, Division of Aging, December 1974, p. 81.
15. William Schwartz, "The Social Worker in the Group," *Social Welfare Forum*, (New York: Columbia University Press, 1961), pp. 146–171.
16. Phyllis Ehrlich, *Elderly Health Advocacy Group: Handbook of Organizing Principles* (Springfield, Ill.: Department of Public Health, 1980).
17. Jessica Getzel, "Social Work with Family Caregivers for the Aged," *Social Casework* (1981), vol. 62, p. 3.
18. Lester Milbrath, *Political Participation* (Chicago: Rand McNally, 1965).
19. Fernando Torres-Gill, "Political Involvement among Member of Minority Groups: Problems and Profits," in R. L. McNeely and John Colen (eds.), *Aging and Minority Groups*, (Beverly Hills, Calif.: Sage, 1983).
20. Ibid, p. 161–162.
21. Robert Hudson (ed.), *The Aging in Politics: Process and Policy* (Springfield, Ill.: Charles C Thomas, 1981).
22. Norval Glenn, "Aging and Conservatism," *Annals of the American Academy of Political and Social Science*, Vol. 4/5, 1974.
23. A. Campbell, "Politics Through the Life Cycle," *Gerontologist*, Vol. II(197), pp. 112–117.
24. Jerry Weaver, "Issue Salience: The Elderly as a Political Community: The Case of a National Health Policy," *Western Political Quarterly*, vol. 29, no. 4, December 1976, pp. 610–619.
25. Ibid.
26. Hudson, op. cit.
27. Gray Panthers, *Statement of Purpose*, 3700 Chestnut St., Philadelphia, Pa., 19104.
28. The preceding quotations are drawn from *The Gray Panther Manual, Vol. 1: Organizing*, 2nd ed. (Philadelphia, Pa.: Gray Panthers, April 1980), pp. 1–27, 61–63.
29. *Gray Panther Statement of Purpose*, op. cit.
30. Perlman and Gurin, op. cit. p. 145.
31. Ibid., pp. 80–81.

14

The Role of Social Work in Developing a Social Policy on Aging; The Social Work Profession and Aging

Society, rather than social work alone, is ultimately responsible for dealing with the problems of the aging. However, the profession shares responsibility for discovering what is needed, communicating that information, and fulfilling the role of advocate both in services to individuals and in social planning. The decade of decision is at hand. If social workers are to participate fully in making and carrying out plans to deal with the social consequences of this massive contemporary challenge, they need specific information as well as values as a basis for their positions and actions. The capacity of the profession to develop hard predictive data—both quantitative and qualitative—about the social and economic costs and the effectiveness of the services required will determine whether policy makers accept the role of social work.[1]

Analytic Approaches to Policy

Paul Kershner and Ira Hirschfield posit that outcomes of social policy are a direct result of four prevailing dichotomous approaches to the legislative process: (1) categorical versus generic, (2) holistic versus segmented, (3) crisis versus rational approach, and (4) political context versus future planning. It is their contention that social policy in this country has usually been formulated in a categorical, segmented, and crisis-oriented way—influenced not by long-range goals and comprehensive approaches, but by political expedience.

Categorical versus Generic

The question is whether the aged should be singled out as a group for specific age-oriented action or whether they should be treated as one segment of a larger generic grouping: Should our policy be to create housing for all segments of our population or to develop housing for the elderly?

Kershner and Hirschfield point out the following:

[By] accepting the generic approach, whereby the aged are one among many groups to be affected by legislation, public policymakers can use a more general data base than would be necessary if they were solely applying a categorical approach. For example, in the development of a mass transit system serving a total (generic) population, there is a need to know the specific preferences of the aged (routes, times, costs, accessibility). Given the limitations in available resources, however, these preferences may be disregarded in an effort to serve the larger population.

If, on the other hand, one utilizes the categorical approach, whereby legislation and programs are tailored exclusively to the requisites of older adults, then the data base must be absolutely accurate as well as focused, or it may well be destructive to the well-being of the user population. For example, a mass feeding program designed for the elderly should be structured around a detailed knowledge of age-related issues such as diet, eating periods, and group versus individual preferences.

Legislation affecting the aged has been neither wholly categorical nor wholly generic in approach. What has occurred is a continual shifting between the two approaches, resulting in chaos within the public policy process. It would not be inappropriate to use the analogy of an individual who constantly is having to shift between cooking for one person and cooking for a family of ten. It should be easily recognized that one would be dealing with two distinct types of data bases with varying needs for specificity and accuracy. The Social Security Administration, like the alternating chef, once served primarily the aged, but not has expanded its scope to also include the blind, poor, disabled, and dependent survivors. It, like many organizations, has had to reorient itself to serving a more comprehensive poulation. Such a reorientation often results in greater inefficiency and inadequate delivery of services to its recipients.[2]

Holistic versus Segmented

In a segmented approach, aged individuals are divided into segments and categorized into selective needs, and then we devise programs and address these needs separately, rather than viewing persons as whole units. Thus we have either nutrition, or health, or income programs. This approach manifests itself in segmented service delivery as people get shunted from one agency to another.

Crisis versus Rational Approach

Most social policy is formulated as a result of crisis. For example, the Social Security Act of 1935 was a direct result of the crisis of the Depression of the 1930s.

The three major health programs serving the elderly, as well as other age groups, also resulted from the onset of a crisis. The Medical Assistance for the Aged Program, Title XIX of the Social Security Act (Medicaid—for the medically indigent), and Title XVIII of the Social Security Act (Medicare—for those 65 and over) grew from the health-care cost crisis sweeping the nation in the 1960s.

An additional example is the Supplemental Security Income Program (Title XVI of the Social Security Act) which provided federal control of the state-operated payment programs for the aged, blind, and disabled. The Supplemental Program was hastily enacted in part to calm the dismay resulting from the failure to enact the far broader Family Assistance Proposal.

This demonstration of the "crisis reaction" process contradicts the administrative purists who deny the crisis theme and yet continue to rail against the poor conceptual framework of public policy. They somehow are convinced that public policy emerges out of a rational examination of the available facts and pertinent data. We posit this to be far from accurate, since experts cannot even agree on what is considered to be a sound conceptual framework. In analyzing a series of issues like the economy, the antiballistic system, and age-related topics, we immediately can line up experts on each side of the debates, who all claim patents on the key to rational planning.

Scientific data [are] useful, but [are] not the magic word to opening the door to rational policymaking. We can listen to economic experts like Schultz, Samuelson, Friedman, and Galbraith. We can examine pages of statistical facts verifying the overwhelming numbers of older Americans suffering from malnutrition, and we can read about the mortality rates in the Sudan. Yet the hard-core facts are not simply the statistics or the deaths. Facts can reveal crisis situations daily, but change cannot occur unless this information gets into the right hands, and is subsequently communicated to and accepted by the general public.[3]

Political Context versus Future Planning

Public policy and legislation is reactive; it is a response to a crisis or a prevailing mood of the present; it is not a thoughtful, rational response to potential future needs. "The tragic elements of this approach are that most legislation in aging evolves not from a group of policy scientists drafting programs for the future, but rather from some pragmatic assumptions about what will be tolerated by the dominant forces in the society."[4]

Policymakers respond to pragmatic, political realities instead of the real needs of the aged population. Despite accumulated evidence through research data that indicate overwhelmingly a need for comprehensive and reimbursable outpatient health services for the elderly, the Medicare Act focuses almost solely on inpatient hospital care. "Aging legislation has been caught in a morass of conflicting and competing interests and issues. The result . . . of these fragmented approaches is that in most cases involving major aging legislation, policymakers have abdicated moral responsibility by passing laws based on flimsy and often inaccurate data."[5]

In Social Policies and Programs on Aging, this author cited a series of agenda items for social policies on aging.

1. Assurance of an adequate income for every older person through a federally administered system of income security which is protected against inflation, devaluation of the dollar, and pension loss.
2. Reduction or abatement of federal, state, and local taxes for older persons and also a reduction of rates of public utilities such as transportation, telephone, gas, electricity, and so forth.

3. Reorganization and reordering of the health delivery system with stress on early detection: treatment, rehabilitation, prevention, group practice, and home assistance; development of an all-inclusive prepaid national health insurance system to remove financial worries and to assure cost control.
4. Provision of increased public social services divorced from financial needs.
5. Development of additional social and community services (as proposed by the Senior Citizens' Community Planning and Service Act of 1963) which would include many additional social services for older people and for research and demonstration projects leading to newer or improved programs to aid them.
6. Increase in senior citizens' housing projects in urban and rural areas and eligibility of single persons for moderate income and rental housing which is now only available to couples. In addition, automatic inclusion of a battery of social services in all public housing projects designed for the elderly.
7. Inclusion in the national service corps opportunity for older people who are able and willing and in a position to provide services for people with problems in all age groups.
8. Expansion of the Manpower Development and Training Act and the Area Development Act in order to launch a series of experimental and demonstration projects to help older workers and those in the middle years make the best possible use of training opportunities in communities and to prepare for second careers.
9. Provision of a pool for [full- and] part-time employment opportunities for older people and preretirement counseling services sponsored under industry, management, and labor.
10. Increase in the federal contribution for the building of nursing homes and provision of more uniform standards for nursing homes and more uniform standards for nursing home care with enforcement possibilities. Removal of institutional stigma from institutions for the aged who are chronically ill.
11. Development of increased geriatric treatment facilities for the mentally ill and halfway houses for those who are released from hospitals and mental health institutions.
12. Provisions of increased home health and medical care services for the mentally ill as well as for the physically ill in their own homes or homes of relatives.
13. Provision of an increased program of foster and boarding care for the elderly.
14. Development of day care centers, recreation centers, and outreach programs for those who cannot take advantage of existing recreational facilities.
15. Increase in educational opportunities under adult-education auspices.
16. Development of a more uniform statutory program of social services, particularly homemaker, protective, consumer information, legal assistance, friendly visitor, meals-on-wheels, and multi-service centers.
17. Creation of more nutritional programs coupled with social and recreational services to improve the nutrition of older people [out-of-home as well as in-home] and to assist in alleviating incipient personal problems.
18. Provision of improved transportation facilities to counteract physical isolation and to advance the mobility of older persons.
19. Development of short-range and long-range plans by all professions and organizations (governmental and nongovernmental, including older people themselves), on planning bodies to design plans for the well-being of the

elderly in all walks of life, taking into account that the aged are not a homogeneous group. Creation of opportunities for choice!

20. Expansion of research projects and facilities and provision for the utilization of research findings as soon as possible in the planning and development of social welfare programs and services.

21. Development of new, and improvement of existing, educational and training programs for professionals, paraprofessionals, nonprofessionals, and volunteers working with the elderly.

22. Development of a system whereby the existence of projects can be readily communicated to the public and where the results of successful demonstration projects can be made part of programs and services as quickly as possible.[6]

These goals are as valid today as at the time when they were set forth.

Dimensions of Social Welfare Policy

There are two basic types of social worker: those engaged in the provision of direct services to clients (individuals, families, groups, members of community organizations) and those engaged in offering services indirectly (planners, administrators, social policy shapers). In addition, some social workers are researchers involved in knowledge testing and building and some are educators transmitting knowledge and skills to others. Neil Gilbert and Harry Specht see social welfare policies as "choices among principles or guidelines to determine what benefits are to be offered to whom, how these benefits are to be delivered and how they are to be financed." Their dimensions are the following:

1. Bases of social allocations: What are the guiding principles that determine the benefits, programs, or services allocated to older persons in our society? E.g., older persons whose incomes are below a certain amount per month are eligible for Supplemental Social Security Income.

2. Nature and types of social provisions: What are the forms in which the benefits, programs, or services are to be received by older persons? E.g., those eligible for SSI receive benefits in cash, not in kind or in vouchers; or transportation is made available regularly via a cab service contracted by an agency at a flat-rate nominal price to the elderly person for hospital visits.

3. Delivery of provisions: How are benefits, programs, or services to be delivered to the elderly in the community? E.g., meals-on-wheels are delivered to the older person in his [or her] home five days a week if he or she is incapable of leaving the residence; or meals are available at specially designated nutrition sites (at a service center) for all older people (whether ambulatory or not).

4. Sources and methods of financing: How are these benefits, programs, or services paid for? Through taxes via federal and state governments, contracts for services with private agencies? E.g., SSI is paid for via a mix of federal and state funding; nutrition programs on-site are federally financed via Title III of the Older Americans Act, as amended; meals-on-wheels may be funded via contract for service agreements through a mix of public tax and private philanthropic monies.[7]

Social workers in direct practice must be aware of these dimensions as their clients and services are affected by them (see Chapter 7) and as they may affect the allocation and flow of such provisions in turn—as Brody and Brody pointed out already in 1984:

> While social security benefits were .5 percent of the gross national product (GNP) in 1940, they were 4 percent of it in 1972. SSI is expected to at least double the number of aged recipients on public assistance. Together with a special SSI increase and that program's tie-in to the cost of living index, transfer payments to the aged from these two programs should be stabilized at 5 percent of the GNP in the 1980s, modified only by radical shifts in the population or special increases authorized by Congress.
>
> Several results of this development concern social work:
>
> Is the base grant enough to guarantee an end to poverty for the aged? The 1972 poverty threshold was $1994 for an older individual and $2505 per couple, against a base SSI individual grant of $1680 and $2540 per couple. Considering the consumer price increase from 1972 to 1974 and, further, the definition of near-poor set at 125 percent of the poor threshold, one concern of the social workers will be to make sure that the level of the nationally guaranteed income promises to eliminate poverty for the aged. What percentage of national income is the public willing to allocate for the aged? How will that percentage be allocated between income and services?[8]

Or take health social service needs. Again, Brody and Brody spoke to this issue then:

> Physical, mental, and environmental factors together determine the health of the aged. Developmental understanding of the aging process suggests that varying degrees of dysfunctioning or health status result from the accumulated insults of life crises interacting with universally present chronic illness. This process evolves within the framework of the genetic mold and the characteristics of personality. Medical care operates to stablize physical or mental impairment. The availability of the family network and other social supports assures that medical care will be utilized and that the prescribed regimens will be carried out. Accordingly, any projection of the health needs of the aged would have to consider prospective knowledge, probable deliverty systems, and predicted age spread. . . .
>
> The Medicare system, as presently administered, makes short shrift of social services related to health. Those who apply for reimbursement for such services under Medicare must be sick enough to require acute inpatient care before they can receive the services at home. Virtually all the insurance proposals before Congress build on the Medicare experience, and the few that are not specifically modeled on it do not include a broad spectrum of home health services. More particularly, social services are not covered as appropriate for vendor payments under third-party pay arrangments. . . .
>
> The hospital—focal point of the health delivery system, with over one third of its bed days used by the aged—pays little attention to the social needs of patients. . . . The new emphasis on health maintenance organizations (HMOs) as a preferable delivery system is also built on experience that has not included health social services. For the most part, HMOs have not served the aged in their

proportion to the total population. A significant breakthrough was achieved in the Health Maintenance Organization Act of 1973 when medical social services were made a requirement of "qualified" HMOs. It remains to be seen how this law will affect both the provision of health social services benefits and the enrollment of the aged.

In preparing for the decades ahead, social workers concerned with the aged have a major interpretive responsibility to heighten the awareness of health institutions and providers in meeting the needs of the elderly. Providers will not be able to respond, however, until they have an economic base on which they can plan to expand home-health and institutional social services. This, in turn, requires providing policymakers with hard information as to the economic and social cost-benefit of these services. Task defining and pricing of home health services and determining the incidence of their need on an actuarial basis must precede the extension of prepay mechanisms to these services.[9]

What can the social worker rendering direct services do to participate in shaping social policy amid such substantive areas and issues? Let us turn to the prophetic Brodys again:

A critical role of social workers with respect to the aged for the decade of the eighties is fulfilling the primary responsibility of advocacy. Advocacy in turn must be supported by research, education, and service. Hard information must be available for the brief that backs up the value commitment. Social work education similarly needs research data in preparation for training professionals to work with the aged. The practitioner, in giving service, fulfills the promise of the advocate.

While any schism in social work between planners, practitioners, and action groups on the one hand and direct service practitioners on the other is to be deplored for all age groups, it is particularly inappropriate for the elderly. Certainly, the broad goals are to reduce socially induced risks: negative attitudes, poverty, vulnerability due to minority group status, environmental stresses such as poor housing and dangerous neighborhoods, and neglect in health services.

Within the framwork of the broad goals, the social worker must determine and distinguish what his [or her] particular agency can provide directly, what the larger community (that is, other agencies and the three levels of government) must provide, and what linkages are necessary among them. To focus on planning and delivering the specific services that a particular agency can develop and control does not mean avoidance or denial of the broad social changes needed as a context for those services.

Paralleling those broad-gauged efforts, there must be preventive, therapeutic, restorative, and prosthetic services for those elderly individuals and families who inevitably are vulnerable in any society: those who through illness, loss, and psychological vulnerabilities lack the personal resources to deal with the pressures that all are subjected to as part of the human condition. There is no absolute protection from the distress attendant on such experiences, and no programmatic substitute for skilled human help.

The rendering of social work services will depend increasingly on third-party payments either for services rendered by the social worker practicing as an individual or in a group, or as part of organizations with a variety of missions. More likely, social work services for the aged will be available under the health rubric, as much for the convenience, accessibility, and acceptance of the aged consumer as for the provider.[10]

Hard data to back up claims and to provide documentation for positions taken; projections as to present and future needs of the young, middle, and older population; articulation of ideas based on research findings that are properly evaluated; presentation of viewpoints that counteract stereotypical myths of the aging; convincing arguments based on reflected experience with older people in daily practice—be this in a community agency or a residential institution—all this is needed and can be supplied by social workers to decision-making groups in the private and public sectors, as well as to organizations of elderly citizens, such as the AARP or Gray Panthers, to add ammunition to their arsenal.

Take the case for or against mandatory retirement. This social policy issue has enormous implications for the country as a whole, as well as for each person, whether of retirement age or not. The changes in retirement laws enacted in 1978 have far-reaching effects for industry, trade unions, government agencies, and people of all ages. However, *mandatory* retirement for employment in the private sector has not been abolished nationally, though several individual states have taken steps to ban legally *mandatory* retirement.

Social workers have dealt with people and their various experiences with retirement—people who anticipate retirement, suffer from it, or adjust to it to varying degrees. Some have opinions about it, love it or hate it; some experience stress and family conflict; some have prepared for it, and some have been traumatized by it. Data are vital; they need to be systematically brought together and conveyed in discussions with management and unions, with governmental agencies, with lawyers, and with legislators. Social workers must write and speak on such a subject; it should be on the agenda of social agency staff meetings. The case now becomes a cause!

Strategies and Techniques

To participate in the social policy formulation and shaping process and to intervene effectively, "retail" social workers must be cognizant of strategies and techniques that are based on an analysis of the problem and policy. The four-dimensional framework discussed earlier is a useful way to approach such an analysis. Like the problem-solving model outlined in the previous chapter, strategies and techniques follow the appropriate assessment. Literature on the "planning of change" distinguishes three major types of strategies: (1) empirical-rational, (2) normative-reeducative, and (3) power-coercive.[11]

Empirical-Rational

The assumptions of the empirical-rational strategy may be summarized as follows: Fundamentally, people are rational and they follow their rational self-interests once this is revealed to them. First, a change must be proposed by some person or a group that knows of a situation that is desirable, effective, and in line with the self-interests of the person (group, organization, or community) that will be affected by the change. Because persons or groups are assumed to be rational and moved by self-interest, they will adopt a proposed change if it can be rationally justified and if they can be shown that they will gain by the change. This strategy includes certain techniques:

Collecting Data. In daily practice with the aged, social workers must gather and record information about their clients and groups, not only for agency purposes or as a tool for supervisory conferences, but to make these data available to policymakers in the agency (executives, board members), to members of the legislature, to community lobby groups, to special interest associations, and to the public media.

Expert Testimony. Often, social workers who know the magnitude of their clients' problems fail to speak of them frankly in the political and public arenas. Social workers should testify as professionals and as representatives of their agencies.

Case Conferences with Other Agencies. These conferences can be used by agencies that are familiar with the treatment of their clients by a second agency. They should be held in the presence of the clients involved and should be conducted with decision makers as well as line workers.

Education. This technique includes using informational meetings, panels, exhibits, literature, and press campaigns, all of which are aimed at educating segments of the community to a particular issue.

Demonstration Projects. Although recent examples of this form have been focused directly on specific problems of the poor, other long-range implications are possible. Further advocacy in usually needed to carry the message of the demonstration project into institutional changes, which affect the total population involved.

Direct Contacts with Officials and Legislators. The agency may want to be a resource of information about community problems for officials. It may want to have individual or group meetings with legislators on a regular basis, so that elected officials can be exposed to views on current issues that affect their clientele.

Normative-Reeducative

The normative-reeducative strategy does not deny the rationality and intelligence of people; however, it focuses on the belief that patterns of action and practice are supported by social-cultural norms and by commitments on the part of individuals to these norms. Social-cultural norms are supported by the attitude and value system of individuals on normative outlooks that undergird their commitment. Change in a pattern of practice or action, according to this view, will occur only as the persons involved are brought to change the normative orientation to old patterns and develop commitments to new ones; and changes in normative orientations involve changes in attitudes, values, skills, and significant relationships, not just changes in knowledge, information, or intellectual rationales for action and practice. Techniques mostly involve *group-sensitizing programs* (e.g., T-groups) that involve members of agency staffs, clients, and interagency committees and that start by consciousness-raising efforts and activities.

Coalition Groups. This technique involves the agency's becoming a member of an ad hoc group that is committed to a specific objective. The advantages of this form of involvement are that the agency is less vulnerable to direct attack and is involved with disparate types of organizations in concerted action. The problem with this type of involvement, however, is that the issue at hand may become too generalized to meet the wishes of member organizations. This is especially true if there is a high orientation among the members for "consensus" or "cooperation."

Client Groups. This is a development in which consumers of services or potential consumers form groups for social change. The common interest among the members is the identification of a mutual problem. The social service agency initiates the group, gives it impetus, assists it to obtain certain information or access to selected people, and mounts collaborative efforts with other community groups.

Power-Coercive

The power-coercive approaches emphasize political and economic sanctions in the exercise of power as well as moral power, playing upon sentiments of guilt and shame. Strategies are nonviolent and involve the use of political institutions to achieve change and the use of changing power elites. Certain techniques are called for.

Position Talking. The more effective stand will be related to the "position" of the person or agency. To take a stand on an issue has both external and internal values since the clients and staff note the record of an agency's position.

Petitions. Petitions can be used to call attention to an issue, assist group members in making public contacts, and help members formulate points and rebuttals.

Persistent Demands. This technique involves bombarding officials and legislators and going beyond the usual channels of appeal. This tactic stays within the limits of the law, but it may be a precursor to actual harassment or even extralegal means.

Demonstrations and Protests. These include marches, street dramas, vigils, picketing, and other forms of nonviolent direct-action public demonstrations. Social work advocates should be equipped to conduct and guide such efforts, and their agencies must be committed to the support of such activities prior to their initiation. The agency must consider whether other means have been exhausted fully and, if so, whether the other available means are too far behind the firing line from which the decisions must be made. Advocacy by board and staff in these matters might call for financial, political, and technical assistance in such a struggle. This strategy must not be utilized without broad commitment and clearance with those on whose behalf advocacy action is contemplated and carried out.

Social Workers in Planning and Policy Roles

Based on the interplay of the roles of social workers as enablers, brokers, advocates, therapists, teachers and experts, their tasks are to use a variety of techniques of intervention to effect changes in the social policy arena. While much of what has been said so far has direct applicability for "wholesale" social workers as well, there are specific functions incumbent upon them that arise out of role expectations and role prescriptions. In the capacity of planner and policy maker, the social worker devotes a major portion of his or her professional life to influencing social policy on aging.

Perlman and Gurin's problem-solving model (reviewed in Chapter 13) applies to the organizational context of planning organizations when the social worker and planner in the field of aging engage in the tasks of (1) studying needs and identifying problem areas (such as housing); (2) setting goals and policies (what type of housing, for whom, at what cost, and where); (3) implementing the policies and plans (building the housing units); (4) monitoring and feedback (examining to what extent implementation is in accord with goals, policies, plans and changing needs). An exposition of these tasks and application in practice addresses itself primarily to the role of social policy analysts and implementors—that is, administrators in the field of aging.

An Illustration

This example describes the role of professionals in social policy in a state unit on aging in Massachusetts. As such, it illustrates the kind of contributions that can be made. It is excerpted from an article by this author in the journal *Aging and Human Development*.[12]

> On August 31, 1970 Governor Francis Sargent of Massachusetts signed an Act establishing the Executive Office of Elder Affairs. As a result, Massachusetts had become the first state in the nation to have a cabinet level office that deals solely with the affairs of the elderly . . . chartered to be a "program and advocacy agency." Soon afterwards, the Governor appointed a Secretary to head this office and two advisory committees as recommended by the White House Conference on Aging Planning Group in the Commonwealth: a Citizens Advisory Committee composed of elderly in the state and a Professional Advisory Committee, henceforth to be named Professional Task Force Committee. The State Unit on Aging, that is, the

Executive Office of Elder Affairs, was to engage in planning, monitoring and delivering service programs and in advocacy functions on behalf of the elderly.

Subsequently, the newly appointed secretary asked this author to chair the Professional Task Force Committee. In consultation with the Secretary, 25 professionals in gerontology and geriatrics were appointed by the Governor based on three criteria: (1) functional competence; (2) leadership potential; and (3) representativeness. As a result, professionals were included who [were] working with the elderly in institutional and noninstitutional service programs—students, academic [experts] (teachers and researchers), policymakers, and administrators. Because the Chairman of the Committee and the Secretary viewed it as essential that this Committee should be involved in social policy shaping by providing advisory input to the Secretary and his staff, various and different competencies [were to] be represented so that the Secretary and his staff would get the best possible advice that would aid them in designing policy for the aging.

In order to facilitate this task, several Committee members assumed chairmanships of [subsidiary] task forces that were reflective of particular areas of concern that came up in the life of the Executive Office or among gerontologists. Professionals in the Commonwealth were asked to join such subcommittees and to work with them on a specific task. In this way, a number of talents were tapped and their know-how could be made available to the total Professional Task Force Committee. As of the present time, the following [subsidiary] task forces have been created: Community Health Nursing, Elderly Housing, Employment, Information and Referral, Legislation, Preretirement, Training, Nutrition, Home Care, Nursing Homes, Education of the Elderly, Image, Transportation, and Reorganization of the Executive Office Implementation. To establish an ongoing link with the Citizens Advisory Committee, its cochairmen were made members of the Professional Task Force Committee. They attend regularly its monthly meetings and on two occasions the two Committees met jointly.

ANALYSIS OF OPERATION OF THE PROFESSIONAL TASK FORCE

In order to analyze the operations of the Task Force, I would like to use three major patterns of activity or strategies that have served as a framework for a study at Brandeis University: (1) systemic reallocation; (2) regional and local advocacy; and (3) service delivery. Systemic reallocation is primarily directed at state legislatures. In addition to authorizations and allocation of funds for the aging, this strategy seeks legislation that affects eligibilities, standards, operating authority for programs and services.

In this respect, the Professional Task Force Committee was performing advocacy functions to marshal support for legislative programs, particularly during the reorganization phase of the State Government in Massachusetts. It was vital for the elderly that the Governor-appointed Executive Office of Elder Affairs became a "Department of Elder Affairs" by statutory legislation. This was achieved in December 1973 when the General Court voted to this effect.

Systemic reallocation functions were also involved when professional expertise, status, and prestige were utilized by the committee in order to help set standards for community health nursing, to appoint an ombudsman for nursing homes, and to support guaranteed income legislation (passed by the legislature and signed into law in December 1973). The second major pattern, regional and local advocacy, is designed to proliferate the number of regional and local organizations that can serve as generalized advocates for the aging in local communities. At this stage, the Professional Task Force Committee has been less involved in this activity, though it has been related to existing Councils on Aging in the State.

With regard to service delivery to benefit older persons, the Committee was perhaps most instrumental, as it designed a proposal for setting up a Home Care Service Delivery System as an alternative to institutionalization of older people. Home Care, subsequently, has become one of the major program foundations of the Executive Office of Elder Affairs. The design was hammered out by members of the Professional Task Force in many hours of deliberations and then submitted to the Citizens Advisory Committee. After their modifications had been incorporated, it was finally adopted by the Executive Office and has since become basic policy in the Commonwealth to provide alternatives to institutional care for the elderly.

The Committee has also developed a set of standards for housing of the elderly, participated in developing nutrition standards for Title VII programs, and is presently in the process of planning a conference to create an appropriate image of the elderly in the community. The Professional Task Force also has acted as a review committee for the State plan under Title III of the Amended Older Americans Act of 1973.

In summary, the activities carried out so far have included: (1) input of ideas and shaping program designs, such as the Home Care Proposal; (2) testing of plans and ideas put forth by the Executive staff, such as a review of the Title III State Plan; (3) dissemination of information affecting the elderly to the professional community in the Commonwealth; (4) lending support to the advocacy roles of the Executive Office by providing expert testimony in the State Legislature and by mobilizing professional community support to influence Congress and the State Legislature in support of particular legislation benefiting the elderly; (5) providing a liaison between professionals and older persons through link-up with the Citizens Advisory Committee and having the cochairmen of the Citizens Advisory Committee as members of the Professional Task force; (6) providing a critical perspective to the Executive Office, its staff, and its operation. This function is very important, and though it has been underplayed in the early stages since everybody was concerned with getting the Department of Elder Affairs on its feet in the first place, it will become a most significant function in the immediate future.

LIMITS AND CONSTRAINTS

Several limitations in the functions of the Committee can be discerned as of now: (1) Professionals are busy people; therefore their time is limited and they cannot always be available when they are needed most. (2) To design a new role and at the same time to perform is difficult at best; while advisory committees have existed before, the task force approach through which various committee members act also as chairmen of their own subcommittees and thereby increase and enlarge the range of activities of the overall Committee, had few models to follow. (3) No monitoring and evaluation unit had been placed in the Executive Office so far, and the Professional Task Force Committee was in no way equipped to fulfill an evaluative function although it was urgently needed. (4) Communication of data from the Office to the Committee was sporadic and the Professional Task Force Committee was not equipped to provide an inflow of communication to the Office as regularly as it should have. Staff and clerical services were minimal; the relationship with the Citizens Advisory Committee was sporadic, despite the fact that a linkage was provided in the structure. (5) The inevitable tension between operating out of political necessity and using a more deliberate approach created stress. When immediate action had to be forthcoming on the policymaking level, the professional group would have preferred to contemplate longer and to reflect more upon the action to be taken.

PRESENT EVALUATION AND A HYPOTHESIS

(1) Linkage of professionals and the elderly themselves has become closer but there are still wide gaps. Many professional interests and perceptions are not necessarily in harmony with the way older people view themselves and view professionals. There has been some attempt to provide such a linkage, which has resulted in greater appreciation of what professionals actually do and potentially can do. In many respects, such appreciation is still a one-way street. It is essential that both advisory committees develop closer ties. With the reorganization of the Executive Office accomplished, both advisory committees are now anchored in legislation and are sanctioned in their respective functions. This evidences recognition that advisory groups of professionals and of elderly citizens are essential to provide input and to make their voices heard in shaping policy by the Department of Edler Affairs.

(2) The influence of professionals upon State Units on Aging can be effectively utilized. Based upon the experience over the past two years, this author submits the following hypothesis: the degree of influence of professional as a group on a State Unit on Aging will be mediated by the following variables:

(a) A commitment of professionals to the work of the State Unit that is expressed through (i) commitment of their time on a regular basis and (ii) commitment of professional competence to the work of the State Unit, that includes a recognition of limitations of their knowledge, available and accessible data, and professional competence. Competence used is competence believed!

(b) Legitimation of a professional group as an advisory body which is sanctioned by the executive and legislative branches of government.

(c) Establishment of a continuous, professional relationship with the head and key staff of the State Unit, based on mutual respect which allows for a critical give and take.

(d) Acceptance by the professionals of the nature of an advisory (in contrast to a decision-making) relationship, recognizing that besides expert power, other sources of power, such as political, economic, senior power, will be utilized by many interest groups to influence policymaking in the State Unit.

(e) Maintenance of a clear focus on limited goals to be pursued at any one time, coupled with a flexible stance to adapt to changing conditions that demand an immediate response.

(f) Existence of an appropriate structure to allow for long-term goal pursuits and an immediate action response.

To what extent the State Unit will be able to make successful use of expert power to shape policy for the elderly and thereby effect a better quality of life for them is a major research question which we expect to pursue more systematically in the immediate future; the hypothesis advanced will guide us in this undertaking.

SOME CONCLUDING THOUGHTS

The experience in Massachusetts has demonstrated that a body of professionals linked together through an appropriate structure . . . can shape and effect policies that a State Unit on Aging eventually promulgates. To what extent the aged themselves will be beneficiaries of such efforts can only be indirectly assessed because the Professional Advisory Committee targets in on the State Unit on Aging, and not on the elderly themselves. The experience, know-how, and competence of professionals will be reflected in the kind of policy questions that they tackle, to the degree to which they apply themselves to such particular questions, and in the approach they take to these questions and issues. In the give and take of an advisory committee, individual professionals who are strongly beholden to a particular professional viewpoint tend to modify their positions without compromising their principles, to benefit the policymaking process. This became clear when we worked on designing the Home Care Proposal. In this instance, the output of various professionals was solicited, collected, and put into working papers, which were disseminated among the other members of the Committee. They related [the papers] to their particular areas of competence and finally an editing committee, composed of the chairman and other members, worked over the proposal and finally submitted it in draft form to the Secretary and then to the Citizens Advisory Committee. This procedure showed us that a cross-fertilization approach can yield significant results if people are enthusiastic enough to give of their time and competence.

At the beginning of the creation of the Executive Office there was great interest in participation of and by the professional community. Whether this will continue now when the Department becomes more institutionalized and more bureaucratized is another question. Presently there is still a good deal of enthusiasm and a strong interest by the members of the Committee; both have to be preserved because without them the commitment may flounder. What professionals offer must primarily accrue to the benefit of the elderly, although the professional community may reap secondary gains because of an advancement in their status. However, like all sources of power, expert power is also subject to abuse. Therefore, the checks and balances provided by citizens groups or organized elderly [are] essential to avoid "blind spots" and "notions of superior knowledge" which are inherent in an expert approach to policy shaping. [Experts] can and should make [their] expertise available in policy analysis, policy development, and in policy implementation. But, at the same time, [they] must recognize that, like everybody else, [they need] a corrective; otherwise, expert power will be guiding too much the direction of a State Unit on Aging (or any other government department) and this may not always be in the interest of those who are going to receive services and to be the beneficiaries of social programs. It has been said that the "functional approach emphasizes professionalization in the administration of public policy leading to bureaucratic autonomy from popular majorities and their elected representatives."

This Task Force under its new name, "Professional Advisory Committee to the Mass. Dept. of Elder Affairs," has continued ever since and though its objectives and tasks have changed in accordance with the changing and growing operations of the State Unit, it has played a significant role in the life of the Department until today.

Agency Policy and Social Policy

Social workers in the field of aging, as in other fields of practice, have a number of roles to play in the arena of social policy shaping—and not merely in carrying out the results of a haphazard, crisis-engendered and politically motivated *nonpolicy* that places them into a position of a passive *repair person*. While social workers are deliverers of social services, in the broadest sense of its definition, they are also coarchitects in the shaping of our social policies. Since values, knowledge, and power affect the making of such policies, social workers on any level of practice must be engaged in this enterprise.

> Regardless of whether a social worker devotes his [or her] career to practice as a caseworker, group worker, or community organizer, as administrator, researcher or teacher, he [or she] should have professional commitment to promote social change or reform. In order to develop such a commitment [the worker] needs corresponding attitudes, knowledge and skills which equip him [or her] to be motivated to understand the issues and problems involved and to be able to act in accordance with the knowledge and understanding gained.[13]

Kahn has phrased it succinctly: Practice enacts policy as much as policy enacts practice. All too often, social workers have allowed policy to enact practice without realizing that their very actions and activities in practice do indeed make policy. Nowhere is this so clear as in the microcosm of the agency. After all, most social work practice is taking place within and through a bureaucratic agency; and agencies set their own policies and adopt their own procedures. As a social system, an agency responds to its environment and influences that environment in turn. While bureaucratic structural imperatives and social work professional norms are sometimes at odds and not infrequently give rise to conflicts, the agency as a resource in the community also has influence and, if properly mobilized, may wield power.

A long-term care institution, a senior center, a day-care facility, or a home health care agency consists of policymakers, administrators, staff members, and clients—members or residents that can be galvanized into action. Their combined know-how, their experiences, and their sentiments can be a vital source in influencing social policies affecting the elderly beyond those who use these services. Whether they are aware of this potential, and whether leadership exists and is forthcoming to initiate action are vital questions.

Without leadership, the chances of doing something about a social condition or problem are slim, indeed. It is crucial ingredient in the struggle for social policy development. Sicne charity begins at home, however, social workers must begin to assess the degree to which agencies that employ them meet criteria of adequacy, availability, accessibility, acceptability, and accountability regarding the services that they render to older persons in the community. If nursing homes, family service agencies, multiservice centers, and protective service agencies do not fulfill the mandate of the community, or if clients, residents, and patients feel that the mandate itself is wanting, then social workers have a responsibility to challenge the policy, program, and services rendered and to seek changes in accord with the value positions of the social work profession.

The same arsenal of change strategies and techniques as have been reviewed in this chapter now come into play for deployment. An article called "Changing the Agency from Within"[14] offers an excellent distillation of three phases of intraorganizational change: formulation of goals, mobilization of resources, and use of interventive strategies and activities. A critical role for all social workers, regardless of position, function, or type of organization or service with which they are affiliated, is performing the role of advocate. Increasingly, all social workers engaged in work with older people must support and strengthen the activities and movements of and by the elderly and act as coalition partners to secure the "bicentennial rights" promised to older persons by translating them into societal obligations that are manifest in tangible benefits, programs, services, and validated roles:

I. The Right to Freedom, Independence and the Free Exercise of Individual Initiative. This should encompass not only opportunities and resources for personal planning and managing one's life-style but support systems for maximum growth and contributions by older persons to their community.

II. The Right to an Income in Retirement Which Would Provide an Adequate Standard of Living. Such income must be sufficiently adequate to assure maintenance of mental and physical activities which delay deterioration and maximize individual potential for self-help and support. This right should be assured regardless of employment capability.

III. The Right to an Opportunity for Employment Free from Discriminatory Practices Because of Age. Such employment when desired should not exploit individuals because of age and should permit utilization of talents, skills, and experience of older persons for the good of self and community. Compensation should be based on the prevailing wage scales of the community for comparable work.

IV. The Right to an Opportunity to Participate in the Widest Range of Meaningful Civic, Educational, Recreational, and Cultural Activities. The varying interests and needs of older Americans require programs and activities sensitive to their rich and diverse heritage. There should be opportunities for involvement with persons of all ages in programs which are affordable and accessible.

V. The Right to Suitable Housing. The widest choices of living arrangements should be available, designed and located with reference to special needs at costs which older persons can afford.

VI. The Right to the Best Level of Physical and Mental Health Services Needed. Such services should include the latest knowledge and techniques science can make available without regard to economic status.

VII. The Right to Ready Access to Effective Social Services. These services should enhance independence and well-being, yet provide protection and care as needed.

VIII. The Right to Appropriate Institutional Care When Required. Care should provide full restorative services in a safe environment. This care should also promote and protect the dignity and rights of the individual along with family and community ties.

IX. The Right to a Life and Death with Dignity. Regardless of age, society must assure individual citizens of the protection of their constitutional rights and opportunities for self-respect, respect and acceptance from others, a sense of enrichment and contribution, and freedom from dependency. Dignity in dying includes the right of the individual to permit or deny the use of extraordinary life support systems.[15]

The Social Work Profession and Aging

As has been evident throughout the history of American social work with the aging, the reluctance of the profession to assume a significant role and function in working with older adults has been as pronounced as the reluctance of social work professionals, and change in this direction is coming slowly, though quite markedly. We have delineated the value base that impinges upon social work practice, its goal continuum, the knowledge areas that are a foundation for working with the elderly, the existing programs and those yet to be created, and the skills and methods that must be mastered to accomplish the goals envisioned and to carry out the tasks. We have looked at the role of social workers in shaping social policy on aging; now we shall identify a few salient frontier issues facing social work with the aging from the perspective of the social work profession.

1. Social work with the aging: specialized field of practice or generic social work?
2. Direct clinical practice versus policy and management functions
3. Differential use of manpower and womanpower in providing services and career opportunities
4. Volunteerism

Specialization versus Generic Social Work

Social work is still involved in a discussion of what constitutes generic practice and what constitutes specialization. It was Harriet Bartlett who dealt with this controversy in the 1950s and assumed a leadership role in the debate. It was her constellation view of social work that lead to the working definition (see Chapter 4) in which she and her colleagues postulated that the components (values, purpose, sanction, knowledge, and method) are generic, but that practice is specific to person, situation, and environment. She subsequently delineated fields of practice such as social work in mental health, corrections, group services, etc.

Carol H. Meyer, writing in *Shaping the New Social Work*, uses a *systems framework* to conceptualize a practice that is holistic because it "allows for flexible modes of help as needed" and does not fit clients "into a single methodology."[16] She also asserts the specificity of practice, but overcomes the specialization of practice according to "social work methods." Specialization, respectively "concentration," now emerges according to problems (e.g., mental illness), status (e.g., migrants), age (e.g., youth, aging), or function (e.g., planning, direct service provision).

This author has developed five curriculum organization models for content on aging in social work education, detailed in Figure 14.1. These models span the continuum between incorporation of aging content into the core social work education curriculum, and specialization in aging.

Social work with the aging makes use of specialized knowledge about aging and the aged but deploys generic methods and skills in performing the social work tasks incumbent upon the practitioner in settings that are germane to older persons in our society today.

The National Association of Social Workers recognized this fact when it created a Council on Social Work Services to the Aging in 1976 that was similar to councils for other fields of practice. In the light of mandated reorganization of the NASW structure, the council recommended that a NASW task force unit on aging be continued for the following reasons:

> [It] makes manifest the Association's recognition of the rising political and social importance of the elderly in American society and their need for a share of the human services. Moreover, to sustain a continuing organizational unit within the Association recognizes the existence of an increasing number of retired social workers in NASW and offers some reassurance to them of the Association's interest in potential utilization of this relatively untapped pool of professional expertise.[17]

Specific recommendations by the Council to the NASW Board of Directors included that a task force on aging be appointed by the president to give leadership within NASW and to serve as a focal point on issues of social policy and practice related to the elderly in American society; that the task force on aging serve as the specific body in NASW charged with the development and recommendation of policies, positions, and strategies to the board in all pertinent areas of concern within the Association relating to the elderly in general and the elderly membership of NASW; and that the task force on aging concentrate its activities within six specific areas: long-term care of impaired elderly, geriatric day programs, effective use of retired social workers, mental health of the aging, legal problems of the elderly, and transportation of the aging.

In October, 1983, the Council on Social Work Education (CSWE) received a fourteen-month grant from AoA to "expand and strengthen the capability of social work faculties and programs to prepare practitioners and to train students at the master's and baccalaureate levels for practice with an increasingly larger aged population."[18] In this national curriculum and faculty development project in gerontology, the CSWE is seeking to assure that social workers are adequately trained to provide the following services to this country's elderly:[19]

- Mental health counseling
- Administration and planning in area agencies on aging
- Health services
- Housing arrangements

Figure 14.1. Major Curriculum Organization Models for Content on Aging in Social Work Education.

Dimension	Model 1 Incorporation within Curriculum (Integration)	Model 2 Incorporation and Addition of Special Courses or Clusters	Model 3 Specialization in Curriculum (Concentration)	Model 4 Multi-disciplinary Gerontology Program (Centers or Consortia)	Model 5 Dual Degree with Aging Specialty in Social Work and other Field
Educational Objectives: Attitudes Toward Aging/Aged	Appreciation of aging as development of values of aged people and as resource in society. Commitment to eliminate ageism as another form of prejudice and oppression.				
Knowledge about Aging/Aged	bio-psycho-socio-cultural aspects of aging and aged in breadth		Understanding of: bio-psycho-socio-cultural aspects of aging and aged: in greater depth	in greater depth and breadth	in greater depth and breadth
Skills in Working with Aging/Aged on Micro and Macro Levels	General ability to work with any age group, including the aged.	General ability to work with any age group, yet more specifically with aging.	Specific competence to work with the aging and general ability to work with other age groups.	Specific competence to work with the aging and general ability to work with other age groups.	Specific competencies to work with the aging and general ability to work with other age groups. Additional skills beyond social work.
Orientation to Learning/Teaching	From generic	to specific	From specific	to generic	Variable
Priority of "Aging" in Educational Institution	Low to Medium	Medium	Medium to High	Medium to High	Medium to High
Career Interests and Goals of Students	General social work practitioner		Gerontological social worker	Gerontological social worker and social gerontologist	Gerontological social worker and social gerontologist

Source: Louis Lowy, "Incorporation and Specialization of Content on Aging in the Social Work Curriculum," *Journal of Gerontological Social Work*, vol. 5(4), summer 1983, p. 39.

- Advocacy
- Group work
- Long-term care
- Family therapy

An advisory committee of social workers has been formed to assist Dr. Robert L. Schneider, Virginia Commonwealth University, School of Social Work, the Project Director, with the project's implementation. The following are committee members: Dr. Marion Beaver, School of Social Work, University of Pittsburgh; Dr. Marjorie Cantor, Graduate School of Social Services at Lincoln Center; Dr. Fred Ferris, American Association of Retired Persons; Dr. Florence Kohn, School of Social Work, Adelphi University; Dr. Marvin Kaiser, Undergraduate Social Work Program, Kansas State University; Dr. Louis Lowy, School of Social Work, Boston University; Dr. Lee Rathbone-McCuan, Department of Special Education and Social Work, University of Vermont; Dr. Gary M. Nelson, School of Social Work, University of North Carolina at Chapel Hill; Dr. Kermit Schooler, School of Social Work, Syracuse University; Dr. Barbara Silverstone, Lighthouse New York Association for the Blind.

As of November 1984 the Project finished its tasks. As a result, a network of faculty liaisons has been established in each graduate school of social work. They are assisting in the dissemination of information and the promotion of gerontology. Many undergraduate program directors are serving the same role.

A survey of all graduate programs has been completed by Drs. Gary Nelson and Robert L. Schneider which provides clear evidence that most administrators, faculty and students are aware of the importance of education for gerontological social work practice, although several issues of concern as to quantity and quality of educational offerings are suggested by the findings.

For the use of undergraduate faculty and advisors, a *Directory of Study Opportunities in Gerontology in Graduate Schools of Social Work* has been prepared, and four other volumes have been developed: 1. *The Integration of Gerontology into Social Work Educational Curricula*; 2. *Specialized Course Outlines for Gerontological Social Work Education*; 3. *A Curriculum Concentration in Gerontology for Graduate Social Work Education*; and 4. *Gerontology in Social Work Education: Faculty Development and Continuing Education*.

Direct Clinical Practice versus Policy and Management Functions

This dichotomy is rather academic today, since it is recognized that both functions and activities are essential. The issue is rather one of deciding whether these functions can be carried out by one and the same practitioner or whether they call for specialization within the field of aging or specialization within social work. If specialization is called for within the field of aging, would practitioners specialize along direct services and in planning and management? If specialization along these lines is called for within social work, would practitioners divide along the same sectors but encompass all substantive areas, such as direct service providers for families, children, and aged, and planners and administrators in areas of child services, family programs, and services to the aged?

The division of the pie has implications for the deployment of education and training of personnel as well as for knowledge and skill development, and design of social policies and programs. Therefore cogent and rational discourse on these issues coupled with the field-of-practice controversy will continue and not find easy resolution. Meanwhile both options are being pursued with implications for personnel and educational policy formulation and implementation.

As far as direct services are concerned, the issues today evolve around the questions: What are direct services to the aged? Are they means-tested social services or social utility social services? Are they intensive-treatment oriented services or care-managerial services? Are they supportive or protective services? Are they personal social services or social care services? (Social services include treatment, adjustment, protective services; social care includes helping measures such as hygiene, home health, homemakers and home chores, shopping escort services, etc.) Kamerman and Kahn capture this issue well:

> The real issue would seem to be that given some criteria of need and preference, what kinds of service and facilities programs best satisfy or are most appropriate for those needs? One major problem is the need to develop some standardized, consistent criteria for assessing individual needs, and a standardized classification of functional impairment, and then to provide a continuum or spectrum of facilities and services as appropriate. One objective should be to permit people to remain in their own homes as long as they can and want to. When this is no longer possible, protected or congregate housing facilities with varying amounts of personal and medical care should be available in reasonably close proximity to relatives and friends. . . .
>
> In reviewing community services for the aged, one is struck by the absence of a satisfactory, consistent organizing principle. Traditional formulations tend to utilize discrete, often dichotomous categories, such as institutional versus community-based provision, medical versus nonmedical care, long-term versus short-term care. Not only are the boundaries unclear but the distinction is often dysfunctional because this is not how needs are felt in the real world, where the needs of the aged are often cumulative and increase gradually over time. What is required in planning services for the aged is the development of a conceptual framework that encompasses a continuum or spectrum of needs. Moreover, we note [that the] major users of services other than socialization and recreational programs are those aged 75 and over. The most heavily used services are those involving a mix of health and social services. Regardless of whether they are provided in the home or outside the home, what characterizes these services is the element of practical personal care and help.
>
> In searching for an accurate formulation to describe these services we employ a term used in Britain which we think is particularly appropriate: the social care services. More precisely, social care is a term describing a particular cluster of practical helping measures, including personal care and hygiene (assistance with bathing and dressing); home health services (light practical nursing, assistance in

taking medication); homemaker services (meal preparation, light cleaning and laundry); shopping, chore, and escort services; and visiting and reassurance services.

Where the aged are concerned, social care services can encompass both in-home and out-of-home services, delivered in ordinary or congregate housing, provided from either a medical or a social service facility. They do not represent all the personal social services. Clearly, other types of services are needed for the "young" aged adjusting to retirement, for those wanting leisure-time programs, and so forth. Yet it seems equally apparent that these services are essential in caring for the aged (and also for the handicapped).

In fact, it would seem that social care services could become the cornerstone of a personal social services system for the aged.[20]

Differential Use of Manpower and Womanpower in Providing Services

The field of aging offers many creative opportunities to deploy a range of personnel—professional, paraprofessional, and volunteer. Professional social workers on the M.S.W. and B.A. levels are called upon to perform many interventive tasks in practice that have been discussed so far. Differential competencies of trained social workers with M.S.W. and B.A. degrees have been delineated by NASW, though it is admittedly quite difficult to arrive at satisfactory demarcation for each. In general, it is noted that B.A.-level workers in the provision of direct services should be able to communicate confidently with other people to convey accurately observations, analyses, and plans; establish and maintain purposeful relationships through which their clients' problems may be examined and effective helping strategies developed; function responsibly as team members and also independently within an agency; and work effectively with individuals, groups, or community structures.

Depending on the complexity of the tasks, the extent of and degree of supervision by an M.S.W. will be adjusted. Workers on the M.S.W. level in the provision of direct services should be able to carry out advanced practice functions: complex cases, groups, community problems, and in the management of service delivery, supervisory functions, administrative tasks, consultation, team management, staff training and development.

There are still many overlaps of functions between the two types of professional social workers, since it was only in 1970 when the NASW and the Council on Social Work Education recognized that the B.A. in social work was the first professional degree for entry. Thereupon, differential use of manpower and womanpower was officially recognized, although this recognition merely satisfied a long-existing direction in practice, particularly in the field of aging where relatively few M.S.W.s provided direct services. Semiprofessionals are usually classified under the job category of social service assistant, and many of them hold associate degrees after two years of study at junior colleges.

Notably in the field of aging were social service assistants employed, since the shortage of professional social work personnel and a reluctance of many to work with the elderly left little choice. The Benjamin Rose Institute, for example, had been experimenting with the use of social service assistants since the early 1960s.

> In setting up the project, the job of the nonprofessional worker was carefully defined as to role, scope, qualifications, and relation to professional staff. Use of the title "social service assistant" further served to designate the nonprofessional worker's role and relation to the caseworker; quite literally, [he or] she assists, facilitates, augments, and supplements the professional services, and [this person] and the caseworker operate as a closely knit team. It is always the professional worker's responsibility to define the service goals, exercise professional judgment, and represent the agency in situations in which such judgment is required.
>
> While the institute's experience in use of nonprofessional workers in accordance with the present pattern is still quite limited, the caseworkers to whom the social service assistants have been assigned express real conviction that the present plan provides improved service to clients. It also frees the professional worker to concentrate on those areas that require professional service and to increase the total number of clients given professional service. From the beginning of this project, emphasis has been on the social service assistant's job as one in its own right—facilitative, challenging, productive, and rewarding.[21]

A large number of services to the elderly are provided by volunteers. Thousands of hours are devoted to the myriad tasks that volunteers undertake in hospitals, extended care facilities, day-care and multi-service centers, home health programs, etc. They perform patient-care roles, help with letter writing and personal errands, and serve as recreational leaders, tutors, confidants, homemakers, shoppers, foster grandparents, board members, and advocates. The scope is practically unlimited. Proper recruitment, preservice and in-service training, supervision, and monitoring are imperative features in any volunteer program.

The demarcation lines among volunteer, semiprofessional, and professional are unclear and still changing. Using a team organization, people with a variety of skills and interests work together to offer a series of services, such as meals-on-wheels, homemaking, counseling, personal health care, friendly visiting, and recreational activities through group programs.

> Viewing the field of the aging through the perspective of differential use of manpower illuminates the complexity of the work to be done. Whether the practice task is to be case-finding, help in decision making, development of transactions between the aged person and his [or her] family, peers, or institutional contacts, or mobilizing essential resources, these interventions would be empty gestures without personnel available to carry out the tasks. Therefore, as case and program planning evolve in this field, manpower allocations will have to be integrated into the planning to deliver effective services.[22]

Pioneers can still reap the rewards of their search for adventure and for meeting challenges. Since aging as a field is not yet overcrowded, there is room to maneuver and room for experimentation.

Volunteerism

Older persons have traditionally been thought of as recipients of services instead of volunteers or providers of services.[23] As Perry points out, Havighurst's (1954) suggestions for incorporating certain functions of work into leisure to make it meaningful (social participation, routinization of life activity, creative self-expression, interesting experiences, and source of self-respect) may be accomplished through playing the role of volunteer. In his survey of fifty-six elderly persons, he found that 59 percent expressed a willingness to "contribute their time without pay to non-profit organizations in the community."[24] The most frequent response given for not volunteering at present was simply "no one asked me!" National programs such as the Retired Senior Volunteer Program, Foster Grandparent Program, Peace Corps/VISTA, and local programs such as "Across the Generations" of the Capital Children's Musuem in Washington are capitalizing on this potential for reciprocity. The older volunteers gain opportunities for self-affirmation and community agencies, and programs gain valuable resources in a time of severe budget cuts. Perry points out that an emerging role for human service workers could be that of volunteer coordinator.[25] The author would add to that the role of peer counselor trainer and the role of "broker" between our country's elderly, who have so much to gain from volunteering, and agencies and programs, who have so much to gain from enlisting their help.

Learning about Human Dignity

Many older people engage in learning about themselves and the world around them and about how to cope as well as how to understand. Educators as well as social workers have a ready market and a significant role to play in meeting the demands for learning, teaching, and training. Will we be ready to quench this thirst for information, knowledge, and help and the appetites for more learning and inquiry? The answer is not yet given.

Some years back Bertolt Brecht wrote a story called *The Undignified Old Lady*. It gives us a glimpse of a person's two lives in her past. Let us read and reflect upon it.[26]

THE UNDIGNIFIED OLD LADY

By Bertolt Brecht
Translation by Ditta Lowy

My grandmother was seventy-two years old when my grandfather died. He had a small printing shop in a small town in Baden where he worked with two assistants until his death. My grandmother had taken care of the old shaky house, cooked for the men and the children, all without help.

She was a small, thin woman with lively lizard's eyes, but slow of speech. She had raised five children on a mere pittance; she had given birth to seven.

She seemed to have shrunk over the years. Two of the children, the girls, went to America and two of the boys also moved away. Only the youngest, a sickly boy, remained in town. He became a printer and had a large family of his own. So she was alone in the house after my grandfather died.

The children exchanged letters dealing with the problem of what to do with her. One of them was willing to have her move in with him, and the printer wanted to move with his family into her house. But the old lady rejected all these suggestions and only wanted to accept a small monetary contribution from each of her children, whoever could afford it. The printing shop, long obsolete, brought almost nothing when sold and there were also debts to pay. The children wrote to her that she really could not live all by herself, but when she simply did not respond to that, they gave in and sent her a small monthly allowance. After all, so they thought, the printer had remained in the small town. So it was the printer who took it upon himself to inform his siblings about his mother's doings. The letters he wrote to my father and [what my father learned] two years later on the occasion of [his] visit there after my grandmother's funeral gave me an idea of what had transpired in those preceding two years.

It seems that, from the very beginning, the printer had been disappointed by my grandmother's refusal to welcome him into the rather large and now empty house. He lived with his four children in three rooms. But the old lady kept the contact with him to a minimum. She invited the children every Sunday afternoon for coffee. That was actually all.

She visited her son once or twice every three months and helped her daughter-in-law with preserving berries. The young woman inferred from some of her remarks, that the old lady found the small flat of the printer too confining. He, in turn, couldn't refrain from underlining such remarks in his report to my father.

To a written inquiry by my father what it was that the old lady was doing now to keep busy, the printer answered rather curtly: "She goes to the cinema." One must realize, that this was not a common pastime, not in the eyes of her children anyway. Thirty years ago the cinema was not what it is today. The theaters were miserable, poorly ventilated places, often located in old bowling alleys. Sensational posters at the door were advertising murders and tragedies. Mostly teenagers went there or loving couples because of the dark. Surely an old lady was an unusual sight there. And there was another aspect to the cinema as such. The ticket price was cheap enough, but pleasure was considered a frill, a waste of money, and wasting money was not respectable. My grandmother not only did not visit her son regularly, she also neither visited nor invited any of her friends. She never joined any of the *Kaffeeklatsches* in the town either. She chose to visit, often, the workshop of a cobbler located in a small street of doubtful repute where all kinds of unemployed people loitered about. The cobbler was a middle-aged man, who had traveled all over the world, but had not achieved anything worthwhile. People said that he drank a lot. Anyway, he was no company for my grandmother. The printer mentioned in a letter that he had pointed this out to his mother, but that she had replied coolly: "But he has seen the world." And that was all she had to say. It was not easy to discuss problems with my grandmother that she was unwilling to talk about.

About six months after my grandfather died, the printer wrote to my father that their mother was eating at the local inn every other day. What news! Grandmother who all her life had cooked for a dozen people and only ate the leftovers eating at an inn! What had gotten into her?

Soon after that, my father went on a business trip and took the opportunity to visit his mother. He arrived just as she was about to leave the house. She took her hat off again and offered him a glass of red wine and a zwieback. She seemed to be in a serene mood. She inquired about all of us but did not go into too much detail. Mainly she wanted to know if there were churches for the children. She was her usual self. The house was spotless of course and she looked healthy. The only indication of her changed life-style was that she did not take my father to visit my grandfather's grave. "You can go by yourself; it is the third one on the left in the eleventh row. I have an errand to do." The printer explained later that she probably had to see her cobbler. He complained a lot. "I sit here in this dump, with my family, have only five hours' work a day and that poorly paid, on top of that my asthma is bothering me again and there her house on Main Street is empty."

My father took a room at the inn but had somehow anticipated an invitation from his mother, if only going through the motion; but she did not mention anything. When the house used to be full, she always objected to his going to the inn to waste all that money!

Now, however she seemed to have finished with family obligations; she went her own new way in the evening of her life. My father, who had a good sense of humor, found her "quite cheery" and said to my uncle to let the old lady do what she wanted.

But what did she want?

The next report about her said that she had ordered a "Bregg," a horse-drawn carriage for an excursion into the country, and that just on an ordinary Thursday. The few times when we grandchildren had come to visit, grandfather had rented a Bregg like that. At that time, grandmother had always stayed at home, declined to come along. And after that came the trip to K, a bigger town two rail hours away. There were horse races there, and to the horse races my grandmother went.

The printer was thoroughly alarmed by now. He wanted to consult a doctor. My father shook his head when he read that letter, but rejected the idea of the consultation.

My grandmother had not gone to K by herself. She had taken along a young girl, a semi-imbecile, as the printer wrote, a kitchen maid from the inn where my grandmother ate every other day. This "cripple" played a very important part from now on.

My grandmother seemed to have taken to her in a big way. She took her to the cinema and to the cobbler, who by the way, turned out to be a Social Democrat and rumor had it that the two women played cards in the kitchen while drinking wine.

"She bought a hat for the cripple, with roses on top," wrote the printer, "and our Anna doesn't even have a communion dress." My uncle's letters got quite hysterical, dealt only with "the unworthy behavior of our dear mother" and nothing else. The rest I heard from my father.

The innkeeper whispered to him with a wink in his eye, "Mrs. B. is amusing herself now, one hears."

In reality my grandmother did not live these last years in wealth at all. When she did not eat at the inn, she only made herself some scrambled eggs, a little coffee, and her favorite zwieback. Other than that she treated herself to some cheap red wine which she imbibed from a small glass with her meals. She kept the house very clean, not only the kitchen and her bedroom, the only rooms she used. However she took a mortgage on the house without the knowledge of her children. Nobody ever knew what she did with the money. It seemed she had given it to the cobbler. After her death he moved to another town and supposedly opened a larger store for custom-made shoes.

Looking at it closely, she actually lived two lives, one after the other. The first one as daughter, wife, and mother; the second simply as Mrs. B., a single person without responsibilities, with modest, yet adequate means. The first life lasted six decades, the second no more than two years.

My father found out that during the last half year of her life she took certain liberties that ordinary people were not even aware existed. During the summer months, she rose at three o'clock in the morning just to walk through the quiet empty streets of the town that she had all to herself this way. And when the priest came to see her to help the old woman dispel her loneliness, she invited him—so they say—to the cinema.

She was not at all lonely. At the cobbler's, evidently lots of sociable people liked to spend their time and tell stories. A bottle of her own red wine was always there; she drank her small glassful of it while the others talked and gossiped about the prominent people in the town. This wine was only for her, although occasionally she brought some stronger stuff for the others.

She died unexpectedly on an afternoon in the autumn in her bedroom; not in her bed, but on a wooden chair at the window. She had invited the "cripple" for the evening at the cinema and so the girl was with her when she died. My grandmother was seventy-four years old. I saw a photo of her that showed her on her deathbed. It had been taken for her children. On it one can see a tiny wrinkled face with a thin wide mouth. Every feature small, yet not smallish. She had savored the long years of servitude and the short time of her freedom and eaten the whole "loaf" that is life to the very last crumb.

Has the old woman found the "sense of integrity" of which Erikson speaks, and put it all together? What does she teach social workers, what can we learn from her? . . .

Occupational Outlook for Careers in Working with the Aging

A growing variety and number of employment settings are provided primarily or exclusively for services to older persons. These include but are by no means limited to:

- Senior citizens, adult day-care centers
- Nursing homes and intermediate-care facilities
- Senior housing sites, retirement communities
- Nutrition sites, older worker employment programs, community care agencies
- State and area agency components of the national aging network
- Family service and counseling agencies
- Hospices

- Veterans Administration hospitals
- Legislative bodies
- Community planning agencies.

Recognition of the importance of designing and providing specialized programs, facilities, and services addressed to the older population has also been spreading rapidly among organizations and institutions serving the general population. Thus, personnel with relevant knowledge of social aspects of aging can also be found in:

- Banks and investment institutions
- Group medical practices, dental clinics
- Community health and mental health centers
- Travel agencies
- Personnel offices of large corporations and quasigovernment agencies
- Educational institutions
- Employment agencies
- Newspapers, publishing and broadcasting agencies.

Private social work practitioners are also building a clientele based upon their specialized knowledge and skills for working with older adults.

Employment Opportunities

There is no available estimate of the number of social workers working in the field of aging. Employment opportunities in this field are closely related to state and federal government funding for services to the elderly. Even though state and local governments have faced increased pressure from the federal government to keep spending for new programs at a minimum, the field of aging does not seem to be affected. The mandate contained in the 1978 and 1984 amendments to and funding authorizations of the Older Americans Act testifies to the continuing interest of Congress in assuring the availability of qualified manpower to perform the multiplicity of tasks and services found in the expanding field of aging. (*Newsweek* in October 1982 listed the field of gerontology as one of the growth industries of the future.)

Job opportunities for social workers in general vary widely by geographic area. It is difficult to predict the long-run job market conditions of any profession. Nonetheless, reports indicate that compared to the overall situation for social workers, social work graduates with training in the field of aging have fared well in the job market. A high percentage of graduates have found employment in aging-related settings. Some educators have reported receiving requests from around the country for graduates with a concentration in aging. Future job-market conditions for graduates educated in both social work and gerontology depend on the relationship between supply and demand. Compared to the services for other groups, however, aging services are largely in their infancy. Thus, the future demand for social workers in the field of aging is largely a function of a continual healthy expansion of aging services at a time when other services are faced with small growth and are even being cut back.

. . . And Now the Future

Statistical projections for the year 2000 point to a population of people over 65 of over 35 million, against a population of 87 million in the under 5-to-19 age bracket; in the year 2050, it is expected that over 67 million Americans will be over 65 as against 87 million in the under 5-to-19 age category out of a total population of over 310 million people. By 2050 the ratio of older persons will probably be one in five. Also, the older segment of the elderly population, those over 75, will increase at a faster rate than those between 60 and 75 years of age and claim a sizable share of the health and social resources for their care. Three and four generations of people and/or families alive together will create new intergenerational life pattens, relationships, and life-styles. With this demographic shift, the needs of the old and the economic problems they create for the proportionally decreasing number of young are becoming social concerns. At the same time, the political influence of the aged has to be reckoned with: they go to the polls in larger numbers than younger people.

Donald Cowgill and Lewelyn Holmes postulate several universals about the aged in every society. For example, they constitute a minority within the total population, and since females outnumber males, widows constitute a high proportion of the older population. There is a tendency of people classified as old to shift to more sedentary, advisory, supervisory roles, involving less physical exertion and more concern with group maintenance than with economic production. In all societies, they point out, some older persons continue to act as political, judicial, and civic leaders; and mores prescribe some mutual responsibility between old parents and their adult children. All societies value life and seek to prolong it. But they find that variations are pronounced and differ from culture to culture, from society to society.[27] As Butler states:

> Sociocultural attitudes, events, and institutions, transitory and enduring, affect the psychological experience of aging. Indeed, some sociocultural phenomena are so intense in their effects that they handicap recognition and study of the basic processes of aging, biological as well as psychological. Moreover, personal issues, which may often be traced in more superficial sociocultural phenomena, potently affect both the concept and the experience of aging. Public attitudes may reflect an older person's struggle with his [or her] fear of aging and death, or lead to sentimental over-reaction to, or grim rejection of, the older person by the younger generation. Adults may be troubled by aspects of their residual dependence on their parents and by their pain at seeing those upon whose judgment they so long depended deteriorate into states of incoherence and incontinence.[28]

We can assume that the aged cohort of tomorrow will be affected by their historical heritage and will respond differently to the challenges of their days.

> The politicalization of older people that reemerged in the late 1960s when it was recognized that "senior power" has the potential for effecting essential changes through collective action will continue. The first major attempt in the 1930s which culminated with the Townsend Movement had lost its momentum in the 1940s for a variety of reasons (see Chapter 2).

However, the elderly of today and tomorrow are less likely to accept with resignation and gratitude a reduced status and a reduced standard of living, lack of opportunities, and a sense of powerlessness than did their forebears. Over 20 million voters will participate in the political and legislative processes; and senior citizens' organizations, self-help groups, and social action movements are emerging to counteract the neglect of the aged by the dominant power groups in American society. If anything, the appearance of older adult organizations with the intent to produce social action on behalf of the elderly toward improving their status and social and economic conditions may have heralded a new dawn in the life of older people. Binstock thinks that, at most, only some roles in the political system may be exchanged, and aging interest groups may merely achieve incremental gains rather than power for the elderly as a whole.

The changing nature of the older population will contribute toward this trend. In the future, more older people will be native born, better educated, will have better access to improved health care and also will have had a higher standard of living. It is, therefore, likely that they will have higher expectations in terms of health care, living facilities, and the amenities of life. During their young and middle years, they will have been more aware of the prospects of retirement. They will be more sophisticated about availing themselves of organized programs of assistance, about educational and recreational activities, and about their group potential in social action. They will also have reached a milestone period in world history as they have been exposed to rapid postindustrial social and economic changes. Therefore, any social policy with regard to the aged has to anticipate what the future needs of our present younger population will be like.

Perhaps the most important item on the agenda of tomorrow is a serious commitment to research on aging as a lifelong process and on social policy questions that affect the young and the old. The Gerontological Society [of America] has stated some of the most basic research issues as follows: Who are the elderly? What needs do they have? What kind of services are best suited to meet their needs? How can they be delivered and by what kind of people? Do such services, when provided, effect positive changes among the elderly? Social welfare research is essential in order to base plans on a more rational footing and to provide services that are commensurate with the needs and tasks of older people.[29]

Carol Meyer summarizes the implication for social work:

As social work itself ages and goes through its developmental crises, one discovers that experimentation is among the essential tasks of a maturing profession and the citing of what is not known as well as what is known. As with manpower utilization, an evolving field has the opportunity to build in research at the beginning to demonstrate and evaluate effectiveness. Needless to say, the field of aging cannot be the only field in social work to develop research methodology. Fortunately, maturing is a generalized process that is occurring social work at large, in spite of all obstacles, just as it occurs in normal life.

The field of aging contains in microcosm all the elements found in the field of social work at large. It may even have a special quality in that it is a field open to new investigation and innovation. What is known for sure is that aged people survive with greater health and integrity when they are engaged in life. The influence of social workers, using their special knowledge and skills to sustain and at times create pathways between the aged person and his [or her] immediate world, has the potential of becoming a modern-day social invention that will exact intellectual as well as emotional excitement for the practitioner in search of a developing field.[30]

We have come full circle. Beginning with the history of social work's encounter with older persons, we have looked at its value base and its effect on practice; at its goal continuum; its source of knowledge—tentative and hypothetical as are all findings in gerontology till now; and at its intervention stances, working with individual older persons, with families and groups, with community organizations and social-action bodies. We have reviewed the role of social workers in influencing our social policy toward the aged and have outlined a series of issues in the profession that have bearing upon the role of working not just with older people, but with people of all ages today and tomorrow, since at any age there are challenges to be met, potentialities to be discovered, and promises to be fulfilled.

References

1. Elaine Brody and Stanley Brody, "Decade of Decision for the Elderly," *Social Work*, vol. 19 (September 1974), p. 545.
2. Paul Kershner and Ira Hirschfield, "Public Policy and Aging," in *Aging—Scientific Perspectives and Social Issues* (New York: Van Nostrand, 1975), p. 354.
3. Ibid., pp. 356–357.
4. Ibid., p. 356.
5. Ibid., p. 357.
6. Louis Lowy, *Social Policies and Programs on Aging* (Lexington, Mass.: D. C. Heath, 1984), pp. 8–9.
7. Neil Gilbert and H. Specht, *Dimensions of Social Work Policy* (Englewood Cliffs, N.J.: Prentice-Hall, 1974), p. 29.
8. Brody and Brody, op. cit., p. 6.
9. Ibid., pp. 6–7.
10. Ibid., p. 9.
11. Kenneth Benne and Robert Chin, "General Strategies for Effecting Changes in Human Systems," in K. Benne, W. Bennis, and R. Chin (eds.), *Planning of Change* (New York: Holt, Rinehart and Winston, 1969), pp. 31–32.
12. Louis Lowy, "The Functions of Professionals in Gerontology in Policy Making: A Case History from Massachusetts," *Aging and Human Development*, vol. 6, no. 1 (Farmingdale, N.Y.: Baywood, 1975).
13. Louis Lowy, "Social Work and Social Statesmanship," *Social Work*, vol. 5, no. 2 (April 1960), p. 99.
14. Rino Patti and H. Resnick, "Changing the Agency from Within," *Social Work*, vol. 17, no. 4 (July 1972), pp. 48–57.
15. Bicentennial Charter for Older Americans, prepared by The Federal Council on the Aging, January 1976.
16. Carol H. Meyer, "Direct Service in New and Old Contexts," in A. Kahn, ed., *Shaping the New Social Work* (New York: Columbia University Press, 1973), p. 51.
17. "Council on Social Work Services to the Aging." Mimeographed, 1976.

18. *Social Work Agenda*, vol. 3, no. 1, January 1984, p. 2.
19. Schneider, Robert L., *Memorandum Regarding National Curriculum Project in Gerontology*, Council on Social Work Education, New York, January 30, 1984.
20. S. Kamerman and A. Kahn, *Social Services in the United States* (Philadelphia: Temple University Press, 1976), pp. 383–384.
21. Marcella Farrar and Mary Hemmy, "Use of Nonprofessional Staff in Work with the Aged," NASW Reprints, *Social Work*, vol. 8 (July 1963), p. 7.
22. Meyer, NASW, op. cit., p. 7. *Social Work with the Aging.* Compendium of articles published by the National Association of Social Workers. ed. Carol Meyer (New York: Columbia University Press, 1973), p. 7.
23. Perry, William H., "The Willingness of Persons 60 or Over to Volunteer: Implications for the Social Services," *Journal of Gerontological Social Work*, vol. 5, 4, Summer 1983, pp. 107–118.
24. Ibid., p. 110.
25. *Journal of Gerontological Social Work*, vol. 5, 4 (Summer 1983).
26. Bertolt Brecht, *The Undignified Old Lady*, (Frankfurt, W. Germany: Suhr Kamp Verlag, 1919), translation by Ditta Lowy.
27. Donald Cowgill and L. Holmes, *Aging and Modernization* (Englewood Cliffs, N.J.: Appleton-Century-Crofts, 1972).
28. Robert Butler, "Some Observations on Culture and Personality in Aging," *Social Work*, vol. 8 (January 1963), p. 79.
29. Louis Lowy, "Social Welfare and the Aging," in M. Spencer and J. Dorr, eds., *Understanding Aging* (Englewood Cliffs, N.J.: Appleton-Century-Crofts, 1975), p. 173.
30. Meyer, NASW, op. cit., p. 7.

Bibliography*

Abraham, K., "A Short Study of the Development of the Libido Viewed in the Light of Mental Disorders," in *Selected Papers on Psychoanalysis*, vol. 1 (New York: Basic Books, 1954), pp. 418–501. (Cited in Ralph J. Kahana, "Grief and Depression," p. 28, and in United Nations, *The Aging: Trends and Policies*).

Abramson, Marcia, "Ethical Dilemmas for Social Workers in Discharge Planning," *Social Work in Health Care*, vol. 6, no. 4 (Summer 1981), pp. 33–41.

Adams, James P., Jr., "Service Arrangements Preferred by Minority Elderly: A Cross-Cultural Survey," *Journal of Gerontological Social Work*, vol. 3, 2 (Winter 1981), pp. 39–57.

Adams, Mary, Caston, Mary Ann, and Davis, Benjamin G., *A Neglected Dimension in Home Care of Elderly Disabled Persons: Effect on Responsible Family Members*. Paper presented at the 32nd annual scientific meeting of the Gerontological Society, Washington, D.C., November 1979.

Aisenberg, Ruth, and Kastenbaum, Robert, *The Psychology of Death* (New York: Springer, 1972).

Allen, R. E., "A Study of Subjects Discussed by Elderly Patients in Group Counseling," *Social Casework* (July 1962), pp. 360–366.

Altman, Kerry Paul, "Psychodrama with the Institutionalized Elderly: A Method for Role-Reengagement," *Journal of Group Psychotherapy, Psychodrama and Sociometry*, vol. 36, 3 (Fall 1983), pp. 87–95.

Anderson, John Edward, and Kastenbaum, Robert (eds.), *Contributions to the Psychobiology of Aging* (New York: Springer, 1965).

Archbold, Patricia, "Impact of Parent-Caring on Women," *Family Relations*, 32 (1983), pp. 39–45.

* This bibliography contains all references cited in the first and second editions.

410

Association for Gerontology in Higher Education (A.G.H.E.) Newsletter, vol. 4, no. 3 (Fall 1981).

Atchley, Robert C., *The Social Forces in Later Life: An Introduction to Social Gerontology* (Belmont, Calif.: Wadsworth, 1972). See also edition, 1977.

Austin, C. D., "Case Management in Long Term Care" *Health and Social Work*, vol. 8, no. 1 (1983).

————, *The Sociology of Retirement* (Cambridge, Mass.: Schenkman, 1976).

Babcock, Charlotte. "Inner Stress in Illness and Disability," in Howard J. Parad and Roger R. Miller (eds.), *Ego-Oriented Casework* (New York: Family Service Association of America, 1963), pp. 45–64.

Barns, Eleanor K., Lack, Ann, and Shore, Herbert (eds.), "Guidelines to Treatment Approaches," *Gerontologist* (Winter 1973).

Barresi, Charles, and Brubaker, Timothy, "Clinical Social Workers' Knowledge About Aging: Responses to the 'Facts on Aging Quiz,'" *Journal of Gerontological Social Work*, vol. 2, 2 (Winter 1979), pp. 137–146.

Barrett, Carol J., "Effectiveness of Widow's Groups in Facilitating Change," *Journal of Consulting and Clinical Psychology*, vol. 46, no. 1 (1978), pp. 20–31.

Bartlett, Harriett, *Common Base of Social Work Practice* (New York: NASW, 1970).

Barton, M. G., "Group Counseling with Older Patients," *Gerontologist* (March 1962), pp. 51–56.

Beaulieu, Elise Martini, and Karpinski, Judith, "Group Treatment of Elderly with Ill Spouses," *Social Casework* (1981).

Beauvoir, Simone de, *The Coming of Age* (New York: Putnam Press, 1972).

Bengtson, Vern L., *The Social Psychology of Aging* (Indianapolis: Bobbs-Merrill, 1973).

————, and Treas, J., "The Changing Family Context of Aging and Mental Health," in J. E. Birren and R. B. Sloan (eds.), *Handbook of Mental Health and Aging*, (Englewood Cliffs, N.J.: Prentice-Hall, 1978).

Benne, Kenneth, Bennis W., and Chin, R., *Planning of Change*, 2nd ed. (New York: Holt, Rinehart and Winston, 1969).

Bennett, Louis L., *Adult Protective Services and Law: Some Relevant Socio-Legal Considerations* (New York: American Public Welfare Association, 1965).

Berezin, Martin A., and Cath, Stanley, *Geriatric Psychiatry* (New York: International Universities Press, 1965).

Berger, M., and Berger, L., "Psychogeriatric Group Approaches," in C. Sager and H. Kaplan (eds.), *Progress in Group and Family Therapy* (New York: Brunner/Masel, 1972), Chap. 42, pp. 726–736.

Berl, Fred, "Growing Up to Old Age," *Soc. Work* (January 1963).

Berlatsky, Marjorie N., "Some Aspects of the Marital Problems of the Elderly," *Soc. Casework*, vol. 43, no. 5 (May 1962), pp. 233–237.

Binstock, Robert, "Aging and the Future of American Politics," *Annals Amer. Academy Political Soc. Sci.*, vol. 415 (Sept. 1974), pp. 199–212.

————, and Shanas, Ethel, *Handbook of Aging and the Social Sciences* (New York: Van Nostrand Reinhold, 1976).

Birren, James E., *The Psychology of Aging* (Englewood Cliffs, N.J.: Prentice-Hall, 1964).

————, (ed.), *Relations of Development and Aging* (Springfield, Ill.: Charles C. Thomas, 1964).

————, and Sloane, R. Bruce (eds.), *Handbook of Mental Health and Aging* (Englewood Cliffs, N.J.: Prentice-Hall, 1980).

Blenkner, Margaret, "Developmental Considerations and the Older Client," in James E. Birren (ed.), *Relations of Development and Aging* (Springfield, Ill.: Charles C. Thomas, 1964), pp. 247–266.

———, "Social Work and Family Relationships in Later Life with Some Thoughts on Filial Maturity," in Ethel Shanas and Gordon F. Streib (eds.), *Social Structure and the Family* (Englewood Cliffs, N.J.: Prentice-Hall 1965), pp. 46–59.

———, "Social Work and Family Relationships in Later Life with Some Thoughts on Filial Maturity," in E. Shanas and G. Streib (eds.), *Social Structure and the Family Generational Relations* (Englewood Cliffs, N.J.: Prentice-Hall, 1965).

Block, M., "Exiled Americans: The Plight of Indian Aged in the United States," in D. Gelfand and A. Kutzik (eds.), *Ethnicity and Aging* (New York: Springer, 1979).

Blonsky, Lawrence E., "Formation of a Senior Citizen Tenants Council," *Soc. Work*, vol. 18, no. 5 (September 1973), pp. 76–83.

Boehm, Werner, *Curriculum Study of the Council on Social Work Education*, vol. I, New York, 1959.

Branch, L. G. and Jette, A. M., "A Prospective Study of Long-term Care Institutionalization among the Aged." *American Journal of Public Health* 1984 (in press).

Brearley, C. Paul, *Social Work, Aging and Society* (London: Routledge & Kegan Paul, 1975).

Brecht, Bertolt, *Die Unwürdige Greisin*, Ditta Lowy (trans.) (Frankfurt-am-Main: Suhrkamp Verlag, 1919.

Brieland, Donald, *Contemporary Social Work* (New York: McGraw-Hill, 1975).

Britton, J., *Personality Changes in Aging* (New York: Springer, 1972).

Broberg, Merle, Melching, Dolores E., and Maeda, Daisaku, "Planning for the Elderly in Japan," *Gerontologist*, vol. 15, no. 3 (June 1975), pp. 230–235.

Brody, Elaine, "Institutionalization of the Aged: A Family Crisis," *Family Process*, vol. 5, no. 1 (1955), pp. 76–90.

———, "The Aging Family," *Gerontologist*, vol. 6, no. 4 (December 1966).

———, "Serving the Aged: Educational Need as Viewed by Practice," *Soc. Work*, vol. 15, no. 4 (October 1970), pp. 42–51.

———, *Long Term Care for Older People* (New York: Human Sciences Press, 1977).

———, "'Women in the Middle' and Family Help to Older People," *Gerontologist*, 21, 5 (1981), pp. 471–480.

———, and Brody, Stanley, "Decade of Decision for the Elderly," *Soc. Work*, vol. 19, no. 5 (1974), pp. 544–554.

———, et al., *A Social Work Guide for Long-Term Care Facilities* (Rockville, Md.: NIMH, 1974).

Brotman, Herman B., "Summary Table 'A': Middle Series Projections, All Ages and 65 +, By Race and Sex, 1982–2050 (Numbers in Thousands)." (November 1982).

Buckley, Mary, *The Aged Are People Too.* (Port Washington, N.Y.: National University Publications Press, 1972).

Bull, Naomi, "Basic Knowledge for Work with the Aging," *Gerontologist*, vol. 9, no. 3 (Autumn 1969).

Burns, Jennifer, and Miller, Naomi, "Changing Ego Functions of the Aged and Their Implications for Social Group Work Intervention." Unpublished paper, Boston University, 1968.

Burnside, Irene Mortenson, "Loss: A Constant Theme in Group Work with the Aged," *Hospital Community Psychiatry*, vol. 21 (June 1970), pp. 173–177.

_____ , "Sexuality and Aging," in Irene Mortenson Burnside (ed.), *Sexuality and Aging* (University of Southern California Press, 1975), pp. 42–53.

_____ , *Working with the Elderly: Group Process and Techniques* (Belmont, Calif.: Duxbury Press, 1978).

_____ , *Working with the Elderly: Group Process and Techniques*, 2nd ed. (Monterey, Calif.: Wadsworth, 1984).

Busse, Edward W., and Pfeiffer, Eric, *Behavior and Adaptation in Late Life* (Boston: Little, Brown, 1969).

Butler, Robert, "Some Observations on Culture and Personality in Aging," *Soc. Work*, January, 1963. (Also in Carol H. Meyer, ed., *Social Work with the Aging.*)

_____ , *Sex After Sixty: A Guide for Men and Women in Their Later Years* (New York: Harper & Row, 1976).

_____ , *Why Survive? Being Old in America* (New York: Harper & Row, 1975).

_____ , and Lewis, Myrna L., *Aging and Mental Health, Positive Psychosocial Approaches* (St. Louis: Mosby, 1973).

_____ , and Lewis, Myrna, *Aging and Mental Health: Positive Psychosocial and Biomedical Approaches* (St. Louis, Mo.: Mosby, 1982).

_____ , and Lewis, Myrna, *Aging and Mental Health* 3rd ed. (St. Louis, Mo.: Mosby, 1983).

Cameron, Paul, and Henry Beber, "Sexual Thought Throughout the Life Span," *Gerontologist*, vol. 13, no. 2.

Campbell, A., "Politics Through the Life Cycle," *Gerontologist*, vol. II (197), pp. 112–117.

Carpa, Frances (ed.), *Retirement* (New York: Behavioral Publications, 1972).

Carr, A. C., *A Lifetime of Preparation for Bereavement* (New York: Foundation of Thanatology, 1969).

Carter, Beryl, and Siegel, Sheldon, *An Annotated Selective Bibliography for Social Work with the Aging* (New York: CSWE, 1968).

Cath, Stanley, "Some Dynamics of Middle and Later Years," *Smith College Studies in Soc. Work*, vol. 33 (February 1963), pp. 97–126.

Cicirelli, Victor, *Helping Elderly Parents: The Role of Adult Children*, (Boston, Mass.: Auburn House, 1981).

Clark, Margaret, "The Anthropology of Aging," *Gerontologist*, vol. 7, no. 1 (1970).

_____ , and Anderson, Barbara, *Culture and Aging* (Springfield, Ill.: Charles C. Thomas, 1967), pp. 294–301.

Coleman, Peter G., "Social Gerontology in England, Scotland and Wales: A Review of Recent and Current Research," *Gerontologist*, vol. 15, no. 3 (June 1975), pp. 219–229.

_____ , "Social Gerontology in the Netherlands: A Review of Recent and Current Research," *Gerontologist*, vol. 15, no. 3 (June 1975), pp. 257–263.

Collins, Alice, and Pancoast, Diane, *Natural Helping Networks* (New York: N.A.S.W., 1976).

Community Organization and Planning for Older Adults. (Waltham, Mass.: Brandeis University, 1961).

Compton, Beulah R., and Burt Galaway, *Social Work Processes.* (Homewood, Ill.: Dorsey Press, 1975 and 1984).

Council on Social Work Education, *Toward Better Understanding of the Aging: Social Work Education for Better Services to the Aging* (1958).

Cowgill, Donald, and Holmes, L., *Aging and Modernization* (Englewood Cliffs, N.J.: Appleton-

Century-Crofts, 1972).

Cryer, Philip E., "Decisions Regarding the Provision on Withholding of Therapy," in Natalie Abrams and Michael Buckner (eds.), *Medical Ethics: A Clinical Textbook and Reference for the Health Care Professions* (Cambridge, Mass.: M.I.T. Press, 1983).

Cumming, Elaine, and Henry, William, *Growing Old—the Process of Disengagement* (New York: Basic Books, 1961).

Delgado, Melvin, "Politics Among Elderly Hispanics," *Journal of Gerontological Social Work,* vol. 6, no. 1 (September 1983).

Dickman, Irving R., *Making Life More Livable* (New York: American Federation for the Blind, 1983).

Diggs, B. J., "The Ethics of Providing for the Economic Well-Being of the Aging" in Robert J. Havighurst and B. L. Neugarten (eds.), *Social Policy, Social Ethics and the Aging Society* (Chicago, Ill.: University of Chicago Press, 1976), pp. 55–65.

Dobrof, Rose, and Litwak, Eugene, *Maintenance of Family Ties of Long-Term Care Patients: Theory and Guide to Practice.* DHEW Publication, number (ADM) 79-400, 1977 and 1979.

Donahue, Wilma, "Age with a Future" (NCWS Proceedings), *Soc. Work in the Current Scene,* vol. 77 (1950), pp. 70–86.

———, Gottsman, Leonard, and Coons, Dorothy, *A Therapeutic Milieu for Geriatric Patients.* Unpublished paper, University of Michigan, 1969.

Dowd, James, "Aging as Exchange: A Preface to Theory," *J. Gerontology,* vol. 30, no. 5 (1975).

Dowling, Rupert A., and Copeland, Elaine J., "Services for the Black Elderly; National or Local Problem?" *Journal of Gerontological Social Work,* vol. 2(4) (Summer 1980), pp. 289–303.

Downey, Gregg W., "Resident Councils Give Patients the Vote." *Modern Nursing Home,* October 1971, pp. 58–60.

———, "Panthers Striking for Power," *Modern Health Care,* vol. 2, no. 2 (1974), pp. 65–69.

Dynamic Factors in the Role of the Caseworker with the Aged. Insitute Sponsored by Central Bureau for the Jewish Aged, 1960.

Ehrlich, Ira F., and Ehrlich, Phyllis D., "A Service Delivery Model for the Aged at the Communal Level," *Gerontologist,* vol. 14, no. 3 (June 1974), pp. 241–244.

Ehrlich, Phyllis, *Elderly Health Advocacy Group: Handbook of Organizing Principles* (Springfield, Ill.: Department of Public Health, 1980).

Ehrlich, Phyllis, "Elderly Health Advocacy Group: An Interpretative Planning Model of Elderly Consumers and Service Deliverers," The Gerontologist, vol. 23, no. 6 (December, 1983).

Eisdorfer, Carl, and Powell, L. M., *The Psychology of Adult Development and Aging* (Washington, D.C.: APA, 1973).

Emergy, Marian, "Casework with the Aging—Today's Frontier," *Soc. Casework,* vol. 39, no. 8, pp. 455–458.

Encyclopedia of Social Work, vol. 16 (New York: NASW, 1971).

Encyclopedia of Social Work, vol. 17 (Washington, D.C.: NASW, 1977).

Epstein, Leon J., "Symposium on Age Differentiation in Depressive Illness, Depression in the Elderly," *J. Gerontology,* vol. 31, no. 3 (May 1976), pp. 278–282.

Erikson, Erik H., "Identity and the Life Cycle," in *Papers by Erik H. Erikson* (New York: International Universities Press, 1959).

Estes, Caroll L., *The Aging Enterprise,* (San Francisco, Calif., Jossey Bass, 1979).

Euster, Gerald, "A System of Groups in Institutions for the Aged," *Soc. Casework*, vol. 52, no. 8 (October 1971), pp. 523–529.

Evaluative Research on Social Programs for the Elderly. Washington, D.C.: U.S. Dept. of HEW, Publication No. 77-20120, 1977.

Every Ninth American (1982 Edition). An Analysis for the Chairman of the Select Committee on Aging, House of Representatives, 97th Congress, 2nd Session, July, 1982.

"Every Tenth American." *Developments in Aging*, 1975 and January–May 1976. U.S. Senate Report (Washington, D.C.: U.S. Government Printing Office, 1976, 1977).

Facts About Older Americans. Department of HEW (Washington, D.C.: U.S. Government Printing Office, 1977).

Falck, Hans. S., "The Membership Model of Social Work," *Social Work*, no. 29 (1984), pp. 155–160.

Families: Aging and Changing. Hearing Before the Select Committee on Aging, House of Representatives, 96th Congress, 2nd Session, November 24, 1980, San Diego, California. (Washington, D.C.: United States Government Printing Office, 1981).

Farrar, Marcella, and Hemmy, Mary, "Use of Nonprofessional Staff in Work with the Aged." *Soc. Work*, July 1963. (Also in Carol H. Meyer, ed., *Social Work with the Aging*).

Federal Programs Benefiting the Elderly, revised edition. A Reference Guide by the Select Committee on Aging, House of Representatives, 98th Congress, First Session. (Washington, D.C.: United States Government Printing Office, 1983).

Feil, Naomi, "Group Therapy in a Home for the Aged," *Gerontologist*, September 1967, pp. 192–195.

Felstein, Ivor, *Sex in Later Life* (Baltimore: Penguin Books, 1973).

Ferrari, Nelida, "Assessment of Individuals in Groups of Older Adults," in *Social Group Work with Older People* (Washington, D.C.: NASW, 1961).

Fisher, Leon D., and Solomon, Jeffrey R., "Guardianship: A Protective Service Program for the Aged," *Soc. Casework*, December 1974, pp. 618–621.

Ford, S., "Ego Adaptive Mechanisms of Older Persons," *Soc. Casework*, vol. VI, no. 3 (January 1965), p. 16.

Forman, Mark, "Conflict, Controversy and Confrontation in Group Work with Older Adults," *Soc. Work*, vol. 12, no. 1 (January 1967), pp. 80–85.

Fraley, Ivonne, "A Role Model for Practice," *Soc. Serv. Rev.*, vol. 43, no. 2 (June 1969).

Frankel, Charles, "Social Values and Professional Values," CSWE; *J. Education Soc. Work*, vol. 5, no. 1 (spring 1969).

Frankfather, Dwight L., Smith, Michael, and Caro, Francis G., *Family Care of the Elderly: Public Initiatives and Private Obligations* (Lexington, Mass.: Lexington Books, 1981).

Freed, Ann O., "The Family Agency and the Kinship System of the Elderly," *Soc. Casework*, vol. 56(10) December 1975, pp. 579–586.

Frey, Louise, and Meyer, M., "Exploration and Working Agreement in Two Social Work Methods," in S. Bernstein (ed.), *Explorations in Group Work* (Boston: Milford House, 1969).

Furukawa, Chiyoko, and Shomaker, Dianna, *Community Health Services for the Aged* (Rockville, Md.: Aspen Systems Corp., 1982).

Gadow, Sally, "Medicine, Ethics and the Elderly," *Gerontologist*, vol. 20, no. 6 (1980), pp. 680–685.

Garland, James, "The Relationship Between Social Group Work and Group Therapy: Can a Group Therapist be a Social Group Worker, Too?" Paper presented at the fifth annual Symposium on Social Work with Groups, Detroit, Michigan, October 21, 1983.

———— , Kolodny, R., and Jones, H., "A Model in Stages of Development of Social Group Work," in S. Bernstein (ed.), *Explorations in Group Work* (Boston: Milford House, 1969).

Geist, Harold, *The Psychological Aspects of the Aging Process* (St. Louis: Green, 1968).

Gelfand, Donald, *The Aging Network*, 3rd edition (New York: N.Y. Springer Publishing Co., 1983).

Gelwicks, Louis E., *Transportation and Its Influence upon the Quality of the Older Person's Relationships with the Environment.* Unpublished paper, University of Southern California Gerontology Center, 1970.

Germain, Carol B., and Gitterman, Alex, *The Life Model of Social Work Practice*, (New York: Columbia University Press, 1980).

Getzel, George, "Social Work with Family Caregivers to the Aged," *Social Casework* (1981) pp. 201–209.

———— , and Mellor, M. Joanne, "Introduction: Overview of Gerontological Social Work in Long Term Care," *Journal of Gerontological Social Work*, vol. 5, no. 1/2 (New York: The Haworth Press, 1982).

Getzel, Jessica, "Resident Councils and Social Action," *Gerontological Social Work Practice in Long Term Care* (New York: Haworth Press, 1983), pp. 179–185.

Gilbert, Neil, and Specht, H., *Dimensions of Social Welfare Policy* (Englewood Cliffs, N.J.: Prentice-Hall, 1974).

Glenn, Norval, "Aging and Conservatism," *The Annals of the American Academy of Political and Social Sciences*, vol. 4/5 (1974).

Goldfarb, Alvin, "Psychodynamics and the Three-Generation Family," in Ethel Shanas and Gordon F. Streib (eds.), *Social Structures and the Family.* (Englewood Cliffs, N.J.: Prentice-Hall, 1965), pp. 10–45.

Goldman, Elaine B., and Woog, Pierre, "Mental Health in Nursing Homes Training Project 1972–1973," *Gerontologist*, vol. 15, no. 2 (April 1975).

Goldstein, Louis, "Implications for Social Group Work with Older People," in *Social Group Work with Older People.* NASW, 1963.

Gordon, Susan Krauss, "The Phenomenon of Depression in Old Age," *Gerontologist*, vol. 13, no. 1 (spring 1973), pp. 100–105.

Gordon, William, "A Critique of the Working Definition," *Soc. Work*, vol. 1, no. 4 (1962).

Grabowski, Stanley N., and Mason, W. Dean, *Learning for Aging* (Washington, D.C.: Adult Education Association, 1973).

Gray Panthers, 1973 *Statement of Purpose.* 3700 Chestnut Street, Philadelphia.

———— , *Gray Panther Manual, Vol. 1: Organizing*, 2nd ed. (Philadelphia, Pa.: Gray Panthers, 1980).

Guide for In-Service Training for Developing Services for Older Persons. Report of the American Public Welfare Association California Project, 1961.

Gustafson, Elizabeth, "Day Care for the Elderly," *Gerontologist*, vol. 14, no. 1 (February 1974), pp. 46–49.

Haggerty, Judith, "Suicidal Behavior in a 70-Year-Old Man: A Case Report," ACSW, *J. Geriatric Psychiatry*, vol. VI, no. 1 (1973), pp. 43–51.

Hall, Selma, "Understanding of Developmental Goals of Older Adults as an Imperative in Group Work Practice," in *Social Work Education for Better Services to the Aging* (New York: CSWE, 1959), pp. 23–40.

Hamilton, G. V., "Changes in Personality and Psychosexual Phenomena with Age," in E.

V. Cowdry (ed.), *Problems of Aging*, 2nd ed. (Baltimore: Williams & Wilkins, 1952), pp. 810–831.

Harlow, Minnie, "Program Content of Group Experience in a Psychiatric Hospital," 1965. (Unpublished.)

Harris, Louis, and Associates, *Aging in the Eighties: America in Transition*. Study for the NCoA, 1981.

Havighurst, Robert, Neugarten, B., and Tobin, S., "Disengagement, Personality and Life Satisfaction." International Congress of Gerontology, Copenhagen, 1963.

Haynes, J., and Serkin, J., *Community Organization Planning and Resources for the Older Poor*. NCoA Monograph, no. 1 (Washington, D.C., 1968).

Henriques, Fernando, *Family and Colour in Jamaica* (London: Eyre and Spottiswoode, 1953).

Hilliard, Raymont, "Planning Services for the Aged: Part I, by the State Welfare Department," *NCSW Proceedings*, 1947, pp. 402–410.

Hirayama, Hisashi, "Group Services for the Minority Aged," in R. L. McNeely and John L. Colen (eds.), *Aging in Minority Groups* (Beverly Hills, Calif.: Sage Publications, 1983), pp. 270–280.

Hollis, Florence, *Casework: A Psychosocial Therapy* (New York: Random House, 1972).

Holmes, Lowell D., *Other Cultures, Elder Years: An Introduction to Cultural Gerontology* (Minneapolis, Minn.: Burgess Publishing Co., 1983), pp. 147–151.

Holzberg, Carol S., "Ethnicity and Aging: Rejoinder to a Comment by Kyriakos S. Markides," *Gerontologist*, vol. 22, no. 6 (1982), pp. 471–472.

Horowitz, Amy, and Dobrof, Rose, *The Role of Families in Providing Long Term Care to the Frail and Chronically Ill Elderly Living in the Community*. Methodological Report, Health Care Financing Administration, August, 1982.

Howell, Sandra C., and Loeb, Martin B., "Community Organization," *Gerontologist*, vol. 9, no. 3 (autumn 1969).

Hess, Beth B., and Elizabeth W. Markson, *Aging and Old Age*, Macmillian Publishing Co., New York, 1980.

Hudson, Robert (ed.), *The Aging in Politics: Process and Policy* (Springfield Ill.: Charles C Thomas, 1981).

Hulicker, I., "Participation in Group Conferences by Geriatric Patients," *Gerontologist*, March 1963, pp. 10–13.

Ikels, Charlotte, "Old Age in Hong Kong," *Gerontologist*, vol. 15, no. 3 (June 1975), pp. 230–235.

Jackson, Claire L., "The Grief Process in Physical Illness," *Smith College Studies in Soc. Work*, vol. 33 (February 1963), pp. 127–144.

Jackson, Hobart, "Crisis in our Nursing Homes," *Urban Health J.*, August, 1975.

Jackson, Jacquelyne Johnson, "The Blacklands of Gerontology," *Aging and Human Development*, vol. 2 (1971), pp. 156–171.

———, "Guest Editorial—the National Center on Black Aged: A Challenge to Gerontologists," *Gerontologist*, vol. 14, no. 3 (June 1975), pp. 194–196.

Janicki, Matthew, et al., "Service Needs Among Older Developmentally Disabled Persons," in M. P. Janicki and H. M. Wisniewski (eds.), *Aging and Developmental Disabilities: Issues and Approaches*. (Baltimore, Md.: Paul H. Brooks Publishing Co., in press).

Jenkins, Shirley, *The Ethnic Dilemma in Social Services* (New York: Free Press, 1981), pp. 43–74.

J. Communications, vol. 24, no. 4 (Autumn 1974).

J. Geriatric Psychiatry, vol. III, no. 2 (Spring 1970).

Kadushin, Alfred, "Content on Aging in the Human Growth and Behavior Sequence." Aspen Conference, 1958.

Kahana, Ralph J., "Grief and Depression," *J. Geriatric Psychiatry*, vol. VII, no. 1 (1974), pp. 26–47.

Kahne, Merton, J., et al., "Discussion," *J. Geriatric Psychiatry*, vol. VI, no. 1 (1973), pp. 52–69.

Kalish, Richard A. (ed.), *The Dependencies of Old People*. University of Michigan (Wayne State: Detroit), Institute of Gerontology, August 1969.

———, *Late Adulthood: Perspective on Human Development* (Monterey, Calif.: Brooks/Cole, 1975). Copyright © 1975 by Wadsworth Publishing Company, Inc. Reprinted by permission of the publisher, Brooks/Cole Publishing Company, Monterey, California.

———, "The New Ageism and the Failure Models: A Polemic," *Gerontologist*, vol. 9, no. 4 (1979), pp. 398–402.

Kalson, L., "The Therapy of Discussion," *Geriatrics*, May 1965, pp. 397–401.

Kamerman, Sheila, and Kahn, A., *Social Services in the U.S.* (Philadelphia: Temple University Press, 1976).

Kaplan, Gerome, *A Social Program for Older People* (Minneapolis: University of Minnesota Press, 1953).

———, "Evaluation Techniques for Older Groups," *American J. Occupational Therapy*, vol. XIII (1959), pp. 222–225.

Kart, Gary S., "In the Matter of Earle Spring: Some Thought on One Court's Approach to Senility," *Gerontologist*, vol. 21, no. 4 (1981), pp. 417–423.

Kastenbaum, Robert (ed.), *New Thoughts on Old Age* (New York: Springer, 1964).

Keith-Lucas, A., *Giving and Taking Help* (Chapel Hill: University of North Carolina Press, 1971).

Kent, D., Sherwood, S., and Kastenbaum, R., *Research Planning and Action for the Elderly* (New York: Behavioral Publications, 1972).

Kershner, Paul, and Hirschfield, I., "Public Policy and Aging," in *Aging—Scientific Perspectives and Social Issues* (New York: Van Nostrand, 1975).

Kessler, Judy, *Cohesiveness and Aging: An Empirical Test*. Unpublished manuscript, University of Nebraska Center for Urban Affairs, 1969.

Kimmel, Douglas C., *Adulthood and Aging: An Interdisciplinary Developmental View* (New York: Wiley, 1974).

Klein, W. H., Shan, L., and Furman, E. J., *Promoting Mental Health of Older People Through Group Methods: A Practical Guide* (New York: Mental Health Materials Center, 1965).

Kosberg, Jordan I., "The Nursing Home—a Social Work Paradox," *Soc. Work*, vol. 18 (March 1973).

———, "A Social Problems Approach to Gerontology," *J. Soc. Work Education* (fall 1976), in J. Kosberg (ed.), *Working with and for the Aged*. Compendium of 26 articles reprinted from *Social Work* 1979, Nat. Assoc. of Social Workers, Washington, D.C.

Kramer, Charles H., and Johnston, Grace F., "Correcting Confusion in the Brain Damaged," *Professional Home Nursing*, May 1965.

———, and Kramer, Jennette R., "Managing the Hostile Patient," *Geriatric Nursing*, May–June, 1966.

Kramer, Ralph, and Specht, H. (eds.), *Readings in Community Organization Practice* (Englewood Cliffs, N.J.: Prentice-Hall, 1969).

Kreps, Juanita Morris, *Preparation for Retirement* (annotated bibliography). New York, 1965.

Social Security Administration, Washington, D.C.

Krueger, Margaret, and Chellan, Grace (compilers), *Social Group Work with the Aged* (Cleveland: Benjamin Rose Institute, 1963).

Kubie, Susan, and Landau, G., *Group Work with the Aged* (New York: International Universities Press, 1953).

Kübler-Ross, Elisabeth, *On Death and Dying* (New York: Macmillan, 1969).

Kushner, N., and Bunch T., "Graduate Education in Aging Within the Social Sciences." Washington, D.C.: Government Publication, 1963.

Kutner, Bernard, David Fanshel, Alice M. Togo, Thomas S. Langner, *Five Hundred over Sixty* (New York: Russell Sage Foundation, 1952).

Lampe, Helen, "Diagnostic Considerations in Casework with Aged Clients," in *Casework with the Aging* (New York: Family Service Association of America, 1961), pp. 22–26.

Lang, Abigail, and Brody, Elaine, "Characteristics of Middle-aged Daughters and Help to their Elderly Mothers," *Journal of Marriage and the Family* (1983), pp. 193–202.

Lawton, M. Powell, "Assessment, Integration and Environments for Older People," *Gerontologist*, vol. 10 (Spring 1970), pp. 38–46.

Leach, Jean M., "The Intergenerational Approach in Casework with the Aging," *Soc. Casework*, vol. 45 (March 1964), pp. 144–149.

_____ , "Counseling with Older People and their Families." *Soc. Casework*, vol. 45 (1964).

Lehmann, Virginia, "Guardianship and Protective Services for Older People," *Soc. Casework*, vol. 42, nos. 5–6 (May–June 1961), pp. 252–257.

Leonard, Lois E., and Kelly, Ann M., "The Development of a Community-Based Program for Evaluating the Impaired Older Adult," *Gerontologist*, vol. 15, no. 2 (April 1975), pp. 114–118.

Lettieri, Dan J., "Empirical Prediction of Suicidal Risk Among the Aging," *J. Geriatric Psychiatry*, vol. VI, no. 1 (1973), pp. 7–42.

Levin, Morris, "Selected Implications for Social Group Work Practice with Older Adults," in *Social Group Work with Older People.* (New York: NASW, 1963).

Levin, Sidney, "Depression in the Aged: A Study of the Salient External Factors," *Geriatrics*, vol. 18 (April 1963), pp. 51–60.

Levine, Harry, "Day Centers for Older People." Unpublished manuscript, New York Department of Public Welfare, 1952.

Liderman, P., and Green R., "Geriatric Outpatient Group Therapy," *Comprehensive Psychiatry*, vol. 6 (February 1965), pp. 51–60.

_____ , and Liderman, V., "Outpatient Group Therapy with Geriatric Patients," *Geriatrics*, vol. 22 (January 1967), pp. 148–153.

Lindemann, Erich, "Symptomatology and Management of Acute Grief," *Amer. J. Psychiatry*, September 1944, pp. 141–148.

Linden, Maurice E., "Significance of Dual Leadership in Gerontological Group Psychotherapy: Studies in Gerontological Human Relations III," *International J. Group Psychotherapy*, vol. IV (1954), pp. 262–273.

_____ , "Transference in Gerontological Group Psychotherapy: Studies in Gerontologic Human Relations IV," *International J. Group Psychotherapy*, vol. V (1955), pp. 61–79.

_____ , "Geriatrics," in S. R. Slavson (ed.), *The Fields of Group Psychotherapy* (New York: International Universities Press, 1956), pp. 129–152.

_____ , "Emotional Problems in Aging." Unpublished paper, University of Pennsylvania, 1961.

Lindey, Ella (ed.), *A Crucial Issue of Social Work Practice: Protective Services for Older People*

(New York: NCoA, 1966).

Little, Virginia, "Open Care for the Aging: Alternate Approaches" *Aging*, Washington, D.C. U.S. Depart. HH5, Nov. Dec., 1979.

Locker, Rose, "Institutionalized Elderly: Understanding and Helping Couples," *Journal of Gerontological Social Work*, 3(4) (1981), pp. 37–49.

Lokshin, Helen, "Casework Counseling with the Older Client," *Soc. Casework*, June 1955.

Lowenthal, Marjorie Fiske, and Haven, C., "Interaction and Adaptation: Intimacy as a Critical Variable," in Bernice L. Neugarten (ed.), *Middle Age and Aging* (Chicago, Ill.: University of Chicago Press, 1968), pp. 220–234.

Lowy, Louis, "Social Work and Social Statesmanship," *Social Work*, vol. 5, no. 2 (April 1960).

———, "The Group in Social Work with the Aged," *Social Work*, vol. 7, no. 4 (October 1962), pp. 43–50. (Also in Carol H. Meyer, ed., *Social Work with the Aging*.)

———, "Meeting the Needs of Older People on a Differential Basis," in *Social Group Work with Older People* (New York: NASW, 1963).

———, "The Role of Social Gerontology in the Development of Social Services for Older People." Paper presented at the 19th meeting of Gerontological Society, New York, November 1966.

———, "Roadblocks in Group Work Practice with Older People: A Framework for Analysis," *Gerontologist*, vol. 7, no. 2 (June 1967), pp. 109–113.

———, *Training Manual* (Boston: Boston University Press, 1968).

———, "Models for Organization of Services to the Aging," *Aging and Human Development*, vol. 1, no. (1969).

———, "Notes on Theory, Research and Practice: Fundamentals of a Training Program of Workers with the Aging," *Gerontologist*, vol. 9, no. 2 (Summer 1970), pp. 148–150.

———, *The Function of Social Work in a Changing Society* (Boston: Milford House, 1974).

———, "The White House Conference on Aging: Two Years Later," *Aging and Human Development*, vol. 5, no. 2 (Spring 1974).

———, "The Functions of Professionals in Gerontology in Policy Making," *Aging and Human Development*, vol. 6, no. 1 (1975).

———, "Social Welfare and the Aging," in M. Spencer, and J. Dorr (eds.), *Understanding Aging.* (Englewood Cliffs, N.J.: Appleton-Century-Crofts, 1975).

———, "Adult Children and Their Parents: Dependency or Dependability?" *Long Term Care and Health Services Administration Quarterly*, (Fall 1977).

———, "Social Group Work with Vulnerable Older Persons: A Theoretical Perspective," *Social Work with Groups*, vol. 5, no. 2 (Summer 1982), (New York: Haworth Press), pp. 21–32.

———, "Continuing Education in the Later Years: Learning in the Third Age," *Gerontology and Geriatrics Education*, vol. 4(2) (Winter 1983/84), (New York: Haworth Press).

———, "The Older Generation: What is Due, What is Owed," *Social Casework* (1983), pp. 64–66.

———, *Social Policies and Programs on Aging* (Lexington, Ma.: Lexington Books, 1983).

———, "A Social Welfare Viewpoint" (Review Symposium Final Report, 1981 White House Conference on Aging.), *Gerontologist*, vol. 23, no. 2, 1983.

———, "Sozialarbeit/Sozialpädagogik als Wissenschaft im angloamerikanischen und deutschsprachigen Raum" (West Germany: Lambertus-Verlag, 1983).

_____ , Book Review of "The Late Freedom," *Gerontologist* (October 1984), vol. 24, no. 5.

_____ , and Miller, Leo, "Toward a Greater Movement for Gerontology in Social Work Education," *Gerontologist*, vol. 14, no. 6 (December 1974), pp. 466–467.

_____ , and Mogey, John, *Theory and Practice in Social Work with the Aging*. Boston University Council on Gerontology, Conference Paper Series, no. 1, 1966.

Lynes, Jerry, *The Evaluation of Protective Services for Older People* (San Diego: California Community Welfare Council, 1970).

Lysman, Aaron, "Conference on the Potential for Japanese-American Cross-National Research on Aging," *Gerontologist*, vol. 15, no. 3 (June 1975), pp. 248–253.

Lysner, Joan, and Sherman, Etta, "Hip Fractures in the Elderly—a Psychodynamic Approach," *Soc. Casework* (February 1975), pp. 97–103.

Maas, Henry S., and Kuypers, Joseph A., *From Thirty to Seventy* (San Francisco: Jossey-Bass, 1970).

Maldanado, David, Jr., "The Chicano Aged," *Social Work*, vol. 20, no. 3 (May 1975), pp. 213–216.

Manney, James, Jr., *Aging in American Society*. University of Michigan (Wayne State), Institute of Gerontology, 1975.

Mansery, Ellen P., *The Family Advocacy Manual* (New York: Family Service Association of America, 1972).

Markides, Kyriakos S., "Ethnicity and Aging: A Comment," *Gerontologist*, vol. 22, no. 6 (1982), pp. 467–470.

Markson, ELizabeth W., and Cumming, John H., "The Post-Transfer Fate of Relocated Mental Patients in New York," *Gerontologist*, vol. 15, no. 2 (April 1975), pp. 104–108.

Markson, Elizabeth W. (ed.), *Older Women: Issues and Prospects* (Lexington, Mass.: D.C., Heath & Co., 1983).

Maslow, Abraham, *Motivation and Personality* (New York: Saunders, 1954).

Maxwell, Jeanne, *Centers for Older People* (Washington, D.C.: NCoA, 1966).

McHugh, Rose, "A Constructive Program for the Aged," *NCSW Proceedings*, 1947, pp. 391–401.

McKain, W., *Retirement Marriage* (Storrs: University of Connecticut Press, 1968).

McMahon, Arthur W., and Rhudick, Paul J., "Reminiscing—Adaptational Significance in the Aged," *Archives of General Psychiatry*, vol. 10 (March 1964), pp. 292–298. (Cited in Allen Pincus, "Reminiscence in Aging and Its Implications for Social Work Practice, pp. 1–7.

Meerloo, Joost, "Contributions of Psychoanalysis to the Problems of the Aged," in Marcel Heiman (ed.), *Psychoanalysis and Social Work* (New York: International Universities Press, 1953), pp. 321–337.

Meyer, Carol (ed.), *Social Work with the Aging*. (Collection from *Soc. Work*.) (New York: Columbia University Press, 1973).

Milbrath, Lester, *Political Participation* (Chicago, Ill.: Rand McNally, 1965).

Miller, Dorothy, "The Sandwich Generation: Adult Children of the Aging," *Social Work* (1981), pp. 419–423.

Miller, Irving, and Solomon, Renee, "The Development of Group Services for the Elderly," *Journal of Gerontological Social Work*, vol. 2, no. 3 (Spring 1980), pp. 241–257.

Millet, Nina, "Hospice: A New Horizon for Social Work" in Charles A. Corr and Donna

M. Corr (eds.), *Hospice Care: Principles and Practice* (New York: Springer, 1983), pp. 135–147.

Milloy, Margaret, "Casework with the Older Person and His Family," *Soc. Casework*, vol. 45, no. 8 (October 1964), pp. 450–456.

———, "Family Treatment when Difficulties Relate to Families Which Include Older Persons." Presented at Biennial meeting of Family Service Association of America, Detroit, November 1965.

Mishara, Benan L., Robertson, Barbara, and Kastenbaum, Robert, "Self-Injurious Behavior in the Elderly," *Gerontologist*, vol. 13, no. 3, pt. I (Autumn 1973), pp. 311–314.

Monk, Abraham, "Social Policy and the Aged," *Soc. Work*, vol. 16, no. 3 (July 1971).

Monk, Abraham, "Social Work with the Aged: Principles of Practice," *Social Work* (January 1981), pp. 61–68.

Monk, Abraham, Ed., *Handbook of Gerontological Services* (New York, N.Y.: Van Nostrand Reinhold Co., 1985).

Moody, Harry R., "Ethical Dilemmas in Long Term Care," *Gerontological Social Work Practice in Long Term Care* (New York: Haworth Press, 1983), pp. 97–111.

Morris, John N., and Sherwood, Sylvia, "Informal Support Resources for Vulnerable Elderly Persons: Can They Be Counted On, Why Do They Work?" *International Journal of Aging and Human Development*, 18(2) (1984), pp. 81–98.

———, ———, and Gutkin, Claire E., *Meeting the Needs of the Impaired Elderly: The Power and Resiliency of the Informal Support System.* Technical Report, Hebrew Rehabilitation Center for the Aged, Boston, Mass., 1981.

Morris, Robert, "Aging and the Field of Social Work," in M. Riley, J. W. Riley, Jr., and M. E. Johnson (eds.), *Aging and Society*, vol. 2 (New York: Russell Sage Foundation, 1972), chap. 2.

———, Papers; Levinson Gerontological Policy Institute, Brandeis University, Waltham, Mass., 1972–1976.

———, "Identifying Problems in Long Term Care" in James Callahan and Stanley Wallack (eds.), *Reforming the Long Term Care System* (Lexington, Mass.: Lexington Books, 1981).

Morrison, Barbara Jones, "Sociocultural Dimensions: Nursing Homes and the Minority Aged," *Journal of Gerontological Social Work*, vol. 5, nos. 1/2 (fall/winter 1982), pp. 127–145.

Moss, Gordon, and Moss, Walter (eds.), *Growing Old* (New York: Pocketbooks, 1975).

Moss, Sidney Z., and Moss, Miriam S., "When a Caseworker Leaves an Agency: The Impact on Workers and Client," *Soc. Casework* (July 1967), pp. 433–437.

Motenko, Aluma K., *Family Support for the Elderly: What Price Glory?* Paper presented at the annual scientific meeting of the Gerontological Society of America, November 1982, Boston, Mass.

National Council of Senior Citizens, *Law and Aging Manual.* Washington, D.C., July 1976.

National Council on Aging, *The Myth and Reality of Aging* (Washington, D.C.: NCoA, 1975).

National Council on Aging, *Directory: National Organizations with Programs in the Field of Aging* (Washington, D.C.: NCoA, 1971).

National Council on Aging, *Resources for the Aging: An Action Handbook* (New York: NCoA, 1969).

National Council on Aging, *Triple Jeopardy: Myth or Reality* (Washington, D.C.: NCoA, 1971).

National Institute on Aging, *Age Page* (Bethesda, Maryland, 1980).

Nelson, Gary, "A Role of Title XX in the Aging Network," the *Gerontologist* (1982) vol. 22, no. 1.

Nelson, Gary, "Tax Expenditures for the Elderly" *The Gerontologist* (1983) vol. 23, no. 5.

Neugarten, Bernice, "Personality Changes in Adulthood and Old Age." *Proceedings of Seminars, 1959–1961.* Durham: Duke University Council on Gerontology, February 1962, pp. 22–34.

———, (ed.), *Middle Age and Aging* (Chicago: University of Chicago Press, 1968).

Neussel, Frank H., "The Language of Ageism," *Gerontologist*, vol. 22, no. 3 (1982), pp. 273–292.

Occupational Outlook Quarterly. U.S. Dept. of Labor, Bureau of Labor Statistics, Fall 1976. Special Issue: "Working with Older People."

Palmore, Erdman B., "Attitudes Toward the Aged: What We Know and Need to Know," *Research on Aging*, vol. 4, no. 3 (September 1982), pp. 333–348.

Papell, Catherine, and Rothman, Beulah, "Social Group Work Models," *J. Education for Soc. Work*, no. 2, Fall 1966.

Parry, Joan K., "Informed Consent: For Whose Benefit," *Social Casework* vol. 56, no. 5 (1975).

Patti, R., and Resnick, H., "Changing the Agency from Within," *Soc. Work*, vol. 17, no. 4 (July 1972), pp. 48–57.

Peck, Robert, "Psychological Developments in the Second Half of Life," in John E. Anderson (ed.), *Psychological Aspects of Aging* (Washington, D.C.: APA, 1956).

Perchansky, P. and Thomas, T. W., "The Concept of Access: Definition and Relationship to Consumer Satisfaction," *Medical Care*, 19(2) (February 1981), pp. 127–140.

Perlman, Robert, and Gurin, Arnold, *Community Organization and Social Planning.* (New York: Wiley, 1971).

Perry, William, "The Willingness of Persons 60 or Over to Volunteer: Implications for the Social Services," *Journal of Gerontological Social Work*, vol. 5(4) (Summer 1983), pp. 107–118.

Petersen, James A., "Marital and Family Therapy Involving the Aged." *Gerontologist*, vol. 13, no. 1 (Spring 1973), pp. 27–30.

Phillips, Helen, *Essentials of Group Work Skill* (New York: Association Press, 1957).

Pincus, Allen, "Toward a Developmental View of Aging for Social Work," *Soc. Work*, vol. 12, no. 3 (July 1967), pp. 33–41. (Also in Carol H. Meyer, ed., *Social Work with the Aging.*)

———, and Minahan, A., *Social Work Practice, Model and Method* (Itasca, Ill.: F. E. Peacock, 1973).

———, "Reminiscence in Aging and Its Implications for Social Work Practice," *Soc. Work*, July 1970. (Also in Carol H. Meyer, ed., *Social Work with the Aging.*)

———, Posner, William, "Adapting and Sharpening Social Work Knowledge and Skills in Serving the Aging," *Soc. Work*, vol. 2, no. 4 (October 1957), pp. 37–42.

———, "Retrospect and Prospect in Social Work with the Aged," *J. Jewish Communal Service*, vol. 36, no. 2 (Winter 1959).

———, "Casework with the Aged: Development and Trends," in *Social Work Education for Better Services to the Aging* (New York: CSWE, 1958).

Power, Cynthia T., and McCarron, Lawrence, T., "Treatment of Depression in Persons Residing in Homes for the Aged," *Gerontologist*, vol. 15, no. 2 (April 1975).

Proceedings of the Institute on Provision of Social Services for Nursing Home Patients, September

23–25, 1964. Chatham, Mass. Reprinted by the U.S. Public Health Service, Department of HEW.

Rachlis, David, *How to Obtain Grants for Programs for the Aging Poor* (New York: NCOA, 1968).

Ramm, Dietoff, and Gianturco, Daniel T., "Computers and Technology: Aiding Tomorrow's Aged," *Gerontologist*, vol. 13, no. 3, pt. I (Autumn 1973), pp. 322–326.

Rathbone, Eloise, McCuan, "Older Women Mental Health and Social Work Education," *Journal of Education for Social Work* vol. 20, no. 1 (1984).

Rathbone, Eloise, McCuan and Joan Hashimi, *Isolated Elders* (Rockville, Md.: Aspen Publication, 1982.)

Ratzan, Richard M., "Being Old Makes You Different: The Ethics of Research with Elderly Subjects" in Natalie Abrams and Michael Buckner (eds.), *Medical Ethics: A Clinical Textbook and Reference for the Health Care Professions* (Cambridge, Mass.: M.I.T. Press, 1983), pp. 219–523.

Reichard, Susan, Livson, F., and Peterson, P., *Aging and Personality: A Study of Older Men* (New York: John Wiley, 1962).

Riley, Matilda W. (ed.), *Aging and Society*, vols. 1, 2, 3 (New York: Russell Sage Foundation, 1968, 1972, 1973).

———, "The Family in an Aging Society: A Matrix of Latent Relationships," *Journal of Family Issues*, vol. 4, no. 3 (1983), pp. 439–454.

Rose, Arnold, and Peterson, Warren, *Older People and Their Social World* (Philadelphia: Davis, 1965).

Rosenmayr, Leopold, *Die Späte Freiheit.* (Berlin, West Germany: Severin und Siedler Verlag, 1983).

———, and Kockeis, Eva, "Propositions for a Sociological Theory of Aging and the Family," *International Social Science Journal*, 15 (1963), pp. 410–426.

Ross, M., "A Review of Some Recent Group Psychotherapy Methods for Elderly Psychiatric Patients," in M. Rosenbaum, and M. Berger (eds.), *Group Psychotherapy and Ground Function* (New York: Basic Books, 1963), chap. 39.

Rubinow, I. M. (ed.), *The Care of the Aged.* Proceedings of the Deutsch Foundation Conference, 1930.

Runciman, Alexander, "Problems Older Clients Present in Counseling About Sexuality," in Irene Mortenson Burnside (ed.), *Sexuality and Aging* (Los Angeles: University of Southern California Press, 1975), pp. 54–66.

Russell Sage Foundation Library, *Provisions for Care of the Aged* (a selected bibliography). Bulletin no. 75, 1926.

Sager, Alan, *Planning Home Care with the Elderly: Patient and Family and Professional Views of an Alternative to Institutionalization.* (Cambridge: Mass.: Ballinger, 1983).

Santore, Anthony F., and Diamond, Herbert, "The Role of a Community Mental Health Center in Developing Services to the Aging," *Gerontologist*, vol. 14, no. 3 (June 1974), pp. 241–244.

Saul, Shura, *Aging—an Album of People Growing Old* (New York: John Wiley, 1974).

———, et al., "The Use of the Small Group in Orienting New Residents to a Home for the Aged." Unpublished paper.

Scharlach, Andrew E., *Relief of Role Strain Among Women with Aging Mothers.* Paper presented at the annual meeting of the Gerontological Society of America, San Francisco, California, November, 1983.

Schechter, Irma (ed.), *Aging Services News*, August 1982.

Schneider, Robert L., *Memorandum Regarding National Curriculum Project in Gerontology*. Council on Social Work Education, New York, January 30, 1984.

Schneider, Robert L., "Behavioral Outcomes for Administration Majors", *Journal of Education for Social Work* (1979), vol. 14, no. 1.

Schulz, James H., *The Economics of Aging* (Belmont, Calif.: Wadsworth, 1976).

Schwartz, William, "The Social Worker in the Group," *Social Welfare Forum* (New York: Columbia University Press, 1961), pp. 146–171.

Schwarzmann, Betty, "Observations on the Dynamics at Play in a Group of Older People," *Medical Social Work*, vol. 19 (September 1966), pp. 159–165.

Seltzer, Marsha Mailick, and Seltzer, Gary B., "The Elderly Mentally Retarded: A Group in Need of Services," *Journal of Gerontological Social Work*, (in press).

Seltzer, Marsha Mailick, Simmons Kathryn, Ivry Joann, Litchfield Leon, "Agency-Family Partnerships: Case Management of Services for the Elderly," *Journal of Gerontological Social Work*, vo. 7, no. 4, (1984), pp. 57–74.

Seltzer, Mildred, Corbett, S., and Atchley, R. (eds.), *Social Problems of the Aging: Readings* (Belmont, Calif.: Wadsworth, 1978).

Shanas, Ethel, *The Health of Older People: A Social Survey* (Cambridge: Harvard University Press, 1962). (Cited in Margaret Blenkner, "Social Work and Family Relationships in Later Life with Some Thoughts on Filial Maturity.")

Shanas, Ethel, "Social Myth as Hypothesis: The Case of the Family Relations of Older People," *Gerontologist*, 19, 1 (1979), pp. 3–9.

———— , "Older People and Their Families: The New Pioneers," *Journal of Marriage and the Family*, 1980, pp. 9–15.

———— , and Streib, Gordon F. (eds.), *Social Structure and the Family: Generational Relations* (Englewood Cliffs, N.J.: Prentice-Hall, 1965).

———— , and Sussman, Marvin, "The Family in Later Life: Social Structure and Social Policy," in Robert Fogel et al. (eds.), *Aging: Stability and Change in the Family* (New York: Academic Press, 1981).

Sharkey, Harold B., "Sustaining the Aged in the Community," *Soc. Work*, vol. 7 (January 1962).

Shere, E. S., "Group Therapy with the Very Old," in R. Kastenbaum (ed.), *New Thoughts on Old Age* (New York: Springer, 1964), chap. 10.

Sherwood, Sylvia (ed.), *Long Term Care, A Handbook* (New York: Spectrum Publishers, 1975), p. 253.

Sherwood, Sylvia, and Morris, John N., *Alternative Paths to Long Term Care*. Final Report to the Administration on Aging, June 1982.

Shore, Herbert, "The Application of Social Work Disciplines to Group Work Services in Homes for the Aged," *Soc. Serv. Rev.*, vol. 26, no. 4 (1952), pp. 418–422.

———— , "Group Work Program Development in Homes for the Aged," *Soc. Serv. Rev.*, vol. 26, no. 2 (1952), pp. 181–194.

Sibulkin, Lillian, "Special Skills in Working with Older People," *Soc. Casework*, vol. 40, no. 4 (1959).

Siegel, Sheldon (ed.), "Social Work Practice with the Aging and Its Implications for Mental Health." Proceedings of a Workshop, May 6–8, 1964, St. Clair, Michigan.

Silverstone, Barbara, *Establishing Resident Councils*. New York Federation of Protestant Welfare Agencies, Division of Aging, December 1974.

———— , and Burack-Weiss, Ann, *Social Work Practice with the Frail Elderly and Their Families: The Auxiliary Function Model* (Springfield, Ill.: Charles C. Thomas, 1983).

———, and Hyman, Helen Kandel, *You and Your Aging Parent: The Modern Family's Guide to Emotional, Physical and Financial Problems* (New York: Pantheon Books, 1976).

———, and Miller, Sarah, "Isolation in the Aged: Individual Dynamics, Community and Family Involvement," *Journal of Geriatric Psychiatry*, 13, 1 (1980), pp. 27–47.

Simos, Bertha G., "Adult Children and Their Aging Parents," *Soc. Work*, May 1973. (Also in Carol H. Meyer, ed., *Social Work with the Aging.*)

———, and Kohls, Margot, "Migration, Relocations and Intergenerational Relations: Jews of Quito, Ecuador," *Gerontologist*, vol. 15, no. 3 (June 1975), pp. 206–211.

Siporin, May, *Introduction to Social Work Practice* (New York: Macmillan, 1975).

Skelskie, Barbara E., "Grief in Old Age," *Smith College Studies in Soc. Work*, vol. XLV, no. 2 (February 1975), pp. 159–182.

Slover, Daniel, *The Gerontology Concentration in the School of Social Work* (Syracuse School of Social Work Paper, Syracuse, N.Y., 1977).

Social Work Agenda, vol. 1, no. 1; vol. 2, no. 1; vol. 3, no. 1 (January 1982, 1983, 1984).

Social Work Yearbook, vol. 1; vol. 8; vol. 10 (1929, 1945, 1949).

Solomon, Renee, "Serving Families of the Institutionalized Aged: The Four Crises," in George S. Getzel and Joanne M. Mellor (eds.), *Gerontological Social Work Practice in Long Term Care* (New York: The Haworth Press, 1983).

Soskis, Carole W., "Teaching Nursing Home Staff about Patient's Rights," *The Gerontologist*, vol. 21, no. 4 (1981), pp. 424–430.

Southwood, V., "Closing a Policy Services Gap for the Aging." Mimeographed paper, 1970.

Spencer, Marion, and Dorr, J. (eds.), *Understanding Aging: A Multi-Disciplinary Approach* (Englewood Cliffs, N.J.: Appleton-Century-Crofts), 1975.

Special Committee on Aging, U.S. Senate, *Developments in Aging, 1982: Vol. I.*

Stabler, Nora, "The Use of Groups in Day Centers for Older Adults," *Social Work with Groups* vol. 4 (3/4) (fall/winter 1981), pp. 49–58.

Steinberg, Raymond M., and Carter, Genevieve W., *Case Management and the Elderly* (Lexington, Mass.: Lexington Books, 1983).

Stern, K., Smith, J. M., and Frank, M., "Mechanisms of Transference and Countertransference in Psychotherapeutic and Social Work with the Aged," *J. Gerontology*, vol. 8 (1953), pp. 328–332.

Stern, Max, "Community Organization Process in Planning for the Aged Across Social Agency Lines," *J. Jewish and Communal Service*, vol. 40, no. 4 (1964).

Sterns, Harvey L., E. F. Ansello, B. M. Sprouse, R. Layfield-Faus, *Gerontology in Higher Education* (Belmont, Calif.: Wadsworth Publishing Co., 1982).

Streib, Gordon F., and Thompson, Wayne, "The Older Person in a Family Context," in Clark Tibbits (ed.), *Handbook of Social Gerontology* (University of Chicago Press, 1960), pp. 447–475. (Cited in Margaret Blenkner, "Social Work and Family Relationships in Later Life with Some Thoughts on Filial Maturity,") p. 48.

Taub, Harvey A., "Informed Consent, Memory and Age," *Gerontologist*, vol. 20, no. 6 (1980), pp. 686-690.

"The Family is All Generations," *Family Serv. Highlights*, vol. 25 (September, October, November, 1964).

Third National Conference of Senior Centers, "Planning Today for Tomorrow's Older People." Chicago, Ill., 1970.

Thune, Jeanne M., Webb, Celia R., and Thune, Leland E., "Interracial Attitudes of Younger and Older Adults in a Biracial Population," *Gerontologist*, vol. 2, no. 4, pt. I (winter 1971), pp. 305–309.

Tibbits, Clark, *Handbook of Social Gerontology* (Chicago: University of Chicago Press, 1959).

Tine, Sebastian, "Process and Criteria for Grouping," in *Social Group Work for Older People* (Washington, D.C.: NASW, 1963).

———, Deutschberger, Paul, and Hastings, K., "Generic and Specific in Social Group Work with the Aging," in *Social Group Work for Older People* (Washington, D.C.: NASW, 1963).

Tobin, Sheldon "The Educator as Advocate: The Gerontologist in an Academic Setting," *J. Education for Soc. Work*, vol. 9, no. 3 (fall 1973).

Tobin, Sheldon and Lieberman, Martin, *Last Home for the Aged* (San Francisco: Jossey Bass, 1976).

———, "Planning Welfare Services for Older People." *Gerontologist*, vol. 12, no. 2 (1975).

Torres-Gill, Fernando, "Political Involvement among Members of Minority Groups: Problems and Profits" in R. L. McNeely and John Colen (eds.), *Aging and Minority Groups* (Beverly Hills, Calif.: Sage, 1983).

Toseland, Ron, Sherman, Edmund, and Bliven, Stephen, "The Comparative Effectiveness of Two Group Work Approaches for the Development of Mutual Support Groups Among the Elderly," *Social Work with Groups*, vol. 4 (1/2) (spring/summer 1981), pp. 137–153.

Townsend, Claire, *Old Age, The Last Segregation* (New York: Grossman, 1971).

Townsend, Peter, *The Family Life of Old People* (London: Routledge & Kegan Paul, 1957). (Cited in Blenkner, Margaret, "Social Work and Family Relationships in Later Life with Some Thoughts on Filial Maturity," p. 48.

Training. 1971 White House Conference, background paper.

Tull, Anne, "The Stresses of Clinical Social Work with the Terminally Ill," *Smith College Studies in Soc. Work*, vol. XLV, no. 2 (February 1975), pp. 137–158.

Turner, Francis Helen, "Use of the Relationship in Casework Treatment of Aged Clients," *Soc. Casework*, vol. 47, nos. 5–6, May–June 1961, pp. 245–252.

———, "Serving the Older Person: A Multiple Approach by the Family Agency," *Soc. Casework*, vol. 35, no. 7 (1954), pp. 299–308.

Twente, Esther, *Never Too Old* (San Francisco: Jossey-Bass, 1970).

United Nations, *The Aging: Trends and Policies* (New York: United Nations, 1975).

United Nations Secretariat, Social Development Branch, *Bulletin on Aging*, vol. VI, no.1 (1981).

Van Beugen, M., *Agogische Intervention* (Freiburg i/Br.: Lambertus, 1972).

Van Mering, Otto, "Value Dilemmas and Reciprocably Evoked Transactions of Patient and Worker." Reprinted from *Psychoanalysis and the Psychoanalytic Rev.*, vol. 49, no. 2 (Summer 1962).

Vernick, Joel J., *Selected Bibliography on Death and Dying* (Washington, D.C.: U.S. Government Printing Office, 1970).

Vickery, Florence, *Creative Programming for Older Adults: A Leadership Training Guide* (New York: Association Press, 1972).

Videbeck, Richard, "Psychological Aspects of Aging." Unpublished paper, Department of Psychology, Syracuse University, 1973.

Warren, Roland, "Types of Purposive Social Change at the Community Level." *Papers in Social Welfare* (Waltham, Mass.: Brandeis Univeristy, 1965).

Wasser, Edna, "Responsibility, Self-Determination and Authority in Casework Protection of Older Persons," *Soc. Casework*, vol. 42, nos. 5–6 (May–June, 1961), pp. 258–266.

———, *Selected Bibliography for Casework with Older Persons* (New York: Family Service

Association of America, 1963).

———, "The Phenomenon of Aging: A Review of the Literature," in M. Jahn, M. Blenkner, and Edna Wasser (eds.), *Serving the Aging: An Experiment in Social Work and Public Health* (New York: Community Service Society, 1964), pp. 212–243.

———, "The Sense of Commitment in Serving Older Persons," *Soc. Casework*, vol. 65 (October 1964), pp. 443–449.

———, *Casebook on Work with the Aging* (New York: Family Service Association of America, 1966).

———, *Creative Approaches in Casework with the Aging* (New York: Family Service Association of America, 1966).

———, "Family Casework Focus on the Older Persons," *Soc. Casework*, vol. 47, no. 1 (July 1966), pp. 423–431.

———, "Protective Practice in Serving the Mentally Impaired Aged," *Soc. Casework*, vol. 52, no. 8 (October 1971), pp. 511–522.

Weaver, Jerry, "Issue Salience: The Elderly as a Political Community: The Case of a National Health Policy," *Western Political Quarterly*, vol. 29, no. 4 (December 1976), pp. 610–619.

Weinberger, Paul E. (ed.), *Perspectives on Social Welfare*, 2nd ed. (New York: Macmillan, 1974).

Weisman, A., *On Dying and Denying* (New York: Behavioral Publications, 1970).

White House Conference on Aging 1971, *Towards a National Policy on Aging*, vols. 1 and 2.

White House Conference on Aging 1981, *Chartbook on Aging in America.* (Washington, D.C. US Government Printing Office, 1981).

White House Conference on Aging Mini-Conference on Housing for the Elderly, June 1981 (Washington, D.C.: United States Government Printing Office, 1981).

Wickenden, Elizabeth, *The Needs of Older People and Public Welfare Services to Meet Them* (Chicago: American Public Welfare Association, 1953).

Wineburg, Robert J., "The Elderly Blind in Nursing Homes: The Need for a Coordinated In-Service Training Policy," *Journal of Gerontological Social Work*, vol. 4 (3/4) (spring/summer 1982), pp. 67–81.

Wolf, Bee R., "Explaining Retirement in a Small Group," *Soc. Work*, vol. 20, no. 6 (November 1975).

Woodring, Paul, "Why 65? The Case Against Mandatory Retirement," *Saturday Review*, August 1976.

Woodruff, Diana, and Birren, James E. (eds.), *Aging: Scientific Perspectives and Social Issues* (New York: D. Van Nostrand, 1975).

"Working Definition of Social Work Practice," *Soc. Work*, vol. 3, no. 2 (April 1958).

"Working Statement on the Purpose of Social Work," *Social Work.* (January 1981).

Zimberg, Sheldon, "Outpatient Geriatric Psychiatry in an Urban Ghetto with Nonprofessional Workers," *Amer. J. Psychiatry*, vol. 125 (June 1969), pp. 1697–1702.

———, "The Elderly Alcoholic," *Gerontologist*, vol. 14 (1974), pp. 221–224.

Sinberg, Norman, and Kaufman, Irving (eds.), *Normal Psychology of the Aging Process* (New York: Intenational Universities Press, 1963).

Zuniga-Martinez, Maria, "Social Treatment with the Minority Elderly," in R. L. McNeely and John L. Colen (eds.), *Aging in Minority Groups* (Beverly Hills, Calif.: Sage, 1983), pp. 260–269.

Index